ANDREW PICKNELL first visited Japan as an English teacher after working at the National Maritime Museum and the BBC following graduation. He returned many times to travel, teach and spend time in places as varied as Hokkaido, Kyushu and Tokyo. Now teaching History and Politics in Britain, he goes back regularly to explore Japan's past and present and continue his passion for the language.

ANNA UDAGAWA was born in Sussex but after graduating and then working at the BBC in London she headed off to explore the world, gradually travelling further east. Her interest in Japan began with a visit to a friend living in the country and soon inspired her to prolong her stay, working as an English teacher. She met her husband while there but

after marrying they came back to Britain. However, Anna returns to Japan whenever she can.

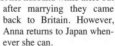

RAMSEY ZARIFEH was born in the UK but has spent most of his working life abroad. After graduating from Magdalene College, Cambridge, with a degree in English, he spent two years in Japan on the Japan Exchange and Teaching (JET) scheme, before spending a year researching and writing the first edition of *Japan by Rail*. He currently works as a broadcast and online journalist, and his travels take him as often as possible back to Japan.

Japan by Rail
First edition: 2002; this third edition September 2012

Publisher
Trailblazer Publications
The Old Manse, Tower Rd, Hindhead, Surrey, GU26 6SU, UK
Fax (+44) 01428-607571, info@trailblazer-guides.com
www.trailblazer-guides.com

British Library Cataloguing in Publication Data
A catalogue record for this book is available from the British Library

ISBN 978-1-905864-39-3

Maps © Trailblazer 2002, 2007 & 2012
Colour photographs © as indicated: J&RL = © Jill & Roderick Leslie
AU = © Anna Udagawa, KU = © Kazuo Udagawa
MA = © Mamie Air, AP = © Andrew Picknell
B&W photographs: p51 & p375 © Andrew Picknell; p353 © Anna Udagawa;
all other B&W photographs © Kazuo Udagawa

The haiku at the start of each chapter in this book is reproduced with the permission of:
Tohta Kaneko: p8; Minako Kaneko: p412; Kazuko Konagai: p68; Professor Makoto Ueda
and University of Toronto Press (*Modern Japanese Haiku – An Anthology*): p31 & p361

Editor: Lucy Ridout
Cartography: Nick Hill
Layout: Anna Jacomb-Hood
Proofreading: Jane Thomas and Kazuo Udagawa
Index: Anna Jacomb-Hood and Jane Thomas

Printed on chlorine-free paper by D'Print (☎ +65-6581 3832), Singapore

Japan

BY RAIL

RAMSEY ZARIFEH

THIRD EDITION RESEARCHED AND UPDATED BY
RAMSEY ZARIFEH, ANNA UDAGAWA
ANDREW PICKNELL & ANTHONY ROBINS

TRAILBLAZER PUBLICATIONS

Acknowledgements

From Ramsey: Thanks are due to the Central Japan Railway Company (JR Central/JR Tokai), without whose generous support the first edition of this book would never have been written, and to the Japan National Tourist Organization (JNTO).

For this edition particular thanks are due to Anthony Robins in Nagoya for helping to update the Takayama and Nagoya city guides, to Kenichi Adachi in Osaka, Yoshiko Minami in Nara, Keiji and Hiromi Shimizu in Kyoto, and Kenichi Anazawa in Tokyo. I am grateful to everyone else I met along the way for giving me advice and telling me about their own experiences of travelling in Japan.

Special thanks to Anna Udagawa for masterminding this edition and for her hard work on the road and back home updating much of the book, to Andrew Picknell for his invaluable contribution, and to Kazuo, Kenichi and Rikki Udagawa for their assistance.

For the haiku (poems) at the start of each chapter I should like to thank: the President of the Modern Haiku Association (Japan), Tohta Kaneko; the President of the British Haiku Society, David Cobb, whose introductions, haiku suggestions and general advice were invaluable; Kazuko Konagai for supplying and translating a wide range of appropriate haiku; and the late Patricia Major for liaising with everyone above and for making the final selection. I am also very grateful to Ichie Uchiyama for providing the calligraphy for the book title. Thanks also to my parents and to my brothers, Alex and Andrew.

From Anna: Thanks to everyone at JR East (in particular Hirotaka Naruse & Yoshiyuki Nagasaka), Yoshitaka Ito at JR Hokkaido, Kosuke Hayakawa at JR Central, Yuko Baba at JR Kyushu, Kylie Clark and everyone at JNTO, Akira Sirai at Oigawa Steam Railway; Kohei Ohno, Tourism Representative in London for Tokyo, and Keiji Shimizu in Kyoto.

I am particularly grateful to Joe Woodruff, and also to Laura & Ross Nixon, for recommendations on Hokkaido, to Clive & Abigail Allnutt, Paul Giangrande, Mamie Air, Charlotte Steggall, Madhvi Harvey and Michael Jay for tips and comments on places in Honshu. Thanks also to Jill and Roderick Leslie for their company on one of my trips to Japan, and to Etsuko Usui in Tokyo.

Special thanks to Kazuo, Kenichi and Rikki for all their support and help – and to Ramsey for giving me the opportunity to spend more time in this amazing country.

From Andrew: Thanks to Tomokiyo Oka and his family who provided me with wonderful food, lodgings and company when travelling in Kyushu, and also to Ramsey for giving me an opportunity to explore Shikoku for the first time as well as the excuse to return to my beloved Kyushu.

For help with producing this edition the authors would jointly like to thank: Anthony Robins for answering so many rail-related queries; Lucy Ridout for her thorough editing and for improving the book in many ways; Nick Hill for the maps; Jane Thomas and Kazuo Udagawa for proofreading; Kazuo Udagawa, Mamie Air, Jill & Roderick Leslie for the photos, and also the publisher, Bryn Thomas.

A request

The author and publisher have tried to ensure that this guide is as accurate and up to date as possible. Nevertheless things change. If you notice any changes or omissions that should be included in the next edition of this book, please write to Ramsey Zarifeh at Trailblazer (address on p2) or email him at ramsey.zarifeh@trailblazer-guides.com. A free copy of the next edition will be sent to those making a significant contribution.

Updated information will be available on 🖳 www.trailblazer-guides.com

Cover photograph: Mt Fuji (3776m/12,388ft) seen
from the tea fields of Shizuoka (see p133) (Photo © JNTO)

CONTENTS

INTRODUCTION

Think of Japan and one of the first images you're likely to conjure up is that of a bullet train speeding past snow-capped Mt Fuji. For many, what lies beyond this image is a mystery. But hop on board that train and you'll quickly discover what the country has to offer.

The fascination of Japan lies in its diversity: remote mountain villages contrast with huge neon-lit cities that never sleep; the vast natural landscape of unspoilt forests, volcanoes and hot springs more than compensates for the occasional man-made eyesore; the silent oasis of a Shinto shrine or a Buddhist temple is not far from the deafening noise of a virtual-reality games arcade. Nowhere else in the world do past and present co-exist in such close proximity as in this relatively small country.

The ideal way of seeing it all is by rail, whether on one of the famous bullet trains (*shinkansen*), on the wide network of local trains, or even on one of the many steam trains. An early 20th-century guidebook advised visitors to 'make travel plans as simple as possible. The conditions of travel in this country do not lend themselves to intricate arrangements'. Today, however, nothing could be further from the truth. Trains run not just to the minute but to the second, so itineraries can be as complicated or minutely timetabled as you wish. Or you can simply turn up at the station and plan your journey as you go.

The real secret to touring the country is the Japan Rail Pass, deservedly recognised as the 'bargain of the century'. Rail-pass holders can travel easily almost anywhere on the four main islands.

Japan need not be too expensive as, apart from your rail pass, you can cut costs by staying in hostels, *minshuku* (Japanese-style B&Bs), or business hotels (Western or Japanese style). For those with a larger budget, staying in *ryokan* (upmarket B&Bs) can be an amazing experience, but if you prefer there are world-class five-star hotels throughout the country.

Unexpected pleasures also await the traveller: where else do railway staff bow to you as they enter the carriage and also look as smart as they do in Japan? And where else can you buy cans of hot coffee from a vending machine at the top of a mountain or sip sake whilst sitting in an open-air hot spring bath? It's said that no *gaijin* (outsider) can ever fully know Japan but only by visiting and seeing for yourself can you discover what the country is really like: somewhere between the images of traditional past and hi-tech future which flicker worldwide on the small screen.

1 PLANNING YOUR TRIP

Routes and costs

ROUTE OPTIONS

So you know you're going to Japan: the next step is to work out what you want to see and how much ground you want to cover once you've arrived. This guide shows you how travelling around Japan by rail is the best way of seeing the country close up and in full colour. And there are few places in the world where the trains virtually always run on time – travelling at speeds of up to 300kph (190mph) and up to 320kph (198mph) from 2013 – and where it really can be as much fun to travel as it is to arrive. Welcome to Japan by rail.

Using this guide

Japan Rail (JR) boasts that its network covers every corner of Japan's four main islands. If you look at the maps in JR's timetable you'll see what appears to be something like a bowl of spaghetti. The choice of routes is, if not infinite, at the very least overwhelming.

To simplify travel planning and to reassure the first-time visitor that a qualification in orienteering is not needed, this guide splits the largest island, Honshu, into regions – Central Honshu, Kansai, Western Honshu and Tohoku (North-eastern Honshu) – and suggests (connecting) routes for each of these as well as for the other three main islands: Hokkaido, Kyushu and Shikoku. For example, if you are following the route round Western Honshu you will pass through Okayama, the starting point for the route guide around Shikoku.

Each section begins with an introduction to the area, with information on regional highlights and suggested stopping-off points. Routes can be followed in reverse but in this case all points of interest from the train will be on the opposite side.

Though it's possible to travel every route by local train, it's assumed that most travellers will have a rail pass so will use the shinkansen and/or limited express (LEX) services. It is not possible to mention every station so, as a rule of thumb, only stops served by limited expresses (or by shinkansen if the route follows a shinkansen line) are included. Stations served solely by local trains are listed if they, or the area around them, are of particular interest. The fastest point-to-point journey times are provided for each section of the route.

きょお！と喚いてこの汽車はゆく新緑の夜中

Kyoh! screaming aloud this train runs into the fresh green midnight
(TOHTA KANEKO)

Even though each route has been divided into different sections it may not be necessary to change trains as you go from one section to the next. Occasionally, however, it is essential to change trains in order to complete the route described. Such instances are denoted by the following symbol ▲. Places which are served by local trains only are marked ♦. Sample itineraries are provided on pp20-5.

There are also guides for Tokyo and Osaka (the gateway cities) as well as for all the other main towns and cities on the islands covered; details of side trips from each of these are also given.

COSTS

Contrary to popular belief, a visit to Japan doesn't have to be expensive but it is important to plan your budget as it is an easy country to spend money in.

Package tours which include travel by rail (see pp16-18) rarely offer better value than organising an independent trip. From the UK you're probably looking at a minimum of £3000 for a 14-day tour including return flights, rail travel, accommodation in basic Japanese inns, some meals and the services of a tour

---

❏ SAMPLE DAILY BUDGETS

Note: The budgets below do not include travel costs because they assume you have a Japan Rail Pass. The exchange rates are rounded up/down for convenience.

Low

Accommodation	¥2600+ (£20/US$31+): dorm bed in a hostel, no meals
Breakfast	¥500 (£4/US$6): coffee and toast
Lunch	¥500 (£4/US$6): sandwich or snack and drink
Dinner	¥1100 (£8/US$13): noodles/pasta or a hostel meal
Sightseeing	¥1700 (£13/US$20): less if you mainly visit free attractions
Total	**¥6400+ (£49/US$77+)**

Mid-range

Accommodation	¥5000 (£40/US$60)+ for a single room, ¥8000 (£61/US$96)+ for two sharing in a business hotel (breakfast is usually included); ¥7000pp (£54/US$84)+ in a minshuku (half-board)
Breakfast*	¥890 (£7/US$11): egg, ham, toast and coffee
Lunch	¥1100 (£8/US$13): lunch deal in a café/restaurant
Dinner	¥1600 (£12/US$19): set evening meal at a restaurant
Sightseeing	¥1700 (£13/US$20): more if you visit lots of galleries/museums
Total	**¥10,590+ (£80/US$128+)**

High

Accommodation	¥12,000+ (£92/US$145+) for a single room, ¥20,000+ (£153/US$241) for two sharing in an upmarket hotel; ¥16,000+ (£120/US$190) per person half-board in a ryokan
Breakfast*	¥2140 (£16/US$26): buffet breakfast
Lunch	¥3570 (£27/US$43): a three-course meal
Dinner	¥6250+ (£48+/US$75+): à la carte meal
Sightseeing	¥9000+ (£69+/US$108+): guided city tours and entry fees
Total	**¥32,960+ (£282/US$397+)**

* If not included in room rate

P L A N N I N G   Y O U R   T R I P

guide. Given the price of a 14-day rail pass (¥45,100: £345/US$544), it would certainly be more cost effective (and more fun) to organise your own trip.

Though the cost of a Japan Rail Pass (see box p12) may seem high, a pass can often pay for itself in just one journey. For example, a return ticket on the shinkansen between Tokyo and Kyoto costs ¥26,840 (£205/US$324), while a 7-day rail pass costs ¥28,300 (£216/US$341); the return fare from Tokyo to Hiroshima by shinkansen is way over that at ¥36,500 (£279/US$440). A return journey to Sapporo from Tokyo by shinkansen and limited express works out at ¥46,940 (£359/US$568), more than the cost of a two-week pass.

When to go

In general, Japan has a mild climate, though it's difficult to talk at all generally about a country which stretches for some 3000km north to south. It can be below freezing and snowing in Hokkaido while southern Kyushu is enjoying sunshine and mild temperatures.

April and May are often considered the best months to visit, when the worst of the Hokkaido winter is over and the rest of Japan is not yet sweltering in humidity. **Cherry-blossom viewing** takes place March to May. However, try to avoid the school/university holidays at the end of March/early April and

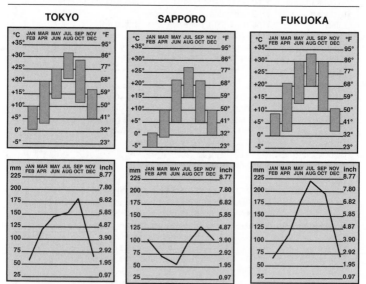

MAX/MIN TEMPERATURE CHARTS (°F/°C) AND AVERAGE RAINFALL (MM/INCH)

so-called **Golden Week** (29th April to 5th May), which includes four national holidays and can feel as if the entire country is on the move; hotels and trains are booked out and prices rise to meet demand. See pp64-5 for a calendar of national holidays and pp65-6 for details of some of the many festivals in Japan.

The **rainy season** in June/July (with occasional typhoons) marks the change from spring to summer but the showers are soon replaced by heat and humidity. Humidity is high throughout the summer months so carry bottled water if you are planning long days of sightseeing at this, the hottest, time of the year. Hokkaido is by far the coolest and least humid place in summer, which also makes it one of the busiest. The school holiday season in August is another busy time, particularly around mid August during the Obon festival, when people head back to their home towns.

The high temperatures and – particularly in the south – blistering heat can last well into September and often there is a lot of rain then. **Typhoons** strike coastal regions, particularly in Shikoku and Kyushu, in late summer. Fortunately these are usually predicted a day or two before they hit so it's unlikely you will be taken unawares. Things usually cool down and dry up by the beginning of October.

Late October and November are the '**autumn-leaves-viewing**' months. If you don't mind the cold, this can be a wonderful time to visit. The sky is often clear so views are better and you have more chance of seeing Mt Fuji.

New Year is another major holiday period so even though the weather may be fine many places get crowded. The main areas for skiing (November/December to April/May) are north-eastern Honshu and Hokkaido.

For further information visit the Japan Meteorological Agency's website 🖥 www.jma.go.jp/jma.

Rail passes

The original and still the best-value rail pass available to visitors is the Japan Rail Pass, which covers the whole country. Apart from JR Central (JR Tokai; see box p14) all companies in the Japan Rail (JR) Group offer their own range of passes. These are available for shorter periods and are useful if you're intending to focus on a specific area. With some exceptions JR passes must be purchased before arrival in Japan. For details of other rail passes/special tickets see pp13-15.

Travel by rail becomes much more expensive without the rail pass, but there are still some discounts and bargain tickets to be had (see p79).

THE JAPAN RAIL PASS

The Japan Rail Pass is truly the bargain of the century. It entitles the pass holder to travel freely on almost all JR services, including most shinkansen (bullet trains) – the only exceptions are the Nozomi (Tokyo to Hakata) and Mizuho (Hakata to Kagoshima) – without needing to buy a ticket.

JR RAIL PASS PRICES

Japan Rail Pass

	Ordinary Class	Green Class
7-day	¥28,300 (£216/US$341)	¥37,800 (£289/US$455)
14-day	¥45,100 (£345/US$544)	¥61,200 (£467/US$737)
21-day	¥57,700 (£441/US$695)	¥79,600 (£608/US$958)

JR East

	Class	Adult	Youth (12-25)
5-day	Ordinary	¥20,000 (£152/US$241)	¥16,000 (£122/US$192)
	Green	¥28,000 (£213/US$337)	n/a
10-day	Ordinary	¥32,000 (£244/US$385)	¥25,000 (£190/US$301)
	Green	¥44,800 (£341/US$539)	n/a
4-day	Ordinary	¥20,000 (£152/US$241)	¥16,000 (£122/US$192)
(flexible)	Green	¥28,000 (£213/US$337)	n/a
3-day	Kanto Area Pass ¥8000 (£61/US$96)		n/a

JR West
Sanyo Area Pass

4-day	¥20,000 (£152/US$241)	8-day	¥30,000 (£228/US$361)

Kansai Area Pass/Kansai Wide Area Pass

1-day	¥2000 (£15/US$24)	3-day	¥5000 (£38/US$60)
2-day	¥4000 (£30/US$48)	4-day	¥6000 (£45/US$72)

4-day Kansai Wide Area Pass ¥7000 (£53/US$84)

JR Hokkaido

	Ordinary class	Green class
3-day	¥15,000 (£114/US$181)	¥21,500 (£164/US$259)
4-day (flexible)	¥19,500 (£149/US$235)	¥27,000 (£206/US$325)
5-day	¥19,500 (£149/US$235)	¥27,000 (£206/US$325)
7-day	¥22,000 (£168/US$265)	¥30,000 (£229/US$361

JR Kyushu

	Northern Kyushu Area Pass	All Kyushu Area Pass
3-day	¥7000 (£53/US$84)	¥14,000 (£107/US$168)
5-day	¥9000 (£69/US$108)	¥17,000 (£130/US$204)

JR Shikoku
All Shikoku Rail Pass

2-day	¥6300 (£47/US$78)	4-day	¥7900 (£60/US$95)
3-day	¥7200 (£54/US$87)	5-day	¥9700 (£75/US$117)

JR West, JR Shikoku & JR Kyushu
Sanyo-Shikoku-Kyushu Pass

5-day ¥25,000 (£190/US$300) for all Kyushu
5-day ¥22,000 (£168/US$265) for Northern Kyushu only

Note: Children aged 5 and under travel free providing they do not occupy a seat; those aged 6-11 pay half the adult rate. Prices are fixed in yen, but the charge is payable in local currency. The prices in brackets are for rough guidance only. The exact cost depends on the exchange rate in your home country at the time of purchase. It's worth shopping around as travel agencies apply different exchange rates.

PLANNING YOUR TRIP

JR has a dedicated website (💻 www.japanrailpass.net) which provides up-to-date information about the Japan Rail Pass and all regional passes.

Who can use the pass?

The rail pass can be used by any non-Japanese tourist visiting Japan under 'temporary visitor' status. Some Japanese nationals not residing in Japan can use a rail pass but other Japanese cannot. The pass cannot be used by anybody arriving in Japan for employment.

Buying the pass

The most important rule concerning use of the rail pass is that it **cannot be purchased in Japan**. It is sold, in the form of an Exchange Order, at authorised agents (see pp15-18) outside Japan.

First you need to decide whether you would like a **7-day**, **14-day** or **21-day** pass (see box opposite). The pass runs on consecutive days from the date you start to use it but there is no limit to the number of passes you can buy.

The next step is to choose which class you'd like to travel in. There are two types of rail pass: the **Ordinary Pass** is valid for standard-class rail travel, which is likely to be more than adequate for most people. Seats in Ordinary Class are very comfortable and have ample legroom; on some trains they are as good as first-class rail travel elsewhere in the world.

The **Green Pass** is for those wishing to travel in more style. Green-class carriages (known as 'Green Cars') offer wider seats and even more legroom; they also often include extras such as slippers, personal TVs, laptop power points as well as free tea and coffee. However, there are no Green Cars on most services on the Sanyo shinkansen line (Shin-Osaka to Hakata) or on Tsubame (Series 800) shinkansen (Hakata to Kagoshima-chuo) in Kyushu. Most limited expresses have Green Cars but local/rapid trains generally only have Ordinary Class.

REGIONAL JR RAIL PASSES

The regional JR rail passes outlined below can either be purchased before arrival in Japan (see pp15-18, or in some cases online through the company's website), or at the main airports and at some mainline stations in the relevant region and sometimes in other regions. For most passes you need to have a 'temporary visitor' stamp in your passport. Every now and then the companies introduce special promotional passes/tickets so check also on their websites.

One of the advantages of a regional rail pass is that some allow travel on trains not covered by the Japan Rail Pass, such as the Nozomi from Shin-Osaka to Hakata (JR West Sanyo Area Pass and Sanyo-Shikoku-Kyushu Pass) and Mizuho (JR Kyushu Pass and Sanyo-Shikoku-Kyushu Pass). (The Nozomi between Tokyo and Kyoto/Shin-Osaka cannot be used with any rail pass.)

JR East

The **JR East Pass** (see box opposite) is valid for travel on the JR East network, which extends north and east of Tokyo and includes the route around Tohoku (see pp267-300) as far as the northern tip of Honshu, but does not include Hokkaido. The pass is also valid on JR services to some of the places covered

PLANNING YOUR TRIP

> ❏ **JR Central**
> JR Central (JR Tokai), which operates the Tokaido shinkansen line between Tokyo and Shin-Osaka, is the only JR company not to offer a rail pass. However, it does offer a wide range of shinkansen tour packages, from ¥21,000, including to Kyoto and Fuji, as well of course in Tokyo. Some of the packages include accommodation (three or five nights) but some are for travel only; the e-vouchers for these must be bought before arriving in Japan. For further details see 🖳 english.jr-central.co.jp/shinkansen).

in the Central Honshu section, such as Nagano and Matsumoto, as well as on JR services in the Tokyo metropolitan area (including the hot-spring resort of Atami) and on the Narita Express (N'EX) train from Narita airport and Tokyo Monorail from Haneda airport. Passes are available in **5-** and **10-day** varieties, or the **flexible 4-day** ticket is valid for any four days within one month from the first date of use. The pass is an especially good deal if you're aged between 12 and 25 because there is a youth rate.

JR East's newest pass is a 3-day **Kanto Area Pass** (see box p12) permitting unlimited travel on JR East's shinkansen (except the Hayabusa) and limited express services in the designated area as well as on some private lines. The designated area includes Nikko, Karuizawa, the Fuji/Lake Kawaguchi area, the Izu peninsula, Narita and Haneda airports, and the Tokyo metropolitan area.

For more details see 🖳 www.jreast.co.jp; for itinerary suggestions see p23.

JR West

(See also box p12) JR West's **Sanyo Area Pass** (4-day or 8-day) is valid only for stops on the Sanyo line between Shin-Osaka and Hakata (Kyushu). The pass permits travel on all shinkansen services on this route (including the Nozomi) as well as local trains, the JR ferry service to Miyajima, and trains from Kansai Airport to Osaka. It is **not** valid for journeys to Kyoto.

The **Kansai Area Pass** is useful if you're spending only a few days in and around Kyoto and plan to make a couple of short excursions. It covers travel on local trains only between Kyoto, Osaka, Kobe, Nara, Himeji and Kansai Airport. It is also valid for non-reserved seats on the Haruka LEX to Kansai Airport. The pass is available for 1-4 days. To buy this pass, visit a JR travel centre at either Kansai Airport, Kyoto or Shin-Osaka station. The **Kansai Wide Area Pass** (4 days) is valid for unreserved seats on the Sanyo shinkansen (Shin-Osaka to Okayama) and several limited express trains in the Kansai region.

In partnership with JR Shikoku and JR Kyushu, JR West also offers 5-day **Sanyo-Shikoku-All Kyushu** and **Sanyo-Shikoku-Northern Kyushu** passes which permit travel on all Sanyo/Kyushu shinkansen (including Nozomi and Mizuho) as well as all JR rail services in Shikoku and Kyushu.

For more details see 🖳 www.westjr.co.jp; for itinerary suggestions see p23.

JR Kyushu

(See also box p12) There are two main pass options for Kyushu: one is valid for JR services, including the shinkansen, in the **northern part of the island only** (including Nagasaki and Kumamoto), and the other covers the **whole island**.

Both passes can be used for travel on Mizuho services, which the Japan Rail Pass does not permit. However, neither can be used on the Sanyo shinkansen linking Fukuoka/Hakata with mainland Honshu. There is no Green Car pass.

See opposite re the Sanyo-Shikoku-All Kyushu/Northern Kyushu passes.

For more details see 🖥 www.jrkyushu.co.jp; for itinerary suggestions see p25.

JR Hokkaido

(See also box p12) JR Hokkaido's passes are valid on all JR Hokkaido trains but not for the journey from Honshu to Hokkaido. As well as **3-, 5- and 7-day passes**, and a **flexible 4-day pass** that can be used on any 4 days in a 10-day period from the date of issue, JR Hokkaido also sells a **7-day Hokkaido Free Pass** (Hokkaido Furii Passu), which costs ¥25,500 (£197/US$310). The ticket – which, unlike the other rail passes, can be purchased by anyone – offers 7-day unlimited rides in the unreserved carriages of express trains and limited expresses as well as on some JR Hokkaido buses. You can make up to six seat reservations for free during the validity of the ticket. However, the pass cannot be used during peak holiday seasons: Golden Week (29thApril-5th May), Obon (mid August), and New Year. (See p79 for details of passes for people with student/working holiday visas).

See also 🖥 www.jrhokkaido.co.jp and for itinerary suggestions see p24.

JR Shikoku

(See also box p12) The **All Shikoku Rail Pass** permits unlimited travel (2-5 consecutive days on all JR Shikoku services (up to Kojima station on Honshu) as well as those provided by private rail companies (Kotoden, Iyotetsu, Tosaden, Tosa Kuroshio Railway and Asa Kaigan Railway). It can only be used by foreign visitors with temporary visitor status. However, it can either be bought before arriving in Japan or when in Shikoku.

See opposite for details of the passes JR Shikoku operates in partnership with JR West and JR Kyushu.

JR Shikoku also offer passes (three consecutive days only) for residents in Japan. The **Shikoku Free Kippu**, which costs ¥15,700 (£120/US$189), permits unlimited travel on all trains in Shikoku. However, if you are travelling in the month of your birthday you can get a **Birthday Kippu** for ¥10,000 (£76/US$120); one person travelling with you can also have this pass. The **Saihakken Kippu** for ¥5500 (£42/US$66) is for use on local trains only.

See also 🖥 www.jr-shikoku.co.jp and for itinerary suggestions see p25.

GETTING A RAIL PASS

The Japan Rail Pass has to be bought outside Japan but some regional passes can be bought on arrival.

The travel agencies listed below **are all authorised to sell the Japan Rail Pass** (some also sell the regional passes); most also book flights and accommodation, operate tours to Japan and can organise tailor-made holidays. If flying with either ANA or JAL it is possible to get a rail pass through the airline. The full list of authorised agents is available at 🖥 www.japanrailpass.net.

In the UK and Republic of Ireland

● **AWL Travel** (UK ☎ 0845-222 6200, Ireland ☎ 01-679 5340; 🖥 www.awlt. com) offer guided, self-guided and tailor-made tours.

● **Discover Japan** (☎ 020-3327 2780, 🖥 www.discover-japan.co.uk, London) arranges tours for the luxury end of the market.

● **Ffestiniog Travel** (☎ 01766-772030, 🖥 www.ffestiniogtravel.com, Gwynedd) operates a self-guided 3-week tour (with a 21-day Japan Rail Pass).

● **H.I.S. Europe Ltd** (☎ 020-7484 3337, 🖥 www.his-euro.co.uk, London) has branches all over Japan; sells the JR West, JR Hokkaido and JR Kyushu passes.

● **Inside Japan Tours** (☎ 0117-370 9751, 🖥 www.insidejapantours.com, Bristol) offers self-guided tours, guided adventures with a variety of themes such as anime and manga, and tailor-made tours. It also sells the JR East, JR West Sanyo, JR Kyushu and JR Hokkaido passes.

● **International Rail** (☎ 0871-231 0790, 🖥 www.internationalrail.com) sells the JR East pass and the JR West Sanyo and Kansai area passes.

● **Into Japan Specialist Tours** (☎ 01865-841443, 🖥 www.intojapan.co.uk, Oxon) has an office in Japan and will meet you at the airport and help you orientate. They offer fully escorted (luxury) tours, which coincide with major festivals, a unique In the footsteps of the Samurai tour as well as tailor-made tours which come with a rail pass.

● **Japan Journeys** (☎ 020-7766 5367, 🖥 www.japanjourneys.co.uk; London) arranges special-interest tours such as manga, bonsai, gardens of Japan.

● **Japan Travel Centre** (☎ 020-7611 0150, 🖥 www.japantravel.co.uk; London) offers a variety of tours. Their 11-day Japan Rail Pass Plus Tour includes flights, hotels and a 7-day Japan Rail Pass.

● **JRPass** (🖥 www.jrpass.com) is an internet-based agency with a very useful travel tips section, videos and a forum.

● **JTB** (Japan Travel Bureau; ☎ 020-8237 1605, 🖥 www.japanspecialist.co.uk, London) has a Japan Rail Pass starter pack which includes flights to Tokyo, two nights' accommodation and a 7-day pass; it also has branches all over Japan.

● **My Bus** (☎ 020-7976 1191, 🖥 www.mybus.co.uk, London) is part of the JTB group. It is authorised to sell the JR Kyushu and JR West passes as well as tickets for Studio Ghibli (see box p92).

● **The Travel Bureau** (☎ 08448-156212, 🖥 www.thetravelbureau.co.uk, Wolverhampton) See box p71.

● **Trailfinders** (🖥 www.trailfinders.com; has offices nationwide) operates a 14-day tour of Japan which requires a 14-day Japan Rail Pass.

● **Unique Japan Tours** (London ☎ 020-3239 2519, Dublin ☎ 01-678 7008; 🖥 www.uniquejapantours.com) arranges small-group tours as well as tailor-made and self-guided tours, most of which include the Japan Rail Pass.

In continental Europe

● **Austria** H.I.S. Travel (🖥 www.his-austria.at); JTB (🖥 www.jtbeurope.com).

● **Belgium** Japan P.I. Travel (🖥 www.japanpitravel.be).

● **Denmark** JTB (🖥 www.japanspecialisten.dk).

● **France   Destination Japon** (🖥 www.destinationjapon.fr); **H.I.S. International Tours** (🖥 www.his-tours.fr); **Jalpak** (🖥 www.jalpak.fr); **JRPass** (🖥 www.jrpass.com/fr); **JTB** (🖥 www.jtb-uni.com); **Nippon Travel Agency** (🖥 www.nta-france.com).

● **Germany   H.I.S.** (🖥 www.his-germany.de); **Jalpak** (🖥 www.jalpak.de); **JRPass** (🖥 www.jrpass.com/de); **JTB** (🖥 jtbgermany.com).

● **Italy   H.I.S** (🖥 giappone.hisitaly.com); **Jalpak** (🖥 www.jalpakroma.com); **JRPass** (🖥 www.jrpass.com/it; see opposite); **JTB** (🖥 www.jtbitaly.eu).

● **The Netherlands   JRPass** (🖥 www.jrpass.com/nl); **JTB** (🖥 www.japan tours.nl); **Tozai Travel** (🖥 www.tozai.nl).

● **Spain   JALTour** (🖥 www.jjtour.es); **JRPass** (🖥 www.jrpass.com/es; see opposite); **JTB** (🖥 www.jjpak.es).

● **Sweden   JTB** (🖥 www.japanspecialisten.nu).

● **Switzerland   Harry Kolb Travel** (🖥 www.harrykolb.ch); **H.I.S** (🖥 www. his-swiss.ch); **Japonica Travel** (🖥 www.japonica.ch).

In the USA
Some of the agencies have branches nationwide: where no phone number is given, check the website for details of your nearest office.
● **H.I.S** (🖥 his-usa.com/en) offers a range of tours and can arrange homestays.
● **IACE Travel** (☎ 1-877-489-4223, 🖥 www.iace-usa.com) operates escorted and unescorted tours.
● **Inside Japan Tours** (☎ 1-303-952-0184, 🖥 www.insidejapantours.com, Colorado). See opposite.
● **Japan For You** (🖥 www.japanforyou.com) offers many packages and tours including a World Heritage one.
● **Japan Rail Travel Network** (☎ 1-866-631-2785, 🖥 www.JapanRailTravel. com, Illinois) offers packages, tourist information and a photo gallery of Japanese trains.
● **JRPass** (🖥 www.jrpass.com). See opposite.
● **JTB USA** (🖥 www.jtbusa.com) arranges some festival-based tours and homestays and are authorised to sell tickets for Studio Ghibli (see box p92).
● **Nippon Travel Agency** (🖥 www.ntainbound.com) operates a wide range of tours.
● **Sankei Travel** (🖥 www.sankeitravel.com) offers several 1-/2-day tours.
● **TTA** (🖥 www.ttasfo.com) can tailor-make holidays.

In Canada
● **H.I.S** 🖥 www.his-canada.com/en) See opposite.
● **IACE Travel** (🖥 www.iace-canada.com/us) has branches in Vancouver (☎ 1-866-987-4223) and Toronto (☎ 1-800-931-4223) and can arrange homestays.
● **JTB International** (☎ 416-367-5824, 🖥 jtbi.ca/en) offers a Japan Explorer package (flight and rail pass) as well as other tours.

● **Kintetsu International Express** (☎ 905-670-8710, toll free ☎ 1-800-463-7723, 🖥 www.kiecan.com/toronto) has a fly'n rail package.

● **Nippon Travel** (🖥 www.nippontravel.ab.ca) has branches in Calgary (☎ 403-294-0694) and Edmonton (☎ 780-429-4545) and offers a wide range of tours.

● **Tokyo Tours Ltd** (☎ 905-305-1222, tollfree ☎ 1-877-TYO-TOUR, 🖥 www.tokyotours.ca) arrange tours for 1-16 days.

● **In Singapore**
Diners World Travel (🖥 www.dinerstravel.com.sg); **JTB** (🖥 www.jtb.com.sg).

● **In South Africa**
AWL Travel (☎ 011-268 0614, 🖥 www.awlt.com/southafrica).

In Australasia
● **Japan Package** (☎ 02-9264 7384, 🖥 www.japanpackage.com.au) offers packages for every interest and budget.

● **JTB Australia** (☎ 1300 739 330, 🖥 jtboi.com.au) and **JTB New Zealand** (☎ 0800 525 725, 🖥 www.jtboi.co.nz) sells all the rail passes, can book flights and accommodation and run some rail-based escorted tours.

● **Kintetsu International Express** (🖥 www.kintetsu.com.au) has branches in Sydney (☎ 02-8251-3300) and Melbourne (☎ 03-9654-3320).

● **Rail Plus** (Australia ☎ 03-9642 8644, New Zealand ☎ 09-377 5415, 🖥 www.railplus.com.au) sells all the rail passes and also operates a Guided Japan Train Enthusiasts Tour.

● **Sachi Tours/Nippon Travel Agency** (☎ 02-9275-9645, 🖥 www.nta.com.au) offer the JR West, JR Hokkaido and JR Kyushu passes.

● **Travel Japan by H.I.S** (Australia: ☎ 1800 802 552, 🖥 www.traveljapan.com.au; New Zealand (☎ 09-336 1336, 🖥 www.traveljapan.co.nz) sells all the rail passes and offers a wide variety of holidays.

EXCHANGE ORDERS

When you buy the national rail pass (and any regional pass bought outside Japan), what you actually receive is an exchange order, which you turn in for the real thing once in Japan.

Exchange orders are valid for three months from the date of issue, so only purchase one less than three months before you plan to start travelling by rail. When purchasing the exchange order you will receive a guide to using the pass.

How and where to turn in the exchange order
Once in Japan, take your exchange order to any **JR Travel Service Center** authorised to handle the Japan Rail Pass. The most obvious ones are at the JR stations in Narita/Haneda (Tokyo) and Kansai (Osaka) airports.

Major JR stations such as Tokyo, Nagoya, Kyoto, Osaka, Shin-Osaka, Sapporo and Hakata have travel service centres, but, except at peak holiday periods, it's often easiest to sort your pass out at the airport offices, even if you're not going to start travelling immediately. Staff there are used to handling rail-pass requests and are extremely efficient. However, be prepared for long queues at busy periods (March/April and November); staff may also only book journeys for that day in busy periods.

At the time of exchange you will need to complete a form giving the date you want to start your pass (this can be any day within one month of the day you turn in the exchange order) and other details. This form can be downloaded from the Japan Rail Pass website (see p15) so it is recommended you complete it before arriving at the office. JR staff will ask to see your passport to check that you have been admitted on 'temporary visitor' status. Once a date has been stamped on the rail pass it cannot be changed. JR will not replace lost passes.

HOW TO USE THE RAIL PASS

Once you've received the pass, all you do is show it whenever you pass a ticket barrier and JR staff will wave you through. Since the pass is not computerised it cannot be fed through automatic wickets, but there is always a manned gate on one side of the entrances/exits to the platforms.

⛩ Overcoming the language barrier

One of the biggest worries for first-time visitors to Japan is the language barrier. How difficult is it to make yourself understood and navigate your way around the country? The answer is that it's surprisingly easy; most Japanese can understand some English, even if not everybody speaks it.

You don't need to be able to read Japanese characters (*kanji*) to find your way around; **station names** are written in English on every platform, and on-board

announcements are made in English on all shinkansen and many limited express trains and even on local trains in tourist areas; the vast majority of hotels and ryokan have their names written in English outside, and in most towns and cities, road signs and street names are in both Japanese and English. However, it's always useful to have the name of the place you're heading for written on a piece of paper, so you can show it to taxi drivers or passers-by when asking for directions. Ask hotel reception or tourist information staff to write down in Japanese all the places you're planning to visit during the day.

If you're travelling with a smartphone or tablet you can make use of some very useful **Japanese-language apps**. Touchscreens allow you to draw kanji to find out their meaning as well as look for definitions in the normal way. The *Kotoba* app (free on iTunes) has a comprehensive dictionary of words and kanji. It is very easy to use and can be fascinating simply to type in random English words and see what kanji are used to make up the Japanese word. A similar app called *JED* is available for Android smartphones.

There are also various phrasebook apps with useful recorded **sound files**: try *Japanese Phrases & Lessons* (free on iTunes, or £6.99 with a much-expanded set of phrases).

For a list of railway-related words and phrases see p452.

Unless you are boarding a train which contains reserved carriages only (see p81), seat reservations are not necessary as you can just turn up for any train and sit in the unreserved carriages. However, on some trains, and at certain times of the day/year (see pp10-11), it's a good idea to make a reservation in order to guarantee a seat and avoid the hassle of having to find one, especially if you are not getting on at the first station. Since rail-pass holders can make any number of seat reservations for free (see pp80-1 for details) it's worth doing so in any case.

A few JR trains run on sections of track owned by private companies and rail-pass holders are supposed to pay a supplement to travel on these sections. In practice you will only have to pay if a conductor is checking tickets at the time the train is running along the non-JR track. Where relevant, this is highlighted in the route descriptions.

Suggested itineraries

With such a vast network of rail services, one of the hardest tasks in planning a trip to Japan is working out how much you can fit in. **One week** is really too short to attempt anything more than a quick shuttle between Kyoto and Tokyo, with perhaps a day trip to Nara or Hiroshima. To get anything like a sense of what the country is really about, and to give yourself time to get over jet lag and/or culture shock, plan for at least **two** but preferably **three** weeks.

The following itineraries are neither prescriptive nor are they intended to be the last word on rail travel in Japan. Their purpose is to give a flavour of what can be accomplished. When planning an itinerary it is worth choosing certain cities as a base and doing side trips from there rather than moving on every night. See also pp65-6.

GENERAL ITINERARIES

The following general itineraries are for holders of **7-, 14- and 21-day Japan Rail Passes** and do not include days before/after the rail pass is used.

Seven-day itinerary: the classic route
● **Day 1** Spend the morning in **Tokyo**, Japan's dynamic capital, then go north to **Nikko**, home to the opulent Toshogu Shrine, for the night.
● **Day 2** Spend the morning in Nikko and then return to Tokyo and take the shinkansen west to **Kyoto**, Japan's ancient capital and known for its temples.
● **Day 3** Spend the day and night in Kyoto.
● **Day 4** Pick up the shinkansen to **Hiroshima** and visit the Peace Memorial Park, perhaps stopping along the way for half a day in **Okayama** where you can see Korakuen, one of Japan's 'three great gardens'. Overnight in Hiroshima.
● **Day 5** Take a Sanyo line train to Miyajima-guchi, then transfer to the JR ferry for **Miyajima Island** famed for its scenic beauty, Itsukushima shrine and for the

torii gate that rises out of the sea. Return to Hiroshima and then go by shinkansen to Shin-Osaka (**Osaka**) for the night.

● **Day 6** Take a shinkansen east to Mishima to see some of the **Hakone region** (Mt Fuji and Lake Ashi) and then continue on to Tokyo for the night.

● **Day 7** Spend the day in Tokyo, or have a day trip to **Kamakura** to see the second largest statue of a Buddha in Japan.

Seven-day itinerary: off the beaten track

● **Day 1** Take a shinkansen from **Tokyo** to Sendai and then transfer to a local train to visit **Matsushima**, one of Japan's most famous scenic spots. Return to Sendai and continue to Ichinoseki for the night.

● **Day 2** Hop on a train to **Hiraizumi**, a compact town with some historic temples in scenic surroundings. Return to Ichinoseki for the night.

● **Day 3** Take a shinkansen back to Tokyo and then transfer to the Asama (Nagano) shinkansen and go to Nagano for the night.

● **Day 4** Pick up the Wide View Shinano LEX to Nagoya and stop off at **Narai**, one of the traditional post towns in the Kiso Valley. Continue on to Nagiso and then take a bus to **Tsumago**, another former post town, for the night.

● **Day 5** Walk to **Magome**, along the path used in the past to go between Kyoto and Edo (now Tokyo), and then pick up a bus to Nakatsugawa, or return to Nagiso and take the train to Nagoya from there. Spend the night in Nagoya.

● **Day 6** Pick up a Kodama shinkansen as far as Kakegawa. Transfer to the conventional JR Tokaido line to Kanaya for a side trip on the **Oigawa steam railway**. Return to Kakegawa, reconnect with the shinkansen and overnight in **Tokyo**.

● **Day 7** Have a day trip to **Narita Town** to experience the Goma (Sacred Fire), ceremony at Naritasan Shinsho-ji.

Fourteen-day itinerary: into the mountains and along the coast

● **Day 1** From **Tokyo**, Japan's dynamic capital, go north to **Nikko**, home to the opulent Toshogu Shrine, for the night.

● **Day 2** Spend the morning in Nikko and then return to Tokyo and take the Asama shinkansen to **Nagano** and spend the night there.

● **Day 3** After a dawn visit to **Zenko-ji temple**, take the Shinano LEX to **Matsumoto**, site of one of Japan's best-preserved castles. Overnight here.

● **Day 4** On the Shinano again, continue south to Shiojiri and change to a local train to reach the old post town of **Narai**. By late afternoon, carry on to **Nagiso**, from where it's a short bus ride to **Tsumago**, another post town where a number of traditional inns cater for the weary (rail) traveller.

● **Day 5** After an early morning wander around Tsumago, return to Nagiso and continue south to Nagoya. Then take a shinkansen to **Kyoto** for the night.

● **Day 6** Spend the day in and around Kyoto, Japan's ancient capital. Take in a couple of the city's famous sights or follow one of the suggested side trips by rail from the city.

● **Day 7** Spend a second day in Kyoto or take the train to nearby **Nara**, and visit its deer park and Todai-ji, which houses Japan's largest statue of the Buddha. Overnight in Kyoto or Nara.

● **Day 8** Spend another day in Kyoto or make the brief hop by shinkansen to **Osaka**. Though a city of commerce rather than tourism, Osaka is worth a visit; theme-park enthusiasts will enjoy **Universal Studios Japan**. Overnight in Kyoto or in Osaka/Shin-Osaka.

● **Day 9** Hop back on the shinkansen and spend some time in **Himeji**, fêted for its picture-postcard castle (a visit is recommended even though restoration work is going on until 2015). Continue by shinkansen to **Okayama** for the night.

● **Day 10** Early morning is the best time to visit Okayama Castle and **Korakuen** the city's famous garden. In the afternoon pick up a westbound shinkansen and alight in **Hiroshima**. Overnight here.

● **Day 11** Take a Sanyo line train to Miyajima-guchi, then transfer to the JR ferry to reach **Miyajima Island** famed for its scenic beauty, Itsukushima shrine and for the torii gate that rises out of the sea. Then return to Hiroshima.

● **Day 12** Pick up a westbound shinkansen to **Hakata** (Fukuoka) in Kyushu and then transfer to a Kamome LEX train to Nagasaki; overnight there.

● **Day 13** Spend the day in **Nagasaki**, a beautiful port city but probably better known as the location for the dropping of the second atomic bomb in 1945.

● **Day 14** Finally retrace your steps by riding the shinkansen all the way back to **Tokyo** (you'll have to change at Okayama or Shin-Osaka), covering a distance of 1175km in just over six hours.

Itinerary for a 21-day pass: to Kyushu, Shikoku or Tohoku
Make the most of a 21-day rail pass by combining the 14-day itinerary outlined above with a week focusing on one of the regions described below.

The 14-day itinerary gets you to Nagasaki on Day 13 so you're perfectly placed to continue with a third week of travel around **Kyushu** (see p25). If you prefer to spend the extra week exploring the island of **Shikoku** (see p25), the starting point is Okayama (reached on Day 9 of the 14-day itinerary). Another option would be to return to Tokyo (as on Day 14) and then continue north and explore the **Tohoku** region (see opposite).

Alternatively, consider the three-week itinerary (see box below) followed by a couple of readers.

❏ **A 21-day itinerary including hot springs, Kyoto and a mountain temple**
Using a 21-day Japan Rail Pass and the Hakone Freepass we started our holiday in **Tokyo** and visited Shinjuku, the Meiji Shrine and Ueno, **Yokohama** and **Kamakura**. We then had two nights at a ryokan in **Takaragawa-onsen** (wonderful hot springs and forest/river walks) and one night in **Okayama** before continuing to **Nagasaki** for two nights. Back east to **Kyoto** for five nights (we would have been happy to stay even longer) and then on to **Koya-san**, a mountain retreat, for two nights in Jofukuin Temple. This enabled us to experience *shojin ryori*, the delicious vegetarian food associated with Buddhist temples. From Koya-san we went to Odawara and then used the Hakone Freepass to explore the **Hakone/Mt Fuji region** and had a night in Moto-Hakone, on the shores of Lake Ashi. We then moved on to **Nikko** for two nights before returning to Tokyo from where we had a fantastic day trip to **Narita**. A great way to end the trip.
Jill Rowe and Roderick Leslie

REGIONAL RAIL PASS ITINERARIES

The following itineraries are designed to be used with the various regional rail passes (see pp13-15) but can also be followed with the Japan Rail Pass. If you buy a 5-day JR Sanyo-Shikoku-Kyushu Pass (see box p12 & p14) you can plan your itinerary using those outlined below for JR West, JR Kyushu and JR Shikoku.

PLANNING YOUR TRIP

JR East Pass: Tohoku (North-eastern Honshu) highlights

This itinerary is for a 10-day pass (see pp13-14); recommended stops for a 5-day pass are Nikko, Matsushima (or Sendai), Kakunodate (or Morioka), and Hirosaki or Aomori; for a 4-day pass Tokyo, Nikko, Kakunodate and Hirosaki; and for a 3-day Kanto Area Pass are Tokyo, Nikko and the Mt Fuji area. See the Tohoku (North-eastern Honshu) route guides (pp268-300) for full details.

● **Day 1** From Tokyo, take a shinkansen to **Utsunomiya** and change to the JR Nikko Line for **Nikko**, home to the opulent Toshogu Shrine; overnight here.

● **Day 2** Return to Utsunomiya and pick up the shinkansen to **Sendai**.

● **Day 3** Do a side trip to **Matsushima**, considered one of the most scenic spots in Japan. Return to Sendai and then pick up a shinkansen to Ichinoseki.

● **Day 4** Have a day trip to the temple town of **Hiraizumi**, a compact town with some historic temples in scenic surroundings; return to Ichinoseki for the night.

● **Day 5** Take an Akita shinkansen to **Kakunodate**, a former samurai town, for the day and return to Morioka for the night.

● **Day 6** Hop back on the shinkansen to Shin-Aomori. Spend the day and the night in **Aomori**, Honshu's northernmost city.

● **Day 7** Take a train to **Hirosaki**, a castle town but also worth visiting for the Edo-period garden. Stay in Hirosaki.

● **Day 8** If here at a weekend or in a holiday period try to allow time to do the alternative route to Akita on the Gono Line, or spend another day in Hirosaki.

● **Day 9** From Akita pick up the Inaho LEX which runs south to Niigata. Possible stops include **Sakata**, with its art museum and traditional garden, and **Tsuruoka**, access point for the Dewa Sanzan mountains. Overnight in Niigata.

● **Day 10** Spend the morning in **Niigata** visiting Hakusan shrine and Enkikan, a merchant's house, before completing the rail loop around north-eastern Japan by picking up a Joetsu shinkansen back to Tokyo.

JR West Pass: Western Honshu highlights

This itinerary is for an 8-day Sanyo Area pass (see p14). Recommended stops for a 4-day pass are Osaka, Hiroshima, Okayama and Kobe. See the Western Honshu route guides (pp226-41) for full details.

● **Day 1** Starting in **Osaka** (Shin-Osaka), take a westbound shinkansen as far as **Hiroshima**. Overnight here.

● **Day 2** Spend day (and night) in Hiroshima or go to **Miyajima**.

● **Day 3** In the afternoon continue west to **Shin-Yamaguchi**, access point for an excursion across Honshu. Overnight here.

● **Day 4** Take the Super Oki LEX (at weekends and in summer a steam locomotive operates on this route) which runs inland along the Yamaguchi line to the picturesque town of **Tsuwano**; overnight here.

‘Stamping’ around Japan

‘Stamp’ collecting is a popular pastime in Japan, though the most popular stamps are not of the postage kind. Virtually every tourist attraction here has its own stamp and ink pad at the entrance. Some towns organise seasonal ‘stamp rallies’, when tourists are invited to follow a trail from one attraction to another, collecting stamps as they go. Small souvenir prizes are sometimes doled out to those who completely fill their ‘stamp cards’ (a gesture of thanks for contributing to the local tourism industry). In Japan, it’s almost as if you only know you’ve really been somewhere when you can bring back the stamp to prove it.

Stamps are particularly popular on the railway. JR East has created a 77-station stamp series for all the stations in the Tokyo metropolitan area. Even the tiniest rural station will more than likely have a stamp in the waiting room or by the ticket desk. Paper is not provided so pack a blank notebook in your luggage, try to forget your image of the nerdy stamp collector, and by collecting stamps as you go you’ll have an instant souvenir of your rail trip around Japan, as well as a useful record of your personal itinerary.

● **Day 5** From Tsuwano the Super Oki heads east following the San-in coast to **Matsue**, known as the ‘city of water’. Two possible stops en route are the aquarium in **Hashi**, and **Nima**, site of the unusual Sand Museum. Night in Matsue.

● **Day 6** Spend day exploring Matsue before taking a sunset cruise around **Lake Shinji**. Spend a second night in Matsue.

● **Day 7** From Matsue, pick up the Super Yakumo LEX which cuts across Honshu to **Okayama** and spend the night here.

● **Day 8** Spend last day in Osaka.

JR Hokkaido Pass: Hokkaido highlights

The itinerary below is for a 7-day pass (see p15); recommended stops for a 5-day pass are Sapporo, Hakodate, Onuma-koen, Otaru and Asahikawa, for a 4-day pass are Sapporo, Otaru, Hakodate and Asahikawa, and for a 3-day pass are Sapporo, Hakodate and Otaru. See the Hokkaido route guides (pp317-42) for full details.

● **Day 1** Explore **Hakodate**, a port town with a wonderful morning market.

● **Day 2** Spend additional day and night in Hakodate, or take a train to **Onuma-koen** for the night and to visit the lakes which overlook Mt Komagatake.

● **Day 3** From Hakodate/Onuma-koen go to Oshamambe and then take a local train via **Niseko**, a centre for outdoor sports including skiing, to **Otaru**, a port town with a picturesque setting and lovely canals and old stone warehouses.

● **Day 4** Take a train to **Sapporo**, known for its snow festival and clock tower, and spend the day and night there.

● **Day 5** Get an early train to **Asahikawa** and either spend the day there visiting the zoo or make an excursion to **Asahidake** in Daisetsuzan National Park.

● **Day 6** Head to **Furano**, known in winter for its snow and in summer for the fields of lavender, and spend the night there.

● **Day 7** Return to Sapporo/Hakodate via Shintoku.

JR Kyushu Pass: Kyushu highlights

The itinerary below is for a 5-day pass (see pp14-15); recommended stops for a 3-day pass are Nagasaki and Kumamoto or Kagoshima. See the Kyushu route guides (pp361-80) for full details.

● **Day 1** Starting from Kyushu's capital, **Fukuoka/Hakata**, take the Kamome LEX west to **Nagasaki**, a beautiful port city but probably better known as the location for the dropping of the second atomic bomb in 1945.

● **Day 2** Spend the morning in Nagasaki. Back-track towards Fukuoka/Hakata as far as Shin-Tosu, and pick up a Tsubame shinkansen to **Kumamoto**. Visit Kumamoto Castle and stay overnight.

● **Day 3** Spend the day in Kumamoto or take a day trip to **Kagoshima**, access point for both the island of **Sakurajima**, with its active volcano, and **Ibusuki** for its natural hot-sand bath. Return to Kumamoto for the night.

● **Day 4** Head inland to the **Aso tableland**. Peer over the side of this active volcano before continuing on to **Oita** for the night.

● **Day 5** Take a Nichirin LEX back to Hakata/Fukuoka.

All Shikoku Pass: Shikoku highlights

The itinerary below is for a 5-day All Shikoku Pass. Recommended stops with a 4-day pass are Takamatsu, Tokushima, Kochi & Matsuyama, with a 3-day pass, or any of the Shikoku Kippu (see p15) passes, Takamatsu, Tokushima & Matsuyama, and with a 2-day pass Takamatsu & Matsuyama. Details of all routes and sights are given in the Shikoku route guides (pp412-27).

● **Day 1** At **Takamatsu** visit the magnificent Ritsurin-koen,

● **Day 2** Travel to the nearby roof-top plateau of **Yashima**, and **Tokushima**, known for its summer dance festival, with a side trip to the whirlpools at **Naruto**.

● **Day 3** Go to Awa-Ikeda, change trains and head for **Oboke Gorge**. Spend the night in **Kochi** and look down on the city from its 17th-century castle.

● **Day 4** At Kubokawa transfer to the scenic Yodo line for the bull-fighting city of **Uwajima**. Head to **Uchiko**, with its well-preserved old quarter and Noh theatre.

● **Day 5** Continue to **Matsuyama**; be sure to go to **Dogo-onsen** to relax in the historic hot springs before completing the rail circuit back to Takamatsu.

Before you go

BOOKING A FLIGHT

Most people will fly to Japan. However, it is possible to take ferries from ports in China and South Korea to Osaka, Kobe, Fukuoka and Shimonoseki.

Flights to Japan can be booked direct through an airline (see box p26), through a travel agency (see pp16-18), or online through discounted ticket outlets such as: Cheap Flights (🖥 www.cheapflights.com), Expedia (🖥 www.expedia.com) or Opodo (🖥 www.opodo.com). Discounted fares for students are also offered through STA Travel (🖥 www.statravel.com/worldwide.htm)

❏ **Airlines flying to Japan**

Airlines that fly to more than one destination in Japan offer the possibility of flying into, say, Narita (Tokyo; NRT; see p100) or Haneda (Tokyo; HND; see p101) and out of Kansai (Osaka; KIX; see p117). Some of the airlines listed below have codeshare flights to Japan and do not fly directly there themselves.

Some of the listed airlines also fly to Nagoya (Central Japan International Airport; 🖥 www.centrair.jp/en), Hiroshima (🖥 www.hij.airport.jp), Sapporo (New Chitose Airport; 🖥 www.new-chitose-airport.jp), Sendai (🖥 www.sdj-airport.com) and Fukuoka (🖥 www.fuk-ab.co.jp) as well as other destinations. At the time of research there were no direct international flights to the island of Shikoku.

Airlines with flights to Japan include: **Aeroflot** (NRT; 🖥 www.aeroflot.com); **Air Asia** (KIX, HND; 🖥 www.airasia.com); **Air Calédonie** (NRT, KIX; 🖥 www.aircalin.nc); **Air Canada** (NRT; 🖥 www.aircanada.com); **Air China** (NRT, KIX, HND; 🖥 www.airchina.com.cn/en); **Air France** (NRT, KIX; 🖥 www.airfrance.com); **Air India** (NRT, KIX; 🖥 www.airindia.com); **Air New Zealand** (NRT, KIX; 🖥 www.airnewzealand.com); **Alitalia** (NRT, KIX; 🖥 www.alitalia.com); **All Nippon Airways/ANA** (NRT, KIX, HND; 🖥 www.anaskyweb.com); **American Airlines** (NRT, KIX, HND; 🖥 www.aa.com); **Asiana Airlines** (NRT, KIX, HND; 🖥 us.fly asiana.com); **Austrian Airlines** (NRT; 🖥 www.aua.com); **British Airways** (NRT, HND; 🖥 www.britishairways.com); **Cathay Pacific** (NRT, KIX, HND; 🖥 www.cathaypacific.com); **China Airlines** (NRT, KIX, HND; 🖥 www.china-airlines.com); **China Eastern Airlines** (KIX, HND; 🖥 en.ceair.com); **Continental** (NRT, KIX; 🖥 www.continental.com); **Delta** (NRT, KIX, HND; 🖥 www.delta.com); **Egypt Air** (NRT, KIX; 🖥 www.egyptair.com.eg); **Emirates** (NRT, KIX; 🖥 www.emirates.com); **EVA Air** (NRT, KIX, HND; 🖥 www.evaair.com); **Finnair** (NRT, KIX; 🖥 www.finnair.com); **Garuda Indonesia** (NRT, KIX; 🖥 www.garuda-indonesia.com); **Hawaiian Airlines** (KIX, HND; 🖥 www.hawaiianair.com); **Hong Kong Airlines** (NRT, KIX; 🖥 www.hkairlines.com); **Japan Airlines/JAL** (NRT, KIX, HND; 🖥 www.jal.com); **Jet Airways** (NRT; 🖥 www.jetairways.com); **KLM** (NRT, KIX; 🖥 www.klm.com); **Korean Air** (NRT, KIX, HND; 🖥 www.koreanair.com); **Lufthansa** (NRT, KIX; 🖥 www.lufthansa.com); **Malaysia Airlines** (NRT, KIX, HND; 🖥 www.malaysiaairlines.com); **Peach** (KIX; 🖥 www.flypeach.com); **Qantas** (NRT, KIX; 🖥 www.qantas.com); **Qatar Airways** (NRT, KIX; 🖥 www.qatarairways.com); **SAS** (NRT; 🖥 www.flysas.com); **Singapore Airlines** (NRT, KIX, HND; 🖥 www.singaporeair.com); **South African Airways** (NRT, KIX; 🖥 www.flysaa.com); **Swiss Air** (NRT; 🖥 www.swiss.com); **Thai Airways** (NRT, KIX, HND; 🖥 www.thaiair.com); **United** (NRT, KIX; 🖥 www.united.com); **US Air** (NRT, KIX; 🖥 www.usairways.com); **Virgin Atlantic** (NRT; 🖥 www.virgin-atlantic.com).

and Travel CUTS (🖥 www.travelcuts.com). In 2012, Peach (Pan-Asian, Energetic, Affordable, Cute & Cool, Happy; 🖥 www.flypeach.com) started Japan's first international budget flights from its base at Kansai Airport. Other low-cost airlines with international services to Japan are Jet Star (🖥 www.jetstar.com) and AirAsia (🖥 www.airasia.com).

PASSPORTS AND VISAS

All visitors to Japan must have a passport that's valid for at least six months from the date of entry to Japan. If visiting for the purposes of tourism, citizens of the following countries do not need to apply for a visa and can stay in Japan for up to 90 days under the 'reciprocal visa exemption' scheme: Australia, Austria, Belgium, Canada, France, Germany, Ireland, Italy, Netherlands, New Zealand, Singapore, Spain, Switzerland, UK, USA. Many other countries come under the same scheme, but exceptions include citizens of Hong Kong and Malaysia, who need to apply for a tourist visa from the Japanese embassy in their home country.

Citizens of Austria, Germany, Ireland, Switzerland and the UK can apply for a further 90-day extension while in Japan.

Visa requirements change periodically, so before making travel arrangements check with the Japanese embassy in your home country.

A complete list of Japanese embassies and consulates can be found at 🖥 www. mofa.go.jp. See pp42-3 for details of arrival procedures.

❏ TOURIST INFORMATION

The best source of tourist information prior to arrival in Japan is the **Japan National Tourist Organization** (🖥 www.jnto.go.jp), which has a comprehensive website and a YouTube channel (🖥 www.youtube.com/visitjapan). JNTO's worldwide offices are information centres only – they do not sell any tickets or rail passes.

The main thing JNTO produces which isn't available online is a very useful map of Japan. However, your local branch will send you one, and other brochures, on request.

Branches include: **Australia** (☎ 02-9279 2177, 🖥 www.jnto.org.au); **Canada** (☎ 416-366-7140, 🖥 www.ilovejapan.ca/en); **China** (Beijing ☎ 010-5971 2736, Shanghai ☎ 021-5466 2808, 🖥 www.welcome2japan.cn; Hong Kong ☎ 2968-5688, 🖥 www. welcome2japan.hk); **France** (☎ 01.42.96.20.29, 🖥 www.tourisme-japon.fr); **Germany** (☎ 069-20353, 🖥 www.jnto.de); **Korea** (☎ 02-777 8601, 🖥 www.welcome tojapan. or.kr); **Singapore** (☎ 6223-8205, 🖥 www.jnto.org.sg); **Thailand** (☎ 02-261-3525, 🖥 www.yokosojapan.org); **UK** (☎ 020-7398 5678, 🖥 www.seejapan.co.uk); **USA** (🖥 www.japantravelinfo.com); New York (☎ 212-757-5640) and Los Angeles (☎ 213-623-1952).

At the time of research the Canada (Toronto), UK (London) and USA (New York and Los Angeles) branches were open to visitors.

Other online sources of information

● 🖥 www.att-japan.net Extensive information for visitors and residents; also produces a quarterly magazine which is distributed to tourist information offices;

● 🖥 www.japanvisitor.com Information about all aspects of travelling – and living and working – in Japan;

● 🖥 www.japan-guide.com Comprehensive tourist information and a lively forum;

● 🖥 japanican.com A JTB Group website which is primarily an accommodation-and tour-booking site but also has various travel guides;

● 🖥 jin.jcic.or.jp Has information on fashion, anime and entertainment plus some general travel guides;

● 🖥 www.japantrends.com A fascinating website with links to articles about all the new trends and technological developments in Japan;

● 🖥 www.japan-zone.com Features pages on popular and traditional culture as well as practical information and a forum;

● 🖥 www.newsonjapan.com Compiles news stories on Japan from both the Japanese and international press and gives a great insight into what is current and contemporary.

HEALTH AND INSURANCE

No vaccination or health certificate is required to enter the country (except for those arriving from a yellow fever zone) and there's no need to worry about diseases such as malaria, which are not endemic in Japan.

Unless specified (such as on trains), tap water is safe to drink everywhere in Japan. However, bottled water is readily available in convenience stores (sparkling/carbonated water is harder to find than still) and from vending machines.

Don't arrive in Japan without a comprehensive travel insurance policy. Japanese hospitals invariably offer high standards of care and most doctors speak English, but diagnosis, treatment and prescriptions can be prohibitively expensive.

If you're on medication, bring a copy of your prescription. This may be needed if Customs inspect your bags but will also be useful if you need a repeat prescription. Note that many international drugs are sold under different brand names in Japan.

WHAT TO TAKE

The best advice is to **pack as little as possible**. Travelling light makes life much easier when you are getting on and off lots of trains; it also means you'll have no problem fitting your luggage into a locker (see p82) at the station. Lifts and/or escalators are available at most stations, though not at all the smaller ones.

If planning to stay mostly in Japanese-style accommodation it's worth bringing **slip-on shoes** as you're expected to take your shoes off in the entrance hall. Guests walk around either in the slippers provided or, if these are too small, just in **socks** (pack a few pairs without holes!). Guests in most Japanese-style accommodation, as well as business hotels, are provided with a small towel which doubles as a flannel; if you prefer a large towel it might be better to bring one.

Nightwear is not essential as guests in most forms of accommodation, apart from hostels, are provided with a *yukata* (a cotton robe tied with a belt) that can be worn in bed and which is used as a dressing gown to go between your room and the bathroom. Yukata (and Japanese-style towels) can often be rented or purchased from the front desk if they are not provided.

Pack according to the season and the region in which you're likely to be travelling (see pp10-11). As a general rule, shorts and T-shirts are fine in the summer, though you'll probably need a sweater or two in the spring and autumn. Take warm clothes for the winter, especially if travelling in north-eastern Japan.

At any time of the year, it's worth packing **a few smart clothes** – older Japanese people in particular are generally well-dressed (even when on holiday themselves). If you forget anything, clothes and shoes are relatively cheap as long as you avoid the designer-label boutiques, but it's not always easy to find large sizes. **Don't bother packing an umbrella** as disposable ones are readily and cheaply available in convenience stores. Outdoor tourist attractions, as well as minshuku and ryokan, usually have a supply of umbrellas for visitors to borrow.

If you want an unusual souvenir of your trip, take a notebook (see box p24).

MONEY

Japan is a **cash-based economy** so when travelling around it's best to ensure you always have a supply of cash. Easiest access to cash is via the thousands of post office **ATMs** around the country, all of which accept foreign-issued debit cards (including Maestro and Visa) and have instructions in English.

Travellers' cheques (in ¥ or US$ only) are a useful way to carry money but ensure you cash them before heading off the beaten track. Also be prepared for a long wait when you go to a bank to exchange them.

Credit cards are accepted in most major tourist places but don't rely on this. Upmarket hotels tend to accept credit cards but cash is the preferred currency in hostels, minshuku, budget ryokan and business hotels. (See also pp56-7).

SUGGESTED READING

History
● Goto-Jones, Christopher *Modern Japan, A Very Short Introduction* (OUP, 2009) Covers the period from the early 1800s, when Japan started to open up, to the modern day – useful as a background read before you arrive.
● Henshall, Kenneth *A History of Japan: From Stone Age to Superpower* (Macmillan, 2012) Scholarly but very readable.
● Tames, Richard *A Traveller's History of Japan* (Interlink Publishing, 2008) A great, pocket-sized, book that's ideal to dip into as you travel around.

Travel narratives
● Booth, Alan *The Roads to Sata* (Kodansha, 1997) The late Alan Booth walked the length of Japan, from Hokkaido to Kyushu, looking for beer. Equally absorbing is his *Looking for the Lost: Journeys Through a Vanishing Japan* (Kodansha, 1995), a series of travel narratives taking in parts of Japan that most foreigners never see.
● Bouvier, Nicholas *Japan Chronicles* (Eland 2008) The chronicles are based on three decades (1950s-70s) of living and travelling in Japan.
● Carey, Patrick *Rediscovering the Old Tokaido: In the footsteps of Hiroshige* (Global Oriental, 2000) The story of a nostalgic journey on foot along what remains of the road that linked Edo and Kyoto in the days before the Tokaido railway line.
● Ferguson, Will *Hokkaido Highway Blues* (Canongate, 2003) Ferguson travels from southern Kyushu north to Hokkaido following the path of the cherry blossom; an irreverent account of life on the open road.
● Ingrams, Elizabeth *Japan Through Writers' Eyes* (Eland, 2009) Arranged according to place and includes extracts from travellers' experience through a wide variety of historical periods.

Life in Japan (non-fiction)
● Dalby, Liza *Geisha* (Vintage, 2000) Based on Dalby's year as a geisha in the 1970s. She was subsequently a consultant on the film adaptation of *Memoirs of a Geisha* (see p30).

PLANNING YOUR TRIP

● Downer, Lesley *Geisha: The Secret History of a Vanishing World* (Headline, 2001) This is a personal account of the months Downer spent in the Gion tea houses, befriending the *mama-san* who hold the purse strings and manage the careers of trainee geisha. She gets closer than any commentator to a revelation of life behind the enigmatic smiles and painted faces of geisha in Kyoto.

● Garcia, Hector *A Geek in Japan: Discovering the Land of Manga, Anime, Zen and the Tea Ceremony* (Tuttle Shokai, 2011) An insight into life in contemporary Japan, with plenty of photos and illustrations.

● Hearn, Lafcadio *Kokoro: Hints and Echoes of Japanese Inner Life* (Tuttle, 2011) The best introduction to Irish writer Lafcadio Hearn's experiences of life in Meiji-era Japan (see p34).

● Kaji, S, Hama, N, and Rice, J *Xenophobe's Guide to the Japanese* (Oval Books, 2010) A pocket-sized humorous guide to what makes the Japanese tick.

● Murtagh, Niall *The Blue-Eyed Salaryman: From World Traveller to Lifer at Mitsubishi* (Profile Books, 2006) Amusing insight into what office life is like for a foreigner working in Japan.

Life in Japan (fiction)

● Downer, Lesley *The Last Concubine* (Corgi, 2009) A tale of Japan in the 1860s and the life of Sachi, a village girl, who becomes the last concubine of the reigning shogun.

● Golden, Arthur *Memoirs of a Geisha* (Vintage, 1998) Golden's novel about a trainee geisha's life has become a modern classic and a Hollywood blockbuster. Sayuri is born in a fishing village but she is sold to a Kyoto geisha house from where she rises to become one of the city's most famous and sought-after geisha.

● Mitchell, David *Number 9 Dream* (Sceptre, 2002) The British novelist, who taught English in Hiroshima for eight years, presents an extraordinary post-*Blade Runner* Japanese world which has been variously described as terrifying and exhilarating.

● Murakami, Ryu *In the Miso Soup* (Bloomsbury, 2005) A gritty, frightening story about life in the backstreets of Tokyo.

The railway

● Free, Dan *Early Japanese Railways 1853-1914: Engineering Triumphs That Transformed Meiji Japan* (Tuttle, 2009) A well-illustrated and detailed account of the railway's early days.

● Hood, Christopher *Shinkansen: From Bullet Train to Symbol of Modern Japan* (Routledge, 2006) A comprehensive and readable account of the history of the bullet train. See also 🖥 www.hood-online.co.uk/shinkansen.

Fauna of Japan
A useful website about the wildlife of Japan is 🖥 wildwatchjapan.com. Information includes a calendar guide as well as a regional guide. Mark Brazil, who lives in Hokkaido, also operates birding tours (🖥 www.birdingpaltours.com) in Japan and he is the author of *Birds of East Asia* (Helm/Princeton Field Guides, 2009), a comprehensive, well-illustrated guide.

JAPAN

Facts about the country

GEOGRAPHY

Japan is made up of over 3000 islands, a total land mass almost as large as the state of California. The four main islands are **Honshu**, the largest, followed by **Hokkaido**, the most northern and also the least populated, then **Kyushu**, the southernmost, and **Shikoku**. Stretching 3000km from north to south, the northernmost regions of Japan are subarctic, while the extreme south is subtropical.

Four-fifths of the land surface is mountainous and rural; most of the 127 million people who live on the four main islands are packed into the coastal plains. This has led to the development of so-called 'urban corridors', the longest of which, and perhaps the most densely inhabited in the world, is the Tokaido belt between Tokyo and Osaka.

Japan is a hotbed of **volcanic activity**; even world-famous Mt Fuji, which last erupted in 1707, is actively monitored as even though many don't think it will erupt again, if it did it could cause massive damage. Hokkaido in particular has several active volcanoes but there's no need to panic as the island's hiking routes and paths are always closed at the first sign of smoke. Sakurajima, off the coast of Kagoshima, in Kyushu is also active.

Earthquakes

Japan is located where the Eurasian and Pacific plates meet so is prone to earthquakes. The most powerful (8.9 on the Richter scale) since records began happened on 11th March 2011 off the north-east coast of Honshu and caused a devastating tsunami (see box p275).

Earthquakes, of course, are not seasonal, nor can they be accurately predicted. They are, however, a fact of life in Japan and most cities have an earthquake centre equipped with a simulator room where Japanese can prepare for any eventuality by experiencing the full force of the Richter scale. There are monitors all along the shinkansen tracks, which means that trains can stop within 70 seconds if signs of an earthquake are detected.

Minor quakes/tremors are very common but unless you're particularly sensitive you'll probably only hear about them the

To the butterfly in the sky
all buildings on the temple ground
are upside down
(BOSHA KAWABATA)

蝶の空七堂伽藍さかしまに

next day. In the very unlikely event you find yourself waking up to a sizeable quake, the best thing to do is to **get under something solid, such as a table**. Major quakes are extremely rare and not worth becoming paranoid about – they occur roughly once a century.

HISTORY

Space permits only a condensed 'bullet points' history of Japan. For recommended books on the history of Japan, see p29.

Birth of a nation: myth and reality

Nobody knows exactly when Japan was first inhabited by humans but estimates range from between 500,000 and 100,000 years ago. The **Jomon period**, named after a rope pattern found on the oldest form of pottery in the world, began around 10,000BC but the country was not unified until the 4th century AD, when the **Yamato dynasty** was established and the title of emperor first used.

A capital is established: 710-794

Up until the 7th century, tradition dictated that the capital was changed every time a new emperor ascended the throne. But in 710, the Imperial Court decided to settle in Nara, a city still proud that it was the capital of Japan and the home of seven emperors in just 77 years before the court was moved to Nagaoka in 784 and then to Kyoto in 794. The **Nara period** was marked by influences from China and the growing popularity of its imported religion, Buddhism. The main Chinese influence is visible today in Todai-ji: this temple boasts the largest wooden building in the world and contains Japan's biggest Buddha statue, a bronze image cast in 752. Religious riches and treasure aside, hunger and poverty were commonplace outside the Imperial Court, though there was worse to come in later centuries.

Flourishing of the arts but rivalry outside the court: 794-1185

Nara was soon overrun with Buddhist temples and Shinto shrines, and Emperor Kammu could no longer bear being closeted there. So a new capital was established, in 794, in Heian (present-day Kyoto), where it was to remain until 1868. A symbolic fresh start was assured by a complete reconstruction of the city on a grid layout.

Japan's most famous literary work, *The Tale of Genji* by Murasaki Shikibu, was written during the **Heian period**, as was *The Pillow Book*, a revealing account of life at the Imperial Court by a woman very much on the inside, lady-in-waiting Sei Shonagon. It was not just literature that flourished, but painting, sculpture and poetry; the emperor hosted outdoor parties at which guests would be invited to compose haiku over cups of sake.

Outside the walls of the Imperial Court, far from the parties and poetry gatherings, a new warrior class was emerging: the **samurai**. The bloodiest military campaign of all for national supremacy raged between two rival clans the Minamoto (also known as Genji) and the Taira (or Heike). The epic war, now steeped in as much legend as historical fact, finally climaxed in a decisive sea battle in 1185, and the Tairas were routed. But peace was short-lived and the feudal era had begun.

The first shogun: 1185-1333

The bloody corpses of the defeated Taira had hardly washed away before Minamoto no Yoritomo, victorious leader of the Minamoto clan, moved the capital to Kamakura and was sworn in as the country's first shogun. The Imperial Court remained in Kyoto but real power had shifted geographically and politically to the samurai. Government of the country remained in the hands of successive shoguns for the next 700 years, until the Meiji Restoration of 1868.

The popularity of Buddhism grew during the **Kamakura period**. The Zen sect in particular, with its emphasis on a life of simplicity and austerity, appealed to the warrior class, which had always been ill at ease with the effete world of Heian culture. Instead of ushering in a new era, Yoritomo's death in 1199 prompted his widow and her family to assume control. The political capital remained in Kamakura until 1333, when Emperor Go-Daigo succeeded in overthrowing the shogunate.

Eruption of civil war, West and East meet: 1336-1575

The Emperor's moment of triumph turned out to be unexpectedly brief. He was soon booted out of Kyoto by Takauji Ashikaga, the military turncoat who had defected from the Kamakura court in time to become the Emperor's right-hand military man and assist in the rebellion against the Kamakura shogunate. Rightly or wrongly expecting credit for this assistance and anticipating the title of shogun as due reward, Ashikaga was aggrieved when Go-Daigo completely overlooked him. Seeking revenge, Ashikaga forced Go-Daigo into mountain exile and appointed a new emperor, who was gracious enough to name him shogun.

The Golden and Silver pavilions, two of Kyoto's major tourist draws, were constructed as villas for the shoguns during this period. As in the Heian period, culture and arts took centre stage, with Noh theatre, the tea ceremony and flower arranging all being established in the latter half of the **Muromachi period**. But war was also becoming commonplace as rival feudal lords clashed over territory and isolated skirmishes spiralled into full-scale civil war.

As the nation fought with itself, Christianity made its first appearance in Japan when the missionary Francis Xavier sailed into Kagoshima in 1549, carrying with him enormous ambition: to convert emperor and shogun alike. He failed, but relations with the West developed further in Nagasaki, where the port was opened to trade with the Portuguese.

Reunification: 1575-1603

The long road to reunification began in 1568 when **Nobunaga Oda** descended on Kyoto. Nobunaga soon cemented his authority by building the first castle stronghold and setting a trend that was to be repeated by feudal lords all over Japan. Castles, each one grander and its defences safer than the last, became a must-have for every lord needing to prove his power over the people he ruled. Sadly, only a few original examples remain intact today, notably at Himeji and Matsumoto.

Nobunaga hardly had time to settle into his own castle before he was assassinated in 1582. His successor, **Hideyoshi Toyotomi**, picked up where Nobunaga had left off and continued with efforts to reunite the country, a task largely completed by 1590. Flushed with success at home, Hideyoshi rebranded himself as an international warrior during two ill-fated attempts to capture Korea. After his death, his son and heir, Hideyori, was swept aside by the warlord **Tokugawa Ieyasu**, who went on to establish his own government in Edo (present-day Tokyo).

Closing down on the outside world: 1603-1853

The Kamakura shogunate had shown itself open to attack from rival clans but Ieyasu and his successors tolerated no intruders. Some 300 feudal clans across Japan were forced to travel to Edo for regular audiences with the shogun. The expense and length of such journeys, nearly three centuries before the rail network would shuttle anyone to Tokyo within a day, ensured that feudal lords were never able to build up the power or finances to mount a challenge to the Tokugawa shogunate.

Strict laws of personal conduct were enforced and a social hierarchy developed with the shogun at the top and peasants and merchants at the bottom. Sandwiched in between were the samurai, though they too were restricted in movement and activity by their own strict code. In 1639, Japan suddenly closed all its ports to international trade, with the exception of a tiny Dutch enclave in Nagasaki. The policy of self-seclusion also prohibited all Japanese from leaving the country. Despite, or perhaps because of, the 'no vacancies' sign held up to the outside world, the **Edo period** was one of the most peaceful in Japanese history. Once again, the arts flourished, kabuki theatres opened and merchants traded in lacquerware and silk. But peace and prosperity at the price of national isolation could not last forever; by the middle of the 19th century, the feudal system was looking increasingly outdated. Not for much longer could the shogun keep the outside world at bay.

The era of modernisation: 1853 to the present

Commodore Perry's arrival in 1853 accompanied by the 'Black Ships' of the US Navy was to alter the course of Japan's history for ever. The ships were laden with gifts but Perry's visit was anything but a social call. The Americans demanded that the ports be opened to trade and it became increasingly clear that the authorities would not be able to resist the influx of technology from the outside world. The Tokugawa shogunate clung desperately to power for another decade but was finally overthrown in 1867. In the following year, **Emperor Meiji** was restored to the throne, ushering in what was to become known as the **Meiji Restoration**. The Emperor himself remained politically powerless but he presided over a period of astonishing and fast-paced change. Edo, by now renamed **Tokyo**, became the official capital and Japan embarked on a long period of modernisation. One of the most notable achievements was the building of a national railway, an account of which begins on p68. But the education system was also completely overhauled, inspiration for which came from the

French and German models. The period was also marked by the introduction of universal conscription, and there was wholesale overhaul of the army and navy.

As the country began to catch up with the rest of the world, the last remnants of the *ancien régime* were cast away. The land owned by feudal lords was carved up into the prefectures that still exist today. Swordless samurai were deprived of their status and forced to find work elsewhere – even their trademark top-knot hairstyle had to go. A new Western-style constitution was instituted in 1889 and compulsory education introduced. Wealthy Japanese parents sent their children to Oxford or Cambridge university, while engineers from the West were drafted in to provide the initial technology which would one day turn Japan into an economic superpower.

However, by the end of the first decade of the 20th century, British and other foreign engineers had all but disappeared (the Japanese learned the skills, then learned how to do better themselves). An increasingly confident Japan sought to gain a foothold in Asia; by the time of Emperor Meiji's death in 1912, the country had already engaged in wars with China and Russia. These wars were inspired, in part, by the fact that Japan saw how Britain – an even smaller island nation – had managed to acquire a huge empire and imagined it could do the same.

Elsewhere in the world, Japan was keen to promote its culture and traditions; for six months in 1910, the new international face of Japan was displayed to an intrigued British public at White City in west London. Over 8,000,000 visitors caught a glimpse of a country in transition. There were demonstrations of judo, kendo, karate and sumo. A tea house, replica Japanese gardens and Ainu village were constructed, along with a white-knuckle ride called the Flip-Flap, which gave visitors a bird's eye view of London.

The end of the first half of the 20th century was dominated by Japan's involvement in **WWII**. When France fell to Nazi Germany in 1940, Japan moved to occupy French Indo-China. Japan's attack on the US Pacific fleet at Pearl Harbor in 1941 – which led the US and its allies to declare war on Japan – remains one of the most infamous chapters of the country's WWII history. In the following year Japan embarked on an expansionist campaign across Southeast Asia, occupying a succession of countries including The Philippines, Dutch East Indies, Burma and Malaya. The war culminated in the devastating atomic bomb attacks on the cities of Hiroshima (6th August) and Nagasaki (9th August) in 1945. It is estimated that over 140,000 people had died in Hiroshima by the end of the year, and more than 70,000 people in Nagasaki. **Emperor Hirohito**, who had ascended the throne in 1926, announced Japan's surrender.

Under American occupation after the war, the country embarked on another period of sweeping reform. By the time the **Tokyo Olympics** opened in 1964, and the bullet train was speeding between Tokyo and Osaka, Japan's rise to economic superpower was complete.

Over the next two decades, the rest of the world could only watch in amazement as the country that had been closed to outsiders for more than two centuries became the fastest growing economy in the world.

The economic downturn of the late 1990s worried the Japanese and put pressure on politicians to produce a magic formula and wipe away the lingering recession in an instant. By the early years of the 21st century it became clear that there would be no quick fix, and the real challenge was to try and stem what appeared to be a long and painful process of economic decline. The other formidable challenge is the increasing economic and political might of China. The regional battle for global influence and economic supremacy has only just begun.

POLITICS

For over 50 years Japanese politics was dominated by the ruling **Liberal Democratic Party (LDP),** founded in 1955. Though the LDP has been widely credited for Japan's economic success, it has also been dogged by accusations of cronyism and corruption.

Kakuei Tanaka, prime minister in the 1970s, was dubbed the LDP 'kingmaker' and the country's political powerbroker. He was also seen as one of the most corrupt politicians of modern times; his greatest achievement – having a shinkansen line built from Tokyo to Niigata solely because Niigata was his constituency – bankrupted the entire national railway.

Throughout the 1990s, as the country was searching for a way out of the economic doldrums, the LDP showed no signs of reforming itself. Change finally arrived in 2001, in the figure of Junichiro Koizumi, Japan's 11th prime minister in just 13 years. Considered an outsider, Koizumi remained popular with voters for his maverick style and reformist agenda and lasted for nearly five and a half years (the longest-serving prime minister in modern Japanese history) before passing the baton to Shinzo Abe in 2006. Abe – who became the country's youngest prime minister at the tender age of 52 – brought a return to a more familiar political era, one where grey-suited prime ministers came and went with relative speed and anonymity.

By 2009 the country seemed ready for a genuinely new direction. In the election that year, the opposition **Democratic Party of Japan** swept to power, with the bouffant-haired Yukio Hatoyama – nicknamed 'space alien' for his prominent eyes and at times otherworldly ideas – at the helm. But he was to last barely nine months before throwing in the towel. His successor, Naoto Kan, faced the biggest political challenge of a generation when he had to respond to the devastating 2011 earthquake and tsunami as well as the ensuing nuclear fallout (see p275). Within months of the quake he too resigned, leaving his successor Yoshihiko Noda to set the path to recovery. In his first speech as Prime Minister, Noda confirmed plans to phase out nuclear power. But, in a country so dependent on nuclear energy and still mired in economic uncertainty, charting a course for the future appears far from easy.

ECONOMY

When Japan's bubble economy finally burst in the early 1990s, the nation and world reeled in shock. Throughout the previous decade the country's economy had seemed unstoppable. At 2.5%, interest rates were the lowest in the world, making money easy to borrow. Banks assisted in pumping up the bubble by offering loans to virtually anybody with little or no scrutiny of their personal finances. As a piece of real estate, Japan was worth the whole of the US seven times over. The value of land was pushed artificially high and companies staked their livelihood solely on the soaring price of the square feet they owned. This made them profitable on paper but bankrupt the moment the bottom fell out of the property market. The gloomy economic outlook extended well into the 21st century, but by the middle of the first decade there were signs of cautious optimism and a renewed sense that Japan was finally back in business. This mood did not last long. Japan may have remained in self-imposed isolation from the outside world for hundreds of years, but it could not shield itself from the impact of the global recession at the end of the first decade of the new century. In 2010, the country suffered a huge psychological blow when the Chinese economy officially overtook the Japanese economy for the first time in history.

In the 1980s – at the time Japan was buying up swathes of Lower Manhattan with loose change – Japanese manufacturers were teaching the world to be competitive, and the country's industries were global bywords for quality and efficiency in the workplace. Three decades on, productivity has slowed and global names such as Toyota and Sony have suffered from the twin effects of the global slowdown and increased, cheaper competition. And yet, despite all the odds – including the economic downturn in the Tohoku region following the 2011 tsunami and nuclear disaster – nobody is yet writing off Japan Inc.

RELIGION

The two main religions in Japan are **Buddhism**, imported from China, and **Shinto** (literally, 'the way of the gods'), Japan's indigenous religion. Shinto's origins extend as far back as Japanese mythology, to the belief that all aspects of the natural world (water, rocks, trees and wind, for example) have their own spirit/deity (*kami*). Shinto was the official state religion until 1945, up to which time the emperor himself was considered to be a divine being. There is no founder nor are there any scriptures.

Buddhist places of worship are temples, the names of which in Japanese always end with the suffix '-*ji*'. In Shinto, places of worship are shrines and are much plainer in design than the often brightly coloured temples. Shinto shrines are most obviously distinguished from temples by the *torii* (gate) which marks the entrance to the shrine precinct. The names of shinto shrines end with a variety of suffixes but the most common are *-jinja*, *-gu* and *-taisha*.

Despite numerous attempts by foreign missionaries over the centuries, **Christianity** has made few inroads into Japan, though the Western white wedding is considered a fashionable way to tie the knot. Some of the churches and chapels you might see in Japan have been built solely for white weddings and are not consecrated for religious services.

> **Longevity record**
> Japanese women are the world's longest lived – and have been for over two decades. They enjoy an average life expectancy of 86.4 years, while Japanese men can expect to live 79.5 years. The health ministry puts this down to a healthy diet, rich in vegetables and fish products and relatively low in animal fats. But the figures may not remain so impressive, given the high number of smokers and the Westernisation of their eating habits. And the long life expectancy is not all good news: combined with a falling birth rate, it is creating considerable problems in the economy.

THE PEOPLE

Of the **127 million** people living in Japan, the vast majority are Japanese by birth. Commentators liken Japan to an exclusive club; only rarely is anyone from outside the circle given the much sought-after membership card – a Japanese passport. History disputes the much-touted fact that the Japanese are an entirely homogenous people since the country is said to have been first settled by migrants from various parts of mainland Asia. The Ainu, an ethnic minority who are culturally and physically distinct from the Japanese, are further proof that Japan is much more multicultural than it may at first seem. Believed to have inhabited northern Honshu and Hokkaido since the 7th century, the Ainu began to dwindle in number as the Japanese colonised the north of the country. For more on the Ainu, their cultural heritage and battle for survival, see box p356.

It would be wrong to assume that the 'closed shop' nature of Japanese nationality means the people are hostile. On the contrary, it would be hard to find a more friendly and welcoming country. The traditional image of the polite, but formal, hard-working Japanese is only partially accurate. Indeed, generalisations about the Japanese rarely hold water. Even the briefest (rail!) journey here proves that the people are as diverse as the landscape is varied.

SPORT

Traditional sports

Perhaps the best-known traditional Japanese sport is **sumo wrestling**. Two wrestlers (who usually weigh between 90kg and 160kg each) attempt to push each other out of a 4.55m-diameter clay circle; the winner is decided when any part of a wrestler's body apart from the soles of his feet touches the ground, or if he steps or is pushed out of the ring. Sumo wrestlers are divided into six divisions, the highest rank being that of *yokozuna* (grand champion). There are six sumo tournaments (known as *basho*) every year and each lasts for 15 days. Basho are held in Tokyo (January, May and September), Osaka (March), Nagoya (July) and Fukuoka (November). Tickets for ringside seats are expensive and usually sell out weeks in advance but the public broadcaster NHK provides live coverage of the tournaments. For more information visit 🖥 www. sumo.or.jp/eng.

Of all the martial arts, **aikido** is perhaps the one most steeped in religion. Created in Japan by Morihei Ueshiba (see p196), aikido combines the disciplines of judo, karate and kendo. Practitioners of aikido attempt to harness an opponent's *ki* (spiritual power), which is said to enable them to throw their adversary to the ground with little effort. **Judo** follows a similar principle though the techniques are very different. Much of the basic judo training involves throwing your opponent to the floor and holding them down. Judo has been a regular Olympic event since the Tokyo Olympic Games in 1964 and is now practised worldwide. There are 10 ranks, called *dan*, which are internationally recognised.

Karate originated in China and only reached mainland Japan in the early 1920s; today it exists in many different styles. **Kendo** (literally, 'the way of the sword') is sometimes known as Japanese fencing. Opponents wear protective masks, chest gear and gloves while using a bamboo stick *(shinai)* or metal sword *(katana)* to strike each other. **Kyudo**, or Japanese archery, is one of the oldest martial arts and can be performed on the ground as well as on horseback, when it is known as **yabusame**.

JNTO (see box p27) publishes a *Traditional Sports* leaflet (💻 www.see japan.co.uk; search for Traditional sports) which has details of where and when it's possible to observe practice sessions for the sports mentioned above, as well as information on how to apply for sumo tournament tickets.

Modern sports

Baseball is taken as seriously as it is in the USA, with professional teams divided into Central and Pacific leagues. All major cities have a professional team but the sport also attracts large numbers of students at school and university clubs. Traditionally the sport is associated with men but a professional women's league started in 2010.

Rugby has a smaller following but is growing in popularity as the country makes its mark on the international stage. Japan narrowly missed out on the chance of hosting the 2011 Rugby World Cup, when it was pipped to the post by New Zealand.

Soccer has taken off in a big way since the launch of the J-League in 1993. A measure of the sport's success came when Japan successfully co-hosted the 2002 World Cup with South Korea.

CULTURE

Japan is known as much for its ancient traditions as its futuristic technology. The following is a brief guide to the country's highly distinctive culture.

Traditional culture

Ikebana Perhaps the most celebrated of Japan's ancient cultural traditions is ikebana, or the art of flower arranging. Ikebana was once synonymous with the formality of the tea ceremony, when participants would contemplate the beauty and careful positioning of the flowers decorating the tea room. Just as there are different schools of judo and karate, so too there are some officially recognised schools of ikebana in Japan. Both men and women practise ikebana; indeed, it was even considered an appropriate pastime for the samurai. For more information visit the Ikebana International (🖳 www.ikebanahq.org) website.

Chanoyu Commonly known as the tea ceremony, chanoyu is one of the country's most highly regarded aesthetic pursuits. Considered to be a form of mental training as well as a means of learning elegant manners and etiquette, *sado* ('the way of the tea') is much more than just an elaborate way of pouring a cup of tea. While the powdered green tea is whipped up with boiling water using a special bamboo whisk and poured into the serving bowl, guests are offered a small cake or sweetmeat to prepare themselves for the bitter taste of the tea. The ceremony, which can last a couple of hours, is held in a simple tatami-mat room decorated with hanging scrolls and discreetly positioned flowers. Some top-end hotels in cities such as Tokyo and Kyoto offer tea-ceremony demonstrations and even provide stools for guests who aren't used to sitting on their heels for long.

Kabuki, Bunraku and Noh Probably the most accessible form of traditional theatre in Japan is **kabuki**, a kind of dance drama with music, which dates back to the 17th century. A knowledge of Japanese is not necessary to enjoy the colourful performances, where men dress as women, the make-up is as bright as the costumes are lavish, and members of the audience frequently shout out their appreciation when actors take to the stage, strike a dramatic pose or deliver a famous line. The kabuki theatre comes equipped with a *seridashi*, a trap door in the floor which allows actors to enter the stage from below, as well as a gangway through the audience which lets the actors make a dramatic, sweeping entrance, their silk costumes rustling behind them as they step gracefully towards the stage. It would be hard to find a more lively or entertaining theatrical experience in Japan.

Also originating in the 17th century and closely related to kabuki is **bunraku** (puppet play). Puppets up to two-thirds the size of humans are dressed in costumes which are just as elaborate as those worn by actors on the kabuki stage. The puppets are operated by three stage hands while a fourth narrates the story to the tune of the traditional *shamisen* (see below).

Less immediately accessible than kabuki is **Noh**, a classical form of theatre which dates back more than 600 years. Performances combine music and dance: movements are highly stylised and the dancing is choreographed to represent actions such as crying and laughing and is accompanied by flutes and drums. Most of the actors wear masks depicting a range of expressions and emotions. Performances, on a special raised stage with a roof and a sparse set, often take place by firelight during the summer months in the precincts of Shinto shrines.

Shamisen, koto and taiko Proficiency on traditional Japanese instruments such as the **shamisen** (a wooden instrument covered in cat skin with three strings made of silk) and the **koto** (Japanese harp) was once as much a test of a geisha's talent as her ability to dance. Partly because of the cost of purchasing and maintaining such instruments, their popularity has faded. But one

---

🏮 **Geisha in the 21st century**

Maiko, apprentice geisha, train for up to six years for the right to be called a geisha (*geiko* in Kyoto). During this time the maiko-san will learn how to play traditional instruments, such as the shamisen and koto (see opposite), how to dance and how to dress in a kimono. Above all the trainee is required to become skilled in the manners and comportment associated with the geisha world, since every one of them will be judged by the customers whom they are sent to entertain in the evenings. Up until WW2 a maiko's virginity was auctioned and they had little control over their sexual relationships but nowadays any relationships they have are up to them.

In the 1920s there were about 80,000 geisha and a steady flow of new trainees. Today, fewer than 5000 brave the long hours and difficult working conditions. However, more and more young professional women, dressed in platform heels and forever chatting on their mobile phones by day, are now moonlighting as a new breed of geisha after only the briefest crash course in technique. Customers unwilling or unable to pay for an evening with a traditional geisha can opt instead for one of this new breed who charge a fraction of the price. They are different from hostesses in a bar in the sense that they dress in a kimono and go to their client's premises rather than the client going to a bar.

---

traditional instrument that remains popular for its infectious rhythm is the **taiko** drum. Bare-chested taiko drummers beating a furious rhythm while drenching themselves and their instruments in sweat are a staple sight and sound at most Japanese festivals, where the noise is the perfect accompaniment to a summer parade through the streets. Shaped like a cylinder, the body of the taiko drum is hollow and covered at both ends with leather. Smaller hand drums, known as *tsuzumi*, are often used in Noh and kabuki.

Popular culture

Manga and anime Comic books (manga) are big business in Japan, with an annual turnover of about ¥400 billion; they cover every theme and genre and so appeal to all sections of the population. *Manga kissa* (manga cafés) are popular places for people to read manga but these days manga are also available online as webmanga.

One of the best-known manga is **Tetsuwan Atomu** (called Astro Boy outside Japan) by Osamu Tezuka; he is also credited as the father of anime as he adapted this manga for the television screen. **Doraemon**, a blue robot from the 21st century, is another manga character that was developed into anime. The genre was then expanded by Miyazaki Hayao and Studio Ghibli (see box p92), which has created some of the most successful anime movies.

Pachinko parlours Another popular form of entertainment is a trip to the pachinko parlour. Players sit in front of upright pinball machines and feed them with tiny silver ball bearings. The machines then rattle a lot and, with luck (little skill seems to be involved), more silver balls pour out through the slot into a tray; these can be exchanged for prizes like washing powder and tins of ham. These unglamorous prizes are then traded in for cash at a semi-hidden booth outside. It's illegal to play for cash in the pachinko parlours so owners get

> **卄 Toylets**
> Sega has come up with a novel new line in hi-tech games. Consoles called 'Toylets' (🖥 toylets.sega.jp) have been installed in selected urinals across Tokyo. Each urinal has a built-in pressure sensor, and an LCD screen above it offers access to a variety of games. 'Mannekin Pis' – the least complicated of the challenges – simply measures how hard you can urinate.
>
> In another game you take the role of a gust of wind trying to blow a girl's skirt up: the harder you urinate, the harder the wind blows. Most bizarre is 'Battle! Milk From Nose', where you compete against the person who last used the urinal. The strength of your urine streams are compared, and translated into milk spraying out of your nose. If your stream is stronger, your milk stream knocks your opponent out of the ring. If you wish to retain a record of your win (or loss) you can even save the information to a USB stick, assuming you have one to hand.

around the law by allowing customers to exchange the prizes for money off the premises. The noise coming from the parlours mean they are not hard to find.

Music There is no greater music phenomenon in Japan than **J-Pop**. Most pop artists disappear as quickly as they rise to fame; longevity is counted in months not years. Those who have survived longer than most include the kings of pop, Tsuyoshi Domoto and Koichi Domoto (not actually related), better known as the KinKi Kids, and the boy bands SMAP, V6 and Arashi.

Girl-band Morning Musume ('Morning Daughters'), known simply as MoMusu, was formed when producer Tsunku trawled round search-for-a-star contests, literally picking out losers as he went. The group quickly proved that lack of talent was no impediment to commercial success. Whenever one member of the group faded in the popularity stakes she was simply replaced by another person from the bottomless talent pool. AKB48, another girl band, has the record of being the world's largest pop group with 59 members in all, divided into four 'teams', and is unusual in that they have their own theatre (in Akihabara, Tokyo), where one group performs live every day. Artists with staying power include R&B pop sensation Utada Hikaru, known in Japan as 'Hikki', and rock band L'Arc en Ciel, who have sold over 25 million singles and albums.

Practical information for visitors

ARRIVING IN JAPAN

Japan has three major international gateways: Narita Airport (see p100), east of Tokyo, Haneda Airport (see p101), near Tokyo, and Kansai Airport (see p117), near Osaka and Kobe. Don't confuse Kansai Airport with Osaka (Itami) Airport; the former is the one you are likely to arrive at even though the latter has some international flights. Most large cities have an airport, some of which have international flights but mostly only from Asian countries.

Immigration and Customs are efficient at all the airports but don't expect to rush through the formalities. All foreigners entering Japan (apart from diplomats, children under 16 and US military personnel serving in Japan) are fingerprinted and photographed at immigration, whether or not they have a visa. Tourists will have a 'Landing Permission' stamp confirming their 'Temporary Visitor' status put in their passport.

If you're planning to travel throughout Honshu it makes sense to fly into Kansai and out of Narita or Haneda or vice versa if you can. All airports offer ample facilities for changing money and are connected to the Japan Rail network, so you can exchange your rail pass and begin your journey soon after touching down.

TOURIST INFORMATION

The staff in the main **tourist information centres (TICs)** at the airports and in Tokyo, Osaka and Kyoto speak English and can provide information on onward travel throughout Japan. Most towns and cities have a tourist information office (look for the 'i' logo), though it may be called something else, such as 'Question and answer office'. Though the staff at offices in less touristy areas do not always speak English they can almost always provide maps and town guides in English.

A network of **'goodwill guides'** operates in a number of towns and cities. These are English-speaking volunteers who guide foreign tourists around local sights; the service is free but volunteers generally ask for their expenses to be covered. They can usually be contacted via the local tourist information office, or for a guide interpreter search the online database at 🖥 www.guidesearch.jp.

> ❑ **TIC information line**
> If you're stuck anywhere in Japan and need assistance in English, call the JNTO Tourist Information Center (TIC; ☎ 03-3201 3331; daily 9am-5pm, except 1st Jan). The staff are very knowledgeable and will help with any travel or tourism enquiry.

GETTING AROUND

By rail See pp74-82.

By air
If you're pushed for time and are planning to travel long distances it can make sense to combine use of the rail pass with a domestic flight. However, it may work out quicker to take a shinkansen once you factor in the time it takes to get to and from the airports.

Japan's two major airlines, All Nippon Airways (ANA; 🖥 www.ana.co.jp) and Japan Airlines (JAL; 🖥 www.jal.co.jp), operate a comprehensive network of domestic flights. Smaller domestic airlines include Skymark Airlines (SKY; 🖥 www.skymark.co.jp) and Starflyer (🖥 www.starflyer.jp). Two new airlines offering low-cost flights domestically and internationally are Peach and Air Asia (see box p26); Jet Star (🖥 www.jetstar.com) has domestic flights only at present.

⛩ Smart cards

JR East's Suica (Super Urban Intelligent Card) is a cashless smart card for use on JR East trains as well as on buses, subways and non-JR lines, in some shops and convenience stores, and even for vending machines and coin lockers – anywhere showing the Suica logo. A Suica can be bought at Narita and Haneda airports (for details see pp100-1), or at any JR station in the Tokyo Metropolitan area. A basic Suica costs ¥2500 (preloaded with ¥2000 plus ¥500 refundable deposit). You will see machines where you can top your card up all over stations in the area. To use it just place your card over the IC card sign and wait to hear the beep showing it has been recognised.

There are now several smart cards: JR Tokai introduced the Toica, JR West the Icoca, JR Hokkaido the Kitaca and JR Kyushu the Sugoca. Another well-known card is the Pasmo. However, the Suica is still the most useful as it is accepted in most parts of Japan.

In recent years the price of domestic flights has fallen as a result of more competition, but it still pays to book ahead for the best deals. Both ANA and JAL offer discount 'air passes' for foreign visitors, which are worth considering if you are planning to take two or more flights.

By bus or tram

The **bus** service in Japan is almost as efficient as the rail service. In fact, some urban buses are operated by JR, which means Japan Rail Pass holders travel free on those.

On most urban buses, you enter at the back and take a ticket from the machine by the door. In cities there is usually a flat fare but in rural areas the fare depends on the length of your journey. To work out how much the fare is, just before your stop, match the number on the ticket with the fare underneath the corresponding number on the board at the front of the bus.

Leave the bus at the front, throwing the exact fare and your ticket into the box by the driver; if you don't have the correct money and your fare is less than ¥1000 you must change a note to coins by using the change machine nearby.

Several cities and large towns still have a **tram** (streetcar) service. On most trams fares are collected in the same way as on buses. However, it is often

⛩ JR bus and ferry services

In addition to its rail services, JR operates some **Highway Bus** routes (🖥 www.jrbuskanto.co.jp), though they hardly compete with the trains in terms of speed and are prone to getting snarled up in traffic. They are also less user-friendly than the trains since announcements are usually in Japanese only. The main JR Highway Bus route, for which rail passes are valid, runs from Tokyo railway station to Nagoya, Kyoto and Osaka railway stations. Seats for this service should be booked in advance at the JR bus ticket office at the relevant train station. Further details are not included because it's faster and more convenient to travel by train. However, JR bus services to places of interest not accessible by rail are included in the suggested routes.

Rail passes are also valid for the JR **ferry service** between Miyajima-guchi (near Hiroshima) and Miyajima Island (see pp258-60).

❏ **Cable cars and ropeways**
An important point to note is that a **cable car** in Japan is a funicular/mountain railway and a **ropeway** is what many others consider a cable car (ie carriages suspended from a cable).

---

possible to get a one-day bus/tram pass which makes life easier and is often good value. But you still may need to pick up a ticket as you enter the tram and also put your pass in the ticket machine as you leave.

For information about JR's inter-urban bus services, see box opposite.

By taxi

Taxis are usually available outside even the tiniest of stations but it's also fine to flag one down in the street if the red light in the lower right-hand corner of the windscreen is on. The starting fare is around ¥650 for the first 2km plus ¥100 for each additional 500m; a surcharge (up to 30%) is added between 11pm and 5am. Though taxis are not cheap if you are on your own, they can be very good value if there are three or four of you, especially in rural areas where bus services are limited. Most drivers wear white gloves and peaked caps, and you don't even have to open the door yourself because the driver operates the rear passenger doors from the front.

By bicycle

It is possible to rent a bike at many stations; details are given where relevant. If you rent a bicycle in an urban area, note that there are strict rules about parking, so always check for signs saying parked bikes may be removed and impounded.

Hitchhiking

'There is no reason to hitchhike. That's why we built the bullet train.'
Will Ferguson *Hokkaido Highway Blues* (abridged edn 2003)

The extensive rail network in Japan does mean it is easy to get around but railway lines do not go everywhere. So, if you want to head off the beaten track hitchhiking is worth considering, especially as the chances are high that anyone who offers you a lift will do their best to get you as close as they can to where you want to go. However, as in most countries, you should be particularly careful if hitchhiking on your own.

ACCOMMODATION

There is a wide range of possibilities and accommodation is almost always of a high standard. Unless stated otherwise, rates quoted throughout this guide are generally the lowest you should expect to pay. However, many places offer internet booking and this usually offers the best rates. Rates can increase considerably in holiday periods.

It's wise, though not essential, to book your first couple of nights' accommodation before you arrive in Japan. However, if you are planning to visit places such as Kyoto in March/April (cherry blossom time) or October/November

JAPAN

❏ **Online accommodation agencies**

Most of the agencies listed below offer both Japanese- and Western-style accommodation and also online reservation.

● **Jalan** (🖳 www.jalan.net) – the listings on the English page are not as comprehensive as on the Japanese but it is still a useful resource;

● **Japanese Guest Houses** (🖳 www.japaneseguesthouses.com) – focuses on ryokan but also lists some of the temple lodgings on Koya-san;

● **Japan Hotel Association** (🖳 www.j-hotel.or.jp/en) – a wide range of upmarket hotels offering Western-style accommodation;

● **Japan iCan** (🖳 www.japanican.com) – part of the JTB group and the site lists over 4000 hotel and ryokan;

● **Japan Ryokan and Hotel Association** (🖳 www.nikkanren.or.jp/english) – lists independently owned places;

● **Selected Onsen Ryokan** (🖳 selected-ryokan.com) – over 200 ryokan and hotels that have hot-spring facilities. However, the website does not always say how to reach the onsen by train even though this is often possible; a bus journey may be necessary also.

(autumn leaves) it is worth booking well in advance. Whenever you book it's best to do so either through the relevant hotel/ryokan website or by email, clearly stating dates and room requests. Telephoning may be complicated and anyhow hoteliers much prefer to have your requirements in writing; places that don't have email may prefer to receive a fax. Always make sure you receive written confirmation and take that with you to show at check-in.

The city guides and, where relevant, route guides feature places to stay and contact details. Alternatively, see box p48 for details of the main hotel chains in Japan and the box above for details of online accommodation agencies.

If you do turn up without a place to stay most tourist information centres have an accommodation list and some can make same-day reservations. Staff will also be able to tell you where the closest **JTB** (Japan Travel Bureau) office is as they can make reservations for the whole of Japan.

If you book online you are likely to have to give credit card details. However, many places still prefer payment in cash.

Check-in usually starts **from 4pm** and **check-out** is **by 11am** (10am in many business hotels); most places let you leave your luggage with them for free if you arrive or leave outside those times, so you don't always have to fork out for a locker. Most ryokan and minshuku prefer, or even insist, that you reserve ahead, especially if you want meals.

For general information on accommodation in Japan visit 🖳 www.jnto.go.jp/eng/arrange/accomodations. **Accessible Japan** (🖳 www.tesco-premium.co.jp/aj) has useful information on hotels which offer specially adapted rooms for the disabled.

Hostels and temple lodgings

The cheapest places, particularly if you are on your own, tend to be **hostels**.

The majority of hostels belong to **Japan Youth Hostels** (JYH; 🖳 www.jyh.or.jp), which is part of Hostelling International/YHA (🖳 www.hihostels.com).

Expect to pay ¥2000-3500 per person (pp); non-members may have to pay about ¥600 extra per night so bring your card if you are a member. A few hostels accept members only but you should be able to join (¥1500) on the spot.

Hostels are great if you want to meet other travellers as many organise a programme of events, evening sing-songs and the like. However, JYH hostels in particular get booked up with young Japanese during Golden Week (see p10) and in the summer. Also, if there are two or more of you it may be as cheap to stay in a business hotel by the time you have factored in the almost inevitable cost of getting a bus to and from the hostel (most are not centrally located). Having said that, some of the hostels in rural areas are very atmospheric.

All hostels provide dormitory accommodation; some also offer private rooms (ideal for families travelling together). Most provide breakfast and an evening meal; some have communal kitchen facilities. It's wise to call ahead and make a booking since managers may not appreciate it if you turn up unannounced.

There are now several **backpacker hostel chains** with branches in the main tourist cities – these are often more centrally located than JYH hostels. Expect to pay about ¥3000pp for a bed in a dorm, ¥5000-6000pp half-board. Chains include: J-hoppers (💻 j-hoppers.com); K's House (💻 www.kshouse.jp) and Sakura House (💻 www.sakura-house.com). In Hokkaido it is worth checking out the Toho Network (💻 www.toho.net).

A few JYH hostels, such as those in Takayama and Nagano, are attached to, or in, **temples**. At these it may be possible (if you ask) to join early-morning prayers or participate in a session of Zen meditation with resident monks. Certain temples which are not hostels also accept paying guests, offering an excellent insight into Japanese culture. Koya-san (see pp223-5) has many options but also consider Yoshino-yama (see p223) and Dewa Sanzan (see p298).

Camping

A drawback for rail travellers is that nearly all campsites are a long way from stations. However, for details about campsites in Japan visit 💻 www.jnto.go.jp/eng/attractions/rest) and click on Camping.

Minshuku and pensions

Minshuku are small, family-run inns where the rate usually includes half-board (an evening meal and breakfast); expect to pay ¥6000-8000pp with a reduction for children. Room-only, or bed & breakfast, rates are often available.

Urban minshuku are usually fine but are often less personal and characterful than rural ones, which might be in old farmhouses and so offer a great

---

❏ **Japanese Inn Group**

The Japanese Inn Group (💻 www.japaneseinngroup.com) is a nationwide directory of ryokan and minshuku (not a chain of inns) that are used to dealing with foreign guests and also often accept credit cards. Reservations should be made by letter, fax or email direct to the place you want to stay, using the form on the website. Alternatively, when in Japan, for the price of the phone-call the proprietor of the inn where you are staying will also happily call other Inn Group members and book accommodation for you.

experience of being in a traditional Japanese home. Rooms are Japanese style (futons on tatami-mat flooring); see box p50. There are no en suite facilities and you may not be provided with a towel or yukata (see p28), though you can probably rent one. Most have a TV in the room and many now offer internet access/wi-fi. Meals are eaten at set times (usually 6 or 6.30pm for supper and about 7.30am for breakfast), occasionally with the family. Invariably the food is

❏ HOTEL CHAINS

Business hotels

The majority of the hotel groups listed below have branches all over the country and offer online booking through an English website. If a hotel's name includes 'ekimae' it may literally be opposite, or less than a 10-minute walk from, the station.

● **APA Hotels** (🖳 www.apahotel.com) APA (Always Pleasant Amenity) provide a Japanese buffet-style breakfast and their hotels have a common bath as well as en suite facilities in the room.

● **R&B Hotel** (🖳 www.randb.jp) R&B is short for 'Room and Breakfast'; they offer freshly baked croissants, orange juice and coffee for breakfast.

● **Route Inn** (🖳 www.route-inn.co.jp) Offers a buffet-style breakfast. All branches have a common bath, some of which are onsen (natural hot springs).

● **Super Hotel** (🖳 www.superhotel.co.jp) Rates include a bread-based breakfast. Worth looking out for are their hotels with onsen. Some branches close completely between 10am and 3pm and some have automated check-in and check-out facilities (payment by cash only). They have a student rate for those with valid ID but it is not possible to book this through the English website.

● **Tokyu Hotels** (🖳 www.tokyuhotelsjapan.com) The Tokyu group has hotels for all budget groups: Tokyu Bizfort, Tokyu Resort, Tokyu Inn, Excel Hotel Tokyu, Tokyu Hotel as well as The Capitol Hotel Tokyu. They also have a membership scheme (Comfort Members; ¥500 to join) offering discounts on rates and check-out up to noon.

● **Toyoko Inn** (🖳 www.toyoko-inn.com) One of the best hotel chains in Japan, where virtually all the staff (including management) are women and where the aim is to replicate the welcome of a traditional ryokan in a modern hotel setting. They serve a Japanese breakfast (based on *onigiri*), though often some form of bread is available; some branches also offer a free curry-rice evening meal. The furnishings are the same in every branch and rooms are always clean and well equipped.

For ¥1500 you can become an 'International' Toyoko Inn Club member, which entitles you to discounted rates, one free night's stay for every ten, and early check-in.

Upmarket hotels

The majority of hotel chains listed below offer upmarket accommodation but some also have brands offering more reasonable options. In many cases breakfast is not included in the rate though packages including breakfast may be available.

Japanese chains include: **JAL Hotels** (🖳 www.jalhotels.com/domestic) includes the Nikko and Okura brand; **Mielparque** (🖳 www.mielparque.jp); **Richmond Hotels** (🖳 www.richmondhotel.jp); **Solare Hotels** (🖳 www.solarehotels.com) includes the Chisun and Loisir brands; and **Washington Hotels** (🖳 www.wh-rsv.com).

Also at the top end of the market are Western hotel chains such as **Hyatt** (🖳 www.hyatt.com), **Hilton** (🖳 www1.hilton.com) and **Marriott** (🖳 www.marriott.com). Other Western hotels groups in Japan include **Best Western** (🖳 www.bestwestern.com), **Comfort Inn** (🖳 www.comfortinn.com) and **Holiday Inn** (🖳 www.holidayinn.com).

Japanese, so be prepared for (raw) egg, fish and miso soup at breakfast! However, many minshuku in touristy areas also offer a Western breakfast.

Pensions are the Western-style equivalent of minshuku and are becoming increasingly popular with Japanese. Like minshuku, pensions are usually small, family-run affairs but they offer beds rather than futons. Rates start from around ¥6000pp and usually include a Western breakfast but not an evening meal.

Hotels

A little more expensive and often conveniently located near railway stations, **business hotels** always have plenty of single rooms in addition to twins and doubles. They should not be confused with Japan's infamous capsule hotels, since you get a proper room rather than a sleeping compartment.

Most rooms are Western style, en suite, and are clean and tidy, but, as they cater for business travellers, they rarely have much space to move about in or hang your clothes. A yukata, TV, internet access/wi-fi and coffee-/tea-making facilities are almost always provided. The (compact) toilet/bath units generally include towels, toiletries and a hairdryer; shaver sockets are less common.

Facilities in the hotel usually include vending machines (soft drinks, beer, sake, and perhaps pot noodle and ice cream), a coin laundry, a couple of computers with internet access, and there may be a café where you can get an evening meal. Guests may also be able to use a microwave oven and trouser press. Some of the newer ones offer a no-smoking floor and a few have a women-only floor or rooms specifically for women. The newest even boast an automatic check-in where you feed your money into a slot and receive an electronic key card in return.

Rack rates (usually including breakfast) vary from ¥5000 for the most basic singles up to ¥8000 for a room with slightly more breathing space. Expect to pay ¥8000-13,000 for a twin or double room. Online rates are often less than rack rates and since many business hotels accept online bookings and have websites in English it is worth booking in advance. Many business hotel chains operate nationwide; for more details, see the box opposite.

Other **Japanese hotel chains** include the JR Hotel group (see box below) and those listed in the box opposite. In addition there are many **Western hotel chains** (see also box opposite) in Japan. The best way to find out about independently owned hotels is through an accommodation agency (see box p46).

❏ **The JR Hotel group**

Anyone with a Japan Rail Pass will receive a list of JR-run hotels (the main brand names are Mets, Metropolitan, Associa and Granvia). Pass holders get a small discount (usually around 10% off the rack rate). The hotels are all Western style and range from standard business (Mets) to top-class luxury hotels (Granvia). Rooms always have a good range of amenities and include wired (LAN) internet access; most hotels also have at least one restaurant.

JR hotels are particularly convenient since they're nearly always right outside the station (or in some cases, above it). See the city guides for individual hotel details or check the website 🖳 www.jrhotelgroup.com.

Ryokan

Ryokan offer the most traditional Japanese accommodation and you really should plan to stay at least one night in one. They are more upmarket and have better amenities than minshuku. Rooms are more spacious than those in business hotels and may include *shoji* (sliding paper-screen doors) and an alcove (*tokonoma*) or two containing a Japanese fan, vase or scroll.

In luxury ryokan particularly, where per-person (pp) rates start from around ¥20,000, every guest is a VIP. From the moment you arrive you're waited on by your own kimono-clad maid, who will pour tea as you settle in, serve you meals (usually in your room) and lay out your futon. You may also have en suite facilities and your own Japanese-style bath. But you don't have to stay in a

⛩ Ryokan and minshuku etiquette

A stay in a Japanese inn is a wonderful experience and thoroughly recommended, but it's worth bearing the following in mind. You'll find a row of **slippers** waiting in the entrance hall; this is where you're expected to leave your outdoor shoes. The slippers can be worn anywhere except on the tatami-mat floor of your room and in the toilet/bathroom. If you're heading out for a stroll around the local area, *geta* (wooden clogs) may be provided as an alternative to putting on your outdoor shoes.

Before you enter the toilet or bathroom make sure you take off the house slippers because toilets in particular have their own slippers. These are hard to miss as they are usually plastic, have 'toilet' written on them, and come in bright blue or pink. Don't forget to switch back to your other slippers when you leave.

The **bedding** is stored in cupboards in the rooms. At most ryokan staff lay your futon out each night and put it away in the morning (usually while you are having breakfast/supper), while at minshuku you're expected to do it yourself. Don't be surprised to find that the pillow is very hard – traditionally pillows are filled with rice husks – and, in winter, that a blanket is put below the duvet part of the futon. Also in the room you'll find a hand towel and a yukata (a dressing gown/pyjama combo). Remember to cross the yukata left over right (the opposite way is for the deceased). In winter months a *hanten* (a jacket) may also be provided.

Bathrooms are nearly always communal but this doesn't necessarily mean you have to share your bath time with complete strangers. In the majority of places used to foreign guests the bathroom can be locked from the inside. The bath is often large enough to accommodate two or three and made of stainless steel though in a ryokan it may be made of cedar-wood and the water scented with pine or mint. The golden rules for **having a bath** are: wash outside the tub, only climb in once you're clean (staff will already have filled the tub with piping hot water), and never let the bath water out! When you enter the bathroom you will find bowls, stools and taps/shower heads; pick up a bowl and a stool and sit in front of a tap. Soap and shampoo are usually provided; use your small towel as a flannel and scrub as hard as you can.

Tipping is not encouraged but if you've enjoyed exceptional service you might want to leave a small amount of money (notes only) in an envelope or wrapped in tissue paper in your room; it is considered rude to give something without wrapping it up.

If you have **breakfast** in a ryokan or minshuku the meal is likely to be Japanese (miso soup, grilled fish, pickles, some kind of egg, and rice). If you see a bowl with an egg in its shell it is almost definitely a raw egg. The Japanese break that into their rice bowl and mix it with soy sauce and then eat it.

鳥 **Hi-tech attention to the call of nature**
Most toilets (restrooms) in Japan are now Western style, though on some older
trains, particularly local services, and in public loos you'll still find Asian squat toilets.
Toilet paper is increasingly found in public loos, particularly Western-style ones.

Most Western-style toilets have a control panel as there are usually several functions; many of these now have English translations but if they don't the following may
be useful.

On even the most basic models the seats are heated and there are at least two
buttons to press: one is for the flush (流す) and the other activates a warm-water spray
(おしり洗浄) – you really don't want to get these two mixed up. There may also be a
switch so you can adjust the pressure of the spray (水勢調節つまみ) and move its
position/angle (おしり洗浄用ムーブスイッチ). On some toilets there are two lev-
els of flush, though the effect of using the wrong one is not so dramatic. Other functions you may find are: power deodoriser (パワー脱臭), nozzle-cleaning (ノズルク
リーンランプ); a choice of background music (音姫) or a flushing sound (洗水音),
to hide your own natural noises; and a built-in bidet (ビデ). When you have had
enough of any of these press the stop switch (止スイッチ).

Big hotels try to outdo their rivals by fitting guest rooms with futuristic lavatories
so expect to experience even more amazing functions. See also box p42.

luxury property to enjoy first-class service. Standard ryokan charge around
¥9000-12,000pp including half-board (breakfast and an evening meal).

Most ryokan have a garden and some have their own *onsen* (hot spring),
which may or may not include a *rotemburo* (outdoor hot-spring bath), the perfect place to unwind after a hard day's sightseeing. Many do not have internet
access in the rooms as the idea is you are there to relax.

Meals are nearly always Japanese and the dishes are prepared so that they are
as much a visual treat as a gastronomic one and often feature local produce/
specialities. A typical meal might include some tempura, sashimi/sushi, grilled
fish, a meat dish, vegetable dishes and pickles, and will always include miso soup
and rice; dessert is likely to be slices of fresh fruit. All this can be washed down
with beer or sake (for which there will be an additional charge) and/or Japanese
tea. Some ryokan offer a choice of Japanese- or Western-style breakfast.

Other accommodation options

A new development are **Aparthotels**, which offer the
convenience of standard hotel facilities with the additional benefit of a basic kitchen and sitting/dining area;
expect to pay ¥10,000 per night for two people. Try
Citadines (🖳 www.citadines.com) in Kyoto and Tokyo
or Asahi Homes (🖳 www.asahihomes.co.jp/e) in Tokyo.

If all else fails and you're stuck for accommodation
in a city, find out the location of the nearest **capsule
hotel** (¥3000-4000pp), good for a one-off novelty but
not recommended for claustrophobics and the majority
are for men only. However, in places such as Kyoto and

Capsule hotel

Tokyo, capsule hotels for tourists have opened; women can usually stay in these but men and women may be in separate sections.

Alternatively, consider a **manga kissa** (manga café) – these are meant for people who want to play computer games so aren't necessarily the quietest place, and you will need to 'sleep' in a chair, but they are cheap (¥1000-2000pp) and often soft drinks and light snacks are provided for free.

A final option might be a night in a Japanese **love hotel**. During the day, rooms are rented by the hour, but from around 10pm they can be booked for an overnight stay (¥6000-12,000). Like capsule hotels, you'll find love hotels in big cities and sometimes around mainline stations. They're easy to spot because the exteriors are usually bright and garish. The over-the-top design continues inside with a variety of themed rooms, which may contain bizarre extras such as rotating beds, tropical plants and waterfalls. The service in these places, by contrast, tends to be very discreet and you are unlikely ever to see a staff member. A display board at the entrance lights up to inform guests what rooms are available. You then go to pay at a counter, after which a mysterious hand passes you the key to your room. It is not nearly as seedy as it might sound; the arrival process is designed to protect the customers' anonymity and a night here is just as much an experience of Japan as is a stay in a traditional ryokan.

WHERE TO EAT

Eating out in Japan can seem a daunting prospect but with so much on offer it's also a great opportunity to try a variety of cuisines.

Japanese restaurants tend to specialise in a particular kind of food, so it's more common to find a *sushi* restaurant or *soba* (noodle) shop than a generic 'Japanese restaurant'. Note that many restaurants close early, often by 10pm; for late-night eating head to a bar or an *izakaya*.

Japanese food

For a guide to Japanese food and drink, see pp447-9.

A quick and cheap breakfast is served in **coffee shops** advertising 'morning service' or 'morning set' – usually coffee, toast and a boiled or fried egg. Chains to look out for include Pronto, UCC, Tully's and Doutor; Starbucks continues to spread inexorably across Japan. There also seem to be branches of Mister Donut everywhere – the doughnuts are good but of more interest is the bottomless coffee cup.

⛩ Vegetarians

Vegetarians are rare in Japan so be sure to make any dietary requirements clear to restaurant staff. It may be assumed, for example, that as a vegetarian you eat fish or even chicken. It's advisable to explain exactly what you can eat rather than simply say you're a vegetarian (see Useful Phrases p453). The best place for a truly vegetarian meal is a Buddhist temple. The superbly crafted *shojin ryori* prepared by monks can be tried at the temple town of Koya-san (see pp223-5), for example.

⛩ **Eating out and how to order**

Most restaurants hang a *noren* (split curtain) at the entrance whenever they are open. In the evenings, bars show they are open by hanging or illuminating a red lantern outside. Before entering the restaurant take a look at the window display showing plastic models of the dishes on offer.

As you go in, don't be alarmed by the loud greeting that is often shouted not just by the waiters but by the entire kitchen staff. After the chorus of 'Irasshaimase' ('Welcome') dies down you'll be taken to a table and handed the menu along with hot towels and glasses of cold water or Japanese tea (all part of the service). If you're lucky the menu will contain pictures of what's on offer. If not, staff are usually happy to go outside with you to see which of the plastic models has tickled your fancy.

At some (noodle) places you choose what you want from a list on a machine at the entrance, buy a ticket, hand it to the person behind the counter and then take a seat. At other places you have to ring the bell that is on your table when you are ready to order.

For help reading a menu in Japanese see the food glossary on pp447-9.

To save time and money for lunch, **convenience stores** (known as *konbini*) are a good bet; all stock sandwiches, *onigiri*, noodles and the like, and nearly all are open 24 hours and have microwaves to heat up the food. Major convenience-store chains include Lawson/Natural Lawson, 7-Eleven, Heart-in, ampm and Family Mart; in Hokkaido, look out for Seicomart. Other good places for snack-style food are **bakeries** (every large station has at least one), **supermarkets** (Ito Yokado, Daiei, Jusco and Fresco; these also often have a microwave for customers so you can easily heat up anything you buy), and department store **food halls** *(depachika),* usually in the basement. Snacks nearly always come with the appropriate eating implement. In supermarkets, food halls, and stations, you'll find take-out **lunch boxes** *(bento)* which are cheaper than eating at a restaurant. For details on the *ekiben* (railway station lunch box), see box p82.

The cheapest sit-down meals are at counter-service noodle shops selling **ramen**, **soba** and/or **udon**. A bowl of ramen costs about ¥400. Alternatively, try a **shokudo**; these restaurants serve a variety of economical dishes (plastic models of which are displayed outside) and are often found in and around station areas. Other inexpensive places to eat include the nationwide chains of *gyudon* **restaurants** (bowls of rice with beef and onions cooked in a slightly sweet sauce) such as Yoshinoya and Sukiya, where dishes cost from ¥300.

The **canteens** in city halls are subsidised and meant for the staff but are open to anyone. They're often on the top floor, which means you get a cheap meal and a decent view thrown in.

Look out for **stalls** in the evenings and at festivals which sell savoury snacks such as *yakitori, yaki-imo, takoyaki, okonomiyaki, tomorokoshi* and *yakisoba* as well as sweet things such as candy floss (*wata-ame*) and *kakigori*. (See pp447-9.)

Japan's best known culinary export is sushi; the cheapest **sushi restaurants** are *kaiten-zushiya*, where you sit around a revolving counter and help yourself to plates of sushi (different colour plates denote different price bands). At the end of the meal the restaurant staff count how many plates you've taken and tell you how much to pay. It's usually possible to eat your fill for less than ¥1500.

Vending machines
Vending machines (*jidohan-baiki*) are on every street corner, as well as in unexpected places such as mountain tops, temple precincts and remote villages. The vast majority sell drinks, both hot and cold, with a bewildering range of options. However, you are unlikely to find white coffee without sugar; only the black coffee in cans has a sugar-free option. Check that fruit juices say '100% juice' or you might get a sweet syrupy concoction. Beer and sake vending machines close at 11pm.

In Tokyo, particularly at Shinagawa station, some 'acure' machines are touch screen and have a camera which identifies the age and sex of the person, predicts what they would like and then suggests it – though the full range of drinks is still available if the recommendation doesn't appeal. When no one is near the machine it shows two eyes. Not surprisingly these machines accept smart cards (see box p44) but for the moment at least they also accept cash. Many machines now have energy-saving features and another new development is machines that still work if there is a power cut.

Few vending machines sell food other than ice cream and snacks but in Tokyo some now sell bananas!

Restaurants specialising in *tonkatsu* and *kare-raisu* (curry-rice, see p447; look out for the CoCoCurry chain) are also a culinary mainstay; there are usually one or two in large stations. *Tempura* restaurants tend to be a bit more expensive than these.

All **department stores** have at least one 'restaurant floor' where you'll find a variety of Western and Japanese eateries; most offer a daily set lunch which can be very good value. Restaurant floors tend to stay open until 10pm, though the department stores themselves close earlier. At main meal periods there is almost always a queue at the popular places.

Other foods

In major cities you'll rarely be far from **restaurants** serving ethnic cuisine, the most popular being Chinese, Indian, Italian and French. Italian places tend to be cheap but bland, while Indian restaurants serve relatively authentic curries, though you may prefer to try the Japanese version (see above). French food is considered classy and therefore is expensive. Luxury hotels invariably have at least one French restaurant, where a bottle of imported Perrier costs nearly as many yen as it has bubbles. Malaysian and Thai restaurants are popular, though the spiciness you might expect is often toned down to suit the Japanese palate.

For **fast food**, McDonald's is everywhere, but look out too for the Japanese chain Mos Burger, and also Wendy's. In big cities you'll find branches of Lotteria and KFC.

Don't reject out of hand the large number of so-called '**family restaurants**' that seem to be everywhere. The menu at these places is a mix of Western and Japanese, such as spaghetti, steaks, pizza, noodles, tonkatsu and curry rice. Some places also offer a salad bar and all-you-can-drink soft drinks bar. Popular family restaurant chains include Royal Host, Jonathan's, Denny's, Gusto, Ringer Hut and others which are found only in specific regions. An advantage of family restaurants is that they always have picture menus which makes ordering easy. You may have to sign in at busy times to ensure that queuing diners are assigned tables in the correct order. At your table you will often find a bell to ring when you are ready to order.

NIGHTLIFE AND ENTERTAINMENT

Japan has its fair share of clubs, discos and bars. Some are ultra-exclusive and expect you to part with a wad of cash in the form of a cover charge before you even see the drinks menu but many more offer good value for money. Every town and city has its own entertainment district, which often radiates out from the area around the main railway station. To find the nightlife look for the large numbers of businessmen staggering about at dusk in search of their favourite karaoke bar or izakaya. For details of traditional Japanese entertainment see p40.

Karaoke bars Some people have never forgiven Japan for inventing karaoke but its presence in every town and city is unavoidable. You'll know you've stumbled into a karaoke bar if you see television screens strategically placed around the room and rows of whisky bottles stacked up behind the bar (most bars operate a 'bottle keep' system for regulars). If you do visit a karaoke bar, sooner or later you'll be invited to sing. Protest in these situations is futile and it's at least reassuring to know that virtually all karaoke machines have some English songs programmed into them (usually a mixture of the Beatles, the Carpenters, Bob Dylan and *We are the World*).

Izakaya and robotayaki **Izakaya** are small atmospheric Japanese-style pubs (bars). They are often filled with locals who go along after work for a few beers and an evening meal. A typical izakaya consists of seating along a counter, with tables squeezed into any other space available. The menu changes according to what the owner (known as the 'master') has bought in from the market but there's nearly always a choice of fresh fish and meat, as well as salads, tofu dishes and *edamame* (soy beans). Everything is served in snack-size portions so it is a good chance to try a variety of things; dishes usually cost ¥300-600 each. Keep track of what you are ordering if you are bothered about your budget as it is easy for the bill to mount up. If the menu is only in Japanese you will probably find the kanji in the food glossary (see pp447-9) useful; alternatively you can look at what others are eating and point at that. Izakaya are great places to meet people and it is unlikely anyone will mind you pointing at their food; in fact it may be a great way to start a conversation. These places don't tend to open much before 6pm and close around 1am or even later; to find them, look for the tell-tale red lanterns hanging outside.

    Robotayaki offer similar food and drink; the main difference is that the food is cooked in front of you.

Beer gardens The name is a bit of a misnomer because beer gardens are almost always on the roof of department stores and large hotels rather than on the ground. For a fixed price (around ¥3000) most places offer an all-you-can-eat-and-drink beer-and-buffet deal for a set time (90-120 minutes).

Beer gardens are open only from the end of May to early September and are highly recommended as places from which to escape the summer humidity.

Cinema The multiplex rules in Japan so you're rarely more than a short walk from a cinema. The good news is that films are shown in their original language and subtitled in Japanese. The downside is that tickets tend to be expensive (approx ¥1800). Avoid the high prices by going in the afternoon or early evening, booking early, or try showing a student card. Most cinemas also offer reduced prices once a month on 'movie day' and women can take advantage of half-price tickets on the weekly 'ladies day' (often a Wednesday).

MEDIA

Four English-language daily **newspapers** are published in Japan, of which the best are the *Japan Times* (🖥 www.japantimes.co.jp) and the *Daily Yomiuri* (🖥 www.yomiuri.co.jp/dy); you can find copies at kiosks in most large stations. Outside the Tokyo metropolitan and Kansai areas, they're usually a day late.

The main national broadcaster of **television** programmes is NHK (Nippon Hoso Kyokai; 🖥 www3.nhk.or.jp/nhkworld), the Japanese equivalent of the BBC. NHK operates two digital channels, NHK-G (the main channel) and NHK-E, which broadcasts mainly educational programmes. The nightly news programme on NHK-G at 7pm is simultaneously broadcast in English and Japanese but you can pick up the English only if the TV in your hotel has a 'bilingual' button. Private broadcasters such as TBS, Fuji and TV Asahi fill the rest of the airwaves with game shows and soaps. Both the *Daily Yomiuri* and *Japan Times* carry TV listings in English.

Radio is not as popular as TV and most programmes are broadcast only in Japanese. A few cities produce selected pop music shows in English.

ELECTRICITY

The electric current in Japan is 100 volts AC, but there are two different cycles: 50Mhz in eastern Japan (including Tokyo) and 60Mhz in western Japan. Plugs in Japan are of the flat two-pin variety (the same size and shape as American plugs).

TIME

Japan is GMT + 9 so at 9pm in Tokyo it is noon in London, 7am in New York, 4am in California and 11pm in Sydney (all same-day times, not taking summer daylight-saving times into account).

BANKS AND MONEY MATTERS

The unit of **currency** is the Japanese yen (¥). Bank notes are issued in denominations of ¥10,000, ¥5000, ¥2000 (though you are unlikely to see these) and ¥1000. Coins are ¥500, ¥100, ¥50, ¥10, ¥5 and ¥1; the ¥50 and ¥5 coins have a hole in the middle.

For such a sophisticated economy, banking practices remain somewhat archaic. Banks are open Monday to Friday from 9am to 3pm only. The section dealing with currency exchange (**travellers' cheques**) often operates even more limited hours. Always take your passport and expect the exchange process to take at least 30 minutes.

❏ **Exchange rates**	
£1	¥125
€1	¥101
US$1	¥80
Can$1	¥78
Aus$1	¥82
NZ$1	¥64
To get the latest rates of exchange check: 🖥 www.xe.com/ucc	

Japan has always been a **cash-based society** and although things are changing credit cards are nothing like as popular as they are in many other countries so check that any hotel, restaurant or shop accepts them before you go in. However, you can use foreign-issued credit cards to buy JR train tickets. If you are expecting to use lockers and buses and don't have a smart card (see box p44), it is worth keeping a supply of ¥100 coins, though buses do have change machines.

Many **ATMs** at banks do not accept foreign-issued cards and, with very few exceptions, ATMs in Japan are not open 24 hours. The good news is that all 26,000 post office ATMs across the country (including small branch offices) as well as branches of 7-Eleven convenience stores accept Visa, MasterCard, Diners Club, American Express, Cirrus, Plus and Maestro cards issued outside Japan. On-screen instructions are available in English. The normal hours for post office ATMs are Monday to Friday 9am-7pm, Saturday 9am-5pm, Sunday 9am-noon (some ATMs are closed on Sunday; for more information see 🖥 www.jp-bank. japanpost.jp and click on 'Service information). ATMs at 7-Eleven stores are open 24 hours a day.

POST AND TELECOMMUNICATIONS

Post
Post offices open Monday to Friday 9am-5pm; main branches also offer a limited service in the evening and at weekends. Post offices in Japan are identifiable by a red '〒' sign outside.

Japan's **postal service** is fast and very efficient but not all that cheap. Postcards cost ¥70 to send abroad and ¥50 within Japan.

❏ **Taxes and tipping**
A **5% consumption tax** (called *shohizei*) is levied on nearly all goods and services in Japan, but you won't necessarily notice it in shops because the tax is already included on price tags. Hotel rate-cards will usually show room charges both before and after tax – the latter is the only one you need to worry about. As a rule, hotel charges quoted throughout this guide refer to the room rate after tax. See also box p103.

Additionally, upmarket hotels levy a **service tax** of between 10 and 20% on top of the 5% consumption tax. Room rates quoted in this guide are mostly on a per-room basis and do not include taxes unless otherwise stated.

There is no culture of **tipping** in Japan but see box p50.

Japanese write addresses with the country first, then the post code and the name of the recipient last; for any postcards you send make sure the destination country is clear and you add an airmail sticker. You may also be charged more if anything other than the address is written on the address side of the postcard.

Internet access

Wired (LAN) internet access is available in most Western-style hotel rooms, but not always in Japanese-style places; it is generally free for guests (except in some upmarket hotels). You may need to borrow a LAN cable from the reception desk.

Wireless access has exploded in Japan in recent years. However, free, publicly available wi-fi is rare, so, if you are bringing your laptop, iPhone or smart phone to Japan, you'll need to register with a wi-fi service. Companies worth trying are Wi300 (⌨ 300.wi2.co.jp; ¥800/day, ¥2000/week) and NTT (⌨ www.hotspot.ne.jp/en; ¥500/day); both offer unlimited wireless access. Once registered you will be able to surf the internet in most hotels, airports and fast-food restaurants such as McDonald's, as well as in some cafés, railway stations and public buildings. Go to ⌨ www.hotspot-locations.com for a list of wi-fi hot spots. Softbank (see below) also offers iPad SIM rental (from ¥1575/day). Alternatively, Skype WiFi (⌨ www.skype.com) enables you to log on to wi-fi hotspots all over Japan and pay for the time you are online with your Skype credit.

In every city and town it won't take you long to find an **internet café**. The rate (around ¥400 per hour) often includes free soft drinks and snacks. A few places require you to become a member by paying an additional charge (¥100 or ¥200) and by showing proof of identity such as a passport (a copy of the relevant pages is usually accepted).

Manga kissa (comic-book cafés) are good places to access the internet. They are often near railway stations and usually open 24 hours a day; they can also be a good place to crash for the night (see p52).

Phone

Mobile (cell) phones (*keitai denwa*) are the ultimate everyday accessory in Japan as around the world. Unfortunately you won't be able to use your own phone if it is GSM because there is no GSM network in Japan. If this is the case the best option is to rent a Japanese mobile with a SIM card.

If your phone has 3G it can be used via international roaming though this is the most expensive option. If you have an unlocked iPhone you can rent a 3G SIM card from a Japanese provider. However, this option is usually only available at airport counters but it is a much cheaper way of staying in touch. If your phone has wi-fi you can use VoIP or Skype (see above).

Phone company SoftBank (⌨ www.softbank-rental.jp) has counters at the main airports, and branches throughout the country. If you book at least three days before you arrive, you can be informed of the number for your rented phone/SIM and you can then give that to friends/relatives before you leave for Japan. A similar service is provided by NTT DoCoMo (⌨ roaming.nttdocomo.co.jp). Both companies also have roaming agreements with phone companies in most countries; see their respective websites for details.

You'll need to provide proof of identity (such as your passport) when you pick up any phone/SIM card you rent.

On almost every railway line in Japan mobile phones must be on **silent mode**; if you really need to talk to someone you need to go to the area between carriages.

The proliferation of mobile phones has not yet led to a decrease in the number of **public telephones**. Public telephones are installed on all shinkansen and some limited express services, though a surcharge is levied and you may get cut off in tunnels. Both national and international calls are possible from some green phones and the newer grey ones. Both these phones accept ¥10 and ¥100 coins and/or telephone cards. It's best to use only ¥10 coins for local calls since change is not given. Local calls cost ¥10 per minute.

マナーモードに
設定の上、通話は
ご遠慮ください。

Please set your mobile phone to silent mode
and refrain from talking on the phone.

Prepaid telephone cards (¥1000) are sold at shops, kiosks, and from vending machines inside some phone boxes. Many cities and individual tourist attractions sell their own souvenir phone cards, which make great collectibles.

Making a call When calling **city-to-city** in Japan dial the area code first (all telephone numbers in this guide include the area code). The area code can be omitted if calling a local number (for example, if you call a Tokyo number from within Tokyo omit the 03). Numbers starting 0120 or 0088 are toll free.

Three telecom operators provide **international services** at broadly similar rates. To make an international call, dial the relevant access codes – SoftBank Telecom: 0061-010; NTT: 0033-010; or KDDI: 001-010 – followed by the country code, area code (minus the initial '0') and telephone number. Making overseas calls is cheaper at night as well as at weekends and on public holidays.

Two alternative but expensive options are to place a direct-dial call from your hotel room or to look for one of the public phones in major cities which accept credit cards.

LANGUAGE

Japanese is one of the most difficult languages to learn to read and write, mixing as it does Chinese characters, known as *kanji*, with two different syllabaries, *hiragana* and *katakana* (the latter is used exclusively for writing words which the Japanese have borrowed from other languages); see pp450-1 for a guide to these scripts. That said, basic greetings and phrases are not difficult to remember (see pp450-3) and any efforts to speak Japanese will be appreciated. The Japanese always seem amazed and impressed that foreigners can speak their language, especially given the various levels and subtle nuances that need to be used in certain situations.

English or Japlish?

'English' is everywhere you look in Japan, on vending machines, advertising hoardings and in shops, though it doesn't take long to realise that this is not the English you may know. The Japanese use of English to sell products or simply look trendy has been dubbed 'Japlish'. Here is a selection of signs spotted around the country:

● Outside a pachinko parlour in Sapporo: 'The heart of the people here is burning hotly. It is for holding a chance. I am praying your fortune. This is the space filled with joy and excitement.'

● Outside a funeral parlour in Nagoya: 'Your good times are only just beginning.'

● On a vending machine in a hotel lobby in Nagasaki: '"Hot Gour Ben"' is epoch-making dishes for gourmets. It gets warm in about 8 minutes by a chemical reaction between lime and water.'

● A café sign in Matsuyama, Shikoku: 'This is the space which it is made that you get along slowly in.'

● On a vending machine in Shizuoka: 'When you have felt thirst in your heart, you are in need of an oasis for quench your thirst. Your heart are thirsting for a good feeling of place.'

● On the front of a notebook: 'This notebook having horizontal ruled lines and being able to fold up is the best for arranging sentences.'

● Inside a restaurant in Kyoto advertising its 'Steak rice in summer' dish: 'This is so hearty that you will not spend without summer lethargy. Tomato sauce must tempt the taste buds of you. This one is a full volume dish.'

● On a pack called 'Shape up Gel' given out at a business hotel: 'I can't join the party due to my ugly body. I am now in shape-up mode. Some day I will do it with dress up. Body Seleb (sic) is willing to help you to achieve it. The success gives you self-confidence. Let's go to the party where a lot of celeb gather. You will see yourself changed drastically.

A misunderstanding sometimes arises over the meaning of the Japanese word 'hai' which is translated into English as 'yes'. Anyone who has had contact with the Japanese business world knows that the Japanese do not like to commit immediately to a straightforward 'yes' or 'no' answer to a proposal, at least during a first meeting. Thus, 'hai' often means 'yes, I am listening' (this also applies when talking on the phone) rather than 'yes, I agree'.

Although nearly everyone in Japan learns English at school, this does not mean they can speak it. Despite efforts to bring more native English speakers into Japanese schools as 'assistant language teachers', the classroom emphasis continues to be on written English and grammar, rather than spoken skills. If you need help, try talking to school or university students.

If you can't make yourself understood, try writing your question down; many Japanese find reading English much easier than listening to, or speaking, it. And consider downloading a dictionary app or two on to your smartphone or tablet (see box p19).

ASSISTANCE

You'll almost certainly find that the Japanese are delighted to go out of their way to help you: all you need to do is ask. For general information see box p43

⛩ **Cultural tips**

Perhaps the most important piece of advice to remember when visiting Japan is that foreigners are not expected to know the conventions that dictate how the Japanese behave in public. Nobody's going to care, for example, if you haven't mastered the art of bowing. Indeed, people would probably be more concerned if you did know exactly how low to bow on every occasion since it might suggest you know more about the culture than the Japanese themselves (which is a far greater sin). The following tips may help, however.

● The Japanese prefer consensus over disagreement and rarely show strong emotions. Flaring into a temper if your hotel room is not ready, for example, would be considered inappropriate behaviour and people might not know how to react.

● Take your shoes off as you enter a minshuku, ryokan, temple, or someone's home; shoes and slippers are never worn on tatami mats.

● It's understood that foreigners are unable to sit on their knees for long periods of time so if you have to sit on the floor it's fine to sit cross-legged; just don't point your legs towards anyone.

● Chopstick etiquette is important to the Japanese. Pitfalls to avoid include 'spearing' food with chopsticks, allowing them to cross over each other or using them to rummage through dishes. Avoid passing food between pairs of chopsticks and never stick them upright in a bowl of rice as these actions are associated with ceremonies observed after a cremation.

● Slurping noodles is supposed to improve the flavour and is encouraged; it's also common to bring the bowl up to your mouth to ensure you don't spill the liquid.

● If drinking beer or sake with a group, it's polite to pour someone else's glass and wait for yours to be filled.

● Eating while walking along the street is becoming less taboo, but should be avoided if possible. However, eating at a festival is OK.

● Blowing one's nose in public used to be considered rude – sniffing was seen as a demonstration of your ability to resist temptation. However, nose-blowing is much more common now.

● Business cards (known as *meishi*) are almost sacred. Though tourists are not expected to carry a supply, they're still worth bringing with you. If you are offered a business card, it's considered very bad form to put it straight in your pocket and even worse if you get out a pen and scrawl notes on it. It's best to look at it for a while before putting it away.

● If you're expecting to visit someone's home, a souvenir from your home country is appreciated: tea, chocolates, biscuits, and coasters or tea towels or other things with famous landmarks on, would be perfect.

For details of etiquette in a ryokan/minshuku, see the box on p50.

and for rail information see p75. If you have lost your passport you will need to contact your embassy (see box p62). Though few **police officers** outside cities speak English, you can expect them to be polite and helpful. Even the smallest villages have a street-corner *koban* (police box), where you can ask directions.

Pharmacies are everywhere and can be recognised by the green cross outside the store. Few pharmacists speak much English but sign-language will generally do the trick.

❏ **Emergency numbers**
Police (emergencies) ☎ 110
Fire/Ambulance ☎ 119

❏ **Embassies and consulates**
All the below have embassies in Tokyo; consulate offices are listed where relevant.
Australia (☎ 03-5232 4111, ☐ www.australia.or.jp) Fukuoka, Osaka and Sapporo;
Austria (☎ 03-3451 8281, ☐ www.austria.or.jp); **Canada** (☎ 03-5412 6200, ☐ www.
canadainternational.gc.ca/japan-japon) Hiroshima, Nagoya, Sapporo; **France** (☎
03-5798 6000, ☐ www.ambafrance-jp.org) Kyoto; **Germany** (☎ 03-5791 700, ☐
www.tokyo.diplo.de) Fukui, Fukuoka, Nagoya, Osaka, Sapporo, Sendai; **The
Netherlands** (☎ 03-5776 5400, ☐ japan.nlambassade.org) Osaka; **Ireland** (☎
03-3263 0695, ☐ www.irishembassy.jp); **Italy** (☎ 03-3453 5291, ☐ www.ambtokyo.
esteri.it/ambasciata_tokyo) Fukuoka, Osaka, Sapporo; **New Zealand** (☎ 03-3467
2271, ☐ www.nzembassy.com/japan); **Switzerland** (☎ 03-5449 8400, ☐ www.eda.
admin.ch/tokyo); **UK** (☎ 03-5211 1100, ☐ ukinjapan.fco.gov.uk/en) Osaka; **USA** (☎
03-3224 5000, ☐ japan.usembassy.gov) Osaka.

SHOPPING

Department stores open daily from 10am to around 7 or 8pm, but are closed
one day a month (usually Wednesday or Thursday but rarely Sunday). If you
arrive as the store opens, dozens of eager staff will be standing in position to
greet and bow to you. If you can negotiate your way through their ranks (realis-
ing as you go that this is how Japan achieves its low unemployment figures),
you'll eventually find departments that sell everything from furniture to food,
from digital cameras to kimonos. The biggest stores often encompass several
buildings and the variety of goods can be overwhelming but they are great
places for discovering Japan's latest fashions and craziest inventions. Souvenir
hunters will certainly not be disappointed: watches, silks, bamboo and lacquerware, pottery, woodblock prints, Japanese fans, dolls, kimonos, and chopsticks
can all be found under one roof. As if selling goods were not enough, department stores also stage exhibitions of art or ikebana and sometimes even fashion
shows. Some have roof-top playgrounds, amusement arcades and beer gardens
(see p55) in the summer.

If you prefer to stay on ground level, Japan also boasts a wide range of **speciality shops** and stores. Every town or city has its own shopping area, often
identified by plastic flowers (the colour of which varies according to the season)
suspended from lamp posts; many precincts are pedestrianised and under cover.

Worth looking out for are the **hyaku-en** (¥100) shops. Strictly speaking this
is a misnomer as goods cost ¥105 (the ¥5 is the consumption tax). There are
thousands of these shops all over Japan and they offer some great bargains and
are a useful place to pick up souvenirs and presents.

❏ **Floor confusion**
A point of confusion, particularly for the British, is the way floors in departments
stores and other multi-storeyed buildings are numbered. '1F' means the ground floor,
and is not the same as the '1st floor' (which is really the 2nd floor). 'BF' indicates the
basement and B1F the first floor of the basement (there are often two).

The many **open-air markets** provide another great shopping experience. As at most markets they sell locally made goods, traditional handicrafts and fresh produce. Tourist information offices can provide details of the market day(s) in a particular town or city. Fresh fruit and vegetables are inevitably good buys; melons, for example, are one of the most expensive kinds of fruit in Japan, but you'll often be able to buy one for a quarter of the price you'd pay in a department store (though you have to forego the fancy wrapping paper, beautifully packaged box and gold ribbons).

MUSEUMS AND TOURIST ATTRACTIONS

Most museums and tourist attractions are open on Sundays and national holidays but closed on Mondays. If a public holiday falls on a Monday, museums are closed on Tuesday instead. Typical opening hours are 9.30am-5pm with last admission 30 minutes before closing. The opening hours quoted in this guide are for the full day so bear this in mind when planning your day.

Admission prices quoted are for standard adult tickets. The child rate (up to age 16) is usually 50% of the adult rate. University students sometimes qualify for small savings so it's worth showing an ISIC card at the entrance.

⛩ Japanese gardens: a potted history

Japanese gardens (*teien*) were first developed during the 8th century, in what is now Nara Prefecture. Inspired by Buddhists from China and Korea they were designed to imitate **natural scenes**, in particular the seashore, and often featured ponds large enough to go boating on, with rocks for islands and stones representing sand.

In the Heian era (794-1185), when the capital moved to Kyoto, gardens became simpler though the boating ponds remained and waterfalls were added; gardens in this period were not intended for walking around. Background, or **'borrowed' scenery** became an important design feature and one which pertains to this day; Korakuen (see pp248-9) is an example of this, making fine use of Okayama Castle for its backdrop.

The **dry garden** (*kare-sansui*) came to the fore in the Muromachi period (1333-1568). In these gardens sand and fine gravel were used to represent water, and rocks and stones symbolised islands. Dry gardens were common in Zen temples, the idea being that they should be viewed from a particular place and used for contemplation. Probably the best-known example is Ryoan-ji (see p203) in Kyoto.

The **tea-ceremony garden** developed in the Momoyama period (1568-1603). It was only then that gardens were designed to be walked through – on the way to a tea ceremony. Konchi-in in Nanzen-ji (see p205), Kyoto, is a well-known example.

The concept of the **stroll garden** evolved further in the Edo period (1603-1868), this time incorporating a variety of areas, each with a different view, for *daimyo* (feudal lords) and their guests to wander around. Many gardens also had a teahouse and ponds but the latter were by now too small for boating. These were 'secular' gardens in that they were not associated with temples. The main feature of the Meiji era (from 1868) was the spread of Western influences throughout every aspect of Japanese life. In gardens this was seen through the introduction of lawns and parks; a good example of a stroll garden is Fujita Memorial Japanese Garden (see p291) in Hirosaki.

In general in Japanese gardens, trees are trained and pruned so show their best qualities and natural landscapes are reproduced in miniature.

⛩ **Welcome cards**
   Welcome cards are free and they entitle non-Japanese to discounts (10-50%), small gifts or special services in some hotels, restaurants, museums and tourist attractions in certain parts of Japan. If you are planning to travel all over Japan it would be simplest to get the **Visit Japan Card** (🖥 www.visitjapan.jp). However, if you are only travelling in a few regions you may prefer to get the card for that region.

   The cards are available either from the tourist information offices in these areas or at the main airports; alternatively most can be downloaded and printed from the websites: Take/print out one per person.

   ● **Fukuoka** (🖥 www.welcome-fukuoka.or.jp/english) This guidebook card is valid at about 20 places in Fukuoka City.

   ● **Kobe** (🖥 www.feel-kobe.jp/_en) The Welcome Coupon entitles the holder to discounts at over 60 facilities including on the City Loop bus.

   ● **Kagawa** (🖥 www.21kagawa.com/visitor/kanko) This card is valid around Takamatsu in Shikoku and offers discounts at about 130 sites and facilities.

   ● **Kitakyushu** (🖥 www.kcta.or.jp/pdf/welcomecard.pdf) Welcome at over 80 sites/ facilities in and around Kitakyushu City, Kyushu.

   ● **Mt Fuji** (🖥 www.mtfuji-welcomecard.jp) Only available as a website printout and it is welcome at over 200 places in the Fuji, Hakone and Izu region.

   ● **Narita City** (🖥 www.chiba-tour.jp/eng/airport) Welcome at 110 places in the Narita City and surrounding area.

   ● **Northern Tohoku** (🖥 www.northern-tohoku.gr.jp/welcome) Accepted at 164 places in the region.

   ● **Tokyo Handy Guide/Map** The card/map offers discounts at 37 museums, parks and gardens in Tokyo.

   You may have to show your passport (with a 'temporary visitor' stamp in) when you apply for the card if in a tourist information office and/or when you use it.

NATIONAL HOLIDAYS

Japan observes 15 national holidays when all banks, offices and post offices, and most shops are closed. Museums and tourist attractions are usually open but will close the next day. If a holiday falls on a Sunday, the following day is treated as a holiday.

   Nearly everything, apart from public transport and larger shops, closes from 31st December to 3rd January for the **New Year** holiday. The period from 29th April to 5th May is called **Golden Week** and is a prime holiday time, as is **Obon** (mid August), even though there is no national holiday then.

● **1st January** Shogatsu (New Year's Day) – traditionally people visit a shrine; many women dress up in a kimono

● **Second Monday in January** Seijin no hi (Coming of Age Day) – girls who have reached the age of majority (20) don gorgeous kimonos and visit their local shrine

● **11th February** Kenkoku Kinenbi (National Foundation Day) – commemoration of the legendary enthronement of Japan's first emperor, Jimmu

● **20th March** Shunbun no hi (Vernal Equinox Day) – graves are visited in the week around this day

- **29th April** Showa no hi (the late Emperor Hirohito's birthday)
- **3rd May** Kenpo kinenbi (Constitution Day)
- **4th May** Midori no hi (Greenery Day) – to celebrate the former Emperor's (Emperor Hirohito) love of plants and nature.
- **5th May** Kodomo no hi (Children's Day) – kite-flying events are held all over the country
- **Third Monday of July** Umi no hi (Ocean Day)
- **Third Monday of September** Keiro no hi (Respect-for-the-Aged Day)
- **Around September 23rd** Shubun no hi (Autumnal Equinox Day)
- **Second Monday in October** Taiiku no hi (Health and Sports Day) – commemorates the opening day of the 1964 Tokyo Olympics
- **3rd November** Bunka no hi (Culture Day)
- **23rd November** Kinro kansha no hi (Labour Thanksgiving Day)
- **23rd December** Tenno no tanjobi (The Emperor's Birthday)

FESTIVALS AND EVENTS

Japan is truly a land of festivals (*matsuri*); hardly a day goes by when there is not a celebration taking place somewhere. These can be huge, lively, atmospheric events attracting thousands of visitors, such as Sapporo's Snow Festival, Aomori's Nebuta Festival or Kyoto's Gion Festival, or local festivals in towns and villages which are little known outside the area.

Parades of large floats, street processions to the tune of taiko drummers, firework displays, and colourful costumes are all part of the festival experience. Eating and drinking while walking around in public is generally frowned upon but this rule is broken at festival time; street stalls serve yakisoba, takoyaki, okonomiyaki, as well as grilled squid and octopus.

Festivals and events that are worth including in your itinerary if you are in Japan at the correct time of year are listed below. For more details see the relevant city guides. JNTO publishes a comprehensive list (🖥 www.jnto.go.jp/eng/location/festivals) which is useful if you want to plan your itinerary to include one or more.

The dates for religious festivals, which are based on the lunar calendar, vary every year but other festivals are held on the same dates.

February Yuki Matsuri (Snow Festival), **Sapporo**, Hokkaido; Fuyu Matsuri (Winter Festival), **Asahikawa**, Hokkaido. **Setsubun** (3rd Feb) is held in temples and shrines everywhere; people throw soy beans around to celebrate the end of winter (by banishing the evil spirits) and welcome the start of spring.

March-May The **cherry blossom season** is eagerly anticipated and the Japan Meteorological Agency (JMA; 🖥 www.jma.go.jp) has an internet page dedicated to reporting when the blossoms are forecast to flower. Although each year is different, the season generally starts in Kyushu in mid to late March and progresses northwards, climaxing in Hokkaido in May. Families, friends and colleagues gather to celebrate the fleeting appearance of the blossom with *hanami* (blossom-viewing) parties, sitting on plastic mats under the trees to drink and eat.

Popular spots for hanami include: Ueno Park and Shinjuku-gyoen, **Tokyo**; **Kamakura**; Philosopher's Path, Heian Jingu and Maruyama-koen in **Kyoto**; **Yoshino-yama**; **Nagoya** Castle area; **Kakunodate**; and **Hirosaki**.

April **Takayama** town festival; Yayoi Festival, **Nikko**; **Kamakura** town festival; Yabusame Festival (horseback archery), Washibari-Hachimangu Shrine, **Tsuwano**; Hi-watarishiki (fire-walking ceremony), Daisho-in Temple, **Miyajima**.

May Hakata Dontaku Festival, **Fukuoka**, Kyushu; Sanja Festival, Asakusa, Tokyo; Aoi Matsuri, **Kyoto**.

June Hyakumangoku Festival, **Kanazawa**; Yosakoi Soran Festival, **Sapporo**.

July Hakata Gion Yamakasa Festival, **Fukuoka**; Gion Matsuri, Yasaka Shrine, **Kyoto**; Tenjin Matsuri, **Osaka**. Soma-Nomaoi, **Minami-Soma** (see box p316).

Late July and August **Fireworks (hanabi) festivals** Spectacular firework displays are a feature of most summer festivals. They are often staged as a competition between rival pyrotechnic groups. The largest in **Tokyo** is the Sumida River Fireworks Display. The National Japan Fireworks Competition is held in **Omagari**, Akita, at the end of August.

August Nebuta Matsuri, **Aomori**; Neputa Matsuri, **Hirosaki**; Kanto Matsuri, **Akita**; Tanabata Matsuri, **Sendai**; Yosakoi Festival, **Kochi**; Awa Odori Festival, **Tokushima**; Yosakoi Soran Festival, **Sapporo**; Asakusa Samba Carnival, **Tokyo**.

September Yabusame at Tsurugaoka Hachimangu Shrine, **Kamakura**.

October **Takayama** town festival; Toshogu Shrine Autumn Festival, **Nikko**; Jidai Matsuri, Heian Jingu, **Kyoto**.

October to December **Autumn leaves' viewing** The autumn colours begin their magnificent display in Hokkaido and move south through the islands, in the opposite direction to the cherry-blossom wave. Well-known places for viewing autumn leaves include: **Daisetsuzan**, Hokkaido; **Nikko**; **Hakone**; **Miyajima**; Arashiyama and Philosopher's Walk, **Kyoto**.

November Hi-watarishiki (fire-walking ceremony), Daishoin Temple, **Miyajima**; International Balloon Festival, **Saga**, Kyushu.

December Kasuga Wakamiya's On-matsuri, **Nara**.

ACTIVITIES

Japan's mountainous terrain provides opportunities for a wide range of adventure activities. The Japanese Alps (Central Honshu) and Hokkaido offer the most spectacular **hiking**; routes and paths are nearly always well signposted and almost always well trodden. See 🖳 www.japanhiking.com for more details.

It's worth trying **skiing** in Japan, if only for half a day – where else in the world can you get bowed off a chair lift? There are ski resorts throughout the

🏯 **Relaxing in a hot spring or public bath**

Hot springs, known as **onsen**, are hugely popular among Japanese, who consider the chance to relax in a hot tub the perfect escape from the stresses of life. Hokkaido in particular is full of natural hot springs, where the water is often pumped direct from a bubbling pool of volcanic rock. Diehard onsen lovers travel the country in search of the perfect hot spring, and open-air baths, or **rotemburo**, are the ultimate. Some ryokan and minshuku in rural areas have rotemburo, and there are also some free, public ones, usually high in the mountains, which are mostly mixed and without facilities. At the other extreme are Japan's infamously gaudy onsen resorts, such as Beppu (see p375) in Kyushu, where luxury hotels operate themed bath houses and the water is really only a sideshow.

Onsen generally include several indoor baths of varying temperatures, a sauna, plunge pool, Jacuzzi, and, where possible, a rotemburo. If you're lucky with the location, this will afford sweeping views of the mountains and surrounding countryside.

At a public onsen you will need to pay to enter (at the counter or from a vending machine) and to rent a flannel-sized towel if you don't have one. Then head for the segregated changing rooms (for the Japanese characters for male and female see p451). As when taking a bath in a minshuku or ryokan, you're expected to wash before entering the water (see box on p50); soap is always provided. Swimming costumes are not worn but you can use your towel to protect your modesty when walking around. The onsen experience does not end the moment you step out of the bath. Changing rooms are often equipped with massage chairs, weighing machines, combs, brushes, aftershaves, scents, industrial-sized fans to help you dry off, and vending machines.

With so many hot springs scattered around Japan, it's hard to know where to start, though JNTO's leaflet *Japanese Hot Springs* (🖥 www.jnto.go.jp/eng/attractions/rest; click on Hot springs) contains a useful region-by-region guide to the country's best-known onsen. Also worth looking at is the forum on 🖥 www.secret-japan.com/onsen. Many of the reports are in French but enough are in English to make it useful.

A place on Shikoku that is definitely worth considering, because it is both traditional and easily accessible, is Dogo-onsen (see pp444-5). For an unusual bathing experience in a holy hot spring by the ocean, take a trip to the island of Sakurajima (see pp410-11) on Kyushu. Rail enthusiasts might prefer to head for the Kansai area where, in Nachi, there's a chance to soak in a tub which affords views of a railway track (see p194) and for wonderful ryokans head to Takaragawa-onsen (see box p138) or Bessho-onsen (p140).

Another option is to go to a **public bath-house** (*o-sento*). Here the water is not naturally hot but in other respects the experience is the same. Unlike onsen most people in a sento are likely to know each other and thus they can have a very communal feel. One sento that is particularly recommended is Hakusan-yu (see p202) in Kyoto. For further information visit 🖥 www.sentoguide.info.

Japanese Alps and also in Hokkaido. For everything you need to know check 🖥 www.snowjapan.com. JNTO also publishes a mini-guide called *Skiing in Japan* (🖥 www.jnto.go.jp/eng/attractions/rest; click on Skiing), which provides details of the best ski resorts in the country. Also worth looking at is: 🖥 www.skijapanguide.com.

Hokkaido, in particular, offers a huge range of other possibilities year-round – from **white-water rafting** to **canyoning**, **mountain-biking** to **snowboarding**. For more information on the great outdoors, see 🖥 www.outdoorjapan.com.

3   **THE RAIL NETWORK**

Railway history

When Commodore Perry appeared off the coast of Japan in 1853 with the US Navy's 'Black Ships' (see p132), the country, like many others, had no railway whatsoever. But in the years since Japan ended its policy of self-isolation, its rail network has become the envy of the world. This transformation, given the country's topography and history of devastating earthquakes, is nothing short of extraordinary.

PIONEERING EARLY DAYS

One of Perry's gifts on his second trip to Japan in 1854 was a quarter-size steam locomotive and accompanying track. However astonishing the sight of this miniature railway set up on the beach must have been, it would be a mistake to believe that the Tokugawa shogunate was entirely ignorant of technological developments outside Japan.

From the tiny Dutch enclave in Nagasaki, the only point of contact with the outside world in 265 years of self-imposed isolation, the Shogun had received an annual report on developments in the rest of the world. In 1865 Thomas Glover (see box p390) brought the first steam railway locomotive to Nagasaki and tested it on a line he built there. But it was not until the Meiji Restoration of 1868 (see p34) that the idea of constructing a proper railway in Japan began to take root.

The Japanese government employed a number of British engineers and pioneering railwaymen to assist in the development of the country's rail network, notably Edmund Morel (1841-71); Morel was appointed chief engineer but died a year before the opening of Japan's first railway line, between Shimbashi (Tokyo) and Yokohama, on 12th October 1872. An American, Joseph Crawford (see p322), helped build the first railway in Hokkaido.

Ninety-two years before the inauguration of the Tokaido shinkansen between Tokyo and Osaka, Emperor Meiji and his entourage set off on the country's first official train ride, a 30km journey from Shimbashi, in Tokyo, to Yokohama. The driver for this historic journey was British and the coach the Emperor rode in was made in Birmingham. Some Japanese guests, it is reported, upheld tradition by taking off their shoes before

蒸気機関車マリゴールドの野を過ぎる

The steaming locomotive passing across the field full of marigold at night (KAZUKO KONAGAI)

boarding and so travelled to Yokohama in their socks.

The use of foreign engineers was not without its complications, not least of which was the language barrier. British railwaymen accustomed to grey skies and drizzle also found it hard to adapt to Japan's hot and humid climate. Edmund Holtham, writing about his time as a railway engineer, describes how the summer heat made work 'rather a burden...in spite of running down to Kobe for a game of cricket and a plunge in the sea, I fell out of condition' (*Eight Years in Japan*, 1883).

A significant turning point came in the spring of 1879, when Japanese drivers were allowed to operate the trains between Tokyo and Yokohama – though on about one-sixth of the salary. However, it wasn't long before the Japanese were taking over from the British and other Western engineers. By 1904, as the last British railwayman set off for home, the country had embarked on an unprecedented expansion of the railway network.

❏ The Golden Age of steam?

The JR network may now be one of the most reliable in the world but it would appear from Kelly and Walsh's *Handbook of the Japanese Language* (Yokohama, 1898) that rail travel in Japan used to be far from trouble-free. The following phrases appear (together with their Japanese equivalent) in a section entitled 'A Journey By Railway' and are a useful gauge of the state of the nation's railway in its early days:

When will the train start?
　Immediately, Sir.
Didn't you tell me 'immediately' half an hour ago?

The Railroad Department seems to be asleep!
The whole railroad system is disorganised and upset.
The Railroad Department doesn't seem to care the least for the convenience of the Public.

They don't yet realise the value of time.
Are we not behind time?
　That is the usual thing in Japan.

We are now at last at our destination.
We are three hours late.

NATIONALISATION AND EXPANSION

As the railway expanded, people began to move around at previously unimaginable speeds. The old Tokaido road, for centuries the only way of getting between Edo (Tokyo) and Kyoto, was quickly abandoned after the opening of the Tokaido line in July 1889. A journey which had taken 12 or 13 days could now be completed in just 20 hours. By 1906, when a 'super express' was introduced, the journey time was cut still further to 13 hours 40 minutes. The year 1906 was significant in another way; 8000km (5000 miles) of track had been laid in just 34 years, though the majority of this was in the hands of private rail companies.

Under pressure from the military, who were finding it increasingly difficult to move around the country at any speed when they had to wait for connections between the private railways, the government passed the 1906 Railway Nationalisation Act, giving itself the authority to purchase the 'trunk' lines, while allowing private railways to own local lines. The railway (Japan National Railway; JNR) was to remain a nationalised industry until 1987.

THE RAIL NETWORK

ARRIVAL OF THE 'BULLET TRAIN'

Electrification

A nationwide network of trunk lines was well on its way to completion by 1910 but major electrification of the railway had to wait until after WWII, during which many lines sustained severe damage from bombing raids. In the early 1950s the journey between Tokyo and Osaka took most of a day and there was an observation car at the back with armchairs for passengers to enjoy the view. The Tokaido line, running through what had become Japan's major industrial corridor, was electrified in 1956. It was also in the mid 1950s that the idea began to surface for a new, high-speed link between Tokyo and Osaka. The proposal was not just for an upgrade of the existing line but for a completely new railway that would allow a top speed of 250kph. Crucially, businessmen in Tokyo and Osaka would be able to commute between the cities and return home the same day.

Picking up speed

There is no more instantly recognisable symbol of modern Japan than the *shinkansen* (literally 'new main line'), known throughout the world as the bullet train. When the government finally gave its approval for the project in 1958, Japan National Railways (JNR) had six years to prepare the line in time for the opening ceremony of the 1964 Tokyo Olympics. The deadline was made and the ribbon cut at precisely 6am on October 1st 1964, but the construction bill had spiralled from an original estimate of ¥200 billion to ¥380 billion. Initial design faults also meant passengers experienced ear pain whenever the train darted into a tunnel and, more alarmingly, gusts of wind blowing up through the toilets.

The foreign press corps was taken for a test run, however, and appeared suitably thrilled. A *Times* journalist gushed on cue to his readers, remarking that the shinkansen fully lived up to the boast of a 'new dimension in train travel': 'In the airliner-style seats one groped subconsciously, but in vain, for the safety belt as the train hummed out of Tokyo, rather like a jet taking off in a narrow street. Bridges, tunnels, even passing trains flash by, thanks to the air-tight doors, as in a silent film. It is uncannily smooth...So much tends to the vulgar in modern Japan that it is pleasant to report the superb fittings and finishing in this train...Ablution facilities dazzle, with winged mirrors, and three lavatories per car set, one of them Western-style' (*The Times*, 28th September 1964).

Two services began operation in 1964: the *Hikari* ('Light'), which initially took four hours and stopped only in Nagoya and Kyoto, and the stopping *Kodama* ('Echo'), which took five hours. The new line was an instant success and tickets sold out weeks in advance; Queen Elizabeth II and Prince Philip went for a ride during their 1975 state visit to Japan – though only after a railway strike was called off at the last minute. The construction deficit was overturned and the line was soon extended west to Okayama (in 1972), and on to Hakata (in 1975). Expansion east of Tokyo on the Tohoku shinkansen quickly followed.

Out of control

As the shinkansen spread further and sped faster, JNR's debt grew larger. Though the Tokaido shinkansen was a financial success, the rest of the network was in meltdown. The railway's total deficit year on year throughout the 1970s and '80s spiralled into thousands of billions of yen. Fares became daylight robbery, particularly in comparison with those offered by private railways, the network was grossly over-staffed, labour relations were poor and morale low. Some pointed the finger at greedy politicians. Such was the glamour of the shinkansen, reported *The Times* in January 1987 (23 years after it had enjoyed that free test ride), that 'every politician of note feels he needs a shinkansen station in his district…Over the years, promises of shinkansen services have brought in innumerable votes for the ruling Liberal Democratic Party. And with every new shinkansen put on to a marginal or loss-making line, JNR's deficit has increased.'

At midnight on April 1st 1987, the whistle was finally and literally blown on all this by the president of JNR, who rode a steam locomotive back and forth near Shimbashi in Tokyo (the starting point for Japan's first railway in 1872) on a symbolic last journey for the nationalised industry. JNR, undeniably the ultimate political pork barrel in Japan, had not made money for 20 years. Its liabilities on that April Fool's Day stood at ¥37 trillion (£160 billion), more than the combined debts of Brazil and Mexico, and £12 billion more than the US budget deficit of the previous year.

Privatisation of the railway was achieved by carving up the network into six regional passenger railway companies and one nationwide freight company, to be known collectively as the JR Group. In a bid to reduce some of the debt, unprofitable lines were closed, railway land was sold and staffing levels reduced. No longer constricted by the rules governing a nationalised company, the JR companies have since diversified into everything from department stores to hotels, hospitals and helicopters.

Future expansion

In the 21st century, expansion of the shinkansen continues apace: an under-sea link north from the Tohoku shinkansen line's current terminus in Shin-Aomori to Shin-Hakodate in Hokkaido is under construction and should be open by spring 2015. The hope is to then extend this line as far as Sapporo. The Hokuriku shinkansen extension from Nagano to Kanazawa is also due to open by spring 2015 and may then be extended to (Shin-)Osaka which would make a circular route possible. In Kyushu, a branch line from Shin-Tosu to Nagasaki is also being contemplated.

THE RAIL NETWORK

❏ **The Japanese Railway Society**
Rail enthusiasts might be interested in joining the Japanese Railway Society (🖥 www.japaneserailwaysociety.com), which has members all over the world. The society takes an interest not just in the old steam days but in the state of Japan's railway today as well as how it might look in the future. Members receive a quarterly journal, *Bullet-In*.

The society organises occasional **rail trips** to Japan through UK-based The Travel Bureau (☎ +44 1902-324343, 🖥 www.thetravelbureau.co.uk). Since the trips are not frequent they are not shown on The Travel Bureau's website so contact the society or the bureau direct for further information.

❏ **Rail museums**
Rail museums of varying size and interest are spread throughout Japan but space does not permit a nationwide listing. Worth visiting, even if you aren't a particular rail fan, are:
● **Honshu**: Railway Museum, Omiya (see p270); Tobu Museum, Tokyo (see p98); Linear Tetsudo Kan (Linear Railway Hall; also known as SCMAGLEV and Railway Park), Nagoya (see p160); Modern Transportation Museum, Osaka (see p115); Umekoji Steam Locomotive Museum, Kyoto (see p202); Usuitouge Tetsudo Bunkamura, Yokokawa, accessible from Takasaki (see p138).
● **Hokkaido**: Otaru Transportation Museum, Otaru (see p324).
● **Kyushu**: Kyushu Railway History Museum, Moji (see p366).

But new technology is not the preserve of the shinkansen. Fuel-cell trains powered by hydrogen are being tested in the hope that they can one day replace diesel services on lines not yet electrified. And one JR company, JR Central (JR Tokai), is already looking beyond the shinkansen towards the next generation of high-speed travel. It's hoped that the **Maglev**, or 'superconducting magnetically levitated linear motor car', will one day travel at over 500kph along an as yet only partially constructed Chuo shinkansen line, bringing Shinagawa (Tokyo) and Nagoya to within 40 minutes of each other. But arguments persist over funding for the project. The cost of construction of the new line is estimated at ¥17-18 billion per kilometre. The Chuo shinkansen is not expected to open fully until 2027 (with an extension from Nagoya to Osaka to be completed by 2045), but it's already predicted to become the most expensive transport project in the world. That hasn't stopped Yoshiomi Yamada, president of JR Central, comparing his company's future Maglev with the one already operating in Shanghai, saying 'Theirs can be compared to a toy for elementary schoolchildren, while our Maglev train can be compared to an iPad'.

As room to expand at home reaches saturation point, the JR companies are looking to sell their technology and expertise abroad. JR Central is keen to sell its shinkansen system to the United States and JR East has been part of a consortium bidding to build both the railway and trains for a high-speed line between Los Angeles and San Francisco.

STEAM RAILWAYS

In 1936 around 8700 steam locomotives were in operation across Japan. Complaints about the emission of black smoke, along with technological advances, brought about the demise of the commercial steam railway, as more efficient diesel and electric trains were brought into service after **WWII**. By 1976 steam had all but disappeared.

For years, many steam locomotives (known in Japan as SLs) were left to rust away in museums, or were shunted into corners of public parks and quietly forgotten. Perhaps because the Japanese now have the psychological room to look back on the nation's history of modernisation, restored SLs have made a comeback. In the late 1980s and '90s, with the vocal and financial support of nostalgic rail fans and local authorities, steam trains began to reappear as tourist attractions on rural lines. No longer the exclusive preserve of *tetsudo mania/otaku* (rail enthusiasts), of which there are thousands in Japan, preserved steam operations now cater to the tourist trade. But some experts warn that the current nostalgia boom will be short lived. Railway-equipment manufacturers are no longer geared up to supply spare parts for old locomotives and it may only be a matter of time before the SLs are once again shunted away into the sidings, for ever.

❏ Steam locomotive (SL) operations

The following is a list of major preserved steam operations in Japan. JR rail passes are valid for most of the services below but seats have to be reserved; book early as the services are very popular. For up-to-date information in English, contact JR East's information line (see p75) or visit 💻 homepage3.nifty.com/EF57/index.html.

Hokkaido
● **SL Hakodate Onuma (C11 171/C11 207)** Hakodate to Mori (daily 29th Apr to 5th May and weekends in Jul & Aug; 80 mins; one round trip/day). To add to the atmosphere staff dress in period costume.
● **SL Niseko (C11 171/C11 207)** Sapporo to Rankoshi via Otaru and Kutchan (weekends and hols Sep-Nov; one round trip/day). Seat reservations are possible only from Sapporo to Kutchan.
● **SL Fuyu no Shitsugen (C11 171/C11 207)** Kushiro to Shibecha or Kawayu-onsen (one round trip/day late Jan-Feb). A good chance for a ride through the snow!

Honshu
● **Oigawa Railway** (four SLs including the **C12 164**) Shin-Kanaya to Senzu. Operated by the private Oigawa Railway (see p135), this is one of the busiest preserved steam operations in the country and the only one with services throughout the year.
● **SL Banetsu-Monogatari (C57 180)** Niigata to Aizu-Wakamatsu on the Banetsu-Sai line (3hrs 50 mins). See p275.
● **Mooka Railway* (C11 325/C12 66)** Shimodate (JR Mito Line) to Motegi (weekends and hols for most of the year; 90 mins). The chance to experience a nostalgic branch line journey and see the steam-engine-shaped building at Mooka.* (See p270).
● **Chichibu Railway Paleo Express* (C58 363)** Kumagaya to Mitsumineguchi (weekends and hols Mar-Oct; 2 hrs 30 mins) Other trains give you the chance to outpace it for photos.
● **SL Minakami (D51 498 or newly restored C61 20)** Takasaki (see p138) to Minakami (Joetsu Line; 2 hrs; runs quite frequently at weekends and holidays Mar-June).
● **SL Usui (D51 498/C61 20)** Takasaki to Yokokawa (60 mins; runs quite frequently at weekends and holidays Mar-Apr). A good way to reach Yokokawa's museum (see p138).
● **SL Kita-Biwako (C56 160)** Maibara to Kinomoto on the Hokuriku line (typically operates on just a few days including 29th April to 5th May). See p188.
● **SL Yamaguchi (C571, nicknamed Lady of Rank)** Shin-Yamaguchi to Tsuwano on the Yamaguchi line. See p234.

Kyushu
● **SL Hitoyoshi (58654)** Kumamoto to Hitoyoshi (Mar-Nov weekends and some additional days). Originally called the SL Aso Boy; see p404.

* **Note**: reservations for the Chichibu (¥700) and Mooka (¥500) can be made at JR East offices as well as at the companies themselves. Chichibu also has a ¥500 non-reserved supplement for the Paleo Express, but it **does not** guarantee you a seat!

THE RAIL NETWORK

The railway

JAPAN RAIL TODAY

The railway in Japan is one of the most efficient in the world and it reaches nearly all parts of the four main islands. Private railways provide additional coverage but the bulk of the railway network is operated by six regional companies known collectively as the JR Group (hereafter known as JR). For the holder of a Japan Rail Pass, the six companies can be considered one national company because the pass is valid on virtually all trains across the JR network.

Every day, about 26,000 JR trains travel on a network which stretches for 20,000km. These range from some of the fastest trains in the world shuttling businesspeople from one meeting to another, to one-carriage diesel trains on remote rural lines. JR well deserves its reputation for **punctuality**; it is extremely rare for any service to run late. In the UK a train is judged to be on time if it leaves or arrives within five or ten minutes of the scheduled time – and most passengers are just grateful it is leaving (and arriving) at all. In Japan trains are officially late if they are more than one minute off the published schedule. On some lines they are meant to stay within 15 seconds and drivers assiduously check the time and any deviation from the schedule as they pass each station. Most services have a window built in to their schedule so that any lost time can be made up along the way. If there is a delay, likely never to be more than a few minutes, staff will make frequent apologies. The only time when there is a risk of major disruption is after a serious earthquake or in the event of really extreme weather conditions. Warm water is sprayed on to the tracks on the Tohoku shinkansen east of Tokyo to ensure that snow does not affect service, but in north-eastern Honshu and Hokkaido severe snow in winter occasionally does cause problems to these and other services.

❏ Women travellers

Japan is one of the safest countries in the world and it's unlikely women travelling alone will have any problems. However, in crowded commuter trains women might

find themselves being groped. The best thing to do is shout out – the offender will be embarrassed – or try to move away. As a result of this some trains (both overground and subway) have dedicated women-only carriages during peak periods.

The best advice for safe travel is the same as for anywhere else in the world: don't take unnecessary risks, know where you're going if someone invites you out, and always arrange to meet in a public place.

❏ **Japan by rail on the web**

Useful websites include:

● **Hyperdia:** 🖳 **www.hyperdia.com** Input your origin and destination points for anywhere on Japan's rail network and this site will come up with an itinerary, including transfers, journey time and fare. It will also show you the station timetable (ie all the services leaving from that station), the train timetable (ie all the stops on the journey) and the interval timetable (ie how often that service operates).

● **JNTO:** 🖳 **www.jnto.go.jp/eng/arrange/transportation** JNTO's page devoted to rail and air travel around Japan includes a route planner and online train timetable.

● **JP Rail:** 🖳 **jprail.com** An unofficial but extremely useful website about how to make the best use of the Japan Rail Pass but also about rail travel in Japan in general.

● **The man in Seat 61:** 🖳 **www.seat61.com/Japan** General information about all aspects of train travel in Japan, including the Japan Rail Pass (which can also be bought through the website).

● 🖳 **www.shinkansen.co.jp/jikoku_hyo/en** Has timetables for all shinkansen services.

All the companies in the JR Group have websites in English: **JR Central** 🖳 english. jr-central.co.jp; **JR East** 🖳 www.jreast.co.jp; **JR Hokkaido** 🖳 www2.jrhokkaido. co.jp/global; **JR Kyushu** 🖳 www.jrkyushu.co.jp; **JR Shikoku** 🖳 www.jr-shikoku. co.jp; **JR West** 🖳 www.westjr.co.jp. These have details of the rail passes, tickets and package tours available to foreign tourists for their area.

Rail companies around the world must envy JR's track record for **safety**: not a single fatality on the shinkansen since services began in 1964. The only time a shinkansen has ever derailed was in 2004 following a major earthquake near Niigata, but there were no passenger injuries or deaths. After midnight, when the shinkansen closes down for the night, a small army of engineers inspect and repair the track on a special shinkansen nicknamed the 'Dr Yellow'. They have only six hours each night to carry out essential track maintenance.

Not only is JR the most efficient rail network in the world, the trains are also some of the **best maintained**. It's worth turning up early for your shinkansen (at the beginning of a route) to see the swarm of uniformed cleaning staff who have only a few minutes to ensure the carriages are swept, the toilets cleaned, and all the seats turned round to face the correct way. At stations, platforms are always spotless, floors are constantly swept, wiped and disinfected, dustbins emptied before they are ever full and escalator rails wiped (staff seem to be employed exclusively for this task).

JR trains are no longer the paradise for smokers they once were. Some of the rail companies now **ban smoking** entirely, others permit it in certain parts of the train. However, there are dedicated smoking areas on most platforms giving smokers the opportunity for a last puff.

THE TRAINS

For **information** in English on all JR East services call the **JR East Infoline** (☎ 050-2016 1603; daily except year-end/new-year holiday period, 10am-6pm). Operators can provide information on fares and fares, and advise on routes. Seat reservations are not accepted by phone.

THE RAIL NETWORK

Shinkansen

JR's flagship trains are, of course, the shinkansen, better known as the bullet train. At the time of research the Nozomi (N700), which runs between Tokyo and Hakata, and the Hayabusa (E5) used between Tokyo and Shin-Aomori, are the fastest (300kph), but from 2013 the E6 series (to be used on the Akita shinkansen; unnamed at the time of writing) will be the fastest as they will be able to go up to 320kph. The fastest shinkansen in Kyushu is the Mizuho (800 series; up to 260kph), which runs between Hakata and Kagoshima-chuo.

The Hayabusa has (and the E6 will have) an approximately 15m-long nose, making them perhaps the most stylish-looking shinkansen. The E6 is being designed by Ken (Kiyoyuki) Okuyama, who designs Ferraris and, as for the Hayabusa, its service name will be decided by the public.

The shinkansen offers what is almost certainly the smoothest train ride in the world as the train appears to glide effortlessly along the line; this is largely because, apart from the Akita and Yamagata shinkansen, they run on special tracks and the lines were built with as few corners as possible.

The Ordinary Class **seating** configuration is either 3 x 2 or 2 x 2 and, as with most trains in Japan, seats can be turned round so that a group travelling together can face each other. Green Class seating is either 2 x 2 or 2 x 1. The 'Max' (Multi-Amenity Express) shinkansen operated by JR East on some lines are double decker; the views from the Upper Deck are, of course, better.

Facilities on board include telephones, Japanese- and Western-style toilets, and a nappy-changing room which can be used as a sick bay by anyone who is not feeling well – the key is available from the train conductor. Trolley services selling ekiben (see box p82), pastries and hot/cold drinks are found on most services; some trains also have vending machines. However, whichever train you take, it's far cheaper to stock up at a station kiosk or convenience store before you travel. There are no dining cars on bullet trains.

Most shinkansen can be used with the Japan Rail Pass.

Limited expresses

Next step down are limited expresses (LEX; called *tokkyu*), which run on the same tracks as the ordinary trains but stop only at major stations.

Most limited expresses are modern and offer almost as smooth a ride as the shinkansen but a few (mainly diesel-powered ones) are not quite as glamorous or hi-tech. The JR companies constantly try to outdo each other by rolling out ever more space-age-style interiors whenever they upgrade their limited express services. Many trains have on-board vending machines and telephones (though expect to pay a premium rate). Some are called Wide View which not surprisingly means they have extra large windows.

The seating configuration varies but is very often 2 x 2 (2 x 1 in Green Class) and, as with the shinkansen, all seats can be turned around to face the other way. Refreshments trolleys are usually available (a complimentary drink may be served in Green Class) but it is worth buying food and drink in advance as the trolleys have a limited selection. There is generally a mixture of Japanese- and Western-style toilets.

⛩ **Luggage space**
On all shinkansen and most limited expresses there is an area at the back of each car for luggage, as well as airline-style overhead storage bins or racks. Since the seat spacing is usually very good if your luggage is not too large you can probably keep it with you. If it is too big for that, or too heavy to lift up, ask to have a seat at the back of the car if you prefer to sit as close as possible to your luggage.

Local trains do not have dedicated storage areas but as long as you're not travelling during the rush hour there will be space for your luggage.

Express, rapid and local trains

Despite their names, **express** (*kyuko*) and **rapid** trains (*kaisoku*) are much slower than limited expresses and boast few facilities; they are also increasingly rare. Seating is usually 2 x 2, though on some local trains there are long rows of bench-style seats on either side of the train, which leaves plenty of standing room in the middle. There is usually no trolley service but most of these trains have at least one toilet, though this is likely to be Japanese style.

Slowest of all are the **local trains** (*futsu*) which stop at every station. The smallest trains with just one or two carriages are called 'one-man densha' (one-man trains) because the driver also acts as ticket seller and collector. However, even these have a toilet, though it will almost definitely be Japanese style.

A few lines in rural areas, particularly in Hokkaido, are served by local trains only. One of the pleasures of a ride on a local train is the chance to stand right at the front next to the driver's compartment; here you'll see close-up how and why the Japanese rail network is so efficient. Wearing a suit, cap and regulation white gloves, the driver of the smallest local train seems just as meticulous as the driver of a 16-carriage shinkansen. Before the train pulls away from each stop the driver points at the clock as if to confirm the train is indeed leaving on time, then points ahead to check the signals have given him (or her) the all clear to go.

Sleeper trains

In addition to the trains mentioned above, JR operates a (dwindling) number of sleeper services. The main options are private rooms/suites, couchettes, *goron to shito* (couchettes without bedding but which are categorised as seats), *nobinobi* (carpet cars where you lie on the floor), and reserved seats.

On services which are all berths and do not have a reserved seat section, rail-pass holders have to pay both the limited express charge (around ¥3000 – less for services that are expresses rather than limited expresses) and a hefty supplement for use of a berth. This can be anything from ¥6500 for a couchette (a bed in a compartment) to ¥21,500 or more for a private room (twin or single; see box p78); supplements vary according to the distance travelled. Holders of a Japan Rail Pass who use the Hokutosei or Cassiopeia also need to pay an additional supplement of ¥6560 to cover travel over the IGR and the Aoimori Railway (see p286).

The de luxe sleepers (Cassiopeia and Twilight Express) have a toilet and basin in every room as well as on-board showers and a dining car, but don't

THE RAIL NETWORK

❏ **Major sleeper services**
● **Ueno (Tokyo) to/from Aomori (Tohoku, Honshu)** The **Akebono** (daily; 13 hours) has couchettes, private rooms, and goron to shito*, one of which is for women only.
● **Ueno (Tokyo) to/from Sapporo (Hokkaido)** The **Cassiopeia** (3-4/week; 17 hours) has private twin rooms, luxury suites as well as a lounge and dining car.
● **Aomori (Tohoku) to/from Sapporo (Hokkaido)** The **Hamanasu** (daily; 8 hours) has couchettes, reserved seats, non-reserved seats* and nobinobi (some are women only)*; an express service so the supplement is less.
● **Ueno (Tokyo) to/from Sapporo (Hokkaido)** The **Hokutosei** (daily; 17 hours) has couchettes, private rooms, luxury suites and a restaurant car.
● **Osaka to/from Sapporo (Hokkaido)** The **Twilight Express** (4-7/week; 22 hours) has couchettes, private rooms, luxury suites, restaurant and a salon car; this service is usually a charter service for tour operators/travel agents.
● **Tokyo to/from Takamatsu (Shikoku)** The **Sunrise-Seto** (daily; 10 hours) has private rooms and nobinobi*.
● **Tokyo to/from Izumo-shi (Western Honshu)** The **Sunrise-Izumo** (daily; 12 hours) has private rooms and nobinobi*.

The **Moonlight Nagara*** (Tokyo to/from Ogaki, near Nagoya, Honshu) and **Moonlight Echigo*** (Shinjuku, Tokyo, to/from Niigata, Honshu) services are seasonal and they can be used with the JR Seishun Juhachi Kippu ticket (see opposite).

* Available to rail-pass holders without supplement. However, reservations are essential; see also pp80-1.

expect great facilities on other services. Slippers and a yukata are often provided but, surprisingly, buffet cars and vending machines are rare. The best advice is to pick up some snacks and drink before you set off.

TIMETABLES

This guide contains timetables for the main routes described (see pp454-70). Twice a year (Mar & Oct) JR publishes a condensed **timetable in English** (*Railway Timetable*) which covers the major shinkansen and limited express services. If you are intending to stick to main rail routes, this is all the information you will need. However, the Railway Timetable is not easy to find. The best place to ask for one (and to exchange your rail-pass voucher) is at a main airport, shinkansen station, or at the JNTO office in Tokyo (see p102). Bear in mind, however, that timetables can change monthly so you should not rely on the times in either of these timetables; double-check before you travel.

The best option for getting timetable information **online** in English 🖳 www.hyperdia.com (see box p75) as it offers a lot of search options, such as excluding Nozomi services, which 🖳 www.jorudan.co.jp/english/norikae does not do. Be aware, however, that some station names on Hyperdia are shown without hyphens, even when hyphenated in general use and in this guide.

Alternatively, if you can read Japanese, or even if you can't but are up for the challenge, get a copy of the **Japanese timetable** (*Jikokuhyo*/¥1050). The huge volume, which lists everything that moves in Japan (trains, buses, ropeways, cable cars, ferry services, chair lifts) is published monthly. You'll find a well-thumbed copy in every JR ticket office. Much easier to carry around is the pocket-sized version (Pocket Jikokuhyo/¥500), also published monthly; this condensed volume still contains much more information than JR's Railway Timetable in English or the timetables in this guide. Both versions of the Japanese timetable are available from any bookstore in Japan.

For a guide to using the Japanese timetable see p454.

ALTERNATIVES TO A JAPAN RAIL PASS

If you arrive in Japan without a rail pass there are a few other JR pass options, though none is quite such a good deal.

JR West's Kansai Thru Pass (see box p186) allows unlimited travel between Kyoto, Nara, Osaka, Himeji, Koya-san, Kobe and Kansai International Airport.

JR East sells a one-day **Holiday Pass** (¥2300) offering unlimited use on weekends and during holiday periods of local and rapid JR trains in the Greater Tokyo area, including the Tokyo Monorail, Omiya, Yokohama and Kamakura.

JR Hokkaido has a 3-day **Foreign Student Pass** for ¥19,000, or a 5-day pass for ¥22,000, for anyone with Exchange Student or Student visa status; and a 3-day **Working Holiday Pass** for ¥19,000, or a 5-day pass for ¥22,500, for anyone with a Working Holiday visa.

Probably the best buy is the near-legendary **JR Seishun Juhachi Kippu** ('Youth 18 ticket'). This is a seasonal ticket, permitting travel on local trains only, but it is valid everywhere, not just in one JR region. It is aimed at young people travelling around in holiday time, but there is no upper age limit. The ticket (¥11,500) is a card which can be used by one person travelling on any five days within the period of validity, or five people on one day, or any combination of two/three in between; it is stamped per day of use or per person.

The tickets are valid only during three designated periods of the year: for travel between 1st March and 10th April (on sale 20th Feb to 31st Mar); for travel between 20th July and 10th September (on sale 1st July to 31st Aug); and for travel between 10th December and 20th January (on sale 1st Dec to 10th Jan).

BUYING A TICKET

This is the most expensive way of travelling and is not really recommended if you can purchase a rail pass. However, the fare structure in Japan is straightforward.   First

❏ **Sample single fares from Tokyo**

To	Distance	Fare	Supple-ment*	Total
Hakata	1176km	¥13,440	¥8280	¥21,720
Hiroshima	894km	¥11,340	¥6910	¥18,250
Kyoto	514km	¥7980	¥5440	¥13,420
Nagano	222km	¥3890	¥4280	¥7970
Nagasaki	1330km	¥14,810	¥9730	¥24,540
Sapporo	1212km	¥14,770	¥8700	¥23,470
Shin-Aomori	713.7km	¥9870	¥6500	¥16,370
Takayama	533km	¥8510	¥5490	¥14,000

* Includes the standard shinkansen and limited express surcharges (both increase by ¥200-300 in peak periods and drop by ¥200-300 in the low season) and the seat reservation charge (¥510).

THE RAIL NETWORK

there is a basic fare which corresponds to the kilometre distance you travel; this is valid only on local and rapid trains. Supplements (see note in box on p79) have to be paid if using any other train. The fare for a return trip by rail is discounted by 20% if the one-way distance exceeds 600km.

Tickets can be purchased from ticket machines or at JR ticket offices. If buying from a machine and unsure of the fare to your destination, select the cheapest ticket and then pay the difference to the train conductor or at a 'fare-adjustment machine' at your arrival station. Most ticket machines have an option to purchase several tickets for the same journey in one go: simply push the buttons which indicate the number of adults and children in the group.

Ticket counters at major stations accept credit cards issued overseas but in most other places you'll need to pay in cash. Tables of the basic per-kilometre fares and limited express/shinkansen supplements are printed in the condensed English-language timetable; a few sample fares are provided in the box on p79.

MAKING SEAT RESERVATIONS

Seat reservations are free if you have a JR pass so it's always worth making one, particularly if travelling at peak times. Thanks to JR's computerised seat-reservation system, you can book seats up to the very last minute. Only at peak travel times, such as the Golden Week holiday (see p10), are seats booked weeks in advance. Seat reservations can be made from one month before the date of travel, for shinkansen, limited express and express services (rapid and local trains are all non-reserved).

Pass holders are not penalised for not using a seat reservation, so it doesn't matter if you miss the train or change your plans – just cancel your reservation by handing in your seat-reservation ticket. However, if you sit in a reserved carriage without a seat reservation the conductor will charge you the appropriate supplement even if you have a rail pass.

JR East offers **online reservations** (🖥 jreast-shinkansen-reservation.eki-net. com) whether you have a Japan Rail Pass, a JR East Pass or just want to buy a

Midori-no-madoguchi
(Green window reservation office)

ticket. Alternatively, at any JR station, find the **reservations office** ('Midori no Madoguchi'), or, if there are long queues, try a Travel Service Center (TSC). TSCs are JR-run travel agencies which also handle seat reservations; they are found in larger stations – look for the racks of holiday brochures outside. The regional JR companies call their TSCs by different names but they all offer the same service. The names to look out for are JR Tokai Tours (in the JR Central area), View Plaza (JR East), Travel Information Satellite (TiS; JR West), Warp Navi (JR Shikoku), Joyroad (JR Kyushu) and Twinkle Plaza (JR Hokkaido).

You can make a seat reservation at any JR station so at busy periods it may be worth going to smaller stations and/or out of peak hours. If you are planning to book a lot of journeys, it helps staff if you can show them a typed itinerary detailing dates, times and departure and arrival stations, as well as any special requests regarding window or aisle seats and which

---

The Japanese calendar

Traditionally the Japanese have named and counted their years by the length of an emperor's reign. The count starts with each new emperor. The year 2012, for example, is known as Heisei 24; Heisei being the name that refers to the current emperor's era, and 24 being the number of years that have elapsed since he ascended to the throne; the year 2013 will be Heisei 25. While the Western system of counting years is widely used, the Japanese system is often found on official documentation such as train tickets and seat reservations.

---

side of the train. For the classic view of Mt Fuji from the shinkansen, ask for a seat on the right side coming from Tokyo, and on the left side from Kyoto.

Staff usually print seat-reservation tickets for foreigners in English (as well as Japanese). For details of how to read your seat-reservation ticket if it is just in Japanese, see the sample on p453.

It is essential to have a seat reservation for the Narita Express (N'EX), the Hayabusa, Hayate and Komachi trains (all in the Tohoku region) and most sleeper services (see box p78). Also for the Mizumi-go bus between Aomori and Towada-ko and the Oirase-go between Hachinohe and Towada-ko; see pp81-2.

RAILWAY STAFF

JR staff are always impeccably dressed in company uniforms which differ slightly in design from one region to another. Suits are the norm but short-sleeved shirts are worn in summer. JR Central's (JR Tokai) conductors on the shinkansen are given a new tie once a month.

Don't expect all JR staff to speak English, though basic questions concerning platform and destination are usually no problem. At the ticket offices in major stations (such as Tokyo, Osaka and Kyoto), you'll find someone who speaks English. Some train conductors on the bullet train also speak some English. All carry pocket timetables and can advise on connection times and even tell you from which platform your next train will be departing.

Standing in line

The British may be known for queuing but the Japanese have turned standing in line into an art form. At mainline stations, including all shinkansen stops, locator maps of trains are found on each platform. These show the layout and configuration of your train and indicate precisely where you should wait on the platform. Look along the edge of the platform for numbered signs which indicate the stopping point for each carriage. You can be sure that the train will stop where it should and the doors of each carriage will open opposite the appropriate platform markers.

At busy stations there are often a bewildering number of signs telling you where to stand for particular trains. If you've got a seat reservation ticket you could show it to someone and ask them to point you in the direction of the right queue. But don't get unduly stressed about standing in the right line: all the carriages are interconnected so you can easily find the way to the right compartment once you're on board.

THE RAIL NETWORK

STATION FACILITIES

Lockers

Almost every station has lockers which range in price from ¥300 to ¥600; ¥300 lockers are big enough for day packs only, while all but the biggest rucksacks should fit into a ¥500 locker. The majority of lockers have a key and take ¥100 coins (hence they are often called coin lockers) – if you need change ask at a station kiosk. However, increasingly they dispense a password/number which you will need to key into the locker to retrieve your luggage. Also many now accept smart cards (see box p44). The fee is charged on a midnight to midnight basis, so if you store your luggage at 6pm and leave it until the following morning, you have to pay the same fee again to retrieve it. If you have a hotel booking it would be cheaper and probably easier to leave your luggage there.

Food

It is hard not to find food in any station: most have either a bakery, coffee shop, kiosk and/or convenience store; in addition there will probably be at least one noodle stall where you can get a filling bowl of udon or soba for ¥300-500.

The most popular railway food is the ekiben (see box below).

Facilities for the disabled

In the majority of stations now there are lifts (elevators) or stair lifts from platform to concourse level as well as accessible toilets. However, if travelling off the beaten track on local lines it is worth checking in advance what facilities there are. Enquire at the ticket office at least 30 minutes before the departure of your train and staff will bring a ramp and assist with boarding. They will also ring ahead to your destination station and arrange for staff there to help you leave the train.

On all shinkansen and some limited express services there is at least one car with space for a wheelchair (reservations are recommended) as well as an accessible toilet. However, on some trains, the aisles are too narrow for wheelchair use and thus it may be necessary to be lifted into a seat; the wheelchair will be left in the luggage area.

Unless facilities are specifically referred to in the route and city guides, seek assistance from station staff.

For further information visit 🖳 www.tesco-premium.co.jp/aj.

🎏 **Ekiben (station lunch box)**

'Bento' is a generic term for a packed lunch, but the ekiben (station lunch box) is a cut above the rest. There's an ekiben stall (often several) in every station. Ekiben are also sold on shinkansen and limited express trains, but it's much cheaper to buy one at the station before you leave. Most are priced at around ¥800-1500.

The boxes feature local ingredients, which give you a taste of the places you are passing through, and they are all freshly made – some even state what time of the day they should be eaten by. Most ekiben are rice based but it is possible to get sandwiches or noodles. A new development is that some come with a string which, when pulled, heats the food up. Crucial to the success of an ekiben is the shape of the box and whether the contents are pleasing to the eye as the lid is uncovered.

Tokyo

It will come as no surprise to first-time visitors that Tokyo is the most populous city in the world; over 13 million people are packed within its perimeters. There's no denying this makes Tokyo seriously over-crowded. Rumours that staff are employed at some stations to push passengers on to trains are true, at least during peak times. But if you avoid the morning and evening rush hours, it's possible to travel around Tokyo in comfort. And whatever the time of day, there is a frequent and reliable service.

More surprising than the mass of people is the fact that Tokyo became Japan's official capital only in 1868, when Emperor Meiji was restored to the throne (see p34). For centuries before, it was an undiscovered back-water and might have remained so had Tokugawa Ieyasu not decided to settle there. In 1603 Ieyasu chose Edo (which was renamed Tokyo in 1868) as the seat of government for the Tokugawa shogunate. Right up until the collapse of the shogunate in 1867, Japan's official capital remained Kyoto but the Emperor who resided there exercised no real power.

In the years since Edo was renamed Tokyo and snatched the capital prize from Kyoto, the small town has become a thriving city of commerce, industry, entertainment and luxury. Little of the old Tokyo remains but one area worth seeking out for its atmosphere is Asakusa, home to one of Japan's most vibrant temples and packed with narrow streets which are a world and at least a century away from the sky-scrapers of Shinjuku and the city-within-a-city in Roppongi.

Some arrive in Tokyo and never leave, captivated by the neon, designer stores and relentless energy of the place. Others arrive and never leave their hotel rooms, terrified of the noise and sheer number of people who fill the streets day and night.

The answer is somewhere between these two extremes. Stay just long enough to get a feel for the city but get out in time to make full use of the rail pass and discover how much lies beyond this metropolis.

WHAT TO SEE AND DO

The number of things to see, do and experience in and around Tokyo would easily fill the whole of this book. Thus this guide

Ah! what memories!
Myriad thoughts evoked
by those cherry trees!
(MATSUO BASHO)

さまざまの事おもひ出す櫻かな

focuses mostly on places that are near stops on the Yamanote or other JR lines. See also pp106-13 for details of side trips around Tokyo.

If you plan to stay a while in Tokyo consider getting the **Grutt Pass** (🖥 www. museum.or.jp/grutto; ¥2000; valid for two months from the date of issue), a booklet giving free or discounted entry to 75 museums and galleries. It can be bought at any of the sights as well as at the Tokyo Tourist Information Center (see p102) and at branches of Lawson and other convenience stores. The **Tokyo Handy Map/Guide** (free from tourist information centres) also offers some discounts.

On the Yamanote line

JR's Yamanote line runs in a loop around Tokyo; the text below suggests stopping-off points both on and off the line. The route follows an anti-clockwise direction, beginning and ending at Tokyo station. A full circuit of the Yamanote line takes about an hour and is recommended as a way to orientate yourself and get a sense of the different sides to Tokyo, the range of architecture, and the wonderful blend of old and new. Yamanote line trains have on-board colour screens above the doors telling you (in Japanese and English) what the next stop is, how long it will take to get there and even which side of the train the exit is going to be, so it's easy to navigate your way around.

Tokyo Station This is the terminus for most shinkansen services to the city as well as conventional JR lines. The station is divided into **Marunouchi** and **Yaesu** sides; see p98.

The Marunouchi side of Tokyo station is the old half and has a traditional red-brick frontage. The landmark Tokyo Station Hotel (see p104), centrepiece of a multi-billion-yen project to restore this side of the station to its early 20th-century heyday, is due to reopen in October 2012. Until then you can expect building work and scaffolding to obscure much of the outside facade.

A short walk north-west from the Marunouchi exit brings you to the imposing **Imperial Palace** (Kōkyo), surrounded by a stone-wall moat. Home to the Emperor and his family, this is a quiet oasis of green but is mostly off-limits to the public except on two days of the year (23rd Dec and 22nd Jan), when the Emperor, his wife, and other family members wave from the balcony to thousands of enthusiastic flag-waving patriots and tourists. One area the public can visit are the **Imperial Palace East Gardens** (Kokyo Higashi-gyoen; Tue-Thur & Sat-Sun 9am-4.30pm, Nov-Feb to 4pm; free), which include a Japanese-style garden (Ninomaru). From there you can walk to **Kita-no-maru Park**, home to the **National Museum of Modern Art Tokyo** (Tōkyō Kokuritsu Kindai Bijutsukan; 🖥 www.momat.go.jp; Tue-Sun 10am-5pm, Fri to 8pm; ¥420), which showcases contemporary Japanese art and crafts. Also in the park is the **Nippon Budokan** (🖥 www.nipponbudokan.or.jp), a venue for martial arts events and concerts. The park is also a convenient way to get to **Yasukuni Shrine** (🖥 www. yasukuni.or.jp; daily Jan-Feb & Nov-Dec 6am-5pm, Mar-Apr & Sep-Oct to 6pm, Jun-Aug to 7pm; free), where Japan's war dead are remembered.

Yurakucho Alight here for the **tourist information centre** (see p102), which is just beyond **Tokyo International Forum** (🖥 www.t-i-forum.co.jp). The latter mainly hosts conventions but it's worth popping in to see the magnificent architecture.

It is about a five-minute walk to the Ginza area (see pp91-2) from here (take the Ginza exit) if you prefer to save the cost of a subway/private line ticket.

Shimbashi Shimbashi was the birthplace of the railway in Japan and it remains a centre of rail innovation as the starting point for the Tokyo Waterfront New Transit Line, a monorail better known as the **Yurikamome** (see below), which whisks passengers to **Odaiba**, an island of reclaimed land in Tokyo Bay. In the square outside the station is – to quote one rail fan – a 'rather sad, stuffed and mounted' steam locomotive (C11 292), built by Nippon Sharyo in 1945.

Shiodome is near Shimbashi station and is also a stop on the Yurikamome. It used to be a railroad area but has now been redeveloped into a futuristic office and leisure space. However, the district's railway heritage has not been entirely forgotten: the **Former Shimbashi Station** (Tue-Sun 11am-6pm; free), a replica of Japan's first station building, stands on the site of the birthplace of the country's railway system. It houses a small Railway Exhibition Hall, which traces the history of railways and trains (originally called landsteamers) in Japan. Most signs are only in Japanese, but the videos have English dubbing/subtitles. The original building, which served as the terminus for Japan's first 29km rail line from Tokyo to Yokohama in 1872 (see p68), burnt to the ground in the Great Kanto Earthquake of 1923. But Shimbashi, later renamed Shiodome station, rose from the ashes and continued to serve as an important railway junction in various guises – latterly as Tokyo's main freight terminal – until 1986, when it was finally abandoned.

At the adjacent **Shiodome City Center building**, the **Panasonic Living Showroom** (🖥 www.shiodome-cc.com; Thur-Tue 10am-6pm; free) is worth a brief visit to see Panasonic's latest lifestyle products; there are restaurants in the basement. Nearby, in **Caretta Shiodome**, is **Advertising Museum Tokyo** (ADMT; 🖥 www.admt.jp; Tue-Sun 11am-6.30pm; free). The museum, at the headquarters of Dentsu, Japan's leading advertising company, focuses on the history of advertising from the Edo period (1603-1868) to the modern day.

Hama-Rikyu Garden (daily 9am-5pm; ¥300) is one of Tokyo's best-known landscape gardens. The park is peaceful and has a number of ponds which change level with the tide, as well as wooded areas and a teahouse. It is a 10- to 15-minute walk from the station though actually is best accessed on one of the water bus services (see box p87). You can pick up a map here to guide you to Kyu-Shiba-Rikyu garden (see p87).

The Yurikamome monorail to Odaiba

The chance to see Tokyo from another angle makes a trip from Shimbashi to Odaiba worthwhile in itself, but the monorail (🖥 www.yurikamome.co.jp) calls at plenty of tourist attractions along the way. As you leave Shimbashi look to the right for views down onto the shinkansen.

A one-way journey from Shimbashi to the terminus at Toyosu (¥370) takes around 30 minutes. A one-day pass costs ¥800, valid for unlimited travel between Shimbashi and Toyosu. An Odaiba and Ariake area one-day ticket

TOKYO & OSAKA

costs ¥900 and includes the Yurikamome, the water taxi (a limited route around the Odaiba area) and travel on the Rinkai Line (from Osaki to Shin-Kiba via Tokyo Teleport on Odaiba); buy a ticket or pass from a machine in any of the stations. Some of the attractions offer a discount if you have a one-day pass.

From Shimbashi trains stop at **Shiodome** (see p85), **Takeshiba**, **Hinode** (a stop on the water bus route; see box opposite) and **Shibaura-Futo**, after which the train does a loop and crosses the spectacular **Rainbow Bridge**, so called because the lights on it are illuminated at night. If the weather is good it is worth walking across the bridge. Take the east exit from Shibaura-Futo station and then walk straight along the road (about 10 mins) towards Rainbow Bridge. When you get near the bridge turn left and follow the signs to the lift and take that up to the 7th floor. Turn right to walk on the north side and left for the south side. The noise of the traffic means it isn't really a relaxing walk and at first the view is spoiled by the metal grille but there are proper viewing places where there are excellent views of Tokyo's cityscape. It will take approximately 20 minutes to cross the bridge and from there head for Marine Beach (see below).

Odaiba-kaihin-koen Stop here to visit **Marine Beach**, a seaside park with a man-made beach, and **Decks Tokyo Beach**, a vast retail space which includes **Tokyo Joypolis** virtual reality games arcade (🖥 tokyo-joypolis.com; daily 10am-11pm; ¥500, ¥3500/1-day pass) and **Little Hong Kong**, a dozen restaurants set in a themed area and spread across the 6th and 7th floors.

The space-age metallic building with a sphere suspended in the middle belongs to **Fuji Television**. There is an observatory (Tue-Sun 10am-6pm; ¥500) in the sphere.

Daiba Go to **Aqua City Odaiba** or **DiverCity Tokyo Plaza** for shopping and eating options and to **Gundam Front Tokyo**, with a 18m statue of the anime character Gundam in front, and **Mediage**, a cinema complex, for entertainment.

Fune-no-kagakukan Nearest stop for **Miraikan** (Museum of Emerging Science and Innovation; 🖥 www.miraikan.jst.go.jp; daily 10am-5pm apart from some Tuesdays; ¥600), in Tokyo Academic Park, where you can discover the latest in robot technology or just lie back and watch the earth revolve with displays of the sea-surface temperature and projections of future global warming and a global chemical weather-forecasting system.

Telecom Center Alight here for **Telecom Tower**. Inside is an observation deck (Tue-Fri 3-9pm, Sat & Sun 11am-10.30pm; ¥500) which offers views of the city. This is also the stop for **Oedo-onsen Monogatari** (☎ 03-5500 1126, 🖥 www.ooedo onsen.jp/higaeri; daily 11am-8am (no entry 2-5am); ¥2900, or ¥2000 after 6pm), an enormous hot-spring theme park set in the Edo period with more baths than you'll be able to visit in a day. The hot water is pumped up from a natural source 1400m below ground. Massages and other spa treatments are available, there are 16 restaurants and accommodation is planned and may be available by the time you are here. If you're not expecting to visit another onsen in Japan this will give you a good insight into why the Japanese take the art of bathing so seriously.

Aomi From here you can visit **Palette Town**, an entertainment complex which includes the **Mega Web** theme park (🖥 www.megaweb.gr.jp; daily 11am-9pm, occasional closed days), a showcase for Toyota, where you can see and get in all their latest models and, if you have a driver's licence, go for a spin in one. Palette Town also includes **Venus Fort**, an Italianate shopping centre geared towards women and with plazas and fountains. Also here is the tallest (115m-high) **Ferris wheel** (daily 10am-10pm, Fri & Sat to 11pm; ¥900) in Japan, though the one in Sakuragicho (see pp127-8) is not much smaller.

Kokusai-tenjijo-seimon The stop for **Tokyo Big Sight International Exhibition Center** (🖳 www.bigsight.jp). Shows, such as Tokyo Motor Show and the International Robot show, are held here. The Conference Tower is probably architecturally the most unusual building in this area as it is based on an inverted pyramid.

Ariake If you haven't visited the Sony Building (see p92) in Ginza get off here for the **Panasonic Center** (🖳 panasonic.net/center/tokyo; Tue-Sun 10am-5pm; free) where their latest products are displayed.

After Ariake there is little of interest: trains stop at **Ariake-Tennis-no-Mori** (where national and international tennis matches are played), **Shijo-mae** (there is a good view of Tokyo Tower from here), **Shin-Toyosu** and the terminus at **Toyosu**, future site of Tsukiji, Tokyo's fish market (see p92), and home to the Lalaport shopping centre. Toyosu links up with the Yurakucho subway line.

If you have the Odaiba and Ariake area ticket you can take the water bus from Toyosu back to Hinode and then walk a couple of minutes to the ferry passenger terminal where you can catch a water bus (see box below) up Sumida-gawa to **Asakusa** (see p94).

Hamamatsucho The Tokyo Monorail to **Haneda Airport** (see box p101) starts here. Opposite the north exit of the station, **Kyu Shiba-Rikyu** (daily 9am-5pm; ¥150) is a landscape garden (see box p63) that was originally built on reclaimed land and is now surrounded by skyscrapers. It is smaller and less peaceful than Hama-Rikyu (see p85) but quite pleasant in that you can see the whole garden in one view. It is probably not worth making a special trip for but if you combine it with the boat trip to Hama-Rikyu you can then walk here and

---

⛩ **Tokyo from the water**
   A number of companies operate water buses or sightseeing trips. All are a great way of seeing Tokyo from the water and have a recorded English commentary.

Tokyo Cruise Ship (🖳 www.suijobus.co.jp) offers two ways of going by boat between Asakusa and Odaiba. The traditional way is to take the Sumida River Line (daily 10am-6pm; 1-2/hr; 40 mins; ¥760), which operates between Asakusa and Hinode Pier (Hinode is linked with the Yurikamome monorail; see p85) and stops at Hama-Rikyu garden en route. For a more hi-tech journey, take the Asakusa-Daiba Direct Line, which uses the futuristic-looking Himiko water bus (daily except 2nd Tue and Wed of the month; 2-4/day; 50 mins; ¥1520), which runs in a loop from Asakusa (same starting point as the River Line cruise) to Odaiba Seaside Park. It is best to go in the evening when the floor panels on the water bus are lit up.

Mizube Cruise Line (🖳 www.tokyo-park.or.jp/english/business; Tue-Sun 6/day, more in peak periods) operates between Ryogoku (see p94) and Odaiba Seaside Park (60 mins; ¥1000) with stops at Asakusa (10 mins; ¥300) and Hama-Rikyu (25 mins; ¥500; see p85).

thus make a circuit. While in the area you may also like to go up to the Observatory (Seaside Top; daily 10am-8.30pm; ¥620) at the top of **Tokyo World Trade Center Building**. Take the dedicated lift to the 40th floor.

The next stop is **Tamachi**.

Shinagawa A useful station as it is also a stop on the Narita Express (see box p100), the Tokaido/Sanyo shinkansen to Shin-Osaka and several main lines (Tokaido, Keihin-Tohoku, Yokosuka & Sobu) as well as being on the Yamanote line. The station is also worth exploring for its vending machines (see box p54).

The next stops are **Osaki**, **Gotanda**, **Meguro** and **Ebisu**.

Shibuya Follow the signs for the Hachi-ko Exit (see box below), which will lead you to the main shopping area. The zebra crossing in front of the station is always packed with people making a beeline for the shops and boutiques. Head up Koen-dori (the road goes to the right of Starbucks) away from the station to find all the top fashion department stores. The road to the left of Starbucks leads to a pedestrianised area which has plenty of shops and restaurants and the road to the left of that leads to the original branch of **Shibuya 109**, home to over a hundred boutiques with all the latest fashions. **Hikarie** (💻 www.hikarie.jp) is a new, 34-storey complex on the other side (east exit) of the station incorporating a theatre for musicals, galleries (on the 8th floor), shops, restaurants and offices.

Harajuku Opposite Harajuku station is **Yoyogi Park** (daily Apr-mid Oct 5am-8pm, mid Oct-Mar to 5pm), site of **Meiji Jingu** (💻 www.meijijingu.or.jp; daily at least 6.40am-4pm), Tokyo's best-known shrine. It is a 5- to 10-minute walk from the station. Dedicated to Emperor Meiji and his consort, the shrine is divided into Outer and Inner gardens; the Inner Garden (daily 9.30am-4.30/5pm, longer in June; ¥500) is particularly popular in June when the irises are in bloom. Harajuku is just as hip as nearby Shibuya and there are plenty of restaurants, cafés and trendy (read: retro/alternative) clothes and music stores in the streets around the station. On Sundays, particularly in the afternoon, crowds of *cosplay* fans take over Jingu Bashi (Jingu Bridge) and the area leading to Yoyogi Park.

Yoyogi The huge skyscraper you can see looming over Yoyogi station is Nippon Telecom's DoCoMo Tower. It's easier to transfer to the Chuo/Sobu Line for Tokyo and Ryogoku (see p94) here than at Shinjuku. Take an orange train for Tokyo and a yellow one for Ryogoku and beyond.

⛩ The legend of Hachi-ko

Hachi-ko was an Akita dog born in Odate (see p294) in 1923 and brought to Tokyo by its owner, Eisaburo Ueno, the following year. A pet of unflinching loyalty, Hachi-ko bade his master goodbye every morning when he left for work and greeted him at the end of the day at Shibuya station. Such was the dog's devotion, that even after Ueno died in 1925 Hachi-ko continued to return every day for the next 11 years to the station and waited patiently for him. The statue of Hachi-ko which stands today outside Shibuya station (see above) is a popular local landmark and meeting place.

Shinjuku Probably the busiest station in the world, Shinjuku is home not only to JR but also to the private Odakyu (for Hakone, see pp112-13) and Keio railways. There's a certain Jekyll and Hyde character to this district. While the west side of the station is a sea of grey suits and immaculately turned-out business-men, conformity is abandoned over on Shinjuku's east side. The streets around **Kabukicho**, a few minutes' walk north of the east exit, fill up as the sun sets and the neon is switched on. Cinemas, clubs, restaurants, pubs and hostess bars compete for business and cater for all tastes. See also Where to stay (p104).

If you were to follow any of the mass of commuters (taking the west exit) between 6 and 8.30am, you would probably end up heading directly for the **Tokyo Metropolitan Government Building**, completed in 1991 and the work-place of 13,000 bureaucrats. The best reason for visiting here is the free bird's eye view of Tokyo and even as far as Mt Fuji (Dec-Feb is best for this). Even if the weather isn't good enough to see Mt Fuji, it is worth going to see the rooftop tennis courts and helipads as well as Tokyo Sky Tree (see p95). To get to the top, take the direct elevator inside the No 1 Building (go down the steps outside so that you enter the building at basement level) up to one of two 202m-high observatories (daily 9.30am-11pm) on the 45th floor. The South observatory is open during the day and the North at night. Volunteers give free guided tours of the views from the observatory (daily 9.30am-3pm; 20 mins) or of the building (40-50 mins). The cafés on the 45th floor are overpriced but for a reasonably priced meal with a view go to the canteen (Mon-Fri 11am-2pm) on the 32nd floor; it's meant for government employees but is open to everyone. The can-teen is in two areas with different choices in each; when you have chosen select the appropriate number at one of the vending machines, then go and pay; after collecting your food from the relevant counter find a seat with a view.

On your way in or out of the building, call in at the **Prefecture Corner** on the 2nd floor (daily 9.30am-6.30pm) for general information about the rest of Japan and at the **Tokyo Tourist Information Center** on the 1st floor (street level; see p102) for details about Tokyo.

Shinjuku Gyoen (⌨ www.env.go.jp/garden/shinjukugyoen; Tue-Sun 9am-4.30pm; extended hours during the cherry blossom season and for the Chrysanthemum Exhibition in early Nov; ¥200) is a complete surprise in amongst Shinjuku's skyscrapers. Built in 1906 as an Imperial Garden, all 58.3 hectares are open to the public and the site includes an English landscape garden, French garden and traditional Japanese garden. A couple of tea houses serve green tea and Japanese sweetmeats for ¥700. People come here to escape the busy city that surrounds the park; though you never quite feel you've left the metropolis, this is a pleasant temporary escape. Take the east exit from Shinjuku station and walk south-east, following the signs, for about 10 minutes.

The next stops on the Yamanote Line are **Shin-Okubo**, **Takadanobaba** and **Mejiro** (see Where to stay p104).

Ikebukuro On either side of Ikebukuro station are two enormous department stores; **Seibu** is on the east side and its rival **Tobu** is on the west. An underground passageway links both sides of the station. Both Seibu and Tobu have restaurant floors and food halls. See Where to stay p104.

Otsuka Transfer here for the **Toei Toden (tram) Arakawa line** (see pp93-4).

The next stop is **Sugamo**.

Komagome If you decide to stay here (see Where to stay, p104), **Rikugien** (daily 9am-5pm; ¥300), a large landscaped garden, constructed in 1700, featuring a pond, islands, trees, artificial hills as well as several tea houses is worth visiting at any time of the year. It is a seven-minute walk from the station,

The next stops are **Tabata** and **Nishi-Nippori**.

Nippori Nippori is a point of transfer for the private Keisei Railway line to Narita Airport. It is also good for **trainspotting**, with both JR (including the shinkansen) and private line trains passing constantly. Follow the signs first for the North Gate and then for the east exit and then turn left out of the station just after passing the ticket office and cross the road. A poster on the building to the left identifies the trains you might see. See also Where to stay (pp104-5).

Nippori is also one of the few areas in Tokyo where you can get views of Mt Fuji (**Fujimizaka**) without going up a tower. From the North Exit walk uphill for about five minutes; assuming the weather is good (Dec-Feb is usually the best time) you should get views of Mt Fuji between the buildings.

Uguisudani Up until WWII, Uguisudani was a popular geisha quarter but it is now better known as a night-time pleasure area full of love hotels.

Ueno A major rail junction and the second stop after Tokyo for shinkansen services to the north. Ueno is an access point for Asakusa (see p94) as it is the nearest stop for transferring from the Yamanote line to the Ginza subway line.

Right outside the station is **Ueno Park**, Japan's oldest public park and the largest in Tokyo. During the cherry-blossom season in March/April, thousands of Tokyo residents come here armed with portable karaoke machines, picnic hampers and crates of beer. The park is home to a number of big museums including: **Tokyo National Museum** (🖳 www.tnm.jp; Tue-Sun 9.30am-5pm, Apr-Dec Fri to 8pm for special exhibitions, Apr-Sep Sat & Sun to 6pm; ¥600), the country's largest, with exhibits on the history and fine arts of Japan, China and India; and **National Museum of Western Art** (🖳 www.nmwa.go.jp; Tue-Sun 9.30am-5pm, Fri to 8pm; ¥420) displays masterpieces collected by a Japanese business magnate while travelling around Europe in the early 1900s. Also here is **Ueno Zoo** (🖳 www.tokyo-zoo.net/english/ueno; Tue-Sun 9.30am-5pm; ¥600), which opened in 1882 and is the oldest zoo in Japan. The two new pandas (RiRi and ShinShin) from China, who have been on show since March 2011, have boosted the number of visitors dramatically.

The fascinating **Shitamachi Museum** (🖳 www.taitocity.net/taito/shitamachi; Tue-Sun 9.30am-4.30pm; ¥300, English-language guide/leaflet ¥500) features a small display of recreated shops and homes from the Edo and Taisho periods. It is on the south-eastern side of Ueno Park near Shinobazuno pond (Shinobazuno-ike).

Another reason for visiting Ueno is to wander around **Ameyoko Market** (Ameyoko-cho). Take the Shinobazu exit at Ueno station and head for Ameya-dori, a long shopping arcade that extends beneath the elevated rail tracks. Stallholders call out loudly to passers-by and this is one of the few places in Japan where you are expected to haggle. You can buy almost anything here, including (fake?) Prada handbags, Rolex watches, clothes as well as food.

A 20-minute walk along Asakusa-dori from Ueno takes you to **Kappabashi** (see p94).

Okachimachi Okachimachi is known for its cheap jewellery stores.

Akihabara Akihabara is the discount electrical goods district (Electric Town) of Tokyo and the place to see the latest gadgets months before they hit the worldwide market. If you're planning to buy, check that the guarantee is valid overseas and that the voltage requirements are compatible.

While Akihabara has been traditionally associated with cutting-edge technology, the district is increasingly becoming a centre for animation and manga (comics) and is home to **Tokyo Anime Center** (🖳 www.animecenter.jp; daily 11am-7pm; free) on the 4th floor of the UDX Building. Follow the signs to the Electric Town exit, turn right out of the station, cross the plaza and go up the escalator. The Anime Center is a short walk along on the left-hand side. The centre is geared to children but is worth visiting for anyone interested in animation especially as, unlike Studio Ghibli (see box p92), there is a lot of explanation in English. There is a 3D Theater which screens new works as well as other anime-related events.

Change here for the JR Sobu Line to Ryogoku (see p94) and to Kinshicho for the closest JR station to Tokyo Sky Tree (see p95).

The next stop is **Kanda**.

Tokyo Station This completes the loop around the Yamanote line.

Off the Yamanote line
Ginza One stop on the Marunouchi subway line from Tokyo, Ginza is billed in tourist literature as the 'most fashionable shopping paradise in Japan'; the main thoroughfare, Chuo-dori, is lined with upmarket department stores and designer-label boutiques.

Apart from shopping, Ginza's best-known entertainment is kabuki (see p40); however, **Kabuki-za** (☎ 03-3541 3131, 🖳 www.kabuki-za.co.jp), 10 minutes south-east of central Ginza on a corner of Harumi-dori, is being rebuilt and will reopen in spring 2013. Performances have transferred to other theatres; see 🖳 www.tokyokabukiguide.com or 🖳 www.kabuki-bito.jp/eng/contents for details. The new building will retain the original façade but will be connected to an office block. The basement level will be linked to Higashi-Ginza subway station and there will be a large area with shops, restaurants and a tourist information centre. The Harumi-dori entrance will be for the kabuki theatre and Showa-dori will be the entrance for the office block.

Sony Building (🖥 www.sonybuilding.jp; daily 11am-7pm; free) hosts a number of shops and restaurants (11am-9pm) but most interesting are the Sony Showrooms on the 1st-4th floors. It's best to take the lift to the 4th floor and walk down, touching, seeing, hearing and experiencing the latest technology as you go. Take Exit B9 from the subway; alternatively it is a five-minute walk from the Ginza exit of JR Yurakucho station (on the Yamanote line).

Tsukiji Tsukiji (Tokyo Metropolitan Central Wholesale Market; 🖥 www.tsukiji-market.or.jp; Mon-Sat exc public holidays and occasional days; first group entry at 5.25am, second at 5.50am) is Japan's biggest fish market (90% of all fish sold in Tokyo comes from here) and a popular tourist attraction. As this makes life very difficult for the market traders, visitor numbers are now limited to 120 people a day, on a first-come-first-served basis. Queue at the O-sakana Fukyu Center (open from 5am) at the Kachido-ki gate. Tsukiji is two stops from Ginza on the Hibiya subway line. However, that is closed till about 5am so you need to get a taxi or stay nearby.

The market was scheduled to move to Toyosu (see p87), on Odaiba, several years ago but this was delayed because the top layer of the soil there was found to be toxic and needs to be removed. The move is now expected to be in 2014. Check the website or ask at a tourist information centre before you go.

Roppongi Also on the Hibiya subway line (transfer from the Yamanote line at Ebisu), Roppongi comes alive at night when the neon goes on and clubs and bars throw open their doors. The only reason for coming here by day is to climb the landmark 333m-high **Tokyo Tower** (🖥 www.tokyotower.co.jp; daily

---

⌂ Animation museums

If Tokyo Anime Center in Akihabara (see p91) has whetted your appetite for the cartoon world, there are some other places just outside the city centre you might like to consider visiting. The tiny **Suginami Animation Museum** (🖥 www.sam.or.jp; Tue-Sun 10am-6pm; free) hosts special exhibitions and has displays on every aspect of animation as well as a theatre showing some anime classics. Take the JR Chuo line to Ogikubo station, follow signs for the north exit, take a Kanto bus from either stop No 0 or No 1 and get off at Ogikubo Keisatsusho-mae (Ogikubo Police station), a five-minute journey.

Studio Ghibli Museum (🖥 www.ghibli-museum.jp; Wed-Mon 10am-6pm; ¥1000), a celebration of the work of leading Japanese animator Hayao Miyazaki, famous for – among many others – his 2001 film, *Spirited Away*. Explanations are only in Japanese, but it's primarily a visual museum, with many of Miyazaki's original drawings on display, and a screening (approx 20 mins) of one of his short films. The nearest station is Mitaka, on the JR Chuo line from Shinjuku (20 mins); from Mitaka either take the small community bus from outside the south exit (round trip ¥300) or walk 15 minutes along Tamagawa-josui. Entry to the museum is restricted so it is **essential** to get **tickets in advance** – either from a JTB office in your home country (see pp16-18), from any branch of Lawson in Japan, or from the Travel View travel agency near Mitaka station. As long as the foreigner allocation of tickets has not been sold for that day you should get in – but do not go to the museum until you have a ticket.

⛩ **Roppongi in the 21st century**

For a glimpse of 21st-century urban life, it's worth exploring at least one of the cities-within-a-city that are Roppongi Hills (🖥 www.roppongihills.com) and Tokyo Midtown (🖥 www.tokyo-midtown.com). In both, shops, cinemas, restaurants, galleries, museums and offices all converge on one space. They can be accessed directly from Roppongi station on the Hibiya subway line.

Art Triangle Roppongi refers to the National Art Centre, Suntory Museum of Art and Mori Art Museum. If you go to one of these, keep your ticket stub for a discount at the other museums. The walking route between the galleries is well signposted and the guide also gives information about smaller galleries in the area.

Roppongi Hills Roppongi Hills was the brainchild of construction tycoon Minoru Mori, one of the world's richest men. Crowds of well-heeled Japanese flock to the upmarket design stores and restaurants, but there's something here to please visitors of all budgets. An English *Gourmet Guide* lists all the restaurants and cafés, many of which will not break the bank. Once you've shopped and eaten to your heart's content, don't leave Roppongi Hills without visiting the landmark **Mori Tower**, inside which you'll find the **Mori Art Museum** (🖥 www.mori.art.museum; Wed-Mon 10am-10pm, Tue 10am-5pm; admission price varies), a great contemporary art space on the 53rd floor. On the 50th floor **Mori Urban Institute for the Future** (Mon-Thur 10am-8pm, Fri-Sun 10am-10pm) contains, among many other things, magnificent scale models of New York and Tokyo; and on the 52nd floor is **Tokyo City View** (Mon-Thur & Sun 10am-11pm, Fri & Sat to midnight, Sky Deck 11am-8pm; ¥1500 or ¥1200 if bought in advance at a Ticket Pia counter or any convenience store), an observation platform which affords a spectacular 360-degree panorama of the city down below. Sky Deck (an additional ¥300) is an open-air rooftop (270m) observatory and thus may be closed in bad weather.

Tokyo Midtown Apart from shops, restaurants, offices and residences the Tokyo Midtown site includes a *Ritz Carlton Hotel* (☎ 03-5474 5311, 🖥 www.ritzcarlton.com/hotels/tokyo), on the top nine floors of **Midtown Tower**, a 53-storey skyscraper, and three exhibition spaces: **Suntory Museum of Art** (🖥 www.suntory.com/culture-sports/sma; Wed-Mon 10am-6pm, Fri to 8pm), **21_21 Design Sight** (🖥 www.2121designsight.jp; Wed-Mon 11am-8pm; ¥1000), and the **National Arts Centre** (🖥 www.nact.jp; Wed-Mon 10am-6pm, to 8pm on Friday).

9am-10pm), which opened in 1958 as a symbol of Japan's post-war recovery; it is 13m higher than the Eiffel Tower in Paris and is the world's tallest self-supporting steel tower. However, since 2011 it has been dwarfed by the Sky Tree (see p95). Entry to Tokyo Tower's 150m-high observatory costs ¥820; an additional ¥600 gets you up to the 250m 'special observatory'. Mt Fuji can sometimes be seen from here, particularly in the winter months.

Toei Toden (tram/streetcar) Arakawa line One of Tokyo's two surviving tram lines runs between Waseda and Minowa-bashi (29 stops; 50 mins). The line passes through some of Tokyo's oldest neighbourhoods and the best place to join it is outside **Otsuka station** (see p90) on the Yamanote line. The journey isn't massively exciting, but it is a chance to see another side of Tokyo. Sadly, however, the characterful trams dating from 1962 are slowly being replaced and the modern versions aren't as atmospheric. Take the south exit at Otsuka station and turn left. Trains to Minowa-bashi leave on the left side but note that some trains terminate at Arakawa-shakomae. The flat fare is ¥160 (throw the money in the box as you enter), or you can buy a 1-day pass (¥400); see also p103.

Asakusa The best-known landmark in Asakusa, the last stop on the Ginza subway line (take Exit 3 from the subway), is lively **Senso-ji**, also known as Asakusa Kannon-ji. The temple is said to have been founded in the 7th century and was named after Kannon, Goddess of Mercy. The present main hall was rebuilt in 1958. The temple is reached through **Kaminari-mon** (Kaminari gate) and along Nakamise Shopping Street, lined with stalls selling everything from lucky charms to rice crackers. Across the street from Kaminari-mon and in a striking new 8-storey building is **Asakusa Culture Tourist Information Center** (daily 9am-8pm). In addition to providing tourist information (1st floor) and information about the local area (7th floor), there is a foreign exchange counter (1st floor) as well as a tearoom and viewing terrace (8th floor).

The unmissable Golden Flame sculpture on the top of **Asahi Super Dry Hall** is often referred to by locals as the *O-gon-no-Unko* (Golden Poo). **Sumida Park** (Sumida-koen) is on both sides of the river and is particularly popular at cherry blossom time but is also the site of the Sumida River fireworks (see p106).

Kappabashi Dougu Street (🖳 www.kappabashi.or.jp) is well worth visiting. It is home to 170 shops specialising in everything that the restaurant industry needs, including the plastic café and wax food samples that are so commonly seen outside restaurants all over Japan. You can pick up a fake, but amazingly realistic, bit of sushi for about ¥1000. Kappabashi is a short walk from Asakusa station. Alternatively, the nearest station is Tawaramachi on the Ginza subway line; it is also a stop on the Shitamachi bus (see p103).

The aim of the **Sumida River Renaissance project** is to make the river area attractive so walkways are being developed and cafés and other attractions are opening. Ask for details at the tourism centre.

Ryogoku Take the JR Sobu Line from Akihabara and follow signs for the west exit. The Sumo Stadium is straight ahead and Edo-Tokyo Museum to the right. The sumo exhibition in the museum at the **Sumo Stadium** (Ryogoku Kokugikan; 🖳 www.sumo.or.jp; Mon-Fri 10am-4.30pm except when there's a tournament; free) changes every three months but unless you can read some Japanese it is probably not worth going.

Edo-Tokyo Museum (🖳 www.edo-tokyo-museum.or.jp; daily 9.30am-5.30pm, to 7.30pm on Sat; helpful volunteer guides available daily 10am-3pm; ¥600) is far more interesting. The ticket booth is on the plaza underneath the museum. The museum focuses on the politics, culture and lifestyle of people in Tokyo over the years. Everything is on a grand scale: one exhibit is so big it even comes with binoculars to allow visitors to inspect the more distant details. Also look out for the metre-high 'heels' used by fishermen standing in the sea, and displays on the earthquakes of 1855 and 1923. To see actual buildings from the Edo, Meiji and Showa eras go to the Open-air Museum (see p98).

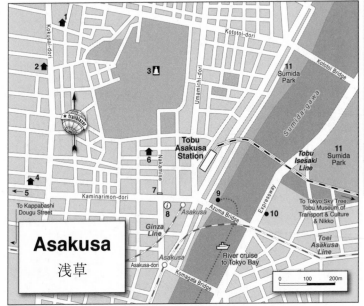

ASAKUSA – MAP KEY

Where to stay
1 Sukeroku no Yado Sadachiyo Ryokan
  助六の宿貞千代旅館
2 Asakusa View Hotel
  浅草ビューホテル
4 Taito Ryokan 台東旅館
5 Tokyo Ryokan 東京旅館
6 Ryokan Asakusa Shigetsu
  旅館浅草指月

Other
3 Senso-ji 浅草寺
7 Kaminari-mon Gate 雷門
8 Asakusa Culture Tourist Information
  Center 浅草文化観光センター
9 Sumida River Line/Himiko Waterbus
  隅田川ライン/ヒミコ水上バス
10 Asahi Super Dry Hall
  アサヒスーパードライホール
11 Sumida Park 隅田公園

Kinshicho Opened in May 2012, **Tokyo Sky Tree** (🖳 www.tokyo-skytree.jp; daily 8am-10pm), a digital TV broadcasting tower, is the tallest building (634m/2080ft) in Japan and the tallest broadcast tower in the world. Its construction, though, was influenced by traditional techniques (see box p98). There is a viewing deck at 350m (¥2000 on the day, no reserved time; ¥2500 advance purchase with reserved date/time) and a viewing corridor at 450m (¥1000, on the day only). Below the tower are **Sumida Aquarium** (🖳 www.sumida-aquarium.com; daily 9am-9pm; ¥2000), **Konika Minolta Planetarium** (🖳 www.planetarium.konicaminolta.jp; daily 11am-9pm; ¥1000, ¥1300 healing planetarium) and a large number of shops and restaurants. *(continued on p98)*

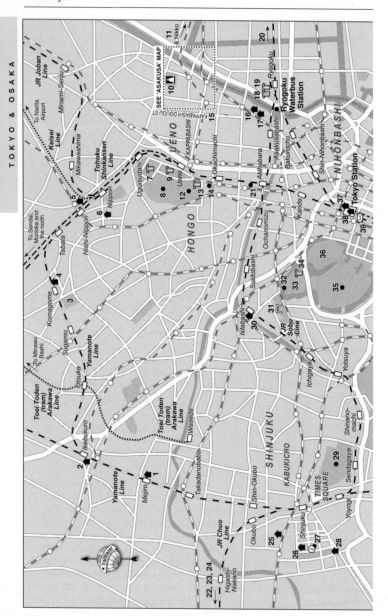

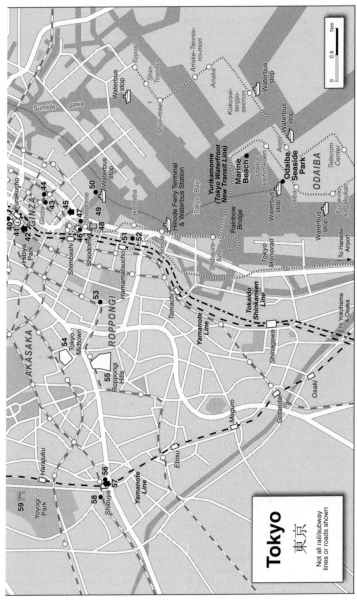

TOKYO & OSAKA

Tokyo

東京

Not all rail/subway
lines or roads shown

Toyosu

Shin-
Toyosu

Ariake-Tennis-
no-mori

Ariake

Waterbus
stop

Kokusai-
tenjijo-
seimon

Waterbus
stop

Sumida-
gawa

Shijo-mae

Aomi
Waterbus
stop

Telecom
Center

Waterbus
stop

Odaiba-
kaihin-koen

ODAIBA

Odaiba-
Seaside
Park

Yurakucho

GINZA

Ginza

50
Waterbus
Stop

Takeshiba

Tokyo Bay

*Yurikamome
(Tokyo Waterfront
New Transit Line)*

Marine
Beach

Daiba

Fune-no-
kagakukan

Hinode Ferry Terminal
& Waterbus Station

Shiodome

Hibiya
Park

Shimbashi

Shiodome

40 41 42
46
38
49
44
43
45
47
48

Hinode

Rainbow
Bridge

Waterbus
stop

51
52

55

To Haneda
Airport

Hamamatsucho

Shibaura-
futo

*Tokyo
Monorail*

53

ROPPONGI

54
Tokyo
Midtown

55
Roppongi
Hills

AKASAKA

*Yamanote
Line*

Tamachi

*Tokaido
Shinkansen
Line*

Shinagawa

To Yokohama
& Osaka

Meguro

Gotanda

Osaki

Harajuku

Ebisu

*Yamanote
Line*

56
57

58

Shibuya

59
Yoyogi
Park

0   0.5   1km

┌───┐

Earthquake-proof design from the 7th century
Tokyo Sky Tree is definitely a 21st-century structure but its design is heavily influenced by traditional Japanese architecture. The tower shares an unlikely affinity with the construction of Horyu-ji's five-storey pagoda (see p222), which was built in the 7th century. Both have a central column, but the main feature is that this is not attached to the frame of the building. It is believed that if both parts can move independently it protects the structure as a whole. No pagoda has been destroyed as a result of an earthquake, though plenty have by fire. The tower's ability to withstand an earthquake was tested far sooner than anyone might have imagined. The tower reached its full height a week after the Great East Japan Earthquake in March 2011 but tests showed it had suffered no damage.

└───┘

(continued from p95) The best way to get here is to take the Tobu Isesaki Line from Asakusa to Tokyo Sky Tree station. However, if you have a JR rail pass and don't mind a walk take the JR Sobu Line to Kinshicho (one stop beyond Ryogoku) and then find the north exit. It is a pleasant 10- to 15-minute walk along the road opposite the station exit; you'll see the Sky Tree in the distance. Be aware that since it is a new attraction it may be hard to get tickets on the day.

Before leaving walk west along the river on the south side of the tower to Jukken Bridge from where you can get a mirror image photo of the tower.

Higashi-Mukojima **Tobu Museum of Transport and Culture** (💻 www.tobu.co.jp/museum; Tue-Sun 10am-4.30pm; ¥200; English pamphlet available) is compact but interesting. Among its rolling stock are two Manchester-built Beyer-Peacock locomotives (one in the museum and one across the road) dating from the end of the 19th century. The company's type 5700 limited express car 5701 for service to Nikko is resplendent in a beautiful maroon livery. There are also bus and train simulators and model train layouts.

To get here take the Tobu Isesaki Line from Asakusa (¥140), past the new Tokyo Sky Tree tower.

Musashi-Koganei **Edo-Tokyo Open-air Architectural Museum** (💻 www.tatemonoen.jp; Tue-Sun Apr-Sep 9.30am-5.30pm, Oct-Mar to 4.30pm; ¥400), a branch of the Edo-Tokyo Museum, is a fascinating place to visit and features both Japanese- and Western-style houses, complete with furnishings. Take the JR Chuo Line from Shinjuku to Musashi-Koganei (25 mins) and then either walk (15-20 mins) or take a bus (Nos 12, 13, 14, 15 or 21; about 10 mins; ¥170) to Koganei-koen Nishiguchi from bus stand No 2.

PRACTICAL INFORMATION
Station guide
Tokyo station may not officially be as busy as Shinjuku station but it is just as complicated to navigate. (See box p102 for details of the platform layout.) If transferring to another line note that the Tokaido and Sanyo shinkansen services (to the west of Japan) have different ticket gates from the shinkansen services to the north-east so you need to go through both sets of ticket gates. If arriving by shinkansen you will need to go through that ticket gate and then the ticket gates for the normal services before reaching the station concourse.

Once here one of the first things you should do is go to an information counter (see p100) or one of the ticket offices to

TOKYO MAP KEY (see map pp96-7)

Where to stay

1 Hotel Mets Mejiro
ホテルメッツ目白
2 Hotel Metropolitan Tokyo
ホテルメトロポリタン東京
4 Hotel Mets Komagome
ホテルメッツ駒込
5 Sunny Hotel ホテルサニー
6 Annex Katsutaro Ryokan
アネックス勝太郎旅館
16 Tokyo Sumida-gawa Youth
Hostel 東京隅田川ユース
ホステル
17 Toyoko Inn Tokyo Akiba
Asakusabashi-eki Higashi-
guchi 東横インアキバ
浅草橋駅東口
25 Nishitetsu Inn Shinjuku
西鉄イン新宿
26 Hyatt Regency Tokyo
ハイアットリージェンシー
東京
28 Park Hyatt Tokyo
パーク ハイアット 東京
30 Tokyo International Youth
Hostel 東京国際ユースホ
テル
37 Hotel Metropolitan
Marunouchi ホテル
メトロポリタン丸の内
38 Tokyo Station Hotel
東京ステーションホテル

Where to stay (cont'd)

42 Peninsula Hotel Tokyo
ペニンシュラホテル東京
45 Mitsui Garden Hotel Ginza
Premier 三井ガーデン
ホテル銀座プレミア
57 Hotel Mets Shibuya
ホテルメッツ渋谷

Other

3 Rikugien 六義園
7 Tokyo National Museum
東京国立博物館
8 Ueno Park 上野公園
9 National Museum of Western
Art 国立西洋美術館
10 Senso-ji 浅草寺
11 Tobu Museum of Transport
and Culture 東武博物館
12 Ueno Zoo 上野動物園
13 Shitamachi Museum
下町風俗資料館
14 Ameyoko Market アメ横
15 Kappabashi Dougu St
かっぱ橋道具街
18 Sumo Stadium & Museum
相撲博物館
19 Edo-Tokyo Museum
江戸東京博物館
20 Tokyo Sky Tree
東京スカイツリー

Other (cont'd)

21 Tokyo Anime Center
東京アニメセンター
22 Suginami Animation Museum
杉並アニメーション
ミュージアム
23 Ghibli Museum ジブリ美術館
24 Edo-Tokyo Open-Air
Architectural Museum 江戸
東京たてもの園
27 Tokyo Metropolitan Government Building/Tokyo Tourist
Information Center 東京都庁/
東京観光情報センター
29 Shinjuku Gyoen 新宿御苑
31 Yasukuni Shrine 靖國神社
32 Nippon Budokan
日本武道館
33 Kita-no-maru Park
北の丸公園
34 National Museum of Modern
Art Tokyo
東京国立近代美術館
35 Imperial Palace 皇居
36 Imperial Palace East Gardens
皇居東御苑
39 Central Post Office
中央郵便局
40 Tokyo International Forum
東京国際フォーラム

Other (cont'd)

41 JNTO Tourist Information
Center 観光案内汐留
43 Sony Building ソニービル
44 Kabuki-za 歌舞伎座
46 Former Shimbashi Station
旧新橋駅展示室
47 Panasonic Living Showroom
(Shiodome City Center
Building) パナソニック
リビングショウルーム
(汐留シティセンタービル)
48 Advertising Museum Tokyo
(Caretta Shiodome) アド
ミュージアム東京
(カレッタ汐留)
49 Hama-Rikyu Garden 浜離宮
51 Tsukiji Market 築地市場
51 Kyu Shiba-Rikyu garden
旧芝離宮
52 World Trade Center Building
世界貿易センタービル
53 Tokyo Tower 東京タワー
54 Tokyo Midtown
東京ミッドタウン
55 Roppongi Hills
六本木ヒルズ
56 Hikarie ヒカリエ
58 Shibuya 109 渋谷109
59 Meiji Jingu (Yoyogi Park)
明治神宮 (代々木公園)

pick up a map of the station! There are two main sides – Marunouchi on the west and Yaesu on the east – and each has a North, a Central, a South and a Nihombashi ticket gate. The shinkansen platforms are on the Yaesu side of the station. There are passageways (north to south) between each side of the station within the ticket gates and on the north side only outside the ticket gates. There are **information counters** in the middle of the station and on the Marunouchi side of the Central passage as well as cafés, restaurants, shops, ticket offices and lockers almost everywhere.

❏ ARRIVING IN JAPAN

Tokyo's two main airports are **Narita**, which is 66km south-east of Tokyo and **Haneda**, which is 19km south of Tokyo.

Narita International Airport

Narita International Airport (🖳 www.narita-airport.jp) is Japan's major international gateway. It has **two terminals** connected by a free shuttle bus. In the Arrivals lobby of each is a **tourist information desk** (daily 8am-8pm), **hotel reservation desk** (7.30am-9/9.30pm) and a **currency exchange counter** (daily 6.30am-11pm) as well as mobile (cell) phone rental (see pp58-9), car hire, baggage delivery and other standard airport services.

Japan Rail and the private Keisei Railway have ticket desks in both Arrivals lobbies. However, to convert a rail-pass Exchange Order (if in Terminal 2) you have to go down to B1 (one floor below the Arrivals hall) and go to the Travel Service Center (daily 10.30am-8pm). In Terminal 1 go to the dedicated 'Exchange Office for Japan Rail Pass' (daily 8.15am-7pm) on the station concourse. Outside these times, in both terminals, go to the normal JR ticket office. Note that the offices can be very busy at peak times. If planning to use the subway buy a Tokyo Metro subway pass (see p102) while here.

Getting to and from Narita Airport The quickest and most efficient way between Narita and downtown Tokyo is by train. JR East operates the **Narita Express** (N'EX; 🖳 www.jreast.co.jp/e/nex; see Table 1, pp454-5), which takes about an hour to downtown Tokyo (¥2940 to Tokyo Station, ¥3110 to Shinagawa, Shinjuku or Ikebukuro); this is the best option for those with a rail pass but the Suica & N'EX package (see opposite) is recommended otherwise. All seats on the N'EX are reserved (reservations are free to rail-pass holders); since the trains often get booked up it is worth making a reservation for your journey back to the airport as soon as possible.

If you are planning to transfer onto the shinkansen west to Kyoto/Osaka, or to somewhere on the Yamanote Line (see pp84-91), it's better to go to Shinagawa (see p88 and p126), rather than Tokyo station. At Tokyo station, the N'EX services arrive and depart from platforms deep underground, which means a slog through the station to find the shinkansen/Yamanote Line platforms which are above ground level. The transfer at Shinagawa is, by contrast, very easy: it's just a short walk from the N'EX platforms (13-15) to the shinkansen platforms (21-24) or the Yamanote Line (1-2). The station itself is less chaotic and you avoid endless escalators.

The privately operated Keisei Railway is worth considering if you don't have a rail pass as this is cheaper and faster than the N'EX. The **Keisei Skyliner** (🖳 www. keisei.co.jp; 2/hr; ¥1200) stops at Nippori station (36 mins; see p90) on the JR Yamanote line before terminating at Keisei Ueno station. The Skyliner Metro Pass (¥2600/2980 for 1-/2-day one-way, ¥4500/4880 for 1-/2-day round trip) includes travel on the Skyliner (either one-way or a round trip) and unlimited travel on the Tokyo metro for the validity period of the pass.

At the time of research both sides of the station, particularly the Marunouchi side, were being redeveloped. The work should be completed in October 2012.

The roof of the original station building on the Marunouchi side is going to be restored to its pre-war design.

Tokyo Station Hotel (see p104) will re-open and there will be a travel service centre with a rail-pass exchange office, a currency exchange counter and an ATM as well as luggage storage facilities and a tourist information centre.

The **Friendly Airport Limousine Bus service** (💻 www.limousinebus.co.jp) connects Narita with major hotels in Tokyo in 80-125 minutes. Tickets (one-way from ¥3000) are available from the Limousine bus counter in the arrival lobby at Narita.

Don't even consider taking a **taxi** from Narita to Tokyo unless you want to part with ¥20,000 before you've even really arrived.

● **Suica & N'EX** At Narita any adult, or child under 12 travelling with an adult, with a foreign passport can buy a Suica smartcard (see box p44) with a N'EX ticket to any JR East station in the Tokyo/Yokohama area; see 💻 www.jreast.co.jp/e/suica-nex for details. The adult package costs ¥3500/5500 (this includes one-way/round-trip travel within two weeks from the airport, ¥1500 on the Suica smartcard and a ¥500 refundable deposit). In addition to the Suica card you will be given a seat reservation ticket for the N'EX. The child package costs ¥1200/2400 but doesn't include a Suica card.

When entering Narita Airport station scan the Suica card on the top part of the machine and put the seat reservation ticket into the ticket machine.

Haneda Airport (Tokyo International Airport)

Haneda (💻 www.haneda-airport.jp) is smaller but closer to downtown Tokyo. If possible, it's preferable to fly into Haneda rather than Narita, particularly if you are transferring to a domestic flight. On the Arrivals floor there is a **tourist information centre** (daily 5.30am-1am), a **hotel reservation desk** (5am-1am) and a **currency exchange counter** (8.30am-8pm) as well as the usual airport services. The **JR East Travel Service Center** (daily 11am-6.30pm) is to the right of the entrance to the Tokyo Monorail (see below). Go here to convert your rail pass Exchange Order.

If you arrive late, are leaving early, or just want somewhere to relax, consider *First Cabin* (💻 first-cabin.jp; from ¥800/hr in day, night from ¥4500/S) in Terminal 1.

Getting to and from Haneda

Tokyo Monorail (💻 www.tokyo-monorail.co.jp; approx every 3-5 mins; ¥470 one-way; free with Japan Rail Pass; see also below) operates between Haneda and Hamamatsucho (see pp87-8; about 20 mins) on the JR Yamanote line. The journey offers a bird's eye view of the port area of Tokyo and is an interesting experience in its own right. Services are either local, semi local, or express (just stopping at the international and domestic terminals).

The **Friendly Airport Limousine Bus service** (💻 www.limousinebus.co.jp) connects Haneda with major hotels in Tokyo in 25-45 minutes. Tickets (one-way from ¥900) are available from the Limousine bus counters in the arrival lobby at Haneda.

● **Suica & Monorail** This is the best option if you don't have a rail pass. Any adult with a foreign passport can buy the Suica & Monorail package (¥2700/round trip valid for 10 days, ¥2400/one-way). As above, use the monorail ticket in the ticket machine for the Monorail, not the Suica card. The ticket is valid to Hamamatsucho but the card also has ¥1500 on it so that part can be used for any onward journey.

❏ **Tokyo Station platform layout**

Overground platforms

1 & 2	Chuo Line for Takao
3	Keihin-Tohoku Line for Omiya
4	Yamanote Line for Ueno
5	Yamanote Line for Shinagawa
6	Keihin-Tohoku Line for Ofuna
7 & 8	Tokaido Line for Atami
9 & 10	Tokaido Line Express and Limited Express services
14-19	Tokaido/Sanyo shinkansen for Shin-Osaka & Hakata
20-23	Tohoku/Akita, Yamagata, Joetsu & Nagano shinkansen

Underground platforms

1-4	Sobu Line, Yokosuka Line, Keiyo Line & Narita Express (NE'X)

Tourist information

The **JNTO Tourist Information Center** (TIC; 🖳 www.jnto.go.jp; Tokyo Kotsu Kaikan; daily 9am-5pm except 1st Jan) is on the 1st floor of Shin-Tokyo Building, on Marunouchi Naka-dori, a five-minute walk from Yurakucho station (take the International Forum Exit). The staff are helpful and clued up about travel all over Japan and there is free wi-fi. Wi-fi and PCs are also available for free at Marunouchi Café Seek (2nd floor of TIC). There is also a TIC at Narita Airport (see box p100).

Tokyo Tourist Information Center (🖳 www.gotokyo.org; daily 9.30am-6.30pm except New Year holiday) is on the 1st (ground) floor of Tokyo Metropolitan Government Building No 1. The staff can provide information on accommodation and almost anything else you want to know. There are also information centres in Haneda International Airport and at Keisei Ueno Station. See also Asakusa, p94.

Getting around

For rail-pass holders the free and most convenient way of getting around is on the JR **Yamanote line** (see pp84-91), which runs in a loop around the city, stopping at virtually all the major points. JR and some private companies also operate lines from suburban areas to stations such as Shinjuku, Shibuya, Shinagawa, Ueno and Tokyo. The Chuo/Sobu Line goes across from Shinjuku and Yoyogi to Tokyo/Akihabara, which may save time if you don't want to go round the Yamanote Line.

If you don't have a rail pass but plan several journeys on JR lines, particularly for travel beyond the Yamanote Line, consider buying a **Tokunai Pass** (¥730/day). It is valid for unlimited travel on local and rapid trains in the Tokyo Metropolitan area. Buy it at a ticket machine (click on Discount Ticket) or a JR ticket office.

The **subway** will get you everywhere else. There are 13 lines: nine are run by Tokyo Metro (🖳 www.tokyometro.jp) and four by a company called Toei (🖳 www.kotsu.metro.tokyo.jp). All operate from 5am to shortly after midnight and fares are based on distance. If in doubt about how much to pay, buy a ticket from a machine for the minimum amount and 'fare adjust' when you arrive at your destination. Fare Adjustment machines are located by the exit barriers at all stations. Insert the ticket and the machine calculates how much extra you have to pay; the machines give change.

A **one-day pass** for use on Tokyo Metro subway lines normally costs ¥710. But if you buy it at Narita Airport when you arrive, it will only cost ¥600; a two-

❏ **Tokyo on the net**
There are dozens of websites dedicated to life in Tokyo. A few worth checking out for everything from restaurant to art-gallery reviews as well as ideas of what to see and do are: 🖳 www.digi-promotion.com, 🖳 metropolis.co.jp, 🖳 www.planettokyo.com, 🖳 www.sunnypages.jp, 🖳 whereintokyo.com.

⛩ Tokyo by bike
Forget the railway, if only for a day, and take to the streets of the capital on two wheels. That's the offer from the Tokyo Great Cycling Tour company (💻 tokyo cycling.jp; 3 mins' walk from Kayabacho subway station, on the Hibiya Line; tours: Sat, Sun, Tue & Thur 9am-3pm; ¥10,000 including bento lunch box; reserve online two days ahead), run by a group of English-speaking bicycle enthusiasts who are keen to show off what the city has to offer when you ditch motorised transportation. The pace on their six-hour tours is gentle, there is no significantly hilly terrain, rest stops are plentiful and the guides very knowledgeable.

---

day pass costs ¥980. These special reduced-price tourist tickets are available from the railway-ticket counter at the Arrivals lobbies in both terminals. A 'Tokyo Combination Ticket' is ¥1580 and can be used on subway lines operated by both Tokyo Metro and Toei, Toei buses, Tokyo's tram line (see pp93-4) and on JR trains in the metropolitan area. Alternatively, the Toei and Tokyo Metro 'Common One-day Ticket' (¥1000) offers unlimited use of all Toei Tokyo Metro lines for one day. However, many of these tickets are not really worth it unless you plan to travel extensively during the day.

JR East and the private companies sometimes introduce special passes for certain periods of time so when you are here it is worth asking if there are any that may be relevant.

Toei Tokyo Shitamachi Bus (💻 www .kotsu.metro.tokyo.jp/bus/shitamachi; 1-2/ hr; ¥200/journey, ¥500/one-day pass) is a **fixed-route hop-on hop-off bus** that provides a convenient way to get around the area it covers. During the week services operate between Ueno (see pp90-1), Kappabashi (see p94), Asakusa (see p94), Azumabashi, Narihira (for Tokyo Sky Tree, p95), Kinshicho (see p95) and Ryogoku (see p94). At the weekend some services start at Tokyo station. See the website for further information.

If you prefer to be guided, **Hato Bus** (💻 www.hatobus.com/en) offers a variety of half- and full-day **bus tours** (¥5000-12,000) in and around Tokyo as well as two walking tours. Services depart from their bus terminal at Hamamatsucho (see pp87-8); from the JR station head for the World Trade Center Building (south exit) and then follow signs for the bus terminal. However, the bus will also pick up/drop off at certain hotels. See their website for details.

Festivals and events
Senso-ji (see p94) has one of the busiest festival calendars in Japan. One of its more unusual events is the **Asakusa Samba Carnival** (late Aug/early Sep), which combines the Japanese tradition of carrying *mikoshi* (portable shrines) with the rhythm of samba. Dancers from Brazil join in the street party.

Other festivals here include **Setsubun** (Feb 3rd; see p65), and **Kiku Kuyo** (Oct), when the temple area is filled with displays of chrysanthemums. **Sanja Matsuri** happens in the Asakusa area in mid May; this is one of the biggest festivals in Tokyo and it features mikoshi processions.

Sumo tournaments are held at Ryogoku Kokugikan (Jan, May & Sep; see p94). The Sumida River is the location for Tokyo's biggest **fireworks display** (Hanabi Taikai) in late July.

❏ **Metropolitan area accommodation tax**
A special accommodation tax is levied on rooms at hotels and inns in the Tokyo metropolitan area charging ¥10,000 or more. The tax is ¥100 for rooms costing ¥10,000-14,999 per night; ¥200 for rooms costing ¥15,000 or more.

TOKYO & OSAKA

Where to stay

Accommodation (see also pp45-52) is available all over Tokyo but this guide focuses on places to stay on the Yamanote Line and in the Asakusa district.

On the Yamanote Line

There are hotels in the station area at virtually every stop on the Yamanote Line (see map pp96-7). A selection of the many are listed below.

Rail-pass holders in particular might like to stay at one of JR's hotels (see box p49) as they will receive a discount.

● **Tokyo Station** JR's *Hotel Metropolitan Marunouchi* (☎ 03-3211 2233, 💻 www. hm-marunouchi.jp; from ¥18,680/S, ¥30,230/D or Tw, online discounts available; buffet breakfast ¥2300) offers the chance to be as close to the station as possible but also to escape the crowds. Reception is on the 27th floor and the stylish, well-equipped rooms with huge windows are above that. Rail fans should ask for a room overlooking the tracks – you won't want to leave the room. You can even book railway tickets at the front desk. The hotel is in Sapia Tower and is closest to the Nihombashi exit.

Tokyo Station Hotel (☎ 03-5220 1112, 💻 www.tokyostationhotel.jp; from ¥30,030/D or Tw) was built in 1911. A huge project to restore the hotel to its original European Classical design (but with modern features) was completed in October 2012. It can't match the views at the Marunouchi, but will offer style, luxury and spacious rooms. Should you wish to really splash out the Royal Suite costs ¥808,500. Take the Marunouchi South exit from the station. The hotel is on the 3rd floor.

● **Yurakucho** The elegant *Peninsula Hotel Tokyo* (☎ 03-6270 2888, 💻 www.peninsula .com; from ¥47,000/S, from ¥62,000/D, inc American breakfast), opposite the Imperial Palace, has all the facilities and services you would expect at a hotel of this calibre. Take exit C4 from JR Yurakucho station.

● **Shimbashi** *Mitsui Garden Hotel Ginza Premier* (☎ 03-3543 1132, 💻 www.gar denhotels.co.jp; from ¥18,900/S, ¥25,200/D), a five-minute walk from the Ginza Exit of JR Shimbashi station, is an elegant, boutique-style hotel. It's great for watching the shinkansen tracks from the 16th floor open-plan lobby, with fine views from the stunning floor-to-ceiling windows.

● **Shibuya** *Hotel Mets Shibuya* (☎ 03-3409 0011, 💻 www.hotelmets.jp/shibuya; ¥13,500/S, ¥22,000/D or Tw, inc buffet breakfast; concept rooms from ¥15,500/S, ¥25,000/Tw) is a JR hotel with standard well-equipped rooms as well as four 'concept rooms', including a manga-themed one, designed by local artists. The concept rooms provide a unique experience and, since they are all on the top floor, a good view as well, but they can only be booked in English over the phone. From the Yamanote Line follow signs for the New South Exit or the Saikyo Line. The walk takes several minutes but there are moving walkways as well as escalators.

● **Shinjuku** has several world-class hotels. One of the best value is *Hyatt Regency Tokyo* (☎ 03-3348 1234, 💻 tokyo.regency. hyatt.com; rooms from ¥16,000/S, ¥22,050/D or Tw), nine minutes on foot from the west exit of Shinjuku station. A free shuttle bus operates between the hotel and the west exit of the station. Rooms are spacious and facilities include several restaurants and a top-floor pool and spa.

A sleek alternative is *Park Hyatt Tokyo* (☎ 03-5322 1234, 💻 www.parkhyatt tokyo.com; from ¥46,800/Tw, check website for packages), used as the location for Sofia Coppola's critically acclaimed film *Lost In Translation*. Closest to Nishi-Shinjuku station on the Marunouchi subway line but in walking distance of Shinjuku station is *Nishitetsu Inn Shinjuku* (☎ 03-3367 5454, 💻 www.n-inn.jp/info/ shinjuku; ¥10,300/S, ¥15,300/Tw), a relatively new place offering standard, clean rooms.

● **Mejiro** *Hotel Mets Mejiro* (☎ 03-5985 0011, 💻 www.hotelmets.jp/mejiro; from ¥9800/S, ¥15,000/D or Tw inc breakfast), a JR hotel, has some single rooms for women only. It is a minute's walk from the station – turn right out of the station and then first right.

● **Ikebukuro** *Hotel Metropolitan Tokyo* (☎ 03-3980 1111, 💻 www.metropolitan. jp/e; from ¥20,790/S, from ¥27,720/D or

Tw) is further from the station than other JR hotels but still conveniently located and it has a wide range of rooms and restaurants. Follow signs for South Exit/Metropolitan Exitå and walk through Metropolitan Plaza between Tobu and Lumine department stores. The hotel is diagonally opposite when you emerge onto the street.

● **Komagome** *Hotel Mets Komagome* (☎ 03-5319 0011; 🖳 www.hotelmets.jp/koma gome; from ¥9800/S, from ¥17,000/D or Tw, inc breakfast) is another JR hotel. Facilities also include a branch of Denny's and a café. Follow the signs for the south exit. Turn left at the exit and then left again.

● **Nippori** By the east exit, *Sunny Hotel* (☎ 03-3807 3200, 🖳 www.hotelsunny.co. jp; ¥6300-7875/S, ¥9975-10,050/D, ¥7875-10,500/Tw; breakfast from ¥500) offers reasonable accommodation and has a restaurant/café (7am-11pm). Several readers have recommended *Annex Katsutaro Ryokan* (☎ 03-3828 2500, 🖳 www.katsu taro.com; ¥6300/S, ¥10,500/D, ¥14,700/Tr), **Yanaka**, for its 'spacious rooms, good price, great neighbourhood, washing-machine and dryer, and internet access'. There are plenty of Japanese restaurants to choose from (unagi, okonomiyaki) nearby as well as a typically Japanese shopping street. It is a seven-minute walk from the west exit of Nippori station.

In Asakusa (see map p95) Apart from being a very atmospheric area to stay, Asakusa has places to suit all budgets and is handy for exploring the city. From Tokyo station take the Yamanote line to Ueno, change to the Ginza subway line and get off at Asakusa (the last stop).

Taito Ryokan (☎ 03-3843 2822, 🖳 www.libertyhouse.gr.jp; ¥3000pp; no meals) has only a few tatami rooms (with common bath) in an old building but is central and a great bargain. The manager is extremely friendly and will help you get the most out of your stay in Tokyo. Guests on their own may be asked to share a room. *Tokyo Ryokan* (☎ 090-8879 3599, 🖳 www. tokyoryokan.com; ¥3500pp) is a very characterful place offering similar hospitality and facilities.

Ryokan Asakusa Shigetsu (☎ 03-3843 2345, 🖳 www.shigetsu.com; Western singles from ¥6700, Japanese-style rooms from ¥8400/S, ¥14,700/Tw; breakfast ¥1300; dinner ¥4200 if ordered ahead) is a great place just off the arcade which leads up to Senso-ji. The top-floor public bath has a view of the temple's five-storey pagoda.

At the luxury end of the market, and highly recommended, is *Asakusa View Hotel* (☎ 03-3847 1111, 🖳 www.viewho tels.co.jp/asakusa; ¥15,000/S, ¥28,000/D).

For an authentic Edo experience try *Sukeroku no Yado Sadachiyo Ryokan* (☎ 03-3842 6431, 🖳 www.sadachiyo.co.jp; from ¥14,000/S, ¥9500pp for two sharing; breakfast ¥1500, evening meal ¥7000-12,000 but special diets not catered for). This ryokan is everything you imagine a Japanese inn to be. Tatami rooms have attached bathrooms and are decorated with antiques from the Edo period. The rooms can sleep up to six people. Look for the rickshaw parked outside.

On the JR Sobu line (see map pp96-7) *Tokyo International Youth Hostel* (☎ 03-3235 1107, 🖳 www.japan-yh.com/eng lish/english2/tokyoI/tokyo.htm; ¥3500pp; breakfast ¥400, evening meal ¥800) has mostly bunk-bed dorms. It's on the 18th and 19th floors of Iidabashi Central Plaza, right outside the west exit of **Iidabashi** station on the JR Sobu line (transfer from Yoyogi or Akihabara on the Yamanote line).

Not far from Asakusa is the 40-bed *Tokyo Sumida-gawa Youth Hostel* (☎ 03-5715 0145; 🖳 www.jyh.or.jp/english/ka nto/sumida/index.html; ¥3000/¥3600pp members/non-members). Meals are not provided. Take the east exit of **Akusabashi** (one stop from JR Akihabara station) on the JR Sobu line.

Take this exit also for *Toyoko Inn Tokyo Akiba Asakusabashi-eki Higashi-guchi* (☎ 03-3851 1121, 🖳 www.toyoko-inn.com; from ¥5980/S, ¥7980/D, ¥8980/Tw), which opened in 2012; it is a three-minute walk from the station.

Around Narita Airport There's no short-age of hotels in the airport vicinity, though most are overpriced. If you prefer to stay in a hotel actually on site, your only choice is *Narita Airport Rest House* (☎ 0476-32 1212, 🖳 www.apo-resthouse.com; ¥8100/S, ¥22,600/Tw, ¥12,200/D, inc buffet breakfast), a somewhat down-at-heel establishment but its proximity to the airport is a great asset especially if you arrive late at night or are leaving early. Another benefit is that the breakfast is very good; evening meals are also available but you may prefer the wider choice in the airport. Some rooms have views of parked aircraft.

The rooms at the *Toyoko Inn Narita Kuko* (☎ 0476-33 0451, 🖳 www.toyoko-inn.com; from ¥5700/S, ¥9800/D or Tw, inc curry rice supper and onigiri breakfast) are much more spacious than in most of their hotels. A shuttle bus to/from the airport operates every 15 minutes in the morning and evening. See also pp111-12.

Where to eat and drink
There are so many good places to eat at all over Tokyo (the city has more Michelin-starred restaurants than any other in the world) that it is hard to recommend anywhere in particular. Tokyo, Shinjuku and Ikebukuro stations have attached department stores with restaurant floors which are usually open until 10pm. Ginza, Harajuku and Shibuya are good areas to wander around in search of cafés and restaurants. And if you're staying in Asakusa, there are plenty of small, atmospheric restaurants that serve all kinds of Japanese food. Tokyo also has some of the best and most expensive restaurants in Japan, many of which are in the top hotels.

Nightlife
Tokyo is very much a 24-hour city, though there are certain areas which really only come alive after dark. You'll never be far from a bar or club in downtown Roppongi (see pp92-3), or in Shinjuku's Kabukicho (see p89). In the summer many hotels and department stores open rooftop beer gardens (see p55) which offer two-hour all-you-can-eat-and-drink deals for around ¥3000.

SIDE TRIPS FROM TOKYO

Yokohama
The port city of Yokohama (see pp127-9) makes for an interesting day trip as its attractions cover the 19th to the 21st century. It can be reached on the JR Keihin-Tohoku/Negishi Line in 35-45 minutes from either Shinagawa or Tokyo station. Alternatively take a shinkansen to Shin-Yokohama (pp126-7), 20-30 minutes from Shinagawa or Tokyo, and transfer to the JR Yokohama Line for trains to Yokohama; the rapid service goes direct but if you take a local train you will have to change to the Keihin-Tohoku/Negishi Line at Higashi-Kanagawa.

Kamakura   [map p109]
Kamakura, a small town by the sea one hour south of Tokyo, is packed with temples and shrines and makes for a relaxed escape for a day or longer from the bustle of the city. Kamakura became the seat of feudal government in the 12th century after the struggle for power between the rival Taira and Minamoto clans was won by Minamoto Yoritomo (see pp32-3).

To reach Kamakura by JR take the JR Yokosuka line from Shinagawa (4-5/hour; 53 mins; ¥690) or Tokyo station (4-5/hour; 63 mins; ¥890); some temples are best accessed from Kita-Kamakura which is the stop before Kamakura station. Even if you are not a particular rail fan it is worth changing to the Shonan Monorail at Ofuna (see opposite). Alternatively, if you are based in Shinjuku it is worth considering the Enoshima-Kamakura pass (see p110).

An alternative rail experience

An interesting way to make a round trip to Kamakura involves getting off the Yokosuka line at Ofuna (look for the Kannon statue on the right as you enter the station) and transferring to the 6.6km long Shonan Monorail (follow the signs; 6/hr, 15 mins, ¥300).

The **Shonan Monorail** is unusual in that the train is suspended below the track so you get the experience of 'flying' but are actually only about 10 metres above ground level. For the best views sit at the front or back of the train. The line ends at Shonan-Enoshima; turn right at the bottom of the steps down from the platform and then left out of the station. Walk straight down until you see Enoshima Enoden station on your left.

The **Enoden line** (🖳 www.enoden.co.jp), a single-track railway opened in 1910, runs between Fujisawa and Kamakura (about 10km). Both old-fashioned and modern train-sets are used so it is pot luck what you get but even so the journey is a pleasant one along the coast – at times the track passes so close to houses it almost feels intrusive. If planning to visit the Daibutsu (see below) it is best to get off at Hase (Enoshima to Hase: 5/hr; 20 mins; ¥250), from where it is a 10-minute walk, otherwise stay on till Kamakura, another five minutes. Enoden Kamakura station is adjacent to JR Kamakura station.

Engaku-ji (🖳 www.engakuji.or.jp; daily 8am-5pm, Nov-Mar to 4pm; ¥300) is a quiet Zen temple with a 700-year history, set on the wooded hills above Kamakura. The original buildings were either burnt down or destroyed in an earthquake but they have all been replaced. Zen courses are held here in the summer months and are open to the public. Turn right out of Kita-Kamakura station and walk along till you see some steps leading up to the temple. There are some lockers (¥100/300) on the left.

After visiting the shrine cross over to the other side of the station; turn left and walk along the road till you see the entrance to Jochi-ji on your right – it is just before the railway line crosses the road and is near a bus stop. **Jochi-ji** (daily 9am-4.30pm; ¥200) is one of the five main Zen temples in Kamakura and dates from the 1280s. For the **Daibutsu Hiking Course** (3.5km; 1¼-1¾hrs) follow the road to the left of the entrance to the temple. Despite this uphill start the walk is mostly downhill. The route is clearly marked but may be a bit muddy after rain. En route you'll pass a Fuji (partial) viewing point, **Hino Toshimoto's grave** (mausoleum style) and **Genjiyama Park** (Genjiyama-koen), but the big attraction and one of the most popular places in Kamakura is **Zeniarai Benten Shrine** (Zeniarai Benten Jinja; daily 8am-5pm; free). At a crossroads on the trail you turn right to stay on the hiking course and cross over to go to this shrine. The entrance is through a tunnel on your right soon after the crossroads. In 1185 Minamoto Yoritomo, the first shogun of the Kamakura government, had a dream in which he was told that if he went and found a spring gushing from the rocks in north-west Kamakura, and worshipped the Shinto gods, peace would come. Since he had this dream on the day, month and year of the snake, the shrine is dedicated to the Buddhist goddess associated with snakes. It is now said that any money that has been washed in the spring's water will increase its value (*zeni* means coins and *arai* means wash); nowadays most people wash paper notes rather than coins. If you want to have a go at 'money laundering' put a note in one of the baskets and follow the crowds.

To continue on the official route to the Daibutsu, retrace your steps to the crossroads and then turn left. However, it is also possible to get to Kamakura and the Daibutsu by continuing on downhill from the shrine.

Although its importance as a national power base faded many centuries ago, Kamakura is known for the **Daibutsu (Great Buddha)**, in Kotokuin temple (daily Apr-Oct 8am-5.30pm, Oct-Mar to 5pm; ¥200). The Daibutsu (built in 1252) is an 11.4m-high bronze statue of the Amida Buddha; it is the second largest in Japan after the one in Nara. For an additional ¥20 it is possible to go inside (daily 8am-4.30pm) the Daibutsu. From the Daibutsu it is an easy walk to **Yuigahama Beach**; despite its grey volcanic sand it is a pleasant, unspoilt place of fishing boats and surfers.

The main sight in Kamakura itself is **Tsurugaoka Hachiman-gu** shrine (daily 6am-8.30pm; free). Take the Hachimangu (east) Exit from the station and walk straight ahead until you reach Wakamiya-oji. In the middle of this is the Dankazura, a raised pedestrian path lined with cherry trees. Turn left and walk along this until you reach the edge of the shrine complex. The main hall is set back in the hills at the top of some steps and at the end of a long, wide approach. On the right of the steps are two ponds and a garden (open seasonally, ¥500), known for its peonies. To return to the station turn right out of the temple complex and walk along Komachi-dori, a street lined with shops, restaurants and cafés.

PRACTICAL INFORMATION
Station guide
At JR Kamakura station the Hachimangu (east) Exit is for the main part of the city, while the west exit leads to a quieter, more local neighbourhood.

One part of the station is for JR services and the other is for the Enoden line (Enoden Kamakura). There are **lockers** (¥300-600) in and around both stations but the ones inside are not available 24 hours/day.

If you don't have a rail pass you can use the underpass (actually at ground level), on the Enoden side of the station, to get to the west side of Kamakura.

KAMAKURA MAP KEY

Where to stay, eat and drink
8 Dolce Far Niente
   ドルチェファールニエンテ
9 Tonkatsu Komachi 豚カツ小町
10 Shitateya, Café La Mille (in Kamakura Komachi) 仕立屋, カフェラミル
   (鎌倉小町)
11 Donburi Café Bowls
   どんぶりカフェBowls
12 Hotel New Kamakura
   ホテル　ニューカマクラ

Other
1 Engaku-ji 円覚寺
2 Jochi-ji 浄智寺

Other (cont'd)
3 Daibutsu Hiking Course
   大仏ハイキングコース
4 Hino Toshimoto's grave
   日野俊基の墓
5 Zeniarai Benten shrine
   銭洗弁財天宇賀福神社
6 Genjiyama Park 源氏山公園
7 Tsurugaoka Hachiman-gu
   鶴岡八幡宮
13 Post Office 郵便局
14 Tourist information 観光案内
15 Rent a cycle レンタサイクル
16 Daibutsu (Kotokuin) 大仏 (高徳院)
17 Yuigahama Beach 由比ヶ浜

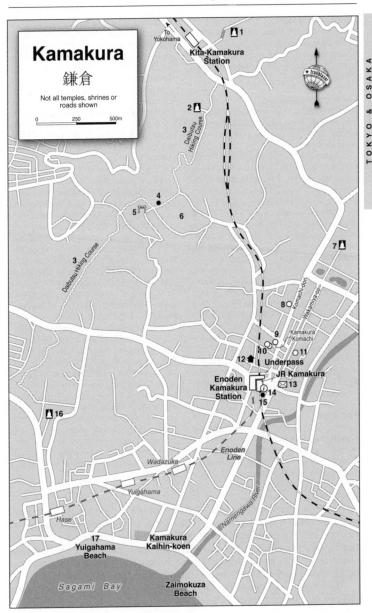

Kamakura

鎌倉

Not all temples, shrines or roads shown

0   250   500m

To Yokohama

Kita-Kamakura Station

1

2

3 Daibutsu Hiking Course

4
5
6

3 Daibutsu Hiking Course

7

8

Komachi-dori
Wakamiya-oji

9 Kamakura Komachi
10
11
Underpass

12

Enoden Kamakura Station

JR Kamakura

13
14
15

16

Enoden Line

Wadazuka

Yuigahama

Hase

17
Yuigahama Beach

Kamakura Kaihin-koen

Namerigawa River

Sagami Bay

Zaimokuza Beach

TOKYO & OSAKA

Tourist information

The tourist information office (🖥 www.city.kamakura.kanagawa.jp; Apr-Sep daily 9am-5.30pm, Oct-Mar to 5pm) is to the right outside the station, by the entrance to a shopping mall.

Getting around

Both Kamakura and Kita-Kamakura are easy to walk around though quite far apart, so use your rail pass to take the **train** between them.

Alternatively, and particularly for the Daibutsu if you don't want a long walk, take a **bus** from in front of Kamakura station: Keihin Kyuko (blue-and-white) buses go from stand No 6 (bus Nos 1, 2 and 4) for the Daibutsu, and stand No 4 for Hachimangu (bus No 20); buses accept Pasmo and Suica cards as well as cash. Enoden Bus (orange-and-beige buses; bus stand No 1) also goes to the Daibutsu.

If you don't have a JR pass it may be worth getting an **Enoshima-Kamakura Freepass** (🖥 www.odakyu.jp), which allows unlimited travel on the Enoden Line (see p107) and the Odakyu Line between Fujisawa and Katase-Enoshima for ¥600, or for ¥1430 including the journey on the Odakyu Line from Shinjuku.

Another option is to **cycle**: Rent a Cycle (daily 8.30am-5pm; from ¥600/1hr, ¥1600/day) is up the stairs on the right side of the east exit of the JR station.

Festivals

Tsurugaoka Hachimangu shrine hosts the **Kamakura Matsuri** in mid April, and in mid September the **Yabusame** festival features archers on horseback, dressed in 12th-century hunting costumes.

Where to stay and eat

Only a minute's walk from the station, *Hotel New Kamakura* (☎ 0467-22 2230, 🖥 www.newkamakura.com; ¥4200-10,000/S, ¥10,000-17,000/D) has both Japanese- and Western-style rooms; some are en suite but most of the rooms in the original wing, dating from the 1920s, share bathroom facilities. Turn right out of the west exit, look for a post box, behind which a small road leads to the road parallel to the railway; walk along for about a minute till you see the sign for the hotel on your left.

On Komachi-dori there are enough cafés and restaurants to satisfy anyone's taste buds or budget. **Kamakura Komachi**, a mini-plaza offering some respite from the crowds, is to the left off Komachi-dori. Here, *Shitateya* (10am-10pm) offers traditional Japanese set meals such as tempura soba (¥1050), while *Café La Mille* has burgers, pasta and cakes. Back on the main street is *Tonkatsu Komachi* (Wed-Mon 11.30am-7.30pm), serving tonkatsu from ¥1580 and a lunch menu from ¥1000. *Dolce Far Niente* (Tue-Sun 11am-9pm) serves pasta and Italian desserts.

An interesting and recommended alternative is *Donburi Café Bowls* (🖥 bowls-cafe.jp; daily 11am-10pm, lunch 11am-3pm; from ¥880) on Wakamiya-oji. It is on the right, after a Catholic church, as you walk to Hachiman-gu from the station. Here you get a bowl of rice – you can have either small, medium or large size – and then you choose what you want on top from a huge range of fish, meat and vegetable options. If, when you finish, you see some Japanese characters at the bottom of your bowl you will get a discount! Wi-fi is also available.

Kawagoe

To step back in time and discover what life was like in Tokyo more than a century ago, make a side trip by rail to the small town of Kawagoe (🖥 www.kawagoe.com). Sometimes called Little Edo (Ko-edo), its streets are lined with historic *kura* (warehouses) that double as traditional confectionery shops, noodle houses and private homes. It takes around 50 minutes on a 'rapid' local train on the JR Kawagoe line from Shinjuku (see p89); Kawagoe is the last stop.

Turn right as you leave the JR ticket barrier and the **tourist information counter** (daily 9am-4.30pm; no English spoken but English leaflet available) is on your right, close to the entrance to the private Tobu Railway. The Tobu Koedo Loop Bus (¥180/journey, ¥500/one-day pass, purchase from the driver; 2/hr, daily approx 10am-4pm), which leaves from stop No 3 outside the station's east exit, takes you to the main town area.

Take the loop bus to **Kawagoe Matsuri Kaikan** (daily exc 2nd & 4th Wed, Apr-Sep 9.30am-6.30pm, Oct-Mar 9.30am-5.30pm; ¥300), where some of the floats used in the festival are displayed and highlights are shown on a big screen. However, the best time to visit Kawagoe is on the third weekend of October, when the highlight of the festival itself is a parade through town with these huge, colourful floats.

A short walk from the museum is Kawagoe's most famous sight, the 16m-high **Toki-no-kane** (Bell Tower). First constructed in 1624, the tower that stands today was rebuilt after a fire in 1893 and is promoted locally if a little incongruously as having 'the same height as the Daibutsu in Nara' (see p216). Sadly, there are no campanologists on hand to ring the bell, but a recording is played four times a day (6am, noon, 3pm and 6pm).

A couple of blocks behind the museum is **Kashiya Yokocho**, a small street famous for its traditional sweet shops. If the streets elsewhere in Kawagoe are deserted, it will be because the hordes of elderly Japanese tourists have made a beeline for the candy stores here, where you'll find them in fits of nostalgia buying bags and boxes of traditional sweets. Morinaga's milk caramels seem particularly popular.

Pick up the bus and take it to **Kita Temple** (Kita-in; daily 8.50am-4pm; ¥400). The star attraction is not the temple itself (the original was destroyed in a fire in 1638), but, in a corner of the temple grounds, **Gohyaku-Rakan** – 500 stone statues of Buddhist monks in a variety of quirky poses and states of emotion, from happy to furious.

Narita town

Most people land at Narita Airport and head straight into Tokyo but it is really worth planning a night in the Narita area in order to visit **Naritasan Shinsho-ji** (⌨ www.naritasan.or.jp; daily 7am-6pm; free) in Naritasan Park (24 hours/day; free). The extensive temple complex, with its two pagodas and many halls, is interesting enough in its own right, but allow time to see the Goma (Sacred Fire) ceremony which is staged several times every day; the temple is often called Narita-no-Fudo-sama (the God of Fire at Narita).

The temple is a 10- to 15-minute walk down Narita's main street, Omotesando, from both the JR and Keisei Narita stations (11-12 mins from Terminal 1 at Narita Airport; ¥230/¥250). There is a **tourist information centre** (daily 8.30am-5.30pm) by the eastern exit of JR Narita.

Omotesando is lined with a variety of shops, including some making and selling crafts, and restaurants (see p112); there is also a tourist pavilion (⌨ www. city.narita.chiba.jp; Tue-Sun Jun-Sep 10am-6pm, Oct-May 9am-5pm; free) with exhibits about the local area and how it would have been in the Edo period.

If you are interested in seeing more of the area, take the **Narita City Round Bus** (7/day, round trip approx 60 mins; ¥200/journey or ¥500/one-day pass),

which calls at the main sights, and consider getting the Narita Welcome Card
(🖥 www.nrtk.jp) for discounts.

APA Hotel Keisei Narita Ekimae (☎ 0476-203111, 🖥 www.apahotel.com;
from ¥7500/S, ¥13,000/Tw; buffet breakfast ¥1000) is right by Keisei Narita
station but on a lower level. Walk down the steps at the east exit and then turn
left. The hotel's shuttle bus to and from the airport is free but only operates
every 90 minutes. The rooms are compact but some have views of the rail tracks.
There's also a spa. In the evening the restaurant, *Sandaime Shigezo*, is an izakaya
(see p55) specialising in tofu dishes (about ¥1500-2000pp). *Mercure Hotel* (☎
0476-237000, 🖥 www.mercurehotelnarita.com; from ¥5500/S, ¥12,127/Tw;
breakfast ¥1500), very near the west exit of Keisei Narita station, has a lovely
Japanese restaurant with unusual (in a good sense!) food. *Torimasa* yakitori
restaurant opposite Mercure Hotel is also very good.

Sushi fans, in particular, should head for one of the two branches of *Edokko
Sushi* (11.30am-2.30pm & 5-10pm) in Narita. The sushi is thought to be some
of the best in Japan and it would be a great place to eat on your last night – or
indeed to celebrate your arrival in Japan. From the JR station, walk past
McDonald's and down the hill a few yards to the Japanese red bridge. Turn left
at the street which runs from the bridge and one branch of Edokko (closed Mon)
is 10m along the street on your right. The other branch (closed Wed) is along
Omotesando; walk along about 200m and Edokko is on the right-hand side.

Eel is on the menu at many restaurants in Narita town, perhaps because they
can be fished from the surrounding rivers and lakes year-round. The Unagi (Eel)
Festival (mid Jul-mid Aug) is possibly the best time to try it.

Tokyo Disney Resort

Only a short journey by train from Tokyo station, but a world away from the
commuter belt which surrounds it, is Tokyo Disney Resort (🖥 www.tokyodis
neyresort.co.jp; Mon-Fri 9am-10pm, Sat & Sun 8/8.30am-10pm). The main
attraction, **Tokyo Disneyland**, opened in 1983 as an almost exact copy of the
original in Anaheim, California, which opened in 1955. **Tokyo DisneySea**
(theme: the myths and legends of the sea) followed in 2001, the highlight of
which – at least for white-knuckle junkies – is the Tower of Terror ride. Tickets
for foreigners must be bought, or collected if reserved in advance, from the
Tokyo Disney Resort Ticket Center on the 1st (ground) floor of Ikspiari opposite JR Maihama station.

A one-day passport to either park costs ¥6200 (12-17 years ¥5300, 4-11
¥4100). A two-day passport, which allows entry to both parks, costs ¥10,700
(¥9400/¥7400). There are also three- and four-day passports and reduced-price
passports for entry after 6pm, or after 5pm at weekends/holidays. The nearest
railway station is Maihama on the JR Keiyo line (take the train direct from
Tokyo station).

Hakone

It's just about possible to visit Hakone (see pp129-31) in a day if you make an
early start, but an overnight stay would be far better. The private Odakyu

Railway (🖥 www.odakyu.jp; JR passes are not valid) runs services to Hakone from Odakyu Shinjuku station (connected to JR Shinjuku). Rail tickets, accommodation and package tours of the region can be booked at the Odakyu Sightseeing Service Center (daily 8am-6pm), on the ground floor concourse by the west exit of Odakyu Shinjuku station. Best value is the **Hakone Free Pass** (Sat & Sun ¥5500; discounted passes outside peak season Mon-Fri ¥4700, valid for two days only), which covers various modes of transport in Hakone as well as return travel by regular Odakyu trains from Shinjuku to Hakone-Yumoto (change trains in Odawara). For an ¥870 supplement each way you can take the more luxurious Romance Car LEX, which runs direct to Hakone-Yumoto and is well worth the extra. Rail-pass holders can save over ¥1000 by taking a Tokaido shinkansen from Tokyo west to Odawara (see p129) and then transferring to the Odakyu railway for the rest of the journey to Hakone-Yumoto.

Nikko

Some 150km by rail north of Tokyo, the temple and shrine town of Nikko (see pp271-2) is well worth an overnight stay but can be seen in a day if necessary. For rail-pass holders the best route to Nikko is by shinkansen to Utsunomiya (see pp270-1).

Without a rail pass, take the private Tobu Railway (🖥 www.tobu.co.jp) direct from Tobu Asakusa station to Tobu Nikko station (160 mins by rapid train, ¥1320; or 110 mins by LEX, ¥2620). A **World Heritage Pass** (¥3600), valid for two days, includes return travel on the rapid trains and admission to two shrines and one temple. Alternatively, the **All Nikko Pass** (¥4400) is valid for four days and includes return travel as well as unlimited travel on Tobu-operated buses in and around Nikko; it also gives some discounts on attractions. Both can be bought at the Tobu Sightseeing Service Center (daily 7.45am-5pm) at Tobu Asakusa station. These tickets are available only to foreign visitors.

Osaka

Osaka is the commercial and industrial centre of western Japan; as such it is of more interest to the business traveller than the tourist. Also, with the ancient capitals of Kyoto and Nara so close, there's no great incentive to stay in Osaka for very long. But with an international airport close by, Japan's third largest city (after Tokyo and Yokohama) functions as a useful gateway to the Kansai area and is less than three hours by shinkansen from the capital. It is also known for its food and as Japan's centre of stand-up comedy.

WHAT TO SEE AND DO

The city's big historical draw is Osaka Castle but as a modern reconstruction it's nowhere near as impressive as nearby Himeji (see p228). However, even a commercial city like Osaka has some surprises.

Osaka Unlimited Pass

If you're going to spend even just a short time in Osaka, it's worth investing in the Osaka Unlimited Pass (⌨ www.pia-kansai.ne.jp/osp). The one-day pass (¥2000) provides unlimited use of private train lines (Hankyu, Hanshin, Nankai, Keihan and Kinki Nippon Railways, but not JR) and city buses. The two-day pass (¥2700) allows unlimited travel on Osaka City subway, the new tram and the city bus but not the railway lines. Both also get you free admission to 27 tourist attractions, including Osaka Castle, the Floating Garden Observatory and Osaka Museum of Housing and Living, as well as discounted entry to Osaka Aquarium and the Modern Transportation Museum, and reductions at selected restaurants, shops and hotels.

The pass can be purchased from all the tourist information offices listed on p120 and from some hotels.

On Osaka Loop Line

Other than **Umeda Sky Building**, behind JR Osaka station, there is little in Umeda in the way of sights but it's a great place to shop and eat. The Sky Building is one of Japan's most imaginative skyscrapers, with a 173m-high '**Floating Garden Observatory**' (⌨ www.kuchu-teien.com/english; daily 10am-10.30pm; ¥700) which connects the two towers. The entrance for the lift is at the first corner of the first tower you reach when walking from the station and emerge from the underpass. It is well signposted. In good weather the views are magnificent and, according to the publicity, the observatory is the venue for 'one of Japan's one hundred most famous sunsets'. As if that were not enough to lure the lovestruck, one corner of the rooftop lookout – the 'Lumi Deck' (daily 7-10pm) – is open exclusively to couples: 'a place especially for lovers. The light on the floor goes through various changes when you sit down on the bench, hold each other's hands tightly, and touch the dome on the right and left. The hearts of the loving couple will be projected...revealing the degree of your love. You can then attach a Heart Lock (sold at Shop Sky 39 on the 39th floor) to the Fence of Vows.'

Osaka Castle (⌨ www.osakacastle.net; daily 9am-5pm; ¥600) was originally built in 1586 by Toyotomi Hideyoshi but was destroyed by fire only a few years later in 1615. It was completely reconstructed in 1629, only for the main tower to be struck by lightning and once again burnt to the ground. A further reconstruction in the 1930s suffered aerial bombardment during WWII. The *donjon* has been fully restored and is worth climbing for the views of Osaka but the displays inside are less impressive. Look out for Tako-ishi (Octopus Stone) by Sakura-mon Masugata (Square); it is the largest single block of stone in the castle – 59 sq metres, 90cm thick and weighing about 130 tonnes. Note that you cannot take photos inside the castle.

The castle is a short walk from Osakajo-koen station. Taking the central exit, you'll see the castle in front of you in the distance. The castle tower has an elevator for wheelchair access.

Osaka Human Rights Museum (⌨ www.liberty.or.jp; daily except Mon & 4th Fri of month, 10am-5pm; ¥250), also known as **Liberty Osaka**, focuses on people who have faced discrimination in Japan, including the country's Korean population and the Ainu (see box p356). One exhibit focuses on people living with HIV/Aids. The museum is 10 minutes on foot south of Ashiharabashi station.

The **Modern Transportation Museum** (💻 www.mtm.or.jp; Tue-Sun 10am-5.30pm; ¥400; ask for the English leaflet as most signs are in Japanese only) is right in front of Bentencho station. It's one of the best-organised transport museums in Japan, with exhibits on the history of the railway from the steam age to the future. It opened in 1962, as an alternative to the Transport Museum in Tokyo (see p98), as it was thought that many people from West Japan would not travel as far as the nation's capital. Boats, planes, buses and cars are given a little space, but the focus is on rail. A huge model railway periodically bursts into life, while outside there's a collection of full-size locomotives and passenger carriages. Steam buffs will be in heaven: there are several locomotives from the late 19th and early 20th centuries, including one – imported from England to run on the original Tokaido line between Kyoto and Otsu – that dates back to 1881. Also on show are four of the original twelve cars, built in 1963, which ran as the first-generation shinkansen between Tokyo and Osaka.

Off Osaka Loop Line

One of Osaka's biggest draws is **Universal Studios Japan** (💻 www.usj.co.jp; variable opening hours; ¥6200/10,700 one-/two-day passport). Modelled on the original Universal Studios theme park in Florida, visitors are offered a similar mix of attractions and can expect long queues (though you can buy a 'Universal Express Pass Booklet' which allows you to avoid the queues for major attractions). The park has a working TV studio, and backstage production tours let visitors see behind the scenes of Japanese drama and variety shows.

Tickets can be purchased at the park entrance but also in advance at JR ticket offices, Lawson convenience stores, and online. The park is about 250m on foot from Universal City station on the JR Yumesaka (Sakurajima) line, which starts from Nishi-Kujo station on the Osaka Loop line. The journey from Osaka station takes 15 minutes.

Other attractions accessible by subway

The **Open-Air Museum of Old Japanese Farm Houses** (💻 www.occh.or.jp/minka; Tue-Sun 9.30am-5pm; ¥500; pick up an English pamphlet at the entrance) is an amazingly peaceful retreat just three stops north of Shin-Osaka. You can walk around this quiet wooded area and look inside 11 farmhouses collected and reassembled from all over Japan. In the houses are displays of craft and farm implements (with bilingual signs) – a great opportunity to see something of rural Japan without having to leave the metropolis. Take the Midosuji subway line from Shin-Osaka to Ryokuchi-koen station and head for the west exit, which leads into Ryokuchi-koen (park). The museum is on the north side of the park, about 15 minutes on foot from the station (follow the signs).

Osaka Museum of Housing and Living (daily except Tue & 3rd Mon of month; 10am-5pm; ¥600; English audio guide available) sounds dull but offers the chance to see what the city was like in the Edo period (see p34). The entrance is on the 8th floor of Osaka Municipal Housing Information Center, which is close to, and signposted from, Tenjinbashisuji 6-chome station on the Tanimachi and Sakai-suji subway lines.

The **National Museum of Art** (⌨ www.nmao.go.jp; Tue-Sun 10am-5pm, Fri to 7pm; ¥420), housed in a swish, modern underground facility in Osaka's Nakanoshima district, focuses on Japanese and foreign modern and contemporary art. Take Yotsubashi subway line to Higobashi, Exit No 2, and walk west for about 10 minutes.

Tempozan Harbor Village is an area of **Bayside Osaka** with several attractions, all of which are within walking distance of Osaka-ko station on the Chuo subway line (connect to the subway line from Bentencho station on the Osaka Loop line). Take Exit No 1 or 2 from Osaka-ko station and head down the shopping street that leads away from the station. The first thing you'll see is the **Tempozan Giant Ferris Wheel** (¥700; daily 10am-10pm; 15 mins). At 112.5m, it's one of the tallest in the world and high enough to afford a 360-degree view of the city and, in the distance, Mt Rokko (see p247). Two of its cabins are completely transparent, including the floors and seats (it's pot luck if you get to ride in one of them), and the wheel itself boasts the 'world's first transmission of weather information by 100m-diameter illumination'. You can get a next-day forecast for the Osaka region by looking at the wheel in the evening: red means sunny, green means cloudy and blue heralds rain. To the left of the entrance to the wheel are some lockers (all sizes, up to ¥600).

Follow the signs to the hugely popular **Osaka Aquarium** (Kaiyukan; ⌨ www.kaiyukan.com; daily 10am-8pm, last entry 7pm; ¥2000 or ¥2900 inc Santa Maria, see below), which gets more than 2.5 million visitors a year. Start on the 8th floor and begin your journey down to the ocean depths, encountering sharks, seals, sea lions, dolphins, penguins and many more along the way. A particular highlight is the Pacific Ocean tank, which extends down several floors; the fluorescent floating jelly fish at the end are fabulous too.

Directly behind the aquarium, and accessed via a waterfront walkway, is the berth from which the *Santa Maria* (⌨ suijo-bus.jp/language/english/santmaria. aspx; daily 11am-6pm; hourly; 50 mins; ¥1600, or ¥2900 inc the aquarium) departs on tours of the bay area, weather permitting. It's apparently modelled on the ship on which Columbus journeyed to the Americas, but is twice as large.

One stop along the Chuo subway line from Osaka-ko to Cosmosquare lies **Osaka Maritime Museum** (⌨ www.jikukan.or.jp; Tue-Sun 10am-5pm; ¥600), in a huge glass dome. Displays explain how ships and ports developed in Osaka and around the world – a celebration of man's triumph on the high seas – and provide a great introduction to the transformation of Osaka into one of the world's leading shipping hubs. The centrepiece is a full-scale reproduction of the *Naniwamaru*, a 30m-long Edo-period cargo vessel. You can board the *Naniwamaru* (which, although it is only a replica, did actually sail on Osaka Bay when it was constructed in 1999) via a ramp on the 2nd floor. It's a great museum for children and adults alike. To find it, take Exit No 1 at Cosmosquare station, and walk for seven minutes along the path which runs parallel to the waterfront.

For a sky-high view take the elevator up to the 55th-floor observation platform inside **World Trade Center Cosmo Tower** (WTC; 🖥 www.wtc-cosmo tower.com; Mon-Fri 1-10pm, Sat & Sun 11am-10pm; ¥800). The 252m-high building is the tallest in Osaka and second tallest in Japan. From Bentencho on the Osaka Loop line, take the Chuo subway line to Cosmosquare then change to the New Tram/Nanko Port Town line and get off at World Trade Center-mae, right outside the entrance.

Access to the observation platform is from the 1st (ground) floor of the tower. Purchase a ticket from the vending machines before taking the express glass lift (which zooms to the top in little more than one minute) to the 52nd floor, from where escalators connect to the 55th floor. On a clear day, you can see the offshore Kansai Airport, Osaka Castle and Mt Rokko; the vast sprawl of the metropolis stops only at the water's edge.

On the 48th-floor of the WTC is the *World Buffet Restaurant* (11am-2.30pm & 5-10pm), a Viking (buffet)-style all-you-can-eat spread (lunch ¥1570, evening ¥3150). A great place to pig out and take in the views. The men's restrooms enjoy a spectacular view of bayside Osaka from the urinals! On the return to ground level you take a different lift, from the 51st floor.

PRACTICAL INFORMATION
Arrival and departure
International flights land at **Kansai International Airport** (KIA; 🖥 www. kansai-airport.or.jp), built on a man-made island in the middle of Osaka Bay. KIA is a more impressive gateway to Japan than Narita – the terminal building (designed by Renzo Piano) was at one time the longest airport terminal in the world. Its efficient Wing Shuttle train (every 3 mins) will take you to the main airport building to collect your luggage and complete the formalities.

Staff at **Kansai TIC** (🖥 www.kansai-japan.net; daily Apr-Oct 8.30am-8.30pm, Nov-Mar 9am-9pm), in the Arrivals lobby, can advise on travel throughout the Kansai region. There are branches of nine banks so there's always at least one open between 6am and 11pm. There are also **ATMs** in the Arrivals lobby which accept foreign-issued credit cards. For somewhere to eat, check out the north side restaurant area on the 2nd floor.

Rail-pass Exchange Orders can be converted either at the small JR West Information Counter (daily 9.30am-7pm) in the Arrivals lobby, or at the JR Travel Center (daily 10am-6pm) or ticket office (daily 5.30am-11pm) at Kansai Airport station on the 2nd floor.

Getting to and from Kansai Airport
The fastest way of accessing Osaka (and Kyoto) is **by rail**; Kansai Airport station is connected to the terminal building. The blue half of the station is run by Japan Rail, the red half by Nankai Railway (see below). JR's Haruka LEX (see Table 2, p455) goes to Kyoto (¥3290; 75 mins) and stops on the way at Tennoji (¥2070; 33 mins) and Shin-Osaka (¥2780; 50 mins) but not at Osaka station. Fares listed are for reserved seats. A 'rapid' service (slower than the Haruka) operates to Osaka station (¥1160; 65 mins). If you are lucky the cleaning staff will line up and wave as the train leaves the station.

Nankai (🖥 www.nankai.co.jp), a private line, operates the 'rapi:t' train from Kansai to Osaka Namba station (¥1390; 29 mins), where you can transfer to the sub-way. *(continued on p120)*

Osaka
大阪

Not all rail/subway
lines or roads shown

0   250   500   750m

Osaka Loop Line

Kyobashi

Osakajo-koen

Morinomiya

Katamachi

13

Sakuranomiya

Yodo-gawa

Temma

Osakajo Kitazume

Temmabashi

Chuo-dori

Osaka Temmangu

1, 2, 3, 4
5 & 6

To Shin-Osaka
station

Umeda

Yodo-yabashi

Midosuji-dori

Kita Shinchi

Osaka
Station

8

9

11

10
Umeda Sky Building

Shin-Fukushima

12

Tokaido Main Line
(Kobe Line)

Fukushima

Dojima-gawa

Tosabori-gawa

Noda-Hanshin

Shin Yodo-gawa

Ebie

Noda

Osaka Loop Line

Yodogawa

Nishi-Kujo

To Kobe

Yumesaka
(Sakurajima)
Line

4

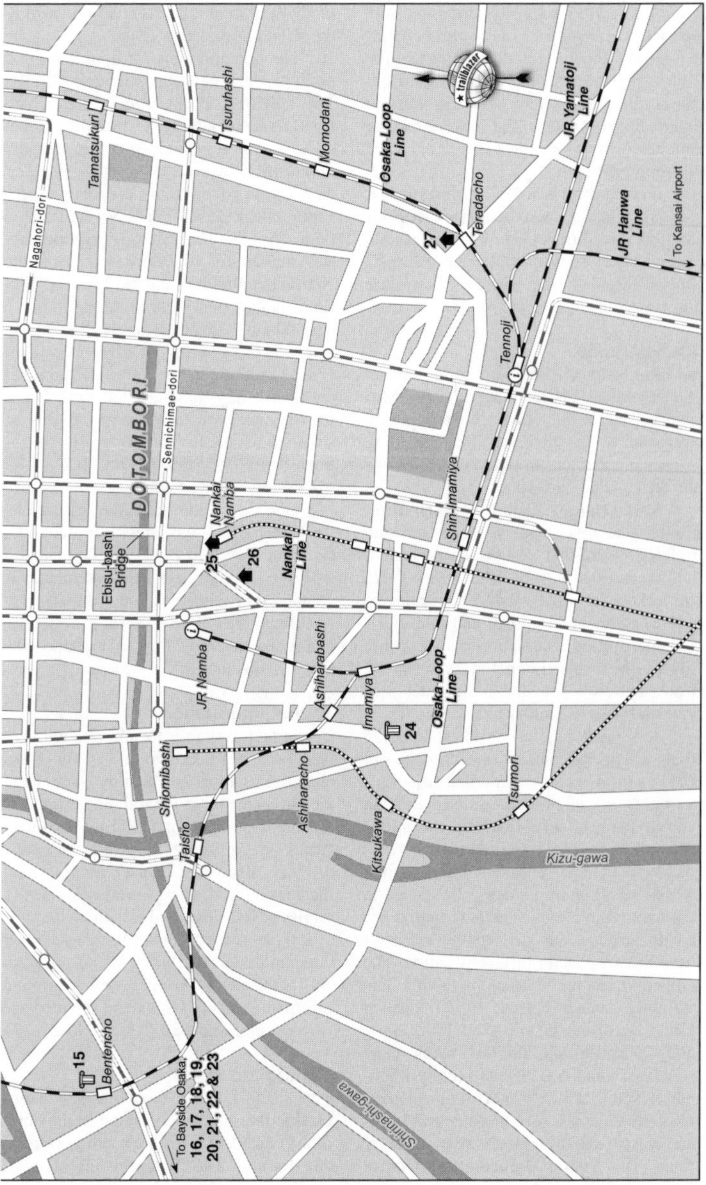

TOKYO & OSAKA

DOTOMBORI

Nagahori-dori

Tamatsukuri

Tsuruhashi

Momodani

Osaka Loop Line

Teradacho

JR Yamatoji Line

JR Hanwa Line

To Kansai Airport

Tennoji

27

Sennichimae-dori

Shin-Imamiya

Nankai Namba

Nankai Line

25

26

Ebisu-bashi Bridge

JR Namba

Ashiharabashi

Imamiya

Osaka Loop Line

24

Shiomibashi

Ashiharacho

Kitsukawa

Tsumori

Taisho

Kizu-gawa

15

Bentencho

To Bayside Osaka,
16, 17, 18, 19,
20, 21, 22 & 23

Shingashigawa

(continued from p117) Limousine **bus services** (🖳 www.kate.co.jp) run between the airport and various destinations in the Kansai region, including Osaka, Kyoto and Nara. Bus stops are located outside International Arrivals and tickets can be purchased from vending machines outside the terminal building.

If heading for Kobe or western Honshu you may like to take the **Kobe-Kansai Airport Bay Shuttle** (🖳 www.kobe-access. co.jp; 1/hr; 31 mins; ¥1800) to Kobe Airport Access Terminal, from where the Port Liner travels into Kobe (see pp241-7).

Station guide

● **Shin-Osaka station** This station marks the western limit of the Tokaido shinkansen and the start of the Sanyo shinkansen. It is also used by the JR Kyoto line providing connecting services to other JR stations in the area, including Osaka.

Shin-Osaka Visitor Information Centre (daily 9am-6pm) is on the left side walking towards the west exit of the station. It is almost opposite a JR ticket office. There are **lockers** (all sizes) all over the station as well as plenty of restaurants and cafés.

● **Osaka station** The station is used primarily by the Osaka Loop Line and the JR Kobe and JR Kyoto lines; the latter provides services to Shin-Osaka.

The rebuilding of Osaka station (🖳 osakastationcity.com) was completed in 2011 and it is now branded a 'city'. Certainly it can provide almost anything you are likely to need – a hotel, restaurants, convenience stores, department stores, ATMs, a cinema, a fitness club, even a wedding hall and a garden – let alone the chance to take a train. The new station has a light, spacious and airy feel but it doesn't have the wow factor of Kyoto station. The railway tracks are between the North Gate Building, which houses JR Mitsukoshi Isetan Department Store (2nd-10th floors; daily 10am-8pm), and the South Gate Building, which has Daimaru (daily 10am-8pm). Note that the elevators for the department stores don't operate when the stores are closed and also don't stop at every floor. The **Visitor Information Centre**

(daily 8am-8pm) is on the 2nd floor, next to the station information office.

The bridge on the 4th floor is a good place to view the trains but even better is Toki-no-Hiroba Plaza, an open area which connects both buildings and where you can sit and have a granita (¥600) at *Bar del Sole Café*. However, if you want internet/ wi-fi access go to *Wired Café* (daily 10am-11pm; lunch menu from ¥850) on the 2nd floor. The other main areas for **restaurants** and cafés are the 10th floor in Lucua in the North Gate Building and the 15th and 16th floors in the South Gate Building.

Take the escalators on the North Gate side up to **Yawaragi-no-niwa** (Yawaragi Garden; 10th floor) for views of Osaka and the Umeda Sky Building. Follow the signs for the 'hiking course' (a few flights of steps up to the 14th floor) to **Tenku-no-noen farm** (vegetable garden) to see a bit of greenery amongst all the concrete.

Don't leave the station without seeing the **Water Clock monument** by the South Gate entrance (3rd floor) on the Daimaru side. As the sign says, 'the monument is composed of numerous water threads representing time [it is a clock in a sense], letters and patterns'. It is hard to believe the patterns are made out of water.

Tourist information

In addition to the visitor information centres (🖳 www.osaka-info.jp) at Shin-Osaka and Osaka stations (see Station guide) there are also branches at Tennoji (8am-8pm), JR Namba (8am-8pm) and JR Universal City (9am-8pm). At any of these, ask for a copy of the 'Explorer Osaka' map, which includes money-saving coupons for certain tourist sights, shops and restaurants.

If you need information on travel outside Osaka, it's better to visit Kansai TIC at the airport. For general background information about Osaka and the area see 🖳 www.pref.osaka.jp.

Getting around

The main railway junctions are **Shin-Osaka**, the shinkansen station to the north of the city; **Osaka**, further south in Umeda; and **Tennoji**. The JR Kyoto line connects

Shin-Osaka and Osaka. Osaka and Tennoji stations are both on the **Osaka Loop line**. The Osaka Loop line (orange-colour trains; departures from platforms 1 and 2 at JR Osaka station) is the most useful means of getting around the city with a rail pass.

The **subway** is convenient for reaching places off the Loop line. The individual fare depends on where you are going. A one-day pass (¥850) allows unlimited use of the subway and city buses.

Festivals

The biggest event in Osaka's busy festival calendar is **Tenjin Matsuri** (24th-25th July). The highlight is a procession of more than 100 brightly coloured boats down Dojima-gawa on the evening of the 25th. Performances of traditional dance and music are staged on a boat lit by lanterns and moored in the middle of the river.

Where to stay

There is plenty of accommodation in Osaka. This guide primarily focuses on places that are near stations but also around Osaka Bay. See also pp45-52.

● **Near Shin-Osaka station** The reception desk for the very clean *Shin-Osaka Youth Hostel* (☎ 06-6370 5427, 🖳 www. osaka-yha.com/shin-osaka; ¥3300/dorm bed; ¥9000/Tw, Japanese-style room ¥4500pp; supper ¥1050, breakfast ¥480) is on the 10th floor of the Koko Plaza Building,

OSAKA MAP KEY (see map pp118-19)

Where to stay

2 Toyoko Inn Shin-Osaka Chuo-guchi Shinkan
東横イン新大阪中央口新館

3 Toyoko Inn Shin-Osaka Chuo-guchi Honkan
東横イン新大阪中央口本館

4 Shin-Osaka Youth Hostel 新大阪ユース ホステル

5 Hotel Shin-Osaka ホテル新大阪

6 Toyoko Inn Shin-Osaka Eki Higashi-guchi 東横イン新大阪駅東口

8 Hotel Granvia Osaka ホテルグランヴィア大阪

11 Hotel Monterey Osaka ホテルモントレ大阪

16 Hyatt Regency Osaka ハイアットリージェンシーオーサカ

22 Cosmosquare Hotel ホテルコスモスクエア

23 Best Western Joytel Osaka ベストウェスタン ジョイテル大阪

Where to stay (cont'd)

25 Swissotel Nankai Osaka スイスホテル南海大阪

26 Hotel Il Cuore Namba ホテルイルクオーレな んば

27 Hotel 1-2-3 Tennoji ホテル1-2-3天王寺

Other

1 Open-Air Museum of Old Japanese Farm Houses
日本民家集落博物館

7 Osaka Museum of Housing & Living
大阪市立住まいの ミュージアム

9 Central Post Office 中央郵便局

10 Umeda Sky Building 梅田スカイビル

12 National Museum of Art 国立国際美術館

13 Osaka Castle 大阪城

14 Universal Studios Japan ユニバーサルスタジオ ジャパン

Other (cont'd)

15 Modern Transportation Museum
交通科学博物館

17 Osaka Aquarium 海遊館

18 Osaka Maritime Museum
なにわの海の時空館

19 WTC Cosmo Tower WTCコスモタワー

20 Tempozan Giant Ferris Wheel
天保山大観覧車.

21 Santa Maria サンタマリア

24 Osaka Human Rights Museum/Liberty Osaka
大阪人権博物館/ リバティおおさか

a short walk from the east exit of Shin-Osaka station; see the website for a useful map.

Hotel Shin-Osaka (☎ 06-6322 8800, 🖳 www.hso.co.jp; from ¥4950/S, ¥7300/D, ¥8,700/Tw, inc breakfast; good online rates) is conveniently located by the east exit of the station. The hotel has a floor with rooms called 'sleeping rooms' as the beds in them are meant to offer a more comfortable and relaxing night than most other beds.

There are several branches of Toyoko Inn (🖳 www.toyoko-inn.com) in the area: *Toyoko Inn Shin-Osaka Chuo-guchi Shinkan* (☎ 06-6303 1045; from ¥6480/S, ¥7480/D, ¥8480/Tw, inc breakfast) and *Toyoko Inn Shin-Osaka Chuo-guchi Honkan* (☎ 06-6305 1045; from ¥5980/S, ¥6980/D, ¥7980/Tw, inc breakfast) are next to each other and are both five minutes on foot from the main exit of JR Shin-Osaka station; if these are full try *Toyoko Inn Shin-Osaka Higashi-guchi* (☎ 06-6160 1045; from ¥4980/S, ¥6980/D, ¥7980/Tw), an eight-minute walk from the east exit of the station.

● **Near Osaka station** JR-run *Hotel Granvia Osaka* (☎ 06-6344 1235, 🖳 www. granvia-osaka.jp; from ¥10,500/S, ¥15,000/D, ¥16,000/Tw, exc breakfast), in the South Gate building, is directly accessible from the station – the cheapest rooms (mostly for single use) don't have a good view but all others do. Front (reception) is on the 1st floor; the rooms are on the 20th-27th floors.

Hotel Monterey Osaka (☎ 06-6458 7111, 🖳 www.hotelmonterey.co.jp/osaka; ¥15,015/S, ¥27,720/Tw) is an upmarket European-style hotel; rooms are spacious with tiled or wooden floors. There is a choice of Italian, French, Chinese and Japanese restaurants.

● **Osaka Bay** For luxury accommodation, try *Hyatt Regency Osaka* (☎ 06-6612 1234, 🖳 osaka.regency.hyatt.com; from ¥11,700/Tw, Regency Club from ¥21,700/Tw). Facilities include indoor and outdoor pools, a state-of-the-art health/fitness centre and a choice of Western and Japanese restaurants. For a taste of extra luxury, ask for a room on the Regency Club floors (25th-27th floors), which have breathtaking views of the bay area and afford access to the Regency Club lounge, offering private

check-in and check-out, breakfast, afternoon tea and pre-dinner cocktails. The Hyatt Regency is an official Universal Studios Japan hotel and packages including entrance to the theme park are available. A limousine bus for Kansai Airport (¥1300) stops right outside the hotel and there's a free shuttle bus (daily 8am-10pm; 2/hr) for guests from outside the Sakurabashi exit of JR Osaka station. Alternatively, from Bentencho on the Osaka Loop line, take the Chuo subway line to the terminus at Cosmosquare and transfer to the New Tram/Nanko Port Town (the terms are interchangeable) line (¥200) for Trade Center-mae or the next stop at Nakafuto; from both stops the hotel is a five-minute walk.

A 5- to 10-minute walk from the Hyatt Regency, but considerably cheaper, is *Cosmosquare Hotel* (☎ 06-6614 8711, 🖳 www.hotel-cosmosquare.jp; ¥7875/S, ¥14,700/Tw; breakfast ¥787). Business-hotel style rooms are the order of the day (all rooms have wi-fi; ask for one with an ocean view), but it's well located in the Osaka Bay area and there is a Family Mart convenience store outside and an in-house *izakaya*-style restaurant/pub, where the menu includes tonkatsu, udon and steak. Lunchtime set meals cost from ¥680. To find the hotel, walk behind the Hyatt Regency, then up the road which runs past/parallel to the Intex Osaka exhibition centre (this should be on your right-hand side as you walk up the road). Cosmosquare Hotel is the building in front of you at the end of this road.

At the eastern terminus of the New Tram/Nanko Port Town Line, right outside Suminoe-koen station, is *Best Western Joytel Osaka* (☎ 06-6684 1231, 🖳 best western-joytel.com/osaka; ¥7000/S, ¥13,000/D, ¥14,000/Tw, inc breakfast), which offers clean, compact rooms. To reach here, either take the same route as for Hyatt Regency Osaka and continue on the New Tram/Nanko Port Town line to the terminus at Suminoe-koen station, or take the Yotsubashi subway line from Nishi-Umeda (accessed from JR Osaka) to the terminus at Suminoe-koen. The lobby and reception desk are on the 9th floor of the adjacent Osker Dream building.

• **Other areas** *Swissotel Nankai Osaka* (☎ 06-6646 1111, 🖳 www.swissotel.com/osaka; from ¥12,500/S, ¥17,000/Tw), directly above Nankai's **Namba station**, is a haven of luxury. Check the website for details of special packages, some of which include treatments at the hotel's top-end Amrita Spa.

Hotel Il Cuore Namba (☎ 06-6647 1900, 🖳 www.ilcuore-namba.com; ¥9000/S, ¥15,000/D, ¥17,000/Tw; breakfast ¥1000) is also conveniently located for Nankai's Namba station, with plenty of economical eating places nearby. Its design has a bit more flair than your average business hotel. The 11th floor is for women only.

A good budget choice is *Hotel 1-2-3 Tennoji* (☎ 06-6770 2345, 🖳 www.hotel123.co.jp/english/tennoji; ¥5145/S, ¥7245/D, inc breakfast), which has clean, compact rooms. Take the Osaka Loop line to **Teradacho**. Leave the station, cross to the other side of the road (McDonald's is opposite the exit) and turn left. The hotel is a minute's walk up the road, on the third street on your right.

• **Kansai Airport** *Hotel Nikko Kansai Airport* (☎ 0724-55 1111, 🖳 www.nikkokix.com; from ¥10,080/S, ¥16,470/Tw, ¥20,925, inc buffet breakfast; room-only rates also available) is an upmarket place five minutes' walk from the terminal building. Book online and as far as possible in advance for the cheapest deals.

Where to eat and drink

Osaka has a reputation as a gastronomic city but mostly at the cheaper end of the market, not fine dining. However, that is not to say there aren't some wonderful restaurants here. There's endless choice at JR Osaka station (see p120) as well as in Umeda, the area around the station, particularly for lunchtime deals, and in the Osaka Bay (see p116) area. Dotombori (see Nightlife) is another area worth looking around. In fact it is associated with *kuidaore* – literally being extravagant with what you spend on food, but also the concept of 'eat till you drop'. So, you shouldn't find it hard to eat well in Osaka.

Specialities of Osaka include okonomiyaki, takoyaki, kushikatsu (deep-fried breaded food on skewers), kitsune-udon (udon served with deep-fried thinly sliced tofu) and kaiten sushi (conveyor-belt sushi). It is also the city where instant ramen (see box below) was invented.

Nightlife

The **Kita area**, around JR Osaka station, is busy after dark and packed with restaurants and bars. However, the main centre for nightlife is **Dotombori**, on the southern side of Dotombori Canal in the Minami (southern) district of the city. A useful point of reference and a good place to start a night out is Ebisu-bashi (Ebisu bridge). From here, the canal is brightly lit up by competing neon signs and the streets surrounding it are packed with cinemas, cheap eateries, clubs and bars.

⛩ Pot-noodle king

Osaka is the undisputed instant-noodle capital of Japan, if not the world. The city's association with this global phenomenon can be traced back to 1958, when Momofuku Ando (1910-2007) launched Chicken Ramen, the world's first instant noodle dish. Generations of students around the world have Ando to thank for inventing the Cup Noodle in 1971, a mass-market product which remains one of the world's most instantly recognisable supermarket-shelf items. Nissin, the company Ando founded in 1948 now sells in excess of 85 billion instant-noodle products in 70 countries each year.

In 1999 Ando opened the **Momofuku Ando Instant Ramen Museum** (🖳 www.nissin-noodles.com; Wed-Mon 9.30am-4pm; free but ¥2000 deposit for audio guide) in his home city of Ikeda, near Osaka, where noodle fans can wallow shamelessly in chicken-ramen nostalgia. The museum is a five-minute walk from Hankyu Ikeda station (20 mins by LEX from Hankyu Umeda in Osaka).

HONSHU

Central Honshu – route guides

Culturally rich and geographically diverse, central Honshu is a vast area stretching from the Pacific Ocean in the south to the Sea of Japan in the north. If this region is Japan's beating heart, the Tokaido line which runs along the southern coast is the country's transportation artery. It is above all a functional rail line – perhaps the most functional in the world, transporting thousands of passengers every day between the business and industrial hubs of Tokyo, Nagoya and Osaka.

But it would be a great shame to restrict your travel by rail only to the Tokaido shinkansen. Much of the area along the Tokaido line is heavily built-up and polluted by factories and heavy industry so, in its own way, a journey along this line offers a real taste of Japan; concrete proof that nature has indeed been spectacularly sacrificed for the industrial revolution. For many visitors who only just have the time to rush between Tokyo and Kyoto, this is all they see of the country. But just a short distance from the industrialised southern coast lie the majestic Japanese Alps, most easily accessed by shinkansen from Tokyo to Nagano. The rail network is fast, efficient and even in the winter months of heavy snowfall almost invariably on time.

Highlights of a tour around this region include **Hakone**, with its wonderful scenery and views of **Mt Fuji**; **Takayama**, a mini-Kyoto in the mountains; the preserved Edo-period 'post towns' of **Narai** and **Tsumago**; and **Kanazawa** which has one of Japan's most celebrated gardens. Between April and November, the **Tateyama-Kurobe Alpine Route** (see p148) offers an opportunity to appreciate the region's astonishing beauty in a day-long journey from the coast to the Japanese Alps, involving as it does a variety of modes of transport.

For details about using this rail route guide see pp8-9.

Foggy drizzle!
Intriguing is the day
we can't see Mt Fuji
(Matsuo Basho)

霧雨や富士を見ぬ日ぞ面白き

❏ **Shinkansen services**
The only shinkansen which run all the way from Tokyo to Hakata in Kyushu are the Nozomi services for which a Japan Rail Pass is not valid. Thus, if you have a Japan Rail pass, wherever you are going, you will need to take a Hikari or Kodama shinkansen. However, Kodama should be avoided if possible because they stop at every station. If you are travelling further west than Osaka you will need to change trains at Shin-Osaka or Okayama.

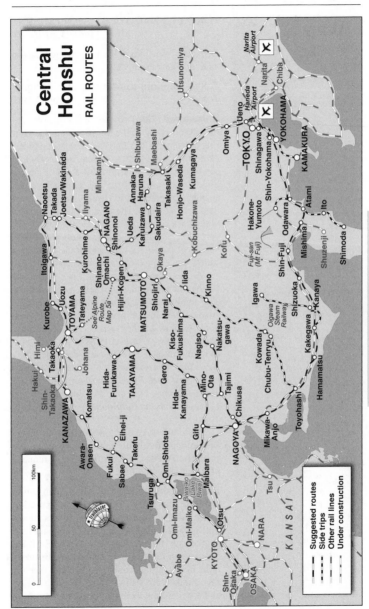

Central Honshu
RAIL ROUTES

Suggested routes
Side trips
Other rail lines
Under construction

HONSHU

KANSAI

MAP 1

To Nagano (Map 3);
to Tohoku
& Hokkaido
(Map 15)

TOKYO
Shinagawa

Yokohama

Shin-Yokohama

Trailblazer

Side trip to
Kamakura

0   10   20km

Odawara

Fuji-san
(Mt Fuji)

Hakone-
Yumoto

Atami

Ashi-ko
(Lake Ashi)

Side trip to
Ashi-ko
by bus

Mishima

Gotemba
For climbing
Mt Fuji
(summer only)

Numazu

Shin-
Fuji

Side trip
to Ito &
Shimoda

Shizuoka

Suruga
Bay

Igawa

Oigawa Steam
Railway
side trip

Kanaya

Kakegawa

To Nagoya
(Map 2)

HONSHU

TOKYO TO NAGOYA BY SHINKANSEN
[Table 3, pp456-7]

Distances from Tokyo. Fastest journey time (on a Hikari shinkansen): 110 mins.

Tokyo (Station) to Atami   [Map 1]
Tokyo   [see pp83-106]

Shinagawa (7km) All the shinkansen services (platforms 21-24) call here. If you are transferring to/from the JR Yamanote line (see pp84-91; platforms 1 and 2), or the Narita Express (N'EX, see box pp100-1; platforms 13 & 14) it makes sense to change here as the station is much smaller and easier to navigate your way round than Tokyo Station. There are **lockers** (all sizes) at the back of the platform side of the main JR concourse as well as toilets. You'll also find a variety of places for food and drink, in an area called 'ecute', on the platform concourse.

A passageway connects the Takanawa (west) exit and Konan (east) exits of the station. The shinkansen tracks are on the Konan side. Also on this side are places to eat such as *New York Grand Kitchen* (daily 7am-10.30pm), which serves pasta and burgers as well as a morning buffet for ¥880. Next door there is a *New York Oyster Bar* (daily 11am-10.30pm) and a *New York Sub's American Diner* (daily 11am-10.30pm). On the 3rd floor in Queens Isetan, is the *Food Boutique* supermarket (daily 10am-8pm).

Rail buffs may like to know that a railway station was first built here and opened to the public on 7th May 1872. Sadly nothing remains of the original building.

Shin-Yokohama (29km) All the shinkansen services call here. The **tourist information office** (daily 10am-6pm) is by the station's north exit, opposite the east exit for the shinkansen tracks. **Lockers** (¥300-600) are available in most parts of the station. Ordinary train lines and the Yokohama subway connect this shinkansen station with Yokohama Port and areas around there (see opposite).

Hotel rates in Shin-Yokohama are often a bit lower than in central Tokyo, so if you have a rail pass you might consider basing yourself here; Shinagawa/Tokyo are only 12/20 minutes away by shinkansen. Attached to the station is the JR-run *Hotel Associa Shin-Yokohama* (☎ 045-475 0011, 💻 www.associa.com/english/syh; from ¥16,000/S, ¥21,000/D or Tw, inc continental breakfast; small discount for rail-pass holders), with smart rooms and compact but stylish bathrooms. *Toyoko Inn* (💻 www.toyoko-inn.com) has two branches, Shin-Yokohama Ekimae Honkan (☎ 045-474 1045) and Shin-Yokohama Ekimae Shinkan (☎ 045-470 1045), near the north exit of the station. Both charge from ¥5480/S, ¥6980/D or Tw.

On the north exit side of the station, **Cubic Plaza** has various restaurants including *Katsukura* (daily 11am-10pm) on the 9th floor, which serves delicious tonkatsu, especially *hirekatsu* (80g for ¥1200). Nearby is a branch of *Harvest* (daily 11am-9.30pm), which does an excellent-value Viking (buffet-style) meal with mostly vegetarian dishes for ¥1500-1800 per person.

The main tourist sight near the shinkansen station is the unusual **Ramen Museum** (💻 www.raumen.co.jp/ramen; Mon-Fri 11am-10pm, Sat, Sun & hols 10.30am-10pm; ¥300), five minutes on foot north-east from the north exit of the station (get a route map from the website or the tourist office). The ground-floor museum tells the story of how noodles rose from humble beginnings to embrace the global market. But the big attraction is the re-created ramen village in the basement, featuring traditional ramen shops from around Japan, most notably from Sapporo in Hokkaido and Fukuoka in Kyushu, the two best-known centres. Each ramen shop has its own machine and you need to order your ramen (¥800-1100) and any drinks and side dishes before going in. After you've eaten, be sure to walk around the back streets in the museum and look at the very educational shop area.

Side trip to Yokohama

The most interesting parts of Yokohama to visit are Sakuragicho, for a taste of the 21st century, and Ishikawa-cho for a bit of history. From Shin-Yokohama take the JR Yokohama line to Yokohama and Sakuragicho (from platform 5; about 20 mins); for Ishikawa-cho it is necessary to change at Yokohama or Higashi-Kanagawa and transfer to the JR Keihin-Tohoku/Negishi Line (about 25 mins in all).

There are **tourist information centres** (💻 www.welcome.city.yokohama.jp; daily 9am-7pm) on the east–west walkway at Yokohama station, in Minato Mirai Information centre outside Sakuragicho station, and in Sangyo Boeki Center (Mon-Fri 9am-5pm) near Yamashita-koen.

● **Sakuragicho** Home to **Minato Mirai 21 (MM21)**, a city within a city featuring hotels, restaurants, shopping complexes and museums, this area all looks very different to how it must have been in 1872, when it opened as a terminus for Japan's first rail line between Shinagawa and Yokohama. **Akai Kutsu** (Red Bus; daily 10am-6pm, 3-4/hr; ¥100/journey, ¥300/one-day pass) does a circuit round the main tourist sights from in front of Sakuragicho station.

From Sakuragicho station it is an easy walk – a lot of it on a moving walkway – to the **Landmark Tower**, where a lift (daily 10am-9pm, to 10pm

⛩ **Yokohama's place in history**

   Yokohama was a small fishing village in the Edo period but its place in history came when it was the location for the signing of the Japan-US Treaty of Peace and Amity in February 1854, less than a year after Commodore Perry (see p34) had arrived in the area demanding the Japanese open their ports to trade. Yokohama port was officially opened to foreign trade in 1859 and it was not long before representatives of other nationalities had also moved into the residential area designated for foreigners.

on Sat and Jul-Aug; ¥1000) will whisk you in seconds to the Sky Garden Observatory (on the 69th floor). *Yokohama Royal Park Hotel* (☎ 045-221 1111, 🖳 www.yrph.com; from ¥34,650/S, ¥39,900/D), on the 52nd to the 67th floor, is the highest hotel in Japan.

Also in the Minato Mirai 21 area is an amusement park, **Yokohama Cosmo World** (Mar-Nov daily 11am-9pm, Dec-Feb weekends only), with Cosmo Clock, a 112.5m-high Ferris wheel, one of the tallest in Japan. At the **Cup Noodles Museum** (🖳 www.cupnoodles-museum.jp; daily 10am-6pm; ¥500) visitors can make their own cup noodles and learn about Momofuku Ando (see box p123); they may also of course try many of the varieties in the food court.

• **Ishikawa-cho** This is the best stop for Yokohama's **Chinatown**; turn left out of the station and follow the signs, which effectively means following the road around, over a bridge and then going straight on. Once in Chinatown proper the street is pedestrianised; follow the signs to **Yamashita-koen** (Yamashita Park) which is also basically straight on; you'll know you're there (15-20 mins) when you see the sea. On Yamashita-koen-dori, the road running alongside the park, you'll see the **Hotel New Grand**, which is the only original hotel building left in Yokohama; the facade is virtually unchanged since it was built in 1927. Beyond the hotel is **Toda Peace Memorial Hall** (daily 11am-7pm; free), which was once English House No 7 and is the only foreign trading house remaining from before the Great Kanto earthquake. Josei Toda, a Buddhist and educationalist, wanted nuclear bombs abolished and the museum here is operated by young people as a museum for peace.

The **Silk Museum** (🖳 www.silkmuseum.or.jp; Tue-Sun 9am-4.30pm; ¥500) is in English House No 1, the former Jardine Matheson and Company building, where exhibits describe the silk production process. From here turn back and walk into the park itself. On the left is the **International Passenger Terminal**. Yamashita Park is a pleasant place for a rest, and for watching the boats and cruise ships coming and going. The *Hikawa Maru* (🖳 www.nyk. com; Tue-Sun 10am-5pm; ¥200) – an NYK Line passenger liner on the Yokohama to Seattle and Vancouver route – is moored permanently at the other end of the park to commemorate the centenary of the port. A combined ticket with the NYK Maritime Museum (same hours; ¥400) is ¥500. Not far away is the **Marine Tower** (daily 10am-10pm; ¥750) which has a 106m-high observatory floor.

Soon after the Marine Tower you pass **Yokohama Doll Museum** (🖳 www.yokohama-doll-museum.com; Tue-Sun 9.30am-5pm; ¥500), which houses over 9000 dolls from around the world. From here follow signs to

Minato no Mieru Oka Koen (Harbour View Park), which is on the other side of Hori-kawa (Hori River). Climb up the steps into the park and you will soon come to the ruins of the **French Consul's house**, which was built in the 1860s. Keep walking through the park but head to the right and then out on to the road. At the junction with the traffic lights turn right and head towards **Yokohama Foreigners Cemetery** (🖳 www.yfgc-japan.com; Mar-Dec weekends and hols only, noon-4pm; donation of ¥200 or more welcome). Over 4000 people from about 40 countries are buried here and even if it is not open it is worth going to look at the inscriptions on the graves you can see from the main entrance. From here it is an easy walk down through Motomachi and back to JR Ishikawa-cho station – just follow the signs.

Odawara (84km)

Some Hikari and all Kodama stop here. In March 1886, the Zusho Jinsha (Human Railway) was opened between Odawara and Atami (the next stop along the shinkansen line), a distance of 25km. It took more than four hours to go between the two towns. The eight-seater coach, pushed by three people, was used for 12 years until the introduction of steam locomotives.

Once an important castle town, Odawara is now a major junction on both the shinkansen and Tokaido mainlines, as well as a terminus for the private Odakyu line from Shinjuku. It's also the main gateway to **Hakone** (see below).

There are **lockers** (¥300-400) by Beck's coffee shop on the main east–west concourse and at the top of the escalators from the shinkansen platforms heading to the east exit. The **tourist information centre** (daily 9am-5pm) is on the left on the concourse; staff can give you a map showing how to reach the castle and the area where the samurai used to live.

A convenient place to spend the night is *Hotel Kunimi Odawara* (☎ 0465-24 8080, 🖳 www.hotelkunimi.com; ¥6300/S, ¥6800-11,550/D or Tw). Follow the signs for the east exit and head straight down the road to the traffic lights. Turn right at Ohoribata-dori and walk along for about five minutes. The hotel is set back from the road on the right-hand side.

On the right-hand side on the main road leading down from the station is a branch of *Café Jr Italian Tomato* (daily 8am-10pm), which serves a delicious spinach and pumpkin pasta (¥580). There are other restaurants and cafés around the station but many of them close early in the evening.

Continue along this road to reach **Odawara Castle** (daily 9am-4.30pm; ¥400), a 1960s reconstruction of the 15th-century original. It is one of the best in the Tokyo area and has an excellent museum (if you like armoury) and a great view from the top.

Side trip to Hakone

The best way to get to Hakone from Odawara is with Odakyu Railway's (🖳 www.odakyu.jp) **Hakone Free Pass**, a package ticket which includes return rail travel from Odawara (or Shinjuku, see pp112-13) to Hakone. The pass is valid for two or three days and for unlimited travel on a switchback (mountain) railway, cable car (funicular) and ropeway (cable car), from which there are excellent views of Mt Fuji if the weather cooperates, and on a boat trip on Lake Ashi.

At Odawara station, buy the pass from **Odakyu Sightseeing Service Center** (daily 6.30am-9pm), on the main concourse by the Odakyu exit.

HONSHU

Passes for weekends year-round and weekdays mid March to early May, mid July to late August, late December to early January cost ¥4130/2070 adult/child; passes for weekdays in the rest of the year are ¥3410/¥1700 but are valid for two days only.

If you're staying for any length of time in the Hakone area get a **Mt Fuji Welcome Card** (see box p64) for discounts on some attractions.

If starting the journey in Odawara the first stage is to take an Odakyu train to **Hakone-Yumoto** (daily 4/hr; 15 mins; ¥300). The station has lockers as well as a **tourist information centre** (daily 8.30am-4.30pm).

If you are staying the night in the Hakone area and would like to sightsee without being laden go to Hakone Baggage Service (daily 8.30am-7pm; ¥700-1000 per bag, ¥100 discount with a Free Pass), behind the stairs on the 1st floor in Hakone-Yumoto station. They will take luggage that has been deposited at their office by noon to your accommodation by 3pm.

If planning to stay in Hakone-Yumoto itself *Kappa Tengoku* (🖳 www.japanhotel.net/kappa), a short but steep walk up behind the station, offers simple accommodation (¥5600pp) and also open-air single-sex baths (daily 10am-10pm; residents free, non-residents ¥750, plus ¥150 for towel rental).

At Hakone-Yumoto transfer to **Hakone Tozan Railway** (daily 3/hr; 40 mins; ¥650), the only full-scale mountain railway in Japan. The train changes direction three times, at switchbacks, en route to Gora; for the best views sit on the left. The line goes up 550m over 15km of track; some of the sections of track on this railway are the steepest in Japan.

Miyanoshita is the closest station to the atmospheric *Fujiya Hotel* (☎ 0460-82 2211, 🖳 www.fujiyahotel.jp; from ¥14,500pp), which opened in 1878. The hotel has Western-style rooms spread over five different houses. Each room has natural hot spring water and the hotel is a Registered Cultural Asset of Japan. Facilities include swimming pools, hot spring baths, and several restaurants. Charlotte Steggall (UK) says: 'It's not for people wanting modern, clean Japan. It's for people who would like to take a look into Japan of yesteryear, see how the richer folk lived. My recommendation to those who stay there is to look out for the "World Facial Hair Championship" photos!'

Hakone Open-Air Museum (🖳 www.hakone-oam.or.jp; daily 9am-5pm; ¥1600), featuring Henry Moore sculptures and over 300 works by Picasso, is a glorious place to walk round, especially if the weather is good. It's a short walk from **Chokoku-no-Mori** station, the last stop before Gora.

At **Gora** take the cable car (funicular; 4/hour; 10 mins; ¥410) to Sounzan, from where the Hakone Ropeway (cable car; 🖳 www.hakoneropeway.co.jp; Mar-Jul & Sep-Oct 8.45am-5.15pm, Aug to 5.30pm, Dec-Feb 9.15am-4.15pm; 30 mins; ¥1330 one way, ¥1470 return) goes to Togendai. The cars have glass sides and seats for up to 18 people. If the weather is good, just before arriving at the Ropeway's first stop, **Owakudani**, look out to the right for views of Mt Fuji. Owakudani (Hell Valley; 🖳 www.owakudani.com) is so called because of the horrible smell coming from the poisonous hydrogen sulphide gas which emerges from gaps (vents) in the ground. Don't let the smell put you off getting out and exploring, though some of the paths are closed now because of concerns about erosion and landslides. A separate cable car brings eggs up to be cooked in the hot water. The shells of these turn black – try one (¥500 for five) – though the hard-boiled egg inside tastes much the same as usual.

Few get out at the next stop, **Ubako**, but it is a chance to have a break from the almost inevitable crowds. Take the left exit to see one of the original cars from the ropeway and the right exit for an observation point (a five- to ten-minute walk), which is an excellent place for a picnic. Fuji san is obscured here but you can see Lake Ashi (Ashi-no-ko) and the boat you will soon be on. At **Togendai**, the final stop, you could rent a swan pedalo, but most people join one of the kitsch but fun sightseeing cruise boats; apart from the scenery this is one of the highlights of the trip. The replica 17th-/18th-century pirate ships operated by **Hakone Sightseeing Ships** (🖥 www.hakone-kankosen.co.jp; Mar-Nov 13/day, Dec-Mar 10/day; ¥1780) convey you around Lake Ashi, a crater lake. The full circuit takes about 100 minutes but most people get off at either Hakone-machi, the first stop, or Moto-Hakone. From Hakone-machi you can walk along the ancient cedar avenue (see pp132-3) to Moto-Hakone.

Moto-Hakone Guest House (☎ 0460-83-788, 🖥 hakone.syuriken.jp/hakone; ¥5250, breakfast ¥840pp) is a friendly place. It is a fairly steep 12- to 15-minute walk along the main road heading inland, or you can take a bus and get off at Ashinokoen-mae. Evening meals are not available but the proprietor can give you a map showing a pleasant way to walk back to Moto-Hakone. Since most restaurants close early it may be best to buy your own provisions from the *7-Eleven* convenience store (at the Moto-Hakone end of the main road).

Atami (105km)

Only a few Hikari stop here. Atami is a famous spa town but, due to its proximity to Tokyo, it often gets unpleasantly crowded. The **tourist information centre** (TIC; daily 9am-5/5.30pm) is on the station concourse. There are lots of **lockers** (¥300-400 inside the station, ¥300-500 outside).

Hot springs abound, with a choice of seven spas; you can pick up a stamp card (see box p24) and trek around the town visiting them all. There is also a free foot hot spring just outside the station.

A well-known sightseeing spot is **Oyu geyser** (see box p132), which claims to be one of the three largest in the world, along with the Great Caesar in Iceland and the Old Faithful in Yellowstone National Park, USA. British travellers, in particular, might want to make a pilgrimage here to see the grave of Poor Toby, a Scottish terrier whose life was tragically cut short after a visit here. To reach it turn right out of the station and walk downhill through a covered shopping street, turn right at the end and follow the road down a bit more; you will soon see signs in the pavement showing the way back slightly up the hill to the geyser. En route you will pass various hot springs; look out for **Kosawa-no-Yu** – the legend here is that the louder you shout the higher the water spurts.

The other main tourist draw is **MOA Museum of Art** (🖥 www.moaart.or.jp; Fri-Wed 9.30am-4.30pm; ¥1600), on a hillside overlooking Atami; it is accessible by bus from the station (bus No 4 from stand 4; 10 mins). It contains a large collection of woodblock prints, ceramics and gold and silver lacquer-ware. Pick up a discount voucher (¥200 per group) from the TIC.

In 1604, the shogun Tokugawa Ieyasu visited Atami to bathe in the hot springs. From that time on, hot spring water was dedicated to the shoguns and transported annually from Atami to Edo Castle, Chiyoda-ku, Tokyo. Celebrations are still held in commemoration of this every 10th February and 10th October.

HONSHU

HONSHU

⛩ **Sir Rutherford Alcock and Poor Toby**
Sir Rutherford Alcock, a British minister, visited Japan in 1859 and the following year climbed Mt Fuji. Clearly not a modest man, Alcock stopped in Atami on his return from Fuji and had a monument built here with the inscription: 'I am the first non-Japanese to have climbed Mt Fuji and visited Atami'. It stands next to the **Oyu geyser**, alongside a monument to Alcock's faithful Scottish terrier, Toby. Having survived the journey from Britain, Toby suffered the misfortune of standing on the piece of ground from where the geyser used to periodically erupt. The inevitable happened; the unsuspecting dog was blasted into the air by the force of the boiling water shooting out from the earth.

A distraught Alcock organised a funeral for his pet in Atami, an event which was almost certainly the origin of Britain's reputation in Japan as a nation of eccentrics. Toby was buried beside the geyser, perhaps as a warning to other mad dogs and Englishmen to beware of the danger that lurks close by. His tombstone reads simply: 'Poor Toby, 23 September 1860'. If the sign at the geyser is to be believed, the dog did not die in vain. 'At that time, Japan had a bad impression of the British people,' it reads. Alcock reported back to Britain that the Japanese had been very kind to him during his period of mourning and advised his country that they should not look upon Japan as an enemy. 'Thanks to his report and advice,' the sign continues, 'Great Britain's public opinion towards Japan turned favourable'.

In Toby's day the spring gushed hot water and steam six times a day, 'shaking the earth with its vigorous blasts'. During the 100 years since Alcock's visit to Atami the geyser gradually gave up and died. In 1962 it was given a new lease of (artificial) life and now goes off for three minutes at four-minute intervals.

Side trip by train to Shimoda
Atami is the starting point for the Ito line south to **Ito** (about 20 mins), where William Adams, the first Englishman to set foot in Japan, spent much of his life after a shipwreck off the coast of Kyushu in 1600. He became known as Anjin-san and his arrival is celebrated during the Anjin Matsuri in August. Beyond Ito, the line continues to **Izukyu Shimoda** (about 80 mins from Atami), but this section is operated by the private Izukyu Railway so JR rail passes are not valid. Shimoda is the place to gaze out over the sea and imagine what it must have been like to behold Commodore Perry's 'Black Ships' in 1854 (see p68). It is the southernmost town on the Izu Peninsula and is known now for its beaches and surfing. The Odoriko/Super View Odoriko LEX (7/day) and local trains (6/hr) operate on this line.

Atami to Nagoya   [Map 1, p126; Map 2, p134]
Mishima (121km) A few Hikari stop here. There are **locker**s of all sizes as well as some cafés outside the north exit. Mishima is an access point for the Hakone region (see below) and Mt Fuji (see box opposite).

Side trip by bus to the Hakone region
Take a Numazu Tozan Tokai bus from bus stand 5, outside the south exit of Mishima station, to Moto-Hakone (hourly; 60 mins; ¥1000). From there you could take one of the sightseeing boats on Lake Ashi, or walk to Hakone-machi along a section of the Ancient Cedar Avenue (cedars were planted to provide shade for travellers on the old Tokaido Highway) passing the Hakone

---

⛩ **Climbing Mt Fuji**

If intending to climb Mt Fuji (3776m), change at Mishima for a local JR train to **Numazu** (2-3/hr; 6 mins), one stop along the Tokaido mainline towards Kyoto. Change at Numazu for the JR Gotemba line to **Gotemba** (1-2/hour; 24-36 mins), from where you can pick up a Fuji-kyu bus to Subashiri 5th station (July to late Sep; 1/hr; 60 mins; ¥1500) on Mt Fuji; buses also run to Gotemba 5th station (40 mins; ¥1080) but less frequently. It's then about 6½ hours on foot to the summit, but don't rush up as altitude sickness can be a problem for some people. Most people climb in the late afternoon and spend the night in one of the huts on the mountain and then get up early in order to go to the summit to see the sunrise. Since the walking season is so limited (Jul-Sep), expect the mountain to be very crowded.

For more information on climbing Mt Fuji, see 🖥 mountfujiguide.com or 🖥 www.shizuoka-guide.com. Mt Fuji Visitor Centre (daily 9am-4pm Dec-Feb, to 6pm Jul & Aug, to 5pm rest of year) is a 10-minute bus ride (on a retro bus) from JR Kawaguchiko station; see 🖥 transportation.fujikyu.co.jp.

Checkpoint/Exhibition en route. Sightseeing cruise boats depart from Hakone-machi (as well as Moto-Hakone). If you don't have time to do the full circuit (see p131) consider taking the Mississippi side-wheeler steamboat (about 40 mins; ¥1220), which covers the southern part of the lake. If the weather is good you should be able to see Mt Fuji from the lakeside without taking this boat trip.

Buses back to Mishima depart from bus stand 4 (by Hakone-machi pier).

Shin-Fuji (146km) Only Kodama stop here. There are hideous smoke stacks everywhere you look as you pass through Shin-Fuji, which is a shame since you expect a place with this name to afford picture-postcard views of Japan's most famous natural wonder. You should start looking out for **views of Mt Fuji** though; on the right side of the train (from Tokyo) or on the left side (to Tokyo).

Shizuoka (180km) One Hikari an hour stops here and all Kodama. A well-known **tea-producing area**, Shizuoka is often overlooked as being too soon after Tokyo to make it a destination in its own right, but it has some attractions.

At JR Shizuoka station the main exit for the city (where all the buses arrive and depart) is the north side. There is normally an English speaker on hand at the **tourist information office** (🖥 www.shizuoka-guide.com; daily 8.30am-6pm), along a passageway behind the JR ticket gate.

Kunozan Toshogu Shrine (May-Oct daily 9am-5pm, Nov-Apr to 4pm; ¥800 inc museum, or ¥1650 inc transport from ropeway descent only, purchased from ropeway top station) is a mausoleum honouring Tokugawa Ieyasu (1542-1616), who spent the last years of his life in Shizuoka; his body, however, is now in Nikko. The shrine is accessed via bus from Shizuoka station and then by ropeway. Take bus No 42 (Mon-Fri 4/day, Sat-Sun 8/day; 35 mins; ¥580) from stop No 19 and get off at Nihondaira (the last stop) for the short ropeway ride (🖥 www.shizutetsu.co.jp/park; daily 9.10am-4pm; ¥550 one way, ¥1000 return). This terminates by the entrance to the shrine. Behind the main shrine, surprisingly ornate and colourful and looking more like a Buddhist temple than an austere Shinto shrine, is the simple mausoleum, surrounded by trees. Also

HONSHU

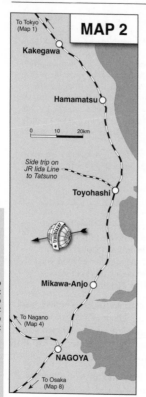

MAP 2

To Tokyo (Map 1)

Kakegawa

Hamamatsu

0   10   20km

Side trip on JR Iida Line to Tatsuno

Toyohashi

Mikawa-Anjo

To Nagano (Map 4)

NAGOYA

To Osaka (Map 8)

here is a small but fascinating museum housing a colourful treasure trove of Ieyasu's possessions, including glittering swords, hanging scrolls, samurai armour and an antique table clock from Madrid.

There are two ways back to Shizuoka from the shrine. Either take the ropeway back to Nihondaira and then pick up the bus back to the station, or walk down the 1159 steps from the shrine to the coast. There are several strawberry farms at the bottom of the steps where, even out of season, you can buy strawberry juice, ice cream and jam. Turn left when you reach the foot of the steps (don't go as far as the main road in front of you) and walk 150m to the bus stop, where bus No 14 (¥470) will return you to Shizuoka station. If you really want to climb the 1159 steps up to the shrine you can catch this bus from stop No 22 outside Shizuoka station.

The highlight of **Shizuoka Prefectural Museum of Art** (🖳 www.spmoa.shizuoka.shizuoka.jp; Tue-Sun 10am-5.30pm; ¥300; English audio guide available) is the Rodin Wing, which boasts an impressive collection of bronze Auguste Rodin casts, including his famous *Thinker* and the *Gates of Hell*. Take bus No 44 from stop No 13, which is across the road from Shizuoka station (take the north exit and cross the road by Hotel Associa Shizuoka) and alight at Kenritsu Bijutsukan (25 mins; ¥350).

The most convenient place to stay is the JR-run *Hotel Associa Shizuoka Terminal* (☎ 054-254 4141, 🖳 www.associa.com/sth; ¥9800/S, ¥10,500/D, ¥14,800/Tw; pass-holders get a small discount), on your right as you take the north exit from Shizuoka station. Rooms are bright and furnished with a minibar and bilingual TV. On the south side of the station, just a couple of minutes from the exit, is *Hotel Privé Shizuoka Station* (☎ 054-281 7300, 🖳 www.hotel-prive.com; ¥5400/S, ¥12,000/Tw). Expect good-value, smart rooms and the usual small bathrooms, though bilingual TV is a nice surprise in this category. The hotel has a faux-European atmosphere, including a somewhat chintzy exterior.

The Wide View Fujikawa LEX (7/day) goes from Shizuoka to Fujinomiya, another possible access point for climbing Mt Fuji (see box p133).

Kakegawa (229km) Only Kodama stop here, the nearest point of access for Oigawa Railway (see opposite), one of Japan's most spectacular steam railway lines. Take the Tokaido line exit from the shinkansen platforms.

Side trip to Oigawa Steam Railway [see Map 1, p126]

The Oigawa Railway began operations in 1926 to transport timber, freight and tea from the mountains along the Oigawa River. During the 1960s revenue from freight began to fall as did the number of people living in the mountainous areas, so the railway turned to tourism. The preserved steam operation (top speed 65kph) runs from Shin-Kanaya to the terminus at Senzu (40km) and really is like stepping back in time. There are four steam engines (including the C12 164), though not all are in use at the same time. Some of the coaches have their original wooden seats and floors, and ceiling fans. The conductor may come through the train playing a harmonica or sing songs over the loudspeaker.

To reach the start point for the Oigawa Railway (🖳 www.oigawa-railway.co.jp), take a local JR train from Kakegawa two stops east to **Kanaya**; there are a few lockers (¥300-500) in the station but little else so if you want any souvenirs of the trip buy them at Shin-Kanaya. The entrance to Oigawa Kanaya station is on your right as you leave JR Kanaya station. You can purchase tickets online through the website or here: Shin-Kanaya to Senzu costs ¥1720 one-way, ¥560 supplement for the steam locomotive; Senzu to Igawa (Abt Line) is ¥1280 one way; the 2-day Oigawa & Abt Line Pass, valid between Kanaya and Igawa, costs ¥4200/5500 Dec-Mar/Mar-Dec. Then board the train and go one stop along the Oigawa line to Shin-Kanaya station, where you transfer on to the steam locomotive for the journey to Senzu (up to 3/day). The local train (1-3/hr) continues all the way to Senzu.

At **Shin-Kanaya** there's a small steam museum (Plaza Loco; daily 9am-5pm) with a few model railways, as well as a gift shop selling Oigawa tea and *ekiben* (railway station lunch box; see box p82); the Oigawa ekiben (¥980) is recommended. Opposite Shin-Kanaya station is a café called *Warau Neko* (daily 10am-8pm), easy to find as it's the only place full of good-luck pottery cats, which according to the owner are supposed to bring in customers – if you're there, it's clearly worked.

The line passes through the Oigawa tea fields and there are good views on both sides so it doesn't really matter where you sit. However, on the left, look out for the raccoon statues and later on in the journey Shiogo suspension bridge. There are also quite a few tunnels – some were built to prevent rock falling on the track and trains – so you may be requested to keep the window closed. There's another small rail museum (10am-4pm; ¥100) at the **Senzu** terminus.

From Senzu an Abt system cog-and-tooth railway travels higher up into the mountains to the very end of the line at **Igawa** (25km); this is the steepest incline for a railway line in Japan. There are several hot springs near stops en route and the line also passes Nagashima Dam.

Hamamatsu (257km)

Some Hikari stop here. Located almost halfway between Tokyo and Osaka, and home to such world-famous companies as Yamaha, Suzuki and Honda. Hamamatsu is known as the 'Music City': it's said that every piano made in Japan is built here.

The **tourist information centre** (🖳 www.hamamatsu-daisuki.net/lan/en/center; daily 9am-7pm) is in front of you as you exit the shinkansen ticket barrier. **Lockers** of all sizes are slightly hidden down a passageway off the main concourse. Immediately above the station is the May One shopping complex with **restaurants** on the 7th floor and take-out food counters in the basement.

On the station concourse itself, try *Tokyo Grill* (beef steak set menu ¥1790) or *Robata* (Japanese-style grilled eel and sashimi). Both are opposite the entrance to the non-shinkansen tracks.

The best place to get your bearings is almost directly in front of the north (Act City) exit of Hamamatsu station and is hard to miss. Standing 212m high, the vast **Act City** complex is home to both the quirky **Museum of Musical Instruments** (🖳 www.gakkihaku.jp; daily except 2nd and 4th Wed of the month 9.30am-5pm; ¥400), which houses more than 2000 instruments from around the world, and the 45th-floor **Observatory Tower** (Mon-Fri 10am-6pm; ¥500), located at a height of 185 metres. This is well worth the admission fee for the chance to take in the surrounding area and – if the weather is good – the spectacular Mt Fuji. Keep an eye out, too, for the imposing black and white façade of **Hamamatsu-jo** (daily 8.30am-4.30pm; ¥150), a castle originally built over 400 years ago by Japan's most celebrated warlord, Tokugawa Ieyasu (see p34). Anyone hoping for promotion at work could do worse than head straight for the castle as soon as they rejoin firm ground. According to legend, Hamamatsu-jo – the present-day incarnation of which dates back to 1958 – gained its nickname 'Castle of Success' by virtue of the fact that every feudal lord who lived inside it later went on to enjoy even higher office.

The best place to stay in Hamamatsu is *Hotel Okura Act City* (☎ 053-459 0111, 🖳 www.act-okura.co.jp; from ¥12,075/S, ¥21,000/Tw), right outside the station. The rooms are on the 32nd floor or higher, so you're guaranteed a good view. The hotel plays on the city's musical theme, with associated motifs on everything from the yukatas to the bathroom walls, and even the up/down lift signs are shaped like grand pianos. Cheaper but reliable alternatives include *Toyoko Inn Hamamatsu-Eki Kita-Guchi* (☎ 053-457 1045, 🖳 www.toyoko-inn.com; ¥6300/S, ¥8400/D or Tw) and *Hotel Century Inn Hamamatsu* (☎ 053-455 0118, 🖳 www.hotelcentury-inn.jp; ¥5900/S, ¥9800/Tw).

Hamamatsu delicacies include eel and *suppon* (soft-shelled snapping turtle), which is usually served as sashimi, in a soup or deep-fried. Local tourist literature even suggests 'turtles from Lake Hamana improve both health and beauty. Try it stewed, deep-fried or in a porridge'.

If you're in the area on 3rd-5th May it's worth stopping for the **Kite Festival**, which sees rival groups armed with giant kites doing battle with each other.

Toyohashi (294km) The view as the train heads towards Toyohashi may discourage you from stopping here but a side trip by rail along the rural Iida Line (see opposite) is well worth considering. Some Hikari and all Kodama stop in Toyohashi, which is also a transfer point for the JR Tokaido line.

Take the east exit for the main part of the city and the tram line. The station has elevators from platform to concourse and street level. Toyohashi Information Plaza (daily 9am-7pm) on the main concourse has maps which include sightseeing details and corresponding tram stops. Close to the tourist information counter, on your right as you head towards the east exit, are lockers (all sizes, up to ¥600).

A tram service has operated in Toyohashi since 1925. Rail fans may enjoy this piece of tramline trivia: the Ihara intersection between the Ihara and

Undokoen-mae tram stops boasts Japan's tightest rail bend, with a radius of just 11m. A single tram line runs through the city (¥150 flat fare) from the Ekimae stop in front of the station to Toyohashi Park (five stops to Toyohashikoen-mae), where you'll find the ruins of **Yoshida Castle** (partially reconstructed in 1954), **Toyohashi City Art Museum** (Tue-Sun 9am-5pm; free) and **Sannomaru** Tea Ceremony Hall (Tue-Sun 9am-5pm; green tea ¥350). There are also walking paths along the Toyogawa River running behind the park.

The most convenient accommodation is the JR-run *Hotel Associa Toyohashi* (☎ 0532-57 1010, 💻 www.associa.com/english/tyh; ¥9000/S, ¥14,000/D, ¥15,000/Tw; small discount for rail-pass holders), attached to the station and accessed directly from the 2nd-floor concourse. A cheaper and more basic option, outside to the left as you take the station east exit, is *Toyoko Inn Toyohashi-eki Higashi-guchi* (☎ 0532-53 1044, 💻 www.toyoko-inn.com; ¥5980/S, ¥7480/D, ¥7980/Tw). Look for the sign in English on the roof. For take-out food options, try the ground floor (one floor below the station concourse level) of Kalmia department store attached to the station. On the station concourse itself, and next to the entrance to Hotel Associa, is *Café Danmark*, with an eat-in and take-out bakery section.

After Toyohashi, Kodama call at **Mikawa-Anjo (336km)** but all other services run non-stop to Nagoya.

Side trip on a rural railway to Iida

The JR Iida Line, local trains for which leave from platform 1 at JR Toyohashi station, is regularly touted as one of the most rural and scenic in Japan. The line stretches over 195km between **Toyohashi** (in Aichi prefecture) and **Tatsuno** (in Nagano prefecture), following the course of the Tenryugawa river. There are more than 90 stations along the way, many of them known as *hikyo-eki* (secluded stations, literally those that are in the middle of nowhere, often with no sign of life or habitation nearby).

Look out along the line for **Kowada** station (83.8km) on the borders of Aichi, Shizuoka and Nagano prefectures. People flocked to this otherwise unremarkable stop with an old wooden station building in 1993 when Crown Prince Naruhito married Masako Owada, because the three kanji characters in the station's name are identical to those in the maiden name of the crown princess. If you venture further along the Iida line, take note of **Kinno** (113.6km): statistics show that it is the station which sees the fewest passengers (no more than 150 people get on or off a train here every year). Aside from the curiosity of deserted stations, the real attraction is the scenery, primarily thick forest and steep tea fields. The green tea cultivated in this area is highly sought after.

To travel the entire length of the line by local trains will take you at least six hours. To speed things up take the Wide View Inaji LEX (2/day), which runs between Toyohashi and **Iida** (129.3km). However, it does not stop at Kowada or Kinno.

Nagoya (366km) [see pp155-63]

All shinkansen services stop here. If continuing to Kyoto, stay on the shinkansen and connect with the route guide starting on p188.

TOKYO TO NAGANO BY SHINKANSEN   [Table 4, p458]

Distances from Tokyo. Fastest journey time: 87 minutes.

Tokyo to Nagano   [Map 3]
Tokyo (0km)   [see pp83-106]
Shinkansen for Nagano depart from platforms 20-24. The Asama fills up
quickly so reserve a seat if possible.

Ueno (3.6km) Most trains make a brief stop here, though definitely reserve a
seat in advance if you're joining the train here.

After **Omiya** (**30km**; see p270) a few shinkansen call at **Kumagaya (65km)**,
change here for the Chichibu Railway (see box p73), and **Honjo-Waseda (86km)**.

Takasaki (105km) Takasaki is the point at which the Joetsu shinkansen line
to Niigata and the Nagano shinkansen line diverge. It is also associated with
Daruma dolls (see box below) and is an access point to the rail museum in
Yokokawa (see below), and for two lines with steam locomotives (see box p73),
as well as for a highly recommended onsen in Minakami.

> ### Side trips by train from Takasaki
> ● **To Yokokawa Usui Pass Railway Heritage Park** (Usuitouge Tetsudo
> Bunkamura; 🖳 www.usuitouge.com/bunkamura; Wed-Mon 9am-4.30/5pm;
> ¥500, discounted if bought from the JR counter in Yokokawa station) is acces-
> sible by local train on the **JR Shin-etsu** line. This line used to continue beyond
> Yokokawa to the mountain resort of Karuizawa, but when the Hokuriku
> shinkansen to Nagano was completed the Karuizawa extension became too
> expensive to operate. The museum is built on the site of the old Yokokawa
> depot and has a good collection of rolling stock. It is a short walk from the
> station (ask at the station for directions).
>
> ● **To Minakami** To reach *Takaragawa-onsen* (☎ 0278-752611, 🖳 www.
> takaragawa.com; from ¥11,700pp half-board) take the **JR Joetsu line** (60
> mins). A courtesy bus to the onsen operates once a day though reservations are
> required. The onsen has five *rotemburo* (open-air baths), both mixed and sin-
> gle sex, and a magnificent setting; it's a world away from city life. If possible
> book a room in one of the original wooden buildings rather than East Building
> which is a concrete structure. The meals here are also recommended.

After Takasaki, a few shinkansen call at **Annaka-Haruna (124km)**. Soon
after you start to feel as if you are going uphill, proof enough that this is now

> ### ⛩ Daruma dolls
> Takasaki is an important production centre for Daruma dolls, modelled on the
> founder of Zen Buddhism in China and popular as lucky charms. The idea is that the
> purchaser of a Daruma paints in one of the eyes at the time of buying it, then makes
> a wish. The other eye is only painted in if the wish comes true. Daruma craftsmen
> receive a rush on orders for the dolls during general election campaigns from candi-
> dates trying to buy themselves some luck.

mountain territory, as the train heads towards its namesake, Mt Asama.

Karuizawa (147km) All the shinkansen call at this thriving mountain resort with top-notch hotels, golf courses and villas for diplomats and celebrities, as well as opportunities to hike and ski. Once also a favourite haunt of John Lennon and Yoko Ono, Karuizawa garnered more international recognition when it hosted the inaugural curling event at the 1998 Nagano Winter Olympics; in fact, Karuizawa station was rebuilt for these Olympics. The original station (Tue-Sun 9am-5pm; ¥200), dating from 1910, has been fully restored and is to the left as you leave the north exit of the station.

The **Visitors Information Office** (🖳 www.karuizawa.co.jp; daily 9am-5pm) is on the right after the ticket barrier. **Lockers** (mostly ¥300, plus a few ¥500 ones) are on the ground floor. Karuizawa Prince Shopping Plaza, a short walk from the south exit of the station, has a selection of restaurants.

The town itself is not much more than a tacky array of gift shops selling mountain honey, jam and pot pourri.

Unless you're on a budget-free trip, don't even think about staying the night at *Mampei Hotel* (☎ 0267-42 1234, 🖳 www.mampei.co.jp), where backpacks will not impress the concierge and if you have to ask the price you should be looking elsewhere; this hotel is for the rich and famous – John Lennon and Yoko Ono stayed here. For everyone else *APA Hotel Karuizawa Ekimae* (☎ 0267-41 1511, 🖳 www.apahotel.com; ¥8500-13,500/S, ¥14,000-27,000/D or Tw) is a convenient option. Take the north exit and it is the building with a black wooden frame that is straight ahead as you come down the stairs.

The journey from Karuizawa to Sakudaira is either mostly in tunnels or the vistas are obscured by steep sides or trees but once you reach Sakudaira you start to get views of the mountains in the distance.

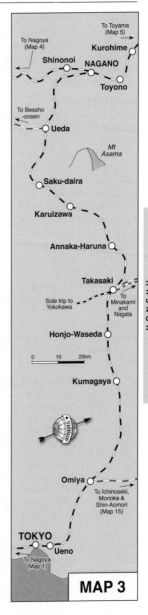

MAP 3

Sakudaira (164km) This small town is a case study for the legacy left by the Olympic Games. Before the opening of the Nagano shinkansen it took over 3½ hours to Tokyo. Now the journey is 80-90 minutes, turning Sakudaira into a satellite commuter town for the capital. If there's no room at the inn in nearby Nagano, *Toyoko Inn Sakudaira-eki Asamaguchi* (☎ 0267-66 1045; 🖥 www.toyoko-inn. com; from ¥5980/S, ¥8190/D or Tw) is outside the Asama exit of the station.

Ueda (189km) Last stop before the Nagano terminus, Ueda is a former castle town. English maps are available at the ground-floor **tourist information counter** (daily 9am-6pm). Go straight as you leave the shinkansen ticket barrier and it's at the end of the concourse. The **JR ticket office** (daily 5.40am-10pm) and View Plaza travel agency (Mon-Fri 10am-7pm, Sat & Sun to 5.30pm) are close to the shinkansen ticket barrier. Reading glasses are thoughtfully provided beside the timetables in the JR office. There are **lockers** (including a few ¥500 ones; closed 11pm-6am) to the left as you exit the station.

The only thing left of **Ueda Castle** (Ueda-jo) is three turrets, located inside a park about 10 minutes on foot north of the station (take the castle exit, Oshiro-guchi). The castle was completed in 1585 and twice saw off attacks by the Tokugawa clan (see p34). According to a sign inside the park, 'there were many other castles in feudal Japan. But no castle was attacked twice in this way and none was so brilliantly defended as Ueda Castle', before revealing – almost as an afterthought – that the castle was indeed 'later destroyed by the Tokugawa troops'. Though there's not much left to see, the park is a pleasant place to stroll and for rail buffs there's a great vantage point from the turrets which overlook the elevated shinkansen track – perfect for spotting and photographing the Asama shinkansen as it glides towards or away from Ueda station.

Toyoko Inn Ueda Eki-mae (☎ 0268-29 1045, 🖥 www.toyoko-inn.com; from ¥5980/S, ¥7480/D or Tw) is to the left as you leave the station.

Side trip by rail to Bessho-onsen
Bessho-onsen (🖥 www.bessyo.or.jp), a hot-spring resort, is just under half an hour away by local train along the Ueda Dentetsu Bessho line (¥570 one way; JR passes not accepted). The tourist information at Ueda station can provide English maps of Bessho, accommodation details and train times to/from Ueda. To reach the platform at Ueda, head up the stairs by the tourist office and take the Hot Springs exit.

The baths at Bessho are said to have healing properties which make the skin smooth. There are several **bath houses** in town; two with a rotemburo (outside bath) are O-yu (6am-10pm, closed 1st and 3rd Wed; ¥150) and Aisome-no-yu (10am-10pm, closed 2nd and 4th Mon; ¥500). *Ryokan Hanaya* (🖥 hanaya. naganoken.jp; from ¥16,800pp inc two meals) is highly recommended.

Look out on your right as you leave Ueda station for the three remaining turrets of what was once Ueda Castle, on a hill overlooking the shinkansen track. Soon afterwards, the train darts into a long series of tunnels.

Nagano (222km)   [see pp163-8]
Nagano is a major gateway to the Japanese Alps.

NAGANO TO NAGOYA VIA MATSUMOTO   [Table 5, p458]

Distances by JR from Nagano. Fastest journey time: 3 hours 7 minutes.

Nagano to Nagoya   [Map 4, p142]
Nagano (0km) From Nagano, pick up the Wide-View Shinano LEX, which runs along the Shinonoi line towards Nagoya. The Shinano has large panoramic windows, hence the name.

Shinonoi (9km) The first stop after Nagano by limited express.

After Shinonoi there are views, to the left, of the valley and towns below the rail line. A few limited expresses call at **Hijiri-Kogen (31km)**. There's one very long tunnel shortly before arriving in Matsumoto.

Matsumoto (63km)   [see pp169-73]
Matsumoto is a historic castle town set amid fine mountain scenery and a terminus for the JR Oito line to Itoigawa (see p146) via the ski resort of **Hakuba**.

Should you wish to return to Tokyo pick up the Azusa/Super Azusa LEX, (1/hr) which takes just under three hours to Shinjuku (see p89).

Shiojiri (76km) If planning to visit Narai (see below), you'll need to change from a limited express to a local train here.

Follow signs for the east exit and take the escalator down to street level for lockers (¥300-500) and the **tourist information office** (🖳 www.city.shiojiri. nagano.jp; daily 9am-5pm) which has information in English though the staff do not speak much English. There is a *café* (Midori) in the station.

From Shiojiri, the Shinonoi line becomes the Chuo West line, though there's no need to change trains as limited expresses run direct to Nagoya. The line runs through the beautiful Kiso Valley, surrounded by the Central Alps to the east and the Northern Alps to the west.

♦ **Narai (97km)** Narai is the first in a series of '**post towns**' along this route that were once used as stepping stones on the journey to Edo (Tokyo). In the days before the railway, a total of 69 post stations lined the Nakasendo highway, a trunk road connecting Edo with Kyoto. Not all the post towns have survived but a handful, including the one here in Narai and two more further down the line, have been preserved. Here you'll find a 1km stretch of road lined with Edo-period houses. Narai was 34th of the 69 towns on the highway and the most

---

⌂ Edo highlights in two days
A great way to fully experience post-town life is to do what those who once travelled the road between Edo (Tokyo) and Kyoto did – stay overnight at a minshuku. A possible two-day itinerary, starting in Matsumoto and ending in Nagoya, might be as follows: on the first day, leave Matsumoto and travel by local train to Narai. Spend the morning there before picking up another local train to Nagiso. Then take a bus to nearby Tsumago (see box p143). After a night in Tsumago, you could return the same way to Nagiso or, better still, hike to Magome (3 hours) and then pick up a bus to Nakatsugawa for a train to Nagoya.

HONSHU

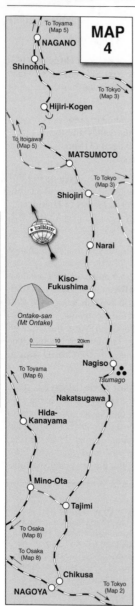

prosperous in the Kiso Valley. Steep slopes and thick forest made this section of the highway the most challenging (it took three days to cross the valley), so Narai became an important stop for weary travellers to rest and stock up on supplies.

The local train service from Shiojiri to Narai (20 mins) operates irregularly but approximately once an hour. The trains, which have two cars, are called 'One-man densha' because the driver also checks (and sells) tickets; at stations he will open the window from his compartment and you will only be able to leave the train from this car.

The old wooden station at Narai sets the tone for what to expect along the main road. Even the benches in the waiting room are fitted with mini tatami mats. More unusually, the station is run not by JR staff but by a local senior citizens' club – members take it in turns to be at the station to meet trains. There are no lockers at Narai station but you can leave your luggage with whoever is on duty until 5pm (¥200).

Turn left out of the station and the main street is straight in front of you. Look out for the odd sake shop (a hangover from the drinking houses that provided Edo-era travellers with some liquid relief) and craft shops, many of which sell locally made *nurigushi* (lacquered combs). Two former residences are open to the public; both are on the right as you walk along from the station: you reach Kamidonya Shiryokan (Apr-Nov 9am-5pm, Dec to 4pm; ¥300) first and then Nakamura Residence (same hours; ¥200).

Several of the old buildings contain small restaurants serving soba. Alternatively, at the far end of the street on the right is **Kokorone** (daily 11am-2.30pm), which does hearty portions of delicious *toki soba* (noodles with vegetables; ¥1350) that will fill you up for the rest of the day. If you order this you will be brought all you need to cook the noodles yourself.

Return to the station and pick up a local train to Kiso-Fukushima (20 mins) from where you can rejoin the main route. There is one very long tunnel just after leaving Narai.

Kiso-Fukushima (118km) Kiso-Fukushima was once a checkpoint on the highway between Edo and Kyoto. Its sights include a temple and rock garden, and the former residence of a local governor who managed the checkpoint in the Edo period. It's also the main rail access point for a visit to **Mt Ontake**, a 3067m volcano, popular with hikers in summer and skiers in winter.

The station here is small and has no lockers. Exit the station and cross the road for the **tourist information counter** (daily 9am-5pm), which can supply basic maps. Buses to Mt Ontake (Jul-Aug 3/day; 50 mins; ¥1360 one way, or ¥4000 return inc Ropeway) drop you at Ontake Ropeway, from where gondolas climb to 2150m (daily 8.45am-5.30pm; ¥2400 return). It's then a 3½-hour hike to the summit. The ticket office counter is opposite the tourist information.

Nagiso (152km) Only a few limited expresses stop here, the nearest station to **Tsumago** (see box below) so you may need to take a local train. Buses run from outside the station to Tsumago (7/day; 7 mins; ¥300) or take a taxi (¥1100). Luggage can be left for the day at the station for ¥410 per item (ask the JR staff). In the station is a **tourist information counter** (🖳 www.town.nagiso.nagano.jp; summer daily 8.30am-5pm; winter hours vary), with guides to Tsumago.

If you have time to spare turn right out of the station and walk downhill for a few minutes. Soon on your left you will see a **double-span wooden suspension bridge** (247.76m long and 13m high). This impressive pedestrian bridge was built in 1922 by Momosuke Fukuzawa in order to make it easier to access the nearby sites where hydro-electric power stations were being constructed.

HONSHU

🏯 **Tsumago and Magome**

The opening of the Chuo railway line in 1911 along Kiso-gawa effectively robbed the post towns of their purpose, as the old highway was abandoned in favour of the locomotive. For decades Tsumago stood forgotten, left behind by the age of the train. But in 1968, a century after the beginning of the Meiji era, a renovation programme began on Tsumago's houses, which had by then fallen into disrepair. Now the old post town has been reconstructed and survives, as it did before, thanks to a steady influx of visitors. Most of the houses are now craft shops, minshuku and restaurants. This doesn't mean that the area is tacky or full of souvenir kitsch but it is more commercial than nearby Narai (see p141) and can feel like you've walked onto an Edo-period film set.

Buses from Nagiso pull in at the terminal just below Tsumago's main street, from where you head up a path to a side entrance. In the early evening, once the day crowds have gone, Tsumago feels much less like a Universal Studios Edo theme park. All the minshuku offer the same rates (¥7500 inc two meals); ask at the tourist office (daily 9am-5pm) along the main street about which have vacancies.

Tsumago is at one end of a popular hiking route through the Kiso Valley to the southernmost post town, Magome. The three-hour walk between the two is not particularly strenuous, though you'd need proper hiking boots in winter when snow can be half-a-metre deep. A luggage-delivery service (daily mid July to end Aug, Sat & Sun Apr to mid July & Sep to late Nov; ¥500 per piece) is available at the tourist information office (and also at the tourist information office in Magome). Drop off your luggage by 9am and it will be waiting for you at the other end.

To rejoin the rail route take a bus (13/day; 25 mins; ¥540) from Magome to Nakatsugawa, the next limited express stop along the Chuo line to Nagoya.

Nakatsugawa (171km) Nakatsugawa is only 10 minutes down the line by limited express from Nagiso but it feels much further away. Business hotels, concrete, the odd factory smoke stack…here are the realities of post-Edo life, an unpleasant warning that you are less than an hour from the industrial heartland of Nagoya. The only reason for stopping here is to take a bus to the post town of Magome (see box p143).

The **tourist information counter** (daily 8.30am-6pm), on the left as you leave the station, has a guide map to this region (Nakasendo) in English. There are **lockers** (mostly ¥300-500) and there's a coffee bar and udon/soba stand in the station waiting room. **Buses to Magome** (14/day; 25 mins; ¥540) depart from stop No 3 outside the station

If you are getting back on a train here and have a Japan Rail Pass you will need to pay a supplement of ¥350 to travel on a Central Liner train to Nagoya.

Tajimi (215km) Tajimi is a terminus for the local Taita line to Mino-Ota on the Takayama line (2/hour; 30 mins). If planning to visit Takayama (see pp174-9), instead of going all the way to Nagoya to change lines, cross via the Taita line here to Mino-Ota (see p150) and pick up the route (in reverse) to Takayama.

The Japanese Alps are a distant memory. Instead there are chimney stacks and pachinko parlours for the last 20 minutes into Nagoya. **Chikusa (244km)** is the final stop on the limited express, just a few minutes out of Nagoya.

Nagoya (251km)   [see pp155-63]
From Nagoya, connect up with the Kansai route guide beginning on p188.

NAGANO TO NAGOYA VIA TOYAMA & TAKAYAMA

Distances by JR from Nagano. Fastest journey time: 6¼ hours.

Nagano to Naoetsu   [Map 5; Table 6a/d, p459]
Nagano (0km)   [see pp163-8]
Pick up a local train along the Shin-etsu line heading for Naoetsu. Trains operate irregularly but approximately hourly; the journey to Naoetsu takes about 90 minutes. Not all stops are mentioned in the route below. One of the joys of this journey is that there are very few tunnels.

Toyono (11km) A couple of local trains terminate here so you may have to change for another local train.

After Toyono, the limited express also calls **Mure (18km)** and at **Kurohime (29km)**. If you can, sit on the right side for the best river views. A few local

---

❏ **Hokuriku shinkansen**
The Hokuriku shinkansen line (Nagano to Kanazawa) is due to open in spring 2015. That will then be the quickest route from Nagano to Toyama. Stations on the line will be Iiyama (currently called Wakinoda), Joetsu, Itoigawa, Shin-Kurobe, Toyama, Shin-Takaoka and Kanazawa.

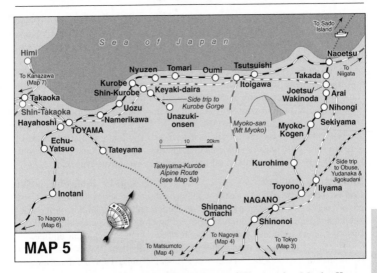

MAP 5

trains from Nagano terminate at **Myoko-Kogen (37km)**. After Myoko-Kogen
most services stop at **Sekiyama (44km)**. On either side of the train there are
spectacular views of the surrounding mountains. On leaving **Nihongi (52km)**,
the train reverses first before continuing along the line.

By the time you leave **Arai (58km)**, the mountain scenery is beginning to
recede. As the line heads towards the coast you can see the height of the mountains gradually drop. Some trains stop at **Wakinoda (64.6km)**.

Takada (68km) The old castle town of Takada merged with the port town of
Naoetsu in 1971 to become, for administrative purposes, Joetsu City.

Takada Castle was built as a stronghold to maintain peace throughout east
and west Japan. A **Lotus Festival** is held in the first half of August along the
moats of Takada Park, the former site of Takada Castle. During the festival, tea
ceremony parties and haiku poetry gatherings are held in the park, and the
moats are completely covered in thick, green lotus leaves. It takes 15-20 minutes on foot to reach Takada Park.

Views from the train around here are likely to be spoiled by the construction
of the Hokuriku shinkansen line from Nagano to Kanazawa.

Naoetsu (75km) Fittingly for a place where land meets the sea, Naoetsu station is styled like a cruise ship, with portholes for windows. The station has a
waiting area with lockers (¥300-500) and a branch of Newdays. Take the north
exit and go down the escalator to leave the station. Walk straight ahead past an
udon and soba bar on the right to reach the **tourist information office** (daily
Apr-Oct 9.30am-5.30pm, Nov-Mar 10am-4/4.30pm). *Hotel Century Ikaya* (☎
025-545 3111, 🖳 www.ikaya.co.jp; ¥6825/S, ¥13,650/D, ¥12,600/Tw), opposite the main station exit, is a decent hotel and a convenient place to stay.

HONSHU

Naoetsu Port runs a car **ferry service** (🖥 www.sadokisen.co.jp; 2-4/day; 2½ hours; passengers ¥2920; cars from ¥19,000) to Ogi on Sado Island. Kodo Village on Sado Island is home to the world-famous Kodo drummers (🖥 www. kodo.or.jp). See also pp311-12.

▲ From Naoetsu you can pick up a Hakutaka LEX east to Echigo-Yuzawa and transfer there to a shinkansen for Niigata (see pp306-11). To follow the route below, change trains at Naoetsu and board either a Hakutaka LEX or Hokuetsu LEX, both of which run west along the Hokuriku line to Toyama (and from there to Kanazawa, see pp180-4).

Naoetsu marks the end of JR East territory. The line and stations west of here are run by JR West (a subtle change in colour of the JR logo from green to blue). JR East passes are not valid for the journey west from Naoetsu.

Naoetsu to Toyama   [Map 5, p145; Table 6b/c, p459]

Don't expect views of the coast as you hurtle through a series of tunnels. There are occasional sightings of mountains on the left and the Japan Sea on the right but mostly the track runs slightly inland past buildings that obscure the coastline. Even the views to the left may soon be blocked by the new shinkansen line.

If you are on a local train you will stop at **Tsutsuishi** (94km). This station is unusual in that the platforms are in a tunnel (Kubiki Tunnel); there are 280 steps up to ground level, and 290 if going down.

Itoigawa (114km) A terminus for the Oito line from Matsumoto (see p141) and a stop on the forthcoming Hokuriku shinkansen line (see box p144).

After Itoigawa some trains stop at **Oumi (121km)**, **Tomari (139km)** and **Nyuzen (144km)**.

Kurobe (161km) Most limited expresses stop here, from where there's a possible side trip by private railway to **Kurobe Gorge** (Kurobe-kyokoku; see below). There are no lockers at Kurobe station, nor is there a tourist information centre but there is a kiosk selling drinks and snacks. A new station, Shin-Kurobe, is being built and it will be a stop on the Hokuriku shinkansen (see box p144) and will connect with the Toyama Chiho line to Unazuki-onsen (see below).

Side trip by rail through Kurobe Gorge

For rail enthusiasts, this is a chance to travel on a narrow-gauge railway which affords sweeping views of the northern Japanese Alps. And anyone into Japan's *onsen* culture should consider taking this side trip as the line passes a number of open-air hot springs. Note that the Kurobe Kyokoku railway is very busy during the summer and in late October for autumn leaves' viewing.

Walk down the road from JR Kurobe station and turn left at the fourth set of traffic lights to reach **Dentetsu Kurobe** station for services on the private Toyama Chiho railway line to **Unazuki-onsen** (1-2/hr; 30 mins; ¥710). A five-minute walk from **Unazuki-onsen** (follow the crowds) takes you to Unazuki station, starting point for the private Kurobe Kyokoku Railway line (🖥 www. kurotetu.co.jp; mid Apr to late Nov 11-20/day). A **'torokko' train** with open-air carriages pulled by a tramcar runs on the stunning 75-minute journey through the gorge to the terminus at Keyaki-Daira (¥1660 one way; a seat in a car with windows, in other words protection from the elements, costs an extra ¥360-630pp). The line was originally built to carry construction materials for the Kurobe dam. An unusual feature of this line is that it is rebuilt every year – the bridges are dismantled before the winter so that they are not destroyed by the snow or avalanches and they are stored in the tunnels.

Uozu (167km) Uozu is also a stop on the private Toyama Chiho Railway (see opposite) linking Kurobe and Unazuki-onsen with Toyama.

After Uozu, some limited expresses also call at **Namerikawa (176km)**.

Toyama (193km) Toyama is a major business city and it will be a stop on the Hokuriku shinkansen line (see box p144) when that opens. The main reason for stopping here is to begin the **Tateyama-Kurobe Alpine Route** (see p148) but an interesting way of getting around the city is the **Portram** (see box below).

Take the central exit for the **tourist information booth** (daily 8.30am-8pm), in a small hut to the left as you go out. **Lockers** of all sizes are to your left as you exit the station.

The best place for a view of the area is the observation platform at the top of **Toyama City Hall**. It's free – just take the lift to the top. This is also a good place to head for a cheap lunch (Mon-Fri 11am-2pm) in the ground-floor canteen, where all the City Hall workers congregate. City Hall is on the left side, 10 minutes on foot up the main street which leads away from the station.

To the left as you exit the JR station is Dentetsu-Toyama, the private Toyama Chiho railway station, from where services depart to Tateyama (for the start of the Alpine Route, see p148) and to Unazuki-onsen (see opposite). Tickets are available from the office (daily 7am-7pm) on the left as you walk into the station.

If beginning the Alpine Route early in the morning it may be necessary to overnight in Toyama. Across the street and to your left as you exit the station is *Toyoko Inn Jr Toyama Eki-mae* (☎ 076-405 1045, 🖳 www.toyoko-inn.com; ¥4980-8380/S, ¥7480/D or Tw). Alternatively try *Comfort Hotel Toyama* (☎ 076-433 6811, 🖳 www.comfortinn.com; ¥6000/S, ¥7500/D or Tw). Turn right out of the station and cross the road at Ekimae-nishi junction, turn right and go along for about 60m; the hotel is on the left.

The 6th floor of the **Marier Building** (🖳 www.marier-toyama.co.jp) by the station has a selection of restaurants including *Volcano Toyama* (daily 11am-9.30pm), which serves a tasty salmon and spinach spaghetti (¥1120), and *Tonkatsu Sabuten* (daily 11am-9.30pm), which offers tonkatsu (¥600-1000).

⛩ **A light-railway experiment**
Rail fans might like to consider riding Portram, the private Toyamako light rail line (tram; 🖳 www.t-lr.co.jp) from Toyama north up to the coast at Iwasehama, a journey of 7.6km (25 mins; ¥200).

This short stretch of line is unique in Japan since it marks the first time that a conventional rail track has been discontinued and converted for use by a light-rail operator. The Toyamako line previously operated by JR West was shut down in 2006 and reopened a month later in its new guise as a light railway.

Tateyama–Kurobe Alpine Route [see Map 5a]

Toyama is a gateway for the 90km Tateyama–Kurobe Alpine Route (🖥 www.
alpen-route.com) from Toyama on the coast through the Japanese Alps and
Kurobe Dam to Shinano-Omachi. More than a million people every year follow this route, which involves a combination of train, cable car (funicular),
bus, ropeway (cable car) and a bit of legwork. The route is accessed by taking
a train on the private **Toyama Chiho Railway** from Dentetsu-Toyama to the
cable car station at Tateyama; services operate roughly hourly throughout the
day though not at regular times.

First opened in 1971, the route climbs to 2450m but its most spectacular section is the 23km bus journey from Bijodaira to Murodo; in April/May this usually means going through a corridor of ice. It takes nearly two months of bulldoz-
ing to carve out this corridor and remove a depth of around 20m of snow.

If any journey in Japan is proof of the Japanese desire to conquer the elements, it must be this one. The route is impassable in winter, when Siberian
winds sweep south across the Japan Sea, dumping snow in blizzards across the
Tateyama mountain range that doesn't melt away until well into July. The only
section of the entire route which requires any footwork is the 20-minute walk
across Kurobe Dam, completed in 1963. The route ends with a bus journey to
Shinano-Omachi, from where you can pick up a limited express (35 mins) or
local train (65 mins) on the JR Oito line to Matsumoto (see pp169-74).

The route is open from around mid April to the end of November (heavy
snowfall can delay the opening). The journey can be completed in a day (6-8
hours) in either direction; a **one-way package ticket** covering all stages
between Dentetsu-Toyama (see p147) and Shinano-Omachi costs ¥10,560; the
return fare is ¥17,730. Check the website for the latest fares/timetable. When
you buy the ticket you should be given an itinerary showing connection times
for the different modes of transport on the route – if not, ask for one.

A **baggage-forwarding service** (¥1200 per bag) is available from
Dentetsu-Toyama to JR Shinano-Omachi (Alps Roman Kan); bags should be
delivered by 9.30am and will arrive between 3 and 6pm.

Since Matsumoto is about another hour away by train you may prefer to
stay here. *Ryokan Nanakuraso* (☎ 0261-221564, 🖥 www.nanakuraso.co.jp;
¥4500/5500/6800pp room only/one meal/two meals) is a short walk from
Shinano-Omachi station.

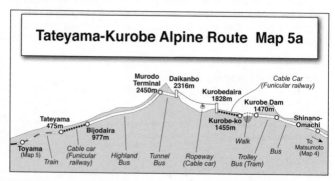

Tateyama-Kurobe Alpine Route Map 5a

Toyama to Nagoya [Map 5, p145; Map 6; Table 7, p460]

Distances quoted are from Toyama.

Toyama (0km) Take the Wide-View Hida LEX (4/day; Takayama Line). Green Car passengers (¥290) can rent headphones for the in-seat audio channels. The panoramic windows are great but tunnels frequently block out the mountainous scenery. All the same, the line to Takayama remains one of the great rail journeys in Japan, as the train runs south from the coast deep into the Hida mountain range.

The train calls at **Hayahoshi (8km)**, **Echu-Yatsuo (17km)** and **Inotani (37km)** but there's nothing to stop off for until Hida-Furukawa, around 80 minutes after Toyama.

Hida-Furukawa (75km) If nearby Takayama is a miniature Kyoto, Hida-Furukawa is an even smaller version of Takayama and is certainly less crowded.

Pick up a map and guide from the **tourist information booth** (daily 9am-5pm; no English spoken) outside the station. **Cycles** can be rented (¥500/3hrs) from Miyagawa taxi office opposite the station, though the town is manageable on foot.

Every April (19th-20th) the peace of Hida-Furukawa is shattered by the town's annual festival, the highlight of which is a parade of floats and a big *okoshi daiko* drum, carried by a team of men dressed in white loincloths. Throughout the year, a few of the floats are on display in the centre of town (10 mins west of the station) at **Hida-Furukawa Festival Hall** (daily 9am-5pm, to 4.30pm in winter; ¥800, or ¥1000 inc the Bunkakan), where you can also watch a 3D film of the festival parade.

Across the street is **Hida-no-Takumi Bunkakan** (daily 9am-5pm in summer, Wed-Mon 9am-4.30pm until end Feb, to 5pm in March; ¥300, or ¥1000 inc Festival Hall), a heritage centre which displays techniques and tools used by local craftsmen. Particularly challenging is a hands-on display of joints, but an enthusiastic staff member will help you.

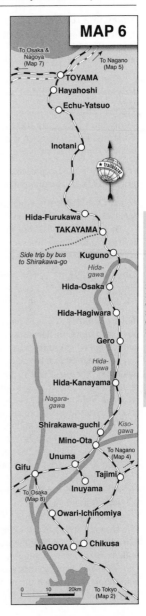

MAP 6

HONSHU

Takayama (89km)   **[see pp174-9]**
From Takayama, the line continues to follow roughly the course of Hida-gawa.
The best part of the journey is the next 50km to Gero, with stunning river and
mountain scenery on both sides of the track.

Some of the Wide-View Hida services that start in Takayama also stop at
Kuguno (103km), **Hida-Osaka (117km)**, and **Hida-Hagiwara (129km)**.

Gero (138km) Gero is one of the best-known spa towns in Japan. This onsen
resort dates back over 1000 years and is mainly popular with elderly Japanese
holidaymakers. The town is also known for its tomato juice, considered to be a
healthy tonic after a day wallowing in a hot tub.

A few limited expresses call at **Hida-Kanayama (159km)** and **Shirakawa-
guchi (193km)**; despite the name this is not an access point for Shirakawa-go.

Mino-Ota (199km) Situated on Kiso-gawa, Mino-Ota is the junction for the
local Taita line to Tajimi on the Chuo line (30 mins).

If planning to visit Matsumoto (see pp169-74), instead of going all the way
to Nagoya to change lines, cross via the Taita line here to Tajimi and pick up the
route to Matsumoto from p144 (though it is described in reverse).

Unuma (209km) A few limited expresses stop here, the nearest JR station to
Inuyama (see p163). Local trains to Inuyama can be caught from the private
Meitetsu Railway's Shin-Unuma station, which is adjacent.

Gifu (226km) Gifu is more of a political and administrative centre than a
tourist destination. The city suffered heavy air raids during WWII. A couple of
attractions which remain are cormorant fishing and Gifu Castle.

Gifu station is a terminus for the Takayama line and a stop on the Tokaido
mainline. The main exit is the Nagara side, outside which the main road heads
north towards Nagara-gawa, and where you could also see a gold statue of famed
warlord Nobunaga Oda (1534-82). There are a few **lockers** in a corner of the
ticket barrier level. There are many **places to eat** in the station and in the adjacent Heartful Square G shopping centre. On the 1st (ground) floor of the station
you'll find a branch of *Osozai + Cafe*, a chain which has mainly vegetarian food.
Plates can be filled at ¥220 per 100 grams and it is a good outlet for bento.

Gifu City **tourist information centre** (🖳 www.kankou-gifu.jp; daily 9am-
7pm, to 6pm in winter) is on the same (2nd) floor as the ticket barrier. Maps are
available and staff will help book accommodation. For further information see
🖳 www.gifucvb.or.jp/en.

Gifu Castle (daily 8.30/9.30am-4.30/5.30pm; ¥200) is perched on top of
Mt Kinka (329m) overlooking Nagara-gawa and accessed via ropeway from
Gifu Park. The concrete reconstructed castle has little to recommend inside – a
video of cormorant fishing and some photos of other castles in Japan. The best
part of the visit is the ropeway, which on a clear day affords views of the city
and the river. To reach the castle from the station (east exit), take either a Gifu
Bus service from stop No 11 marked 'Shinai-Loop-hidari-mawari' (Shinai Loop

anti-clockwise); services except N71-73 and N80 (rapid) from stop No 12; or any bus from stop No 13; and get off at the Gifukoen-mae. From there, take the ropeway (3 mins; ¥1050 return) to the castle.

Cormorant fishing (nightly at approx 7.30pm, mid May to mid Oct; ¥3300), known in Japanese as *ukai*, takes place on Nagara-gawa, 2km north of the station. Fishermen dressed in traditional costume of straw skirt, sandals and black kimono use cormorants to fish for *ayu* (sweetfish). The birds, tied to reins and steered by fishermen standing inside the boats, dive down and catch the fish in their beaks. The rein around each bird's neck prevents it from swallowing any of the

> ❏ **Chaplin and Basho**
> It's little known but often cited by tourism officials in Gifu that silent comedian Charlie Chaplin was a fan of cormorant fishing and was apparently 'so enchanted that he came to Gifu to witness the sight a second time'. Locals recall with pride that Chaplin described the activity as 'the greatest art Japan has to offer'.
>
> He was not alone in admiring the skills of the fishermen. The celebrated Japanese poet Matsuo Basho (see p277) even composed a haiku on the subject:
> *'Cormorant boat, where*
> *Before long, what looks like fun*
> *Perhaps ends in sorrow.'*

catch. Today, the event is geared towards the tourist trade, but when the river is lit up by fire and the cormorants set to work, it's an impressive sight. If you don't want to pay to watch from a boat, there's no charge for standing along the river bank. For fishing schedules and ticket information, contact the tourist information office in Gifu station or the boat office (☎ 058-262 0104) by Nagara-gawa. West of the office are some traditional row houses in Kawara-machi.

A good place to stay the night is ***Comfort Hotel Gifu*** (☎ 058-267 1311, 🖳 www.choicehotels.com; ¥6500/S, ¥12,000/Tw), across the street from the station. Smart rooms and a continental breakfast is included.

After Gifu, some services stop at **Owari-Ichinomiya (239km)**.

Nagoya (256km) [see pp155-63]
To link with the Kansai route guide, see p188 (shinkansen route) or p190 (Kii peninsula route).

TOYAMA AND KANAZAWA TO NAGOYA, KYOTO OR OSAKA

If starting this journey from **Nagano**, follow the route guide starting on p144 as far as **Toyama**, then pick up the route below. This takes you to Tsuruga, where the line divides: south-east for Nagoya, or south-west for Kyoto and Osaka.

Distances by JR from Toyama. Fastest journey time: to Nagoya 3 hours 35 minutes; to Osaka 3 hours 10 minutes.

Toyama to Fukui [Map 7, p152; Table 8, p460]
Toyama (0km) The Thunderbird LEX runs from here to Kyoto/Osaka via Kanazawa. The older Shirasagi LEX (7/day) runs to Nagoya via Kanazawa. Apart from 1/day both the Hakutaka LEX and Hokuetsu LEX terminate at Kanazawa.

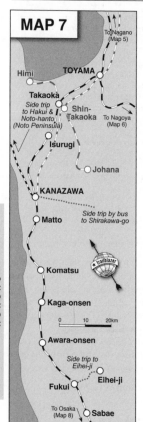

MAP 7

To Nagano (Map 5)

Himi

TOYAMA

Takaoka
Side trip to Hakui & Noto-hanto (Noto Peninsula)

Shin-Takaoka

To Nagoya (Map 6)

Isurugi

Johana

KANAZAWA

Side trip by bus to Shirakawa-go

Matto

Komatsu

Kaga-onsen

0   10   20km

Awara-onsen

Side trip to Eihei-ji

Eihei-ji

Fukui

To Osaka (Map 8)

Sabae

Takaoka (19km) Takaoka feels quiet and uncosmopolitan after Toyama but it has the distinction of being the smallest city in Japan to boast its own tram line. The station was being rebuilt at the time of research but also a new station, Shin-Takaoka, is being built for the Hokuriku shinkansen (see box p144). There's a **tourist information desk** (daily 9.30am-5.30pm) in the station waiting room and a few **lockers** (¥300-600) on your left as you exit the station.

Takaoka is known as a centre for bronze production; the biggest bit of bronze in town is the **Daibutsu**, a 15.85m-high Buddha statue weighing 65 tonnes, the third largest in Japan. The statue is in Daibutsu-ji (daily 6am-6pm) 5-10 minutes on foot from the station's central exit; turn right on to the main road (Sakurababa-dori), go straight to the fourth road on your left (Daibutsu-dori), turn left and go straight until you reach it.

Also worth a look is **Zuiryu-ji** (daily 9am-4.30pm; ¥500), a large temple 10 minutes' walk south of the station's south exit. Originally built 360 years ago, the roof of the temple was made of lead – a rarity in Japan – so that it could be used to make bullets in the event of war. A **Nabe Festival** is held here in mid January. The *nabe*, a stew made with cod, crab and other winter seafood, is cooked in a giant 1200-litre cauldron – enough to serve 3000 people. The cauldron is displayed at Takaoka station.

Daibutsu Ryokan (☎ 0766-21 0075, 🖥 www1.coralnet.or.jp/Buddha; ¥4600/9000/13,200 for 1/2/3 people sharing; breakfast ¥800, dinner ¥1600) is almost opposite the Daibutsu and has spacious if slightly faded tatami rooms. If you prefer a bed to a futon, try *Manten Hotel Takaoka Eki-mae* (☎ 0766-27 0100, 🖥 www.manten-hotel.com; ¥6800/S, ¥11,000/Tw), right outside the station's central exit. It has comfortable rooms and a smart restaurant. Alternatively, *Super Hotel Takaoka* (☎ 0766-28 9000, 🖥 www.superhotel.co.jp; ¥4980/S, ¥6980/Tw or D) is five minutes on foot from the south exit (the exit for Zuiryu-ji).

Tontei (11am-2pm & 5pm to midnight) is on the 2nd floor of the building on the right-hand corner of the main road with the tram line which leads off from the station. It serves excellent tonkatsu, prepared and cooked in front of you. Set meals cost ¥900-1000.

After Takaoka a few services stop at **Isurugi (35km)**.

Kanazawa (60km) [see pp180-5]
Famous for Kenrokuen, a spectacular garden, Kanazawa also boasts lots else to see, including a UFO museum, and is well worth a stop. The station will be the terminus for the Hokuriku shinkansen (see box p144).

After Kanazawa a few services stop at **Matto (69km)**.

Komatsu (88km) Some Thunderbird LEXs do not stop here. Komatsu is not really a sightseeing destination, but since the town is midway between Kanazawa and Fukui it would make a convenient base for visiting both places. Also, it has a hotel whose location right opposite the station is perfect for rail travellers: *Hyper Hotel Komatsu* (☎ 0761-23 3000, 🖳 www.hyper-komatsu. co.jp; ¥5080/S, ¥6800-7150/Tw, ¥7500/Tr, inc breakfast). Even if you don't stay here, it's worth trying the Japanese restaurant on the 2nd floor: *Kamado* (daily 4-11pm; ¥2000-4000pp) is a stylish, modern izakaya serving fresh fish, steaks, cheese fondues, salads and garlic bread.

Kaga-onsen (102km) Not all limited express trains stop here. Look up to the right just before the train pulls into this station (10 mins after leaving Komatsu) and you'll see a giant gold Kannon statue looking down on the station.

After Kaga-onsen, some limited expresses stop at **Awara-onsen (119km)**.

Fukui (136km) History has not been kind to Fukui; the city has been completely destroyed twice, once by war and soon after by an earthquake. The main reason for stopping here is to take a side trip to Eihei-ji (see below).

The **tourist information booth** (daily 8.30am-7pm) is to the left of the central ticket barrier. **Lockers** (all sizes) are available all around the station.

Buses go from in front of the station to **Daianzen-ji** (Wed-Mon 9am-5pm), founded in 1658. The main attraction here is an 11-faced statue of the Bodhisattva of Compassion, which is celebrated for its matchmaking powers. The best place to sit – where the love vibes are strongest – is immediately under the large, sparkling gold lamp shade. Say a prayer here, it is said, and you may not be walking alone for much longer. Zazen introductory meditation sessions are held here twice a month (reserve ahead on ☎ 0776-59 1014, 🖳 www.daian zenji.jp; Fri 6.30-9pm; ¥400); the abbot is said to be a humorous raconteur and foreign visitors are welcome. From the station, take Keifuku bus No 16 (¥400) bound for Kawanishi from stop No 4 and get off at Daianzen-ji Monzen.

Hotel Riverge Akebono (☎ 0776-22 1000, 🖳 www.riverge.com; main building ¥5500/S, ¥6500-6825/Tw, ¥15,750/Tr; new building ¥6825-12,012/ Tw, ¥14,784/D, ¥19,404/Tr), a 10-minute walk from the station, has good-value rooms, a coin laundry, a decent restaurant and a hot spring.

Side trip to Eihei-ji
Eihei-ji (daily 5am-5pm except on festival and ceremony days; ¥400; a booklet in English is available in the temple, not at the ticket booth), built onto a mountainside to the east of Fukui, was founded in 1244 by the Buddhist monk Dogen as a centre for Zen training. The name means 'Temple of Eternal Peace', though with so many tour groups piling through it's best to arrive early to appreciate the tranquillity.

The most sacred building inside the compound is the Joyoden (Founder's Hall), in which Dogen's ashes are kept along with those of his successors. Just as impressive as the fine buildings and beautiful setting is the feeling of how busy and alive the temple remains over 750 years after its foundation. As you walk around you'll almost certainly see monks at work, perhaps practising how to move sacred objects, or trainee monks reciting a sutra.

Rail services towards Eihei-ji start from the private Echizen railway station outside the east exit of JR Fukui station. From Fukui, ride the train as far as Eiheiji-guchi (2/hour; 24 mins; ¥440; no rail passes), then change on to a Keifuku bus for Eihei-ji (🖳 bus.keifuku.co.jp; 6-8/day; 15 mins; ¥410). More practical and cheaper but less frequent is the direct Keifuku bus (6-8/day; 33 mins; ¥720) from Fukui station to Eihei-ji.

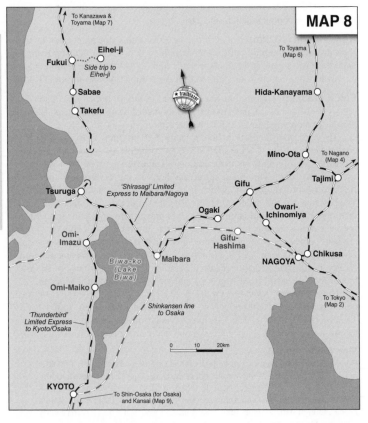

Fukui to Tsuruga   **[Map 8; Table 8, p460]**
The route from Fukui heading south has a number of tunnels. Some limited expresses make a brief stop at **Sabae (150km)**.

After Sabae, some trains also call at **Takefu (155km)**. There's one very long tunnel that lasts around 10 minutes shortly before Tsuruga, just north of Lake Biwa, the largest lake in Japan.

Tsuruga (190km) Tsuruga is a major rail junction, marking the end of the Hokuriku line. This is the last chance to change between the Shirasagi LEX for Nagoya and the Thunderbird LEX for Osaka and Kyoto, but note that the Thunderbird does not always stop at Tsuruga.

Don't worry if your train seems to double back on itself between Tsuruga and Maibara. There is a spiral section on the line so it's part of the route!

Moving on from Tsuruga: to Kyoto, Osaka or Nagoya   **[Map 8]**
Fifteen kilometres after Tsuruga the track divides into two lines which run down either side of Lake Biwa. The **Thunderbird LEX** heads down the west side of the lake, before joining the Tokaido line westbound to Kyoto (284km), Shin-Osaka (323km) and Osaka (327km).

The **Shirasagi LEX** (8/day) runs down the east side of the lake to Maibara (236km; p188), then joins the Tokaido line eastbound to Ogaki (272km), Gifu (286km), Owari-Ichinomiya (299km) and Nagoya (316km).

There are better views of the lake (on the left) on the journey to Kyoto/Osaka but even so trees and tunnels often block the view.

Central Honshu – city guides

NAGOYA

Just over a century ago, Nagoya had a population of 157,000. Today, over two million people live in what has become the fourth largest city in Japan. Much of the city was flattened by WWII air raids, and in 1959 a typhoon struck the southern part of Nagoya, flooding the entire area and destroying over 100,000 buildings. But the city has bounced back to become a major industrial centre with the headquarters of companies including Brother and Toyota, as well as production plants of Toyota, Honda and Mitsubishi, in the immediate area.

Nagoya will never win any awards for the beauty of its architecture, but the city functions as a rail gateway to the Japanese Alps and to Kansai, which means that most rail travellers will pass through at some stage. Osaka and Tokyo may be better known but Nagoya feels more relaxed and easier to manage.

What to see and do
For a bird's eye view of Nagoya, take the express elevator from the 2nd floor of Nagoya station to the 15th, the entrance to Marriott Associa Hotel. What you'll see is a sprawling city, most spectacular when lit up at night.

Glance up as you leave the station: the skyscraper across the street from the Sakura-dori exit is **Midland Square** (🖥 www.midland-square.com), the headquarters for Toyota and the *Mainichi Shimbun* newspaper. The building, completed in 2007, is just under 2m higher than the JR Central Towers (246.9m vs 245m) which loom above the station itself. Midland Square is home to a host of retail and restaurant outlets as well as the multiplex Midland Square Cinema (see 🖥 www.midland-sq-cinema.jp for film listings) on the 5th floor. You'll know the anchor tenant of the building is Toyota because of the gleaming white car showrooms on the 1st (ground) and 2nd floors. Look out for the Toyota staff who spend most of their day cleaning and polishing the cars. The best (and highest) place in Nagoya to see the city is from the 46th-floor Sky Promenade (daily 11am-10pm; tickets ¥700, from the 42nd floor) inside Midland Square, 220m above ground.

Nagoya Castle (🖥 www.nagoyajo.city.nagoya.jp; daily 9am-4.30pm; ¥500) was built in 1612 on the orders of Tokugawa Ieyasu to be a secure base along the main Tokaido Highway. The castle was razed to the ground during a WWII air raid and only three corner towers and gates survived. The donjon was reconstructed in 1959 and is known for the pair of gold dolphins (*kinshachi*) on the roof (which very occasionally are brought down and put on display). Though hard to tell from the ground, the dolphin on the north side is male and the one on the south side is female. It's worth climbing up the tower to reach the 7th-floor observatory and the grounds provide a pleasant respite from built-up Nagoya. To reach the castle take the Meijo subway line to Shiyakusho. Another possibility is the Nagoya Sightseeing Route Bus, which runs on a circular route (Tue-Sun; ¥200/journey, ¥500 one-day pass). It departs from stop 8 outside the Sakura-dori side of Nagoya station, and also serves several of Nagoya's museums as well as the TV Tower. After visiting the castle, look in on the 630-seat **Nagoya Noh Theater** (same times as castle; free), built in 1997. It's open to the public when there are no performances.

Tokugawa Art Museum (🖥 www.tokugawa-art-museum.jp; Tue-Sun 10am-5pm, closed mid Dec to New Year; ¥1200) exhibits treasures that belonged to the Owari branch of the ruling Tokugawa family as well as sections of a 12th-century illustrated scroll of *The Tale of Genji* – though the pieces are too fragile to be kept on permanent display. The gorgeous contents of the museum are matched by an equally extravagant entry fee. Take a local train from JR Nagoya station along the Chuo line four stops to Ozone station. The museum is 10 minutes on foot from the south exit.

In the former headquarters of the Toyoda Spinning & Weaving Company is **Toyota Commemorative Museum of Industry and Technology** (🖥 www. tcmit.org; Tue-Sun 9.30am-5pm; ¥500), much more interesting than it sounds. The Toyota Group was founded by Sakichi Toyoda, inventor of the automatic loom. Automobiles were only added later, by Kiichiro, Sakichi's eldest son. In the Museum of Industry and Technology, the Textile and Automobile Pavilions are interactive in parts, and exhibits are informative about how prototype ideas are turned into reality. The name 'Toyoda', incidentally, didn't change to

'Toyota' until 1935, when it was used as a brand name for export cars. It was thought that Toyota would be easier for foreigners to pronounce. The new spelling also brought the number of katakana strokes in the word to eight, which is considered lucky in Japan; Toyoda had 10 strokes. The museum is a 15-minute walk north from the Sakura-dori exit of JR Nagoya station.

Just before the Toyota Museum, on the same side of the road, is **Noritake Garden**, whose free-to-enter open-plan grounds are home to the **Noritake Craft Center** (🖥 www.noritake.co.jp/mori; Tue-Sun 10am-5pm; ¥500). This world-renowned porcelain company gives visitors the opportunity to follow the manufacturing process from creation and decoration to final inspection. There's also a museum where some of the company's special-order vases, many with price tags of up to ¥10 million, are on display. If those are beyond your budget, there are several shops where mere mortals can purchase more affordable pieces of porcelain.

For car fans, Toyota has just the place for you at its **Automobile Museum** (🖥 www.toyota.co.jp/Museum; Tue-Sun 9.30am-5pm; ¥1000), divided into two parts: the main building, which exhibits 120 cars from some of the earliest models to the present day, and the annex, which traces the history of the motor car in Japan. Take the Higashiyama subway line to Fujigaoka and then the Linimo maglev line to Geidai-dori station.

Sakae area The beating heart of the city may be shifting ever more towards the JR station area, but that doesn't mean that downtown Sakae is giving up without a fight. Aside from the many shops, bars and restaurants, it's also home to the 180m-high **Nagoya TV Tower** (🖥 www.nagoya-tv-tower.co.jp). Now dwarfed by the JR Towers and Toyota headquarters, the tower was a skyscraper when it was built in 1954 as the first television tower in Japan. Climb the 435 steps to the 100m-high Sky Balcony (daily 10am-9/10pm; ¥600) for a panoramic view of life from the centre of city. With the digitalisation of Japanese TV in 2011, the tower's future is uncertain.

Midway between Sakae and Nagoya Station is Fushimi. Reached from Exit 5 at Fushimi station (Higashiyama line), and in Shirakawa Park, is **Nagoya City Science Museum** (🖥 www.ncsm.city.nagoya.jp; Tue-Sun exc 3rd Fri 9.30am-5pm; ¥400 or ¥800 with planetarium). As well as hands-on demonstrations, it also features the world's largest planetarium, with a diameter of 35m.

For fans of Japanese technology, the **Osu area** is Nagoya's equivalent to Akihabara in Tokyo. It's also good for restaurants serving different ethnic cuisines. It is within walking distance of Sakae or take the subway to Osu-Kannon or Kamimaezu.

Nagoya Port area South of the centre of Nagoya city, Nagoya Port has been redeveloped as a 'Leisure Zone'. Attractions in one area of the port include **Fuji Antarctic Museum** (Tue-Sun 9.30am-5pm, daily Jul-Sep; ¥300), on board the *Fuji*. *Fuji* was used for 18 Antarctic expeditions until its retirement to Nagoya Port in 1983. Inside are crew quarters, including kitchen, dentist's surgery and barber shop, as well as operation rooms. *(continued on p160)*

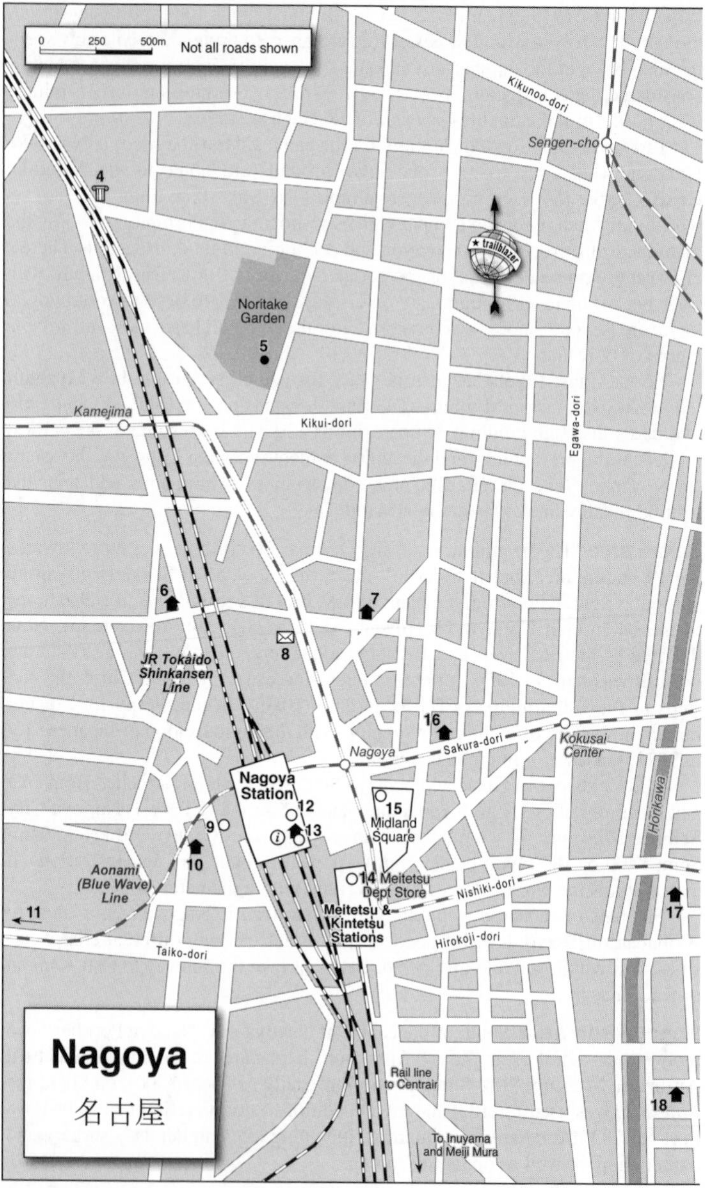

HONSHU

0 250 500m Not all roads shown

Kikunoo-dori

Sengen-cho

4

Noritake
Garden

5

Kamejima

Kikui-dori

Egawa-dori

6

JR Tokaido
Shinkansen
Line

7

8

16

Nagoya

Sakura-dori

Kokusai
Center

Honkawa

Nagoya
Station

12

15
Midland
Square

9

i

13

10

Aonami
(Blue Wave)
Line

14 Meitetsu
Dept Store

11

Meitetsu &
Kintetsu
Stations

Nishiki-dori

17

Hirokoji-dori

Taiko-dori

Nagoya

名古屋

Rail line
to Centrair

18

To Inuyama
and Meiji Mura

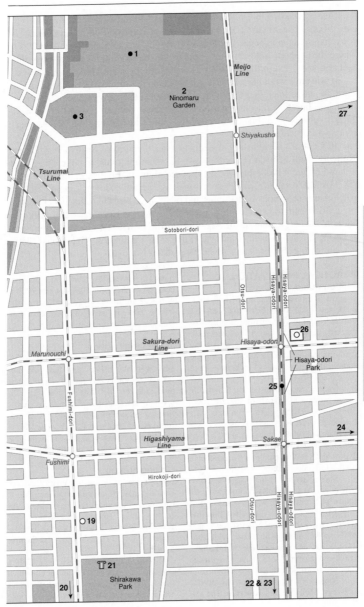

(continued from p157) On the top deck is a small museum about the Antarctic expeditions. The Antarctic theme continues at **Nagoya Public Aquarium** (🖳 www.nagoyaaqua.jp/aqua; Tue-Sun 9.30am-5.30pm, to 5pm in winter; ¥2000), where the penguin tank recreates extreme weather conditions to make the birds feel at home. Next to the aquarium is a stadium for shark and dolphin shows.

If you have a rail pass, to save a few yen on the subway fare to Nagoya Port for these attractions, first take a local train from JR Nagoya station one stop on the Chuo line to Kanayama station, from where you can connect up with the Meiko subway line (branch of the Meijo line) to the terminus at Nagoyako (Nagoya Port; ¥230).

JR Central's new railway museum is in another area of Nagoya Port. **Linear Railway Hall** (Linear Tetsudo Kan; 🖳 museum.jr-central.co.jp; Wed-Mon 10am-5.30pm, ¥1000) but you'll also see signs in English calling the place 'SCMAGLEV and Railway Park'. As well as a prototype linear 'maglev' car (see p72), there are various bullet trains and other more historic rolling stock including a C62 steam locomotive. It is a type that holds the world record of 129km/hr for non-standard-gauge steam. Access from JR Nagoya station (shinkansen side) is by the private Aonami (Blue Wave) line to its terminus at Kinjo-Futo (¥350).

See also p163 for details of side trips from Nagoya.

PRACTICAL INFORMATION

Station guide

Nagoya Station's Towers are a city landmark and home to the city's top hotel and the JR Takashimaya department store. For the city centre take the Sakura-dori exit. Sakura-dori is the main road heading away from the station towards Sakae. Within the station, there are plenty of **lockers** in three main areas (up to ¥700).

On the main concourse you'll find a JR ticket office and branch of the JR Tokai Tours travel agency. To exchange your Exchange Order for your rail pass, or to get any other rail-related information in English, head for the **JR Information Centre** (daily 10am-7pm), in the middle of the concourse on the Taiko-dori side of the station.

Several JR lines run through or terminate at Nagoya: the **Tokaido line** (ordinary trains; platforms 1-6), which heads east to Toyohashi and west to Gifu; the **Chuo line** (platforms 7-10) for Nakatsugawa and Matsumoto; and the **Kansai line** (platforms 11-13) for Matsusaka. The **shinkansen tracks** (platforms 14-17) have an entrance near the Taiko-dori side of the station.

Nagoya is also a hub for two private railways, **Meitetsu** and **Kintetsu**. The stations (first Meitetsu, then Kintetsu) are a couple of minutes' walk from the Sakura-dori side of JR Nagoya. Head out of the station and turn right. The **Aonami line** (see above) also operates from here.

Tourist information

The tourist information office (🖳 www.ncvb.or.jp; daily 9am-7pm) is on the 1st-(ground-)floor concourse of the Sakura-dori side of the station. The English-speaking staff can give you an accommodation list but can't make bookings. Ask also for a copy of the English *JR Nagoya Station Guide*, which details all the shops and restaurants in the vast station complex.

Getting around

Nagoya has an efficient **subway system** with six lines: Higashiyama (yellow), Meijo (purple), Tsurumai (blue), Sakura-dori (red), Meiko (purple and white) and Kamiida (pink). Nagoya station is connected with the Higashiyama and Sakura-dori lines.

A one-day subway **pass** costs ¥740, a one-day bus pass is ¥600 and a combined pass is ¥850. On weekends and on weekdays which fall on the 8th of the month, the price

NAGOYA MAP KEY (see map pp158-9)

Where to stay

6 Super Hotel Nagoya Ekimae
スーパーホテル名古屋駅前

7 The Cypress Mercure Hotel Nagoya
ザ サイプレス メルキュール
ホテル 名古屋

10 Toyoko Inn Nagoya-eki Shinkansen-
guchi 東横イン名古屋駅新幹線口

13 Nagoya Marriott Associa Hotel
名古屋マリオットアソシアホテル

16 Hotel Resol Nagoya
ホテルリソル名古屋

17 Comfort Hotel Nagoya Chiyoda
コンフォートホテル名古屋 チヨダ

18 Aichi-ken Seinen Kaikan
愛知県青年会館

22 Ryokan Meiryu 旅館名龍

Where to eat and drink

9 Yabaton, Kishimen Yoshida (ESCA)
矢場とん, きしめん 吉田 (ESCA)

12 Towers Plaza (JR-Takashimaya)
タワープラザ（JR-高島屋）

13 Mikuni Nagoya, Ka-Un, Sky Lounge
Zenith ミクニナゴヤ, 華雲, スカイ
ラウンジジーニス

14 Maruya Honten まるや 本店

15 Enoteca Pinchiorri
エノテーカ ピンキオーリ

Where to eat and drink *(cont'd)*

19 Shooter's Sports Bar
シューターズスポーツバー

26 Oasis 21 オアシス２１

Other

1 Nagoya Castle 名古屋城

2 Ninomaru Garden 二之丸庭園

3 Nagoya Noh Theater 名古屋

4 Toyota Commemorative Museum of
Industry and Technology
産業技術記念館

5 Noritake Craft Center (Noritake
Garden) ノリタケクラフトセンタ
（ノリタケの森）

8 Central Post Office 中央郵便局

11 Linear Railway Hall リニア 鉄道館

14 Meitetsu Department Store
名鉄百貨店

15 Midland Square
ミッドランドスクエア

20 Osu area 大須

21 Nagoya City Science Museum
名古屋市科学館

23 Nagoya Port Area 名古屋港

24 Toyota Automobile Museum
トヨタ博物館

25 Nagoya TV Tower 名古屋テレビ塔

27 Tokugawa Art Museum 徳川美術館

of the combined pass (called on these days the Do-Nichi Eco Ticket) is reduced to ¥600.

Central Japan International Airport, known as **Centrair** (🖳 www.centrair.jp), is on a man-made island off the coast of Tokoname, a suburb of Nagoya. The private Meitetsu railway (no rail passes) operates a direct service (28 mins; ¥1200) between the airport and Meitetsu Nagoya station (next to the JR station).

Festivals

The biggest festival of the year is **Nagoya Matsuri**, a three-day event in mid October.

Where to stay

Towering above JR Takashimaya in the station is the luxurious *Nagoya Marriott Associa Hotel* (☎ 052-584 1111, 🖳 www.

associa.com/english/nma; from ¥20,000). This world-class hotel certainly can't be beaten for location – from the station concourse a lift whisks you up the twin towers to the gleaming 15th-floor lobby. The rooms are beautifully furnished and have spacious bathrooms. Facilities include a fitness club with an indoor pool and state-of-the-art gym.

Another good upscale choice close to the station is *The Cypress Mercure Hotel Nagoya* (☎ 052-571 0111, 🖳 www.thecy press.co.jp; from ¥20,000/S, ¥25,000/D), which sometimes has good online rates.

A more affordable option is the branch of the reliable *Comfort Hotel Nagoya Chiyoda* (☎ 052-221 6711, 🖳 www.com fortinn.com/hotel-nagoya-japan-JP021; from ¥5880/S, from ¥8925/D.

In the station area, a good bet is another chain hotel, *Toyoko Inn Nagoya-eki Shinkansen-guchi* (☎ 052-453 1047, 🖳 www.toyoko-inn.com; from ¥6980/S, ¥8480/D, ¥8980/Tw). Take the Taiko-dori (shinkansen-side) exit and walk up the main road which leads off from there. The hotel is on the first road on your left after Bic Camera. Also near the station, on the shinkansen side, is *Super Hotel Nagoya Ekimae* (☎ 052-451 9000, 🖳 www.superho teljapan.com/en/s-hotels/nagoya; ¥6090/S, ¥8680/D, inc breakfast) which has the usual functional rooms.

A five-minute walk up Sakura-dori from the station is *Hotel Resol Nagoya* (☎ 052-563 9269, 🖳 www.resol-hotel.jp/resol/ en/hotels/nagoya.html; from ¥7359/S, ¥12,987/Tw or D), which has compact but modern rooms. *Aichi-ken Seinen Kaikan* (☎ 052-221 6001, 🖳 www.aichi-seinenkai kan.or.jp; dorm beds from ¥2992pp for YH/ HI members, rooms from ¥4462/Tw) offers bargain dormitory-style accommodation and a few private rooms. Return after 11pm is discouraged. It's south-east of the station across Hori-gawa towards Fushimi. On the 1st (ground) floor, Kitchen Asama serves lunch and dinner.

Ryokan Meiryu (☎ 052-331 8686, 🖳 www.japan-net.ne.jp/~meiryu; ¥5250/S, ¥8400/Tw, ¥11,025/Tr; breakfast ¥630, dinner exc Sunday ¥2310) is a homely Japanese inn with tatami rooms (none en suite). Services include free internet access and coin-operated laundry. The ryokan is a three-minute walk south-east of Kamimaezu station (Exit 3) on the Meijo/Tsurumai subway lines.

If you're catching an early-morning flight and need to stay the night at Centrair, your best bet is the on-site *Comfort Hotel Central International Airport* (☎ 0569-38 7211, 🖳 www.comfortinn.com/hotel-toko name-japan-JP039; ¥9500/S, ¥13,000/Tw), which is adjacent to the terminal building.

See pp45-52 for general details about finding accommodation.

Where to eat and drink

Inside the station, head for **Towers Plaza** on the 12th and 13th floors of the JR Takashimaya department store, where you'll find nearly every kind of Japanese food as well as Italian and Chinese. The two basement floors are also crammed with food and outlets selling freshly made take-away lunch boxes.

For more upmarket dining, **Nagoya Marriott Associa Hotel** (see p161) has a wide range of restaurants including: *Mikuni Nagoya* (daily 11.30am-2.30pm & 5.30-10pm), a top-class French restaurant on the 52nd floor with views over the city; and *Ka-Un*, the hotel's best Japanese restaurant with sushi and tempura bars, as well as table and tatami seating. If you just want to enjoy an elevated view for the price of a drink, try the hotel's 52nd-floor *Sky Lounge Zenith*, where they do cocktails from 5pm to midnight, as well as a lunch buffet (11.30am-3pm; Mon-Fri ¥3000, Sat & Sun ¥3500).

Across the road from JR Nagoya station at **Midland Square** you'll get the cheapest deals in the restaurants on the basement and 4th floors. But for a splurge, why not book a table with a floor-to-ceiling window view at the upscale modern Italian restaurant *Enoteca Pinchiorri* (🖳 ep-na goya.jp; daily 11am-3pm & 5-11pm). Lunch courses start from ¥4400, but the spectacular views more than repay the expense.

On the 9th floor of **Meitetsu department store** next to JR Nagoya station is *Maruya Honten* (daily 11am-11pm), where the speciality is delicious pieces of grilled eel in soy sauce (from ¥1780).

Yabaton (daily 11am-10pm), a Nagoya-based restaurant chain famous for its *misokatsu* (deep-fried pork cutlet dipped in a delicious miso-based sauce), has several branches around the city. Downtown branches often have long queues – a better bet is to visit the Nagoya station branch in the basement (northernmost part) of the **Esca shopping mall**, the entrance to which is down an escalator right outside the Taiko-dori exit. Dishes include sets with the two main cuts of meat: *rosu tonkatsu* (¥1155) and *hiré tonkatsu* (¥1680). Also in the Esca shopping mall is *Kishimen Yoshida* (daily 11am-9.30pm), where you can try the Nagoya speciality *kishimen* noodles, with a variety of toppings, including tempura (¥785).

In the **Fushimi** district just west of Sakae and popular with foreign residents is *Shooter's Sports Bar*, which has draught beer, pool tables and a variety of lunch menus (¥893) as well as Shooter's Burger (¥1040). **Oasis 21** in Sakae has a good range of cafés and restaurants and attractions include skating on an artificial rink in the winter.

Side trip by rail from Nagoya

A popular side trip is to nearby **Inuyama**, known for its **castle** (daily 9am-5pm; ¥500), perched on a hill overlooking Kiso-gawa. Built in 1537, it was partly destroyed during the division of Japan into prefectures at the beginning of the Meiji era in 1871 and then again after an earthquake in 1891. Four years later, what was left of the castle was handed back to the Naruse family who had originally owned it – this act of charity was, however, tempered by a condition: the castle had to be repaired. Restoration work on the donjon was completed in 1965.

The other big sight here is **Meiji Mura** (⌨ www.meijimura.com; Mar-Oct daily 9.30am-5pm, Nov-Feb daily 9.30am-4pm; ¥1600), an open-air collection of Western-style buildings from the Meiji era, including the 1898 Sapporo Telephone Exchange, St John's Church from Kyoto, and a steam locomotive – currently out of use – that chugs the short distance between 'Tokyo' and 'Nagoya' stations.

Inuyama is on the private Meitetsu Inuyama line from Meitetsu Railway's Nagoya station (frequent services; 30-43 mins; ¥540-890), next to the Sakuradori exit of JR Nagoya. From Inuyama station, a bus service runs to Meiji Mura (3-4/hr; 20 mins; ¥410). For Inuyama Castle, continue on to Inuyama-Yuen station, one stop after Inuyama. If you want to save money and have a JR rail pass, the closest JR station to Inuyama is Unuma (see p150) on the Takayama line. From Nagoya, take a Hida LEX bound for Takayama and change at Unuma (30 mins), where you transfer to Meitetsu's adjoining Shin-Unuma station, from where local trains (3 mins; ¥160) run to Inuyama. Not all Hida LEX services bound for Takayama stop at Unuma; check at the JR ticket office in Nagoya before boarding.

NAGANO

Situated in the centre of Honshu, Nagano is the junction of the northern, central and southern Japanese Alps, and is often referred to as the 'roof of Japan'. The city has expanded from its original site around Zenko-ji. However, the temple, a 20- to 30-minute walk north of the station, remains the focal point of the city. The extension of the shinkansen from Tokyo to Nagano in time for the 1998 Winter Olympics reduced the fastest journey time from the capital to just 85 minutes.

What to see and do

According to the Nagano tourist literature, **Zenko-ji** (⌨ www.zenkoji.jp; daily 5am-4.30pm; free) is regarded as a special temple which one 'must visit at least once even if a great distance must be travelled'. Judging by the number of tour buses that pull up outside, this instruction continues to be followed to this day.

> **From princess to perfume**
> The story of Nagano would not be complete without mention of the legendary
> Nyoze Hime (Princess Nyoze) whose bronze statue (atop a fountain) stands proudly
> on the ground-floor plaza directly outside the Zenko-ji exit of the station. To cut a long
> and rather convoluted story to its bare bones, Princess Nyoze became gravely ill and
> was granted a miraculous recovery by the triad now housed in Zenko-ji. As a mark of
> respect and thanks, the statue of Nyoze offering incense is positioned looking towards
> the temple to the north.
> As if to prove that a legend is nothing if it cannot be commercialised, visitors to
> Nagano can now purchase Princess Nyoze Eau de Parfum (¥3000 a bottle) which is
> promoted locally as having a 'fresh floral fragrance to evoke the healthy and elegant
> figure of Princess Nyoze and the refreshing weather of Nagano'.

To avoid the inevitable crowds, arrive in the early evening or better still at
dawn, when the abbot and abbotess make an appearance to pray for the salvation of visiting pilgrims. The starting time of this daily ceremony depends on
the season – in the summer it's as early as 5.30am, in December at 7am; check
with the tourist office. You can buy a guide for ¥50 at the information office on
the left side of the approach to the temple.

The temple is said to have been founded in the 7th century as a place to
house the golden triad, a sacred image of the Buddha. It is never displayed in
public but every seven years an exact copy is brought out as part of the
Gokaicho ceremony – the next will be in 2015. Inside the main hall, people
gather around the statue of Binzuru, considered to be Buddha's most intelligent
follower; by rubbing the statue, they hope their own aches and pains will be
rubbed away. Access to the pitch-black passage containing the 'Key to Paradise'
is by ticket from vending machines (daily 9am-4/4.30pm; ¥500) inside the main
hall. Anyone who touches the key is assured eternal salvation. Anyone who
doesn't can buy another ticket and try again. Don't go in if you're claustropho-
bic or afraid of the dark.

The 20m-tall **Sanmon Gate**, the main gateway to the temple precinct, was
constructed in 1750 but extensive restoration work was completed in 2007.
Visitors can climb the steep stairs (¥500) inside the gate to the top, for a view
down the long street leading to the temple.

Though it's possible to take a bus to the temple from the station (bus No 6,
from stop No 1 outside the Zenko-ji exit; ¥100), it's easy to walk the 30 minutes
north up Chuo-dori. Heading up the main street, look out on the right for **Saiko-
ji**, a small temple founded in 1199; a leaflet is available. You'll know you've
reached the start of the main path towards Zenko-ji because it's lined with
shops, soba restaurants and stalls. Legend has it that 7777 stones were used to
pave the final 450m leading to the temple's main hall.

Just to the east of Zenko-ji are **Nagano Prefectural Shinano Art Museum**
and the adjacent **Higashiyama Kaii Gallery** (🖥 www.npsam.com; both Thur-
Tue 9am-5pm; ¥500), both worth popping into. The former showcases the work
of local artists, mainly landscapes of the surrounding mountains and countryside.

The latter houses the work of Yokohama-born painter Higashiyama Kaii, who died in 1999. Between the museum and the gallery is *Café Kaii*, with outdoor seating in the summer – a good place to grab a coffee away from the bustle.

The **M-Wave Arena** was the speed-skating venue during the Olympics and is now home to **Nagano Olympic Museum** (💻 www.nagano-mwave.co.jp; Sat & Sun only 10am-5pm; free). Displays include the Japanese Olympic team uniforms, the Olympic torch and the skates used by Hiroyasu Shimizu, who became a national hero when he took gold in the 500m speed-skating event and bronze in the 1000m in the M-Wave Arena. The vast arena has the world's largest wooden suspension roof, which is supposed to resemble ocean waves. In summer, the arena is used for a variety of events including a sumo tournament. The skating rink is open from early October to the end of March (daily 10am-6pm). To reach the M-Wave Arena, take bus No 8 from stop No 1 outside the station's east exit and get out at M-Wave-mae (20 mins; ¥300).

See also pp168-9 for details of side trips from Nagano.

PRACTICAL INFORMATION
Station guide
Rebuilt for the Olympics, Nagano station has two sides: East and Zenko-ji. Take the latter for the city centre and Zenko-ji itself. **Lockers** (a few ¥500, plenty of ¥400 and ¥300) are near both exits. Shinkansen services depart from platforms 11-14 and have a separate entrance to other JR lines. There are elevators to/from the shinkansen platforms and main concourse. There is a transfer area at the top of the escalator from the shinkansen platforms for connecting JR services: the Iiyama line for Nozawa-onsen and the Shin-etsu line for Myoko-Kogen.

There are surprisingly few places to eat at in the station, aside from a couple of convenience stores and a noodle bar (see 'Where to eat', p168) in a waiting room, which also houses lockers.

Tourist information
Nagano City TIC (💻 www.go-nagano.net; daily 9am-6pm) is on the station concourse, opposite the shinkansen ticket barrier. Staff will book accommodation for you (Nagano city only) and can advise on the best places to ski and hike. They have bus timetables and information on late-season skiing and will provide English leaflets on request.

Getting around
The private **Nagano Dentetsu Railway** (💻 www.nagaden-net.co.jp), known as 'Nagaden', operates in the Nagano area. The entrance is outside the Zenko-ji exit of JR Nagano station; the station itself is underground.

The main **bus terminal** is at street level outside the Zenko-ji exit. Stop No 1 is for buses to Zenko-ji. The **Gururin-go city area bus** (daily 9.30am-6.10pm; 3/hr; flat fare ¥100) operates on a circular route round the city.

Where to stay
Mielparque Nagano (☎ 026-225 7800, 💻 www.mielparque.jp/nagano; from ¥7600/S, ¥14,500/Tw; tatami rooms ¥25,000/5 people, ¥17,500/2, ¥15,000/1; breakfast ¥900) is less than five minutes on foot from the station's east exit, in a sleek modern building with glass lifts that whisk you from the lobby to your room. It is part of a chain run by the post office (there's a handy branch office on the ground floor with an ATM). The singles are nothing special, twins are roomy with larger bathrooms but best of all are the Japanese tatami rooms which can sleep up to five people.

The JR-operated *Hotel Metropolitan Nagano* (☎ 026-291 7000, 💻 www.metro-n.co.jp; from ¥9240/S, ¥18,480/D or Tw; rail-pass holders get a small discount) is one of the most luxurious places in town, located to the left as you take the Zenko-ji exit. One of its suites has been fitted out with a 6m (20ft) model railway, the largest indoor model railway of its kind in the country. Also included are miniature versions of tourist attractions in Nagano, including Zenko-ji, and the surrounding snow-capped mountains. The railway boasts four kinds of electric model trains, including the Asama shinkansen. Furthermore, guests staying in the suite can watch the real-life bullet trains pulling out of the station below. The suite does not come cheap (¥88,000/night) but anyone can enjoy the model railway for shorter periods of time (¥3000/1 hr or ¥5000/2 hrs).

Island Hotel (☎ 026-226 3388, 🖳 www.island-hotel.co.jp; ¥6000/S, ¥11,500/Tw) is a smart business hotel. All rooms are en suite, but there is also a hot-spring-style common bath. Twins are reasonably spacious with relatively large bathrooms.

Comfort Hotel Nagano (☎ 026-268 1611, 🖳 www.comfortinn.com/hotel-nagano-japan-JP034; ¥5800/S, ¥9800/Tw) has compact rooms with bright and cheerful common areas.

For something a little more upmarket try *Hotel JAL City Nagano* (☎ 026-225 1131, 🖳 www.jalhotels.com/nagano; ¥6300/S, ¥10,000/D, ¥12,500/Tw), which is closer to Zenko-ji.

Zenko-ji Kyojuin Youth Hostel (☎ 026-232 2768, 🖳 www.jyh.or.jp/english/hokushinestu/zenkoji/index.html; 📄 232 2767; dorm bed ¥3360pp, private room ¥4000pp; additional ¥600 for non members; no meals) is just outside the main temple compound. Bags must be left in the entrance hall lockers so as not to damage the specially hand-made tatami in all the dormitory rooms (the building is over 100 years old). It's 20 minutes on foot from the station up Chuo-dori.

Shimizuya Ryokan (☎ 026-232 2580, 🖳 www.chuoukan-shimizuya.com; from ¥6300pp inc breakfast, dinner ¥2100), on the road leading up to Zenko-ji, is a convenient place to stay for early-morning access to the temple and it has free internet. Tatami bedrooms can sleep up to four people; the price per person is the same whether you are in a single or sharing. There are no en suite bathrooms: as usual in ryokan, the large common bathrooms are shared. Look for the white sign on the street outside the entrance – with the name written in English and kanji.

A good budget business hotel choice is *Smile Hotel Nagano* (☎ 026-226 3211, 🖳 www.smile-hotels.com; ¥4980/S, ¥6980/D or Tw), with standard facilities including coin laundry and in-house café.

NAGANO – MAP KEY

Where to stay
3 Matsuya Ryokan 松屋旅館
4 Zenko-ji Kyojuin Youth Hostel
    善光寺教授院ユースホステル
12 Shimizuya Ryokan 清水屋旅館
15 Smile Hotel Nagano
    スマイルホテル長野
16 Hotel JAL City Nagano
    ホテルＪＡＬシティ長野
18 Island Hotel アイランドホテル
19 Comfort Hotel Nagano
    コンフォートホテル長野
20 Mielparque Nagano メルパルク長野
22 Hotel Metropolitan Nagano
    ホテルメトロポリタン長野

Where to eat and drink
5 Suyakame Miso すやかめみそ
8 Fujiya Gohonjin 藤屋御本陣
10 Fujikian 藤木庵

Where to eat and drink (cont'd)
11 Rakucha Rengakan 楽茶レンガ館
13 Gotokutei ごとく亭
21 Sobatei Aburaya そば亭油や
23 Pronto, Osaka Ohsho
    プロント，大阪王将

Other
1 Zenko-ji 善光寺
2 Zenko-ji (Information) 善光寺案内所
6 Higashiyama Kaii Gallery
    東山魁夷館
7 Nagano Prefectural Shinano Art
    Museum 長野県信濃美術館
9 Post office 郵便局
14 Central post office 中央郵便局
17 Saiko-ji 西光寺
20 Post office 郵便局
24 Bus terminal バスターミナル

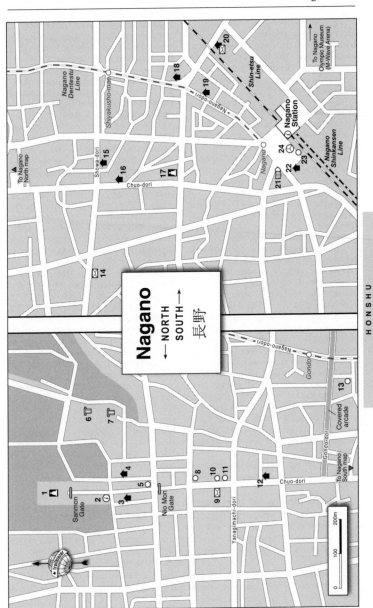

Nagano
← NORTH
SOUTH →
長野

To Nagano
Olympic Museum
(M-Wave Arena)

Shin-etsu
Line

Nagano
Station

Nagano
Shinkansen
Line

Nagano
Dentetsu
Line

Shiyakusho-mae

Nagano-dori

Showa-dori

Chuo-dori

To Nagano
North map

HONSHU

Nagano-dori

Gondo

Covered
arcade

Gondo-dori

To Nagano
South map

Chuo-dori

Yanagimachi-dori

Nio Mon
Gate

Sanmon
Gate

0   100   200m

If you're looking for Japanese-style accommodation, you can't beat *Matsuya Ryokan* (☎ 026-232 2811, 🖳 www14.ocn.ne.jp/~matuya; ¥6300pp, or ¥10,500pp half-board) for location, a small traditional inn within the precinct which leads up to the main gate of Zenko-ji.

Where to eat and drink

Don't overlook the *noodle bar* inside the station, in the coin-locker area on the right before you take the Zenko-ji exit. You select and pay for the type of noodle bowl you want from the vending machine (¥390 for tempura soba), give in your ticket at the counter, and wait to be served.

To the left as you take the Zenko-ji exit of Nagano station, the *Pronto* café turns into a bar in the evenings but also serves pasta dishes during the day from ¥530.

Osaka Ohsho (daily 11am-9pm), opposite Pronto on the left-hand side before you take the escalator to ground level at the Zenko-ji exit, is a good-value Chinese restaurant with an English menu. Steamed pork dumplings are ¥290, vegetable and seafood ramen is ¥630, mango pudding ¥290.

For a more formal place to eat soba, try *Sobatei Aburaya* (daily 11am-11pm), right across the street as you take the Zenko-ji exit. Bowls of soba noodles start from ¥700, or for ¥1400 you get a filling soba and tempura set menu. Take the zebra crossing from the station, and the entrance is to the left of the escalator leading up to Heiando. Look for the blue 'Soba' sign in hiragana hanging over the food display window.

There are plenty of soba restaurants on the approach to Zenko-ji, including

Fujikian, along Chuo-dori opposite a small branch post office. The name is written in kanji in grey letters above the front. Seating is on tatami or at wooden tables. The tempura and soba (from ¥1000) are delicious.

Rakucha Rengakan (daily 11am-8pm), next door to Fujikian (to the right as you face the entrance to Fujikian), is in a brick building with a small red awning above the door. They serve soba set meals (¥1150 for a meal with all the trimmings, including an ice-cream dessert) as well as Western-style meals such as pasta.

Suyakame Miso (daily 10am-5.30pm) does grilled rice balls with miso (soybean paste) for ¥200, and miso-flavoured ice cream (¥250), which sounds awful but tastes good. Also worth trying is the *ama-zake* (¥200), a sweet form of sake usually served warm. It's on a corner as you approach the temple and has a sign in English.

Gotokutei (daily 5-11pm) serves a range of Japanese dishes at reasonable prices (set meals from ¥1260 or splash out on the full 'Japanese dinner course' for ¥3150). They have an English menu and are used to dealing with foreign guests. A wide range of sake is available. It's on a side street which leads off from the Gondo covered arcade. The street is opposite Ito-Yokado department store.

The Fujiya Gohonjin (🖳 www.thefujiyagohonjin.com; Mon-Fri 11.30am-3pm & 6-10.30pm, Sat & Sun 7-10.30pm) occupies an impressive old building that used to house one of Nagano's most upmarket ryokan. It's now a café, bar and wedding hall, serving steak set lunches for ¥2900, chef's special-course lunches for ¥2400, and afternoon tea and cake sets for ¥1000.

Side trips by rail from Nagano

Possible trips by private Nagano Dentetsu (Nagaden) railway are to the small town of Obuse, or to the rail terminus and gateway to the Japanese Alps at Yudanaka. The Nagaden line, which is separate but next to JR Nagano station and accessed by subway from the Zenko-ji exit, starts underground but soon emerges to a very fertile part of Japan. You'll see peach and apple trees as well as grapevines on all sides (all covered in a blanket of snow during the winter months), in addition to the usual rice fields, so even though the train rocks and rolls a bit it is a pleasant journey.

● **Obuse** Obuse (22/33 mins; ¥650/750 one way by local/express train) was a stop on the old highway linking the Japan Sea with Edo (Tokyo) and now boasts a number of museums, temples and gardens. The biggest draw is **Ganshoin Temple** (Apr-Oct daily 9am-5pm, Nov 9am-4.30pm, Dec-Mar 9.30am-4pm; ¥300), which belongs to the same Zen Buddhist sect as Eihei-ji near Fukui (see p153). The temple is renowned for its ceiling painting of a phoenix 'staring in eight directions' by the artist Katsushika Hokusai (1760-1849). The impressive **Hokusai Museum** (Apr-Sep 9am-6pm, Oct-Mar 9am-5pm; ¥500) houses some of the artist's best works of art. Pick up a map of Obuse from the tourist information office at Nagano station. The lockers (¥300) at Obuse station are suitable for day packs. The town is manageable on foot but at the weekend (and on weekdays in high season) a shuttle bus (9.50am-5pm; 1/hr; ¥300/one-day ticket) runs from the station in a loop and stops at all the main sights, including Ganshoin and the Hokusai Museum.

● **Yudanaka and Jigokudani** Yudanaka (50/60 mins; ¥1130/1230 one way by local/express train – it is worth spending the extra money on the express service: sit at the front for spectacular views from the panoramic windows) is an onsen town and a good base for a day trip to Jigokudani (see below). *Yorozuya Annex Yurukuan* (☎ 0263-33 2117, 🖳 www.yurakuan.com; from ¥10,800/S, ¥17,600/Tw half-board) offers spacious Japanese- and Western-style rooms, all of them en suite, though it's an extra ¥1000 for a view. There are public baths as well as a rotemburo and a Jacuzzi (men can use the former in the morning and the latter in the evening; women at other times). Evening meals must be booked in advance (*kaiseki ryori* costs from ¥3000) but there are other places to eat in Yudanaka. There's free internet, and station pick-up provided if you reserve ahead. The most popular side trip from Yudanaka and well worth the visit if you can stand the smell is **Jigokudani Wild Monkey Park** (Jigokudani Yaen-koen; 🖳 www.jigokudani-yaenkoen.co.jp; daily Apr-Oct 8.30am-5pm, Nov-Mar 9am-4pm; ¥500), 7km from Yudanaka and 850m above sea level, where you can see wild monkeys (*Macaca fuscata*) bathing – and stealing food from passing tourists – in the natural hot-spring baths. The local tourist literature contends that it is 'very soothing to watch the adorable monkeys at play', although many visitors would beg to differ: it's for a good reason that Jigokudani Monkey Park is known in English as Hell's Valley. From outside Yudanaka station take a bus to Kanbayashi-onsen (approx 7/day, 10am–6.45pm; 7 mins; ¥210), from where it is around 30 minutes on foot to the monkey park. A very helpful English-speaking guide who lives in Shibu-onsen, a spa resort two kilometres from Yudanaka station, is Zeno Kubicek. He is a Slovakian expatriate and runs his own website (🖳 www. yudanaka-shibu onsen.com), which is a one-stop-shop for local hotel/ryokan reservations and sightseeing tours off the beaten track.

MATSUMOTO

Surrounded by mountains, Matsumoto is an ancient castle town and a gateway to the north-western corner of Nagano prefecture. The 3000m peaks of the Japanese Alps form a backdrop to the west of the city. Locals like to think of Matsumoto as not the heart but the 'navel' of Japan. Whichever it is, thousands visit the city every year to see one of the country's best-preserved castles.

What to see and do

Fifteen minutes on foot north of the station is **Matsumoto Castle** (8.30am-5pm; ¥600, or ¥540 with Town Sneaker pass, inc City Museum) considered to be one of the finest castles in Japan. A small fortress was first built here in 1504 but this was remodelled and expanded in 1593 to become what still stands today. It's a rare example of a Japanese castle which is not a 20th-century concrete reconstruction. The fortification once dominated the city skyline but the view is now obscured by office blocks and the castle remains invisible until the final approach. The five-storey donjon is known as 'Crow Castle' because the outside walls are mainly black. The design is unusual because although the castle is built on a plain rather than a hill it still contains traditional defensive elements: the hidden floor, sunken passageways, specially constructed holes in the wall to drop stones on the enemy below and incredibly steep stairs to make an attack on the castle difficult for intruders. Tacked on to the side is the moon-viewing room, a later addition, where guests could stare up at the moon while enjoying a cup or two of sake. The nearby **Matsumoto City Museum** (8.30am-5pm; free with Castle entry), which is also known as the **Japan Folklore Museum**, focuses on the history of the city and features one or two pieces of pottery and stoneware worthy of inspection, but it's not worth bothering with if you are short of time.

Ten minutes on foot north of the castle is **Kaichi Gakko** (Tue-Sun 8.30am-5pm; ¥300 or ¥250 with Town Sneaker pass), a former elementary school built in 1876 which looks like something out of little England. The oldest Western-style school building in Japan, it remained open for 90 years and is now open to all. Proving that, contrary to popular belief, the education system in Japan was not all work, the school has a room dedicated to extra-curricular activities, which included ice-skating (note the 'geta-skates' that look uncomfortable and dangerous to wear). Upstairs, in the main hall, look out for the coil of rope used in *tsunahiki*, a tug-of-war tournament between classes that took place every year at the school athletics festival.

Matsumoto Timepiece Museum (Tokei Hakubutsukan; Tue-Sun 9am-5pm; ¥300 or ¥250 with Town Sneaker pass; English pamphlet available) is by the river and features a large pendulum clock (supposedly the biggest in Japan) outside. If possible, get here on the hour when you can see many of the clocks on display swing into action and chime. It's a small museum but watch- and clock-lovers will be in heaven. You'll find everything from tiny intricate pocket watches to enormous clocks – look out for the 19th-century cannon-shaped sundial from England. Inexplicably there is also a small selection of antique gramophones.

Even if you're not staying at Marumo Ryokan (see p172), head over to the **Nakamachi district** along the southern side of Metoba-gawa to find old houses, craft shops and cafés.

See also p174 for details of side trips from Matsumoto.

PRACTICAL INFORMATION
Station guide
As trains pull into Matsumoto station, a female voice virtually sings the station's name to arriving passengers. Trains for the JR Shinonoi Line (also known as JR Chuo East, for services to Shinjuku in Tokyo, and JR Chuo West, for services to Nagoya, uses platforms 0-5. JR Oito Line trains arrive at and leave from Platforms 3-6 and the private Matsumoto Dentetsu line (Matsumoto to Shin-Shimashima) uses platform 7 and is on the Alps Exit (west exit) side of the station.

From the platforms, follow the signs for the Castle (Oshiro) Exit. On the station concourse is a branch of JR East's View Plaza travel agency. There are **lockers** (daily 5.15am-12.30am; ¥300, ¥400, and a few ¥500) in the waiting room to your right, opposite the entrance to Midori department store before you take the escalator down to street level. There are also cafés such as *Vie de France* and *Starbucks* in the station.

Tourist information
The tourist information counter (🖳 wel come.city.matsumoto.nagano.jp; daily 9am-5.45pm) is in front of you as you exit the ticket barrier. Friendly, English-speaking staff can assist with same-day reservations and will provide travel information.

Getting around
Matsumoto is compact enough to visit on foot, but if you really need it there is a 'Town Sneaker' bus (¥190 flat fare or ¥500 for a one-day ticket, which gives you reduced-price entry to many of the city's attractions). The bus runs on four different loops at regular intervals during the day, all of which start and finish outside Matsumoto station, but also call at the **bus terminal** beneath Espa department store across the street from the station. Pick up the English-language *Town Sneaker Timetable and Bus Route Map* from the tourist information counter at Matsumoto station.

Festivals
An annual outdoor performance of **Noh** is held in the grounds of Matsumoto Castle on the evening of 8th August. The show is illuminated by bonfires, with the brooding presence of the castle as a backdrop. On 3rd November, **Matsumoto Castle Festival** features a samurai parade and puppet shows.

In October (usually over a long weekend), the annual **Soba Noodle Festival** is marked with over a hundred soba stalls setting up inside Matsumoto Castle Park.

The **Taiko Drum Festival** (last Sat & Sun in July) also takes place next to Matsumoto Castle and attracts some of the country's best taiko drummers.

Where to stay
Ace Inn Matsumoto (☎ 0263-35 1188, 🖳 www.ace-inn.net; from ¥6700/S, ¥11,000/D, ¥13,000/Tw) is a standard business hotel conveniently located right outside the station. Take the main station exit (for Matsumoto Castle) and it's on the corner on your right.

Toko City Hotel Matsumoto (☎ 0263-38 0123, 🖳 tokocityhotel-matsumoto.wise knot.ne.jp; from ¥6800/S, ¥11,000/D, ¥13,000/Tw) is across the street from the station. Reception ('Front') is on the 10th floor and as this is also where guests have breakfast there are wonderful views of the Alps. The rooms are on the 4th-9th floors.

A good alternative is *Toyoko Inn Matsumoto Ekimae Honmachi* (☎ 0263-36 1045, 🖳 www.toyoko-inn.com; from ¥5480/S, ¥6980/D or Tw). From the station's Castle (Oshiro) exit go over the pedestrian crossing and along the bricked road. The hotel is on the far side of the plaza. This branch has one of the better Toyoko Inn breakfasts.

Richmond Hotel Matsumoto (☎ 0263-37 5000, 🖳 www.richmondhotel.jp; ¥10,500/S, ¥13,000/D, ¥17,000/Tw) is just a few minutes on foot from the main station exit and next to Parco department store. It's a hyper-efficient place with automatic check-in, clean, compact rooms and a coin laundry. A more economical option is *Hotel New Station* (☎ 0263-35 3850, 🖳 www. hotel-ns.co.jp; ¥6200/S, ¥11,600/Tw, exc breakfast), only two minutes on foot from the station. The rooms are basic but all have en suite facilities. Just across the street is

Hotel Mor-Schein (☎ 0263-32 0031, 🖳 www.mor-schein.co.jp;¥7350/S,¥11,550/D, ¥13,650/Tw; breakfast ¥650), a standard business hotel.

Marumo Ryokan (☎ 0263-32 0115, 🖳 www.avis.ne.jp/~marumo; ¥5000pp, breakfast ¥1000), a traditional inn in the Nakamachi district by Metoba-gawa, has tatami rooms (none en suite) with a fantastic wooden bath. It gets booked up fast. An alternative is the small and friendly **Nunoya Ryokan** (☎ 0263-32 0545, 🖳 www.mcci. or.jp/www/nunoya; from ¥5000pp but cheaper for doubles, exc meals), one block back from the river. It's a small, traditional Japanese inn with the usual creaking wooden floors and communal (lockable) bathrooms. The owner speaks a little English.

Where to eat and drink

If you're looking for noodles **Ekimae Benten** (daily exc 1st & 3rd Wed, 10am-7pm) does traditional soba dishes for under ¥1000.

Kobayashi (daily 11am-8pm) serves delicious hand-made soba noodles. It's a quaint, traditional place on a quiet street just set back from the river. Meals start at around ¥1000. Look for the white hanging curtain and bench as well as a small display

of plastic food outside. There is another branch outside Matsumoto station.

One of Matsumoto's specialities is *basashi*, raw horsemeat (which is also popular in Kumamoto, see box p403). A good place to try it is **Shinmiyoshi** (Mon-Sat 11.50am-2pm & 5-11pm), a short walk from the station. The restaurant is known for its *sakura nabe* (horsemeat hotpot) as well as basashi, and the décor includes harnesses, saddles, whips and horse-themed calligraphy. Set menus start at ¥1500.

Gusto, a 24-hour family restaurant on the 1st (ground) floor of Hotel Richmond Matsumoto, is open to anyone (not just hotel guests) in need of some late-night sustenance. **5 Horn** (daily 10am-10pm), an Italian café on the ground floor of Parco department store, has an open kitchen and a menu in English. Their four-course tasting menu is ¥2700, or you could go à la carte, with soup (¥470) and bottarga, pecorino cheese and tomato spaghetti (¥1155); portions are minimalist but tasty.

If you're in the **Nakamachi** area, it would be a crime to miss **Kissa Marumo** (daily 8am-8pm), a café attached to Marumo Ryokan (see column opposite), which plays classical music and serves good coffee, ice-cream and mouth-watering cakes.

MATSUMOTO – MAP KEY

Where to stay

6 Marumo Ryokan まるも旅館
7 Nunoya Ryokan ぬのや旅館
9 Hotel Mor-Schein ホテルモルシヤン
10 Hotel New Station
　ホテルニューステーション
12 Richmond Hotel Matsumoto
　リッチモンドホテル松本
14 Toyoko Inn Matsumoto Ekimae
　Honmachi 東横イン松本駅前本町
17 Toko City Hotel Matsumoto
　トーコーシティホテル松本
19 Ace Inn Matsumoto エースイン松本

Where to eat and drink

4 Kobayashi こばやし
5 Ekimae Benten 駅前弁天
6 Kissa Marumo 喫茶まるも
11 Kobayashi こばやし

Where to eat and drink (cont'd)

12 Gusto ガスト
13 5 Horn ファイブホルン
16 Shinmiyoshi 新三よし
17 Doutor ドトール

Other

1 Kaichi Gakko 開智学校
2 Matsumoto Castle 松本城
3 Matsumoto City Museum (Japan
　Folklore Museum) 松本市博物館
　（日本民族資料館）
8 Matsumoto Timepiece Museum
　松本市時計博物館
13 Parco department store
　パルコデパート
15 Post Office 郵便局
18 ESPA dept store; bus terminal
　ESPAデパート; バスターミナル

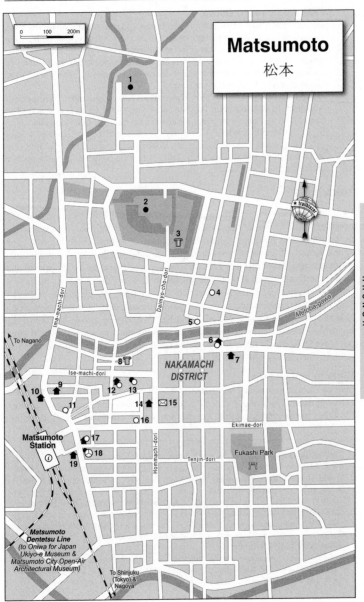

Matsumoto

松本

0   100   200m

1

2

3

4

5

6

7

8

To Nagano

NAKAMACHI
DISTRICT

Ima-machi-dori

Daimyo-cho-dori

Metoba-gawa

Ise-machi-dori

10

9

12   13

11

14

15

16

17

18

19

Matsumoto
Station

Hommachi-dori

Ekimae-dori

Fukashi Park

Tenjin-dori

Matsumoto
Dentetsu Line
(to Oniwa for Japan
Ukiyo-e Museum &
Matsumoto City Open-Air
Architectural Museum)

To Shinjuku
(Tokyo) &
Nagoya

HONSHU

★ trailblazer

Side trip by rail to Oniwa

On the outskirts of Matsumoto is the **Japan Ukiyo-e Museum** (🖳 www.uki yo-e.co.jp/jum-e; Tue-Sun 10am-5pm; ¥1050), a private museum built by the Sakai Family which houses over 100,000 Japanese woodblock prints. Take the private Matsumoto Dentetsu railway from Matsumoto station to tiny Oniwa station (¥170). Ask at Oniwa ticket office for a map with directions to the museum, about 15 minutes' walk away.

While here, stop by the **Matsumoto City Open-air Architectural Museum** (Rekishi-no-Sato; Tue-Sun 9am-5pm; ¥400), which is next door. The main building is an old wooden court house, the only one of its kind still standing in Japan today. Displays focus on the history of Japanese law and court proceedings, and on items used by the police, including *shuriken*, the small but lethal handheld weapon known as ninja stars. One of the other buildings is a reconstructed prison block.

TAKAYAMA

Deep in the mountains, in the region known traditionally as Hida, Takayama is deservedly one of the most popular destinations in central Honshu, combining as it does ancient traditions with a stunning natural setting. Often referred to as 'Little Kyoto', Takayama boasts temples, shrines, small museums, traditional shops and inns. As a result it gets very busy, particularly during the spring and autumn festivals, when 300,000 people come to watch the parade of floats.

The greatest pleasure, however, comes not from the museums or tourist sights but from the chance to wander round the old, narrow streets of wooden houses and discover a side of Japan that has been largely airbrushed out of the big cities. Set aside enough time to simply enjoy the atmosphere; two or three days would be ideal. Takayama is also a good place to hunt for souvenirs, particularly lacquerware, woodcraft and pottery.

What to see and do

One of Takayama's many highlights is a visit to the daily **morning markets** (*asaichi*; daily 6/7am-noon). One is right outside Takayama Jinya (see opposite), the other, more gift orientated, on the banks of Miya-gawa. Every morning,

---

⛩ Sukyo Mahikari – a new religious movement

Look out on the bus ride back to Takayama from the Folk Village for the **Main World Shrine** (daily 9.30am-4pm; free), along Highway 158 at the bottom of the hill and instantly recognisable from its elaborate gold roof with a red sphere perched on top. You won't find this place on any official maps of Takayama because it is home to Sukyo Mahikari, one of Japan's 'new religions' that have sprung up in the post-war years. Mahikari is described as 'true light, a cleansing energy sent by the Creator God that both spiritually awakens and tunes the soul to its divine purpose'.

Anyone is welcome to visit this bizarre shrine; the twin towers at the entrance look like minarets, an enormous fish tank stretches across the inside wall, there's a pipe organ that wouldn't be out of place in a cathedral, and a hall with a seating capacity of 4500. The sheer scale of the place is overwhelming.

women from the surrounding area come here to sell vegetables, flowers and locally made crafts.

During the Edo period, **Takayama Jinya** (Mar-Jul & Sep-Oct daily 8.45am-5pm, Aug to 6pm, to 4.30pm the rest of the year; ¥420; occasional tours in English) was used as the government building for Gifu prefecture. It's now open to the public but most of the rooms are empty. One or two of the rooms need little explanation; the torture room, for example, tells its own story. Look out for the old toilet in one of the rooms, with the helpful 'out of use' sign on it – it would be a desperate visitor who felt the need to relieve him/herself in front of crowds of sightseers.

If you're not here at festival time, you can see four of the large floats at **Takayama Yatai Kaikan** (Float Exhibition Hall; daily 8.30am-5pm, Dec-Feb 9am-4.30pm; ¥820). The floats change three times a year, in March, July and November. Each float would cost the equivalent of US$4 million to replace. A tape commentary in English is available. The attendant shows you a card stating this, rather than daring to tell you!

Takayama's new **Museum of History and Art** (daily 9am-7pm, garden until 9pm; free) is housed in traditional warehouse-type buildings (*kura*), which are probably more of a highlight than the exhibits themselves.

A short walk north of the river you'll find a street of **traditional shops** stretching along three blocks – fruitful for local souvenirs. A good place to rest weary legs is at the nearby **Yoshijima Heritage House** (Yoshijima-ke Jutaku; summer daily 8.30am-5pm, winter Wed-Mon 9am-4.30/5pm; ¥500), built in the Meiji period for a sake-brewing family. The entrance fee includes a cup of mushroom tea. You might also visit **Matsumoto House** (Matsumoto-ke; Sat & Sun only 9am-4.30pm; free) with its attractive garden.

The main temple district is just east of Enako-gawa in **Higashiyama**, which is a little hilly but still a great area to explore on foot. The map available from the tourist information office has a suggested walking tour. The youth hostel (see p178) is part of Tensho-ji.

For more recent history, try **Takayama Showa Kan** (daily Apr to mid Jan 9am-6pm, mid Jan to end Mar to 5pm; ¥500). One of a number of places around Japan catering to nostalgia for the Showa period (1926-89), it features a wide selection of memorabilia, a small cinema shows historic newsreels, and a recreated classroom.

Hida-no-Sato (Hida Folk Village) area Twenty minutes out of town along Highway 158, in the hills overlooking Takayama, is **Hida Folk Village** (daily 8.30am-5pm; ¥700). Over 30 traditional farmhouses and merchant cottages from rural areas have been moved here and restored. On a fine day it's a great mini-escape from the town below but since the village is all open air it's not so much fun in the rain. As well as the buildings, traditional crafts such as wood-carving and weaving have also been preserved and there are displays inside some of the houses. To reach the Folk Village take a bus from stop No 6 at the terminal outside the station. A ¥900 ticket available from the bus terminal includes return bus ride and entry to the village.

⛩ **Poppo-koen**
　Rail fans may like to make a mini-pilgrimage to Poppo-koen, just out to the
west on the other side of Takayama station. In this small park you'll find a well-
preserved steam locomotive (No 19648, to be precise), built in 1917, as well as a 1934
vintage snow plough which – by the time it was taken out of service in 1980 – had
clocked up enough miles to circumnavigate the globe twice.

Young children might like the **Teddy Bear Eco Village** (daily 10am-6pm,
closed some days Jan-Mar; ¥600), a museum full of bears from all over the
world, the oldest of which dates back to 1903. In the ecology corner there's a
display of how real bears are suffering as a result of environmental destruction.
It's a short walk down the hill from the Folk Village.

Hida-Takayama Museum of Art (🖳 www.htm-museum.co.jp; daily 9am-
5pm, closed some days Dec-Mar; ¥1300) has a large collection of glassware
from the 16th to 20th centuries. It's in a modern building two minutes further
down the road from the Teddy Bear Eco Village.

See also pp179-80 for details of side trips from Takayama.

PRACTICAL INFORMATION
Station guide
The small station gives a hint of the scale of
Takayama itself. The **locker** room (daily
7am-9pm) contains large ¥500 lockers.
Turn right as you go out of the station and
it's on the right.

Tourist information
Hida Takayama TIC (🖳 www.hida.jp; daily
May-Oct 8.30am-6.30pm, Nov-Apr to
5pm) is in a wooden booth outside the station. Staff will help book same-day accommodation. Also worth looking at is 🖳 www
.takayama-guide.com.

TAKAYAMA – MAP KEY

Where to stay
  6 Tensho-ji Youth Hostel
　　天照寺ユースホステル
 10 Takayama City Hotel Four Seasons
　　高山シティホテルフォーシーズン
 11 Hida Hotel Plaza ひだホテルプラザ
 14 Country Hotel Takayama
　　カントリーホテル高山
 17 Hida-Takayama Washington Hotel
　　Plaza 飛騨高山ワシントンホテル
　　プラザ
 19 Best Western Hotel Takayama
　　ベストウエスタンホテル高山
 31 J-Hoppers Hida-Takayama
　　J-Hoppers 飛騨高山
 32 Spa Hotel Alpina
　　スパホテルアルピナ
 33 Super Hotel スーパーホテル高山
 34 Hotel Associa Takayama Resort
　　ホテルアソシア高山リゾート
 35 Minshuku Sosuke 民宿惣助

Where to eat and drink
  5 Alice アリス
  8 Masakatsu Tonkatsu 政かつとんかつ
 16 Black Sea Coffee
　　ブラックシーコーヒー
 18 Myogaya 茗荷舎
 20 Maruaki 丸明
 21 Mieux's Bar ミューズバー
 22 Bistro Mieux ビストロミュー
 23 Ebi Hachi えび八
 24 Hanamizuki ハナミズキ
 25 Le Midi ルミディ
 29 Hida Komeya 飛騨米屋

Other
  1 Takayama Yatai Kaikan
　　高山屋台会館
  2 Yoshijima Heritage House
　　吉島家住宅
  3 Morning Markets 朝市
  4 Takayama Showa Kan 高山昭和館

Takayama
高山

Enako-gawa

Miya-gawa

trailblazer

Yasukawa St

Kokubunji-dori

Streets of
traditional
shops

Takayama
Station

Hirokoji-dori

Takayama
Line

Route 158

Hachikenmachi-dori

← 34, 35, 36
& Shirakawa-go

HONSHU

Other *(key continued from opposite)*

7 Higashiyama 東山
9 Takayama Museum of History and Art
   飛騨高山まちの博物館
12 Poppo Koen (park)
   ポッポ公園
13 Hida-Takayama Bus Center
   高山濃飛バスセンター
15 Hida-Takayama TIC
   飛騨高山観光案内所

26 Taguchi Rent a cycle
   田口レンタサイクル
27 Takayama Jinya 高山陣屋
28 Matsumoto House 松本家住宅
30 Central Post Office 中央郵便局
36 Hida Folk Village; Teddy Bear Eco
   Village; Hida-Takayama Museum of
   Art 飛騨高山民族村；テディベア
   エコビレッジ；飛騨高山美術館

Getting around

Takayama is best negotiated on foot or by **bike**. Try Taguchi Rent a Cycle (daily 8am-6pm; ¥300/1 hour, ¥1300/6 or more hours). Since it is a popular place there are plenty of signs in English so it easy to find your way around.

Sarubobo **Bus** (🖳 www.nouhibus.co .jp; 1/hr; ¥100 per journey, ¥550/day pass with discounted entry to certain places) operates a circular route between the bus centre (to the left of the station) and the main sights; another bus operates to Hida-no-Sato (see p175; 2/hr; ¥200). **Tourist rickshaws** (*jinrikisha*; approx ¥5000 for 30 mins/two people) are an emergency standby.

Festivals

Takayama is known for its two annual **float festivals**, when 300-year-old floats are paraded through the streets. One is in spring (14th-15th Apr) and the other in autumn (9th-10th Oct). Around town, signs in English describe the different floats. One reveals that a float puppet show was prohibited in 1892 because a scene involving an 'exotic woman's dance', during which 'a lion's head suddenly comes out of her mid-section' was deemed immoral. The scene was not reinstated until 1984.

Where to stay

The JR-operated *Hotel Associa Takayama Resort* (🕿 0577-36 0001, 🖳 www.associa. com/tky; from ¥17,000/Tw, ¥28,500/Tr; 10% discount with JR rail pass) is the place to head for first-class luxury in the hills overlooking the town. Expect spacious en suite rooms, two high-quality restaurants and impeccable service. The best reason for staying here is the chance to use the extensive in-house spa and hot-spring facilities. The baths are on two separate floors and are open either to men or women on a daily rotating basis. A free shuttle bus service runs between Takayama station and the hotel (10 mins).

Best Western Hotel Takayama (🕿 0577-37 2000, 🖳 www.bestwestern.co.jp/ english/takayama; ¥8900/S, ¥14,800/D, ¥15,750/Tw, inc a good buffet breakfast) is a five-minute walk east of the station and has rooms and facilities you would expect from an international chain. The standard twins are comfortable if not overly large.

Apart from the clean and modern rooms, an additional selling point at *Takayama City Hotel Four Seasons* (🕿 0577-36 0088, 🖳 www.f-seasons.co.jp; from ¥6900/S, ¥16,200/Tw, breakfast ¥800) is the hot spring-style bath. Also featuring a hot spring-style bath, including outside rotemburo section, is *Spa Hotel Alpina* (🕿 0577-33 0033, 🖳 www.spa-hotel-alpina.com/eng lish; ¥7200/S, ¥13,000/Tw). As with other hotels in Takayama, rates are higher at peak times such as during the festivals.

Hida Takayama Washington Hotel Plaza (🕿 0577-37 0410, 🖳 takayama.wash ington.jp; ¥6700/S, ¥15,000/Tw) is convenient for the rail tracks: it's across the street from the station. Close by is *Country Hotel Takayama* (🕿 0577-35 3900, 🖳 www. country-hotel.jp; ¥5900/S, ¥13,000/D or Tw), a relatively new place with compact single rooms and a couple of twins/doubles. The budget *Super Hotel* (🕿 0577-32 9000, 🖳 www.superhoteljapan.com/en/s-hotels/ hidatakayama; ¥5480/S, ¥7980/Tw) chain has a conveniently located branch of a more subdued appearance than usual.

Also worth considering is *Hida Hotel Plaza* (🕿 0577-33 4600, 🖳 www.hida-hotel plaza.co.jp; ¥6930/S, ¥16,110/D or Tw). It has two coin-operated computers in the lobby (¥100 for 10 mins).

The best ryokan in Takayama can set you back up to ¥25,000 (inc two meals) but minshuku are a much more affordable option. *Minshuku Sosuke* (🕿 0577-32 0818, 🖳 www.irori-sosuke.com; ¥5040pp room only, breakfast ¥735, dinner from ¥2000; at festival/holiday periods from ¥8925 half-board), a short walk behind the station, is a homely 13-room minshuku.

Centrally located and converted from a former ryokan is *J-Hoppers Hida-Takayama* backpackers' hostel (🕿 0577-32 3278, 🖳 takayama.j-hoppers.com; dorm beds from ¥2500, en suite twins, triples and quads ¥3200-3800). Daily bicycle rental is available for ¥500.

Possibly the most atmospheric, cheap place to stay is the 95-bed *Tensho-ji Youth*

Hostel (☎ 0577-32 6345, 🖵 www.tenshoji. jp; dorm bed ¥3000, private room ¥4000, breakfast ¥630). Lights go out at 10pm in the dorms. Cycles can be rented here for ¥100/hour and a map of places to eat at around the temple area is available from the front desk. The hostel is 20 minutes' walk east from the station across the Miya-gawa and Enaka-gawa rivers, at Tensho-ji in Higashiyama.

Where to eat and drink

Masakatsu Tonkatsu (Wed-Mon 11am-2pm & 5-8pm), on Yasugawa-dori, is a small place that serves large portions of melt-in-the-mouth tonkatsu (sets from ¥980). Almost directly opposite is *Alice* (Thur-Tue 11am-2pm & 4.30-8pm), also a wedding hall, which serves a variety of set meals from ¥1280. The cheapest deals are the weekday lunch menus (Western or *ten-don* – tempura on rice) for ¥890; the pasta set menu is ¥880.

Restaurants combining Hida beef and French cuisine are popular in Takayama. At *Le Midi* (🖵 www.le-midi.jp; Mon-Wed & Fri 11.30am-3pm & 6-9.30pm, Sat-Sun 11.30am-3.30pm & 5-9.30pm), lunch ranges from the 'Simple' at ¥1800 to the 'Extravagant and Gratifying' at ¥3800. Or try the potato and *nori* (seaweed) soup. Dinner is from ¥2800.

Another choice is *Bistro Mieux* (Thur-Tue 11.30am-1.30pm & 5-9.30pm), a five-minute walk from the station along Kokubunji St. Creative French food is presented with flair and there's a good selection of wines. The dinner course menu is

from ¥4305 but the ¥1350 French lunch is excellent value.

If that sounds a bit pricey, head across the street to the newer *Mieux's Bar* (Thur-Tue 11.30am-2pm & 5-11pm), which has a cheaper menu including a tasty 'plate lunch' for ¥1050. Credit cards are not accepted.

Vegetarians will want to make a bee-line for *Myogaya* (Wed-Sun 8am-4pm, 5-7pm), an organic restaurant serving brown rice and curries from ¥950.

Hida Komeya specialises in Hida beef and *hoba miso*, vegetables cooked with miso on a small stove (meals from ¥2000). *Maruaki*, identified by its cow in a glass case outside, also specialises in Hida beef and has both a restaurant (daily 11am-9pm) and shop where you can see some very marbled meat at up to ¥2000 for 100 grams.

For an economical taste of Hida beef, *Hanamizuki* offers burgers from ¥680, and there is also a 'big secret (*himitsu*) parfait', potentially shareable, at ¥1500.

Ebi Hachi (Thur-Tue 5-10pm) serves tasty tempura freshly produced by the friendly owner who takes pride in the number of international customers, as indicated by a map behind the counter. Tempura sets range from ¥1600 and some feature tempura ice-cream, which can also be ordered separately.

For a quick caffeine fix, try *Black Sea Coffee* (daily 11.30am-6pm), across the street from the station. It is also a bar in the evening, until midnight. Look for the sign written in English.

Side trip to Shirakawa-go

Shirakawa-go (🖵 shirakawa-go.org/english), a World Heritage Site, is known for its *gassho zukuri* (constructed like 'hands in prayer') houses. These have steep thatched roofs to help protect them from the heavy snowfall in this area. Their location also optimises wind resistance and sunlight. Some of the houses are over 250 years old.

With the opening of the final section (Hida-Kiyomi to Shirakawa-go) of the Tokai-Hokuriku Expressway, Shirakawa-go has become much more accessible from Takayama. Seven buses a day (¥2400/4500 one-way/round trip; 50 mins) leave from stop No 4 at the bus centre next to Takayama station, and there are also round-trip sightseeing services (2/day; ¥6500). The latter include a visit to **Gokayama** (Ainokura and Suganuma villages), the other World

Heritage Site with these kinds of houses, over the border in Toyama Prefecture. You can also reach Shirakawa-go from Kanazawa (see p184), terminus of some Takayama buses, and on other services from Takaoka.

The bus stop in Shirakawa is located in **Ogimachi village** near the main information centre (daily 9am-5pm). Near here is **Gassho Zukuri Minka-en** (Apr-Sep & Oct daily 8.30am-5pm, Aug daily 8.30am-5.30pm, Dec-Mar Fri-Wed 9am-4pm; ¥500), a collection of buildings, some of which were rebuilt after being relocated from a more remote part of Shirakawa, Kazura, which its inhabitants abandoned in the 1960s. The buildings contain artefacts illustrating life in the area in the past and one is a rest place where visitors can try *zenzai* (red bean soup) for ¥200.

Across a sturdy suspension bridge is the main street of Shirakawa-go. Many of its houses are now cafés, minshuku or souvenir shops, and **Kanda, Nagase and Wada houses** (9am-5pm; ¥300 each) are open to the public. You can rent bicycles (¥400/hour, ¥1100/day) from near the Kanda and Nagase houses. **Doburoku Festival Museum** (daily Apr-Nov 9am-7pm; ¥300), next to Shirakawa Hachiman Shrine, showcases the festival associated with the local white unrefined sake. A fairly steep walk after passing Wada House brings you to an observatory and a great panoramic view of the village.

KANAZAWA

Though somewhat isolated on the Japan Sea coast, the variety of sights in Kanazawa more than repays the effort of the journey.

In 1580 the Maedas, the second largest clan in feudal-era Japan, settled here. Peace and stability followed and Kanazawa quickly became a prosperous centre for the silk and gold-lacquer industries. As its citizens became wealthy, Kanazawa's arts and culture scene began to flourish. Even today Kanazawa has a reputation for its patronage of 'high-class' arts such as Noh and the tea ceremony.

The city is also curiously proud of another claim to fame: it is allegedly one of the wettest places in the country, with an average of 178 rainy days per year. A local proverb translates as 'Even if you forget your packed lunch, don't forget your umbrella'.

Apart from the much-hyped Kenrokuen garden there are other surprises, such as well-preserved geisha and samurai districts and a working Noh theatre. The city also functions as a gateway to the Noto Peninsula, a knuckle of land that juts out into the Japan Sea north of the city. And just for good measure, a short train ride away is the intriguing UFO town of Hakui (see p184).

What to see and do

The first major stop on the Loop Bus (see p183) is at **Omi-cho**, a daily indoor market with around 170 stalls selling fresh fish, fruit and vegetables. A market is said to have existed here for more than 280 years.

Kenrokuen and around Everyone visits Kanazawa to see **Kenrokuen** (🖳 www.pref.ishikawa.jp/siro-niwa/kenrokuen; Mar to mid Oct daily 7am-6pm, mid Oct to Feb 8am-5pm; ¥300), rated as one of the top three gardens in Japan. Inside, professional photographers wait around for the tour groups but if you can find some space away from the crowds, a couple of hours can easily be spent wandering round the grounds. Constructed 200 years ago as the garden for Kanazawa Castle, Kenrokuen is spread over 11.4 hectares and contains about 12,000 trees. The number six (*roku*) in the garden's name refers to the six attributes of a perfect garden: vastness, seclusion, careful arrangement, antiquity, water and panoramic views. Water features in particular are everywhere, including the first fountain ever placed in a Japanese garden.

Apart from **Ishikawa-mon gate** most of the buildings in **Kanazawa Castle Park** burnt down but some have been reconstructed and the renovation of Ishikawa-mon Gate is due to be completed in 2013. Kenrokuen and Ishikawa-mon gate are the main sights here but if you have time you may like to explore the grounds of Kanazawa Castle Park (daily Mar-Oct 7am-6pm, Oct-Feb 8am-5pm; free). To reach this area take the Loop Bus (see p183) to Stop 9. Maps are available at the entrance. Kanazawa Goodwill Guide Network (🖳 kggn.sakura. ne.jp) has an information booth (Apr-Nov daily 9.30am-3.30pm) by Ishikawa-mon gate and guides will take you around the park and Kenrokuen for free.

Close to Kenrokuen is **Ishikawa Prefectural Museum of Art** (🖳 ishibi. pref.ishikawa.jp/english; daily 9.30am-5pm; ¥350), full of cosmetics boxes, decorated plates, hanging scrolls and *shoji* screens, and well worth a visit. Across the street is **Ishikawa Prefectural Nogakudo** (Noh Theatre; Tue-Sun 9am-4.30pm; free) Performances (some free) are held throughout the year. In July and August performances are held on Saturday evening. If there are no performances or rehearsals it's possible to take a look inside.

A short walk from Kenrokuen is **Kanazawa 21st Century Museum of Contemporary Art** (🖳 www.kanazawa21.jp; Mon-Thur & Sun 10am-6pm, Fri & Sat 10am-8pm, closed occasionally to hang new exhibitions; ¥350), opened in 2004 and billed as the 'world's most advanced art museum'. The design of the building – gleaming white, circular and set in its own landscaped gardens – threatens to overshadow its permanent collection, an eclectic mix of Japanese and foreign contemporary art. There's also a well-stocked contemporary art library, and one of Kanazawa's swankiest **cafés** (Tue-Sun 10am-8pm), just to the right of the main entrance.

Higashi-yama district Across Asano-gawa is Higashi-chaya, a former **geisha quarter**, where you'll find a few streets lined with old geisha houses, instantly recognisable by their wooden latticed windows. Tea and coffee shops are now open in some of the houses but the area still retains a traditional charm and in the early evening there's the chance of spotting a geisha.

More than 90% of Japan's gold leaf is produced in Kanazawa and it's in this area that you'll find **Sakuda Gold and Silver Leaf Shop** (🖳 www.goldleaf-sakuda.jp; daily 9am-6pm), where the most expensive item for sale is a pair of gold-leaf screens for ¥3 million. At the other end of the scale are gold-leaf boiled sweets and telephone cards, but there's no charge at all for using the gold and platinum toilets on the 2nd floor.

A JR bus (rail passes are accepted) leaves from the JR bus stop outside Kanazawa station's east exit; get off just after crossing Asano-gawa. If you don't have a rail pass take the Loop bus and get off at stop 6.

Teramachi district Temple lovers should head south of Sai-gawa to the Teramachi district. The most famous is **Myoryu-ji**, better known as **Ninja-dera** (reservations required for the compulsory tour: call ☎ 076-241 0888; Mar-Oct daily 9am-4.30pm, Nov-Feb to 4pm; ¥800). A defensive stronghold as well as a temple, its rooms contain trick doors, false exits, secret tunnels and pits – no wonder you have to go on a guided tour (in Japanese only, so ask at the tourist office inside Kanazawa station for an English translation). To reach the temple area, get off the Flat Bus (see opposite; Nagamachi route) at Stop 24.

If you're in Teramachi at 6pm on a Saturday, listen out for the bells of six temples ringing together – rated as one of the '100 best soundscapes in Japan'.

Nagamachi district It's a pleasant surprise to stumble upon Nagamachi – an area of narrow, cobbled streets with a few preserved **samurai houses** – just a few minutes' walk west of the busy Katamachi shopping district. The **Nomura family's house** (🖳 www.nomurake.com; Apr-Sep daily 8.30am-5.30pm; Oct-Mar to 4.30pm; ¥500 or ¥800 with tea) contains a shrine, samurai armour and a small but immaculate Japanese garden. To reach the house, get off the Flat Bus (see opposite; Nagamachi route) at Stop 3.

Station area Ishikawa Prefectural Concert Hall (Ongakudo; 🖳 www. ongakudo.jp/english) is the large modern building to your right as you leave the station's east exit, next to the ANA Hotel. It's the home of Kanazawa Orchestra Ensemble but also attracts orchestras from across Japan and abroad. The main hall seats 1500 and is a tremendous concert space. Ask for a performance schedule at the tourist information centre (see opposite) or check the website – with luck there will be something on while you're in town. There's a run-of-the-mill café, *Café Concerto*, on the 2nd floor.

Kanazawa Yasue Gold Leaf Museum (☎ 076-233 1502, 🖳 www. kanazawa-museum.jp/kinpaku; daily except last 2-3 days of month in Feb/May/ Aug/Nov, 9.30am-5pm; ¥300) is a hidden gem, just around the corner from Manten Hotel. The first room describes the process of making gold leaf. All the signs are in Japanese – but don't worry, a member of staff will appear and start to tell you all about the display in English (reading from a manual!). After this you'll be served gold-leaf tea (including edible slivers of gold leaf) and biscuits. Among the many highlights of the upstairs exhibition are the gold-leaf screens and exquisite gold-leaf embroidered kimono. There's also a small shop selling gold-leaf products, including a cream which is said to do wonders for the skin.

See also p184 for details of side trips from Kanazawa.

PRACTICAL INFORMATION
Station guide
There are **lockers** (all sizes) in various locations, including in the corridors off the main concourse.

The east exit – with its enormous steel and glass dome – has become a symbolic gateway to the city. The dome is supposed to keep new arrivals from getting wet in

notoriously rainy Kanazawa. Take the east exit for the bus terminal and city centre.

Kanazawa will be the terminus for the Hokuriku shinkansen (see box p144).

Tourist information
The **tourist information centre** (🖳 www4. city.kanazawa.lg.jp, 🖳 www.kanazawa-tourism.com; daily 9am-7pm) is inside a

shopping mall to the left of the station concourse as you face the main (east) exit. At the far end of the mall you'll find a small branch **post office** with **ATM**.

Getting around

The city centre is a 10-minute bus ride from the station. As its name suggests, **Kanazawa Loop Bus** (5/hr; ¥200/ride or ¥500 for a one-day pass, purchased from the driver) does a circular tour of the main city sights. **Kanazawa Flat Bus** (4/hr, ¥100/ride) operates on four routes. Both services run daily (8.30am-6pm) and the buses leave from stops outside the east exit of the station.

Rent-a-Cycle (daily 8am-8.30pm; ¥800/4hrs) is along the side of the station building, to the left as you take the station's west exit.

Festivals

Hyakumangoku Festival takes place over three days every year around the first Saturday in June. The event celebrates the arrival of Lord Maeda into the city and begins at dusk with a procession of floating lanterns down Asano-gawa. Public tea ceremonies are also held in Kenrokuen, but the highlight of the day is a parade through the streets which mixes acrobatics, horse-riding, period costume and even a 'Miss Hyakumangoku' beauty contest.

Where to stay

Toyoko Inn (🖳 www.toyoko-inn.com) has two branches here: *Kanazawa Eki Higashi-guchi* (☎ 076-224 1045; ¥4980/S, ¥5980/D or Tw inc breakfast, and curry rice supper on weekdays) is very convenient for the station. An older branch, *Kanazawa Kenrokuen Korinbo* (☎ 076-232-1045; ¥4980/S, ¥5980/D or Tw inc breakfast) is in the Korinbo district, closer to the shopping, restaurants and bars.

R&B Hotel Kanazawa Eki Nishi-guchi (☎ 076-224 8080, 🖳 kanazawa.randb.jp; ¥4200-7100/S inc breakfast) is a modern, single-room-only place. Five to ten minutes on foot from the station's west exit, but it's a bit difficult to spot as there are no large signs on the roof. A three-minute walk from the station's west exit is

Kanazawa Manten Hotel (☎ 076-265 0100, 🖳 www.manten-hotel.com; ¥6800/S, ¥12,600/Tw). The rooms are small but well furnished; all rooms feature semi-double beds. *APA Hotel Kanazawa Eki-mae* (☎ 076-231 8111, 🖳 www.apahotel.com; from ¥8000/S, ¥11,000/D or Tw), right outside the west exit, boasts that it is the closest hotel to the JR ticket barrier – it beats even Manten Hotel, only a stone's throw from the station, for location. It's an upmarket place with reasonable rooms and an 'Eki Spa Sauna' (daily 6am-midnight; ¥1000/3 hours, ¥2000/day), a hot spring on the 2nd floor which is free to hotel guests. There's also a branch of Seattle's Best Coffee on the ground floor.

For top-class luxury, choose **Hotel Nikko Kanazawa** (☎ 076-234 1111, 🖳 www .hnkanazawa.co.jp; from ¥11,600/S, ¥16,000/D or Tw). It's outside the station's east exit and can hardly be beaten for its friendly staff and service.

Less than a five-minute walk east of the east exit is *Kanazawa Central Hotel* (☎ 076-263 5311, 🖳 www.centralh.co.jp/eng lish; ¥5000-7140/S, ¥7000-13,650/Tw; best rates online), a good, standard business hotel with clean, comfortable rooms.

If you prefer Japanese-style accommodation, a great choice is *Ryokan Murataya* (☎ 076-263 0455, 🖳 www. murataya-ryokan.com/e; ¥4700/S, ¥9000/ Tw, ¥12,600-13,500/Tr; breakfast ¥500-800). This traditional inn is just set back from the Katamachi district. Some of the rooms overlook a small garden and all are simply decorated with Japanese paper screens and hanging scrolls.

Where to eat and drink

A good place to stop for lunch is one of the sushi restaurants inside **Omi-cho market** as the fish is guaranteed to be fresh.

Porte Kanazawa, a 30-storey building, has several traditional Japanese restaurants as well as a branch of *Saizeriya* (daily 11am-2am), which has an extensive menu of Western-style dishes (pasta from ¥399).

Shiki at APA Hotel (see Where to stay) serves a buffet (daily 6.30-10pm; ¥1365, or ¥1200 if booked ahead) with a mixture of

Japanese and Western dishes. *Akane-doki* (Mon-Thur 5pm-2am, Fri & Sat to 3am, Sun to midnight), on the 2nd & 3rd Floor of **Ito Building**, serves sashimi (¥1380), sushi, steak (¥950) and over a hundred drinks from its English menu.

Plenty of restaurants line the streets of the **Katamachi** shopping district. *Ninnikuya* (daily 5pm to midnight) adds garlic to practically all its dishes and is very busy at weekends.

Side trips by rail from Kanazawa

The JR Nanao line heads north towards the **Noto Peninsula** (Noto-hanto). An intriguing place to visit lies 40km (and 40 mins) along the line at **Hakui** a self-proclaimed 'UFO town'. **Cosmo Isle Hakui** (🖳 www.city.hakui.ishikawa. jp/cosmo/index_e.html; Wed-Mon 9am-5pm; ¥350 admission, ¥500 for Cosmo (Dome) Theater) is an enormous dome containing a UFO museum. On display are assorted space craft, astronaut suits and genuine moon dust. A few of the exhibits (all signed in English), including the Soviet Union's Vostok capsule and a NASA space suit with 24-carat gold helmet, are real. Video booths show interviews with sober and eccentric professors and scientists connected with SETI (Search for Extra Terrestrial Intelligence) and there's also an extensive UFO database. Cosmo Isle Hakui is 10 minutes' walk north of Hakui station's east exit. It's easy to spot as it's the only building with a 26m American rocket parked outside. Cycles (¥300/2 hours, ¥1000/24 hours) can be rented from the JR ticket office at the station.

Nohi Bus (3/day; ¥1800/¥3200 one way/round trip; seat reservations essential) operates services to **Shirakawa-go** (see pp179-80) from outside Kanazawa Station's east exit.

KANAZAWA – MAP KEY

Where to stay

2 R&B Hotel Kanazawa Eki Nishi-guchi
  R&Bホテル金沢駅西口
3 Kanazawa Manten Hotel
  金沢マンテンホテル
4 Kanazawa Central Hotel
  金沢セントラルホテル
6 APA Hotel Kanazawa Eki-mae
  アパホテル金沢駅前
9 Hotel Nikko Kanazawa
  ホテル日航金沢
10 Toyoko Inn Kanazawa Eki Higashi-guchi 東横イン 金沢駅東口
19 Toyoko Inn Kanazawa Kenrokuen Korinbo 東横イン 金沢香林坊
21 Ryokan Murataya 旅館村田屋

Where to eat and drink

6 Shiki 四季
7 Café Concerto カフェコンチェルト
8 Akane-doki 茜どき
9 Saizeriya (Porte Kanazawa)
  サイゼリヤは (ポルテ金沢)
11 Omi-cho Market 近江町市場
22 Ninnikuya にんにくや

Other

1 Kanazawa Yasue Gold Leaf Museum
  金沢市立安江金箔工芸館
5 Rent-a-Cycle レンタサイクル
7 Ishikawa Prefectural Concert Hall
  石川県立音楽堂
11 Omi-cho Market 近江町市場
12 Sakuda Gold and Silver Leaf Shop, Higashi-chaya 株式会社金銀箔工芸
  さくだ本社本店, 東茶屋街
13 Kanazawa Castle Park & Ishikawa-mon gate 金沢城公園 & 石川門
14 Kenrokuen 兼六園
15 Ishikawa Prefectural Noh Theater
  石川県立能楽堂
16 Ishikawa Prefectural Museum of Art
  石川県立美術館
17 Kanazawa 21st Century Museum of Contemporary Art 金沢21世紀美術館
18 Central Post Office 中央郵便局
20 Nomura Family House
  武家屋敷野村家
23 Myoryu-ji (Ninja-dera) 妙立寺

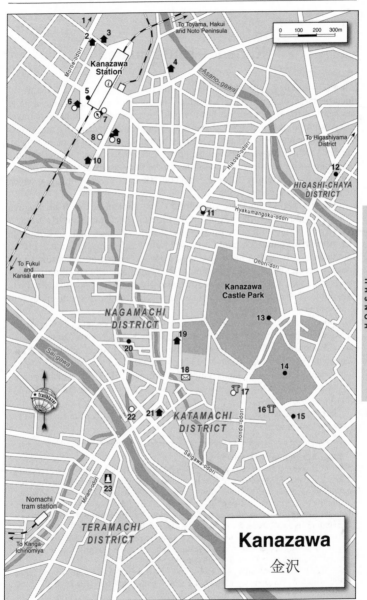

Kanazawa

金沢

Kansai – route guides

All roads lead to Kyoto, at least that's what most tourist brochures and travel documentaries on Japan let you assume. The ancient capital does indeed lie at the heart of the Kansai region but it would be a shame to restrict your travel solely to the well-beaten track. Japan's even more ancient capital, Nara, is less than an hour away by rail and it's easily worth staying a night or two there. Further south, the landscape becomes more rural, the crowds thin out and the views are worth seeking out. Kansai has one of the most extensive networks of rail lines in the country (operated by both JR and private railways), which means it's easy to go exploring.

The first part of this route guide follows the shinkansen line **from Nagoya to Osaka** via Kyoto – there is relatively little to see en route but it's useful if you're in a hurry. With more time, consider a much longer route to Kyoto **via the rural Kii Peninsula**, easily accessed from Nagoya but very much off the traditional tourist trail. Limited expresses operate around the peninsula so the journey needn't be too time-consuming; the countryside and coastline certainly repay the effort. Taking this longer route also gives you the opportunity to go to **Ise**, home of the Grand Shrine and spiritual centre of Japan's indigenous religion, Shinto.

Another spiritual centre, the mountain retreat of **Koya-san**, offers a wholly unexpected change of pace. It can be accessed from Kyoto, Nara or Osaka, and also from Wakayama as part of a longer journey around the Kii Peninsula. The final stage whichever way you come is a hair-raising cable car (ropeway) journey.

If you've arrived in Japan without a rail pass, JR West, which operates services throughout the Kansai area, sells regional passes over the counter. For details, see box below.

For up-to-date information on events throughout the Kansai region, check 🖥 www.kansai.gr.jp.

⛩ Alternative Kansai rail pass

If you're a tourist or Japanese national who lives abroad and don't have a Japan Rail Pass, and are not interested in any of the regional rail passes sold by JR West for the Kansai region (see p14), it's worth considering the **Kansai Thru Pass** (🖥 www.surutto.com). This pass (**2-day**/¥3800, **3-day**/¥5000) gives you unlimited access to most private railways (services other than JR), subways and buses throughout Kansai, including Osaka, Kobe, Kyoto, Nara and Koya-san. It can also be used for the journey from Kansai International Airport to Osaka on the private Nankai railway (but you have to pay a supplement to ride Nankai's 'rapi:t' express service). The ticket also offers discounts at 350 tourist facilities in the region.

The pass can be bought at Kansai Airport, Kyoto Station Bus Information Center and visitor information centres in Osaka. Check the website for other possibilities.

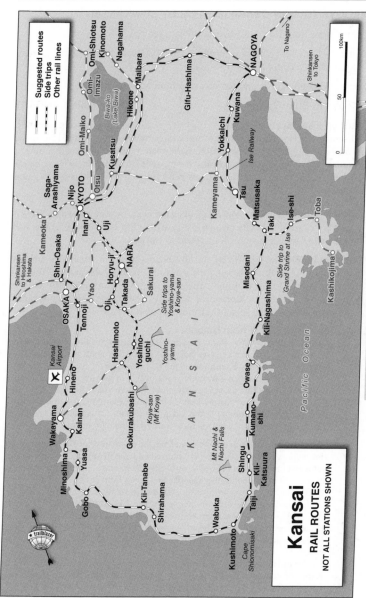

NAGOYA TO SHIN-OSAKA (OSAKA) BY SHINKANSEN

For the route from Tokyo to Nagoya (366km) see pp126-37.

Distances from Tokyo. Fastest journey time on a Hikari to Shin-Osaka: (from Tokyo) 3 hours; (from Nagoya) 55 mins.

Some Hikari and all Nozomi run non-stop from Nagoya to Kyoto.

Nagoya to Shin-Osaka

[Map 9; Table 3, pp456-7]

Nagoya (366km)

[see pp155-63]

All shinkansen stop here. Look out for the huge **Sanyo Solar Ark** (315m wide, 31.6-37.1m high, 13.7m deep) on the right soon after leaving Nagoya. It is a stunning way of making a functional device (a source of solar power) into a work of art. There are 5046 solar panels generating up to 530,000kw/h of green electricity.

Gifu-Hashima (396km) Only Kodama stop here. Despite its name, this station is not close to Gifu city (see pp150-1) at all. Gifu is on the Takayama line on the route from Toyama (or Kanazawa) to Nagoya.

Maibara (446km) Some Hikari and all Kodama stop here. Maibara is a major rail junction: in addition to being a stop on the Tokaido shinkansen, Tokaido mainline trains (Tokyo to Kobe), Biwa-ko line (Maibara to Kyoto) and the Shirasagi LEX (8/day to Kanazawa) call here. The station has some **lockers**, vending machines and a soba bar (*kitsune soba/udon* ¥350).

Side trips by rail from Maibara

On SL Kita-Biwako For a few days each year, typically around Golden Week, the SL Kita-Biwako (see box p73) runs 22km north along Lake Biwa between Maibara and **Kinomoto** on the Hokuriku line.

A ride on this steam locomotive is enjoyable in its own right, but it's also worth stopping along the way at **Nagahama** where you'll find the oldest station building in Japan, dating back to the time when goods were transferred from the Pacific (Tsuruga) to the Japan Sea (Kobe) via Nagahama and Otsu. The original station is three minutes' walk from the current one.

To Hikone Maibara is one stop east from the castle town of Hikone (Biwa-ko line; approx 6 trains/hour; 5 mins), situated on Lake Biwa, Japan's largest lake. A **tourist information office** (🖳 www.city.hikone.shiga.jp; daily 9am-6pm) is to your left at the foot of the stairs leading down from Hikone station.

Hikone is known for its castle, **Hikone-jo** (daily 8.30am-5pm; ¥600 inc garden), a 10-minute walk up the main street, Ekimae Oshiro-dori, from the station. The castle is not quite as dramatic as the one further down the line at Himeji (see pp228-9) but it benefits from the superb natural backdrop of Lake Biwa. **Genkyu-en**, a Japanese garden dating back to 1677, is at the foot of the castle.

From Hikone either backtrack to Maibara and pick up the shinkansen to Kyoto or continue directly along the Tokaido line from Hikone station (the fastest trains take 50 minutes to Kyoto).

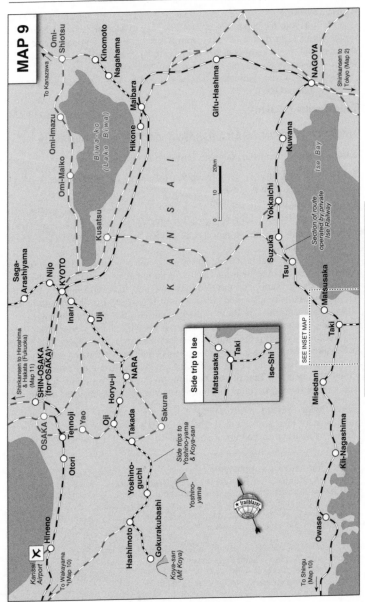

MAP 9

To Karazawa

Omi-Shiotsu

Kinomoto

Nagahama

Omi-Imazu

Maibara

Omi-Maiko

Hikone

Biwa-ko
(Lake Biwa)

Gifu-Hashima

NAGOYA

Shinkansen to Tokyo (Map 2)

Kusatsu

K A N S A I

Kuwana

Ise Bay

Saga-Arashiyama

Nijo

KYOTO

Yokkaichi

Section of route operated by private Ise Railway

0 10 20km

Inari

Uji

Suzuka

Tsu

Shinkansen to Hiroshima & Hakata (Fukuoka) (Map 11)

SHIN-OSAKA
(for OSAKA)

NARA

Horyu-ji

Sakurai

Matsusaka

Taki

SEE INSET MAP

OSAKA

Tennoji

Yao

Oji

Takada

Misedani

Otori

Yoshino-guchi

Side trips to Yoshino-yama & Koya-san

Kii-Nagashima

Side trip to Ise

Matsusaka

Taki

Ise-Shi

Hineno

Kansai Airport

To Wakayama (Map 10)

Hashimoto

Gokurakubashi

Yoshino-yama

★ trailblazer

Koya-san (Mt Koya)

Owase

To Shingu (Map 10)

HONSHU

Kyoto (514km) [see pp198-212]

Change in Kyoto for **Nara** (see pp215-22). Nara is accessible by JR Nara line rapid service (2/hr during the day) from Kyoto station. If you don't have a JR rail pass you may like to consider the private Kintetsu Railway line's services (from its tracks in Kyoto station) to Kintetsu-Nara station.

Look out for the shinkansen 'car park' (*torikai* yard) on the right between Kyoto and Shin-Osaka.

Shin-Osaka (553km) [Osaka – see pp113-23]

NAGOYA TO SHIN-OSAKA (OSAKA) VIA THE KII PENINSULA

Fastest journey time from Nagoya via Shingu to Osaka: 7 hours.

Nagoya to Shingu [Map 9, p189; Map 10, p195; Table 9, p461]

Distances by JR from Nagoya.

Nagoya (0km) [see pp155-63]

From Nagoya board a Wide-View Nanki LEX or the slower Mie 'rapid' train heading towards Tsu and Shingu. The Nanki has lovely big windows and raised seats with foot rests.

If planning to visit the Grand Shrine at Ise (see opposite) it's best to take the Mie train; this is not as luxurious as the Nanki but does run direct from Nagoya to Ise. Both the Nanki and the Mie have reserved and non-reserved cars. The private Ise Railway also runs services from Nagoya to Ise; this would be the most convenient route for those without a rail pass. See also box below.

The journey as far as **Kuwana** (24km) is not particularly scenic. After leaving **Yokkaichi (37km)** the industrial landscape starts to clear. Some trains stop at **Suzuka (48km)**. Change here for Suzuka Circuit Ino station and access to one of the oldest tracks on the Formula One circuit and location of the Japanese Grand Prix in 2012. **Tsu (66km)** has little worth making a stop for but the ride starts to get more interesting as you can see hills in the distance on the right.

Matsusaka (85km) Matsusaka is known for its locally bred cows and in particular for their unusual diet, which is supposed to make them all the more flavoursome when served up in strips on the table. 'If a cow should lose her

---

⛩ Ise Railway supplement

A small section of the track between Nagoya and Tsu is owned by Ise Railway. If you have bought a ticket, the fare will include the supplement for the Ise section between Kawarada and Tsu. Rail-pass holders are supposed to pay the conductor on board the train. If travelling on the Nanki LEX this means paying both the standard fare (¥490) and limited express fare (¥310) just for that section (whatever your total journey is).

On the Mie rapid train, only the standard charge (¥490) has to be paid. You could get away without paying the supplement if you are in a non-reserved seat and if the conductor checks tickets only when the train has left Tsu, since there is no way of telling from the rail pass where you joined the train.

appetite', informs a local leaflet, 'she is given beer to drink as a tonic to activate her stomach, along with a gentle, full-body massage. Every cow receives meticulous care'. Some sushi shops in Matsusaka even do a brisk sale in beef sushi, though in restaurants the most popular dish is either steak or *shabu-shabu*.

A guide map to Matsusaka is available from the **tourist information office** (daily 9am-6pm), in the glass building next to the police box (*koban*), on the right as you leave the station.

The main sights are in or around the castle ruins of **Matsusaka Park**, a 10- to 15-minute walk north-east of the station. Only a few stone walls are left of Matsusaka Castle, so head through the park instead and go out the back to find a preserved street with a number of old houses.

A few of the residents on this street are descendants of the samurai families who once lived in the same buildings. The **Castle Guardman's House** is open to the public (Tue-Sun 10am-4pm; free). It's first on the right as you walk down the street from the park.

To try some of Matsusaka's famous beef, head up the main road that runs straight ahead from the station. On the corner at the first set of traffic lights, and on the right, is *Kameya* (daily 11am-8pm; set lunch 11am-12.30pm), a casual restaurant that serves up good-value set meals, including shabu-shabu. The cheapest meal with beef is a truly delicious *gyudon* (¥2100); the most expensive steak costs ¥18,000. The entrance is next to a butcher's counter, so you can guarantee that the meat is fresh.

Taki (93km) In the Edo Period, Taki was a stop along the pilgrim path to Ise Grand Shrine. Today it is home to Sharp's largest Liquid Crystal Display factory.

▲ Taki is a tiny station but an important rail junction. The track divides here. The route described follows the Kisei line south towards Shingu and the Kii Peninsula (see p193).

However, if you took the Nanki LEX from Nagoya but are planning to do the side trip to visit the Grand Shrine at Ise change to the Sangu line here. This goes to **Ise-shi** (12 mins by Mie rapid train approx 1/hr, 20 mins by local train also approx 1/hr).

Beyond Ise-shi, JR trains run as far as **Toba**, famous for Mikimoto pearls, but the only way of moving on from Ise to continue the rail route described below is to backtrack to Taki.

Side trip to the Grand Shrine at Ise

Ise Grand Shrine (Ise Jingu; 🖳 www.isejingu.or.jp; daily dawn to dusk; free) is the centre of Japan's indigenous religion, Shinto. The town receives over six million visitors annually, many of whom are making a once-in-a-lifetime pilgrimage to the place considered to be the spiritual home of the Japanese.

The complex comprises Outer and Inner shrines, as well as Uji Bridge, which you have to cross to reach the Inner Shrine. One of the main features of Ise Jingu is that the main shrines are completely rebuilt (Shikinen Sengu) every 20 years; ceremonies for the 62nd rebuilding started in 2012 and the whole process will be completed in autumn 2013.

To celebrate the rebuilding a new **information centre** (Sengu-kan; daily 9am-4.30pm; ¥300) is being built and this will in effect become the new entrance to the shrine. The notes below are based on the layout of the shrine in 2012 but may change when the new buildings are complete so check in advance.

A visit to the shrine is necessarily in two parts, since the Outer and Inner shrines are several kilometres apart. You can either take bus No 51 or 55 (10 mins; ¥410) between the two, or hop on a CAN bus (Mie Transit Bus; 🖳 tourismmiejapan.com/travel/michikusa.html; ¥1000/1600 1-/2-day pass), which shuttles between the station, the shrines, Toba (see p191) and other sights in the area. The pass also gives discounts at sights. Near the entrance to the Outer Shrine, and opposite the stop for buses going to the Inner Shrine, is **Ise City TIC** (🖳 www.ise-kanko.jp; daily 9am-5.30pm), which has guide maps and a useful explanatory leaflet about the shrines.

The Outer Shrine, or **Geku**, is an eight-minute walk from JR Ise-shi station. Turn right as you go out of the JR side of Ise station and take the main road that heads straight up until you reach the entrance to the shrine. Devoid of gaudy decorations, and lacking the gold and red colours you find at Buddhist temples, the shrine is simple to the point of austerity.

From Geku, retrace your steps to the entrance, where you can board a bus or make use of the fleet of taxis that wait to take pilgrims and visitors on to the **Naiku**, the Inner Shrine. The sun goddess Amaterasu Omikami, the Imperial family's ancestral *kami* (deity), is enshrined here. A sacred mirror, symbol of the kami, is carefully wrapped up and hidden away in the inner sanctuary and never shown in public. Indeed, there's not a great deal to see at all, since the interior of both shrines is off limits.

To compensate for the lack of 'sights' at the shrines, it's worth visiting at least one of the three museums a short bus ride from the Inner Shrine; all three open Tue-Sun 9am-4.30pm and a combination ticket costs ¥700. The obvious choice is **Jingu Chokokan** (History Museum; ¥300). From the Inner Shrine, take bus No 51 (¥280) that goes to Uji-Yamada and Ise-shi stations via the Chokokan Museum. It's a Meiji-era building that houses a large-scale model of the Inner Shrine, allowing you to see all around the compound. This bird's eye view makes you realise how little of the shrine you see for real when standing at the outer gate. Also on display are some elaborate festival costumes, a selection of *kagura* masks, sacred treasures offered to the deities on the occasion of previous shrine renewals, and a few random paintings of Corsica.

From the Chokokan, go down a flight of steps, and across the road to find **Jingu Bijutsukan** (Museum of Fine Arts; ¥500), opened in 1993 to commemorate the rebuilding of the shrine in that year. Inside are works of art offered to the shrine by Japanese artists; fortunately, instead of hiding them away in the Inner Shrine, they have been put on public display.

Finally, back across on the other side of the road is **Jingu Nogyokan** (Agriculture Museum; ¥300). This is less interesting but does contain a photo of the current Emperor in wellington boots, getting down to a bit of manual labour in a field. After visiting the museums you can pick up the bus at the Chokokan stop and head back either to Ise-shi or Uji-Yamada stations.

A good overnight choice is *Pearl Pier Hotel* (☎ 0596-26 1111, 🖳 www. pearlpier.com; ¥7875-8400/S, ¥15,750/D, ¥16,800/Tw), a five-minute walk behind JR Ise station. The hotel is easily recognisable – it's the building with a steel lifeboat hanging off one side – and has a bakery/café called *Piccolo*

(7am-5.30pm), a more upscale Italian restaurant, *Il Mare* (5-9.30pm), and a Japanese restaurant, *Umi* (5-9.30pm).

When leaving Taki, sit on the left side of the train for the best views of the small mountain ranges and rivers, as well as the rice fields and then tea fields, though the train sometimes dives into a tunnel. Some trains stop at **Misedani (118km)**. Until now the train has followed an inland course. From Misedani the track shadows the Pacific coast, albeit at a slight distance. A couple of minutes out of **Kii-Nagashima (127km)** is the small Nagashima Shipyard out to the left, followed by great views of clusters of rock and small islands.

A few minutes from **Owase (151km)** there are glimpses of lovely bays with fishing villages but also a number of tunnels, some of which are pretty long.

The next stop is **Kumano-Shi (186km)**, a good base for exploring the Kumano Kodo (see box p194) pilgrimage routes. *Kumano-shi Seinennoie Youth Hostel* (☎ 0597-89 0800, 🖹 89 1115; ¥2230pp plus ¥600 for non members; breakfast ¥550, dinner ¥950) is an 8-minute walk from the station.

Shingu (209km)
Shingu, in Wakayama, one of Japan's most rural and isolated prefectures, serves as a useful transport hub. It is also an access point for one of the three Kumano Sanzan (see box p194) shrines.

The station is very small with a few **lockers** (mostly ¥300) to the right as you exit the ticket barrier, an ekiben stand. The **tourist information office** (Fri-Wed 9am-5.30pm) on the left as you exit the ticket barrier has friendly staff, a good map and bus timetables. You can **rent a bicycle** from here or from the shop (Apr-Aug daily 8.30am-6pm, Sep-Mar to 5pm) in Jofuku Park; both charge ¥500/day.

Shingu has a small number of cheap business hotels. Not surprisingly the closest to the station is *Station Hotel* (☎ 0735-21 2200, 🖳 www.rifnet.or.jp/~station; ¥5500-5700/S, ¥10,000-14,000/D or Tw, ¥16,500/Tr); turn right out of the station and then first right and the hotel is a couple of minutes' walk along on the right-hand side. For food, try the local speciality, *meharizushi* – literally 'goggle-eyed sushi', so called because each piece is so large that your eyes are supposed to open wide at the sight. *Mehariya* (Thur-Tue 10am-9pm) is a good place to try some (¥1300 inc soup). Turn right out of the hotel and walk along till you cross the railway line. Then turn first right and Mehariya is on the left after the first set of traffic lights.

Shingu to Osaka/Kyoto
[Map 10, p195; Table 10, p461]
Distances by JR from Shingu.

Shingu (0km) The Kuroshio LEX operates from here along the JR Kisei (Kinokuni) line to Osaka/Kyoto.

For the most part, the line from Shingu to Nachi follows the coast, though the view is often obscured by tunnels and trees. You will, though, see a row of warehouses for stores such as Uniqlo on the left as you leave Shingu.

◆ **Nachi (13km)** Limited expresses don't stop here, so take a local train from Shingu (11/day; 18 mins). Though very small, Nachi station does have its own

HONSHU

⛩ **Kumano Sanzan**
   Kumano Nachi Taisha is one of the three grand shrines in this area which have great significance in the Shinto religion. Indeed, they are so important that they are known as Kumano Sanzan (🖳 www.tb-kumano.jp) and these, along with Koya-san (see pp223-4) and Yoshino-yama (see pp222-3) and the pilgrimage paths between them have been declared part of the World Heritage listed 'Sacred sites and pilgrimage routes in the Kii Mountain Range.' A path on the Kumano Kodo pilgrimage route (see p196) connects this area with Kii-Tanabe.

hot spring (onsen) called **Nishiki-no-Yu** (Tue-Sun 10am-9pm; ¥600 plus ¥200 towel rental); from the bath there are great views out over Nachi Bay and also of the train tracks below, so rail enthusiasts can enjoy the unusual experience of trainspotting from the comfort of a bathtub.

Buses run from outside Nachi station (1-2/hr; 28 mins; ¥540) to the sacred waterfalls of **Nachi-no-Otaki**. Get off at the Taki-mae bus stop, from where you walk under the *torii* (shrine gate) and down a flight of stone steps towards the 133m-high waterfall, where there's an altar. Legend has it that Emperor Jimmu arrived here in the 7th century, having seen the cascading water from the sea-shore, and pronounced it the spiritual embodiment of a *kami* (deity).

A short walk uphill brings you to a Shinto shrine, **Kumano Nachi Taisha** (see box above), and adjacent Buddhist temple, Seiganto-ji. Nachi Shrine Fire Festival (Nachi-no-Hi Matsuri) is held here in mid July; it commemorates Jimmu's arrival here from Kyushu and is one of the three largest fire festivals in Japan.

Kii-Katsuura (15km) Katsuura has a number of onsen, the best known of which is **Boki-do spa** (daily 5am-11pm; ¥1000), inside a cave, from where there are views out to sea. The cave is part of *Hotel Urashima* (☎ 0735-52 1011, 🖳 www.hotelurashima.co.jp). To reach it, first walk 10 minutes from Kii-Katsuura station straight ahead to the boat terminal. From there, take the free ferry to the hotel. Check where the boat is going as there's also a ferry service to another hotel, *Hotel Nakanoshima* (☎ 0735-52 1111, 🖳 www.hotel-nakanoshima.jp), which rents out private indoor/open-air baths for ¥2100 for 50 minutes. Reservations are essential.

Taiji (20km) Some limited expresses stop here. Taiji is known for whaling and, despite calls for a worldwide ban, whale meat still sometimes turns up on the menu around this part of the Kii Peninsula.

For the final part of the journey towards Kushimoto, the train heads inland but the journey is still scenic. After Taiji, some trains stop at **Koza (35km)**. There is an impressive line of rocks on the left as you approach Kushimoto station.

Kushimoto (42km) Kushimoto station is the nearest stop to **Cape Shionomisaki**, the most southerly point on Honshu, a 15-minute bus ride away (¥600 return). There is no tourist information here but the bus stop is right outside the station. There's a small locker area in the station.

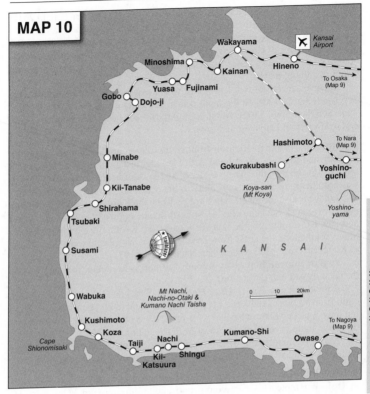

MAP 10

Wakayama
Kansai Airport
Minoshima
Kainan
Hineno
To Osaka (Map 9)
Yuasa Fujinami
Gobo
Dojo-ji
Hashimoto
To Nara (Map 9)
Gokurakubashi
Yoshino-guchi
Minabe
Koya-san (Mt Koya)
Kii-Tanabe
Yoshino-yama
Shirahama
Tsubaki
Susami
K A N S A I
Wabuka
Mt Nachi, Nachi-no-Otaki & Kumano Nachi Taisha
0   10   20km
Kushimoto
Koza
To Nagoya (Map 9)
Cape Shionomisaki
Taiji Nachi
Kumano-Shi
Owase
Kii-Katsuura Shingu

HONSHU

You'll probably only notice **Wabuka (56km)** if on a local train but it's a good vantage point for views of the Pacific Ocean, with waves crashing over rocks. The latter half of the journey towards the next major stop at Shirahama is mostly inland. All trains stop at **Susami** (73km) and some at **Tsubaki** (87km).

Shirahama (95km) Shirahama is a popular summer vacation destination. A fleet of taxis outside the station and regular buses will speed you off to the main resort area (bus No 1; 5-6/hr; 15 mins; ¥380). In the station there are lockers (¥300/400) and a food kiosk. The **tourist information desk** (daily 9.30am-6pm) has accommodation lists but staff are unable to make reservations.

The panda cushions on the seats in the waiting area, the panda painted windows in the station, let alone the panda seats in some of the carriages of Kuroshio train, are a clue to one of the closest attractions to the station: **Adventure World** (🖥 www.aws-s.com; Mar-Nov daily 9.30am-5pm, to 8.30pm in holiday periods, Dec-Feb 10am-5pm, closed approx two Wed/month; ¥3800). The park is divided into zones, including Safari World, Marine World and Panda Land. Twin panda cubs, Kaihin and Youhin, were born here in 2010. A shuttle bus (10 mins) runs to Adventure World from Shirahama station.

This and the large number of onsen in the area mean Shirahama is not the place to come for deserted, unspoilt beaches. Resort hotels, hot springs, glass-bottom boat rides and a 'laser beam studded dance show' turn the bay area into a summer tourist mecca.

However, there are two *rotemburo* worth experiencing: **Shirasuna** (May-Sep 10am-3pm; ¥100), on the main beach, and **Saki-no-yu** (July & Aug 7am-7pm, Sep 8am-5pm; ¥300), which is slightly further away. There are also several *ashi-yu* (foot baths) around town.

Kii-Tanabe (105km)
Right in front of the station are love hotels, pachinko parlours and a whole street lined with bars and restaurants. However, there's more to Tanabe than this. The founder of aikido, Morihei Ueshiba (1883-1969), was born here; his statue stands close to the ocean on the other side of town.

Tanabe is also the junction of three paths on the **Kumano Kodo pilgrimage route** (Kumano Sankeimichi; 🖥 www.tb-kumano.jp/en/kumano-kodo). One path, the Kii-ji route, comes along the coast from Kyoto; the Ohechi route continues south along the coast from Tanabe; and the Nakahechi route goes inland to Koya-san (see pp223-4) and then Nachi (see pp193-4).

Tourist information (daily 8.30am-5.30pm) is available from an office to the right as you exit the station.

A good place to stay is *Altier Hotel* (☎ 0739-81 1111, 🖥 www.altierhotel. com; from ¥5775/S, ¥8400/D, ¥11,550/Tw, inc breakfast). The rooms are small but have attached bathrooms and wide beds. It's on the right side, five minutes down the main street that runs away from the station.

About 10 minutes out of Kii-Tanabe, there are views of the Pacific as the train runs along an elevated track. Some trains stop at **Minabe (114km)**.

♦ Dojo-ji (145km)
Only local trains stop here, from where it's a short walk to **Dojo-ji** temple (🖥 www.dojoji.com; auditorium/museum ¥600; complex free). If on a limited express, the best plan is to get off at Gobo, the next station along from Dojo-ji, and then backtrack one stop on a local train. Services leave Gobo hourly (times vary) and take three minutes to Dojo-ji.

From the station, turn left on to the main road, go to the first junction and turn right. The temple is at the end of the street and is reached by a flight of steps at the end of a row of souvenir shops. Inside the temple is a three-storey pagoda, as well as the main hall. People come here to listen to the monks tell stories with the aid of long, painted scrolls.

The best-known story, handed down by successive generations of monks, is about Kiyohime, a girl who falls hopelessly in love with Anchin, a pilgrim monk. It's a tragic tale of unrequited love with an unusual ending: Kiyohime turns into a serpent and burns the one she most desired to death. For the full story, as well as general information about the temple, ask for the *Brief Guide to Dojo-ji Buddhist Temple* at the office in the new building to the left as you enter the temple compound.

There's a good place to eat at the station, serving noodles and curry rice at reasonable prices, as well as breakfast sets until 11am. The interior is like a log cabin. Look for it on the right just as you leave the station.

Gobo (146km) Rail enthusiasts may want to take a ride on the **Kishu Railway** that runs between Gobo and Nishi-Gobo; some say that this is the shortest railway line (2.7km; 8 mins; 1-2/hr; ¥180) in Japan.

After Gobo the train passes through a number of tunnels.

Yuasa (164km) A few limited expresses stop at Yuasa, notable as the place where soy sauce comes from. The method of making soy-bean paste (miso paste) had reached Japan from China but it was here, in Yuasa, that the liquid version was created. There are now only a few soy-sauce breweries here but some of the old houses where it was made have been preserved.

The stop after Yuasa is **Fujinami (166.5km)**. After that the scenery is just a line of identikit towns and industrial plants. Some limited expresses stop at **Minoshima (175km)**, part of Arida city, which is known for its oranges and for cormorant fishing (June to early Sep) on the Arida-gawa. Just before the train pulls in at **Kainan (190km)** there's a big area of industrial plants out to the left, drawing a final line under the rural part of the peninsula.

Wakayama (201km) Change here for the JR Wakayama line to Hashimoto, the main access point for the mountain resort of Koya-san (see pp223-4). The journey is a pleasant one with the scenery gradually turning more rural, and the joy of a journey with no tunnels.

There's little to see in Wakayama itself, apart from an average **castle** (¥400), from the top of which are views out over Kinokawa River. Originally constructed in 1585, the castle followed the fate of so many Japanese fortresses and was destroyed by fire. The present reconstruction dates from 1958. It's a 10-minute bus ride (¥220) from stop No 2 right outside the station.

To reach the **tourist information office** (daily 8.30am-5.15pm), leave the station and take the escalator down to a soulless basement area; it's over to the right. To find **lockers** (all sizes; ¥300-500), turn left out of the station and look for a room on the side of the station building.

Within the station building there are **restaurants** on the basement level of VIVO department store and a small bakery on ground level. Another place to look is Dining Street in the basement of Mio on the left of the station concourse.

If you need a place to stay, the JR-run *Hotel Granvia Wakayama* (☎ 073-425 3333, 🖳 www.granvia-wakayama.co.jp; from ¥11,319/S, ¥15,939/D, ¥20,212/Tw; discounts for rail-pass holders) is connected to the station.

From Wakayama, trains continue along the JR Hanwa line towards Tennoji and Shin-Osaka.

Hineno (227km) A few LEX stop here (mostly services that started in Shirahama (see note 2 on p461). Change here for the short journey on the Kansai Airport line to Kansai International Airport. A few trains stop at **Otori (247km)**.

Tennoji (262km)   Tennoji is a station on the JR Osaka Loop line (see p121) so if going to Osaka station change here rather than at Shin-Osaka.

Shin-Osaka (277km)   [Osaka – see pp113-23]
Change here for the shinkansen for the route around Western Honshu (see p226) and also for Osaka if you are going there but didn't change at Tennoji.

   If going to Nara (see pp215-22) from Osaka take the JR Yamatoji Line.

   A few limited expresses continue to **Kyoto** (316km; see below).

Kansai – city guides

KYOTO

Kyoto may have lost its status as national capital and Imperial home in 1868, at the time of the Meiji Restoration (see p34), but nobody could dispute its title of modern-day tourist capital. The temples here, many of which are on the World Heritage Site List, let alone the other attractions, make it an essential place to visit on even the briefest of visits to Japan. Arriving by bullet train, the impression is more of a city like so many others: Kyoto has skyscrapers as well as shrines, Starbucks as well as wooden tea houses. But you only need to walk a few minutes north, or south, from the station to reach the first temple and instantly leave the city behind.

   Kyoto is also known for its geisha population but nowadays you're more likely to see a Japanese (or a foreigner) who has paid to be dressed up as a geisha for a day than catch a glimpse of a real one (see box opposite).

   With a superb network of trains radiating out from the city, Kyoto is an excellent base for rail travel around Kansai and beyond; it's also the perfect place to return to, as there's always somewhere else waiting to be discovered.

What to see and do

When planning an itinerary for Kyoto it is important to remember that even though the public transport service is excellent it can take quite a long time to get from one temple, or sight, to another as many are spread out over the city. Also bear in mind that the temples may be very crowded, particularly in spring when people pour in to see the cherry blossom and in autumn for the falling

---

Volunteer guides
   Having a volunteer guide is a great way of seeing Kyoto with someone who knows the place better than anyone else: a local. There are various groups that organise tours, but two worth recommending are Visit Kansai (🖥 www.visitkansai.com), which also offer tours of Kobe, Osaka and Nara; and the Kyoto Good Samaritan Club (🖥 www.geocities.jp/kyoto_samaritan), a student volunteer guide group offering one-day tours of Kyoto for foreign tourists. You need to pay transportation costs, entrance fees and meals for the guide.

⛩ **Getting to know geisha**
Unless you have contacts in extremely high places (no amount of money will do unless you know someone) you are unlikely to meet a geisha while in Japan. The best option is to look for *maiko-san* (apprentice geisha) around 5-6.30pm, along Hanami-koji in Gion and also, on the other side of the river, along the narrow street called Pontocho (see map p207).

Kyoto Tourist Information Center (see p209) can provide you with a list of shops which will dress you up as a maiko or geisha if that appeals; most places require reservations and the cheapest makeovers start at around ¥9975. One good option, with English-speaking staff, is **Studio Shiki** (☎ 075-531 2777, 🖳 www.maiko-henshin. com), which has two branches in Kyoto and also offers men the opportunity to dress up as a samurai swordsman.

If all else fails, Peter MacIntosh, a Canadian expat married to a former geisha, runs guided walking lectures (☎ 090-5169 1654, 🖳 www.kyotosightsandnights.com; ¥3000) of Kyoto's geisha districts.

leaves. But don't let this put you off. This guide lists some sights around the station in case you only have a few hours here, some 'Must sees', but also some 'Optional stops' if you are staying more than a few days.

If you've already started your rail pass before arriving in Kyoto and are planning to stay in the city for more than a couple of days, you'll probably want to use it as much as possible rather than 'waste' days of rail travel you've paid for. With this in mind a couple of suggestions for half-/full-day excursions by rail are also included (see pp212-15).

Kyoto station area The top of the station is a good vantage point for views of the city, since it's free. **Kyoto Tower Observatory** (🖳 www.kyoto-tower. co.jp; daily 9am-9pm; ¥770 or ¥650 with tickets from the TIC and some hotels), the eyesore across the street built in 1964, may be higher but it also costs to take the lift up to the 100m-high observation deck.

A five-minute walk north of the station, the vast and opulent temples of Higashi Hongan-ji and Nishi Hongan-ji serve as the headquarters of two factions of the Jodo-Shin (True Pure Land) sect of Buddhism. **Higashi Hongan-ji** (🖳 www.higashihonganji.or.jp; daily 5.30/6am-5/5.30pm; free) has an enormous Goei-do (Founder's Hall) that boasts 175,000 roof tiles, 90 wooden pillars and 927 tatami mats. Look for the rope on display made of followers' hair; 53 ropes of this kind were used to transport and hang the enormous wooden beams

⛩ **Industrial clean**
If you're in town in December, why not help out at Higashi Hongan-ji's annual clean-up? Every year this event attracts hundreds of volunteers who attack the tatami flooring with bamboo sticks while others blow the dust away using giant fans.

A similar ceremony is held at Nishi Hongan-ji, which has 650 tatami mats in its main hall. The ceremony dates back about 500 years and is supposed to spruce up the temple buildings ready for the New Year festival season.

HONSHU

of the two main halls when they were rebuilt in 1895. Conventional ropes were not strong enough for the task, so human hair was used instead. The Amida-do (Amida Hall) is almost as big, with 108,000 roof tiles, 401 tatami mats and 66 wooden pillars. Note that restoration work on this started in 2011 and may still be going on when you are there. Also, the screens in front of the main statues in the temple are closed at 4pm so it is best to come before then.

A short walk east of Higashi Hongan-ji brings you to **Shosei-en** (daily 9am-4pm; ¥500), a garden belonging to the temple.

Restoration work on the Founder's Hall at the equally impressive nearby **Nishi Hongan-ji** (☎ 075-371 5181, 🖳 www.hongwanji.or.jp; daily 5.30/6am-5/5.30pm; free), a World Heritage site, was completed in 2011. Even though you can see a lot of the temple on your own it is worth joining a tour (10.30am & 2.30pm; free but donation appreciated; bookable by phone; English ability depends on guide), which gives you a chance to see the inside of the temple. The walls of one room depict written documents and since the scent in them is said to attract mice, cats have been painted on the ceiling as a deterrent. There are also two outdoor Noh stages, one of which is the oldest in Japan; plays (about ¥5000) are staged here on 21st May. Leaflets in English are available at the furthest entrance to the temple if coming from the station side.

Ryukoku Museum (🖳 museum.ryukoku.ac.jp; Tue-Sun 10am-5pm; ¥500), to the east of Nishi Hongan-ji, explores the history of Buddhism from its beginnings in India to its spread to Japan.

The main feature at **To-ji** (see map p206; 🖳 www.touji-ennichi.com/info/tohji_e.htm; daily 9am-4.30pm; ¥1000), on the opposite side of Kyoto station,

HONSHU

KYOTO STATION AREA – MAP KEY

Where to stay
2 Tour Club 旅倶楽部
6 Capsule Ryokan Kyoto カプセル旅館
7 Budget Inn バジェット イン
11 Hotel Granvia Kyoto
   ホテルグランビア京都
13 El Inn Kyoto エルイン京都
18 Hotel Station Kyoto West
   ホテルステーション京都西
19 Hotel Station Kyoto
   ホテルステーション京都
20 K's House ケイズ ハウス 京都
21 Kyoka Ryokan 京花旅館
22 Ryokan Kyoraku 旅館京らく
24 Matsubaya Ryokan 松葉屋旅館

Where to eat and drink
4 Second House セカンドハウス
10 Tonkatsu Wako (Eat Paradise, Isetan)
   とんかつ和幸 (イートパラダイス,
   伊勢丹)

Where to eat and drink (cont'd)
17 Tsutsumi つつみ

Other
1 Nishi Hongan-ji 西本願寺
3 Ryukoku Museum 龍谷ミュージアム
5 Coin Laundry コインランドリー
8 Ebisuku supermarket
   エビスクスーパー
9 Central Post Office 中央郵便局
12 Tansuya (Avanti Dept Store)
   たんす屋 (アバンティデパート)
14 Bus information centre
   バス総合案内所内
15 Bus stops バスのりば
16 Kyoto Tower 京都タワー
23 Higashi Hongan-ji 東本願寺
25 Shosei-en 渉成園

Kyoto – Station Area

京都駅周辺

Not all roads shown

HONSHU

Keihan Main Line

Keihan-Shichijo

Kamo-gawa

Kawaramachi-dori

20

25

Rokujo-dori

19

21

22

18

Higashi-notoin-dori

24

Karasuma Line

Karasuma-dori

Kyoto

17

16

14

23

15

11

Kyoto Station

Shinmachi-dori

Shiokoji-dori

8

9

North-south walkway (2nd-floor)

Nishi-notoin-dori

10

Isetan dept store

4

2

Shichijo-dori

JR Nara Line to Uji & Nara

13

12

Aburakoji-dori

3

5

6

Kintetsu Kyoto Line

Horikawa-dori

7

Hachijo-dori

To To-ji (see Kyoto map)

1

JR Tokaido Main Line

JR Tokaido Shinkansen Line

To Umekoji Park for Umekoji Steam Locomotive Museum and Kyoto Aquarium (see Kyoto map)

0   100   200m

is the five-storied, 57m-high pagoda, the highest in Japan. It was first built in 826 but has burnt down four times since then; the current pagoda dates from 1644. An **antiques market** is held in the grounds on the first Sunday of every month and a general market on the 21st of every month.

The temple, a World Heritage Site, is a 15-minute walk from the station; turn right out of the Hachijo exit and walk along Hachijo-dori until you reach the junction with Aburanokoji-dori. Cross the road diagonally and then walk along till you meet Toji-michi on your right. Turn right here and walk along until you reach the temple grounds. Alternatively if you are coming from Nishi Hongwan-ji all you need to do is walk along Omiya-dori.

One more place in the station area that rail enthusiasts will want to seek out is **Umekoji Steam Locomotive Museum** (see map p206; 🖳 www.mtm.or.jp/eng/umekoji; Tue-Sun 9.30am-5pm, daily in holiday periods; ¥400), opened in 1972 on the 100th anniversary of Japan's first railway service. Fans of the railway's golden age will be in paradise as there are a large number of steam locomotives on display, some in working condition. One of the locos runs along a specially constructed track (11am, 1.30pm & 3.30pm; 10 mins; ¥200). This short run can't compete with the growing number of preserved steam locomotives running along real lines but is fun if you haven't had the chance to ride a steam train before. The museum is 20 minutes' walk west of Kyoto station, or take a city bus from outside the station to Umekoji Koen-mae.

Kyoto Aquarium (see map p206; 🖳 www.kyoto-aquarium.com; daily 9am-5pm, longer in holiday periods; ¥2000) opened in Umekoji park in March 2012. It is full of environmentally friendly features and has all the standard aquarium attractions, such as dolphins and penguins, but being an inland aquarium, one of the largest in the world, it also has a section focusing on the eco-systems in Kyoto's rivers.

⛩ **Warm relief for tired legs**

If your feet are exhausted after a long day of sightseeing, the best thing you can do for them is soak in a hot tub. **Hakusan-yu** (🖳 www.hakusanyu.com; Thur, Fri, Mon & Tue 3-11pm, Sat & Sun 7am-midnight; ¥410 plus ¥100 towel rental) is a bath house in walking distance from Kyoto station. It's considered one of the best in Kyoto and uses natural spring water pumped from underground. There are six baths, divided into men's and women's sections, and all with different kinds of water and at different temperatures (avoid the one with cold water!); the women's side also has a *rotemburo* (open-air bath). The bath with royal blue water has a wonderful foot massage. There is also a sauna (with a TV) and a Jacuzzi-style bath, and if that hasn't relaxed you enough there are some massage chairs. It's a wonderful place to soak the stress and pain away and mentally prepare for another day of temples. It is also a good chance to get away from tourists and meet Kyotoites.

From Kyoto station walk along Karasuma-dori, past Higashi Hongan-ji. Turn first left and then take the fourth turning on the right; Hakusan-yu is a little way along on the right after a soba restaurant. These side roads are too small to show on the map on p207 but Hakusan-yu is well known so ask if you have problems.

If you want to try other public baths (*o-sento*) in Kyoto the TIC has a list.

Must sees Kiyomizu-dera (Kiyomizu Temple; daily 6am-6pm; ¥300), a World Heritage Site, is known for its incredible observation platform. The wooden structure juts up and out from the hillside and was built without using any nails. The view out over the cherry and maple trees below and beyond to Kyoto is spectacular. Visit early in the day, or be prepared for the crowds. However, many of the buildings are gradually being renovated so be aware that this may affect your visit. To reach the temple from Kyoto station take Raku Bus No 100 or bus No 206 (approx 15 mins; ¥220) to Kiyomizu-michi bus stop and then walk uphill for about 10 minutes (follow the crowds).

From Kiyomizu-dera head north towards the **Gion District**, known as Kyoto's geisha quarter but also the home of **Yasaka Jinja** (Yasaka/Gion Shrine; open 24 hours; free entry), in Maruyama Park (Maruyama-koen), a Shinto shrine dating back to 656. It becomes the focus of the city for the entire month of July during the Gion Festival (see p210).

As you stand at the entrance to the shrine, Shijo-dori runs west towards the centre of Gion, while Higashioji-dori runs north and south. Head along Shijo-dori for the busy downtown shopping and entertainment district, but look out, just before Shijo Bridge, for **Minami-za**, Kyoto's famous kabuki theatre. There are no tours of the theatre building so to see inside you have to buy a ticket for a performance (see p212). The biggest annual event is in December when some of the country's best-known kabuki actors come here to perform.

Kinkaku-ji (daily 9am-5pm; ¥400), also known as the **Golden Pavilion**, though its proper name is Rokuon-ji, is perhaps Kyoto's most famous sight. The pavilion, its reflection glittering in Kyoko-chi, the Mirror Pond, is deservedly one of Japan's most-photographed buildings. The façade was regilded in 1987 and the roof restored in spring 2003 so it looks magnificent even on an overcast or rainy day. The building was originally a retirement villa for a shogun, Ashikaga Yoshimitsu, but on his death (in 1408) he instructed that it should become a Zen temple. It's in north-western Kyoto, some distance from the centre, but Raku Bus No 101 (see p210) goes there from the station.

From Kinkaku-ji it's a 15- to 20-minute walk south-west to Ryoan-ji, or a ride on the Raku Bus. As you exit, turn right on to the street and go straight. Mid-way between the two temples, look out for a sign pointing towards the 'Museum for World Peace' – not an essential stop but interesting if you have time (see p204). **Ryoan-ji** (🖥 www.ryoanji.jp; Mar-Dec daily 8am-5pm, Jan-Feb 8.30am-4.30pm; ¥500) provides a complete contrast to the showy opulence of the Golden Pavilion. Everyone comes here to sit and gaze out over Kyoto's (and probably the world's) best-known rock garden. Assembled sometime between 1499 and 1507 and measuring about 200 square metres, the garden consists of white sand (raked) and 15 rocks. Visitors are asked to remain silent, though the peace and quiet is regularly interrupted by a recorded history of the temple. The focus here is on the rock garden but a walk round the pond, Kyoyo-chi, and the rest of the grounds is recommended.

Nijo-jo (Nijo Castle; daily except Tue in Dec, Jan, July & Aug, 8.45am-4pm; ¥600) contains beautiful landscaped gardens in addition to Ninomaru

Palace. Originally built in 1603 as an official residence of the first Tokugawa shogun, Ieyasu, it is well preserved and, unlike the former Imperial Palace (see below), visitors are allowed inside. An unusual feature of Ninomaru Palace is the 'nightingale floor', so called because the floorboards that run along the side of the building 'squeak and creak' when you tread on them. On your way out through the gardens, look out for the *koi* (carp) in the central pond.

Nijo station is on the JR Sagano line (see p212). Turn right out of the west exit at JR Nijo, then right again to walk along Oshikoji-dori until you reach the main road, Horikawa-dori. Turn left for the entrance to the castle; the walk takes about 15 minutes. Alternatively, Nijojo-mae station on the Tozai subway line is closer, or take Raku Bus 101 or bus Nos 9, 12 and 50 stop from Kyoto station; these services stop outside the castle.

Optional stops The **Museum of Kyoto** (🖥 www.bunpaku.or.jp; daily except 3rd Wed 10am-6pm, Fri to 7.30pm; ¥500), on Sanjo-dori in central Kyoto, a three-minute walk from Karasuma-Oike subway station, traces the history of Kyoto, focusing on its glory days as the nation's capital and then moving on to the period of modernisation after power shifted to Edo (Tokyo). There are good model displays that let you see what Kyoto once looked like but otherwise not much of a permanent collection. The redeeming factor is an excellent English volunteer guide service; this is very useful as most of the displays are only in Japanese. On the ground floor is a recreated Kyoto street from the Edo period with shops selling traditional crafts, and a couple of restaurants.

Ritsumeikan University's **Museum for World Peace** (🖥 www.ritsumei. ac.jp/mng/er/wp-museum; Tue-Sun 9.30am-4.30pm; ¥400; pick up the excellent brochure at the entrance) is situated between Ryoan-ji and Kinkaku-ji and is well worth a visit. It tackles with astonishing candour the subject of Japan's military aggression during WWII and the country's 'unresolved war responsibilities'. It's unlikely you'd find anywhere else a picture of 'schoolchildren beating the portraits of Roosevelt and Churchill with large sticks in 1943'. The displays are well thought-out and informative, and include images of what Kyoto might have looked like had it suffered the fate of Hiroshima and Nagasaki. Originally on the list of possible A-Bomb targets – the planned epicentre was about 1km west of Kyoto station – Kyoto was later removed as a target for nuclear attack because the US Secretary of War knew it was the ancient capital of Japan, that it was very important for the Japanese, and that it was too beautiful to destroy.

Kyoto Imperial Palace (🖥 sankan.kunaicho.go.jp; Mon-Fri, tours at 10am & 2pm, free; over 20s only) can only be visited on a tour with an official guide. To sign up for a tour, either apply online or take your passport to the Imperial Household Agency office (Mon-Fri 8.45am-noon & 1-4pm), in the outer grounds of the palace, at least 20 minutes before the start of the tour (or the day before to be sure of a place). To reach the palace, take the subway from Kyoto station in the direction of Kokusai Kaikan and get off at Imadegawa (the fifth stop). The entrance to the palace grounds is on Karasuma-dori. The grounds, which include some picture-postcard Japanese gardens, are interesting enough to make the effort of applying to join a tour worthwhile. Rooms have to be viewed from a distance but it's just possible to make out the inside of the throne room. When the present emperor was crowned in Tokyo, the thrones were taken from here and flown by helicopter to the capital. Even though the palace is no longer home to the Imperial Family, tight security remains; an official carrying a walkie-talkie follows the tour group around to make sure nobody sneaks away. The impression is not so much of grandeur but of how much the grounds feel like a prison – or must have done for the Emperor, who hardly ever left the palace.

From the Imperial Palace it is an easy walk to **Heian Jingu** (daily 8.30am-4.30/5.30pm; free, but gardens ¥600). Even though the shrine is not particularly old it is notable because it is the site of the Jidai Matsuri (see p210). Also, the entrance is marked by one of the biggest torii gates in Japan – 24 metres high and with a top rail that's almost 34 metres wide. The gardens are a popular place to see the cherry blossom in spring.

Ginkaku-ji (daily mid Mar to Nov 8.30am-5pm, Dec to mid Mar 9am-4.30pm; ¥500, audio rental ¥500), better known as the **Silver Pavilion**, is on the east side of Kyoto. Like its golden counterpart it was built as a retirement villa but became a Zen temple. However, don't be fooled by this temple's name. The idea was to cover its outer walls in silver; though the plans were never carried out, the name remained. The temple is probably seen as second best compared to the Golden Pavilion but it shouldn't be. The dry sand garden, with the flawless Mt Fuji-like sand cone ('Ginshadan'), and the impressive moss garden are worth seeing, let alone the views of Kyoto from the garden. Either take bus No 5 or 17, or Raku Bus 100 from Kyoto station (40 mins), then walk 5-10 minutes (the Raku Bus stop is closest to the temple).

Ginkaku-ji is at one end of the **Philosopher's Way** (Tetsugaka-no-michi), a walk of about 2km along a section of canal, passing cafés, boutiques and craft shops as well as a number of shrines and temples. The walk is pleasant at any time of the year but particularly in the spring and autumn. The other end of the Way is near **Nanzen-ji** (daily 8.40am-5pm, to 4.30pm in winter; grounds free, temples ¥300-500), one of the most important Zen temples in Japan. As with many temples in Kyoto it started its life as a retirement villa. None of the buildings is the original but it is still an impressive place; there is a rock garden in Hojo Hall as well as a brick aqueduct in the grounds. Also here is Konchi-in Teien (daily 8.30am-4.30/5pm; ¥400) tea ceremony garden.

Kyoto National Museum (🖥 www.kyohaku.go.jp; Tue-Sun 9.30am-6pm, Fri to 8pm; ¥420), opened in 1897, specialises in fine arts and handicrafts, including rare examples of Heian-period pottery and lacquerware. From bus stop D2 outside Kyoto station, take City Bus No 206 or 208 to Hakubutsukan Sanjusangendo-mae, from where the museum is a one-minute walk.

HONSHU

❏ **Seeing red**
Some parts of Kyoto are considered to be of such historical importance that they are protected by laws which prohibit the use of brightly coloured signs. If they are too close to temples, signs for McDonald's and Coca Cola cannot be coloured red.

HONSHU

0   0.5   1km
Not all roads shown

1

3

2

Imadegawa-dori

Takaoguchi Omuro   Ryoanjimichi   Tojiin
Narutaki   Myoshinji   Kitano-
                                 Hakubaicho

Keifuku
Line

Hanazono

Marutamachi-dori

To
Saga-Arashiyama   JR Sagano Line
                       (also known
Uzumasa   as San-in Line)

4

5

Nijo   Nijojo-
            mae

Kaikonoyashiro   Yamanouchi
                                  Sanjoguch
Keifuku   Hankyu-
Arashiyama   Saiin   Omiya
Line
Shiio-dori   Shijo-
                                               Omiya
            Hankyu
            Kyoto
            Line

Nishi-oji-dori

Gojo-dori

Tanbaguchi

Nishikyogoku

6
8
7

Omiya-dori

Katsura   JR Tokaido   JR Tokaido
                  Line   Shinkansen
                                Line

                  Nishioji   Kujo-dori
To Osaka

Kyoto

京都

Kuramaguchi

Mototanaka

Demachiyanagi

Imadegawa

Keihan
Line

9

★ trailblazer

10

12
Tetsugaka-
no-Michi

Keihan-
Marutamachi

11

Marutamachi-dori

Marutamachi

14

Kyoto-
shiyakusho-
mae

15

Karasuma-
oike

Sanjo

Higashiyama

16

13

Keage

Keihan-
Sanjo

17

Hankyu-
Kawaramachi

Shijo

18

19

Maruyama
-koen

Hankyu-
Karasuma

Keihan-
Shijo

20

G I O N

21

21

22

23

Keihan-
Gojo

Gojo-dori

Gojo

24

SEE 'STATION AREA' MAP

Keihan-
Shichijo

26

27

To Nagoya
& Tokyo

JR Tokaido
Line

Kyoto
Station

Kyoto

JR Tokaido
Shinkansen
Line

To Nagoya
& Tokyo

Tofukuji

Tofukuji

28

25

Toji

Kujo

To Uji & Nara

Karasuma-dori

Horikawa-dori

Kawaramachi-dori

Kamogawa

Higashi-oji-dori

Pontocho

Hanami-koji

Shijo-dori

HONSHU

Fans of Japanese animation should fit in a visit to **Kyoto International Manga Museum** (🖥 www.kyotomm.jp; Thur-Tue 10am-6pm, Jul-Aug until 8pm; ¥800). As much a research facility as a museum, the building – a former primary school – is home to 50,000 volumes of Japanese manga and a smaller number of foreign comics. On a fine day, you'll find people sitting on the grass outside, devouring comic books borrowed from the museum's shelves. Inside the adjacent museum café, manga artists have signed their names and left sketches on the walls. Jump on a Karasuma line subway train from Kyoto three stops to Karasuma-oike, and take Exit 2.

Toei Kyoto Studio Park (🖥 www.toei-eigamura.com, Mar-Nov daily 9am-5pm, Dec-Feb 9.30am-4pm, closed late Dec-Jan; ¥2200 or ¥3000 inc the 3D attractions) is about 15 minutes on foot from Hanozono station on the JR Sagano line (see p212). This may be a good antidote for anyone tiring of Kyoto's temples, this very in-your-face thrills and spills entertainment park. The park owners stress that it is a working film set, so there's a chance to see a real samurai film in production, actors running around in full costume, and special effects such as collapsing mountains. You can even dress up and be photographed as a maiko (from ¥6000, or from ¥1800 if you put the costume on over your own clothes).

See also pp212-15 for details of side trips from Kyoto.

PRACTICAL INFORMATION
Station guide
Kyoto station (🖥 www.kyoto-station-building.co.jp), rebuilt in 1997, is one of Japan's most eye-catching modern buildings. Japanese architect Hiroshi Hara suggests that the 27m-wide, 60m-high and 470m-long concourse lets you feel what it's like 'travelling down the side of a mountain into the valley basin'. Certainly it's an impressive sight whether looking up from the main concourse or down from the 12th-floor Sky Garden on to the station atrium.

The shinkansen tracks are on the Hachi-jo (south side) of the station; this is also the side for To-ji. To reach the Karasuma (north) side of the station follow signs for the pedestrian walkway or for the Central Concourse. This is the exit for central Kyoto.

The station has plenty of **lockers** (all sizes; ¥300-600), including some almost opposite the tourist information centre. There's a **meeting point** (Toki-no-akari) opposite the west entrance on the 2nd floor pedestrian walkway, but it hasn't got seats so isn't a relaxing place to wait. However, there is a viewing area (of the trains) just

❏ **Kyoto Station platforms**
Note: all lines are JR except where specified.

Platform Line and destination

Platform	Line and destination
0	Hokuriku line to Fukui & Kanazawa; Tokaido mainline (not shinkansen) to Nagano & Toyama
2	Biwako line to Maibara
3	Kosei line to Omi-Shiotsu (the west side of Lake Biwa)
4 & 5	Kyoto line to Osaka
6	Kinokuni line to Osaka
7	Kinokuni line to Shirahama & Wakayama
8, 9 & 10	Nara line to Nara
11-12	Shinkansen services to Tokyo
13-14	Shinkansen services to Shin-Osaka and Hakata
21 & 22	Kintetsu (private) line to Kintetsu-Nara (Nara)
30	Kansai Airport line to Kansai International Airport
31-34	Sagano (San-in) line to Saga-Arashiyama.

KYOTO MAP KEY (see map pp206-7)

Where to stay, eat and drink
13 Westin Miyako Hotel Kyoto
   ウェスティン都ホテル京都
17 Nishiki Food Market 錦市場
23 Citadines Kyoto Karasuma-Gojo
   シタディーン京都烏丸五条
27 Hyatt Regency Kyoto
   ハイアット リージェンシー 京都

Other
1 Kinkaku-ji 金閣寺
2 Museum for World Peace
   国際平和ミュージアム
3 Ryoan-ji 竜安寺
4 Toei Kyoto Studio Park
   東映太秦映画村
5 Nijo-jo 二条城
6 Umekoji Park 梅小路公園
7 Umekoji Steam Locomotive Museum
   梅小路蒸気機関車館
8 Kyoto Aquarium 京都水族館

9 Kyoto Imperial Palace 京都御所
10 Ginkaku-ji 銀閣寺
11 Heian Jingu 平安神宮
12 Philosopher's way 哲学の道
14 Nanzen-ji 南禅寺
15 Kyoto International Manga Museum
   京都国際マンガミュージアム
16 Museum of Kyoto 京都文化博物館
17 Nishiki Food Market 錦市場
18 Minami-za 南座
19 Yasaka Jinja 八坂神社
20 Yasaka Hall Gion Corner
   三条高倉ギオンコーナー
21 Studio Shiki スタジオ四季
22 Kiyomizu-dera 清水寺
24 Hakusan-yu 白山湯
25 To-ji 東寺
26 Kyoto National Museum
   京都国立博物館
28 Tofuku-ji 東福寺

HONSHU

beyond that. Wi-fi is available in the shinkansen waiting room.

There are plenty of **ATMs** but ATM corner (daily 5.30am to midnight) on the right at the bottom of the stairs to the east exit has a machine for foreign-issued cards. The World Currency Shop (daily 11am-5pm) on the 8th floor of the Kyoto station building exchanges cash and travellers' cheques in most major currencies.

Isetan, the big in-station department store, stretches up both sides of the escalators that run up from the ground floor concourse. On the 7th floor is the **Eki museum** (daily 10am-8pm; ¥700-1000 depending on the exhibition), with changing arts/textile exhibitions; take the south elevator in Isetan.

There are plenty of places to eat in the station. For a snack with a view consider *Café du Monde* on the 2nd floor overlooking the main concourse. However, you may not want to pay ¥410 for a very ordinary chicken sandwich and ¥320 for an orange juice. For delicious bread try *Station Burdigala Express* opposite the central exit on the main walkway.

Musashi (daily 10am-10.30pm) is a *kaiten* (revolving) sushi restaurant on the ground floor of the shinkansen side of the station. The price policy is simple: all pieces of sushi are ¥120. Great value and delicious – the perfect place to grab a bite to eat while waiting for a train. For extra help refer to the restaurant guide on the wall by the TIC. See also Where to eat p212.

And since you are in Kyoto where there are a lot of **World Heritage sites** there's a board outside the station on the left before reaching the bus stands to remind you of what is where.

Tourist information
Kyoto City Tourist Information Center (TIC; 🖥 www.kyotoguide.com; daily 8.30am-7pm) is on the north–south pedestrian walkway on the 2nd floor of the station. Staff can provide you with a *Kyoto City Bus Travel Map* and one-day bus pass (see below), a hotel and ryokan list, a restaurant guide, details of walking and cycling tours as well as information about the many sights. Also worth looking at are: 🖥 www.city.kyoto.lg.jp and 🖥 www.kyoto.travel.

The best guide to what's on in Kyoto is the monthly *Kyoto Visitor's Guide* (🖳 www.kyotoguide.com), available free at the TIC as well as at major hotels. Another good guide to Kyoto and the Kansai region as a whole is 🖳 www.kansaiscene.com.

Getting around

Since Kyoto is so spread out, the best plan is to take buses/subways to the different areas and then explore on foot. There's a flat rate of ¥220 on buses within the city but it's almost always worth investing in the **one-day city bus pass** (¥500) which is valid for buses to all the must-sees and optional sights, and some of the side trips, mentioned in this guide. Alternatively, a **combined subway/city bus ticket** costs ¥1200, or a **two-day ticket** is ¥2000.

All passes are available from the **bus information centre** in front of Kyoto station, near bus stop D1, or from the TIC. Be sure to pick up a *Kyoto City Bus Travel Map*, which details how to get from the station and between the main sights by bus.

If you're following the familiar tourist trail, it's worth considering the special **Raku Bus Kyoto Easy Sightseeing** bus service (signed in English). Fares are a flat ¥220, but the bus passes mentioned above are valid. The *Bus Travel Map* gives full details of routes and stops, and stop announcements are made in English.

To get to/from Kansai Airport take the Haruka LEX (see p117).

Festivals

In a city packed with temples there's nearly always a festival going on somewhere. For details, enquire at any tourist office, or check the *Kyoto Visitor's Guide*.

One of Japan's biggest and most vibrant festivals is **Jidai Matsuri** (Festival of the Ages), which takes place on 22nd October. The highlight is a huge street procession from the Imperial Palace to Heian Shrine. Participants dress in costumes from different periods in Kyoto's history, starting with 1868 (the Meiji era) and going back in time to the Heian period and the founding of Kyoto in 781.

Another major festival is **Gion Matsuri**, the main annual celebration at Yasaka Jinja (see p203). It runs throughout July, with the principal events between the 15th and 17th, when there's a huge procession of floats. At the **Aoi Matsuri**, held in mid May, participants dressed in costumes from the Heian period parade north from the Imperial Palace.

Where to stay

There is accommodation in Kyoto to suit all budgets. However, it's worth booking ahead for peak periods such as cherry-blossom time (late Mar/early Apr) and autumn-leaves viewing (late Oct/early Nov). For convenience this guide focuses on places that are near the station; the TIC will provide a list of accommodation options for the whole of the city. See also pp45-52.

Station area Undoubtedly the best bargain, and conveniently close to the station, are three places under the same ownership. *Capsule Ryokan Kyoto* (☎ 075-344 1510, 🖳 www.capsule-ryokan-kyoto.com; from ¥4980/S, ¥7980/Tw or D; capsule ¥3500pp)

🎏 Bargain hunt

Many visitors to Kyoto have at least one item on their souvenir-shopping list: a kimono. But with top-end garments selling for hundreds of thousands of yen, it's not something that falls within most budgets.

A good option for bargain-conscious shoppers is a small store called **Tansuya** (🖳 tansuya.jp; daily 10am-9pm), in a corner of the 1st (ground) floor of the Avanti department store across the street from the shinkansen side of Kyoto station. This shop (which has other branches in Kyoto and elsewhere) is one of the few kimono outlets in Kyoto which won't burn your credit card. You can pick up new and second-hand kimonos in a range of colours and fabrics from ¥10,000, and *obi* (sashes) from ¥5000.

combines the style of a ryokan with the chance to experience the infamous capsule accommodation. The capsules are in mixed dorms that sleep up to eight people. However, each capsule is private, air conditioned and has a 16" TV. There is lockable storage and a shared bathroom. There are also 32 compact but fantastically well-designed rooms each with monsoon shower, toilet, 32" TV, and clever luggage storage.

There is also a lounge area, kitchenette, laundry facilities, internet access and a very useful file with information about sightseeing and local restaurants. Book early.

Nearby is the spotless *Tour Club* (☎ 075-353 6968, 🖳 www.kyotojp.com; dorms ¥2450pp; ¥6980/D or Tw, ¥8880/Tr; discounts for two-night stays), a small place with four-bed bunk dorms set around a small rock garden as well as a selection of well-maintained Western- and Japanese-style rooms. *Budget Inn* (☎/🖳 075-344 1510, 🖳 www.budgetinnjp.com; ¥10,980/ Tr, ¥12,980/quad, ¥14,980/5 beds) also offers clean, Japanese-style rooms, all with private bathrooms. Both these hotels offer internet access (¥100/20 mins) and have coin laundries.

Further away, but part of a chain of places offering budget accommodation, *K's House* (☎ 075-342 2444, 🖳 kshouse.jp; dorms from ¥2300pp; ¥3500-4200/S, ¥2900-3300/Tw, ¥2900-4400/D) offers a variety of rooms and facilities. There are sitting areas and a roof-top terrace, a kitchen, wi-fi and internet access (¥100/20 mins), as well as a café (daily 8am to midnight).

Four minutes' walk from the station, on Higashi Notoin-dori, is *Hotel Station Kyoto* (☎ 075-365 900, 🖳 www.hotel-st-kyoto.com; from ¥6000pp or ¥5000pp in a triple), with en suite Japanese- and Western-style accommodation, free internet access and nice communal baths. The hotel has another very similar branch on Shichijo-dori, even nearer the station, at *Hotel Station Kyoto West* (☎ 075-343 5000; same website and prices). Both have cafés, but only the West branch serves breakfast (¥800; buffet).

There's cheap, Western-style accommodation at *El Inn Kyoto* (☎ 075-672

1100, 🖳 www.elinn-kyoto.com; ¥6200-7100/S, ¥12,000/Tw) just a couple of minutes' walk south-east of the shinkansen side of Kyoto station. Most rooms are (wide-bedded) singles, though there are a few twins, and there's a coin laundry and a restaurant.

Good-value Japanese inns in the area include the friendly *Matsubaya Ryokan* (☎ 075-351 3727, 🖳 www.matsubayainn.com; ¥4200-6930/S, ¥7770-15,120/D or Tw, ¥17,010-22,680/Tr, ¥21000-26,040/quad), five minutes east along the main road from the station. It has spacious tatami rooms, some of which overlook a small garden. *Kyoka Ryokan* (☎/🖳 075-371 2709, 🖳 up well.jp/kyoka/kyoka.htm; ¥4200pp/S no bath, ¥¥9000-10,500/Tw, ¥13,000-14,500/ Tr) is a bit faded but has tatami room with and without en suite bathrooms. Just around the corner is *Ryokan Kyoraku* (☎ 075-371 1260, 🖳 www.ryokankyoraku.jp; ¥5200-6000/S, ¥9200-12,300/D or Tw, ¥13,800-17,700/Tr; breakfast from ¥700), a rambling but efficiently run place that offers rooms with and without en suite facilities. If none of these ryokan has a vacancy, try the Kyoto Ryokan website (🖳 www.kyoto-ryokan.com).

At the top end of the market and built into JR Kyoto station is *Hotel Granvia Kyoto* (☎ 075-344 8888, 🖳 www.granvia-kyoto.co.jp; from ¥25,410/D, ¥28,875/Tw; discounts and special packages available online), where all the rooms are tastefully furnished, have large bathrooms and free wired internet access. It's a luxurious haven and an ideal base if you're travelling a lot by rail. The indoor pool (for anyone aged over 21) has excellent views of the station's atrium and there are 13 restaurants and bars.

Other areas A good luxury choice in the Higashiyama temple district is *Westin Miyako Hotel Kyoto* (☎ 075-771 7111, 🖳 www.westinmiyako-kyoto.com; from ¥28,900/D but discounted online), which has all the facilities you would expect in a top-class hotel. Also in Higashiyama is *Hyatt Regency Kyoto* (☎ 075-541 1234, 🖳 kyoto.regency.hyatt.com; from ¥40,000/D inc breakfast), which looks very uninspiring from the outside and is minimalist inside but also has everything you would expect and prices to match; wi-fi is free in the lobby but not in the rooms.

If you prefer apartment-style accommodation, consider **Citadines Karasuma-Gojo** (🖳 www.citadines.com/en/japan/kyoto/karasuma_gojo.html; from ¥11,500/night; breakfast ¥735pp), which has studio, double and twin apartments, each with a fully equipped kitchen, wi-fi access, satellite TV and DVD player.

Where to eat and drink

The following places to eat have been chosen primarily because they are in the station area, but you are unlikely to have a problem finding somewhere that suits your tastebuds and budget. If you prefer, the TIC has a restaurant guidebook covering all areas of the city.

At the station, the best place to head for is the 11th-floor **Eat Paradise** in **Isetan** department store, where some restaurants have tables either overlooking the station atrium or with window views of the city. Expect queues outside most restaurants at peak times. **Tonkatsu Wako** (11am-9.15pm) has excellent tonkatsu; a hirekatsu set costs ¥1418. For take-out food, try the food hall in the basement.

Tsutsumi (daily 5pm-midnight), on Shichijo-dori, serves delicious okonomiyaki (around ¥900), side dishes such as corn butter (¥300), and beer and sake.

Second House (🖳 www.secondhouse.co.jp; daily 10am-10.30pm, lunch 11.30am-2.30-pm), in the grey building with pillars and subtitled 'Spaghetti and Cake', serves great Italian food at reasonable prices. It's close to the station and offers free wi-fi.

The best place to hunt for restaurants is in the downtown area. **Nishiki Food Market** (🖳 www.kyoto-nishiki.or.jp; daily 9am-6pm; most stalls close one day a week, usually Wed or Sun) is a covered arcade known as 'Kyoto's kitchen': look out for Nishiki Soyu, a shop which sells delicious soy-milk (*tonyu*) ice cream and doughnuts.

Ebisuku (daily 10am-8pm, closed one Sun/month) is a supermarket that is a great place to go if you are self-catering.

Evening entertainment

Kabuki is sometimes staged at Minami-za in Gion, though it's not a cheap evening out as reserved seats start from ¥4200.

Yasaka Hall Gion Corner (☎ 075-561 1119, 🖳 www.kyoto-gioncorner.com; Mar-Nov nightly 6pm & 7pm, occasionally also 8pm; Dec-Feb weekends only 7pm; ¥3150 from the box office and major travel agencies; ¥2800 with discount coupon from the website) is a tourist-oriented performance of **traditional Japanese arts** featuring an abbreviated tea ceremony, *ikebana* (flower arranging), traditional dances, and excerpts from *kyogen* (traditional comic plays) and *bunraku* (puppetry). They're staged on the 1st (ground) floor of Yasaka Hall in Gion.

Side trips by rail from Kyoto

The first of the two sample excursions described below can be done as a long day or, even better, an overnight trip, while the second, along the JR Nara line (see p214), is convenient as part of a trip to Nara (see pp215-25).

Along the JR Sagano line A trip along the Sagano line to Saga-Arashiyama, only 15 minutes from Kyoto station, offers a complete change of pace and scenery and is a good way of making use of the rail pass but worth doing even if you don't have one. Take a local train (from track Nos 31-34) to follow the route below (distances are from Kyoto station).

Stops before reaching Saga-Arashiyama include **Nijo-jo** (4.2km; see p203), and **Hanozono** (6.9km) for Toei Kyoto Studio Park (see p208).

● **Saga-Arashiyama (10.3km)** Arashiyama may be touristy but it has a lot that is worth seeing, and the scenery is particularly spectacular in the spring and autumn.

⛩ **Riding the Romantic Train**
Expensive but fun is a ride on the **Torokko open-air carriage 'Romantic Train'** (💻 www.sagano-kanko.co.jp; Mar-Dec daily in peak/holiday periods, Wed-Mon at other times; 8-9/day; 25 mins; ¥600 one-way, rail passes are not accepted), which runs along the scenic Hozu River. It gets completely booked out in the autumn when crowds descend on Arashiyama to see the leaves fall, but it's wise to reserve ahead at any time; book at JR ticket counters or the TiS travel agency in Kyoto station.

As an alternative to buying a return ticket, it's possible to take the train one way and then return to Arashiyama by boat (Mar-Nov hourly 9am-3pm, rest of year every 90 mins; 2hr; ¥3900) on the Hozugawa. The course from the starting point in Kameoka (shuttle buses run between the Torokko station at Kameoka and the starting point for the boat rides) back down to Arashiyama is 16km. Accept as hyperbole the description of the journey down the rapids as being the 'most exciting experience not only in Japan but also throughout the world'. It's not the Zambezi but the scenery is still spectacular. And, being Japan, the boat is heated in the winter!

There are ¥300 lockers in the station. Take the north exit for Daikaku-ji and the south exit for the river area. The Torokko train station is on the right by the south exit; the **tourist information centre** here is open (8.30am-5pm) when the Torokko Romantic car (see box above) is operating. The Rental Bicycle shop (daily 9am-5.30pm; ¥300/hr, ¥700/day) is on the right as you walk to the river.

Walk (or cycle) straight down the road from the station until you reach the river. Turn right and walk along until you reach **Togetsukyo-bashi** (Crossing Moon Bridge) on the left; it's a traditional-style bridge first built in 836 though the current bridge dates from 1934. Togetsukyo is a famous spot for cherry-blossom and autumn-leaves' viewing. Cross the bridge and at the end either turn left to explore the area of cherry trees and have a snack from one of the many food stalls (all day in peak season, limited hours at other times), or turn right and walk along the path by the river, or take one of the **boat trips** (daily 9am-3.30pm, Dec-mid Mar 10am-2.30pm; from ¥1100 for about two hours) downriver. Whether walking or in a boat it is not long before you escape the sights and sounds of the city.

A recommended walk (about 1km) is along the river to **Arashiyama Daihikaku Senkou-ji** (daily 10am-4pm; ¥400), a Zen temple which was built in 1614 as a memorial to people who had died in river-control projects. There is a haiku here by Basho (see p277) celebrating the cherry blossom. Signs along the path rightly mention a 'Great View': the final climb to the temple is worth the effort for the panorama over the river, with Kyoto in the distance. If in need of a rest en route there are a few cafés by the river.

On your way back, if the prospect of **Iwatayama Monkey Park** (daily 9am-5pm, Nov-mid Mar to 4pm, closed in bad weather; ¥550) appeals, follow the signs up the hill. Then cross back over the bridge and keep heading straight, along the road lined with tourist shops and restaurants. Turn first left after passing Keifuku-Arashiyama station and follow the signs to Tenryu-ji.

Tenryu-ji (daily 8.30am-5.30pm, Nov to mid Mar to 5pm; garden ¥500, garden and temple ¥600), originally built in 1255 as a palace with a view of Mt Arashiyama, was converted into a Zen temple in 1339 and is now a World

HONSHU

Heritage site. The focal point of the garden is a pond behind which the rest of the garden is spread out on the hillside. When you have seen enough, take the west exit leading to the **bamboo forest** behind the temple. Cool and shady in the summer, the forest offers a number of paths: head left to walk back to the river through Kameyama Park, or right for the small **Nonomiya Shrine**, where Imperial princesses underwent purification rites for three years as part of their training before being sent to the Grand Shrine at Ise (see pp191-3).

From the shrine go back to the main road and turn left. A 10-minute walk brings you to **Seiryo-ji** (daily 9am-4pm; grounds free, temple ¥400), once a country villa and a good place for a special lunch as there's a tiny restaurant, to the right of the main building, called *Chikusen* (Fri-Wed 10am-4.30pm). The ¥3675 lunch served on a tray is a visual delight. On the left of the entrance there is a tea house, where tea and a Japanese sweetmeat cost ¥650.

Just north-east of Seiryo-ji is **Daikaku-ji** (🖳 www.daikakuji.or.jp; daily 9am-4.30pm; ¥500), which has a viewing platform over adjacent Osawa Pond. Originally part of the country villa of Emperor Saga, the complex became a temple after his death in 876. To get there turn left out of Seiryo-ji, go straight over at the crossroads, walk along till you come to a petrol station on the left, then follow the signs.

Along the JR Nara line The fastest service to Nara by JR (rapid train) takes 45 minutes, though most services are local and take over an hour. Trains depart from track Nos 8, 9 or 10 at Kyoto station roughly three times an hour. If you're not in a hurry take a local train, and consider stopping off at one or more of the places described below.

● **Tofuku-ji (1.1km)** Just one stop along the line and barely out of Kyoto station, it's a few minutes' walk south-east of the station to **Tofuku-ji** (see map p207; 🖳 www.tofukuji.jp; daily 9am-4pm, Nov to 4.30pm; grounds free, Tsutenkyo Bridge and Kaisando Hall ¥400, Hojo and gardens ¥400), one of Kyoto's largest Zen monasteries and also known for its stunning foliage in autumn. Tsutenkyo Bridge is one of the most popular viewing spots. The Hojo is where the head abbot used to live and around it are a number of gardens.

● **Inari (2.7km)** The next stop on the line. Right outside this station is the first orange-lacquered *torii* (shrine gate) marking the entrance to **Fushimi-Inari Shrine** (daily dawn to dusk; free). The station itself is bright orange, giving you a taste of what to expect in the shrine.

Fushimi-Inari is a huge complex and contained within the grounds is a long series of tunnels of torii, about 10,000 in all, which you might recognise from the film *Memoirs of a Geisha*. Pilgrims dressed in white are a common sight here. It's only a short walk to the main shrine, behind which paths lead off through the torii tunnels which snake up Mt Inari. Though the walkways are surrounded by trees and mostly in the shade, it's a step up from a gentle stroll, so wear trainers. There are a few tea houses along the way, where you can sit on tatami mats by the window and enjoy views of the mountain on which the shrine complex is built. You are rewarded for your effort when you reach an observation point offering a great view of Kyoto, though from here it's a further walk up to the highest point of 233m (where there are no great views), about 4km in total from the station; you should reach the top within an hour.

Before jumping back on the train, seek out the small **Sekiho-ji** (Mar-Sep daily 9am-5pm, Oct-Feb to 4pm; ¥300), or more precisely the bamboo garden behind it. Five to ten minutes on foot from Fushimi-Inari, but not easy to find, this small temple has one of the most peaceful gardens in Kyoto. Turn right out of Inari station and go straight until you reach the rail track. Don't cross the track but turn left up the road and walk along till you see a graveyard on your right. Turn right and keep walking; soon you will see a sign to Sekiho-ji. The entrance to the temple is on the left but is well hidden; the good thing is that this means few people bother to look for it. The secluded bamboo grove on the hillside behind the main temple building is filled with stone statues of the Buddha and his disciples. The images were created by artist Ito Jakuchu in the late 1700s and are known for their comical facial expressions. The images are supposed to calm the souls of the dead and help relieve the grief of those left behind.

● **Uji (14.9km)** Uji has been a well-known tea-producing area since the Kamakura era (1185-1333) and also features in the last 10 chapters of one of Japan's most famous novels, *The Tale of Genji*. Uji Bridge, mentioned in the book, was first built by a Buddhist monk in 646, though the present construction dates from the 1990s.

There are lockers (¥300-400) to the left of the exit on the 2nd floor and to the right of the exit at street level. There is a **tourist information booth** (Mar-Nov Mon-Fri 9am-5pm, Sat & Sun to 6pm, Dec-Feb daily to 5pm) in the building opposite the station.

Byodo-In (🖥 www.byodoin.or.jp; daily 8.30am-5.30pm; ¥600, plus ¥300 to enter Phoenix Hall, by timed tickets in peak periods), a 10-minute walk down the hill from the station, is a peaceful temple set back from the west bank of Uji-gawa. It's a World Heritage site and is known for the large Buddha statue in its main building, the Phoenix Hall. The shape of the hall, with annexes stretching out either side, is said to 'resemble a phoenix spreading its wings' and is depicted on the ¥10 coin. The main ticket includes entry to the museum (**Hosho-kan**) which displays a wide variety of objects associated with the temple. Byodo-in is the first temple to use iPads to show some of the sculptures in 3D, but also as they would have been when first created. Turn right out of the museum and then left to return to the station; at the riverside **Taiho-an Tea House**, green tea and Japanese cakes are served (Feb-Dec daily 10am-4pm, ¥500; tickets from the adjacent tourist information office). Walk along the river until you reach Uji bridge and then turn left to return to the station.

● **Nara (41.7km)** Rapid services from Kyoto stop at Uji, so you can pick the train up here and continue directly to Nara (journey time: 25 mins).

NARA

Some 40km south of Kyoto, Nara boasts a longer history than its nearby rival. It became Japan's first permanent capital in 710 and, even though its time at the top was short-lived (the Imperial court had decamped to Kyoto by 794), the period was marked by the influence of Buddhism from mainland China.

Nara's tremendous collection of temples, particularly enormous Todai-ji, which houses Japan's largest statue of the Buddha, still stand today as proof of

HONSHU

that influence, and of the great wealth that once poured into the city. Just outside the centre of Nara, Horyu-ji contains the world's oldest surviving wooden structures (particularly impressive when you consider how frequently wooden temples burn to the ground in Japan).

Nara's compact size makes it much more manageable than Kyoto and its vast park is more attractive than Kyoto's urban sprawl. A lightning-fast day excursion can be made from Kyoto but an overnight stay in Nara would allow you time to enjoy the sights at a more leisurely pace.

What to see and do

With just one day here, focus on Nara Park. With more time you could also take in the Naramachi quarter, visit one or two of the museums, or make the short trip out to Horyu-ji. Though it's easy enough to tour Nara Park on your own, it may be worth organising a guided tour of the museum with one of the volunteer guide groups mentioned on p220.

Approaching Nara Park from JR Nara station along Sanjo-dori, look out on your left for the three- and five-storeyed pagodas which belong to **Kofuku-ji** (daily 9am-5pm). Moved here in 710 when Nara became the capital, at the height of its prosperity, this temple boasted as many as 175 buildings but most of them have since burnt down. The three-storeyed pagoda dates from 1143 and the five-storeyed one from 1426. The latter is at its most spectacular when lit up at night (summer only). The Tokondo (Eastern Main Hall; ¥300) and impressive Treasure Museum (¥600), renovated in 2011, display a variety of Buddhist sculptures. The Central Golden Hall is being reconstructed and will be closed until 2015. Performances of Noh take place in the temple precincts in May.

The biggest draw in the park is **Todai-ji** (🖳 www.todaiji.or.jp; Apr-Sep daily 7.30am-5.30pm, Oct to 5pm, Nov-Feb 8am-4.30pm, Mar to 5pm; ¥500 to visit the Daibutsuden, ¥800 inc museum). Its main building, the Daibutsuden (Great Buddha Hall), is the world's largest wooden structure and houses a 16.2m-high, 15-tonne bronze statue known as the 'Great Buddha of Nara'. The small museum (¥500) inside the nearby cultural centre displays the temple's priceless collection of Buddha statues and other historic art.

Nara's most important shrine is **Kasuga Taisha** (Apr-Oct daily 6.30am-5.30pm, Nov-Mar 7am-4.30pm; inner area ¥500), the pathway to which is lined

---

🎋 **Harmonious co-habitation**

Apart from its rich cultural heritage, Nara is known for the harmonious co-habitation of humans and deer. It won't be long before you spot one (they tend to wander in and around the shops along Sanjo-dori in search of food), and it's often not up to you how close you want to get to them. At least this means a picnic in Nara Park will never be lonely. The deer are protected because they are believed to be messengers from the gods (at one point they were even considered to be higher in status than humans). Today the deer population stands at around 1100, a figure which has remained more or less stable for many years (around 200 die and 200 are born every year, and it is an offence to kill one).

with lanterns (there are said to be 3000 in the shrine precincts). Founded in 768 at the foot of Mt Mikasa, this shrine of the Fujiwara family remained influential throughout the Heian Period (794-1185), after the capital had moved to Kyoto. Inside the compound, fortune sticks are available in English for ¥200. Also in the grounds is **Shinen Manyo botanical garden** (Mar-Nov daily 9am-5pm, Dec-Feb to 4pm; ¥525), probably at its best in April and May when the wisteria is in bloom, and a **Treasure House** (daily 9am-5pm; ¥410). The main shrine's annual festival is held on 13th March; other festivals are held here in early February and mid August.

Nara National Museum (Nara Kokuritsu Hakubutsukan; 💻 www.nara haku.go.jp; Tue-Sun 9.30am-5pm, to 7pm on Fri from late Apr to late Oct; ¥500), in the park, opened in 1895 as one of three Imperial museums (the other two were in Kyoto and Tokyo). Nearly all exhibits have brief explanations in English but it's difficult to get a perspective on the wealth of ceremonial objects, paintings, scrolls, statues and sutras without an English-speaking guide. There are two parts to the permanent collection: 'Masterpieces of Buddhist Sculpture' is in the original building (the Sculpture Hall) and 'Masterpieces of Buddhist Art' is in the New West wing. There's a pleasant *café* on the lower-level passageway between the old and new buildings, which does coffee-and-cake sets in the afternoon.

An unexpected attraction in central Nara is **Okumura Commemorative Museum** (💻 www.okumuragumi.co.jp/en/commemorative/index.html; daily exc 3rd Tue 10am-5pm; free), run by the Okumura Corporation, which designs earthquake-prevention systems for buildings and was founded in Nara in 1907. The star attraction is the rather grandly named 'Earthquake and Seismic Isolation Experience Device' – essentially a special chair into which you can be strapped before feeling the full force of a quake. Don't leave the building without visiting the open-air terrace and its great views of Todai-ji. Few tour groups stop here, so it's a welcome break from the hordes. Don't feel bad about lingering, as the museum promotes itself as a 'place to rest while strolling around this historic city'. They even offer free tea and coffee.

Fans of Japanese gardens should make a beeline for **Isui-en** (Wed-Mon 9.30am-4.30pm; ¥650), a stroll garden divided into two sections, each of which has its own pagoda and assorted tea houses. In the classic way of Japanese gardens, Isui-en makes full use of the 'borrowed scenery' of nearby temples and mountains. If you're on a budget, try the adjacent, smaller garden at **Yoshiki-en** (daily 9am-5pm; mid Mar-Dec; ¥250, free to passport-bearing foreign visitors) instead, from where there are views out onto Isui-en, which it overlooks. Yoshiki-en seems less popular than its larger neighbour and is often more peaceful.

The Kintetsu Nara line is the best way to access the grounds of the restored **Heijo Palace** (Heijyo-kyo; Tue-Sun 9am-4.30pm; free), Nara's Imperial Palace now a World Heritage site. This area had its heyday in 710, when Nara became Japan's new capital, but once the palace was moved from Nara to Nagaoka (see p32) in 784, the land was co-opted for paddy fields. The vast palace area – some 321 acres in all – was only restored in time for the 1300th

> ### 🏯 Constructing the past
> It's interesting to note how the quality of building work has changed since Nara's heyday in 710. If you look closely at the wood pillars used in the reconstructed buildings which now make up the Heijo Palace site you'll see the wood is beginning to crack, even though the restoration was only completed in 2010. Contrast this with the more solid workmanship on display in Todai-ji, the most recent incarnation of which has been around for 800 years, and there is no sign of the wood on the huge pillars in this temple cracking. Also very different today are 21st-century concerns about health and safety. The reconstructed buildings had to be built with earthquake-proof steel foundations.

anniversary of its founding in 2010. The main sight is the Imperial Audience Hall (Daigoku-den) and its Takamikura throne, but there is also an Excavation Site exhibition hall, and Nara Palace Site Museum (Heijo-kyo History Museum) containing a full-scale replica of a missionary ship. The East Palace Garden (Toin-teien) is a reconstruction of one thought to have been established here in the 8th century. The closest station on the Kintetsu Nara Line is Yamato-Saidaiji (frequent services; ¥200), from where it is a 15-minute walk east.

Another area of interest is the **Naramachi** district, a very atmospheric old quarter with traditional houses, narrow streets, craft shops, mini museums and cafés. Both **Gango-ji** (daily 9am-5pm), also known as Gokuraku-bo (Paradise Temple) and dating from the 13th century, and **Naramachi-Koshi-no-Ie** (Naramachi Lattice House; Tue-Sun 9am-5pm; free), a typical private house, are worth visiting.

See also pp222-5 for details of side trips from Nara.

NARA – MAP KEY

Where to stay

3 Hotel Nikko Nara ホテル日航奈良
4 Super Hotel Lohas JR Nara Ekimae
　スーパーホテルLohasJR奈良駅前
6 Super Hotel JR Nara Ekimae
　スーパーホテルJR奈良駅前
7 Nara Washington Hotel Plaza
　奈良ワシントンホテルプラザ
8 Hotel Fujita Nara ホテルフジタ奈良
16 Ryokan Seikan-so 旅館静観荘
19 Nara Hotel 奈良ホテル
20 Kikusuiro 菊水楼

Where to eat and drink

10 Bekkan Piatto 別館ピアット
11 Hiten 飛天
12 Ganko Tonkatsu とんかつがんこ
13 Okaru おかる
14 Yamazakiya 山崎屋
19 Hanagiku 花菊
21 Uma-no-Me 馬の目

Where to eat and drink (cont'd)

27 Yume-Kaze Hiroba 夢風ひろば

Other

1 Heijo Palace 平城宮
2 Horyu-ji 法隆寺
5 Eki Rent-A-Car 駅レンタカー
9 Nara City Information Center
　奈良市観光案内所
15 Kofuku-ji 興福寺
17 Naramachi-Koshi-no-Ie
　ならまち格子の家
18 Gangoji Temple 元興寺
22 Nara National Museum
　奈良国立博物館
23 Okumura Commemorative Museum
　奥村記念館
24 Yoshikien 吉城園
25 Isuien 依水園
26 Todai-ji 東大寺
28 Kasuga Taisha 春日大社

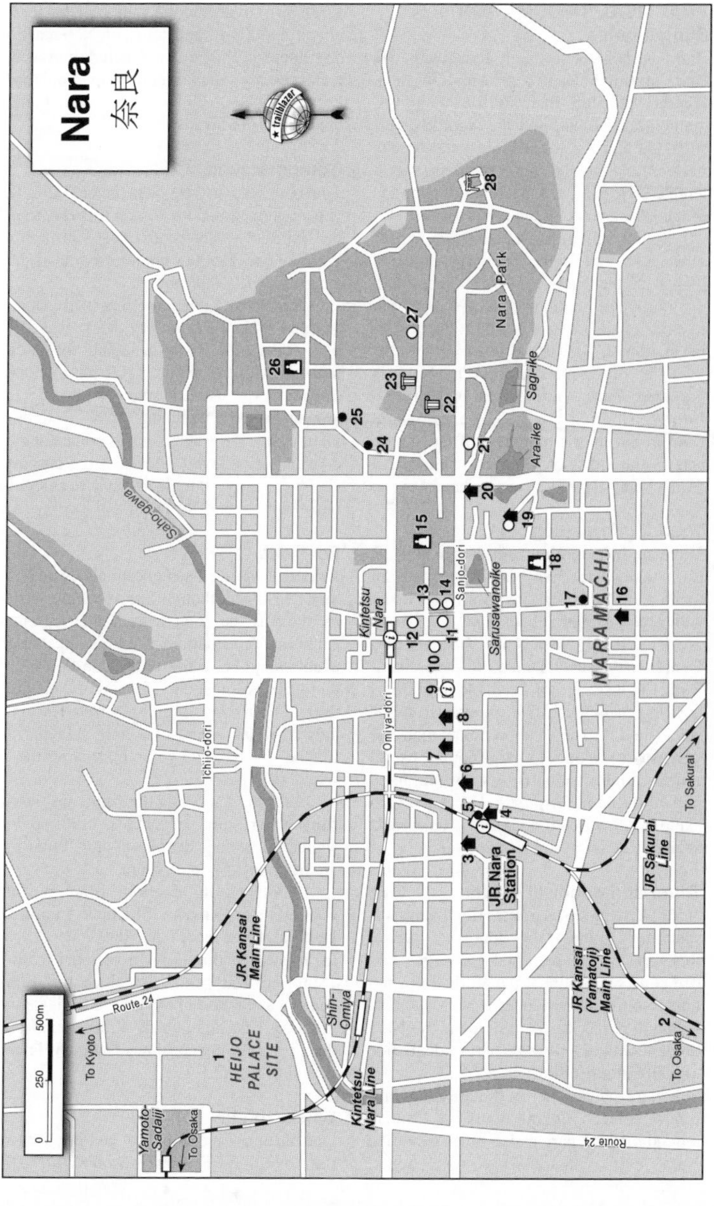

Nara
奈良
trailblazer
0
250
500m
Yamoto-Sadaiji
To Osaka
To Kyoto
Route 24
1
HEIJO PALACE SITE
Shin-Omiya
Kintetsu Nara Line
JR Kansai Main Line
JR Kansai (Yamatoji) Main Line
2
To Osaka
Ichijo-dori
Omiya-dori
3
4
5
JR Nara Station
JR Sakurai Line
To Sakurai
6
7
8
9
10
11
12
Kintetsu Nara
13
14
Sanjo-dori
Sarusawanoike
NARAMACHI
15
16
17
18
19
20
Saho-gawa
21
Ara-ike
Sagi-ike
22
23
24
25
26
27
Nara Park
28
Route 24

PRACTICAL INFORMATION
Station guide
Rail-pass holders are likely to arrive at **JR Nara station**. The two principal JR lines are the Yamatoji line (to/from Horyu-ji, Tennoji and Osaka) and the Nara line (to/from Uji and Kyoto). JR Nara station has been rebuilt; the old station building, with a temple-style roof, is a listed building and is to the left as you exit the new station.

To the right of the station ticket barrier at the east exit is the JR ticket office, a branch of the Nippon Travel Agency and the tourist information counter (see below). Lockers of all sizes are in a building next to the station, to your left as you exit.

The other main station in Nara is **Kintetsu Nara** with services to Kintetsu Namba station in Osaka. There is a *Caffe Ciao Presso* in the basement of the station and on the 3rd floor a branch of *Saizeriya* (daily 11am-11pm) serving pasta and pizza.

Tourist information
There are **information counters** in both JR Nara (daily 9am-5pm) and Kintetsu Nara (daily 9am-5pm) stations. Staff can assist with accommodation bookings.

The main **Nara City Information Center** (🖥 narashikanko.jp; daily 9am-9pm; English speaker available until 7pm) is along Sanjo-dori, five minutes from JR Nara station. They can provide maps of suggested walking tours. Another useful source of information is 🖥 www.pref.nara.jp/nara_e. *Nara Explorer* (🖥 www.naraexplorer.jp), a free bi-monthly magazine, is available at TICs, sights and hotels.

Tours and goodwill guides
Nara YMCA organises free English-speaking guides for tours of Nara. Reservations are preferred (🖥 eggnara.tripod.com) or enquire at the tourist information counters in JR/Kintetsu Nara stations. A similar service is provided by Nara Student Guides (🖥 www.narastudentguide.org/NSG/tourist.html).

Nara Walk (🖥 www.narawalk.com) offers guided walking tours in English around the city, park and temples including Nara Park Classic Tour (3½ hours;

¥2000pp), Great Buddha Tour to Todai-ji (2 hours; ¥1500pp), and tours of Naramachi and Horyu-ji. Prices do not include entrance fees; reserve ahead, online, particularly 21st December to 28th February when tours only run if pre-booked.

Getting around
The best way to see Nara is on foot. If you're pressed for time rent a **bicycle** from the Eki Rent-A-Car booth (daily 9am-5pm; ¥500/1 hour, ¥1000/4 hours), to your right as you exit JR Nara station.

Nara City Loop Line Bus (daily 9am-4.30pm; 2/hr; ¥200/journey, ¥500 one-day pass for central Nara including the sites mentioned in this guide; ¥800 for a wider area) runs – as its name suggests – in a loop around the city, including stops at all the main sights. An English audio commentary is available on board. Catch it from outside JR Nara station; bus stand No 1 for clockwise journeys and No 11 for anti-clockwise.

Festivals
As one of Japan's ancient capitals, Nara has many festivals, though one you may wish to avoid is the annual deer antler-cutting ceremony in the autumn. A more appealing event may be **Shikayose** (Jan/Feb-Mar daily 10am for about 15 mins) when the deer are attracted to an area near Kasuga Taisha by the sound of a horn (playing a Beethoven symphony) and are rewarded with lots of acorns.

July to October is the **'light-up' sea-son**, when some of Nara's best-known sights, including Kofuku-ji and Todai-ji, are lit up nightly until 10pm.

Another illumination time is in February for **Kasuga Shrine's Lantern Festival**, when more than 3000 lanterns are lit. **Kasuga Wakamiya On-matsuri** (15th-18th Dec) has been held since the 12th century and is one of the largest festivals in the area. The highlight is a procession on the 17th featuring costumes from the Heian period to the Edo.

Where to stay
One of the cheapest options, and just across the street from JR Nara, is *Super Hotel JR*

Nara Ekimae (☎ 0742-20 9000, 🖳 www. superhotel.co.jp; ¥5280/S, ¥7280/D), with the usual functional rooms and a free continental breakfast. An alternative, and even closer to – in fact, right outside – the station, is *Super Hotel Lohas JR Nara Ekimae* (☎ 0742-27 9000, 🖳 www.super hotel.co.jp; ¥6980/S, ¥10,800-11,800/Tw or Tr). It has a natural hot-spring spa.

A more appealing area is the historic Naramachi district, with its small lanes and traditional houses. Here you'll find *Ryokan Seikan-so* (☎/🖷 0742-22 2670, 🖳 seikan so@chive.ocn.ne.jp; ¥4450pp; Western breakfast ¥472, Japanese ¥735), an old inn built around a traditional Japanese garden. None of the tatami rooms has an attached bathroom but this is a popular, very reasonably priced place that fills up quickly. It's 15 minutes on foot south of Kintetsu Nara station (part of the way is along a covered arcade) or 25 minutes from JR Nara station.

An excellent mid-range option is *Nara Washington Hotel Plaza* (☎ 0742-27 0410, 🖳 nara.washington.jp; from ¥6900/S, ¥12,000/Tw or D, more expensive in Apr & May, Oct & Nov), five minutes from JR Nara station along Sanjo-dori.

Hotel Fujita Nara (☎ 0742-23 8111, 🖳 www.fujita-nara.com; ¥7200/S, ¥10,200/ D, ¥12,200/Tw) is a little old-fashioned but OK for the price and well located; they offer a number of packages.

The plushest modern place in town, *Hotel Nikko Nara* (☎ 0742-35 8831, 🖳 www.nikkonara.jp; from ¥10,000/S, from ¥17,000/D or Tw), looms up behind JR Nara station (take the west exit). It's a haven of luxury with spacious rooms and a choice of places to eat, including a swish Chinese restaurant: Shuko. The buffet breakfast is ¥1600; some packages include this.

By far the most atmospheric place to stay is *Nara Hotel* (☎ 0742-26 3300, 🖳 www.narahotel.co.jp; ¥16,000/S, ¥25,000/ Tw, exc breakfast, rates discounted for rail-pass holders), opened in 1909 and designed by the architect responsible for the famous red-brick Tokyo Station Hotel (see p102). The old wing has enormous rooms with high roofs and spacious bathrooms. Rooms in the new wing lack the history but are just

as comfortable. The bar is the perfect place to sip a gin and tonic after a hard day's sightseeing and maybe flick through the guest book. Members of the Imperial Family always stay here when visiting Nara (snapshots of their visits line a wall near reception). You too could try the Imperial Suite: a snip at ¥346,500 a night.

You can't get more traditional than *Kikusuiro* (☎ 0742-23 2001, 🖳 www.kiku suiro.com; from ¥47,000pp half-board), a ryokan with creaking wooden floorboards and smart, kimono-clad staff who shuffle along the endless corridors.

Where to eat and drink
Bekkan Piatto (daily 11am-2pm & 6-9.30pm), just off Sanjo-dori, serves tasty pasta dishes (lunch sets ¥1100-1400 plus ¥300 for larger portion), though the normal portions are not large. Its 2nd-floor position gives anyone on the open-air balcony a good view of people passing below.

Along a covered arcade off Sanjo-dori, *Hiten* (daily 11am-3pm & 5-10pm) serves a wide range of Chinese dishes such as dim sum, spicy pork, chicken, shrimps and beef. Lunch sets start at ¥850 but it's still good value in the evening when dishes cost from ¥500. *Okaru* (Thur-Tue 11am-9pm), also in the covered arcade, is a great okonomiyaki place with both tatami and table seating where you choose the ingredients for your pancakes (from ¥680), which are then cooked and served in front of you. *Ganko Tonkatsu* (daily 11am-10pm), also in the covered arcade next to a branch of Mister Donut, serves delicious tonkatsu and does lunch sets cost from ¥880; an English menu is available. They also do take-outs.

Yamazakiya (Tue-Sun 11.15am-9.30pm), the entrance to which is behind a shop in the arcade selling pickled vegetables, is a traditional Japanese place where you can order from the plastic models of sample dishes outside. Lunch from ¥880.

To really empty your pocket pay a visit to *Uma-no-Me* (☎ 0742-23 7784; Fri-Wed 11.30am-2.30pm & 5.30-8.50pm), close to Nara Hotel. This is about as traditional a Japanese place as you are likely to find. It's a very small restaurant decorated with

Japanese *yakimono* (pottery), some of which dates from the early Meiji period. Seating is on tatami mats in the main part of the restaurant or in private rooms with a view over the garden. Lunch costs from ¥3500 and an evening meal (reservation only) from ¥8000. *Hanagiku* (daily 11.30am-2pm & 5.30-9.30pm), in Nara Hotel, serves skilfully prepared box-style lunches (*shokado bento*) for about ¥3700.

If none of these appeals, try one of the regional-produce restaurants in **Yume-Kaze Hiroba** (Yume-Kaze Plaza; 🖳 www.yume-kaze.com; complex open daily 9.30am-10pm though restaurant hours vary), opposite Nara National Museum.

Side trips from Nara

● **To Horyu-ji** Some 12km south-west of Nara lies the temple of Horyu-ji (🖳 www.horyuji.or.jp; daily 8am-4.30/5pm; ¥1000), founded in 607 and now a World Heritage site. Highlights of its western compound are the Five-storeyed Pagoda and the Main Hall, believed to be the world's oldest surviving wooden structure. In the eastern compound, the Hall of Dreams, built in 739, houses a statue of the temple's founder, Prince Shotoku. Its octagonal shape is auspicious, since the number eight is considered lucky in Japan.

To reach Horyu-ji, take a local train on the Yamatoji line from JR Nara station (10 mins). Bus No 72 runs from outside Horyu-ji station to the temple (3/hour; 5 mins; ¥170). Get off at Horyujimon-mae. Horyu-ji is on the Yamatoji Line (part of the Kansai line) between Nara and Osaka so could be visited en route to either city.

● **To Yoshino-yama** Yoshino-yama, together with Koya san (see opposite) and Kumano Nachi Taisha (see p194), are part of the World Heritage site called the Sacred sites and pilgrimage routes in the Kii mountain range. Yoshino-yama is particularly well known for its thousands of cherry trees, which are spread over four areas (Shimo Senbon, Naka Senbon, Kami Senbon and Oku Senbon), and also its ancient Buddhist temples and Shinto shrines.

By JR from Nara take the Yamatoji line to Takada and then the Wakayama line to Yoshino-guchi (sometimes you can stay on the same train; approx 1/hr; 60 mins). At Yoshino-guchi transfer to the Kintetsu line for the journey to Yoshino (35 mins; ¥370). If you don't have a Japan Rail Pass the only direct service to Yoshino is on the Kintetsu Line from Osaka-Benobashi (from 76 mins; ¥950). The journey from Kintetsu Nara to Yoshino (¥1700) on Kintetsu services requires two changes and takes at least 83 minutes.

From Yoshino you can either walk up the hillside (this part, Shimo Senbon, is fairly steep), following the pilgrimage trail to Mt Omine, or take **Yoshino Ropeway** (cable car; ¥350 one way, ¥600 return) to Yoshino-yama station.

Nara Kotsu operates a shuttle bus in the cherry blossom season (April) from Kintetsu Yoshino station bus stop to Naka Senbon-koen bus stop near Chikurin-in temple. Also at this time another shuttle bus operates from Chikurin-in-mae bus stop to Oku Senbon-guchi bus stop right at the top of the mountain. However, the views of the cherry trees are less good from up here.

From Yoshino-yama ropeway station it is about 10 minutes' walk to **Kinpusen-ji Temple** (daily 8.30am-4.30pm; entry to the hall ¥400), which has a 7m-high Buddha statue. This area is called Naka Senbon and it is relatively flat; it is also where most of the sights (including the cherry trees) as well as places to stay and eat are. A half-hour walk brings you to **Chikurin-in Temple** (daily 9am to sunset; ¥300), known for its garden but it also has a *ryokan* (☎ 0746-32 8081, 🖳 www.chikurin.co.jp; ¥13,650-42,000pp half-board). With its open-air bath this would be a wonderful place to spend the night. From the temple it is possible to walk up to Kami Senbon and the Hanayagura viewpoint but the hillside gets steeper again. To walk from Chikurin-in to **Kinbu Shrine** (Oku Senbon), at the top of the mountain, would take at least an hour.

● **To Koya-san** A religious centre was founded on Mt Koya, about 850m above sea level, in 815 by the Buddhist monk Kukai (also known as Kobodaishi) as a place of meditation. Pilgrims and tourists have been flocking here ever since. In 2004 it was added to the UNESCO World Heritage Site list and 2015 will mark its 1200th anniversary. Where once the monks of Koya-san earned an income by begging, today they do so by providing accommodation.

A night spent in a temple, with a superb dinner and breakfast of *shojin ryori* and the chance to take part in early-morning prayers, should not be missed. Think of a visit to Koya-san as an experience in two phases, namely the journey there and then the place itself.

The journey The most direct way to reach Koya-san is from Osaka (see below) on the private Nankai railway (see p223). And the best deal, also if you don't have a JR Pass, is Nankai's **Koya-san World Heritage ticket** (🖳 www. nankaikoya.jp), which offers return travel (outward journey on a limited express), unlimited use of Nankai Rinkun buses on Koya-san and reduced-price tickets on some attractions while you are there for ¥3310 (¥4870 for journeys on Limited Express Koya).

If you plan to travel to Kumano and round Wakayama (see pp193-7) as well get the **W-Pass** (Kansai Wakayama Pass; 🖳 www.wakayama-kanko.or.jp/world/english; ¥3500/2-day, ¥5500 3-day) which is valid on the Nankai Railway from Osaka and buses and trains in Wakayama prefecture (excluding JR services).

JR rail-pass holders can go part of the way to Koya-san by JR but have to transfer on to the Nankai line at Hashimoto station.

From Nara the quickest way is to take a train (1/hr) to Takada on the JR Yamatoji line (45 mins), which then becomes the JR Wakayama line and goes to Hashimoto (51 mins); see below for details from Hashimoto.

From Kyoto take a train to Nara (3/hr) and then follow the route above.

From Osaka take a train from Osaka station (31 mins) or from Tennoji (20 mins), both on the JR Yamatoji line, to Oji. From there, transfer to the JR Wakayama line and get off at Hashimoto (nearly two hours in all). However, if you don't have a JR rail pass take the Nankai Koya line from Nankai Namba station, Osaka, to Gokurakubashi (79 mins on LEX ¥1610 inc seat reservation and cable car; 92 mins by express/local train, ¥850 inc cable car).

From Wakayama (see p197) take the JR Wakayama line direct to Hashimoto (1/hr; 68 mins).

At **Hashimoto** cross via the overhead footbridge to the Nankai platforms and, if you haven't already got a Nankai ticket, buy a ticket to Koya-san (45 mins; ¥810, ¥1310 with seat reservation from Hashimoto to Gokurakubashi) from the booth on the platform. If only staying one night on Koya-san it is possible to buy a return ticket though this only saves time, not money. You might have to hang around a bit at Hashimoto as connections between JR and Nankai services are not always good.

The final part of the route is quite possibly one of the finest rail journeys in Japan. The train rattles and squeaks its way slowly upwards, until the track becomes surrounded by thick, pine-clad forests. As the train climbs (and your ears pop), the temperature starts to drop. Here it's about 10° cooler than on the plains below (pleasant in the summer but freezing in the winter). Inevitably, the train passes through a number of tunnels, though each time it emerges into daylight the scenery becomes more spectacular. Sit on the right-hand side if you can.

The train terminates at **Gokurakubashi**. The last part of the journey is a steep ascent by cable car (funicular) to **Koya-san station**. The five-minute 870m ride is ¥380 but it is included in the cost of the ticket from Hashimoto. From the station buses take about 10 minutes to the centre (2-3/hr). The fare (¥280-320) depends on where you are staying and therefore where you get off; the one-day bus passes are probably not worth the money (¥800) as the town is compact and easy to walk around; stop announcements are in English.

Koya-san Koya-san is small enough to get around on foot. **Koya-san Visitor Information Center** (VIC; ☎ 0736-56 2616, 🖷 56 2889, 🖳 www.shukubo. net; Apr-Nov Fri-Mon & Wed 10am-4pm, Dec-Mar Wed & Fri only), in Daishi Kyokai building in the centre of town, has maps, leaflets about walks in the area and also sells a guidebook (¥1000). Cycles can be rented from here (¥400/ hr, ¥1200/5 hrs), as can a portable audio guide (¥500). They also run free guided tours from outside the VIC (Apr-Oct Wed 8.30am & 1pm), but check in advance. Outside the office there are a few lockers suitable for day packs.

A combination ticket (¥1500) is available from the tourist office but is only worth buying if you intend to visit most of the sights charging admission. The main one to include is **Kongobu-ji** (daily 8.30am-5pm; ¥500), the central monastery in Koya. This is the residence of the High Abbot of Koya-san, who is responsible for the 3000 monasteries across the country that belong to the Shingon Buddhist sect. Next to the monastery is the 6 o'clock bell, rung by a monk every even hour between 6am and 10pm.

Sooner or later, everyone heads for **Okunoin**, part of an enormous ceme-tery with over 200,000 gravestones and monuments, where the body of Kukai is enshrined. According to tradition, on 21st March 835, he entered into 'eternal meditation'; since then he has been known as Kobo Daishi. (Cont'd on p225)

Colour section   **[opposite and pages following]**

● **C1** Geisha (see p41) are renowned for their ability to entertain with music, dance, song and conversation. The women in this photo are maiko (trainee geisha). (© J&RL).

● **C2 Left**: Nishiki food market (see p212), Kyoto, is a great place to find a cheap lunch. (© AU). **Right, top**: Kinkaku-ji (p203), Kyoto's famous Golden Pavilion, shines even on a grey day. (© J&RL). **Right, bottom**: Byodo-In Temple (p215), Uji. (© AU).

● **C3** Morning mist over the pagoda at Kinpusen-ji Temple (p222), Yoshino-yama. (© MA).

● **C4 Left, top**: Relaxing at the foot bath (see p411) outside Ibusuki Station. (© AU). **Left, bottom**: Sunamushi-onsen natural hot sand bath (p411), in Ibusuki. (© AU). **Right**: The Daibutsu (Great Buddha; p108) at Kamakura, an 11.4m-high bronze statue. (© J&RL).

● **C5 Left**: Tokyo Sky Tree (see p95), at 634m the world's tallest broadcast tower, was opened in May 2012. (© AU). **Right, top**: Selling *manju* (a bun made with rice powder), Asakusa (p94, © KU). **Right, bottom**: Busy street crossing in Shibuya (p88), Tokyo. (© KU).

● **C6 Left, top**: The iconic o-torii gate, Itsuku-shima Shrine (see p259), Miyajima © AU). **Btm, left**: Hiroshima's A-bomb Dome (p253), one of the few surviving buildings after the world's first atomic bomb was dropped here on 6th August 1945. (© AU). **Btm, right**: Peace Statue (p391), Nagasaki. (© J&RL). Museums at both bomb sites display tragic reminders such as a child's tricycle (Hiroshima) and a clock stopped at the moment of impact (Nagasaki). (© J&RL). **Right**: The Awa-Odori Dance Festival, Tokushima (p436). (© AP).

C1

C3

C4

C5

(*Cont'd from p224*) It is said he will not wake up until Miroku, the Buddha of the Future, arrives. Okunoin is packed with the tombs and gravestones of Kobo Daishi's followers. It's a good idea to visit early in the morning, when it's a long, peaceful walk from Ichinohashi Bridge on the edge of town through the cemetery towards the Hall of Lanterns, behind which is Kobo Daishi's mausoleum. However, early in the evening can also be very atmospheric. As you enter, turn left for the area with the older graves (the sign later on marking Nakahanohashi cemeteries can be ignored) and return on the lower level where you will see tombstones for companies such as UCC (look out for a tea cup), Toyota, Komatsu, Panasonic and Nissan. The Japan Termite Control Association also has a plaque here in memory of the people whose job it was to get rid of termites; there is also a shrine for the termites to quell their spirits.

● **Where to stay and eat** It's a good idea to book accommodation on Koya-san in advance but tourist-office staff will ring around the temples to see what's available if you arrive without a reservation. Either book directly with the temples or send a fax to the Visitor Center (see opposite) stating dates and preferred accommodation at least two weeks before arrival. They will send confirmation by fax. Payment is in cash only. At all the temples, the evening meal is served about 6pm so ensure you have arrived by about 5pm; overnight guests are invited to attend morning prayers, which usually start at 6 or 6.30am.

The cheapest rates are offered by *Haryoin* (☎ 0736-56 2702; ¥6900pp half-board, or ¥3500pp room only), also called a 'National Lodging House'. Haryoin is a small temple on the edge of town and one of the first stops coming from the cable-car station. All rooms share a common bath.

Almost opposite Haryoin is the larger *Rengejoin* (☎ 0736-56 2233, 🖷 56 4743; from ¥11,000pp half-board). Rooms are larger and better appointed; some have views over a beautiful rock garden. Common bath only.

Sekishoin (☎ 0736-56 2734, 🖷 56 4429; ¥9450pp half-board, plus ¥8000 for an en suite bathroom), founded in 923, is really worth considering. The temple is next to Ichinohashi Bridge, which makes it very convenient for an early morning/evening visit to the Okunoin. Rooms in the new building are modern and more like a hotel than temple lodgings, rooms in the old temple building are more atmospheric; both kinds are available with or without bathrooms. To reach Sekishoin, take a bus heading for the Okunoin from Koya-san station and get off at Ichinohashi-guchi. Also recommended is *Jofukuin* (☎ 0736-56 2109, 🖳 homepage3.nifty.com/koya-jfk; ¥10,000-14,000pp; 10% discount for online bookings, but in Japanese only). Some rooms have en suite toilets and basin, the best also have a massage chair and garden view. Some English is spoken. The room where morning prayers are held can be quite chilly so get there early to be close to the heater. The entrance to Jofukuin is to the left of Konpon Daito (the red pagoda) by bus stop No 8 (Rengedani). Two other good choices are *Shojoshin-in* (☎ 0736-56 2006; from ¥9000pp half-board), which also has easy access to the Okunoin, and *Muryoko-in* (☎ 0736-56 2104, 🖳 www.muryokoin.org; ¥10,500pp half-board).

Most of the temples serve beer and sake. There are several coffee shops, small restaurants and convenience stores around town.

(**Opposite**: **Koya-san**) **Top, left and right**: Two of the many representations of Jizo (bodhisattvas) you can see in Okunoin. **Bottom**: Monks at Kongobu-ji Temple (p224). (© J&RL).

Western Honshu – route guides

Many visitors to Japan take the shinkansen west along the Sanyo coast from Shin-Osaka to Hiroshima, perhaps en route to Kyushu. But western Honshu, also known as **Chugoku** ('the Middle Lands'), has much more to offer than a hurried stop in Hiroshima. The Sanyo coast may have the fastest rail connections and the best-known sights but the less developed San-in (north) coast provides a complete change of pace.

The journey from the Sanyo coast to the San-in offers yet another perspective, with spectacular mountain and river scenery and the chance to see a part of Japan that has not been bulldozed into the industrial revolution. The route along the San-in coast leads to Tsuwano, a picturesque town that offers a chance for a change of pace and also a place with an interesting history, and Matsue, justly famous for the sunsets over its splendid lake, Shinji-ko, and for being the former home of Irish writer Lafcadio Hearn.

Two stations on this route are connection points for other rail journeys: Okayama is the starting point for the Shikoku route guide, and from Shin-Yamaguchi it's only 20 minutes by shinkansen to Kokura, the starting point for the Kyushu route guide.

SHIN-OSAKA (OSAKA) TO SHIN-YAMAGUCHI BY SHINKANSEN

Distances from Shin-Osaka. Fastest journey time: 2½ hours.

This route follows the shinkansen line; regular JR trains go on the Sanyo line which roughly parallels the route described but stops at more stations and takes longer.

Osaka   [see pp113-23]

Shin-Osaka to Okayama   [Map 11, p228; Table 3, pp456-7]
All shinkansen stop here; for notes about the Hikari Rail Star see box below.

☐ Hikari Rail Star

If you have a Green Class Pass be aware that the Hikari Rail Star which runs between Shin-Osaka and Hakata, **doesn't have a Green Car**; however, the seating is 2 x 2 so there is more space than in most shinkansen.

Car No 4 in the Hikari Rail Star has been designated the **'Silence Car'**, a rarity in Japan and a welcome haven from the usual non-stop on-board announcements. Even the staff who wheel the refreshments trolley through the carriage don't say a word. Seats in the Silence Car must be reserved, but don't be put off if JR ticket-office staff try to dissuade you by saying that you might miss your stop because there are no announcements.

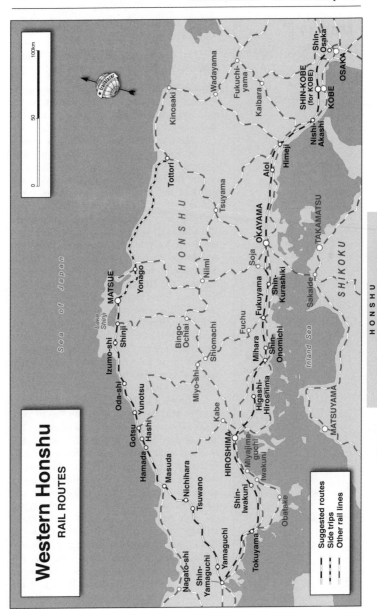

Western Honshu
RAIL ROUTES

Suggested routes
Side trips
Other rail lines

HONSHU

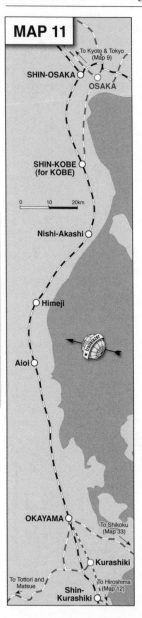

MAP 11

To Kyoto & Tokyo (Map 9)

SHIN-OSAKA

OSAKA

SHIN-KOBE (for KOBE)

0 10 20km

Nishi-Akashi

Himeji

Aioi

Okayama

To Shikoku (Map 33)

Kurashiki

To Tottori and Matsue

To Hiroshima (Map 12)

Shin-Kurashiki

HONSHU

Shin-Kobe (37km) [Kobe, see pp241-7]
All shinkansen stop here.

Only Kodama call at **Nishi-Akashi (60km)**, the next station along the line.

Himeji (92km) All Hikari stop here and some Nozomi. As the train pulls in, look out on the right and you'll see **Himeji Castle** on a hill in the distance.

There's a **tourist information centre** (Himeji Kanko Navi Port; 🖥 www.himeji-kan ko.jp; daily 9am-7pm) opposite the central exit, on the far right of the concourse. There are stacks of **lockers** of all sizes just outside the station's Himeji Castle Exit, on the right. However, the station gets so busy that they may all be taken. If you fancy cycling to the castle, **Eki Rent A Cycle** (daily 9am-4pm, bike must be returned by 6pm; free) is inside the tourist information centre. If you want to see more of the area, the **Himeji Castle Loop Bus** (Mar-Nov daily 9am-5pm; 2-4/hr; ¥100/trip, one-day pass ¥300) is worth considering.

From Himeji station, walk (or cycle) north for about 20 minutes up tree-lined Otemae-dori. About two-thirds of the way along, look out on the left for an udon restaurant, *Menme*, where you can get a filling bowl of noodles and a beer for around ¥1000.

Himeji Castle (🖥 www.himeji-castle.gr .jp; Oct-May daily 9am-4pm, Jun-Sep to 5pm; ¥600, ¥400 during the restoration process, ¥720 inc Koko-en) is truly one of the most picture-postcard buildings in Japan. What makes it so special is that it has never been bombed or reduced to rubble from either a fire or an earthquake. Originally a 14th-century fort, it was rebuilt in its present style at the beginning of the 17th century and has been on the World Heritage list since 1933. It is also known as Hakuro-jo (White Heron Castle) as it resembles a heron with its wings spread out. It is frequently used as a backdrop in samurai movies and even features in the James Bond film *You Only Live Twice* (see p434).

It will take about two hours to explore the castle and the grounds. However, restoration work is continuing until March 2015 and the castle will be hidden under scaffolding until 2014, though parts of the interior will remain open. Visitors can see the restoration work from a special observation deck (🖳 www. himejijo-syuri.jp; ¥200; advance reservations recommended). There are English-speaking **volunteer guides** at the castle (call ☎ 079-285-1146 to arrange one in advance), and their enthusiasm makes a visit to Himeji even more rewarding than a wander around the castle on your own.

Heading through the main gate, Sakura-Mon, you enter the garden where there are plenty of outer fortifications to explore. Inside the main tower, quickly pass through the lacklustre displays of weapons and wall-hangings, and at the end of a flight of very steep, ill-lit steps, you reach the top, from where there's a great view of Himeji city, the station and surrounding area.

Koko-en (Koko Garden; daily 9am-6pm, Sep-Apr to 5pm; ¥300, ¥720 inc castle) behind the castle is recommended – it has nine different gardens and good views of the castle.

A good overnight base in Himeji is *Toyoko Inn Himeji-eki Shinkansen-Minamiguchi* (☎ 0792-84 1045, 🖳 www.toyoko-inn.com; from ¥5480/S, ¥7980/D or Tw), immediately to your left as you take the shinkansen exit of the station (the opposite side to the castle exit). Or try *APA Hotel Himeji-eki Kita* (☎ 079-284 4111, 🖳 www.apahotel.com/hotel/kansai/15_himeji-ekikita; from ¥7500/S, ¥13,000/D, ¥14,000/Tw; Japanese breakfast ¥1000), a few minutes' walk from the station on the castle side.

Only Kodama stop at **Aioi (112km)**.

Okayama (180km) [see pp247-52]

All trains stop at this castle town, famous for it stroll garden, Korakuen.

Okayama to Hiroshima [Map 12, p231; Table 3, pp456-7]
Shin-Kurashiki (206km) Only Kodama stop here. For Kurashiki (see below) transfer to a JR Sanyo line (4/hour; 9 mins). Alternatively take a JR Sanyo Line from Okayama (4/hour; 14 mins).

Side trip by rail to Kurashiki
It's worth coming here to see the preserved **Bikan Historical Quarter** with its quaint old buildings, narrow lanes, small museums and canal.

From Kurashiki station take the south exit for the Bikan Historical Quarter and Eki Rent A Car/Cycle (on street level, to the right as you exit the station; 8am-8pm; bicycles ¥350/4 hours or ¥500/day). There are **lockers** to the right after the ticket barrier (all sizes; ¥300-600). If these are full, there are more by the Eki Rent A Car office.

Staff at the **tourist information centre** (🖳 world.kankou-kurashiki.jp; daily Apr-Oct 9am-7pm, Nov-Mar 9am-5pm) on the station concourse near the ticket barrier speak English and can help book accommodation.

It is less than 1km to Bikan, along Chuo-dori, which leads away from the south exit of the station. Once in the quarter, find your way to the canal and continue to Nakahashi bridge. On the corner here there is another tourist information centre, **Kurashiki-Kan** (daily Apr-Oct 9am-6pm, Nov-Mar to 5pm), which marks the centre of the Bikan district. From here you can either continue walking along the canal or venture into some of the many side streets.

There are several museums and galleries in Bikan. Top priority should be given to **Ohara Museum of Art** (🖥 www.ohara.or.jp; Tue-Sun 9am-5pm; ¥1000, audio guide ¥500). The museum was established in 1930 by Keisaburo Ohara, the then president of Kurashiki Spinning Corporation, to display the works of Western art that his friend Kojima Torajiro had collected on visits to Europe – all this decades before bubble-economy-rich Japanese businessmen were snapping up world-famous Western art work from Christie's by telephone. Since then, the museum has expanded to house not only Western art but also a gallery of Asiatic art and a Craft Art gallery of ceramics and woodblock prints. But the biggest draws are its French Impressionist collection, as well as works by Picasso, Edvard Munch and Andy Warhol.

One of the town's many quirky museums is **Kurashiki Sanyo-do** (also known as **Chokinbako**; 🖥 www.kurashiki.co.jp/chokin/e-cho.htm; Fri-Wed 10.30am-5pm; ¥200), a character bank (piggy bank) museum above an antiques shop. It's on Shirakabe-dori, opposite Kurashiki Ivy Square, which is on the far side of the Historical Quarter – look out for the dalmatian dogs on the roof.

Also worth visiting, but not in the Historical Quarter, is **O-Hashi House** (Tue-Sun 9am-5pm; ¥500), the home of a rice and salt merchant, which dates from about 1796. A bamboo water bucket hangs by the entrance in case there is a fire, though luckily it has never had to be used. Look out also for the Singer sewing machine. To reach the house turn right at the first set of lights at a crossroads on Chuo-dori (before you reach the official entrance to the Bikan Historical Quarter); the house is a short walk along on the left.

Swan Bistro (Thur-Tue 11am-10pm) on the right by the canal and just past the entrance to the Senichi Hoshino Museum (of limited interest unless you are a baseball fan), serves an excellent soup, salad, spaghetti and coffee lunch for ¥1150. The menu at *Kana* (daily 11am-7.30pm) changes according to the season but has something for most budgets; udon costs ¥750, but some dishes cost ¥3600. Take the road to the left on the left side of the canal at Nakabashi bridge; Kana is on the corner at the first crossroads.

APA Hotel Kurashiki Ekimae (☎ 086-426 1111, 🖥 www.apahotel.com/hotel/chugoku/02_kurashiki-ekimae; from ¥7000/S, ¥13,000/D, ¥14,000/Tw) is on the 9th Floor, in West Building – take the Bikan exit and turn right out of the station. Alternatively, *Toyoko Inn Kurashiki-eki Minami-guchi* (☎ 086-430 1045, 🖥 www.toyoko-inn.com; from ¥4980/S, ¥6300/D) is on the left-hand side of Chuo-dori, next to a Lawson convenience store. It's three minutes on foot from the south exit of Kurashiki station.

If continuing west it is best to pick up a JR Sanyo Line train to Fukuyama rather than returning to Shin-Kurashiki.

Fukuyama (239km) All Hikari stop here as well as some Nozomi. As the train arrives look out on the right for a glimpse of Fukuyama Castle. This former castle town suffered extensive damage from WWII bombing raids. The view of concrete blocks as far as the eye can see is not an encouragement to linger but Fukuyama is worth a half-day stop.

There are two sides to Fukuyama station. Take the north exit for the main sights. **Lockers** (¥300-500 plus a few ¥600 ones) are outside and to the right as you take the north exit. Staff at the **tourist information counter** (🖳 www. fukuyama-kanko.com; daily 9am-5pm) on the main concourse give out maps but don't deal with hotel reservations. Within the station is the Suntalk shopping and restaurant mall, where you'll find a range of eat-in/take-away restaurants and cafés.

Fukuyama Castle, built in 1619 and situated in a park by the north exit of the station, has a reconstructed castle tower and museum (Tue-Sun 9am-5pm; ¥200) of no great interest.

Much more fun is **Fukuyama Automobile and Clock Museum** (🖳 www.facm.net; daily 9am-6pm; ¥900), a 15-minute walk north of the station. You're allowed to get in all the cars on display, including a 1954 Mercedes Benz and some original 1960s Mazdas. But it's much more than clocks and cars; there are also gramophones, early TV sets, electric organs, a horse-drawn carriage, light aircraft and waxworks of famous Americans. This is a place where you are encouraged to touch and feel, live and breathe, 1960s America.

There are several hotels near the station but one of the cheapest is *Fukuyama Terminal Hotel* (☎ 0849-32 3311, 🖳 www.fukuyama-t-hotel.jp; from ¥5770/S, ¥9350/D, ¥10,270/Tw), five minutes west.

Side trip to Matsunaga – the 'sole' of Japan

Matsunaga, Japan's top production centre of traditional *geta* (wooden clogs), is between Fukuyama and the next shinkansen station at Shin-Onomichi. To reach it, take a local train two stops (approx 4/hr; about 10 mins) from Fukuyama along the JR Sanyo line.

'As long as footwear continues to be made here,' says a travel brochure, 'Matsunaga will be the "soul" of Japanese feet'. It is not surprising therefore that the town is home to the unique **Japan Footwear Museum** (🖳 www.footandtoy.jp; daily

9am-5pm; ¥1000). Laid out here in pairs is a sweeping history of footwear, from the earliest straw sandals to the latest in high-street fashion boots. Don't miss the glass cabinet that contains a few of the more quirky uses for shoes: a red, stiletto-heeled telephone, a geta-shaped ashtray and a large ceramic boot that doubles as a German beer mug.

The *coffee shop* is a good place to put your feet up, but not for too long since museum staff might just snatch your footwear to add to the collection. Tickets are also valid for the adjacent **Japan Folk Toy and Doll Museum**. Most of the toys, dolls, kites and talismans on display are connected with religious festivals.

The Japan Footwear Museum is five minutes on foot (how else?) from the south exit (to the right as you pass through the ticket barrier) of Matsunaga station. Turn left on leaving the station, walk up to the junction, then turn right; the entrance is just up this road on the right.

From Matsunaga, rejoin the route by taking a train on the Sanyo line four stops to Mihara (approx 20 mins), on the shinkansen line.

Shin-Onomichi (259km) Only
Kodama stop here.

Mihara (270km) Only Kodama stop
here. Mihara is the nearest station to **Buttsu-ji** (🖥 www.buttsuji.or.jp; daily 8am-5pm; free), a centre for training in Zen meditation (see box), 40 minutes to the north by bus (4/day; ¥600).

The temple is surrounded by cedar and maple trees, which attract visitors during the autumn-leaves' viewing season (late Oct to Nov), when admission costs ¥300.

> ❏ **The Holy Grail**
> *Monty Python* star turned globetrotter Michael Palin visited Buttsu-ji during his *Full Circle* travel documentary (episode 2, 14th Sep 1997) for BBC Television and attempted to interview the abbot:
> 'As I am only here for one night, what will I be able to learn in that time from being here, do you think?'
> 'You?'
> 'Yes.'
> 'But that is your problem. You must not ask me.'
> 'Oh well, interviewing never was a Zen activity.'

Higashi-Hiroshima (310km) Only
Kodama stop here.

Hiroshima (342km) [see pp252-8]
All shinkansen stop here. Hiroshima is best known for its Peace Memorial Park but it is also the access point for the unmissable island, **Miyajima** (see pp258-60).

Hiroshima to Shin-Yamaguchi [Map 13; Table 3, pp456-7]
Shin-Iwakuni (383km) Only Kodama stop here. The first major stop after Hiroshima is the town of **Iwakuni**, known for the five-arched Kintaikyo Bridge which spans Nishiki-gawa. The scenery is certainly picturesque and there is the added attraction of a ride by ropeway up to Iwakuni Castle. However, a stop here shouldn't be considered a top priority, more a pleasant diversion if you have the time.

A package ticket which includes the bridge, ropeway and castle costs ¥930. This ticket is sold daily (closed 16th-31st Dec) from 9am and up to 3.30pm, to give you time to get up and down by 5pm.

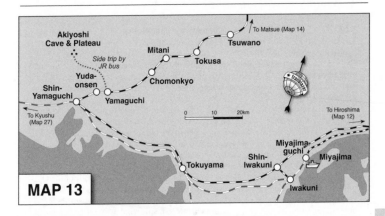

MAP 13

The tourist area is roughly equidistant between Shin-Iwakuni, the shinkansen station, and Iwakuni, which is on the JR Sanyo line: **buses** between Shin-Iwakuni station and Iwakuni station stop at Kintai-kyo bus stop (2-6/hour; about 15 mins from either direction; ¥240 from Iwakuni, ¥280 from Shin-Iwakuni). Tourist information (Tue-Sun 9.30am-4.30pm) is available at both railway stations.

When the feudal lord of Iwakuni constructed **Kintaikyo Bridge** in 1673 his aim was to ensure that it could never be washed away, but it duly has been twice. A return walk across the bridge costs ¥300 when the toll booth is open. Over on the other side you'll see the ropeway (¥540 return trip) up to Iwakuni Castle. Destroyed in 1615 at the time of the Tokugawa shogunate **Iwakuni Castle** (¥260) was rebuilt in 1962 and moved to the top of a hill – not for reasons of military defence but to improve the view. There's little of interest inside (the kind of samurai armour you can see in most castles in Japan and a model of Kintaikyo Bridge, which you can see for real down below), but the top-floor lookout commands excellent views in good weather of Nishiki-gawa, the bridge and the Inland Sea in the distance. In the summer it's a little cooler up here and there are some walking trails.

Tokuyama (430km) A stop for a few Hikari.

Shin-Yamaguchi (474km) Some Hikari stop here. Transfer here to the JR Yamaguchi Line for the route to Tsuwano, Masuda and Matsue (see pp261-6) and for the Lady of Rank steam train (see box p234). If heading for **Kyushu**, continue on the shinkansen and pick up the route guide starting on p362.

The JR ticket office is on the 2nd floor of the shinkansen side, as is the **tourist information office** (daily 8.30am-5pm). *Toyoko Inn Shin-Yamaguchi Eki Shinkansen-guchi* (☎ 083-973 1045, 🖳 www.toyoko-inn.com; from ¥4980/S, ¥6030/D or Tw, inc curry rice supper and breakfast) is outside the station (shinkansen side). For a quick snack there is a branch of the *Vie de France* bakery and café on the ground floor of the station.

♫ **The Lady of Rank – a grand steam experience**
At weekends from March to November, and daily during Golden Week (late Apr to early May), and throughout most of August, the SL Yamaguchi (🖥 c571.jp; C571, nickname: 'Lady of Rank') runs between Shin-Yamaguchi and the picturesque rural town of Tsuwano (see p236). All seats on this 1937 steam-engine locomotive are reserved but there are no additional charges for JR rail-pass holders. Without the pass, the fare from Shin-Yamaguchi to Tsuwano is ¥1650.

The train departs in the morning from the old-fashioned platform 1 at Shin-Yamaguchi and steams along on its 63km journey through the countryside to Tsuwano; it then returns to Shin-Yamaguchi in the afternoon. Rail fans might like to know that the Yamaguchi line was the first in Japan to witness a steam renaissance, when JNR (see p69) introduced the SL Yamaguchi in 1979. Scheduled steam trains had been retired from the same stretch of railway line in 1973.

Apart from the steam locomotive itself, the highlight is a ride in one of the carefully preserved carriages, each designed to recall different eras of Japan's railway history. The best place to sit, however, is at the back of the train, where there's an observation car with (non-reserved) armchairs facing the window. Staff dress up in old railway uniforms and a huge crowd lines up to take photographs as the train pulls out of the station.

SHIN-YAMAGUCHI TO MASUDA
[Map 13, p233; Map 14, p239; Table 11, p462]

Distances by JR from Shin-Yamaguchi. Fastest journey time: 95 minutes.

Shin-Yamaguchi (0km) Take a Super Oki LEX (3/day) or a local train on the JR Yamaguchi line.

Yuda-onsen (10km) This small hot-spring resort is favoured by Japanese looking for a cure for arthritis and other aches and pains. According to legend, 600 years ago a wounded white fox bathed in the hot spring here and was miraculously healed. A large statue of the white fox stands in front of the station.

Yamaguchi (13km) Off the shinkansen track, if not quite off the beaten track, Yamaguchi must be one of the smallest prefectural capitals in Japan. The main reason for pausing here is to take a trip to **Akiyoshi cave and plateau** (Akiyoshi-do and Akiyoshi-dai; see below). However, if you have time to spare it is worth walking along the road north-west from the station (about 15 minutes) to the modern **St Francis Xavier Memorial Church** at the top of Kameyama Park. The original church, built in 1952 to commemorate the 400th anniversary of Xavier's stay in Yamaguchi, burnt down in 1991. It was rebuilt in 1998 and now has a modern, pyramid design with two 53m-high square towers.

Yamaguchi Tourist Association (daily 9am-6pm) is on the 2nd floor of Yamaguchi station. Staff will help book accommodation.

Side trip by JR bus to Akiyoshi cave and plateau
Though not accessible by rail, it's worth considering a trip to Akiyoshi cave and plateau (Akiyoshi-do and Akiyoshi-dai; 🖥 english.karusuto.com; daily

8.30am-4.30pm; ¥1200) since the route from Yamaguchi is operated by JR Bus so rail-pass holders can travel for free. The cave is 100m below Akiyoshi plateau and is the largest limestone cave either in Japan or in Asia – depending on who you talk to, or which leaflet you pick up.

From Yamaguchi station, JR buses run to Akiyoshi-do Bus Center (8/day; 55 mins; ¥1130 one way but free with Japan Rail Pass) close to the cave entrance. You can pick up a guide to the cave and plateau from the **tourist information desk** (daily 8.30am-4.30pm) in the bus centre. From here, follow the signs to the cave entrance, which is a five-minute walk through a parade of shops.After buying an entrance ticket, you enter an area that resembles a rainforest; it's an unexpected scene, especially after the man-made shopping arcade just outside. The entrance to the **cave** is no less impressive. A crashing waterfall (almost) drowns out the noise of microphone-clutching, flag-waving tour guides, who appear to have no fear of wearing high heels inside a slippery limestone cave.

The path is obvious so there's no danger of disappearing down a dark tunnel. Near the entrance there's also a more adventurous track that can be tried for an extra ¥300 (throw your money in the box and pick up a torch). The main path winds its way past various rock formations, some of which have been given unusual names such as 'big mushroom' and 'crêpe rock'. Though it's hard to gush quite as much as the publicity leaflet – 'the colours and shapes of stalactites, stalagmites, flowstones and limestone pools are so fantastic that you feel as if you are in an underground palace' – there's no denying that the interior is breathtaking.

If visiting in the winter it's advisable to put on several layers as the temperature drops considerably inside the cave. In the summer, the temperature is a good reason for heading on in, to beat the humidity.

At the end of the trail inside the cave, an elevator whisks you up 80m to within an easy 300m walk of **Akiyoshi plateau**. The change of temperature hits you as you leave the lift and begin the short ascent towards the plateau, which spans the horizon as if part of an extravagant Scottish Highlands film set (the plateau even boasts its own 'Akiyoshi thistle').

The plateau measures some 130 sq km and dates back 300,000,000 years to the time when a coral reef formed in the sea; the rocks that exist today were once lumps of coral reef. Only 500,000 years ago, rhinoceros, giant deer and elephant roamed around the tree-covered plateau. At the top, there's a lookout observatory, shop and drinks outlet.

To return to Akiyoshi-do Bus Center, you can retrace your steps (¥100 to take the lift back down) and walk back through the cave; alternatively, you can walk, or catch a bus down from the plateau.

♦ **Chomonkyo (32km)** This small station is popular with photographers looking for a suitable vantage point to snap the Yamaguchi steam train (see box opposite). Enthusiasts/photographers should make sure they are on a local train from Yamaguchi (about 30 mins) or Tsuwano (about 50 mins; see p236) so that they can stop here.

After Chomonkyo, the Super-Oki calls at **Mitani (39km)** and **Tokusa (50km)**. The final approach to Tsuwano has some amazing views of the countryside. From the elevated track you can look down on villages of black-roofed houses – a rural side to Japan rarely seen and mostly forgotten.

Tsuwano (63km) Tsuwano is not the only town in Japan to hanker after the name 'Little Kyoto' – Takayama (see pp174-9) also claims that title, as do others – but it is certainly one of the most picturesque stops on a journey through Western Honshu.

A former castle town of samurai lodgings and small canals filled with plump *koi* (carp), Tsuwano can trace its foundation back over 700 years. During the Edo period (1600-1868), a number of persecuted Christians were banished to Tsuwano, a place presumed to be suitably out of the way for the troublemakers to be forgotten about.

The steam locomotive from Shin-Yamaguchi (see box p234) terminates in Tsuwano. **Lockers** (including a couple of large ¥600 ones) are on the left side of the station as you exit. There's a **tourist information office** (🖳 www.tsuwano.ne.jp/kanko; daily 9am-5pm) in a small building to the right as you leave the station; the best source of information is the detailed bilingual English/Japanese booklet and map (¥200).

There's a **Rent a Cycle** (¥500/2 hours, ¥800/day) at the station too. Even though it is possible to get everywhere on foot it is certainly pleasant and easy to get around on a bike so renting one is recommended.

The colourful **Taikodani Inari Shrine** is known for its tunnel of 1000 red *torii* gates; these are spread along the path leading uphill to the shrine. From the top you can walk along to the ruins of **Tsuwano Castle**. At certain places on the walk there are excellent views over the valley and if you are lucky you will be able to see the Lady of Rank steam engine en route to Tsuwano. A **chair lift** (Mar-Nov daily 9am-4.45pm, Dec-Feb weekends and hols only; ¥400) ascends the hill to near the castle ruins, but walking in Tsuwano's many wooded hills is also one of the attractions here.

⛩ **Hidden Japan**

More than just rattling off the main sights, the real pleasure of Tsuwano is to wander around the old streets. With no obligation to tick off a list of must-see historical monuments, you can enjoy watching time pass slowly by. There are no convenience stores, few cars, and hardly any of that mind-numbing noise blaring out from shops, pachinko parlours and restaurants that you find elsewhere in Japan. Not quite frozen in time, Tsuwano has at least decided not to follow slavishly the pace that other parts of Japan rush to keep. Armed with the excellent bilingual guidebook, which contains a comprehensive list of all the town's sights, restaurants, lodgings and cafés, it is very tempting to spend several days here.

Being so picturesque, Tsuwano invites the crowds, but once they've departed, in a puff of smoke as the steam locomotive heads back to ugly Shin-Yamaguchi, it's very gratifying to wander around the quiet roads and savour the atmosphere. Many visitors to Japan justifiably complain that travelling here is never relaxing. Tsuwano is one of the few places to challenge the perception of a fast-paced, hi-tech, can't-wait, non-stop country that, in its desperate haste to meet the future head on, rarely has time to dwell in the past.

The area behind **Washibari-Hachimangu Shrine**, famous as the venue for an annual display of *yabusame* (Japanese horseback archery; 2nd Sun in Apr), is worth exploring, as is the area around the **Chapel of Santa Maria**, which was built in memory of 36 Japanese Catholics who were martyred here in the late 19th century. In town, **Tsuwano Catholic Church**, like others in Japan, is interesting for having tatami-mat 'seating' instead of pews.

Virtually all accommodation in Tsuwano is in a ryokan or minshuku. Staff at the tourist office will make bookings and provide directions; book early if planning to come to the yabusame. *Wakasagi-no-yado* (☎/🖃 085-672 1146; ¥7500pp half-board) is a small, friendly minshuku where English is spoken. It is about a 10-minute walk from the station.

There is no shortage of places for lunch with restaurants catering to the day tourist. *Tsurube* (Sat-Thur 11am-7pm) serves excellent hand-made noodles in huge bowls for around ¥700-800. From the station, turn right on to the road in front of you, walk for about five minutes and look out for it on the right. Most restaurants shut by 7pm, though this isn't really a problem since virtually all the ryokan/minshuku in Tsuwano include an evening meal in the rate.

Nichihara (73km) After Tsuwano, the Super Oki LEX stops briefly at this town of astronomy. Nichihara's link with the stars is evident from the constellation design by the platform. There's no tourist office at the station but there is a 'plaza' with a small branch post office and souvenir stand.

Nichihara Astronomical Observatory (Tenmondai; 🖃 homepage2.nifty. com/tokinokaze/hoshi/tenmondai/place.chugoku/nichihara.htm; Apr-Dec daily noon-10pm; ¥1000) is a 50-minute walk uphill from the station or an eight-minute taxi ride (there is no bus service). During the day you can see the telescope inside the observatory and visit the small museum, but stargazing itself starts after dusk. *Pension Hokutosei* (☎ 08567-41010, 🖃 41647, 🖃 www.sun-net.jp/~p-hokuto; ¥6300pp with breakfast, ¥9450pp half-board), a Western-style pension next to the observatory (under the same management), is a good place to crash out after an evening staring into deep space.

From Nichihara, the train continues north towards the San-in coast, roughly following Takatsu-gawa (Takatsu River) all the way out to the Japan Sea. If you've already travelled around Shikoku, you might notice the similarity of the landscape – lush and green, with rivers, forests and the occasional village and rice field.

A couple of minutes before arriving in Masuda, the scenery changes dramatically. After a slow journey through the rural spine of western Honshu, it's a rude awakening to emerge into a sea of smokestacks and factory buildings.

Masuda (94km) Masuda is an important railway junction, as it marks the end of the line from Shin-Yamaguchi and is the connecting point for lines running along the San-in coast.

There's no need to change trains here for the next part of the route if you're on the Super Oki LEX, which continues east along the San-in coast to Yonago (3/day) and Tottori (1/day). However, it's worth noting that another LEX, the

Super Matsukaze, starts at Masuda and continues along the same route as the Super Oki; all these services go to Tottori.

MASUDA TO MATSUE   [Map 14; Table 11, p462]

Distances by JR from Masuda. Fastest journey time: 2 hours 40 minutes.

Masuda (0km) From here the Super Oki and Super Matsukaze LEXs head east along the San-in line. Two of the three Super Oki continue as far as Yonago, while one of the Super Oki and all the Super Matsukazes go to Tottori (see p241).

A few minutes out of Masuda, the train finally reaches the Japan Sea, which is dotted with rock formations. The sea here is rough and much less inviting than the calm water of the Inland Sea. For coastal views, sit on the left side.

Some services stop at **Mihomisumi (22km)**, then **Hamada (41km)**, beyond which the train heads slightly inland, so views of the Japan Sea are less frequent.

Hashi (51km) This is the nearest stop to **AQUAS** (🖳 www.aquas.or.jp; Wed-Mon 9am-5pm, mid July to end Aug & school hols daily 9am-6pm; ¥1500, English audio guide ¥200), a modern aquarium where you can see white beluga dolphins, seals, crabs, jellyfish and the like. Follow the signs for the 10-minute walk from Hashi station.

Gotsu (60km) Change here to a local train if planning to visit Maji (see below) or Nima (see below). Local/rapid trains (23/34 mins; 4/day). Note: not all rapid services stop at Maji.

Yunotsu (77km) Not all limited expresses stop at Yunotsu, a spa town popular with elderly holidaymakers. Forest surrounds both sides of the track along this section of the route but you might catch the odd glimpse of the sea.

The hot spring here is believed to have been established 1300 years ago by an injured raccoon. The healing waters are supposed to help rheumatism, neuralgia, gout, dermatitis and – of all things – whiplash.

♦ Maji (83km) Nearest station to the 'singing sand' beach of Kotogahama. The beach is named after Princess Koto, a member of the Heike clan who fled north to the San-in coast after the Heike were defeated by the rival Genji clan in the 12th century (see p32).

To thank the people who lived by the beach for offering her protection, she played the *koto* (Japanese zither) every day. According to legend, after her death the sand itself began to make a noise similar to that of the koto. To this day it's said that whoever walks along the beach will hear the sound of the sand 'singing' to them. But beware: tourist literature warns that 'even the slightest dirt will render the sand mute'.

To test this theory, leave Maji station and walk straight ahead to the beach.

♦ Nima (86km) Just before the (local/rapid) train arrives at this small station, you might catch sight of an unusual glass-pyramid building on the left which looks a bit like the entrance to the Louvre in Paris. This is **Nima Sand Museum** (daily except 1st Wed of month, 9am-5pm; ¥700). Beyond the self-playing piano at the entrance there are various machines that revolve and pump sand round and round, displays of coloured sand, and jars of the stuff collected from beaches across Japan and around the world, including a sample from Waikiki Beach in Hawaii.

However, the main attraction is a giant egg timer which towers above the central atrium. It lasts for one year before needing to be turned over again, but as the flow of sand is affected by the outside temperature, a computer is required to regulate the flow and ensure that the year does not end too quickly. Every year at midnight on 31st December, 108 people help to turn the hour-glass round and welcome in the new year; visitors are welcome to join in.

It's an eight-minute walk to the Sand Museum – leave JR Nima station, cross the train tracks and head towards the glass pyramid.

Nima is also an access point for Iwami Ginzan (see below).

Oda-shi (97km) A commuter stop on the limited express but of little interest to the tourist other than also being an access point for Iwami Ginzan (see below).

Side trip by bus from Nima or Oda-shi to Iwami Ginzan

Iwami Ginzan was a silver mine for around 400 years and a large proportion of the silver mined here contributed to the fact that at one time Japan produced a third of the world's silver thanks to the 200,000 or so miners who worked here. The mines and surrounding area were designated a World Heritage site in 2008.

The area can be accessed by bus from either Oda-shi (1-2/hr, 25 mins; ¥560) or Nima (5/day; 15 mins). Buses go to Omori Town and the first stop is Omori-Daikansho. Attractions near this include: **Iwami Ginzan Museum** (daily 9am-5pm; ¥500) in the former Government Office; **Kumagai**

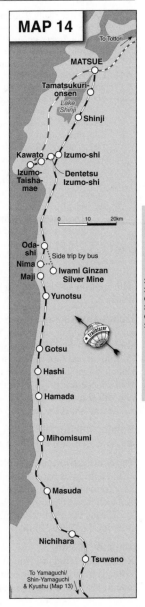

MAP 14

To Tottori

MATSUE

Tamatsukuri-onsen

Lake Shinji

Shinji

Kawato — Izumo-shi

Izumo-Taisha-mae

Dentetsu Izumo-shi

0   10   20km

Oda-shi

Side trip by bus

Nima

Iwami Ginzan Silver Mine

Maji

Yunotsu

Gotsu

Hashi

Hamada

Mihomisumi

Masuda

Nichihara

Tsuwano

To Yamaguchi/ Shin-Yamaguchi & Kyushu (Map 13)

HONSHU

Residence (daily 9.30am-5pm except last Monday of every month; ¥500), a former merchant's house and **Kawashima Residence** (daily 9am-4.30pm; ¥200), a former samurai house. The Kumagai Residence has been restored and is worth visiting. You can then either stroll along the road (1km) popping into some of the shrines, temples and shops along the way, or hop back on the bus (1-4/hr; 5 mins; ¥190) to Omori Town bus stop. **Gohyakurakan** (daily 9am-5pm but irregular closing days; ¥500), a series of man-made caves with about 500 stone statues of Buddha's disciples, is near Omori Town bus stop.

There is no vehicle access beyond Omori Town bus stop to the mining area (about 2km away) so you must either walk (30-45 mins) or rent a cycle. Two of the approximately 600 mine shafts in the area are open to the public. One of them is **Ryugenji Mabu Mine Shaft** (Apr-Nov 9am-5pm; Dec-Mar to 4pm; ¥400), a 273m long tunnel.

Some of the buses go from Omori to Sekai-Isan Center (7 mins; ¥230). This is also known as **Iwami Ginzan World Heritage Center** (🖳 ginzan.city.ohda. lg.jp/wh/en; ¥300; daily 9am-5pm except last Monday of every month) and is the best place to get an overview of the history of the mines and the area.

The entry charges quoted are the standard rates for an adult. However, foreigners receive a discount of 33-50% on production of a passport or Alien Registration Certificate. Alternatively, a combination ticket including all the attractions mentioned above is ¥1500.

There are great views of the Japan Sea on the approach to Izumo-shi as the train runs on an elevated track. You might see the odd fishing boat out in the distance.

Izumo-shi (130km) Izumo-shi is the nearest JR station to **Izumo Taisha** (see p267), a well-known shrine. The shrine can be reached from here by private Ichibata Railway (JR rail passes not valid). From the north exit of the JR station, go straight and turn right on to the main road. The modern Dentetsu Izumo-shi station is just up this road on the right. Take a local train four stops to Kawato, then change trains again for the final leg to Izumo-Taisha-mae. The total journey will take about 25 mins (¥480; approx 1/hr).

Izumo-shi is the last stop on the Yakumo LEX (1/hr) from Okayama.

Shinji (146km) This station is right on the edge of Lake Shinji but trees block all views until just before the train reaches Matsue.

Tamatsukuri-onsen (156km) This popular hot-spring resort, where it is claimed the gods once enjoyed bathing, is on the shore of Lake Shinji. The tourist information office in Matsue (see p264) can provide information on hotels and bath houses here.

During the last few minutes of the journey towards Matsue, there are views of Shinji-ko (Lake Shinji) on the left.

Matsue (163km)   [see pp261-6]
Rather than retracing your steps take a Yakumo LEX from here to Okayama (1/hr; fastest journey time just over 2½ hours). Alternatively, if you take the side trip to Tottori you can return to Okayama from there.

Side trip by rail to Tottori

From Matsue (0km), the Super Matsukaze LEX (4/day) and Super Oki (1/day) continue east to Tottori (122km); the fastest journey time is 85 minutes.

Tottori is known for its sand dunes which extend east to west along the coast for some 16km. The station has lockers should you want to leave your bags there, then take either bus No 4 or 20 (¥360) from outside the north exit – the last stop is the main sand-dune area. Buses run infrequently so be sure to check the timetable for the last bus back. It's hard to believe unless you actually make the effort to travel out here that Japan really does have its own mini desert. Just in case you forget where you are once you've arrived, non-native camels wait on the edge of the dunes for a classic Japanese photo opportunity (for a fee) or to take you for a ride. Horse-drawn carts are also on standby. If you're going to Tottori, think ahead in terms of your footwear – just remember, you'll be walking on sand!

There are several places to stay near the station. *Toyoko Inn Tottori-eki Minami-Guchi* (☎ 0857-36 1045, 🖳 www.toyoko-inn.com; from ¥4980/S, ¥6480/D or Tw) is one minute on foot from the south exit. *Super Hotel Tottori Ekimae* (☎ 0857-22 9000, 🖳 www.superhoteljapan.com; from ¥5280/S, ¥7280/Tw, ¥8280/Tr) is also near the south exit. A more upmarket option is *Hotel New Otani Tottori* (☎ 0857-23 1111, 🖳 www.newotani.co.jp; from ¥9500/S, ¥18,000/D or Tw).

There's a *UCC coffee shop* on the 2nd floor of the station and a variety of **ekiben** are sold on the main concourse: *kanizushi* (strips of crab meat on a bed of rice) is the best known. Daimaru department store, just beyond the north exit, has a basement food hall. The names of the in-house restaurants at *Hotel New Otani Tottori* change every few years, but there's usually an all-you-can-eat buffet lunch (11am-2pm) for ¥1500.

From Tottori, the Super Inaba LEX (6/day) takes under two hours to run south to Okayama. The Super Hakuto LEX (7/day) goes to Himeji, Osaka and Kyoto and the Hamakaze LEX (1/day) goes to Osaka via Himeji. The track between Chizu and Kamigori is operated by the private Chizu Kyuko railway, which means JR rail-pass holders must pay a ¥1260 supplement (payable on board) or ¥1770 if travelling on a limited express in a reserved seat.

Western Honshu – city guides

KOBE

Short on sights for foreign tourists but big on food, shopping and entertainment, Kobe is a good place to break a journey along the Sanyo coast. Like Nagasaki, Kobe developed as an international port city and is today popular as a tourist spot for Japanese interested in seeing the foreign settlements and Western-style houses that lent the city an 'exotic' feel in the decades following the Meiji Restoration (see p34) in 1868.

The biggest event of the more recent past took place at 5.46am on 17th January 1995, when Kobe was struck by the Great Hanshin Earthquake. Over

6000 people were killed, more than 100,000 buildings destroyed, and much of the city and surrounding area reduced to rubble. But few outward signs of this tragedy remain.

What to see and do

There's not a great deal to see in the area around **Shin-Kobe station**, so if you've only got a little time it's best to catch a subway one stop to Sannomiya, the centre of downtown Kobe. That said, a short excursion can be made from Shin-Kobe by taking **Shin-Kobe Ropeway** (🖳 www.shinkoberopeway.com; return trip ¥1000) to Nunobiki Herb Park on a hill behind the station. The herb park is a tourist trap and isn't worth bothering with on a cloudy day, but if the weather is co-operating it's possible to see as far as Kansai Airport. The ropeway (cable car) is a few minutes on foot from the station: head towards ANA Crowne Plaza Hotel just below the station and follow the signs.

To see for yourself what happened to Kobe in January 1995, head for the two museums at the **Disaster Reduction and Human Renovation Institution** (🖳 www.dri.ne.jp/english; Tue-Sun 9.30am-5.30pm, Jul-Oct to 6pm, Fri & Sat to 7pm; ¥600). The Disaster Reduction Museum uses video, dioramas and interactive exhibits to great effect to depict and re-enact the destruction wrought by the earthquake. The Human Renovation Museum, whose theme is the 'preciousness of life', is less effective and could easily be skipped. From JR Sannomiya station, take a local train one stop east to Nada station. The building is a 10-minute walk south from the south exit.

Also south of Nada station, but within the waterfront redevelopment known as HAT Kobe, lies the vast **Hyogo Prefectural Museum of Art** (🖳 www.artm. pref.hyogo.jp/eng; Tue-Sun 10am-6pm; ¥500). Billed as the largest museum in western Japan, the vast space houses an impressive collection of modern art and sculpture, both Japanese and Western. Highlights include print art by Goya, Picasso, Manet, Ernst and Ensor.

North of Sannomiya station lies the **Kitano district** (Kitano Ijinkan-gai), with Western-style buildings from the 19th century such as an 'original Holland house' and 'Wien Austrian house', which are probably of more interest to the domestic tourist. Many of the buildings had to be reconstructed after the 1995 earthquake and aren't really worth seeking out. It is, however, worth visiting **Kitano Tenman Shrine**. The shrine dates from the late Heian period (794-1185) and is popular for the views it offers over the city. On a clear day this is the best place to take in Kobe's geography.

A short walk south of Sannomiya, down the right-hand (west) side of Flower Road, brings you to a flower clock and then to **Kobe City Hall**, which affords great views from the observation point (daily 10am-9pm; free) on the 24th floor, accessed by lifts from the glassed-in area to the left of the main entrance. From the top you can admire the solar-dependent artwork, Duetto, by Fabrizio Corneli, which comprises 16 objects fixed to the outside wall of the nearby Sannomiya Building; at certain times of day the sun makes these objects show up as a silhouette of two people facing each other.

Two stops west along the Sanyo line by local train from JR Sannomiya station is JR Kobe station, access point for **Harborland** (🖥 www.harborland.co.jp) and its shopping malls, department stores and small amusement park with Ferris wheel. Head either underground as you exit the station or overground, walking under the elevated expressway towards the main shopping and entertainment area.

For a good walk, follow the bay around from Harborland all the way to **Meriken Park**, which is popular with young couples searching for a romantic bay view. Unless you are interested in ships and how Kobe port works, as well as its history, you can bypass **Kobe Maritime Museum** (🖥 www.kobe-meriken.or.jp/maritime-museum; Tue-Sun 10am-5pm; ¥600). However, the steel structure on top of the museum, resembling the image of a sail, is impressive.

Sake has been brewed in the Kobe area for many years and several of the breweries now have museums describing the process. The best is **Hakutsuru Sake Brewery Museum** (🖥 www.hakutsuru-sake.com; Tue-Sun 9.30am-4pm; free) as it has useful English-language explanations as well as interesting videos on the 2nd floor, where you can compare the modern brewing process with that of 1928.

To reach the museum take a train from JR Sannomiya along the Tokaido line two stops east to Sumiyoshi station. Turn left out of the station and walk round till you join the main road. Continue left (east) and walk along till the Rokko Liner goes overhead. Cross the road and walk south along the river. Turn right when you meet the private railway line and then left to go under that (through a tunnel), then turn right and keep walking till you see the brewery on your left. It should take 15-20 minutes from Sumiyoshi. If you feel lost, look up: the brewery building has a symbol of a crane on it (Hakutsuru means 'white crane').

Alternatively, if fashion is your thing, transfer at Sumiyoshi on to the Rokko Liner (🖥 www.knt-liner.co.jp) for Rokko Island and alight at Island Center station. Follow the signs for **Kobe Fashion Museum** (🖥 www.fashionmuseum.or.jp; Thur-Tue 10am-6pm; ¥500); the permanent exhibition covers everything from sleek evening dresses to flowing Imperial gowns.

Rokko Island and Port Island are man-made land masses off the coast and are accessible from the centre of Kobe via unmanned light-transit railways. On the larger **Port Island**, caffeine addicts might enjoy **UCC Coffee Museum** (🖥 www.ucc.co.jp/museum; Tue-Sun 10am-5pm; ¥210), which traces the history of the coffee industry and houses an impressive collection of coffee cups. Take the Port Liner from JR Sannomiya to Minami-Koen station, then take the west exit.

See also p247 for details of side trips from Kobe.

PRACTICAL INFORMATION
Station guide

The main JR stations in Kobe city are **Shin-Kobe** (for shinkansen services) at the foot of Mt Rokko, **Sannomiya** in the city centre, and **Kobe**, a gateway to the city's Harborland shopping and entertainment area.

At **Shin-Kobe** the entrances/exits are only on one side as the station is built into the hillside. You'll find **lockers** (all sizes) straight ahead after the ticket barrier, at the end of the station building. The entrance to the **subway** (one stop to Sannomiya station for central Kobe; see p246) is downstairs. On the main station concourse are a few cafés and stalls selling the city's best-known souvenir, Kobe beef.

> ❏ **Shinkansen viewing spot**
> Shinkansen fans should note that Shin-Kobe is a good place to view the bullet trains speeding past. The station is unusual in that it has only two tracks (no middle track for trains not stopping at the station), so the services that don't stop at Shin-Kobe shoot straight past along the platform edge. A barrier on the platform closes automatically whenever a through train is about to go past.

Sannomiya is a major rail junction, with the private Hanshin and Hankyu railways, subway and JR stations all crossing through here. This means that Sannomiya, far more than Shin-Kobe, is the centre for commerce, shopping and entertainment.

Tourist information
Kobe City Information Center (🖳 www. feel-kobe.jp; daily 9am-7pm) is on street level by JR/Hankyu Sannomiya stations. There's also an **information counter** at Shin-Kobe station (daily 10am-6pm), though the staff here don't have as much information.

Kobe Student Guides is a group of volunteer students who guide foreign visitors around sights in Kobe and Osaka as well as Himeji Castle (see p229). You pay only for the guide's transport, admission fees and lunch. To contact the group, pick up a leaflet from the tourist office or check 🖳 www.geocities.co.jp/CollegeLife/3136.

KOBE – MAP KEY

Where to stay, eat and drink
3 ANA Crowne Plaza Hotel; Wakkoqu (Shin-Kobe Oriental Avenue) ANAクラウンプラザホテル神戸 ; 和黒 (新神戸オリエンタル アベニュー)
4 Super Hotel Kobe スーパーホテル神戸
9 Hotel Monterey Amalie ホテルモントレアマリー
10 Hotel Monterey Kobe ホテルモントレア神戸
12 Toyoko Inn Kobe Sannomiya No 2 東横イン 神戸三ノ宮2
13 Toyoko Inn Kobe Sannomiya No 1 東横イン 神戸三ノ宮1
14 Tooth Tooth Garden Restaurant, Kobe International House トゥーストゥースガーデンレストラン, 神戸国際会館
15 Hotel Sunroute Sopra Kobe ホテルサンルートソプラ神戸
18 Kobe Harbor Circus 神戸ハーバーサーカス
19 Mosaic モザイク

Other
1 Kitano Tenman Shrine 北野天満神社
2 Shin-Kobe Ropeway 新神戸ロープウエイ
5 Disaster Reduction and Human Renovation Institution 人と防災未来センター
6 Hyogo Prefectural Museum of Art 兵庫県立美術館
7 Kobe Fashion Museum (Rokko Island) 神戸ファッション美術館 (六甲アイランド)
8 Hakutsuru Sake Brewery Museum 白鶴酒資料館
11 Kobe City Information Center 神戸市総合インフォメーション センター
16 Kobe City Hall 神戸市役所
17 Post Office 郵便局
20 Harborland ハーバーランド
21 Kobe Maritime Museum (Meriken Park) 神戸海洋博物館(メリケンパーク)
22 UCC Coffee Museum (Port Island) UCCコーヒー博物館 (ポートアイランド)

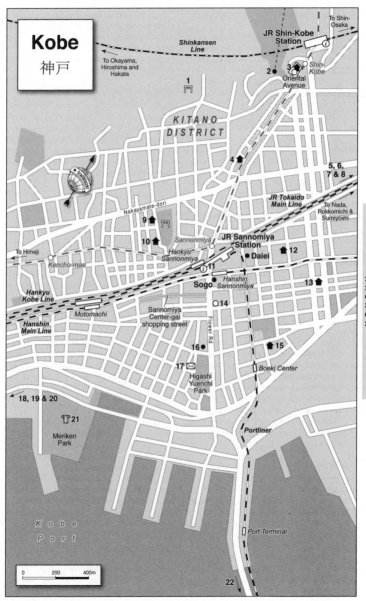

Kobe
神戸

Shinkansen Line

To Shin-Osaka

JR Shin-Kobe Station

To Okayama, Hiroshima and Hakata

2

3

Shin-Kobe

Oriental Avenue

1

KITANO DISTRICT

4

5, 6, 7 & 8

A trailhead

JR Tokaido Main Line

To Nada, Rokkomichi & Sumiyoshi

Nakayamate-dori

9

10

Sannonmiya

JR Sannomiya Station

12

To Himeji

Kencho-mae

Hankyu-Sannonmiya

Daiei

Hankyu Kobe Line

11

Hanshin Sannonmiya

13

Sogo

Hanshin Main Line

Motomachi

Sannomiya Center-gai shopping street

14

Flower Rd

15

16

Boeki Center

17

Higashi Yuenchi Park

18, 19 & 20

21

Meriken Park

Portliner

Kobe Port

Port Terminal

0   200   400m

22

HONSHU

Access to/from Kansai International Airport

If you want to get to Kansai Airport (see p117) by **train** the best way for JR rail-pass holders is to take a shinkansen to Shin-Osaka, one stop along the line from Shin-Kobe, and from there to take the Haruka LEX. Another option is to use the Kansai Thru Pass (see p186).

Alternatively, a direct limousine **bus** service operates from Sannomiya to the airport (65 mins; ¥1800), or if you like the idea of arriving, or leaving, on the water you could take the Bay Shuttle **ferry** (see p120).

Getting around

Kobe has a modern and efficient two-line **subway**, with signs in English. Arriving at Shin-Kobe, it's best to take the Seishin-Yamate subway line (daily 6am-11pm) one stop to Sannomiya (¥200). The newer Kaigan line runs from Sannomiya to the city's main football stadium outside Misaki-koen station before looping back to connect with the Seishin-Yamate line at Shin-Nagata.

The City Loop **tourist bus** service (🖳 www.kctp.co.jp/cityloop.html; 3-4/hr; ¥250/journey, ¥650/day pass), which does a circuit from Shin-Kobe to Sannomiya, Meriken Park and the Kitano area in around an hour, is another option. Route maps are available from the tourist information offices as well as on the bus. Pass-holders get small discounts to some attractions.

The one-day city bus and subway pass (¥1000) permits unlimited travel on the two subway lines and all Kobe city buses.

Festivals

As with most cities there are festivals throughout the year.

The biggest annual event is **Kobe Matsuri**, which is held mid to late May and lasts for about 10 days. On the last weekend there's a big fireworks display and a parade of floats through the city.

In late July there is a **Samba Festa** in the Harborland area and in August **Minato Kobe Fireworks Festival** is held in Meriken Park.

The **Kobe Luminarie** has been held every December since the Great Hanshin Awaji earthquake in 1995. The decorative lights used in the festival were donated by the Italian government. They are turned on for a few hours every evening.

Where to stay

Right outside the main exit of **Shin-Kobe station** is the skyscraper *ANA Crowne Plaza Hotel* (☎ 078-291 1121, 🖳 www.ana crowneplaza-kobe.jp; ¥15,015/S, ¥26,565/ D or Tw), where the best rooms are on the Executive Floor. Facilities include an indoor swimming pool, several restaurants and internet access.

A cheaper option, midway between Sannomiya and Shin-Kobe, but basically only with single rooms, is *Super Hotel Kobe* (☎ 078-261 9000, 🖳 www.superho teljapan.com/en; ¥5460/S inc breakfast). Other good choices are the two branches of the Toyoko Inn chain (🖳 www.toyoko-inn. com): *Toyoko Inn Kobe Sannomiya No 2* (☎ 078-232 1045; ¥6720/S, ¥8820/D or Tw), five minutes south from the Sannomiya railway stations, and *Toyoko Inn Kobe Sannomiya No 1* (☎ 078-271 1045; from ¥5480/S, ¥6980/D, ¥8980/Tw inc breakfast), about another five minutes' walk.

Ten minutes south of Sannomiya is the more upscale *Hotel Sunroute Sopra Kobe* (☎ 078-222 7500, 🖳 www.sunroute.jp/ HotelInfoSVE; from ¥9240/S, ¥17,325/Tw, ¥19,425/D) with reasonably sized rooms and a pleasant coffee shop.

Just below the Kitano area, not far from Sannomiya, is *Hotel Monterey Kobe* (☎ 078-392 7111, 🖳 www.hotelmonterey.co.jp; ¥11,550/S, ¥21,945/Tw). The theme is Italy, with whitewashed walls, patio courtyards and fountains. The guest rooms are less ambitious but pleasant enough with wide beds and wooden floors. Still more intriguing is the annex, *Hotel Monterey Amalie* (☎ 078-334 1711, 🖳 www.hotelmonterey.co. jp; ¥11,550/S, ¥21,945/Tw), which has a nautical theme. (See also pp45-52).

Where to eat and drink

Plenty of restaurants serve the famous Kobe beef. This comes from a breed of

Wagyu cattle and is known for its marbling (partly a result of the cows being massaged) as well as its taste and tenderness. One of the best-known places is *Wakkoqu* (💻 www.wakkoqu.com; daily 11.45am-10pm), on the 3rd floor of **Shin-Kobe Oriental Avenue** adjacent to Shin-Kobe station. An evening meal here doesn't come cheap, with set menus averaging ¥11,000pp, but at lunchtime they start at ¥7500. There are many other restaurants and cafés in the Oriental Avenue, including places specialising in ramen, teppanyaki and tonkatsu.

The area in, around and underneath the railway station in Sannomiya is packed with places to eat. On the 11th floor of

Kobe International House, Flower Road, *Tooth Tooth Garden Restaurant* (daily 11am-10pm; lunch 11am-3pm ¥1200-2000; dinner courses ¥2200-3300) is a café with a relaxing roof-top garden.

The **Harborland** district around JR Kobe station also has countless dining possibilities. Two big shopping and restaurant complexes close to Kobe station are **Kobe Harbor Circus** and **Mosaic**. The latter is the busiest and also has a cinema complex. **Sogo Department Store** and **Daiei supermarket** are also worth visiting if you are self catering.

Side trip from Kobe

Probably the most popular side trip from Kobe is to the **Rokko mountains** behind Shin-Kobe. As with many natural escapes that lie so close to densely populated areas in Japan, the Rokko area has its charms – gentle hikes and views of the Inland Sea – but also shameless tourist traps, such as a museum of music boxes, Mt Rokko pasture and a 'Kobe Cheese Castle' and Japan's first golf course as well as restaurants and shops. Mt Rokko is 931m high.

A trip on a cable car (funicular) and ropeway (cable car) into the mountains can be combined with a visit to **Arima-onsen** (💻 www.arima-onsen. com/eng), one of the 'three most famous springs' in Japan, along with Kusatsu (accessible from Shibukawa in Central Honshu) and Dogo-onsen (see pp444-5). The water quality is meant to be excellent and it has a long history of being visited by the Imperial Family and other members of the elite but the modern hotels that cater to tourists have rather spoiled the atmosphere.

There are a few possible approaches to Arima-onsen. If you have a rail pass, take a local train from JR Sannomiya two stops east to JR Rokkomichi, then city bus No 16 to Cable-Shita station (¥200), the starting point for a 10-minute cable car ride (¥570 one way/¥1000 return) into the mountains. At the top of the cable car you can connect by bus (10 mins; ¥250) with Rokko Arima Ropeway to reach the terminus at Arima station (12 mins; ¥980 one-way, ¥1770 return).

If you don't have a JR rail pass take Hankyu Kobe line from Sannomiya to Rokko station (7 mins; ¥180) and then bus No 16 (10 mins; ¥200) to the base of Rokko cable car.

OKAYAMA

One of the largest cities in western Japan, Okayama faces the Inland Sea, enjoys a mild climate and is particularly known for its large stroll garden, Korakuen. The city expanded politically and economically during the Edo period (1603-1867) but suffered a devastating air raid on 29th June 1945.

The bombing of Okayama has been largely forgotten, even though an area of almost eight square kilometres was razed to the ground, because it happened

HONSHU

> ## ⛩ Momotaro – the Peach Boy
> You can't wander around Okayama for long without coming across one of Japan's most celebrated folk heroes: Momotaro, the legendary Peach Boy. A well-known fairy tale begins with an old woman washing her clothes in a river, when she discovers an enormous peach floating by. She fishes it out and drags it home to her husband. Salivating at the prospect of tucking into a juicy peach, the old man takes a knife and is about to cut it when the fruit suddenly breaks in half and a baby boy jumps out. The 'Peach Boy' grows up with superhuman strength and soon leaves his parents to sail off to the Demon's Isle, where, in the best tradition of good against evil, he defeats the Demon King – with the help of a spotted dog, a monkey and a pheasant he picks up along the way.
>
> Okayama claims the heroic figure of Momotaro for its own, partly because the prefecture is known for peaches but also because the legendary Demon's Isle is thought to be the island of Megishima, in the Inland Sea between Okayama and Shikoku.
>
> A statue of Momotaro and his entourage on their way to fight the demon stands on the plaza outside the east exit of Okayama station, and Momotaro's face appears on some of the city's manholes, on the Momotaro credit card and in most souvenir shops. International mail sent from the central post office receives a Peach Boy stamp and there's even a naked Peach Boy statue (holding a peach) in Korakuen, And every year the town hosts a Momotaro Matsuri (see p250).

just a few weeks before the atomic bomb was dropped on Hiroshima. Over 25,000 buildings – including Okayama Castle – were destroyed and more than 1700 people lost their lives.

What to see and do
Korakuen, part of Okayama's 'Culture Zone', is the city's star attraction. The Culture Zone covers both sides of Asahi-gawa, across town from the station.

It is either about a 15-minute walk from the station to the Culture Zone area. Alternatively rent a cycle (see p250), or take a tram (Higashiyama Line) from the terminus outside the station all the way down Momotaro-dori to Shiroshita (¥100; 5 mins). At this junction, turn left and walk north for a minute to find on the left side the recommended **Okayama Orient Museum** (🖥 www.city.okayama.jp/orientmuseum; Tue-Sun 9am-5pm; ¥300), which houses a collection of ceramics and glassware mainly from Syria, Egypt and Iran. The displays are well lit and there is some English signage; there's a tearoom on the 2nd floor.

Continue north until you see on your right a road leading across a bridge towards the entrance to Korakuen. Constructed on an island on Asahi-gawa,

Korakuen (🖥 www.okayama-korakuen.jp; daily Apr-Sep 7.30am-6pm, Oct-Mar 8am-5pm; ¥400) was commissioned in 1700 by Tsunamasa Ikeda, feudal lord of Okayama, and was one of the first gardens in Japan to include grass lawns. It is also one of the 'three great landscape

> ### ❏ Combination tickets
> Various combination tickets for adults offer modest reductions on individual entrance fees: for example Korakuen plus Okayama Castle costs ¥560. However, this does not include entry to any special exhibitions.

gardens' in Japan – the other two are Kenrokuen (see p180) and Kairaku-en (in Mito). The garden is very spacious and includes a large pond, streams, tea and rice fields as well as plum, cherry and maple trees. However, the highlight of a stroll around the landscaped gardens is the 'borrowed' view – the black façade of Okayama Castle tower looming down from the hill above.

When you leave Korakuen, the easiest access to Okayama Castle is via the smaller south exit (towards the castle). Straight in front of you as you go out is a small path that leads down to the river and a hut where rowing/paddle boats can be rented. Turning to the right once through the south exit, cross Tsukimi Bridge to reach the castle.

Okayama Castle (Okayama-jo; daily 9am-4.30pm; ¥500) is known as *Ujo*, or 'Crow Castle', after its black exterior. The original 1597 donjon was destroyed during a heavy WWII air raid; the present reconstruction dates from 1966. Nevertheless, it's an impressive sight as you approach the donjon, with gold glittering from its roof. The discovery of some historical materials belonging to Teshiroyi Katsuto, who was governor of Okayama after the Meiji Restoration, has provided material for some interesting new exhibitions in the castle. The route starts at the top (the 6th floor), with the first two floors covering the history of the castle, then the final days of the Tokugawa shogunate and finally life in a castle town. The ground floor has a gift shop and a place where you can get soba (¥880), ice cream and coffee.

Okayama Prefectural Museum (Tue-Sun 9am-5pm; ¥350; additional charge for special exhibitions) focuses on art and artists in Okayama.

See pp229-30 for details of the side trip to Kurashiki which can also be accessed from Okayama.

PRACTICAL INFORMATION
Station guide

Okayama station's **east exit** (Higashi-guchi) is the main exit for Momotaro-dori, Korakuen and Okayama Castle; the **west exit** (Nishi-guchi) is the exit for the ANA Hotel, Okayama International Center and Matsunoki Ryokan.

Okayama is a major junction station with lines from here in all directions. The Uno/Seto-Ohashi Line goes to Shikoku, the Sanyo main line and also the shinkansen line has services both west and east. It is also possible to take the Yakumo LEX north to Matsue (see pp261-6) and Izumo-shi (see p240).

Most **lockers** (all sizes) are on the east side. Find them on the far left-hand corner of the ground floor of the station concourse (as you stand inside the station). For something to eat, try *Azuma Zushi*, a branch of a popular sushi restaurant (with take-out) on the main concourse. It's a good place to sample the local speciality, *barazushi*; meals cost from ¥1000.

Beneath the station is **Okayama Ichibangai**, an underground shopping mall, with a selection of cafés, take-out bakeries and restaurants, several of which put on good-value all-you-can-eat lunch buffets.

Tourist information

Staff at the tourist information desk (🖳 okayama-japan.jp; daily 9am-6pm), on the left as you walk towards the east exit, can provide a list of accommodation but will direct you to the NTA travel agency opposite to make bookings.

Getting around

Okayama's **tram** network has a terminus in front of Okayama station. Journeys cost

¥100 within the central area, ¥140 to go further afield; a 1-day pass is ¥400.

There is a JR **Rent a Cycle** office (daily 7am-11pm; ¥300/day) in the passageway between Hotel Granvia and the railway tracks.

Okayama is also easy to walk around **on foot**; it takes about half-an-hour from the station to reach the main sights.

Festivals
Various events are held in Korakuen throughout the year. On the third Sunday in May there is a **tea-picking festival**; the new tea leaves are picked and a dance is performed. From late July to the middle of August the garden is also the location for various illuminations.

The **Momotaro Matsuri** (see box p248) in early August includes a fireworks display in the area by Asahi-gawa river and people dress up in costumes and parade along the streets performing a variety of dances.

Where to stay
The JR-run *Hotel Granvia Okayama* (☎ 086-234 7000, 💻 www.granvia-oka.co.jp/english; ¥13,860/S, ¥21,945/D or Tw; 10% discount for JR rail-pass holders) is an upmarket place right outside the east exit of the station. More luxurious still is *ANA Hotel Okayama* (☎ 086-898 1111, 💻 www.anahotel-okayama.com; ¥13,860/S, ¥20,790/D or Tw), on the west side of the

station; the entrance is at street level. It has plush rooms, facilities galore and a stylish ground-floor café/restaurant.

Turn right out of the west exit and walk parallel to the railway lines to reach the chain hotel *Toyoko Inn Okayama-eki Nishiguchi-migi* (☎ 086-253 1045, 💻 www.toyoko-inn.com; from ¥6090/S, ¥8190/D/Tw, inc breakfast). Some rooms have views of the tracks.

Okayama City Hotel (☎ 086-221 0001, 💻 www.okayama-cityhotel.co.jp; ¥7350/S, ¥12,600/Tw) is a good business-hotel option, with surprisingly spacious rooms. It's a seven-minute walk from the east exit of the station. Opposite is *Mielparque* (☎ 086-223 8100, 💻 www.mielparque.jp; ¥5000-10,000/S, ¥9546-16,000/Tw), one of a chain of hotels run by the post office (hence the post office flags out front and the small branch inside). The cheaper rooms are a lot smaller than the pricier options.

A good choice for the budget traveller is the new *Comfort Hotel Okayama* (☎ 086-801 9411, 💻 www.choice-hotels.jp/cfoka; ¥5800/S, ¥12,000/Tw, inc breakfast) close to Korakuen.

If you're looking for a Japanese inn, *Matsunoki Ryokan* (☎ 086-253 4111, 💻 www.matunoki.com; ¥5250/S, ¥8400/Tw; breakfast ¥700, dinner ¥1300) has tatami rooms with air con and attached bathrooms as well as Western-style rooms. It's a friendly place that attracts a mix of Japanese

OKAYAMA – MAP KEY

Where to stay, eat and drink
1 Toyoko Inn Okayama-eki Nishiguchi-migi
東横イン岡山駅西口右
2 Matsunoki Ryokan
まつのき旅館
3 ANA Hotel Okayama, Fukusa
岡山全日空ホテル、福紗
4 Hotel Granvia Okayama
ホテルグランヴィア岡山
5 Mielparque Okayama
岡山シティーホテル
6 Okayama City Hotel
岡山シティーホテル
8 Cred Building クレド岡山ビル
9 Comfort Hotel Okayama
コンフォートホテル岡山
11 Bar Boccone
ぼーる ぼっこーね

Other
3 Post Office 郵便局
5 Post Office 郵便局
7 Central Post Office 中央郵便局
10 Okayama Orient Museum
岡山オリエント美術館
12 Korakuen 後楽園
13 Okayama Castle 岡山城
14 Okayama Prefectural Museum
岡山県立博物館

Okayama
岡山

岡山

HONSHU

Asahi-gawa

12 Korakuen
Main gate
South gate

14

13

Hotan-bashi

Tsukimi-bashi

Tsukimi-bashi

11

Korakuen-dori

Shiroshita-suji

Shiroshita

10

9

Monotaro-dori

Kenkyoudon

Sadaijicho

Yanagawa

Cred building

8

7

Yanagawa-suji

Tamaichi

Daiunjimae

Yubinkyokumae

Nishi-gawa Kyokudo-koen-suji

Nishigawa

Nishi-gawa (canal)

Kencho-dori

Okayamaekimae

Shiyakusho-suji

1

Okayama Station

4

3

5

6

2

Hokancho (covered arcade)

trailblazer

JR Sanyo Line

0   250   500m

and foreigners. It's two minutes' walk west from the station's west exit. Check-in is from 3pm but guests can leave luggage earlier.

Where to eat and drink

The local speciality in Okayama is *bara-zushi* (a platter of fresh local vegetables with seafood). One place to try this is at the station (see Station guide).

Outside the west exit of the station, the 2nd floor of the complex which houses the ANA Hotel has a section called **Lit Avenue** where you'll find a variety of Japanese and Western restaurants. One of the nicest is *Fukusa* (Wed-Sat 11am-2.30pm & 5.30-10pm, often closed on Sun, Mon or Tue), a modern Japanese restaurant where set lunches start at ¥1500 and evening set meals at ¥2100.

Close to Korakuen, *Bar Boccone* (11.30am to late; lunch 11.30am-3pm) offers a pasta lunch with drink for ¥950 and a selection of cocktails from ¥500. The entrance is up a flight of stairs.

There is also a variety of restaurants on the 20th and 21st floor of the **Cred Building**.

HIROSHIMA

For many visitors, the story of Hiroshima begins and ends with the dropping of the world's first atomic bomb at 8.15am on 6th August 1945. But it was the city's historical importance that made Hiroshima an obvious target to the American military.

The largest castle town in the Chugoku region throughout the Edo period, Hiroshima continued to be a centre of political and economic affairs right up to and beyond the Meiji Restoration (see p34), when the city became the seat of the prefectural government. In the decades following the Meiji Restoration the city grew as a centre for heavy industry, while the nearby port of Ujina expanded to become a base for the Imperial Army.

The atomic bomb wiped out the military garrison in an instant but what is remembered is the human devastation – it's estimated that 140,000 had died as a direct result of the bombing by the end of 1945. Some feared it would be decades before grass would grow again, while others believed the scorched land would remain desolate for ever. Clocks and watches froze at 8.15am but time did not stand still after the blast. It took only 17 days to rebuild the railway between Hiroshima and Ujina, and just three for the first tram line to restart. Many survivors took heart in seeing the trams back in service so soon after the blast.

In the decades since 1945, Hiroshima has reinvented itself as a centre for world peace and now, as you pull into the station by shinkansen, what you see is a thriving city of shops, restaurants and open spaces.

What to see and do

Most people come to see the Peace Memorial Park but Hiroshima has additional attractions, in particular the side trip to Miyajima (see pp258-60).

The Peace Memorial Park area The park is on the west side of the city, sandwiched between the Honkawa and Motoyasu-gawa rivers. Before the A-bomb razed the city to the ground, this area was Hiroshima's main shopping and entertainment district. Now it is home to the **Peace Memorial Museum**

(Heiwa Kinen Shiryokan; 💻 www.pcf.city.hiroshima.jp; daily Mar-Jul & Oct, Nov 8.30am-6pm, Aug to 7pm, Dec-Feb to 5pm; ¥50, audio guide ¥300), the one place everybody should visit when in Hiroshima. Enter the museum on the left side if you are walking towards it with the Cenotaph (the arch-shaped structure; see below) behind you.

Divided into east and west exhibition halls, the first displays you see are two scale models of the city, before and after the explosion.

Just one second after detonation, the bomb created a fireball 280m in diameter; the aftermath and appalling effects of the A-Bomb are detailed in the west hall, where the most powerful exhibits are personal objects, such as a twisted pair of spectacles and a mangled bicycle frame. Don't leave the museum without stopping at the video booths, where some of the A-Bomb survivors – known as *hibakusha* – have recorded their own testimony of the day Hiroshima's sky turned black.

The Peace Park contains over 50 memorial statues and peace monuments. Details are given of the main sights but it is worth allowing at least a day to explore the park properly.

Hiroshima National Peace Memorial Hall for Atomic Bomb Victims (💻 www.hiro-tsuitokinenkan.go.jp; same hours as the Peace Memorial Museum; free), a national memorial for those who either perished in the blast or who died subsequently from the effects of radiation. Just across the river, and clearly visible from the tourist office, is the **A-Bomb Dome (Genbaku Domu)**, the burned-out shell of what was once the Hiroshima Prefectural Industrial Promotion Hall. A car park close by marks the actual hypocentre but the A-Bomb Dome is the only monument to be preserved as a reminder of the devastation. It was added to the UNESCO World Heritage Site list in 1996.

The **Children's Peace Monument** (Genbaku-no-ko-no-zo) is easily identifiable by the colourful paper cranes draped over it. The monument was erected in memory of Hanako Sasaki, a young girl who contracted leukaemia a decade after the bomb and who died in hospital before she could achieve her goal of making 1000 paper cranes. An ancient Japanese legend holds that a person's wish will be granted if they make 1000 paper cranes.

The annual peace ceremony takes place in front of the **Cenotaph**, underneath which is a chest containing the names of all those claimed by the city as atomic-bomb victims. By 6th August 2011 the list of names stood at more than 275,230.

Some of the monuments in the park are more unexpected. Near the tourist information centre lies a large stone, cut from Ben Nevis in Scotland, which was presented to the city as a symbol of goodwill and of the wish for reconciliation and world peace. The base of the **Korean A-Bomb Victims Monument** is a turtle because in Korean legend dead souls are carried to heaven on the back of a turtle. There are 2527 registered Korean victims but it's thought that as many as 20,000 were killed. For years the monument was only permitted to stand outside the Peace Park, on the other side of the river. It was finally allowed into the park in 1999.

Other places of interest in the Peace Park (but not marked on the map) are: the **Peace Bell**, which is rung on August 6th; the **Peace Clock Tower** which rings every day at 8.15am to commemorate the time the bomb exploded; the **Atomic Bomb Memorial Mound**, which contains the ashes of those who were killed but whose remains were not able to be identified; the **Peace Fountain**, which symbolises compassion for those who were unable to get water to drink; and the **Flame of Peace**, which has burned continuously since 1st August 1964.

Away from the Peace Park Try to fit in a visit to **Shukkei-en** (daily Apr–Sep 9am-6pm, Oct-Mar to 5pm; ¥250), a beautiful Edo-period garden originally designed in 1620 and located on the banks of Kyobashi-gawa.

Hiroshima City Transportation Museum (⌨ www.vehicle.city.hiroshima.jp; Tue-Sun 9am-5pm; ¥500) has interactive exhibits geared mostly towards children – the train simulator is the most popular. Serious trainspotters will find the place a bit gimmicky but there's just about enough here – old train posters, tickets, model engines and the like – to make the visit worthwhile.

Pride of place goes to a huge model city, which is either a dream-like vision of how we will all be moving around in the future, or a futuristic urban nightmare, where the quaint idea of walking on foot has long since been abandoned.

Outside, there are 'interesting bikes' and battery-powered cars (chargeable). Rail enthusiasts will enjoy the journey to the museum, by Astramline, Hiroshima's 'new transit system', as much as the place itself; take the Astramline (daily 6am to midnight) from Hondori station in the city centre north to Chorakuji (¥390). The museum is next to the large Astramline office outside Chorakuji station.

A good place for an early evening stroll is **Chuo Park**, just west of the unremarkable **Hiroshima Castle** (daily 9am-6pm, Oct-Mar 9am-5pm; ¥360), a 1958 concrete reconstruction of the 1589 original.

PRACTICAL INFORMATION
Station guide
Hiroshima is a stop on the Sanyo shinkansen line, the Sanyo mainline (for Miyajimaguchi) and the terminus for the Kure Line (to Kure).

There are two sides to the station: the south side for the city centre and the north also known as the 'Hotel Granvia', side for the shinkansen; an underground passageway connects them. On the south side, you'll find Asse department store, with **restaurants** on the 2nd and 6th floors and a food hall in the basement. The **tram terminus** is outside the south exit.

For **lockers** (all sizes) on the shinkansen side, head for the far right-hand corner (as you face the exit). At the south exit, the main bank of lockers (all sizes) is opposite the taxi rank outside: turn left as you exit the station and walk along the station building.

A shop selling scale-model shinkansen trains and the like is tucked away in a quiet corner of the 2nd floor of the shinkansen side of the station.

Tourist information
There are **tourist information offices** on both sides of Hiroshima station. The one on the shinkansen side (daily 9am-5.30pm) is clearly signed on the 2nd floor by the shinkansen ticket barrier. Staff will help with same-day bookings for hotels in Hiroshima. On the south side, the office (daily 9am-5.30pm) is on street level in a corner of the main JR ticket office. Ask for the *Get Hiroshima* English maps.

The main tourist office in the city centre is **Hiroshima City Tourist Information Center** (🖥 www.hiroshima-navi.or.jp/en; daily Apr-Sep 9.30am-6/7pm, Oct-Mar 8.30am-5pm), in the Rest House on the edge of the Peace Park, just after you cross over Motoyasu Bridge.

The World Friendship Center (see p256) can arrange volunteer guides for guests.

Getting around

Hiroshima is one of Japan's best-known **tram** (streetcar/electric railway) cities; provided the trams don't get stuck in traffic, they are by far the best way of getting from the station to the downtown area. Fares are ¥150 per journey in the city centre but it's probably more economical to get a pass (¥600 1/day, ¥2000 2-day pass inc cable car and ferry to Miyajima) from the Hiroden (Hiroshima Electric Railway) terminal outside the south exit.

Pick up a map of the tram network either from the tourist offices or from the ticket booth outside the station. Even if you have a tram pass you will need to put it in the ticket machine when you enter and leave the tram. For further information see 🖥 www.hiroden.co.jp.

The tram routes are numbered 1 to 9 but actually there are eight (there is no No 4, possibly because the kanji for '4' can mean death). The most useful routes are: Nos 1, 2 and 6 from Hiroshima station for the Genbaku (Atomic Bomb) Dome. Route 2 goes to Miyajima-guchi for the ferry to Miyajima. For Shukkei-en take Route 9 from Hatchobori (a stop on routes 1, 2 and 6) and get off at Shukkei-en-mae.

A **river cruise** offers an alternative perspective on the city. Though there are no great views at least the boats don't get snarled up in heavy traffic.

Subject to the weather, Aquanet Hiroshima (☎ 082-240 5955; 🖥 www.aqua-net-h.co.jp) offers a variety of cruises from its terminal near Motoyasu Bridge, including a daytime cruise (10/day; daily Apr-Nov, Thur-Mon Dec-Mar; 25 mins; ¥800), a sunset cruise (daily Apr-Nov; 40 mins; ¥2000; reservations essential) and a World Heritage Cruise incorporating Miyajima (¥1900 one way, ¥3400 return trip).

Festivals

The annual **Peace Ceremony** is held on 6th August inside the Peace Park. In the evening, thousands of paper boats containing lighted candles are set afloat on the rivers and left to drift towards the sea.

Where to stay

Book well in advance if planning to visit Hiroshima for the annual Peace Ceremony on 6th August.

Outside the shinkansen side of Hiroshima station is *Hotel Granvia Hiroshima* (☎ 082-262 1111, 🖥 www.hgh.co.jp; ¥10,741/S, ¥17,902/D, ¥20,212/Tw), an upmarket member of the JR Hotel group (see also box p49). Despite being right next to the station it's a peaceful place with an impressive lobby, spacious rooms and a choice of restaurants.

At the other end of the budget scale, is a branch of *K's House* (☎ 082-568 7244; 🖥 kshouse.jp/hiroshima-e; dorm ¥2500pp, Japanese room ¥2800pp, double en suite ¥3900pp). It has a well-equipped kitchen and is about an 8-minute walk from the station.

Hotel Active! Hiroshima (☎ 082-212 0001, 🖥 www.hotel-active.com/hiroshima; ¥6000/S, ¥9000/D or Tw, inc breakfast) is a gem of a place – a design hotel at budget prices. You'll even find the words 'Welcome home' on the bedspread! Check out the plasma-screen fire in the lobby. The rooms are small but nicely furnished with flat-screen TVs. Nescafé coffee machines on each floor are a nice touch, as are the trouser presses. It's ideally located midway between the station and the Peace Park. The entrance is on the side road, not on Aioi-dori.

Toyoko Inn Hiroshima-eki Shinkansen-guchi (☎ 082-506 1045, 🖥 www.toyoko-inn.com; ¥6300/S, ¥8400/D or Tw, inc breakfast) is a four-minute walk from the north exit (shinkansen side) of the station.

Via Inn Hiroshima (☎ 082-264 5489, 🖥 hiroshima.viainn.com; ¥6825/S, ¥9030/

HONSHU

Tw) is a business hotel bolted on to the end of the station building. It's accessed by turning right out of the south exit. There's a pleasant coffee shop, *Café Di Espresso*, on the ground floor. The entrance to the hotel is next to the Heart In convenience store.

Dormy Inn Hiroshima (☎ 082-240 1177, 🖳 www.hotespa.net/hotels/hiroshima; ¥6300/S, ¥10,500/Tw) is close to the Peace Park and a cut above the usual business hotel. A bonus is the hotel's own hot spring on the 8th floor. The in-house café/restaurant on the 1st (ground) floor is called Big Mamma. Close by is *Comfort Hotel Hiroshima* (☎ 082-541 5555, 🖳 www.comfortinn.com/hotel-hiroshima-japan-JP027; ¥6090/S, ¥7800/Tw), another good budget/mid-range choice.

An upmarket and recommended choice in the downtown area is *Rihga*

Royal Hotel Hiroshima (☎ 082-502 1121, 🖳 www.rihga-hiroshima.co.jp; ¥16,170/S, ¥23,100-40,425/D, ¥24,255-40,425/Tw, exc breakfast). The hotel is in Parcela, a shopping and restaurant complex; the entrance is at street level but the rooms are on the 14th-31st floors; some have good views of the castle.

Ikawa Ryokan (☎ 082-231 5058, 🖹 231 5995, 🖳 www.ikawaryokan.net/en; ¥4725-5775/S, ¥8400-9450/Tw; breakfast ¥735, dinner ¥1365), a 5- to 10-minute walk west of the Peace Park, is a small, modern Japanese inn with friendly owners. All rooms (Japanese and Western) have air con, TV and toilet, some also have a bath.

The *World Friendship Center* (☎ 082-503 3191, 🖳 www.wfchiroshima.net, Japanese-style room ¥3900pp, inc Western breakfast) is a small house run by a very

HIROSHIMA – MAP KEY

Where to stay
1 J-Hoppers　ジェイホッパーズ
2 World Friendship Center　ワールド
　フレンドシップセンター
3 Ikawa Ryokan　いかわ旅館
5 Hiroshima International Youth House
　(Aster Plaza)　広島国際青年会館
　(アステールプラザ)
7 Dormy Inn Hiroshima
　ドーミーイン広島
8 Comfort Hotel Hiroshima
　コンフォートホテル広島
18 Rihga Royal Hotel Hiroshima
　リーガロイヤルホテル広島
24 Hotel Active! Hiroshima
　ホテルアクティブ！広島
26 Via Inn Hiroshima　ヴィアイン広島
28 K's House　ケイズハウス
30 Hotel Granvia Hiroshima
　ホテルグランヴィア広島
31 Toyoko Inn Hiroshima-eki
　Shinkansen-guchi
　東横イン広島駅新幹線口

Where to eat and drink
19 One Coin Bakery
　ワンコインベーカリー
21 Andersen　アンデルセン
22 Mario Espresso　マリオエスプレッソ
23 Okonomimura　お好み村

Where to eat and drink *(cont'd)*
27 Fukuya department store
　福屋店舗情報
29 Asse department store　アッセデパート

Other
4 AquaNet Hiroshima (boat trips)
　アクアネット広島
6 Central Post Office　中央郵便局
9 Hiroshima National Peace Memorial
　Hall for Atomic Bomb Victims
　国立広島原爆死没者追悼平和祈念館
10 Peace Memorial Museum
　平和記念資料館
11 Cenotaph for the A-bomb Victims
　原爆慰霊碑
12 Hiroshima City Tourist Information
　Centre　広島市観光協会
13 Korean A-Bomb Victims' Monument
　韓国人原爆犠牲者慰霊碑
14 Children's Peace Monument
　原爆の子の像
15 A-Bomb Dome (Genbaku Dome)
　原爆ドーム
16 Hiroshima City Transportation Museum
　広島市交通科学館
17 Hiroshima Castle　広島城
20 AquaNet Hiroshima (boat trips)
　アクアネット広島
25 Shukkei-en　縮景園

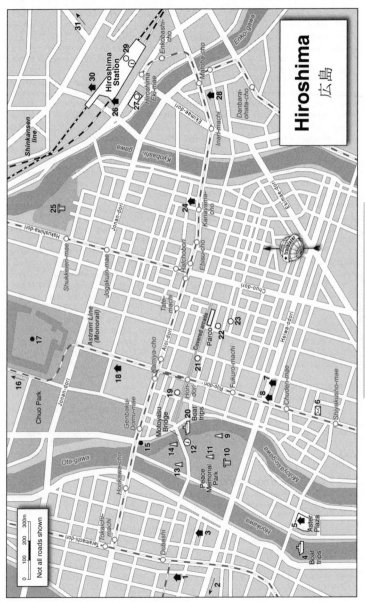

Hiroshima
広島

31

29 Hiroshima Station

30

Shinkansen line

26 27 Hiroshima Eki-mae

Enkobashi-cho

28 Inari-machi

Matoba-cho

Enko-gawa

Danbara-ohata-cho

Ekimae-dori

Kyobashi-gawa

25

24 Kanayama-cho

Jonan-dori

Hakushima-dori

Hatchobori

Ebisu-cho

Shukkeien-mae

Jogakuin-mae

Tate-machi

Chuo-dori

Astram Line (Monorail)

17

Kamiya-cho

Aioi-dori

Covered arcade

Parco 22 23

Ekimae-dori

16 Jonan-dori

18 Chuo Park

Genbaku-Domu-mae

19 Hon-dori

21 Rijo-dori

Fukuro-machi

Heiwa-odori

Chuden-mae

8 7

Ota-gawa

15 14

13

20 Boat trips

12 11 10

9

6 Shiyakusho-mae

Motoyasu Bridge

Motoyasu-gawa

Honkawa-cho

Peace Memorial Park

HONSHU

Ota-gawa

Tokaichi-machi

Teramachi-dori

Dobashi

3

5 Aster Plaza

Honkawa

4 Boat trips

2

1

0   100   200   300m
Not all roads shown

welcoming American couple. The not-for-profit centre, founded in 1965 to promote world peace, has a couple of tatami rooms as well as a living room where guests may sleep if desperate. It's a clean and tidy place with lots of maps and information. There's no curfew and a ¥1000 key deposit gives you the freedom to come and go as you please. See the website for directions. The *okonomiyaki restaurant* next door has dishes from ¥400 and closes at 8pm.

J-Hoppers (☎ 082-233 1360, 💻 hiro shima.j-hoppers.com; dorm beds ¥2300pp, Japanese-style rooms ¥3500/S, ¥2800pp in Tw/D or Tr) has mixed dorms and a female only one. They offer free wi-fi and internet access and also have bikes for rent (¥700/day or ¥500 if you are staying here).

Hiroshima International Youth House (☎ 082-247 8700, 💻 hiyh.pr.arena.ne.jp); discounted rates for foreigners: ¥3620/S, ¥6260/Tw) is just south of the Peace Park in Aster Plaza. The rooms are brightly decorated and an absolute steal for foreign guests. Facilities include a coin laundry and a reasonable restaurant; the only downside is a midnight curfew. Take bus No 24 from stop No 3 outside the south side of Hiroshima station and get off at Kosei Nenkin Kaikan-mae, from where it's one minute on foot to Aster Plaza.

See also pp45-52.

Where to eat and drink
Hiroshima is known for *kaki* (oysters) and also for *okonomiyaki* (savoury pancakes); the best place to try the latter is at **Okonomimura** (💻 www.okonomimura.jp), a building packed with three floors (2nd-4th) of small okonomiyaki places.

Most are open for lunch (daily 11.30am-2pm) and again in the evening (about 5-11pm). Expect to pay ¥500-1200. The entrance is opposite the underground car park on the paved plaza behind Pronto department store.

If you're in or around Hiroshima station, head for the 2nd floor of **Asse department store**, where you'll find a row of okonomiyaki places, the best of which (and hence the one with the longest queues at lunchtime) is *Reichan*, which has a menu in English. Alternatively, try *Oimatsu*; at either expect to pay around ¥1350.

Another recommended place is *Goemon* (11am-10pm) on the 10th floor of **Fukuya department store**. For a kaki-fry set meal (¥1730) try *Ouda* (11am-10pm) on the 6th floor. Ring the bell on your table when you are ready to order. Also try the 11th floor Panorama Food Court.

There are plenty of places to eat along the covered **Hondori shopping arcade**, including the enormous branch of *Andersen* (daily except 3rd Wed 11am-9.30pm), which has a bakery and deli on the 1st floor (street level) and a 2nd-floor restaurant serving a hearty kitchen buffet (Mon-Fri 6-9.30pm, Sat & Sun 5-9.30pm; ¥4500).

The pizzeria *Mario Espresso* (daily 11am-10.30pm) is on three floors opposite a small park, a couple of minutes from Okonomimura. The pizza is home-made and very popular but you can also just stop for a drink at street level.

Don't overlook *One Coin Bakery*, on a street that runs off from Hondori shopping arcade, where all the cakes, buns and rolls are ¥100 (actually ¥105 including consumption tax); great for a cheap meal.

Side trips from Hiroshima
To Miyajima Famous for its iconic red *torii* (shrine gate) that rises out of the sea, Itsuku-shima Shrine is considered one of the top three scenic spots in Japan and is the main attraction on the island of Miyajima (officially actually called Itsuku-shima (Itsuku Island). Other good reasons to make this side trip are the opportunity to hike to the top of Mt Misen, the chance to visit somewhere that has no convenience stores or traffic lights, and, for JR rail-pass holders, a free ferry ride there and back. You can also stay on the island.

From Hiroshima, take a local train eight stops westbound along the JR Sanyo line to Miyajima-guchi (every 10 mins during peak times; 25 mins; free to JR rail-pass holders). Alternatively, tram No 2 takes just less than one hour from Hiroshima station to Hiroden Miyajima-guchi and costs ¥270. The two-day pass (see p255) includes the ferry to/from Miyajima and the ropeway (cable car) up Mt Misen (see below).

At Miyajima-guchi, walk straight down the road from the station to the ferry terminal. From here, JR Ferry services (daily 6am-11pm; 2-4/hr; ¥340 return, free to rail-pass holders) take 10 minutes to Miyajima. JR shares the terminal with Matsudai Ferry, which runs an identical service but doesn't accept rail passes.

The **tourist information desk** (🖳 www.miyajima.or.jp; daily Mar-Nov 9am-7pm, Dec-Feb to 6pm) inside Miyajima ferry terminal can help book accommodation and also has a tide timetable (useful for working out when to see the torii gate at high and also low tide). **Rent a Cycle** (daily 8am-5pm; ¥320/2hrs, then ¥110/hour) is available from the JR ticket office on Miyajima. There are **lockers** (¥200-500) outside the ferry terminal. A free **shuttle bus** runs to the base of the ropeway (see below).

There are deer everywhere where you get off the ferry, so you may be chased if you are carrying food. Gluttons for punishment can even pay ¥200 for deer food and watch the ensuing chaos.

According to legend, **Itsuku-shima Shrine** (6.30am-5/6pm; ¥300) was founded in 593 when three goddesses were led to Miyajima by a crow. It was remodelled in its present structure, with long corridors connecting the main shrine halls, in 1168 and is now a World Heritage Site. Noh performances are occasionally staged at the shrine, which has even seen the occasional fashion show – the 202m-long corridors doubling as the perfect catwalk. The route is one-way only so don't rush through.

The real attraction of the shrine is the vermilion **O-Torii** (Grand Gate), rising out of the sea (or, depending on the tide, sticking out of the silt) 200m from the main shrine. At high tide the gate (16m high) appears to float in the water. It's worth planning several hours on the island so you have a chance to see the gate at both high and low tide. The shrine buildings need constant repair as they are often damaged by the sea and typhoons; the gate is made of camphor wood and is replaced every 100 years.

At 530m, **Mt Misen** is the highest peak on Miyajima and there are excellent hiking trails (see below) to its summit as well as the **ropeway** (cable car; 🖳 miyajima-ropeway.info/en; daily Mar-Nov 9am-5pm, Dec-Feb to 4.30pm; ¥1000/1800 one way/return; closed for safety checks twice a year, usually for about five days in June & Dec) from Momijidani-koen (Park). It is an easy walk up from Itsuku-shima shrine to the base of the ropeway (cable car).

Each of the three main **hiking trails** takes about 1½-2 hours to the top of Mt Misen; the routes are outlined in a map available from the tourist information desk at the ferry terminal. The **Momiji-dani (Maple Valley) route** is the shortest but steepest and is particularly recommended in the autumn but is also lovely at other times of the year. It starts from near the base of the ropeway.

The **Daisho-in route** starts at **Daisho-in Temple**, site of an impressive Fire-Walking Ceremony (Hiwatarishiki) held twice a year (15th Apr & 15th Nov from 11am). It is the least steep route and also offers good views.

The other route, the **Omoto Route** starts from Omoto Shrine, which is beyond Itsukushima Shrine, but meets the Daisho-in route before you reach the

HONSHU

top. The paths are generally easy to follow and not really challenging. However, make sure you stick to them to avoid treading on any snakes and carry water in the summer as it can get very hot.

As you near the top follow signs to the viewing platform (**Shishi-iwa observatory**) which is near the top of the ropeway; from here there are great views out over the Inland Sea. If you are lucky you might also see wild monkeys grooming the deer, especially if the latter are resting. There is a *café* (open during ropeway hours) under the viewing platform as well as a vending machine. Then head to the summit of Mt Misen.

Even if you take the ropeway (in fact a gondola journey followed by a cable car) you still need to walk for about half an hour to reach the very top of **Mt Misen**; the path descends first before climbing uphill so don't worry that you have taken the wrong turn.

If you haven't hiked all the way up, do consider making the descent on foot. The Momiji-dani route (45-60 mins) takes you through Momiji-dani-koen where there are places to eat and stay. *Momiji-so* (☎ 0829-44 0077; ¥8400/pp room only, ¥16,800/pp half-board) is in a lovely setting in the park. One reader said that Momiji-so was 'absolutely wonderful, the room and the food were fantastic – the woman who ran it looked after us so well we called her Mama-san'. It is also open at lunch time and the menu includes a variety of *udon* as well as curry rice (¥500-650); place your order and then sit at one of the tables outside and admire the view.

Also in Momijidani-koen and with an onsen, is *Iwaso Ryokan* (☎ 0829-44 2233, 🖥 www.iwaso.com; from ¥21,150pp half-board). The rooms are in a variety of buildings and not all are en suite. Both these places are close to the ropeway (cable car) which runs up to Mt Misen.

If you prefer to be by the sea, *Miyajima Seaside Hotel* (☎ 0829-44 0118; ¥12,000pp half-board) is recommended; if requested in advance they can pick you up from the ferry terminal. Both Momiji-so and Miyajima Seaside Hotel can be booked online through 🖥 www.gambo-ad.com/english. Right by the ferry terminal, and a place that comes highly recommended, is *Kinsui Villa* (toll free ☎ 0120-44 2193, ☎ 0829-44 2191, 🖥 www.kinsui-villa.jp/en; from ¥15,000pp inc two meals). Online reservation in Japanese only.

There are plenty of other accommodation options on Miyajima; ask at the tourist information office. However, at peak times (autumn and spring) it is worth booking well in advance.

The cheapest place to stay is back **on the mainland** at *Backpackers Miyajima* (☎ 0829-56 3650; 🖥 www.backpackers-miyajima.com; dorm ¥2500pp, Japanese-style dorm ¥3000pp). The hostel has cooking facilities, free wi-fi as well as internet access (¥100/20 mins). Walk down the road from Miyajima-guchi station and keep walking past the ferry terminal. Take the second road to the right and the hostel is on the left.

To Yokogawa Yokogawa is a minor place of pilgrimage for omnibus fans but is also interesting for its shitamachi (old town) district. It can be visited on your way to Miyajima, since local trains from Hiroshima travelling west along the Sanyo line also stop here (it's one stop from Hiroshima). You can also take the tram (Hiroden Yokogawa line) here if you prefer to move at a slower pace.

On February 5th 1905, Japan's first domestically manufactured omnibus went into service here, plying a 15-km route between Yokogawa and nearby

Kabe. A newspaper of the time described the historic event: 'The time has at last matured for the arrival of the Yokogawa-Kabe Automobile Transportation Programme. At 3pm the day before yesterday an opening ceremony was held at the automobile boarding stand in front of Yokogawa station.'

The bus was manufactured in Japan using an American engine and parts, and passengers were charged a fare of 24 sen (by comparison, a horse-drawn carriage cost 15 sen). The maximum load was 12 passengers. Sadly, the tyres could not cope with the bumpy road conditions and the service was halted after just nine months. A replica of the original bus, painstakingly put together by a local club of omnibus enthusiasts from the only surviving photo of the original vehicle, is on display – encased in glass – in front of Yokogawa station. Unlike many old steam engines, which are left to gather dust on sidings in many parts of the country, this replica is kept gleaming.

A sign by the replica suggests that 'we intend to preserve this monument eternally as a symbol of the birthplace of Japan's first omnibus and as a force to breathe new life into the Yokogawa area in future'.

Aside from being the birthplace of the bus in Japan, Yokogawa is an interesting place to explore in its own right, with small restaurants, book shops and even an art house cinema in the station vicinity.

To Kure Another possible side trip by rail is to the sea-side town of Kure, just over 30 minutes south-east of Hiroshima on a rapid train on the JR Kure line. A five-minute walk from Kure station towards the coast is the **Yamato Museum** (🖳 yamato.kure-city.jp; daily mid July to end Aug 9am-6pm; rest of year Wed-Mon, 9am-6pm; ¥500), also known as Kure City Naval History & Science Museum, which displays a 1/10th reproduction of what was at one time the world's largest battleship.

The *Yamato* was launched from Kure in 1941 but sank four years later during a suicide mission to attack the United States fleet on American-held Okinawa. On display are the handwritten wills of some of the 2475 sailors who perished on board. The museum is a bit short of written information in English, but a tape commentary is available.

MATSUE

'There seems to be a sense of divine magic in the very atmosphere, through all the luminous day, brooding over the vapoury land, over the ghostly blue of the flood – a sense of Shinto'.

Thus wrote Irishman **Lafcadio Hearn** of Matsue's Lake Shinji, which glistens to your left as the train pulls into Matsue station from Masuda. The seventh largest lake in Japan is unusual in that it's a combination of fresh and sea water, depending on the tide.

Divided by Ohashi-gawa (Ohashi river), on the shores of Lake Shinji, with a moat around the castle and with one of the highest rainfalls in Japan Matsue well deserves its title 'City of Water'. It is an old castle town and the perfect place to break a journey along the San-in coast. Lafcadio Hearn (1850-1904) took up an English-teaching appointment here in 1890; though he only lived in Matsue for 15 months, his former residence is now one of the city's big draws.

In his time here he met and married Koizumi Setsu, the daughter of a local samurai family, and he also became Japanese. He was unusual enough just being a foreigner in Japan at this time let alone marrying a Japanese. In his books Hearn often voiced his regret that Meiji-era Japan, in its rush to catch up on centuries of isolation from the outside world, was abandoning many of its ancient traditions. He would probably have been dismayed at the tourist industry that has grown up around his name. As well as the usual postcards, souvenir trinkets and T-shirts, more unusual Matsue souvenirs include Hearn chocolates and bottles of locally brewed Lafcadio Hearn beer.

What to see and do

To get orientated and – on a clear day – enjoy a stunning view of Lake Shinji and the castle, take the express elevator up to the 14th floor of the **San-In Godo Bank** headquarters (the tallest building in town), at 10 Uo-Machi, a 10- to 15-minute walk from the station. The lift is hidden in a corner of the ground floor and there are no signs in English, but bank staff will point you in the direction of the observation gallery (daily 9am-5pm). On a bright day you can see as far as Mt Daisen (1711m), over 50km away.

Matsue Castle area The main city sights are all around Matsue Castle. From the station, take the Lakeline Bus (see p264) to the castle and then walk between the sights described below. (See box opposite.)

The **Lafcadio Hearn Memorial Museum** (daily Apr-Sep 8.30am-6.30pm, Oct-Mar to 5pm; ¥300, or ¥150 for foreign visitors) exhibits objects from Hearn's house and his stay in Matsue. Unusual items include a pair of iron dumbbells and a trumpet shell which Hearn 'blew half for fun when he wanted his maid to bring him a light for his tobacco'. Look out also for the high desk Hearn used to compensate for his poor eyesight. Music by Enya plays softly as you walk around.

Next door, **Lafcadio Hearn Former Residence** (Mar-Nov daily 9am-5pm, early Dec & Feb to 4.40pm, closed mid Dec to Jan; ¥350, 20% discount with Universal Pass) is now completely bare but there's a useful leaflet that describes how the rooms would have looked in Hearn's day. The small house looks out on to an even smaller Japanese garden that's similar to the one Hearn enjoyed when he lived in Kumamoto (see pp398-9).

Matsue – City of love as well as City of water?
Izumo Taisha Shrine (see p267) has always been known as a place for people to go if they are looking for luck in love. However, Matsue's main association has been as a 'city of water' (see p261) but it is now developing enmusubi ('good fortune in love') tourism and has created some places for young women and couples to go to in search of romantic reassurance. These are often places that have had no particular romantic associations in the past. Look out for heart shapes as you go around Matsue Castle – one has also been cut into one of the 100-year-old pine trees along Shiomi Nawate, a small street by the north moat of the castle. And a normal postbox in Karakoro Kobo (see opposite) has been painted pink. By the time you reach Matsue there may be many more symbols of love to look for. Given the city's scenic location and its reputation for beautiful sunsets it is not surprising Matsue is developing an association with romance.

> ❏ **Discounted tickets**
> A **Universal Pass** (¥980) includes entry to the Lafcadio Hearn Memorial Museum, Buke-Yashiki samurai residence and Matsue Castle, and offers small discounts at a number of other sights. You can buy it at all three places and it's valid for three days, though you can only enter each property once. Alternatively if you show your passport (non-Japanese), or Alien Registration Card, you will be entitled to a 20-50% discount off most rates.

Further along the same street is **Buke-Yashiki** (daily Apr-Sep 8.30am-6.30pm, Oct-Mar to 5pm; ¥300 or ¥150 for foreign visitors), a samurai house built in 1730. Although you can't actually go into the house, there is an outside path around the rooms which contain displays of samurai swords and other artefacts. If you go up the path behind the house you'll come to a small building where you can watch a film about Matsue's Drum Festival, which takes places every November.

Matsue Castle (daily Apr-Sep 8.30am-6.30pm, Oct-Mar to 5pm; ¥550 or ¥280 for foreign visitors) was built by the feudal lord Yoshiharu Horio in 1611, though what stands today is a 1950s reconstruction. Hearn often climbed the castle tower, which he described as 'grotesquely complex in detail, looking somewhat like a huge pagoda'. On the ground floor of the donjon the original dolphin- and gargoyle-shaped roof tiles are displayed, and other floors contain scale models of the castle and city over which it once presided. But the best part of the climb is the tremendous view from the top-floor observation gallery over Matsue and Lake Shinji.

For a different perspective of the castle take the **Horikawa Sightseeing Boat** (🖥 www.matsue-horikawameguri.jp; see p264) from any of the three boarding points (see map p265).

Other areas **Shimane Art Museum** (Kenritsu Bijutsukan; 🖥 www1.pref. shimane.lg.jp/contents/sam; Wed-Mon 10am-6.30pm; ¥300) is in a modern glass building on the banks of Lake Shinji. Come here just before dusk to watch the sun set over the tiny tree-studded island in the lake. The museum building threatens to overshadow the collection it houses, which includes a few minor works by Monet and Gaugin, and a bronze cast of Rodin's 1897 *Monument to Victor Hugo*.

Karakoro Kobo (daily 9.30am-6.30pm), in the former Bank of Japan building on the north side of Ohashi-gawa, houses temporary art exhibitions, a café, restaurant as well as art and craft shops and a pink post box (see box opposite). The word 'karakoro' comes, of course, from Lafcadio Hearn. It's said that when Hearn woke up after his first night in Matsue, he heard the noise of wooden geta shoes in the street outside his ryokan. To Hearn's ears, the noise each footstep made was 'kara, koro, kara, koro'.

Matsue Shinjiko-onsen is the city's hot-spring resort, on the banks of Lake Shinji close to Ichibata Railway's Matsue Shinjiko-onsen station. The source of the spring is 1250m underground, near the lakeshore. At source, the water temperature is around 77°C, though it's cooled down by the time it reaches the bath houses of the lakeside hotels and ryokan. The best way to enjoy the area is to stay at one of these hotels (see p266), most of which have their own hot spring with a lakeside view. If you can't afford this you can always soak your feet in the **ashi-yu** (foot bath) outside Matsue Shinjiko-onsen station. It's open all hours and has a cover to protect both you and the water if it's raining. To reach the resort, take the Lakeline Bus from outside Matsue station.

See pp266-7 for details of side trips from Matsue.

PRACTICAL INFORMATION
Station guide
Matsue station has two exits; the north exit is the one for tourist information and the bus platforms. You'll find **lockers** of all sizes in a corner of the station concourse. As you leave the ticket barrier, on your left is the **JR ticket office** (daily 5.15am-10.30pm) and in front of you a branch of **TiS travel agency** (Mon-Fri 10am-6pm, Sat & Sun 10am-5pm).

The branch of the *Little Mermaid bakery* in the station offers everything from cakes and buns to slices of pizza – perfect for a lakeside picnic. You'll also find a *UCC Coffee shop* serving simple pasta dishes (in the shopping mall which leads off behind you as you exit the ticket barrier). For details of other restaurants in and around the station see Where to eat.

Tourist information
Matsue International Tourist Information Office (🖳 www.kankou-mat sue.jp; daily 9am-6pm) is in the modern glass building right outside the north exit of the station. Staff can assist with accommodation booking and sell various passes and tours (see Getting around). See also 🖳 matsueguide. com/matsue-what-to-see.

Getting around
The best way of seeing Matsue's sights is to hop on the retro tourist **Lakeline Bus** (daily Mar-Nov 8.40am to sunset, Dec-Feb 9am-4.40pm; ¥200/journey, ¥500 one-day pass), which runs in a loop around the city and stops outside the station.

Cycle rental is available from Nippon Rent a Car, across the street from the tourist information office (¥1000 per day).

However, even though the lake is scenic, cycling along the road around it isn't fun, especially on the north side, as there is a lot of traffic.

As the 'City of Water', Matsue naturally enough offers opportunities for boat rides. **Lake Shinji Boat Tour** (🖳 www. hakuchougo.jp; daily Mar-Nov, 11am-5pm; 5/day; ¥1300) offers one-hour rides and a daily sunset cruise. **Horikawa Sightseeing Boat** (daily Mar-Nov 9am-4/5/6pm, Dec-Feb 10am-3pm; ¥1200 or ¥800 for foreign visitors) does a 50-minute cruise around the moat of Matsue Castle. The boats have to pass under some very low bridges on their way round but this is Japan so a flick of the switch lowers the boat canopy and allows a safe passage underneath. There are three boarding points (see map opposite).

Festivals
At the end of July/beginning of August is the **Suigo-sai Festival**, the highlight of which is a massive fireworks display over Lake Shinji.

The most raucous annual event is the **Drum Festival** on 3rd November.

Where to stay
Directly opposite the station is *Matsue Tokyu Inn* (☎ 0852-27 0109, 🖳 www. tokyuhotelsjapan.com/en; from ¥8200/S, ¥14,100/D, ¥15,300/Tw), a mid-range business hotel with two non-smoking floors.

Also in the station area is *Toyoko Inn Matsue Ekimae* (☎ 0852-60 1045, 🖳 www .toyoko-inn.com; from ¥4980/S, ¥7770/D or Tw inc breakfast), to the left on the main road which runs parallel to the station. The rooms at this chain hotel are spotless. *Hotel Route Inn Matsue* (☎ 0852-20 6211,

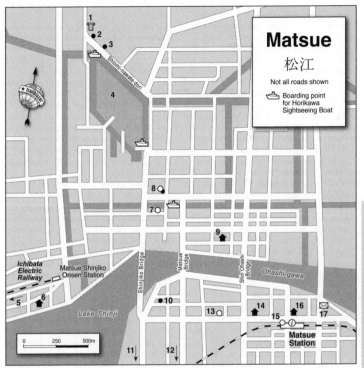

MATSUE – MAP KEY

Where to stay
- 6 Hotel Ichibata ホテル一畑
- 9 Hotel Route Inn Matsue
  ホテルルートイン松江
- 12 Terazuya Ryokan 寺津屋旅館
- 14 Toyoko Inn Matsue Ekimae
  東横イン 松江駅前
- 16 Matsue Tokyu Inn 松江東急イン

Where to eat and drink
- 7 Coffee-kan 珈琲館
- 8 Be-d'oro (Karakoro-kobo)
  びどろ（カラコロ工房）
- 11 Vecchio Rosso ベッキオロッソ
- 13 Shirokiya 白木屋
- 15 Matsue Terrsa 松江テルサ

Other
- 1 Lafcadio Hearn Memorial Museum
  小泉八雲記念館
- 2 Lafcadio Hearn Former Residence
  小泉八雲旧居
- 3 Buke Yashiki 武家屋敷
- 4 Matsue Castle 松江城
- 5 Matsue Shinjiko-onsen
  松江しんじ湖温泉
- 8 Karakoro-kobo カラコロ工房
- 10 San-in Godo Bank 山陰合同銀行
- 11 Shimane Art Museum
  島根県立美術館
- 17 Central Post Office 中央郵便局

🖳 www.route-inn.co.jp; ¥5300/S, ¥9300/D, ¥11,000/Tw) is a smart place a short walk north of the station across Ohashi-gawa.

Terazuya Ryokan (☎ 0852-21 3480, 🖳 www.mable.ne.jp/~terazuya; tatami rooms ¥4200pp, ¥4800 inc breakfast, or ¥7350 half-board) is a small family-run inn. Dinner is a real feast and eaten with the family so there's a very homely atmosphere. Turn left out of the station and follow the train tracks round for about 10 minutes until you hit the ryokan on the left side. Or call for a lift from the station.

At **Matsue-onsen** the top place to stay is ***Hotel Ichibata*** (☎ 0852-22 0188, 🖳 www.ichibata.co.jp/hotel; from ¥12,000/S, ¥15,600/Tw). Ask for a room in the new annex – many of the rooms in the original building are dated and not worth the money. The pricier rooms have views over Lake Shinji. Online booking in English is through JapaniCan (see box p46).

See also pp45-52 for general information about accommodation.

Where to eat and drink

Matsue is known in Japan for the 'seven delicacies of Lake Shinji'. Since the lake is a combination of fresh and sea water, the seven fish are an unusual mix: carp, eel, shrimp, *shijimi* clams, whitebait, bass and smelt. The fish don't all appear in the same season so there are usually only two or three on one plate but it's occasionally possible (for a lot of money) to eat all seven in one sitting. Ask at the tourist information office (see p264) for the best places to try the dish; wherever you go take a wallet full of cash.

On your left as you leave the north side of the station is **Matsue Terrsa**, a glass building whose ground floor *café* serves excellent coffee and cake in a corner of the impressive atrium. On the 2nd floor is ***Capricciosa*** (daily 11am-10pm), a branch of the popular Italian pizza and pasta chain; most main dishes cost around ¥1000.

The upmarket Italian restaurant at Shimane Art Museum, ***Vecchio Rosso*** (Tue-Sun 10am-9pm, last orders 7.30pm), takes advantage of its lakeside location with floor-to-ceiling windows and makes a great spot for watching the sunset. Dinner is expensive, with set meals costing ¥3675-5250, but lunch deals are more reasonable at ¥1600-3200.

A few minutes up the main road past Toyoko Inn you will come to ***Shirokiya*** (daily 5pm-5am), an izakaya-style place. It's open until the early hours and serves everything from *basashi* (raw horsemeat, see p403) to pizza and garlic bread, plus a good selection of beer and sake. You can even sing karaoke here in one of the back rooms. It's cheap, friendly and there's a chance of bumping into some of Matsue's resident gaijin. Look for the red sign with 'Shirokiya' written in white kanji above the entrance and the words 'Public house for enjoyable people' on the door.

The French café/restaurant ***Be-d'oro*** (daily 5.30-11pm & Mon-Sat 11.30am-3pm, Sun 11.30am-4pm) is in **Karakoro Kobo** (see p263). The lunchtime menu (from ¥1000) usually includes soup and a choice of fish or meat; the dinner is more pricey (from ¥3000).

A good place to stop for coffee across the river from Karakoro Kobo is ***Coffee-kan***, which has tables overlooking the water.

Side trips from Matsue
To Adachi Museum of Art A short train and bus ride away from Matsue is Adachi Museum of Art (🖳 www.adachi-museum.or.jp; daily 9am-5/5.30pm; ¥2200 or ¥1100 for foreign visitors; ¥300 for English audio tour), considered one of the top cultural attractions in Japan, as famous for its stunning and immaculate landscaped gardens (which have won several awards and are frequently named the best in Japan) as for its collection of contemporary Japanese art.

To reach the museum, take a local or limited-express train from Matsue east towards Yonago and get off at **Yasugi**. Local trains from Matsue take 25 minutes and limited-express services take 15 minutes. A free shuttle bus (about 9/day; 20 mins) runs from outside Yasugi station to the museum; see the website for the timetable.

To Izumo Taisha Some 30km west of Matsue, at the foot of Yakumo Hill, is Izumo Taisha. It is Japan's oldest shrine and is dedicated to Okuninushi, the God of Marriage. Expect to see lots of happy couples, but also unhappy ones trying for a spiritual repair job. Lafcadio Hearn (see pp261-2), who himself found love in Matsue, visited Izumo Taisha twice and became the first foreigner to be allowed to enter the *honden* (inner shrine). The main hall is under renovation until 2013 (it will be hidden by scaffolding) but the rest of the site is still open.

Izumo Taisha is accessible from Matsue Shinjiko-onsen station via the private Ichibata Railway (55 mins; ¥750). Change trains at Kawato for the final leg to Izumo-Taisha-mae. To save money, rail-pass holders need to backtrack along the JR San-in line from Matsue to Izumo-shi (see p240), and from there transfer on to the Ichibata Railway for the last part of the journey.

Other side trips Other possible day trips from Matsue are to **Tottori** (see p241) if the idea of seeing Japan's only desert appeals and, given an early start, to **Iwami Ginzan Silver Mine** (see pp239-40).

Tohoku (North-eastern Honshu) route guides

This region came to the world's attention on 11th March 2011 as a result of the devastating Great East Japan earthquake and tsunami (see box p275). Undoubtedly there are parts of Tohoku where life will never be the same again, but it is still possible to visit almost everywhere in this region and you are likely to get a warm welcome and have an extremely rewarding visit.

A trip around this region offers a rare chance in an overcrowded island to go off-the-beaten track. When Japanese TV programmes poke fun at rural life and local accents, more often than not their targets are the 'country folk' of Tohoku. Some Japanese will only reluctantly venture into the region, fearing that the dialects they encounter will be so strong that they might as well be speaking a different language. Such is the power of television.

In contrast to other parts of the country, Tohoku offers little in the way of famous temples or shrines. Volcanoes, lakes, mountains and rivers predominate, a geography which explains why north-eastern Honshu lagged behind in the industrial race of the late 20th century. But, the region is not without its attractions: Kakunodate and Hirosaki are known for their cherry blossoms in spring; in summer the festivals here, particularly in Aomori and Hirosaki, are some of the best in Japan; and in autumn Nikko is at its most stunning, though it should be a must whenever you visit.

Rail access to this region is fast and efficient, thanks in particular to the number of shinkansen routes. Beyond these is a network of ordinary lines served by both limited express, rapid and local trains; these are the best means of seeing Tohoku close up – the

> If you're planning an extended tour around Tohoku it's worth downloading and printing off the **Northern Tohoku Welcome Card** (see box p64).

shinkansen is fast but due to the proliferation of tunnels the views are nearly always fleeting. At the time of research services for all the routes described below were working normally.

The following route loops around the region, starting with the journey north from Tokyo, along the eastern side of Tohoku, to Aomori at the northern tip of Honshu and the rail gateway to Hokkaido; then back towards Tokyo down the less-travelled western side. Several side trips heading inland from either coast are suggested; these also make it possible to crisscross the region easily and ensure you never need to double back on yourself.

TOKYO TO SHIN-AOMORI

The fastest shinkansen from Tokyo to Shin-Aomori is the Hayabusa (see box below); the Hayate also operates on this route. The Yamabiko runs from Tokyo as far as Morioka; the Komachi also operates to Morioka but then heads west to Akita; the double-decker Max Yamabiko goes to Sendai; and the Nasuno terminates at Koriyama.

The Hayabusa, Hayate and Komachi are reserved seating only.

Hayabusa – a Gran(d) experience
Whatever shinkansen journey you take you are almost guaranteed a smooth, comfortable ride. For anyone from Britain at least that is an exciting prospect. However, the Hayabusa, with its new **Gran Class**, has taken shinkansen travel into a

new league.

There are only 18 seats (2 x 1) in Car 10 so you immediately feel special. The car attendant will greet you and show you through the space-age carriage done out in a tastefully understated livery. Make your way to your leather seat and slip off your shoes (slippers are provided). Then you need to get comfortable –

there are several buttons enabling you to recline and shape the seat to whatever suits you best. Once you are settled you will be given an *oshibori* (hot towel) and then served a meal (a *bento* lunch box or sandwiches, both of which will include local products) and a drink of your choice. Then it's time to relax and enjoy the feeling of being cocooned from the world – with the attendant only a button's press away.

Anyone with a JR Pass must pay the full express supplement and also pay for a Gran Class ticket. Since the complimentary meal and a drink is provided whatever the length of your journey the best-value way to have a taste of this luxury is to do a short stretch, such as from Morioka to Shin-Aomori (from ¥9520 with a JR Pass, without a rail pass it will cost ¥15,490).

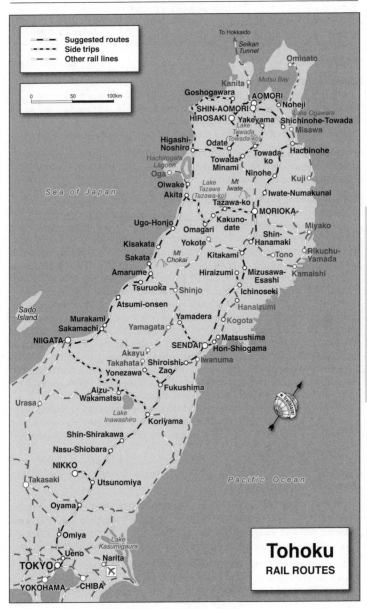

Tohoku
RAIL ROUTES

Tokyo to Ichinoseki

[Map 15; Map 16, p273; Map 17, p279;
Table 12, pp462-3]

Distances from Tokyo by shinkansen. Fastest journey time: 2 hours 21 minutes.

Tokyo (0km)

[see pp83-106]

Ueno (4km) Most trains call here (see pp90-1), Tokyo's main terminal for the north. If joining the train here rather than at Tokyo, it's worth reserving seats because at certain times the non-reserved cars are full by the time the train leaves Tokyo. The shinkansen tracks start underground (allow at least 10 minutes if transferring from the Yamanote Line) but you soon get good views of Tokyo.

Until they reach Omiya, shinkansen don't go at full speed because there are noise restrictions due to the residential neighbourhoods; the bonus is that it is easier to look out of the window.

Omiya (30km) Almost every service stops here. Omiya is so close to Tokyo it's impossible to see where one ends and the other begins.

Even though some of the exhibits are geared to children a visit to the **Railway Museum** (Tetsudo Hakubutsukan; 🖥 www.railway-museum.jp; Wed-Mon 10am-6pm, last entry 5.30pm; ¥1000) is recommended. The museum, operated by JR East, focuses in particular on the history of the railway, both abroad and in Japan. The history zone has 35 real train cars including two of the first shinkansen – even these had seats that could be changed to face the opposite way, a chilled water dispenser and a bottle opener – as well as royal cars used by former emperors. Some labels are in Japanese only but if you have a smart phone you will be able to use it to scan the mobile barcodes and then read labels in English. One of the highlights is the railway model diorama; this has 80 sets of trains with 1002 cars and it runs continuously. Children may be keen to try driving a miniature train (¥200); options include a shinkansen and the Narita Express. Another attraction is the local train driver-training simulator (¥500; reservations required) but, at the time of writing, this was available in Japanese only.

There is a *restaurant* on the ground floor but it is much more interesting to have a picnic in the View Deck on the 3rd floor. Here you can watch real shinkansen speed past – there is a special timetable showing which train will pass by and when.

To get to the museum, take the Saitama Shintoshi Kotsu (New Shuttle) train (2 mins; ¥180; rail passes not valid) to Tetsudo-Hakubutsukan station. The museum is a minute's walk away.

Omiya is the last chance to change to the Asama shinkansen for Nagano (see pp163-9). After Omiya, all Nasunos and some Yamabikos call at **Oyama (81km)**. Transfer at Oyama for the JR Mito line to Shimodate and then to Mooka to see its steam-engine-shaped station building (see box p73).

Utsunomiya (110km) All Nasunos and most Yamabikos stop here. The main reason for coming here is that it is the access point for **Nikko** (see opposite), a beautiful shrine and temple town, thus you need to change trains here.

Look to the right before you walk out of the shinkansen part of the station for the *ekiben* (station lunch box; see box p82) cart; this station was where ekiben were first sold at the end of the 19th century and is one of the few that still sells them from a cart rather than from a kiosk or on the train.

Utsunomiya City Information Centre (daily 8.30am-8pm), on the left as you exit the shinkansen tracks, has information about Nikko and can advise about accommodation but to book a hotel you need to go to View Travel Agency (daily 6am-10pm) nearby. **Lockers** (¥300-500) are down the corridor by the north exit to the right of the stairs, and also by the south exit.

Side trip by train to Nikko

Nikko is at its most stunning in the autumn but even in the rain at any time of the year the colourful opulence of the shrine complex, as well as the intricate carving, make this an unforgettable place. Its location, in the mountains and surrounded by lakes and waterfalls, is also a highlight.

For anyone with a JR rail pass the easiest way to reach Nikko is to transfer at Utsunomiya onto a JR Nikko-line train (approx 1/hour; 50 mins). Follow signs from the shinkansen tracks to platform 5; there is no need to exit Utsunomiya station first. However, note that not all trains from platform 5 go to Nikko.

See p113 for details about reaching Nikko from Tokyo if you don't have a JR rail pass.

JR Nikko Station has no detailed information about Nikko. For that you will need to go to the tourist information centre (see p272). It is about a 30-minute walk uphill from the station towards the shrine area so if you have luggage and are staying near the shrine area it is worth taking a taxi (about ¥710) or a bus (3-4/hr; ¥190 to Shinkyo Bridge); if you expect to use the bus quite a bit consider getting a Sekai-isan-meguri pass (¥500/day) from Tobu Nikko station, a short walk from the JR station. This pass is valid for unlimited travel on Tobu buses in

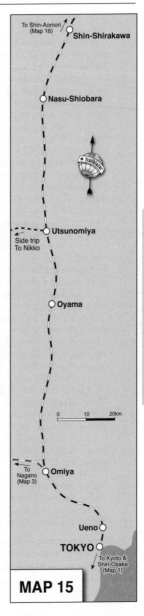

HONSHU

MAP 15

central Nikko for two consecutive days. The **tourist information centre** (🖥 www.nikko-jp.org; daily 9am-5pm, English-language speaker Apr-Nov 10am-2pm), on the left-hand side almost midway between the stations and the shrine area, has very useful maps of the shrine area and accommodation leaflets but staff are unable to make bookings. Internet access is available (¥100; 30 mins).

The vast area known as **Nikko Sannai** (daily Apr-Oct 8am-5pm, Nov-Mar to 4pm; combination ticket for three main sights ¥1000, valid for two days: much better value than individual tickets), on the World Heritage Site list since 1999, contains the three main sights (as listed below).

The original gateway to the Nikko Sannai area was the red-lacquered **Shinkyo Bridge** across the Daiya River. It is still possible to cross this bridge (daily 8am-4pm; ¥300; not part of the combination ticket) but it is free to use the road and that way you can admire the bridge properly.

Rinno-ji (¥900), one of the three main temples in the Tendai sect of Buddhism, dates back to 766. The star attraction, however, is the grand **Toshogu Shrine** (¥1300, plus ¥520 for outlying areas), originally built in 1616 as a mausoleum for Tokugawa Ieyasu, founder of the Tokugawa shogunate. The first shrine was rebuilt a few years later in 1636 on the orders of Iemitsu, who wanted an even more majestic and everlasting memorial to his grandfather.

Look out for the famous monkeys, carved in relief, on the **Shinyosha** (Sacred Stable), which depict 'See no evil', 'Speak no evil' and 'Hear no evil'. **Futarasan Shrine** (¥200) is home to the patron god of Nikko and is dedicated to Mt Nantai, a nearby mountain.

Tsurukame Daikichi Inn (☎ 0288-54 1550; online booking through 🖥 www.japanican.com; from ¥11,500pp inc two meals) has a good location near Toshogu Shrine and has river and mountain views; it also has indoor and outdoor baths and delicious meals. *Johsyu-ya Ryokan* (☎ 0288-54 0155, 🖥 www.johsyu-ya.co.jp; from ¥5500pp; dinner ¥2000, breakfast ¥1000) is situated on the right-hand side near the top of the road to Toshogu Shrine. The rooms are large (some can sleep up to four) but can be noisy as the main road is busy. It also has a (single-sex) hot-spring bath. Meals must be booked in advance.

On the same side of the road as Johsyu-ya but downhill is a branch of the *Skylark/Gusto* restaurant chain (daily 9am-11pm), serving both Western and Japanese dishes, as well as a soba and ramen noodle restaurant, a Chinese restaurant, and *Hi no Kuruma*, where a vegetable okonomiyaki costs ¥470.

On the opposite side and up the hill, *Hippari Tako* serves a wide range of dishes including yakisoba (¥700) and yakitori (¥800). Most of the restaurants open daily from around 11am to 7/8pm.

Yayoi Festival (Futarasan Shrine, 13th-17th Apr) involves portable shrines being carried to and from shrines in the area as well as dance performances; **Toshogu Grand Spring Festival** (Shunki Reitaisai) is held on 17th-18th May as well as in October (Shuki Taisai; 17th Oct) and both events feature a procession of men dressed in samurai costumes.

After Utsunomiya all Nasunos and some Yamabikos call at **Nasu-Shiobara (158km)** and at **Shin-Shirakawa (185km)**. However, there is little reason to stop at either. Soon after Shin-Shirakawa a brief succession of tunnels blocks out the view before opening up again and turning decidedly ugly with a sprawling city as the train approaches Koriyama.

Koriyama (227km) All Nasuno and almost all Yamabikos stop here.

There is little to see in Koriyama but you should change here for the samurai-castle and sake-brewing town of Aizu-Wakamatsu (see below), which is on the Banetsu-sei line that runs some 190km across Honshu from Koriyama to Niigata. There is also the chance to ride the SL Banetsu Monogatari (see p300) from Aizu-Wakamatsu to Niigata.

At Koriyama station there is a **Travel Service Center** (daily 5.20am-11pm) and beyond that a **Question and Answer Office** (💻 www.city.koriyama.fukushima.jp; daily 9.30am-5pm), where staff can provide both tourist and rail service information and have a map of Koriyama. On this floor there is a **restaurant zone** (daily 11am-10pm) and at street level there is a Food Bazaar with a selection of fast-food stands sharing an eating area. In the morning they do coffee and breakfast sets here.

If you decide to stay in Koriyama, rather than Aizu-Wakamatsu, *Washington Hotel* (☎ 024-923 1311, 💻 www.washington-k.co.jp; from ¥7000/S, ¥14,000/D or Tw, inc breakfast) is a good choice as it is conveniently located a short walk from the station. However, the rooms are rather dated. To reach it take the central exit and walk straight ahead. Cross the main road and continue past the Lawsons store on the corner; turn right at the first set of traffic lights at a crossroads. The hotel is on your right after a branch of 7-Eleven.

Alternatively, there's a *Toyoko Inn* (💻 www.toyoko-inn.com; ¥4480/S, ¥5980/D, ¥6980/Tw, inc breakfast) about a seven-minute walk parallel to the railway tracks heading west from the station's west exit.

Side trip by rail to Aizu-Wakamatsu
Aizu-Wakamatsu is known for its castle and as a place where sake is brewed but it was also one of the samurai's last strongholds in Japan; it only lost its influence when the Meiji government took over and ended the feudal era.

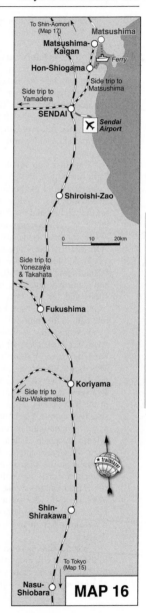

HONSHU

MAP 16

Trains to Aizu Wakamatsu depart from platform 1. The **Aizu Liner** (3/day; about 70 mins) is the quickest service but local trains operate (approx hourly) on this line.

There is an **information centre** (💻 www.city.aizuwakamatsu.fukushima.jp; daily 9am-5pm) on the right by Aizu-Wakamatsu station exit. From there walk straight out to the bus ticket centre on the left; buses stop to the right of that.

The **Aizu Loop Bus** (daily 8am-6.30pm; ¥200, day pass ¥500, combination ticket inc the castle, its tea house and Oyakuen ¥1360) is the best way to get round town as the attractions are spread out. The green bus (daily 2/hr) operates the full route, the red bus (6/day) takes a more limited route. Show your pass as you leave the bus. You will be given a timetable when you buy the pass.

Your first stop should be **Aizu Buke-Yashiki** (Aizu Samurai Residence; daily Apr-Nov 8.30am-5pm, Dec-Mar to 4.30pm; ¥850, ¥750 with bus pass). Even though all the buildings are reconstructions everything has been recreated to look as it would have done in the Edo era. The residence includes areas for the samurai and his family and staff as well as guest rooms, gardens, a tea house, an archery range and a rice mill. Mannequins in the rooms bring it all to life. En route to the castle you may like to stop at **Oyakuen** (daily 8.30am-5pm; ¥310), a landscape garden with a pond and a medicinal-herb garden.

Wakamatsu Castle (Wakamatsu-jo also known as Tsuruga-jo; daily 8.30am-5pm; castle ¥400, castle and tea house ¥500) was first built in 1384 and the original building lasted until 1868. This reconstruction dates from the 1960s and for non-Japanese speakers is chiefly of interest for its unique, 'original-style' red roof. From the castle bus stop, cross the road, take the narrow path to the right of the souvenir shop and then follow the signs.

Sake requires good-quality rice, pure water and a cold climate, and as Aizu-Wakamatsu has all three it is not surprising that there are several sake breweries here. A short walk from the castle is **Aizu Sake Museum** (daily May-Oct 8.30am-5pm, Nov-Apr 9am-4.30pm; ¥300); originally a brewery, it now exhibits both modern and traditional brewing methods. **Suehiro Sake Brewery** (daily 9am-5pm) was founded in 1850 and produces not only some of the best sake in Japan but also sparkling sake, sake jelly, sake cakes and a sake bath extract. The hourly tours take in the brewing area and a sake museum as well as a museum of film cameras (¥300) that houses over 500 cameras. The scientist Noguchi Hideyo, whose portrait is on the ¥1000 note, was born in Aizu Wakamatsu and knew the Suehiro family well so some of his letters and pictures can be seen at the brewery. He became famous as a result of his medical research, particularly into syphilis.

If planning to stay the night, try *Toyoko Inn Aizu-Wakamatsu Ekimae* (☎ 0242-32 1045, 💻 www.toyoko-inn.com; from ¥5480/S, ¥6480/D, ¥7480/Tw, inc breakfast), to the left of the station, or *Alpha 1 Hotel* (☎ 0242-32 6868, 💻 www.alpha-1.co.jp/aizuwakamatsu; from ¥5000/S, ¥9800/D, ¥10,300/Tw) to the right.

When returning to Koriyama, if you take the north exit and want to return to the central exit area (also called the west exit), you need to turn left out of the exit and walk alongside the shinkansen concourse to the central area, or alternatively transfer to the shinkansen area and then find your way to the central exit.

Alternatively, and assuming you are here at the right time of the year, it is worth taking the **SL Banetsu Monogatari** (Mar-Nov weekends only, daily during Aug; 3 hrs 50 mins) from here to Niigata. All seats on this steam train are reserved so you'll need to book ahead at any JR travel agency (reservations are free to JR rail-pass holders). Tickets go on sale one month in advance and are often sold out within the day. A good part of the route follows the Agano river, making for a scenic journey, with photo stops included. The train also has an observation car.

It's only after Koriyama, over 200km from Tokyo, that the scenery start to improve as the landscape becomes more rural, offering the first glimpses of what Tohoku has to offer. The view, however, is frequently blocked by tunnels.

Fukushima (273km)   All the Yamabiko services stop here. Since the Yamagata line branches off here some trains divide. If on a Max Yamabiko you should make sure you're in the right part of the train (if you have a seat reservation you will be); the Yamabiko part continues on to Sendai and Morioka, and the other part, the Tsubasa, branches off to Yamagata (see map p269) and

---

⛩ The Great East Japan Earthquake

Few outside Japan had heard of Fukushima before a 9.0-magnitude quake struck off Tohoku's Pacific coast on the afternoon of 11th March 2011. But within minutes this rural backwater of north-eastern Japan became the epicentre of a tragedy that continues to unfold to this day.

The quake was the most powerful ever to have hit Japan, dwarfing the 1995 Great Hanshin Earthquake which flattened the city of Kobe (see p241). Tsunami waves more than 10m in height powered inland along 530km of the coastline, destroying villages, communities and at least 20,000 lives.

The worst affected areas were north from Choshi, in Chiba, up to and including the southern and eastern coastline of Hokkaido. The tremors were felt west of Tokyo and as far north as Sapporo in Hokkaido. Regional railway services were paralysed, and JR East – the company which manages the rail network in Tohoku – was left with a bill of more than ¥100 billion to repair seven damaged rail sections along a combined total of 325km of track.

But the lasting legacy of the quake and tsunami – beyond the tragic loss of life – remains the damage inflicted on the Fukushima Daiichi nuclear power plant. Its cooling systems were knocked out, which led to a series of explosions and meltdowns, and Fukushima prefecture became the scene of the world's worst nuclear accident in 25 years. Tokyo Electric Power Company, operator of the nuclear plant, struggled for months to contain the disaster, before achieving a state of cold shutdown. It is likely to be several decades before the stricken plant is fully decommissioned. The accident rekindled a debate – which some said was long overdue – about Japan's reliance on nuclear energy, and about the safety of nuclear plants built along earthquake fault lines.

Tens of thousands of residents who lived within what became known as the exclusion zone around the nuclear plant were evacuated in the days following the quake, and many are unlikely ever to return. The long-term impact on the regional economy continues to be felt. Local industries and farmers say their livelihoods have been destroyed because of the association of the name Fukushima with nuclear contamination.

beyond on the extension to **Shinjo** (**421km**; see p297) via **Yonezawa** (**313km**; see below), **Takahata** (**322km**) and **Yamagata** (**360km**). Yamagata is a jumping-off point for the pilgrimage site of **Yamadera** (see p306), which can also be accessed as a side trip by rail from Sendai.

It is worth noting that Fukushima City, and thus the shinkansen station, is 62km (about 38 miles) from the Fukushima Daiichi nuclear power plant.

For details about the Soma-Nomaoi (Soma Wild Horse Chase) see box p316.

Side trip by shinkansen to Yonezawa

The Tsubasa shinkansen's route offers some spectacular scenery, pine forests, rivers (and a few tunnels) but it does make you wonder why a shinkansen was built here, since it's not exactly a teeming metropolis. However, for a pleasant diversion from Fukushima take the Tsubasa shinkansen to Yonezawa (approx hourly; 35 mins), or continue on to Sakamachi (see opposite).

At tiny Yonezawa station, to your right as you exit the ticket barrier is the **JR ticket office** (daily 6.30am-9.15pm) and adjacent View Plaza travel agency. A **tourist information desk** (🖳 www.yonezawa-kankou-navi.com; daily 8am-6pm) is to the left. **Lockers** (including a few ¥500 ones) are outside and to your left as you exit the station, at the end of the building and by the bus stops. Also here is an Eki Rent A Car booth, which also offers **cycle rental** (¥500/4 hours, ¥1000/day).

Yonezawa is most associated with the Uesugi clan, generations of which ruled the area. Two of the most important sights are Uesugi Mausoleum and Uesugi Jinja, both a fair distance from the station (the shrine is 2.3km, a 30-minute walk, and the mausoleum is 3.5km), but **buses** (blue or yellow; 1-2/hr; ¥200/ride) run in a loop around the town, stopping at both places. Or you can save on the bus fare by taking a local JR Yonesaka line train from Yonezawa two stops to Nishi-Yonezawa, from where the mausoleum is 10 minutes on foot.

Uesugi Gobyo-sho (Uesugi Mausoleum; daily summer 9am-5pm, winter 11am-4pm; ¥200; English information sheet available), the last resting place for the feudal lords of the Uesugi clan, is set in a quiet, residential part of town and surrounded by pine trees.

Uesugi Jinja (Uesugi Shrine; free), on the site once occupied by Yonezawa Castle, is dedicated to Uesugi Kenshin (1530-78), the first feudal lord of the Uesugi clan. It burnt down in 1919 and was rebuilt four years later. The entrance is across a moat filled with *koi* (carp) but don't feed them as the staff are concerned they are getting too fat. Next to the statue of Kenshin is a stone memorial upon which is written his motto in life: 'If there is the will, anything that can be imagined can be done'. It is reported that when John F Kennedy was asked about the politicians he admires, he mentioned Uesugi Yozan. Within the shrine precinct is the **Keisho-den** (Treasure House; ¥400), which contains swords, armour and other remnants of the Uesugi reign.

A good place to stay the night is *Toyoko Inn Yonezawa Ekimae* (☎ 0238-22 2045, 🖳 www.toyoko-inn.com; ¥4515/S, ¥7140/D or Tw, inc breakfast), four minutes on foot from the station. Look for it on your left as you exit.

Yonezawa is known for its beef, which comes at a premium price – upwards of ¥10,000 for a meal. One place that's not too expensive, and where Yonezawa beef is the only thing on the menu, is *Toyokan*, across the street from the station. The restaurant name is written in black kanji on the side of the building (on the right-hand corner of the main street which runs away from the station). Look for the picture of a black bull. Its cheapest set menu, with steak, is ¥2800. If your budget is more limited, try the yakiniku (¥1800) or sukiyaki (¥2000) at *Zane* (daily 11am-8pm), on the 2nd floor (above a coffee shop) to the left side of the main road heading away from the station. A map showing the various restaurants is available at the tourist information desk. However, it is in Japanese so ask staff to point out the best ones. A cheaper option is the delicious beef *domamaka* (¥1100) ekiben at the station.

Rail fans might like to consider a further side trip from Yonezawa along the scenic JR Yonesaka line to **Sakamachi** on the coast (from where you can connect with the route guide on p299). The trains are mostly local services, but once a day there is a rapid service called Benibana which runs all the way to Niigata (see pp306-11). This is a scenic journey, particularly when the weather is good and in late autumn when the snow is new; towards the end of the winter it can look rather dirty which spoils the view. It is probably best to sit on the right-hand side if you can, but there are good views on both sides.

There are several tunnels on the route between Fukushima and Sendai. After Fukushima some shinkansen stop at **Shiroishi-Zao (307km)**.

Sendai (352km) [see pp300-6]

All services stop here. Change here for a side trip to the extremely scenic Matsushima Bay (see below).

Side trip by rail to Matsushima

Over 260 islands are scattered around Matsushima Bay; collectively they count as one of the top three scenic spots in Japan, along with Miyajima (see pp258-60) and Amanohashidate.

For centuries, poets have journeyed here in search of inspiration – indeed, the islands themselves are sometimes compared to verses of a poem. In the station there is even a small haiku box where travelling poets can deposit their own work. Matsuo Basho visited on his epic journey through the region and wrote that Matsushima was the 'most beautiful spot in the whole country of Japan'. He was reportedly left speechless by the beautiful scenery and abandoned plans to write a haiku in honour of his visit in 1689.

The mainland was protected from the worst of the March 2011 tsunami by the islands. However, some parts suffered damage though at the time of writing most, apart from Oshima Island, had been repaired.

From Sendai, take the Umikaze rapid train (approx 1/hr; 27 mins) on the JR Senseki Line (from platform 9). Local trains (also approx 1/hr) take 40 mins.

There is enough to see and do in Matsushima but if the idea of going by boat one way appeals leave the train at **Hon-Shiogama (16km)**. At the time of research Hon-Shiogama station was being rebuilt and the tourist information office (Mon-Fri 10am-16pm) had temporarily opened near the Jinja-sando exit of the station. From the station take the Aqua Gate exit, turn left and walk past a branch of Baskin Robbins and then Aeon department store. If you keep going straight you will reach the Marine Gate Terminal. Here you'll find seafood restaurants with harbour views and an observation platform. Marubun Matsushima Kisen offers a Basho cruise (💻 www.marubun-kisen.com; daily

9am-4pm; 1-2/hr; 50 mins; from ¥1400) between Hon-Shiogama and Matsushima as well as round-trip cruises from both Shiogama and Matsushima. All go past some of the many tiny islands that are a familiar sight along this coastline but the journey is marred by the occasional chimney stack, and by the non-stop commentary in Japanese that pours out of speakers around the boat. There's a tourist information desk (daily 8.30am-5pm) at the boat pier in Matsushima, but the staff here don't speak English.

If you stay on the train you will get your first proper view of the islands – and will understand why you have come here – after Higashi-Shiogama station, but the view is fleeting and after that it's tunnels for most of the journey to **Matsushima-Kaigan**.

Matsushima Information Center (💻 www.matsushima-kanko.com; daily 8.30am-5pm) is in a booth to the right as you exit Matsushima-Kaigan station. From here it is an easy walk to the main sights.

A few of the islands just off the shore are linked by bridges to the mainland. The most popular is tiny **Godaidojima**, on which stands a hall containing five Buddhist statues which are put on view only once every 33 years (the last time was in 2006, so the next viewing won't be until 2039). Pleasant though it is, the tranquillity is spoilt by the souvenir stalls set up along the approach to it.

Much more relaxing is nearby **Fukurajima**, connected to the mainland via a long, red footbridge (¥200 to cross). This island has wooded paths free from souvenir stands and (almost) out of sight of any vending machines. From here, there are views to some of the other islands.

Set just back from the port area is **Zuigan-ji** (daily 8am-6pm, to 5pm in winter, art museum to 5pm, or 3.30/4.30pm in winter; ¥800), a Zen Buddhist temple built in 828 and later reconstructed by Date Masamune (see p300). On the right as you walk through the pine trees towards the temple entrance are some caves inside which monks used to train before the temple was built. Look out for the rail monument near the caves, a tall column flanked by railway wheels on pieces of track. It was built to remember those who died during the construction of the railways or in rail accidents. The main temple buildings are closed for restoration work until March 2016 but some others are open. However, next door, **Entsuin** (Mar-Nov daily 8.30am-5pm, Dec-Feb to 4pm; ¥300) includes a rock garden, a moss and maple garden, a rose garden (best Jun-Sep) and Sankeiden, the mausoleum for Date Mitsumune, who died aged 19. The mausoleum is unusual because it has Western as well as Buddhist symbols as the family was interested in Western technology.

For an overnight stay and wonderful views head to *Resort Inn Matsushima* (☎ 022-355 0888, 💻 www.resort-inn.jp; from ¥8000/S, ¥14,000/Tw, family room ¥5000pp) up behind Matsushima-Kaigan station. The rooms in this hotel, operated by JR East, are Western style and feel very homely. Turn right on leaving the station, then sharp right under a short rail bridge and follow the road up for about three minutes. It is on your left.

Before the Great East Japan Earthquake (see box p275) this guide recommended taking a train on the JR Tohoku Line from Matsushima station (not Matsushima-Kaigan) to Ichinoseki rather than backtracking to Sendai. At the time of research this line was not operating but it is now open (approx 1/hr; 72 mins; change at Kogota) and thus it may be worth considering. Matsushima Station is 30 minutes on foot from Matsushima-Kaigan – pick up a map from the tourist information centre, or take a taxi (5 mins).

Look out for the shinkansen 'car park' on the right about three to five minutes after leaving Sendai. Soon after that the train dips into several tunnels, but otherwise the view of rural Japan to the left and right is superb.

Most Hayate services run non-stop from Sendai to Morioka (see pp281-2), but Yamabiko services stop at **Furukawa (395km)** and **Kurikoma-Kogen (416km)** before reaching Ichinoseki.

Ichinoseki (445km) Ichinoseki developed as a castle town in the Edo period; the name literally means 'first gate' and it symbolises that this is the start of the rural north-east. The city is divided by the Iwai-gawa (Iwai river) and is a transport hub with both the Tohoku shinkansen and main lines calling here as well as the Ofunato Line to the coast which was damaged in the 2011 earthquake and tsunami and at the time of writing was still not fully operational. It is also a departure point for a side trip to the temple town of Hiraizumi (see pp280-1) but otherwise has little of interest to the tourist.

An overhead passageway connects the shinkansen (east) side of the station with the (west) side for the local JR lines. The **tourist information office** (daily Apr-Oct 9am-5.30pm, Nov-Mar to 5pm) is to the left of the station's west exit. There are **lockers** outside the station and on the shinkansen concourse.

If you decide to stay here rather than in Hiraizumi, *Toyoko Inn Ichinoseki Ekimae* (☎ 0191-31 1045, 🖳 www.toyoko-inn.com; ¥6090/S, ¥8190/D/Tw, inc breakfast) is modern and has clean, comfortable Western-style rooms. To reach the hotel walk out of the station's west exit and turn first right. The Inn is soon on the left.

For **food** there are several izakaya-style restaurants in the station area but otherwise little choice other than a bakery (daily 7am-8pm) and a soba/ramen/curry rice stand in the station; buy a ticket from the machine (around ¥480). On the shinkansen side there's a coffee shop serving pizza (¥800) and Guinness (¥600).

MAP 17

To Shin-Aomori (Map 28)

MORIOKA

Side trip to Tazawa-ko & Kakunodate

trailblazer

Shin-Hanamaki

Kitakami

0   10km

Mizusawa-Esashi

Hiraizumi

Side trip

Ichinoseki

Kurikoma-Kogen

Hanaizumi

Furukawa   Kogota

Shinkansen route   Matsushima

Mátsushima-Kaigan

Side trip to Yamadera

Hon-Shiogama

Matsushima Bay

SENDAI

To Tokyo (Map 16)   Sendai Airport

HONSHU

Side trip by rail to Hiraizumi   [see Map 17, p279]

Hiraizumi is eight kilometres north of Ichinoseki and reached in less than 10 minutes by hourly local train along the JR Tohoku line. At first glance it's hard to believe that this rural town once boasted a population of over 100,000. In the 12th century it was a major centre of politics and culture, a period dominated by the wealthy Fujiwara family, who ruled for four generations. Today, a couple of historic temples remain as a reminder of the place that once rivalled Kyoto in wealth and national influence. These were granted World Heritage Site status in 2011.

Hiraizumi station is small with a few ¥300 **lockers**. The **tourist information office** (🖳 hiraizumi.or.jp; daily 8.30am-5pm, to 4.30pm in winter) is in the small house with wooden doors to the right as you leave the station.

Next door is a small **Rent-a-Cycle booth** (¥500/2 hours, ¥1000/day) which provides maps of a recommended three-hour cycling route, including stops at both the temples described below. However, the area is hilly so you may prefer to take the **Hiraizumi Run Run Loop bus** (mid Apr-Nov daily 2-3/hr; ¥140, ¥400 day pass), which goes to all the main sites from the station (bus stand 1). There is also a local bus service which operates year-round but less frequently.

Even though it doesn't make sense in terms of the bus route, it is worth going to **Hiraizumi Bunka Isan Center** (Culture Centre; daily 9am-5pm; free) first to get an overview of the history of the area.

Chuson-ji (daily Apr-Oct 8am-5pm, Nov-Mar 8.30am-4.30pm; grounds free, ¥800 inc for Konjiki-do, Sankozo and a few other temples) was established in 850 and once comprised over 300 buildings. Not all have made it into the 21st century but the temple is still an impressive sight. There's no fee to enter the compound and there are plenty of places, including the Honden (Main Hall), that don't charge admission.

The most important surviving building is the **Konjiki-do** (Golden Hall; daily Mar-Nov 8.30am-5pm, Dec-Feb to 4.30pm; ¥800), which was completed in 1124. The theme here is light (as that is believed to drive evil away) and everything, apart from the roof, is covered with gold leaf and filled with gold, silver and mother of pearl. Hiraizumi is the northernmost place that Basho (see p277) visited. After visiting Konjiki-do he wrote a haiku (see box).

Entry tickets also allow access to the modern **Sankozo**, a treasure house with, somewhat bizarrely, an attached ATM.

> *Early summer rains*
> *Fall not here*
> *Temple of light.*
> Matsuo Basho (1644-94)

If you go as far as is possible along the tree-lined avenue through the temple compound and then take a path off to the right, you'll reach **Hakusan Shrine**. After the opulence of Konjikido, the austerity of this Shinto shrine is a pleasant surprise. From a corner of the shrine area there are great views down below of plains typical of the Tohoku region. Also here is the temple's thatched-roof **Noh stage** (Noh is performed here on the evening of 14th August but other events are also held here throughout the year).

Motsu-ji (daily 8.30am-5pm, to 4.30pm in winter; ¥500) was founded in 850 and is known today for its 'Pure Land garden' (see box p63) centred around a pond (Oizumiga-ike). Few of its 40 buildings have survived but it is still an impressive place, particularly for the feeling of space. Look out for the stream which every spring is the site of a poetry festival (Gokusui-no-En). Participants, dressed in traditional costumes, have to create a short poem while a sake cup is floating down the stream towards them. Once they have read their poem they can drink the sake.

Maizuruso (☎ 0191-46 3375, 🖳 www6.ocn.ne.jp/~maiduru; from ¥3500pp, plus 10% for single occupancy; half-board also possible) offers Japanese-style accommodation and is a short walk from the station. Head straight out of the station and take the first turning on the right. The minshuku is a short way along on the right.

Soba fans in particular should not leave Hiraizumi without going to the very popular *Basho-kan* (daily 10am-5pm, Dec-Mar closed Thur); tempura soba costs from ¥750 and wanko soba (see p282) from ¥1800. It's at the railway station by the bus stand for the Loop Bus.

Ichinoseki to Shin-Aomori
[Map 17, p279; Map 18, p287; Table 12, pp462-3]
Distances from Ichinoseki. Fastest journey time: if you are joining the shinkansen at Ichinoseki and wish to travel to Shin-Aomori, you will probably have to take a Yamabiko to Morioka (see below; 42 mins) and change there onto a Hayate service (54 mins to Shin-Aomori).

Ichinoseki (0km) See p279.
After Ichinoseki, all Yamabiko shinkansen but very few Hayate stop at **Mizusawa-Esashi** (25km) and **Kitakami** (42km).

Shin-Hanamaki (55km) All Yamabiko and a few Hayate call here, a small city known for its hot springs and as the birthplace of the poet Kenji Miyazawa, who achieved popularity as a writer of children's stories such as *Night on the Milky Way Train*. The city's major annual event is the three-day Hanamaki Festival held on the second weekend of September, when large floats and portable shrines are carried through the streets in time to music. On February 11th, Hanamaki is also the location for the 'All Japan Noodle Eating Contest', where contestants gorge on bowls of soba until they can eat no more; the record is 188 bowls in five minutes. To reach **Hanamaki** city take a local train two stops west along the Kamaishi line.

The previous edition of this guide included a side trip east from Shin-Hanamaki on the Kamaishi line to the coast at Kamaishi and then north to Miyako and back west to Morioka (see rail routes map p269). However, at the time of research this route was not possible due to the devastation caused by the 2011 earthquake and tsunami.

Morioka (90km) The Yamabiko shinkansen terminates here, while Hayate and Hayabusa services stop before continuing to Shin-Aomori. Consider indulging yourself and going Gran Class in the Hayabusa from here to Shin-Aomori (see box p268). The Komachi shinkansen runs west from here to Akita (see pp294-5).

HONSHU

Shinkansen services depart from the 2nd floor of the station. Also on this floor is the **Northern Tohoku TIC** (daily 9am-5.30pm); staff can help with accommodation bookings in Morioka. There are **lockers** in various corners of the station including large ¥500 ones in the passage between the north and south sides of the station.

The entrance to the private Iwate Ginga Railway (IGR, also known as Iwate Galaxy Railway line; 💻 www.igr.jp) is in a corner of the ground floor of the station. This operates from Morioka to Metoki, on the former Tohoku main line.

Morioka calls itself the 'Castle town of northern Japan' but only the ruined stone walls remain. Apart from a possible side trip to Lake Tazawa and Kakunodate (see opposite), there's little reason to hang around in the city – unless you're passing through between August 1st and 4th, when **Sansa-odori** is held. Groups dressed in traditional costumes dance down the main street to the accompaniment of taiko drums and flutes. Festival stalls line the streets and there's a real street-party atmosphere.

If you do have time here it is worth walking to **Kaiunbashi** (this literally means 'Open up your luck' bridge) for a good view of **Mt Iwate** (2038m) – the northern equivalent to Mt Fuji. Head to the right out of the station and walk down the main road (with Washington Hotel on your left) and you will soon reach the river. Some years ago the bridge featured in a TV soap called *Dondohare*, as a result of which the number of visitors to Morioka increased considerably.

For Japanese-style **accommodation** try the friendly *Ryokan Kumagai* (☎ 0196-51 3020, 💻 kumagairyokan.com; ¥4200/S, ¥8000/Tw or ¥11,100/Tr; breakfast ¥800pp, dinner ¥1500pp). It is an eight-minute walk from the station across Kitakami-gawa. For a Western-style hotel, *Toyoko Inn Morioka Ekimae* (☎ 0196-25 1045, 💻 www.toyoko-inn.com; ¥5460/S, ¥7140/D, ¥8190/Tw) is two minutes on foot from the station's central exit: look for the tall building with 'HOTEL' written in blue neon above 'Toyoko Inn' in Japanese.

More upmarket is the JR-run *Hotel Metropolitan Morioka* (☎ 0196-25 1211, 💻 www.metro-morioka.co.jp; from ¥9240/S, ¥17,325/D, ¥17,902/Tw, inc breakfast; JR rail-pass holders get a discount), which also has a New Wing (not actually that new), with more spacious – and more expensive rooms – and access to the Central Fitness Club next door (¥500/day). The attention to detail means you are likely to have an English newspaper outside your room in the morning. To find the hotels follow signs for the north exit and then for the IGR. Turn left when you reach street level. The entrance to the Hotel Metropolitan is soon on the left and the New Wing is on the left side down the road opposite the main branch.

In terms of **food** Morioka's most famous culinary export is *wanko soba*, bowls of good-quality soba, served with side dishes and traditionally eaten in a competition where diners race to scoff the most noodles. Try it at *Mikakuichi* (10 bowls ¥1050, 20 bowls ¥1570) in the Gourmet Town section of the basement of Fesan department store, on the left of the main station exit; they also serve tempura soba and vegetable soba (both ¥895). Alternatively, if you prefer ramen, head to *Morioka Ramen* (daily 9am-10pm) in the Menkoi Yokocho part of Fesan.

Side trips by shinkansen from Morioka   [see Map 18, p287]

The Komachi shinkansen (to Akita; 1/hr) makes it easy to do day trips from Morioka to either **Tazawa-ko** (32 mins) or **Kakunodate** (about 42 mins), though it would be hard to see both in one day.

Alternatively, you could create a circular route around the northern part of Honshu by continuing on the line to **Omagari** (see p284; 55mins) and then **Akita** (pp294-5; 90 mins) and from there proceed to Aomori by doing the Aomori to Akita route (see pp289-94) in reverse, and finally return to Morioka (or Tokyo).

An added attraction to this side trip is that for the first part of the journey there are good views of the volcanic peak of **Mt Iwate** (see p282).

Tazawa-ko (Lake Tazawa) This is the deepest lake in Japan (423.4m) and is renowned for being a nearly perfect circle. It also attracts more than its fair share of legends, such as the following: 'Once upon a time, a village girl named Tatsuko drank the water of Lake Tazawa as instructed by the goddess Kannon, in order to make her wish of perpetual beauty come true. In the end, she was transformed into a dragon, whereupon she sank into the depths of the lake and was never seen again.'

The **tourist information centre** (🖳 www.tazawako.org; daily 8.30am-5.30pm) is on your right after going through the ticket gate. Staff have bus timetables for the lake, and there's a huge topographical model of the area. The bus ticket counter is to the right of the exit. There are lockers in front of the station.

Several buses go to the lake area; services operating year-round include the Nyuto Line bus (12/day; 15 mins; ¥350), which continues to Nyuto-onsen, and the Tazawako Isshu Line (6/day; ¥350), which operates a circular route. Additional lines operate in the summer months. Tazawa-ko Yuran-sen (Apr-Nov 4-8/day; 40 mins; ¥1170) operates round-trip cruises on the lake.

Kakunodate A former samurai town, this makes an interesting destination at any time of the year but is especially worthwhile in late April when hundreds of *shidarezakura* (weeping cherry trees) are in blossom along the river bank. A lot of the crafts in this area are made from the bark of the cherry trees (*kabazaiku*).

Pick up a map from the **tourist information centre** (🖳 kakunodate-kanko.jp; daily 9am-5.30pm), the white building with a wooden base to the right of the exit. There are lockers around the station but the staff here will keep luggage (¥200 per bag) during their opening hours.

The sights are all easily reached on foot. Most people head straight to the samurai district, but do visit the merchant district as well. It's about a 10-minute walk to **Nishinomi-ya** (daily Apr-Oct 10am-6pm, Nov-Mar to 5pm; free), a former warehouse for rice and pickles that is now a museum, shop and restaurant. The museum displays household objects in glass cabinets, including a radio and sewing machine; there is a general leaflet about the place in English but no captions for the actual exhibits. Don't leave without looking around the former warehouses or trying the truly delicious sushi containing home-made pickles (¥100).

Make your way then to **Ando Jozo Miso** (daily 10am-5pm; free) a miso-and soy-sauce brick storehouse and shop; visit the warehouse with its wonderful screens and then go to the back of the shop where you will be able to try some pickles, tea and *dashi* (soup) for free.

From here continue in the same direction and you will soon come to the **samurai district**. About 80 families used to live here and the descendants of some still do. Several houses can be visited for free. However, this only means you can walk around the outside and for the most part they have souvenirs rather than anything interesting to see.

The two samurai houses you have to pay for are worth seeing. **Aoyagi-ke** (daily Apr-Oct 9am-5pm, Nov-Mar to 4pm; ¥500) has a wide variety of exhibits including armoury, household objects such as sake cups, miso and rice bowls, and dolls (to see these, take the steep stairs on the right as you leave the armoury). There's also a display of military uniforms and a Folk Gallery containing Edison voice-recording machines and record players as well as masses of records – everything from Duke Ellington to *La Traviata*.

The other house, **Ishiguro-ke** (daily 9am-5pm; ¥300), also has samurai armoury and clothing but has less to see overall.

To reach the riverbank go to the end of the road and turn left at the traffic lights. There is a 2km tunnel of cherry trees on this side of the river. To get back to the station turn left along the riverbank and walk along till you reach the first bridge; from there it is about a 20-minute walk to the station.

The most convenient place to stay is *Folkloro Kakunodate* (☎ 0187-53 2070, 🖥 www.jre-hotels.jp/e/folkloro/523.html; from ¥7350/S, ¥11,340/Tw, inc buffet breakfast; discounts for JR rail-pass holders); it is to your left as you leave the station. Some of the hotel's twin rooms can sleep up to four people. Book early in peak seasons (spring and autumn), when rates usually rise.

Omagari   Omagari's claim to fame is that the Omagari National Japan Fireworks Competition is held here, by Omono River, on the 4th Saturday in August (5-5.50pm for 'day' fireworks and night fireworks 6.50-9.30pm); it takes 20-25 minutes to walk there from the station.

The new firework collection is shown on the fourth Saturday in October. Pick up a map of the town from the **tourist information centre** (daily 9am-6pm) to the right of the stairs to the west exit as you leave the ticket barrier.

After Morioka, some Hayate services stop at **Iwate-Numakunai (121km)**. You don't take this route for the views. It is almost exclusively tunnels so there is little to report in the way of sights. Every so often the train emerges from the tunnel but before you have time to take in the view it darts into another.

Ninohe (156km)   Some Hayate stop here. 'Ichinohe' means the 'first door'. In medieval times, the northern part of Iwate and southern part of Aomori prefectures were divided into different political districts. Each district was known as a 'door', meaning the door or gateway to that district. So, in this case, 'Ninohe' means the 'second door'. The next 'door' to be found on the train line is the shinkansen terminus at Hachinohe (the eighth door).

Hachinohe (187km)   All Hayate stop here. Hachinohe is an industrial and port city but not a major tourist centre. There is little reason to stop here unless you are either planning to go to Towada-ko (see pp289-91), or would like to embark on an unusual side trip into the mountains to a small village where it's claimed Jesus Christ is buried (see box below), or you are coming to the Sansha Taisai festival (see p286).

The 'South Bridge' waiting area as you come up from the shinkansen platforms overlooks the tracks so is good for trainspotters. The **JR ticket office** (daily 5.30am-10.50pm) and **View Plaza travel agency** are on the 3rd-floor main concourse. **Hachinohe Tourism Information Plaza** (daily 9am-7pm) is on the 2nd floor by the east exit. **Lockers** (with a few large ¥500 ones) are behind you on your right.

The most convenient place to stay, since it's built into the station, is the JR-operated *Hotel Mets Hachinohe* (☎ 0178-70 7700, 🖳 www.hotelmets.jp/hachinohe; ¥6300/S, ¥12,600/Tw, inc breakfast). The entrance is to the left of the escalators down to the east exit.

⛩ Jesus in Japan?

The journey to the remote village of **Shingo**, deep in the mountains west of Hachinohe, certainly feels like a pilgrimage. There is no rail line and the only way of reaching the village is to take two buses. Your destination is the Christ Park, so called because locals claim that it contains the grave of none other than Jesus Christ. The story goes that instead of dying on the cross, Jesus escaped at the last minute, fled to Siberia, made his way to Alaska and finally boarded a boat bound for Japan, where he landed at the port of Hachinohe. He quickly found his way to the village of Herai (now called Shingo) where he married a Japanese woman called Miyuko, had three daughters and lived to 106. In his latter years, Christ is said to have travelled around Japan, 'endeavouring to save the common people, while observing the language, customs and manners of the various regions'. He is described in village records as being 'grey haired and rather bald with a ruddy complexion and high nose and [he] wore a coat with many folds, causing people to hold him in awe as a long-nosed goblin.'

The extraordinary story only came to light in 1935 when two graves were found in a bamboo thicket at the top of a small hill in the village. It wasn't until May 1936, when Christ's 'last will and testament' mysteriously turned up in the village, that the significance of these graves was revealed: one of the graves was Christ's, the other belonged to his brother, called Isukiri. Or rather, just his brother's ear. Supposedly Jesus managed to avoid crucifixion thanks to his brother who 'casually took Christ's place and died on his cross', allowing him to escape to Japan clutching one of Isukiri's ears along with some 'hair of the Virgin Mary'. Further 'proof' can be found down in the village: Herai, the ancient name of the village, is said to be a corruption of 'Hebrew' and a villager who died some years ago 'looked not like a Japanese, his eyes were blue like those of a foreigner'. Curiously, there has been little attempt to cash in on the story by turning the park into a tacky tourist trap. Indeed, there's so little publicity that it's almost as if the village is embarrassed by the legend and doesn't quite know what to do with its two graves up on the hill.

The **Christ Park**, which contains the two graves as well as a small museum (Thur-Tue 9am-5pm) telling the story in Japanese and English, is open to the public. Take a Nanbu Bus from stop No 5 outside Hachinohe station to Gonohe (36 mins; ¥800). From Gonohe, connect with a bus that takes you direct to the Christ Park just outside Shingo Village (33 mins; ¥800). Tell the driver you want to get out at Kuristo-koen. The Tourist Information Plaza at Hachinohe station (see above) can advise on bus times and connections to/from Shingo; they also have an information sheet in English.

H O N S H U

> **Changes for the Japan Rail Pass, Seishun Juhachi Kippu and sleeper services**
> With the completion of the Tohoku Shinkansen, JR East transferred the original railway tracks between Hachinohe and Aomori to Aoimori Railways, a non-JR company. This results in the unique situation where the JR Ominato Line (from Noheji to Ominato on the Shimokita Peninsula) is now completely isolated from the rest of the JR network and the JR Hachinohe line remains connected to the JR network only through a shinkansen line. In order to keep these two lines accessible to holders of the Japan Rail Pass, JR East Pass and Seishun Juhachi Kippu (Seishun 18 Kippu), a special rule was introduced, allowing pass holders to ride the Aoimori Railway 'for free' if they only get on or off at Aomori, Noheji or Hachinohe stations. If getting on or off at any other station along the line the regular fare has to be paid.
> This also caused the sleeper services (see box p78) between Tokyo and Sapporo to use a longer non-JR section than before. Consequently the supplement to be paid by rail-pass holders increased.

There is a **soba/udon** counter on the main concourse (to the right as you exit the ticket barrier). Alternatively there's a reasonably cheap revolving **sushi restaurant** opposite the lift which takes you to Hotel Mets. And if you take the escalator down to the east exit and turn left, you'll see a line of **yatai/izakaya-style places**, which get packed out with businessmen at the end of the working day but are recommended for the atmosphere.

It is well worth trying to be in Hachinohe for the **Sansha Taisai festival** (31st July to 3rd Aug). This is about 300 years old and the festival is designated one of Japan's National Important Intangible Folk Cultural Assets. There are parades of 27 floats, each of which is made by a different area of the city, and three Mikoshi (portable shrines). One mikoshi comes from each of the three shrines (san-sha), Ogami, Shinra and Shinmei, taking part in the festival.

If you can't be here for the festival you can still see at least one of the enormous floats in **You Tree Plaza** (daily 9am-7pm): turn right as you leave the station and you will see the large building straight ahead. Regional products are sold here and there are more lockers. There's a restaurant on the 2nd floor, which tends to be less busy than those in and immediately outside the station.

Alternative route by rail to Aomori

The new shinkansen line is undoubtedly the quickest way to reach Aomori from Hachinohe but the original line offers better scenery and if you have a Japan Rail Pass (see box above) you can do this journey for free if you stay on the train. If you don't have a pass it will cost ¥2220. The journey takes 91 minutes and services operate frequently in the early morning and evening but only about once every two hours during the day.

For the first part of the journey, the view on both sides is blocked by a line of trees. When the view does open out, the countryside consists of wide green fields and hills, interrupted by small towns. About five or six minutes after leaving **Misawa (21km)** look out on the right for the blue water of Lake Ogawara in the distance. It really is blink-and-you'll-miss-it, since for the most

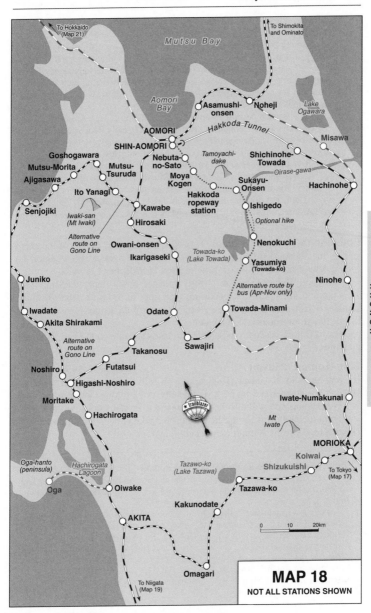

To Hokkaido (Map 21)

To Shimokita and Ominato

Mutsu Bay

Aomori Bay

Asamushi-onsen

Noheji

Lake Ogawara

AOMORI

Hakkoda Tunnel

Misawa

SHIN-AOMORI

Nebuta-no-Sato

Tamoyachi-dake

Shichinohe-Towada

Goshogawara

Mutsu-Tsuruda

Moya Kogen

Sukayu-Onsen

Oirase-gawa

Mutsu-Morita

Hachinohe

Ajigasawa

Ito Yanagi

Kawabe

Hakkoda ropeway station

Ishigedo

Senjojiki

Iwaki-san (Mt Iwaki)

Hirosaki

Optional hike

Alternative route on Gono Line

Nenokuchi

Owani-onsen

Towada-ko (Lake Towada)

Ninohe

Ikarigaseki

Yasumiya (Towada-ko)

Juniko

Odate

Alternative route by bus (Apr-Nov only)

Iwadate

Akita Shirakami

Towada-Minami

Sawajiri

Alternative route on Gono Line

Takanosu

Futatsui

Iwate-Numakunai

Noshiro

Higashi-Noshiro

Moritake

Hachirogata

Mt Iwate

MORIOKA

Koiwai

Shizukuishi

To Tokyo (Map 17)

Oga-hanto (peninsula)

Hachirogata Lagoon

Tazawo-ko (Lake Tazawa)

Oga

Oiwake

Tazawa-ko

AKITA

Kakunodate

0   10   20km

To Niigata (Map 19)

Omagari

MAP 18

NOT ALL STATIONS SHOWN

HONSHU

part trees block the view. **Noheji (51km)** is a point of interchange for the JR Ominato line (see p316) that runs part of the way up the Shimokita Peninsula.

Leaving Noheji, look out to the right for views over Mutsu Bay. It's frustrating at first, since thanks to the ever-present trees along the track you don't get a full view of the bay. It's not until just before the train approaches Aomori that the track gets close enough to the shore for a sweeping view of the bay. Look out for a beautiful pine-clad island that is impressive enough to make people look up from their newspapers.

Right outside **Asamushi-onsen (79km)** station is Yusa Asamushi, a modern building which contains a great hot spring (daily 7am-9pm; ¥350) with views over Mutsu Bay. Small towels are sold but bring your own soap. There is also a free foot bath right in front of the station. (However, you can't get off here if you have a Japan Rail Pass unless you are prepared to pay).

It's a shame after the brief views of Mutsu Bay that the final approach into **Aomori (96km)** is less impressive, with the usual city glut of concrete buildings. Look out for the most famous landmark in Aomori, the triangular ASPAM building (see p312), in the distance on your right as the train pulls into the station.

Shichinohe-Towada (223km)

This new station, built as part of the extension to the shinkansen line, has a View Plaza travel agency and a Midori-no-Madoguchi reservation window but little else at the time of research.

However, Towada Kankou Dentsu operates buses (daily 9.05am, 10am, 11.10am and 12.30pm) to **Towada-ko** (see opposite); buses depart from the south exit. However, if you have a JR rail pass it would be more sensible to take the JR bus from Aomori, or Hachinohe.

Buses from Towada-ko to Shichinohe-Towada depart at 8.25am, 2pm, 4pm and 5pm.

Shin-Aomori (268km)   [see pp312-16 for Aomori]

If continuing to Hakodate (Hokkaido) you will need to transfer here to a Hakucho or Super Hakucho LEX. For details of the through journey, see p318.

For Aomori you will also need to transfer from the shinkansen part of the station to the platforms for the JR Ou line and take either a local line train or a Hakucho LEX to JR Aomori (approx six mins).

⛩ The difference a shinkansen line makes

The fastest journey between Hachinohe and Aomori before the shinkansen line opened was 58 minutes; with the shinkansen the journey takes 28 minutes (to Shin-Aomori).

The considerable time saving is possible because of the large number of tunnels on this section – in fact one-third of the journey is in tunnels, the majority being in the **Hakkoda Tunnel** between Shichinohe-Towada and Shin-Aomori. This tunnel took 6½ years to construct and at 26.5km was for a brief period the world's longest tunnel. But its claim to fame was short lived, since it was soon eclipsed by the 34.6-km long Lötschberg Tunnel in Switzerland. However, Hakkoda Tunnel can still claim to be the longest land-based tunnel if the specification 'double-track' is added.

If you come out onto the general concourse at Shin-Aomori you will see **Aomori TIC** (daily 8.30am-7pm) on the left. However, it has little information in English so it is better to go to the TIC in Aomori, though it does offer internet access (¥100/10 mins). There is also a Travel Service Center (daily 10am-5.30pm) and a Midori-no-Madoguchi reservation window (daily 5.30am-22.40pm). At the time of research there were no hotels here but there are several places to eat. *Café de Tsugaru* (7am-7.20pm) in the ticket area serves sandwiches and cakes (¥300-500). Far more interesting though, even if you aren't hungry, is **Aomori Shunmi-kan** (daily 10am-9pm). It is on street level – go down the stairs to the left of the shinkansen exit and opposite the ticket office area – and is designed to resemble a typical traditional street with stands selling local foods as well as restaurants offering sushi, yakisoba and ramen.

AOMORI TO AKITA AND NIIGATA

The route described below goes across Tohoku and then down the western side. In addition to this a predominantly coastal route (see pp292-3) from Aomori/ Hirosaki to Akita is included as it offers magnificent views and at weekends and national holidays a unique rail experience.

Aomori to Odate   [Map 18, p287; Table 13, p464]
Distances by JR from Aomori. Fastest journey time: 65 minutes.

There are two possible routes for this section of the journey. The first (described from p291) is all by rail and includes a stop in the ancient town of Hirosaki. Alternatively, but only between April and November, you can take the route to Towada-ko described below and from there continue to Odate. However, it would be a very long day and wouldn't allow you to have time to enjoy the scenery.

Alternative (summer) route to Odate via Towada-ko (Lake Towada)
This route (see map p287) is served by JR buses (🖳 www.jrbustohoku.co.jp/ towada) and is free (subject to a prior seat reservation) for anyone with a Japan Rail Pass, but not with a JR East Pass. Reservations should be made at the JR bus counter outside Aomori station or at any Midori-no-Madoguchi or JR travel agency. Services operate throughout the year to Yasumiya (for Lake Towada) from Aomori (bus stand 11) and Shin-Aomori (both Mizumi-go bus; Apr-Oct 3-7/day, Nov-Mar 3/day; 4-4¾ hours; ¥3000) and from Hachinohe (Oirase-go bus; 3-4/day, 4-4¾ hours; ¥2600).

On the way, the bus calls outside **Hakkoda Ropeway station**, from where gondolas (🖳 www.hakkoda-ropeway.jp; daily 9am-4.20pm, occasional closures, ¥1150 one way, ¥1800 return) take 10 minutes to climb Mt Tamoyachidake (1326m), one of the main mountains in the Hakkoda range. On a clear day, it's possible to see as far as Hokkaido. In winter this is a busy skiing area.

The bus journey continues along the winding mountain road, stopping at a number of rural hot springs, the best known of which is **Sukayu-onsen**, known for its mixed-bathing giant cypress-wood bath house (7am-5.30pm; ¥500) that can fit 1000 people – not that you'll see many of them through the steam.

It's possible to stay on the bus all the way to the lake but it's more fun to get off at **Ishigedo**, from where an 8.9km (2-3hr) hiking trail begins, following the course of Oirase-gawa to its source, Lake Towada. At the Ishigedo bus stop is a rest centre with toilets, a scale model of the path to the lake and a small snack bar where you can get noodles and stock up on water. The path leads off from behind the rest area (it's very obvious). Ishigedo means 'huge slab of rock' – you'll see the rock supported by a tree at the trail start. According to the sign, an evil but beautiful woman who once lived here 'would kill travellers and steal their possessions'.

Assuming you survive this first obstacle the remaining kilometres are unproblematic; the route is mostly sheltered under a canopy of trees and passes a number of waterfalls. It's a very popular trail, but unless you're here during high season (Jul & Aug, and Oct for the autumn leaves) there should be room to breathe. The only downside is that the path sometimes connects up with the main road, which means you have to compete with lorries and cars.

The hike ends with a set of stone steps leading up to a bridge and your first view of Lake Towada, formed from a volcanic crater. You are now at the small lakeside resort of **Nenokuchi**, from where boat cruises cross the lake to the main resort centre of **Yasumiya** (Apr-Nov up to 15/day; ¥1400). Alternatively, pick up the JR bus from Nenokuchi for the 20-minute ride to Yasumiya (in the timetable Yasumiya may just be called Towada-ko; either way it's the last stop).

The lake is right in front of you and all around are hotels, restaurants and souvenir shops. ***Towada-ko Lakeside Hotel*** (☎ 0176-75 2336, 🖳 www.towada kolakeside.jp; from ¥24,500/Tw half-board) is two minutes from the bus terminal and has both Japanese- and Western-style rooms. Alternatively email 🖳 folake@tazawako.org with details of what kind of accommodation you would like and they can make a reservation. The best-known lakeside sight is the **Statue of the Maidens** (known locally as 'Two old women in the buff reaching out for each other'), created by Kotaro Takamura in 1953. Takamura's wife is said to have been the model for the statue, a 10-minute walk around the lake from the bus terminal (called JR House). The temperature here can fall as low as -20°C in winter but because of its depth (327m), the lake never freezes.

To continue the journey take an Iwate Shuhoku Bus (Apr-Nov 3/day; ¥1130) from Yasumiya to **Towada-Minami station**, from where you can pick up a local train on the JR Hanawa line west to Odate (5/day; 40 mins). Along the way, the train will call at **Sawajiri**, an unremarkable place save for the fact that it is close to what is believed to be Japan's only major shrine dedicated to a dog.

The story goes that during the Edo period a hunter named Sadaroku lost his way in heavy snow while hunting deep in the mountains and was arrested because he did not have his hunting licence with him. He told his faithful four-legged friend, who rushed back through the snow to his master's home.

The hunter's wife couldn't understand why the dog was barking and the household pet had to return to his master without the document he required. But the hunter repeated his urgent appeal, and the dog raced back home and barked again at the family shrine. His wife finally understood and fastened the licence securely to the dog's collar, all the while praying for her husband's safe return.

The dog ran back to his master for the second time, but all was lost. The hunter had been executed. Legend has it that the dog died soon after, as if following his master. To this day on April 17th every year a ceremony to remember the hunter's dog is held at a special canine shrine located on the mountainside of Kuzuhara, near Sawajiri station.

From **Odate**, pick up the route starting on p294.

Aomori (0km) [see pp312-16]

From Aomori, take a train on the JR Ou line towards Akita – the Tsugaru LEX operates 4-6/day.

The first part of the journey is through a residential area but gradually the landscape opens up. The main sight from the train is **Mt Iwaki**, spiritual symbol of the area. It has three peaks and many different profiles, which means everyone claims their region has the best view. Look out for it in the distance to the right about 20 minutes after leaving Aomori.

If on a local train and planning to do the coastal route (see pp292-3) you could change train at **Kawabe (31km)** but it may be easier to go to Hirosaki.

Hirosaki (37km) All trains stop here. If on a Tsugaru LEX change here for the JR Gono line and the coastal route to Akita described on pp292-3.

Hirosaki flourished from the early 17th century as a castle town of the Tsugaru feudal lords. It is now known as an area of apple production; 20% of the apples grown in Japan come from this area. It won't be hard to find apple products: the sparkling apple wine (*cidre*) is very refreshing.

Follow signs for the central exit, turn immediately left as you leave the station and walk to the end of the building to find **lockers** (up to ¥600 size). At the **tourist information office** (🖳 www.hirosaki.co.jp; daily 8.45am-6pm, to 5pm in winter), to the right as you go out of the station, staff will help book same-day accommodation. **Hirosaki Sightseeing Information Center** (daily 9am-6pm), in a modern building opposite Hirosaki Park, offers similar services.

The best way to get around is the **Dotemachi Loop bus** (daily 6/hr; ¥100/ journey, ¥500 day pass). The bus stops at or near all the main sights but the 'loop' ends at the bus terminal, not the railway station, so you need to walk to the station (5 mins).

Top priority on a visit to Hirosaki should be **Fujita Memorial Japanese Garden** (Fujita Kinen Teien; daily mid Apr to late Nov 9am-5pm; ¥300), a typical Edo-period stroll garden but built on two levels. From the upper level, Mt Iwaki can be seen in the distance.

Across the street from the garden is **Hirosaki Park**, inside which is the site of Hirosaki Castle, completed in 1611. The original five-storeyed castle tower was struck by lightning in 1627 and burnt to the ground, so what stands today is a replacement three-storeyed tower (built in 1810) that has been turned into a **Museum of Samurai Artefacts** (daily Apr to late Nov 9am-5pm, later during the cherry blossom festival; ¥300, ¥500 inc botanical garden). The park has over 2500 cherry trees and is one of Japan's most popular cherry blossom-viewing spots (late Apr to early May).

HONSHU

From the park it is a short walk to the **Sightseeing Information Center** (see p291), at O-temon Square, and in a separate building an exhibition (daily 9am-6pm; free) of floats used in the Neputa as well as the old library and missionaries' house plus a display of miniature models of original buildings in the city. Neputa Mura (daily 9am-5.30pm; ¥500) also contains some of the festival floats as well as other symbols of Hirosaki. Get off at Tsugaruhan Neputa Mura. This is also the stop for the Ishiba Residence, a **merchant's house** (daily 9am-5pm, closed irregular days; free except central area ¥100) and three **samurai residences** (Ito & Umeda houses July-Oct Mon, Wed-Thur, Sat & Sun 10am-4pm; Iwata house July-Oct Tue-Wed, Fri-Sun 10am-4pm, Nov-June all houses Sat-Sun 10am-4pm; free).

The big festival of the year, **Neputa Matsuri**, rivals Aomori's Nebuta Matsuri (see p313) and takes place at the same time (1st-7th Aug). There is a nightly procession through the town of colourful floats.

For accommodation, right outside the station try *Route Inn Hirosaki Ekimae* (☎ 0172-31 0010, 🖳 route-inn.co.jp/english/pref/aomori.html; ¥5900/S or D, ¥10,000/Tw, inc buffet breakfast). Rooms are compact but quite stylish and include a fridge. The only downside is that the beds are firm – almost hard. The hotel also has an onsen, massage chairs (¥100/10 mins) and an izakaya-style restaurant, *Hana Hana Tei* (daily 6-9pm), serving sashimi, tonkatsu, udon and kara-age (¥300-880). On the left side in front of the station is *Best Western Hotel Newcity Hirosaki* (☎ 0172-37 0700, 🖳 www.bestwestern.co.jp/hirosaki; from ¥9000/S, ¥16,000/Tw or D, inc buffet breakfast), an upmarket hotel with a wide variety of rooms and restaurants.

Alternative route: by Resort Shirakami from Aomori or Hirosaki to Akita via Senjojiki [Map 18, p287]

It's a sad fact in Japan that many local railway lines are struggling to survive, but several of the JR companies have hit on an idea to both boost tourism in rural areas and maintain a transportation service for local communities. To do this they introduced so-called 'Joyful Trains'. JR East (🖳 www.jreast.co.jp/train/joyful/index.html) operates these on the Ominato/Tsugaru line (see p316), the Uetsu line (see p297), and the JR Gono line as described below.

The JR Gono line's original Joyful Train went into service in 1997 under the name Resort Shirakami, though these days there are actually three tourist trains operating on this line: the orange Kumagera (Woodpecker), the green Buna (Beech Tree), and the blue Aoike (Blue Pond).

Each train has four carriages with a variety of seating areas, the main feature being large windows and lounge areas. At least one of the carriages has

a number of compartments seating four people in each. The seats in these can be pulled out so that passengers can sit as if sitting on the floor.

Not only do passengers get the chance to see some wonderful scenery, they are also treated to live *shamisen* (see p40) music and traditional Japanese storytelling as they travel.

One reader describes the journey: 'I am not usually keen on touristy things like this, but the Resort Shirakami service on the local Gono Line was fantastic! In particular you get one of the best sunset views from the railway'.

Resort Shirakami trains only operate on the Gono line at weekends and in holiday periods (New Year; Golden Week in late Apr/early May; and late July to end Sep). The journey from Aomori to Akita (or vice versa; 3-4/day) takes about 5 hours 10 minutes.

Shamisen players on a Resort Shirakami train

Rail-pass holders can travel for free but you must have a **seat reservation**; ask for Seat A if you would like a sea-side view. Without a rail pass, Aomori to Akita (or vice-versa) on the Resort Shirakami costs ¥4310 plus ¥310 or ¥510 for the seat-reservation (depending on the dates).

The train runs first from Aomori to **Hirosaki**, where it changes direction and heads for the coast via **Kawabe**, where the traditional storyteller gets on (and stays until **Mutsu-Tsuruda**). The shamisen players get on at **Goshogawara** and leave at **Mutsu-Morita**. They sing and play in Car 3 (occasionally Car 4), but the TV monitors in each car also broadcast the entertainment, and you can walk along to Car 3 whenever you like. When the entertainers are not playing the monitors are used to show the driver's view – straight tunnels become much more fun when you can see a small circle of light ahead which slowly gets larger and larger.

The route is inland until just after **Ajigasawa** and then mostly runs parallel to the coast until Higashi-Noshiro. The train stops for about 15 minutes at **Senjojiki** so that everyone can get out and take photos. Senjojiki ('Thousand Tatami Mats') is so named because the flatness of the beach around here made a former emperor think it was as big as a thousand tatami mats.

Steam fans should look out on the right at **Wespa-Tsubakiyama** (not on Map 18) to see a SL78653. The train slows down when you are passing places of scenic interest such as between **Juniko** and **Akita-Shirakami**.

The coastline is certainly very dramatic in parts but don't forget to look inland as there are also great views of Mt Iwaki and Shirakami-Sanchi, a UNESCO World Heritage Site because of its unspoiled areas of virgin forest, particularly beech trees.

At **Higashi-Noshiro** (technically the end of the JR Gono line) the train changes direction; you then pass Hachirogata Lagoon en route to **Akita**, but scenically this is not as interesting as the coast line already passed. For this reason it is worth considering doing the journey from Akita to Aomori so the best bit is at the end.

Owani-onsen (49km) Only 10 minutes down the line by limited express, this is a popular stop for skiers in winter thanks to nearby **Mt Ajara** (709m), which even boasts its own ski shrine.

It's apple-tree, rice fields and pine-tree territory on both sides of the line between Owani-onsen and Odate. A few trains stop at **Ikarigaseki (57km)**.

Odate (82km) This station is a terminus for the JR Hanawa line from Towada-Minami (see p290) and Morioka. Odate looks and feels a bit run down, and there's little reason to spend time here unless you are particularly interested in Akita dogs, the most famous of which is probably Hachi-ko (see box p88).

Odate to Akita **[Map 18, p287; Table 13, p464]**
Distances by JR from Odate. Fastest journey time: 85 minutes.

Odate (0km) Continue along the JR Ou line towards Akita.

Takanosu (18m) Takanosu once won a place in the *Guinness Book of Records* by building the world's largest drum, measuring 3.71m in diameter, 4.32m deep and weighing in at 3.5 tonnes.

The train may then stop at **Futatsui (30.7km)**. The track, which has been roughly following Yoneshiro-gawa towards the coast, turns south at **Higashi-Noshiro (48km)** on its way to Akita.

The scenery around **Moritake (58.3km)** is mostly rice fields with pine trees in the distance.

Hachirogata (75km) There is a major land reclamation area out to the right (west) along this stretch of the journey. Although there's not a great deal to see, it's an amazing project on paper: Hachirogata Lagoon, once the second largest lake in Japan, was reclaimed and is now a vast expanse of rice paddies – an area equal in size to the space inside Tokyo's Yamanote line.

♦ **Oiwake (91km)** Limited expresses don't stop here but this is the nearest point of interchange for the Oga line that heads west to **Oga Peninsula** (Oga-hanto; 27km, 40 mins).

Oga is known for its Namahage Festival on 31st December when men, wearing demon costumes and masks and wielding large kitchen knives and wooden buckets, come down from nearby Mt Shinzan and invade the town. They knock on doors looking for new residents, such as wives or young children, and 'encourage' them to work and study hard in the New Year.

Akita (104km) Akita is a large industrial city with a bright, modern rail station which was rebuilt when the Komachi shinkansen opened along the Tazawa-ko line, linking Akita with Morioka.

The station has a number of exits (including Topico and Metropolitan) but it is easiest to follow signs for the central exit and once through the ticket barrier head for the West Gate. **Lockers** (including a few ¥500) are in the waiting room adjacent to the JR ticket office on your right as you exit the main ticket barrier.

There's a **View Plaza travel agency** (Mon-Fri 10.30am-6pm, Sat & Sun to 5pm) opposite the JR ticket office. The **tourist information office** (daily Apr-Oct 9am-7pm, Nov-Mar to 6pm) is directly opposite the ticket barrier. Topico department store is built into the west side of the station.

About the only reason for stopping in Akita is if you're passing through during the **Kanto Matsuri** (4th-7th Aug), when men parade through the streets balancing bamboo poles topped with heavy lanterns (weighing 5-30kg) on their foreheads, shoulders, chins, heads and other parts of the body. During the rest of the year, drop by the **Neburinagashi-kan** (Kanto Museum; daily 9.30am-4.30pm; ¥100, ¥250 inc Akarenga-kan) to see a film of the action and a display of some of the weighty lanterns and poles. At weekends from April to the end of October, volunteers demonstrate the astonishing pole-balancing act (visitors are welcome to join in). The lack of labels in English make this museum less interesting than it might otherwise be. More appealing is the preserved **mud-walled storehouse**, home and shop for the Kameko family – go out through the door next to the lift, not the door you came in by. The museum is 20 minutes on foot west from the station.

Also of limited interest is **Akarenga-kan Museum** (daily 9.30am-4.30pm; ¥200), a striking white-and-red brick building which served as the headquarters of Akita Bank from 1912-69. It is said to have survived several earthquakes. The teller windows on the ground floor are still there. Inside are some fine examples of Akita *hachijo* (naturally dyed silk fabric), lacquerware and dolls. It's a 20-minute walk across town, on the other side of the Asahi River.

A convenient choice for an overnight stay is the JR-run *Hotel Metropolitan Akita* (☎ 018-831 2222, 💻 www.metro-akita.jp; ¥11,000/S, ¥20,500/Tw, ¥22,000/D inc buffet breakfast), right outside the west exit of the station – take the stairs down to the right at the start of the covered walkway. The premium rooms have a chaise longue so you can recline and look down on life around the station area. The rooms are stylish and have 42" TV screens.

A cheaper option is *Toyoko Inn Akita-eki Higashi-guchi* (☎ 018-889 1045, 💻 www.toyoko-inn.com; ¥6090/S, ¥8190/D or Tw). Turn left as you exit the main ticket barrier and then follow signs for the east exit. Take the lift or stairs to M2F and enter AL*VE (sic) building; the Toyoko Inn is on the right. Reception is on the 2nd floor but the rooms are on the 8th to 19th floors.

Offering a similar deal is *Hotel Alpha 1* (☎ 018-836 5800, 💻 www.alpha-1. co.jp/akita; from ¥4580/S, ¥7300/D, ¥8300/Tw; buffet-style breakfast ¥880-950), on your left as you take the west exit – look for the 'α-1' sign on the roof.

For **food**, the local specialities are *inaniwa udon* and *kirininpo-soba* noodles, made with seasonal ingredients. You can try both at *Sato Yosuke* (daily 11am-10pm) on the basement floor of Seibu department store outside the west exit. Menus cost from ¥1000. *Dining Manyo* (11am-2pm & 5-11pm) in Hotel Metropolitan serves a set lunch menu (¥1500) using local produce as well as pasta dishes from ¥900. *Hotel Alpha 1* (11.30am-4.30pm & 5pm to midnight) also has a good restaurant. On the same floor as the Toyoko Inn, *Nonbe-Kube* (daily 11am-2.30pm & 5.30-11pm) does set meals including tonkatsu (¥1050) and soba (from ¥1250); *Chanboy's Café* (9am-6pm) sells bagels and muffins; and *Italian Tomato Café Jr* (9am-8pm) serves pasta dishes.

If in a hurry to return to Tokyo take the Komachi shinkansen that runs east to Morioka – effectively the side trip from Morioka (see p284) in reverse – and from there on to Tokyo. Alternatively it would be easy to visit either Omagari or Kakunodate and also possibly Tazawa-ko as a day trip from Akita.

The train travels 'backwards' as far as Omagari (see p284), the first stop after Akita – don't bother to turn the seats around, though, because the direction of the train reverses after leaving Omagari.

Akita to Niigata [Map 19; Map 20, p298; Table 14, p464]

Distances by JR from Akita. Fastest journey time: 3½ hours.

Akita (0km) This part of the route continues south towards Niigata along the Uetsu line on the Inaho LEX. Fifteen minutes after leaving Akita there are glimpses of the Japan Sea out to the right. These views last for another 15 minutes, before the line heads back towards more rice fields.

Limited expresses stop at both **Ugo-Honjo (43km)** and **Nikaho (57km)** but the surrounding area is not particularly noteworthy.

Some trains stop at **Kisakata (68km)**. The coastline round here is very dramatic in parts and until the beginning of the 19th century it was similar to Matsushima (see pp277-8), with tiny islands scattered along the coast. The islands disappeared forever after a huge earthquake in 1804 pushed up the sea floor.

For the next 40km or so there are great views to the left of the mountains in Chokai Quasi National Park. The rail line skirts around the park, at the centre

> *Although little more than a mile in width, this lagoon is not in the least inferior to Matsushima in charm and grace. There is, however, a remarkable difference between the two. Matsushima is a cheerful laughing beauty, while the charm of Kisakata is in the beauty of its weeping countenance.*
>
> **Matsuo Basho**, *The Narrow Road To The Deep North*, trans Nobuyuki Yuasa, Penguin, 1966

of which is **Mt Chokai** (2236m), a semi-dormant volcano known as the Mt Fuji of Akita. Gradually the focus shifts towards the coast, with views out to sea on the right side. The train stops then at **Yuza (93km)**.

Sakata (105km) Sakata is a large port town at the mouth of Mogami-gawa. The area around the station is rather drab and depressing but Sakata does boast a good example of the classic Japanese stroll garden, worth a look if you haven't visited one.

Only small ¥300 **lockers** are available at the station, though ask at the JR ticket counter and they may keep your bags for ¥410. The **tourist information office** (daily 9am-5pm) is on the right after passing the ticket barrier. To reach the unexceptional **Homma Museum of Art** (🖳 www.homma-museum.or.jp; Mar-Oct daily 9am-5pm, Nov-Feb Tue-Sun 9am-4.30pm; ¥900), turn right on to the main road that runs in front of the station and go straight (about 5 mins) until you reach a large junction with traffic lights; the museum is diagonally opposite. The Homma family were one of the wealthiest in Japan thanks to rice production on their land, and they remained the most influential family in the area until WWII brought an end to their power.

Far more interesting is the adjacent small Japanese garden, **Kakubuen**, and wooden guest house. Tea is served inside at tables overlooking the garden; go up to the 2nd floor for better views. A highlight of the garden used to be the 'borrowed' view of Mt Chokai in the distance; this has now been blocked out by buildings. At the top of the stairs turn right and look at the blank screens on the left. Then walk to the window and turn back and see if they are still blank.

Note: The **Kirakira Uetsu Joyful train** (see p292; Apr-Jun Fri-Sun and bank holidays) runs on the Uetsu line between Sakata and Niigata. The carriages are painted so colourfully it would be hard to miss the train if it is operating.

Amarume (117km) Amarume is a stop on the Uetsu line and also a terminus for the Riku Saisen line running east to Shinjo. There is little reason to stop here unless you happen to be passing through on January 15th (see box below).

A quick way of returning to Tokyo from here would be to take a local train to **Shinjo** (50 mins), from where you can pick up the shinkansen which runs via Yamagata and Fukushima south to the capital.

♦ **Fujishima (126km)** Limited expresses don't stop here but this is the venue for the annual Fujishima-gawa Zenkoku Tsuna-Watari Taikai (National River Rope-Crossing Tournament) in August; contestants attempt to cross from one side of the river to the other via a series of ropes. Anyone who falls in is, well, out.

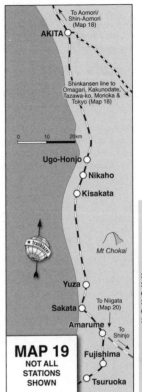

⛩ **Yaya Festival**

If you're passing through Amarume on January 15th it would probably be more sensible to watch than participate in the annual Yaya Matsuri (Festival). At the coldest time of the year men, but particularly boys aged 6-14, meet at Yawata Jinja (Yawata Shrine), strip off and put on straw skirts and sandals. They have buckets of cold water thrown over them by officials at the shrine and are then required to walk around the neighbourhood. When they return to the shrine offerings are made to the gods and prayers are said for good health in the coming year.

This is by no means the only festival in Japan where men wear nothing other than straw skirts and sandals so you may well see a similar festival elsewhere; and in some other festivals, such as at Kanda Myojin Shrine, near Akihabara in Tokyo, women pour icy water over themselves.

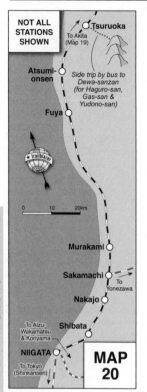

NOT ALL STATIONS SHOWN

Tsuruoka
To Akita (Map 19)

Atsumi-onsen

Side trip by bus to Dewa-sanzan (for Haguro-san, Gas-san & Yudono-san)

Fuya

trailblazer

0   10   20km

Murakami

Sakamachi
To Yonezawa

Nakajo

To Aizu-Wakamatsu & Koriyama

Shibata

NIIGATA

To Tokyo (Shinkansen)

MAP 20

Tsuruoka (132km) Tsuruoka station has ¥300 and ¥500 **lockers** (in the waiting room). The staff at the **tourist information office** (daily Apr-Oct 9.30am-5.30pm, Nov-Feb 10am-5pm), to the right as you go out of the station, don't speak English but will help book accommodation.

Tsuruoka city (🖳 www.tsuruokakanko.com/english) has only a few sights but the main reason people stop here is to go to Dewa Sanzan (see below). The most interesting of the sights in Tsuruoka city is the **Chido Bijutsukan** (Chido Museum; 🖳 www7.ocn.ne.jp/~chido; daily Mar-Nov 9.30am-5pm, Dec-Feb to 4pm; ¥700). There's an odd architectural mix of buildings here, including the former Tsuruoka police station, a Western-style building from the late 19th century and the retirement residence of the former ruling Sakai lords. There's also a small Japanese garden. All signs inside are in Japanese, though a leaflet in English is available. Take a bus from the station and get off at the Shiyakusho-mae stop (12 mins; ¥260), then keep following the road past the park and look for the entrance on the right.

For accommodation, immediately opposite the station is *Tsuruoka Washington Hotel* (☎ 0235-25 0111, 🖳 www.tsuruoka-wh.com; from ¥6930/S, ¥11,500/Tw).

Side trip by bus to Dewa Sanzan

Most people who stop at Tsuruoka are on their way to **Haguro-san** (Mt Haguro; 🖳 www.hagurokanko.jp), part of a chain known as Dewa Sanzan (Three Mountains of Dewa). The mountains are considered to be the home of the *kami* (spirits), and pilgrims visit year-round to undertake spiritual cleansing: first to be climbed is Haguro-san (414m), which represents birth, followed by **Gas-san** (1984m), which represents death, and finally **Yudono-san** (1504m), representing the future or re-birth. The easiest to access, and possible as a day trip from Tsuruoka, is Haguro-san. Shonai-Kotsu operate buses from the stand to the left of the station exit to the base of Haguro-san (7-9/day; 45 mins; ¥800) and to the top (4/day; 50 mins; ¥1150). Get off at the base (Haguro Center bus stop) if you want to follow the pilgrim's route to the top through a cedar forest with over 2400 stone steps; the walk takes about an hour.

It is possible to stay in temple lodgings at the top but bookings must be made through Haguro Tourist Association (see website) or the tourist information office in Tsuruoka (see above).

Atsumi-onsen (162km) More than 1000 years ago, Atsumi served as a border checkpoint for travellers entering Tohoku. Sandwiched between mountains and the coast, Atsumi is nowadays a busy hot spring resort. According to legend, the spring in question was discovered by none other than Kobo Daishi, the monk who founded the Shingon sect of Buddhism and established its headquarters on Koya-san (see pp223-5). The hot spring water flows from the river into the sea. The main onsen area (🖥 www.atsumi-spa.or.jp) is by the sea, a bus ride (7/day; 6-8 mins; ¥230) from the station. There are a few foot baths in town as well as real baths.

After Atsumi-onsen, some limited expresses call briefly at **Fuya (176km)**. From here to Murakami the rail line runs along the coast, though views are limited due to the proliferation of tunnels (of various lengths) along this line.

Murakami (212km) Murakami (🖥 www.murakami.in/murakami) is the closest station to **Senami-onsen** (🖥 www.senami.or.jp). This onsen was discovered in 1904 when the area was being drilled for oil and hot water started pouring out of the earth. Other than that there is little reason to stop here though it could be a convenient place for a night, especially if you have arrived from, or are going to, Yonezawa (see pp276-7).

There isn't a tourist information office here but useful leaflets including a map of the town are available in the station. There is, as always, a JR ticket office and travel service centre.

Murakami Town Hotel (☎/🖨 0254-53-2363) is on the left about a 5-minute walk down the road from the station. It is set back from the road between Good Square Murakami and a petrol station. The rooms in the hotel are spacious but a bit rundown; unusually the beds have a sheet and blanket rather than a duvet/futon. A LAN cable and hairdryer can be borrowed from reception.

There is a **convenience store** further down the road on the hotel side and a branch of the Fujiya Ginza *cake shop* almost opposite that.

From Murakami the train heads inland and after 15 minutes passes a major industrial complex. The views gradually deteriorate as the surrounding area becomes more built up on the final approach into Niigata.

Before arriving in Niigata, there are stops at **Sakamachi (224km)**, the junction with the JR Yonezawa line from Yonezawa (see p277), **Nakajo (233km)** and **Shibata (246km)**.

Niigata (273km) [see pp306-11]
If not returning to Tokyo from here, Niigata also has direct rail connections with **Kanazawa**, just under four hours away by Hokuetsu LEX along the Hokuriku line. Pick up the route guide to Kanazawa from p145 as you pass Naoetsu (100 mins from Niigata).

Niigata to Tokyo
The fastest (100 mins; 1-2/hr), though least scenic, way of returning to Tokyo from Niigata is by Joetsu shinkansen. Single- and double-decker trains (the Toki/Max Toki) run on this line; it's worth reserving a seat on the upper deck of

the latter (book early in peak periods) for the snatches of mountain views in between all the tunnels.

This shinkansen line is especially useful in the winter months as it offers easy access to good **skiing** areas – particularly Gala Yuzawa (🖳 www.gala resort.jp/winter/english), an additional stop on shinkansen services in the winter months, Echigo-Yuzawa (🖳 www.e-yuzawa.gr.jp), and Jomo-Kogen (the Tanigawa ski area is a 15-minute bus ride from the station). The Tanigawa/Max Tanigawa shinkansen (approx 1/hr) operate from Echigo-Yuzawa to Tokyo.

If you have more time and are prepared to change trains you might consider the local Banetsu-sei line that runs inland from Niigata, via the castle town of **Aizu-Wakamatsu** (see pp273-5), to **Koriyama** (see p273) on the Tohoku shinkansen line; from Koriyama you can take a shinkansen back to Tokyo.

A good reason for taking the Banetsu-sei line is the chance to take the **SL Banetsu Monogatari** (see p275) to Aizu-Wakamatsu. From Koriyama, you can complete the journey by jumping on a southbound shinkansen to Tokyo.

Tohoku (North-eastern Honshu) – city guides

SENDAI

Tohoku's largest city, Sendai, is on the Pacific coast and shares the same latitude as Washington DC, USA, and the same longitude as Melbourne, Australia. The city was razed to the ground during WWII and consequently has few sights of historical interest.

Sendai's history is dominated by the figure of Date Masamune (1567-1636), a feudal lord who earned the nickname 'one-eyed dragon' after he contracted smallpox during infancy and lost the sight in his right eye. Most visitors stop here briefly before heading to Matsushima (see pp277-8).

What to see and do
The best way of seeing the main sights is to take the **Loople Sendai** (see p304). The loop runs one way around the city, with 12 stops (announced in English) en route; ring the bell if you want to alight. The following is a guide to the most interesting places along the way. A map at each bus stop shows the route to the place of interest. At the time of research the route had changed around Sendai Castle due to earthquake damage; ask staff at the TIC for an update.

At stop No 4, **Zuihoden** (daily 9am-4.30pm, to 4pm in winter; ¥550 or ¥450 with Loople pass) is a temple-style mausoleum of the Date family reconstructed in 1985. There's a pleasant wooded area you can wander around and a museum with statues, artefacts and video – but the only English is in the guide you receive at the mausoleum.

Sendai City Museum (🖳 www.city.sendai.jp/kyouiku/museum; Tue-Sun 9am-4.45pm; ¥400) at stop No 5 is more old-fashioned than the hi-tech video

> ### ∏ Sendai Shiden Hozonkan (Streetcar Museum)
> Rail fans might like to pay a visit to this museum, also known as **Sendai City Train Museum** (🖳 www.kotsu.city.sendai.jp/shiden; Tue-Sun 10am-4pm; free), located close to Tomizawa subway station, the southern terminus of the Namboku subway line. The museum traces the history of streetcars in Sendai, which for half a century were the main form of public transport in the city. The first four-wheeled wooden streetcar went into service in 1926 and at the height of its popularity the system was carrying more than 100,000 passengers a day. But the age of the automobile heralded the demise of the streetcar, which was finally taken out of service on March 31st, 1976, almost exactly 50 years after it was inaugurated.
>
> The museum exhibits some of the original carriages as well as a collection of mechanical parts, period photographs, tickets and signs. A free shuttle bus operates from outside the north exit of Tomizawa station to the museum.

show at Sendai Castle, but is very informative about the Date family, with brief captions in English and an impressive scale model of the castle.

Stop No 6 is **the site of the former Sendai Castle**, also known as Aoba Castle, built on top of the 132m-high Aoba Hill in 1602 by Masamune Date. Destroyed in 1945, it has now been resurrected as a massive tourist arcade and includes a restaurant and modern shrine. The only reason for heading out here is the panorama over Sendai – an impressive view of an ordinary city. An exhibition hall (daily 9am-5pm; ¥700 or ¥500 with Loople pass) shows the history of the castle with a computer-generated reconstruction video, but it's not particularly informative and could easily be skipped.

Finally, stop No 8 is **Miyagi Museum of Art** (Miyagi Bijutsukan; 🖳 www. pref.miyagi.jp/bijyutu/museum; Tue-Sun 9.30am-5pm; ¥300 or ¥240 with Loople pass), 500m north of Sendai City Museum. The main gallery exhibits the work of 20th-century local artists and some minor works by foreign artists, including three early figurative paintings by Kandinsky. There's also a pleasant modern sculpture garden and café.

For **views of the city** and the Pacific Ocean pay a visit to the 31st-floor viewing terrace (daily 10.30am-8pm; free) of the office (rather than the shopping) part of AER Building; alternatively, head for the 30th-floor observation gallery (daily 7am-11pm; free) of the SS30 Building, where you also get a great view of Sendai by day or night.

Families might enjoy a trip to **Sendai Yagiyama Zoological Park** (🖳 www.city.sendai.jp/kensetsu/yagiyama; Mar-Oct daily 9am-4.45pm, Nov-Feb Tue-Sun 9am-4.45pm; ¥400), home to more than 145 species including the African lion, Sumatran tiger, polar bears and a hippo. In the winter months there is also the unusual sight of elephants playing in the snow. Take a bus from stops No 9, 11 or 12 outside Sendai station to Dobutsu-koen-mae (25 mins; ¥250).

See p306 for details of side trips from Sendai.
See p306 for details of side trips from Sendai.

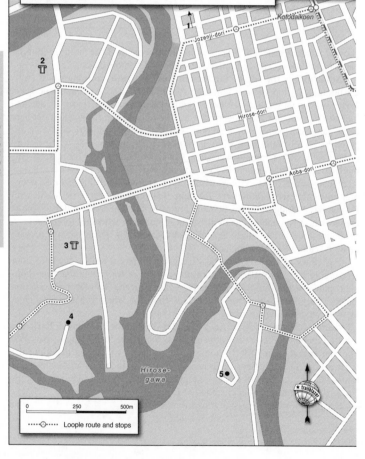

Where to stay
1 Bansuitei Ikoi-so Ryokan 晩翠いこい荘
6 Sendai Chitose Youth Hostel 仙台千登勢ユースホステル
7 Richmond Hotel Sendai リッチモンドホテル仙台
8 Toyoko Inn Nishiguchi Hirose-dori 東横イン仙台西口広瀬通
11 Richmond Hotel Premier Sendai Eki-mae リッチモンドホテルプレミア仙台駅前
13 Toyoko Inn Higashi-guchi No 2 東横イン仙台東口2号館
14 Toyoko Inn Higashi-guchi No 1 東横イン仙台東口1号館
16 Hotel Metropolitan Sendai ホテルメトロポリタン仙台
17 Hotel Monterey Sendai ホテルモントレ仙台
20 ANA Holiday Inn Sendai ANAホリデイイン仙台

Kotodaikoen

Jozenji-dori

Hirose-dori

Aoba-dori

Hirose-gawa

0   250   500m

······○······ Loople route and stops

Where to eat and drink
9 Kirara-zushi きらら寿し
10 Italian Tomato Café Jr
   イタリアントマトカフェJr
11 Hana 波奈
12 Parco パルコ
15 S-Pal エスパル
18 Restaurants (SS30 Building)
   レストラン（SS30ビル）

Other
2 Miyagi Museum of Art 宮城県美術館
3 Sendai City Museum 仙台市博物館
4 Site of Sendai Castle 仙台城跡
5 Zuihoden 瑞鳳殿
19 Central Post Office 中央郵便局
21 Sendai Yagiyama Zoological Park
   仙台市八木山動物公園
22 Sendai Shiden Hozonkan (Streetcar) Museum
   仙台市電保存館

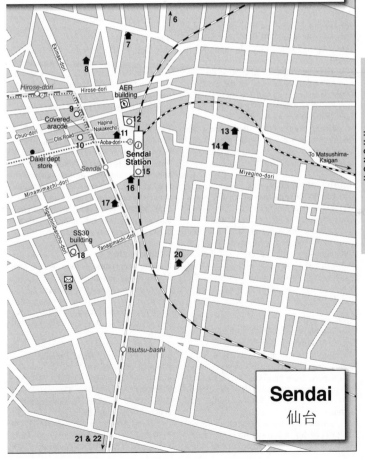

HONSHU

Sendai
仙台

PRACTICAL INFORMATION
Station guide
There are both east and west sides to Sendai station. The main exits into the city are on the west side.

On the 3rd floor is the central shinkansen entrance and main JR ticket office (daily 5.30am-10.30pm). Platforms 11 and 12 are for shinkansen services north and platforms 13 and 14 are for Tokyo-bound trains.

On the 2nd floor is the central entrance for all other JR lines, including the Tohoku, Senseki (for Matsushima) and Sendai Airport lines. Also on this floor is the JR-operated View Plaza travel agency (Mon-Fri 10am-7pm, Sat-Sun 10am-6pm) where rail-pass vouchers can be exchanged.

There are **lockers** all around the station as well as large ones on the 1st floor (street level) right outside the station building. See Where to eat for details of restaurants and cafés in the station.

Heading out of the station from the 2nd floor brings you to the overhead walkways that run above the central streets in front of the station.

Tourist information
The **tourist information office** (🖥 www.city.sendai.jp/kanko; daily 9am-7pm) is in a large booth one floor down from the shinkansen level at Sendai station, by the exit. Staff will not book accommodation (although they will call the youth hostel) but will direct you to the View Plaza travel agency (see Station guide). Next to the booth are two coin-operated internet terminals (¥100/15 mins).

Getting around
The **Loople Sendai** (daily 9am-4pm; 3-4/hr; ¥250/journey, 1-day pass ¥600 inc small discounts at some attractions) is a retro-style tourist bus service (in various colours) that departs from platform No 15-3 of the bus pool outside the west exit of the station. Buy tickets from the driver or at the bus terminal.

Sendai also has a network of **buses** (from ¥180) and a **subway line** (city centre ¥200/journey). The Namboku line runs from Izumi city in the north through the city centre to the southern suburbs. A second subway line, the Tozai line, is under construction and when it opens in 2015 will cross the city from east to west. For further information about travel in Sendai see 🖥 www.kotsu.city.sendai.jp.

Sendai Airport (🖥 www.sdj-airport.com), with connections to a number of Asian cities, was extensively damaged in the 2011 tsunami but is now fully operational. A **limousine bus** runs from stop No 15-2 at Sendai station bus terminal to the airport (40 mins; ¥910). Alternatively, take the Sendai Kuko Access Tetsudo (**Airport Transit rail link**; 17-23 mins; ¥630). The final part of the journey, from JR Natori station to the airport terminal, is on an elevated rail track. Rail fans might like to know that the train used on this line is a two-car electric set (type E721). The airport station is right alongside the terminal building.

Festivals
Sendai's biggest annual bash, and one of the largest summer events in Tohoku, is the **Tanabata Matsuri** (6th-8th Aug). This attracts around two million visitors (so book early if coming then). Colourful paper streamers and decorations are hung from bamboo poles along the main streets and in the station and there are also fireworks, parades and concerts.

Where to stay
Next to the station is the JR-run *Hotel Metropolitan Sendai* (☎ 022-268 2525, 🖥 www.s-metro.stbl.co.jp; from ¥12,705/S, ¥21,945/Tw, ¥23,100/D; discounted for rail-pass holders; breakfast ¥1800), which has comfortable if not overly luxurious rooms.

Across the street from the station is the upscale *Richmond Hotel Premier Sendai Eki-mae* (☎ 022-716 2855, 🖥 www.richmondhotel.jp/sendai-ekimae; ¥9400/S, ¥12,800/D, ¥19,800/Tw). The lobby/reception is on the 5th floor and a restaurant (see Where to eat) in the basement.

Hotel Monterey Sendai (☎ 022-265 7110, 🖥 www.hotelmonter.co.jp/sendai; ¥12,705/S, ¥20,790/Tw; breakfast ¥1700) is a good-value mid range hotel with a European feel – it has a brick façade. A one-day pass for the hotel's 17th-floor Saleya Terrena spa is ¥1515 for hotel guests. The Monterey is less than five minutes on foot from the central exit of Sendai station.

A newish place offering rooms of a high standard is *ANA Holiday Inn Sendai* (☎ 022-256 5111, 🖳 www.anaholidayinn-sendai.jp; ¥10,972/S, ¥19,057/D, ¥20,212 / Tw, ¥23,677/Tr; online discounts available); it's a six-minute walk from the station's east exit.

There are several branches of the popular **Toyoko Inn** hotel chain (🖳 www.toyoko-inn.com; ¥5980/S, ¥6980/D, ¥7480/ Tw, in breakfast) in Sendai. Two are next to each other and close to the station's east exit: *Toyoko Inn Sendai Higashi-guchi No 1* (☎ 022-256 1045) and *Toyoko Inn Sendai Higashi-guchi No 2* (☎ 022-298 1045). Alternatively, on the west side try *Toyoko Inn Nishiguchi Hirose-dori* (☎ 022-721 1045). Take the 2nd floor exit from the station and use the overground walkways to reach the other side of the main road (Ekimae-dori). Turn right and walk along Ekimae-dori and then left down Hirose-dori and take the first right just before Basilica di Santo Stefano, a church built specifically for Western-style weddings. Walk along and the Toyoko Inn is on the left.

A 10-minute walk north of the station is *Richmond Hotel Sendai* (☎ 022-722 0055, 🖳 www.richmondhotel.jp/sendai; ¥4980/S, ¥7950/D, ¥9990/Tw), another branch of the Richmond Hotel chain, with reasonably spacious singles, as well as doubles and twins, a coin laundry and 24-hour restaurant. You pay at a machine in the lobby, though human staff are also on hand.

Bansuitei Ikoi-so Ryokan (☎ 022-222 7885, 🖳 www.ikoisouryokan.co.jp; room ¥5250-6300/S, ¥9450-11,550/Tw; breakfast ¥840pp) has a smart wooden interior with tatami and Western-style rooms. A big selling point is that the common bath turns into a Jacuzzi (which has, according to the owner, 'an ultrasonic massaging effect on your body recognised by the Health and Welfare Ministry'). It's near Kita Yobancho

subway station, three stops from Sendai station. Take North Exit 2, turn right at the top of the steps that lead to street level, and walk for about eight minutes. The ryokan is on a quiet road off to the left, just before you reach Tohoku University Hospital.

Sendai Chitose Youth Hostel (☎ 022-222 6329, 🖳 ryokanchitoseya.co.jp/english; dorm bed ¥3225-3825pp, breakfast ¥735, dinner ¥1260) is a good budget option with tatami rooms sleeping up to six people. They also offer private rooms (room only/ one meal/two meals ¥5460/6300/7560 single occupancy, ¥4935/5670/7035pp for two sharing a room); It's in a residential area about 20 minutes' walk from the station (get a map from tourist information).

See pp45-52 for general information about accommodation and about facilities in chain hotels.

Where to eat and drink

Turn right as you take the central shinkansen ticket exit and double-back on yourself to reach **Gyutan-dori** (Beef Tongue St) and **Sushi-dori**, parades of beef-tongue and sushi restaurants. Grilled beef tongue, known as *gyutan-yaki*, is a Sendai delicacy. Gourmets say the tongue loses fat and develops its taste when it is charcoal roasted. At street level there is a branch of Starbucks, as well as bakeries and cafés that do good-value morning sets.

Built into the station is the **S-Pal department store**, in the basement of which are restaurants (10am-11pm) and take-out food counters (10am-9pm). The floor is divided into three areas: S-Pal Kitchen (takeaway food items), S-Pal Sendai Miyage-kan (gifts and souvenirs) and the restaurant zone.

A very cheap and popular conveyor-belt sushi place close to the station is *Kirara-zushi* (daily 11am-2am), where all the fish dishes are ¥90 each.

For a great variety of Japanese dishes at reasonable prices try *Hana* (daily 11am-2.30pm & 4.30-11pm) in the basement of Richmond Hotel Premier Sendai Eki-mae.

A branch of the popular pasta chain *Italian Tomato Café Jr* (daily 11am-8pm, Sat & Sun to 11pm) is on the left along the

HONSHU

covered Clis Road arcade. Spaghetti with smoked salmon and prawn is ¥580, and with mozarella and tomato cream sauce ¥630.

On floors 28 and 29 of the **SS30 Building** there are several restaurants offering everything from sushi to tonkatsu; some

of the restaurants offer views over the city as well.

Also worth trying is the 9th floor of **Parco**, where *Trattoria La Verde* (11am-11.30pm) offers typical pasta dishes as well as hit-and-miss fusion versions; expect to pay around ¥1000 for a main course.

Side trip by rail to Yamadera

Some 50km west of Sendai lies Yamadera, a hillside temple founded in 860 by the monk Jikaku Daishi and considered to be one of the holiest sights in northern Japan. The temple complex is 50 minutes by 'rapid' train (1/hr; ¥820 without a rail pass) along the JR Senzan line to Yamadera.

Once you pass the urban sprawl of Sendai city, the scenery begins to change. Unlike some rural rail routes that tend to be shut in by dense forest, along this line the views open up as the train weaves between the hills and passes from village to village. Yamadera station is small and has mostly ¥300 lockers. There's an overhead walkway from one side of the single-track line to the exit. There is no tourist information in the station but go to the ticket office and ask for a guide to Yamadera.

From the station, follow the signposted route up towards Yamadera (also known as Risshaku-ji; daily 8am-5pm; ¥300), crossing Hoju Bridge; it's a two-minute walk to the entrance. Give yourself an hour to climb the '1100' steps (it's easy to lose count); there's a handrail but some people buy wooden sticks to help with the ascent. The best views into the valley are from about two-thirds of the way up, at **Godai-do**, a temple built like a stage, which doubles as a useful viewing platform. Your goal at the top is **Okuno-in Temple**, which contains a large golden Buddha.

If you need somewhere to overnight, *Yamadera Pension* (☎ 0236-95 2134, 🖳 www.yamadera-onoya.jp; ¥10,980pp/half-board) is immediately to the left as you leave the station. All the rooms are Western style with low beds and en suite bathrooms; the staff are friendly and speak some English. It's popular and as there's not much else in Yamadera is often booked up in the summer.

NIIGATA

Niigata is the largest city on the Japan Sea coast and was one of the first ports to welcome foreign trade when Japan reopened to the outside world in 1869 after nearly 230 years of self-imposed seclusion. It is known in Japan for the quality of its rice and seafood, and for its sake, which is produced in a number of breweries scattered across Niigata prefecture.

Visitors are put off spending time here because it is a major industrial city, and most press on without delay to nearby Sado-shima (Sado Island). But it's difficult to write the place off as just another identikit Japanese city when it's home to a huge performing arts centre, a coastal area as well as a river which offers another dimension to sightseeing, quiet back streets and, a short distance away, a giant kite museum.

Winters here are cold (the average temperature in January is 2.1°C) but summers tend to be hot and humid.

What to see and do

A good place to start is across Showa Ohashi bridge, on the other side of the city to the station, at **Hakusan Park (Hakusan-koen)**, reached by City Loop bus (see p310) from the station. Here stands **Hakusan Shrine (Hakusan-jinja)**, a place of worship for more than 400 years, which is frequented by couples seeking the support of a God of Marriage enshrined within. Also within Hakusan Park, but entered from a street just outside, is **Enkikan** (daily except 1st and 3rd Mon, 9am-5pm; free), an old merchant's home that was moved here and transformed into a house for traditional Japanese arts such as tea ceremony and *ikebana* (flower arranging). It's a beautiful example of a traditional Japanese house and enjoys a view of the lotus pond. For ¥300 you'll be served a cup of Japanese tea in one of the tatami rooms.

Walking through the park and leaving the other side you'll come to the **Prefectural Government Memorial Hall** (Tue-Sun 9am-4.30pm; free) which dates back to 1884. Used as the prefectural parliament for 50 years, it was apparently constructed in the same style as the Houses of Parliament in London, with Shinano-gawa in place of the River Thames. Old photos of assembly delegates show how the dress code has changed. In a group shot dated 1911 almost all the delegates are in traditional Japanese clothes. By 1931 the vast majority were in Western-style suits.

From here, it's an easy 10-minute walk to the central shopping area of **Furumachi**, where you'll find plenty of places for lunch. For a (free) bird's eye view of the city, the sea and on a clear day Sado Island (see p311-12), head for the 19th floor of the **Next 21 Building** (daily 8am-11.30pm), a landmark that's easy to spot because it's shaped like a pencil. Even better, go to the 31st-floor **observation gallery** (daily 8am-10pm; free; see p311), in Hotel Nikko Niigata, for the highest viewing point on the Japan Sea coast. The gallery is accessed via a dedicated express elevator from the 1st (ground) floor. On the 5th floor of this building is **Niigata Bandaijima Art Museum** (🖥 www.lalanet.gr.jp/banbi; Tue-Sun 10am-6pm; ¥310 or ¥240 with shuttle-bus pass), a modern gallery space with a small permanent collection including a 1970 Andy Warhol painting. Take the City Loop bus operating on the Toki Messe route; Hotel Nikko Niigata is the third stop from the station.

If the weather is cooperating, there can be no better way of seeing Niigata than on a relaxed cruise along the Shinano River. Ferries plough the water on a regular basis, stopping at various embarkation/disembarkation points along the way. Riding the full length of the **Shinano-gawa Water Shuttle** (🖥 www.watershuttle.co.jp) takes just under one hour and costs ¥1100 one way. A one-day water shuttle pass costs ¥1500.

Particularly in the summer, a good mini-escape from the city is down by the coast in the area around **Niigata City Aquarium** (Marinepia Nihonkai; 🖥 www.marinepia.or.jp; daily 9am-5pm, to 6pm late July to Aug; ¥1500 or ¥1200 with the City Loop bus pass). The largest aquarium on the Japan Sea coast, it is home to 450 species of sea life, including a large number of endangered Humboldt penguins, and stages dolphin shows. Both tourist City Loop bus services stop outside.

Near the aquarium, drop by the Sea West 3 complex to sample what's probably the best hand-made ice cream in Japan, at ***Popolo Gelateria***. Down here, and with trees covering the concrete blocks behind, it's hard to believe you're in a major industrial city. Don't miss **Gokoku Shrine**, surrounded by pine trees, just a couple of minutes from the aquarium. It was built in 1945 to console the souls of the war dead. Instead of taking the bus back to the station from here, it's a very pleasant walk back into the city through quiet back streets filled with old wooden houses and privately owned craft shops.

A bus ride away from Niigata, but well worth the trip, is **Shirone Giant Kite History Museum** (Odako to Rekishinoyakata; Thur-Tue 9am-4.30pm; ¥400), which exhibits rare kites from Japan and around the world; the largest are the size of 24 tatami mats (7m×5m), which makes you wonder how they can ever take to the skies (see Festivals p310). The museum – the biggest of its kind in the world – even boasts its own wind tunnel, where you can try flying a kite without going outside. To reach the museum, take a bus (¥630 one way) from stop No 15 outside Niigata station bound for Katahigashi-Eigyosho, and get off at the Shirone Kensei Byoin-mae bus stop, from where the museum is a signed 10-minute walk.

See pp311-12 for details about side trips from Niigata.

NIIGATA – MAP KEY

Where to stay
10 Hotel Nikko Niigata
ホテル日航新潟
13 Comfort Hotel Niigata Eki-mae コンフォート ホテル新潟駅前
14 Shinoda Ryokan 篠田旅館
15 Niigata Tokyu Inn
新潟東急イン
17 Toyoko Inn Niigata Ekimae
東横イン 新潟駅前
20 Dormy Inn Niigata
ドーミーイン新潟
21 Hotel Leopalace Niigata
ホテルレオパレス新潟

Where to eat and drink
1 Popolo Gelateria
ポポロジェラテリア
8 Essa 越佐
10 Serena セリーナ
15 Kurumiya 胡桃屋
18 Immigrant's Café
イミグランツカフェ

Other
2 Niigata City Aquarium/ Marinepia Nihonkai
新潟市水族館/マリンピア 日本海

Other (cont'd)
3 Gokoku Shrine 護国神社
4 Hakusan Shrine/Park
白山神社/白山公園
5 Enkikan 燕喜館
6 Prefectural Government Memorial Hall
県政記念館
7 Next 21 Building
Next 21 ビル
9 Shinano-gawa Water Shuttle
信濃川ウォーターシャトル
10 Niigata Bandaijima Art Museum
新潟市万代島美術館
11 Niigata Ferry terminal (for Sado Island)
新潟フェリーターミナル
12 Niigata Port Intnl Passenger Terminal
新潟港国際旅館ターミナル
16 Tourist Information Center
観光案内センター
19 Central Post Office
中央郵便局
22 Shirone Giant Kite History Museum
しろね大凧と歴史の館

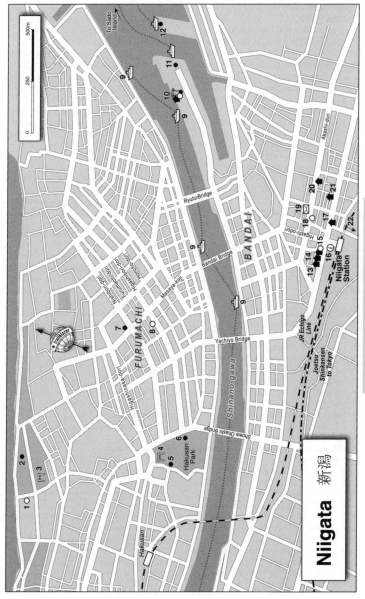

Niigata

新潟

PRACTICAL INFORMATION
Station guide
Niigata is the terminus for the Joetsu shinkansen to/from Tokyo. The other main rail lines are the local Echigo line to Yoshida (this is the line to take for the side trip to Iwamuro (see p312), the Shinetsu line to Nagano via Naoetsu, the Joetsu line to Ueno (Tokyo) and the Uetsu line that runs north to Akita.

The station is divided into the shinkansen side and regular JR lines side.

For the city centre, follow signs for the Bandai Exit. The shinkansen side has the most shops and restaurants, including the *CoCoLo* department store with several places to eat. Lockers are available on both sides.

On the Bandai side of the station, just across from the TIC, is a station waiting room called – inexplicably – 'Banana', where you'll find seats, **lockers** (mainly of the small ¥300 variety, but also a few ¥500) and computer terminals with free **internet access** (daily 11am-7pm; 30 mins per person).

Tourist information
A **tourist information centre** (TIC; 💻 www.nvcb.or.jp; daily 9am-6pm) is to the left as you take the main Bandai exit. The staff here have information about ferries to Sado Island and can book same-day city accommodation. Pick up a copy of the monthly *Niigata English Journal*, which contains restaurant reviews and listings for concerts, exhibitions and movies.

Getting around
The central point for crossing over Shinano-gawa is Bandai Bridge. It's easy enough to walk around central Niigata but all city buses depart from the bus terminal outside the Bandai exit of the station.

A better bet for getting to the main sights is to take one of the **Niigata City Loop Buses**, which operate on different circular routes around the city. Both services start and finish outside Niigata station. Individual tickets are ¥200 or a one-day pass costs ¥500. The one-day pass also offers small discounts at many tourist

facilities in the city. An alternative means of transportation is the water shuttle (see p307) along the Shinano river.

Niigata Airport (💻 www.niigata-airport.gr.jp) has flights to Vladivostok (for connections to the Trans-Siberian Railway) and other places in Russia as well as some Asian destinations including Shanghai and Seoul. A limousine bus to Niigata airport (¥400) departs from bus stop No 5 at the bus terminal outside the station's South Plaza Exit (opposite side to the main Bandai Exit for the city centre).

Festivals
Niigata Matsuri (7th-9th Aug) started as a festival to pray for the prosperity of the port and growth of the city; it still involves a procession and folk dancing over Bandai Bridge (on the 8th) and ends with a huge fireworks display over Shinano-gawa on the evening of the 9th.

In 2002 **Niigata Soh-Odori** (💻 www.soh-odori.net), which was first celebrated 300 years ago, was revived, and has been staged annually ever since in mid September. The highlight is a series of traditional and modern dances performed by large groups; the purpose of all the festivity is to wish for a good harvest.

If you're in town on the first Thur-Sun of June, you'll be able to witness the unusual spectacle of the **Shirone Kite Fighting Festival**, when rival groups of kite fanatics gather on either side of the 80m wide Nakanokuchi River and fight to bring down the opposing team's kites. It's an at times dangerous tradition that dates back to 1740.

Where to stay
Closest to the station is *Toyoko Inn Niigata Ekimae* (☎ 025-241 1045, 💻 www.toyoko-inn.com; from ¥4980/S, ¥8610/D or Tw), immediately on your right as you take the Bandai Exit. Reception is on the 4th floor.

On the left side of the Bandai Exit is *Niigata Tokyu Inn* (☎ 025-243 0109, 💻 www.tokyuhotelsjapan.com; from ¥6900/S, ¥12,600/D, ¥13,400/Tw; ¥1000 discounts Dec to end Mar; buffet breakfast ¥1200). Some of the rooms are for women-only, with extra amenities including humidifier, face lotion, brush and hairband. Also near the station is *Hotel Leopalace Niigata* (☎ 025-249 8100, 🖥 www.leopalacehotels.jp/english/niigata; ¥8400/S, ¥11,800/D, ¥14,800/Tw), a good mid-range choice.

Five minutes on foot north of the station is *Dormy Inn Niigata* (☎ 025-247 7755, 🖥 www.hotespa.net/hotels/niigata; from ¥5450/S, ¥6650/D), a good bet for basic business hotel accommodation. It's clean and efficiently run and the hotel even boasts its own onsen.

Comfort Hotel Niigata Eki-mae (☎ 025-242 0611, 🖥 www.comfortinn.com/hotel-niigata-japan-JP071; ¥6500/S, ¥9000/D, ¥12,000/Tw, inc breakfast) is a good mid-range option with rooms that are a cut above the usual business-hotel standard. Rates include free cycle rental. The hotel is three minutes on foot from the Bandai Exit of JR Niigata station.

For Japanese-style accommodation, a good option is *Shinoda Ryokan* (☎ 025-245-5501, 🗋 025-244 0902; from ¥6000pp), offering basic tatami rooms in a low-rise building just along from the Niigata Tokyu Inn. Look for the white signboard on the corner of the building with the name of the ryokan written in kanji and hiragana. There is also a sign in kanji directly above the sliding doors that lead into the ryokan's *genkan*.

At the top end is *Hotel Nikko Niigata* (☎ 025-241 0808, 🖥 www.hotelnikkoniigata.jp; from ¥13,860/S, ¥27,720/D or Tw, exc breakfast), centrepiece of the redeveloped harbour area which includes the Toki Messe international convention centre. The tallest hotel on the Japan Sea coast enjoys a superb waterfront location set back from the city centre. The rooms are spacious, have large windows and there's a choice of restaurants.

Where to eat and drink

To sample two of Niigata's specialities – seafood and sake – head for *Kurumiya* (daily 11.30am-1.30pm & 5-11pm), a modern restaurant just across the street from the station's Bandai Exit, on the ground floor of the Tokyu Inn building. Their sake 'tasting set' (from ¥1000) allows you to select from different breweries and at lunchtime the set menu is reasonable value at ¥2000; dishes feature local produce including fish, beef and pork.

An unusual dining experience is possible at *Essa*, on a corner of the WITH building along Higashibori-dori (look for the moving crab on the wall outside, then take the stairs down to the basement). The speciality here is ultra-fresh seafood; you eat at a counter around a big pool, from which staff pull out your chosen fish, then serve it to you within minutes.

In the harbour area, it's worth taking lunch at *Serena* (11.30am-10pm), a modern all-day dining place on the 3rd floor of Hotel Nikko Niigata, where there are spectacular panoramic waterfront views through the bay windows. Buffet lunches and set meals are good value (lunch from ¥2000; dinner from ¥3300).

A popular evening haunt is *Immigrant's Café* (🖥 immigrantscafe-med.com; Tue-Sun 5.30pm to late) on Akashi-dori just across from the central post office, five minutes on foot from the station. It's popular with Niigata's foreign community as the staff (Japanese and foreign) all speak English. The café's tag line is 'Come and experience the world'. Certainly the menu offers a great selection of international dishes – everything from skewered pork wrapped around green pepper (¥590) to Mexican taco salad (¥630) – as well as more predictable bar snacks. Most dishes are under ¥1000 and there are regular happy hours.

Side trips from Niigata

● **Sado Island** The most popular trip is to Sado Island (🖥 www.visitsado.com), once a place of exile and now home to the world-famous Kodo drummers (🖥 www.kodo.or.jp). Ferries (🖥 www.sadokisen.co.jp; 2½ hrs; ¥2190 one way) and jet foils (1 hr; ¥6090 one way, ¥10,990 return) depart from

Niigata Port bound for Ryotsu on the island. To reach Sado Ferry Terminal, take a bus from stop No 6 outside the station to its terminus at Sado Kisen. Before leaving Niigata station, pick up the English map of Sado Island, which contains information on bus routes on the island as well as sights, accommodation and restaurants.

● **Iwamuro** Hot spring fanatics might like to take a 30km side trip by rail from JR Niigata on a local train along the JR Echigo line to Iwamuro (1/hr; 12 stops; 45 mins), a hot spring resort which – according to legend – was founded in 1713 after a village elder discovered a wild goose nursing a wound by bathing in the local spring water. Several centuries on, people still flock to the hotels and hot springs, which are believed to help heal cuts and skin diseases. It's a great escape from the city. From JR Iwamuro station, walk along the road north-west for 20-30 minutes.

AOMORI

The last major city before Hokkaido, Aomori is known for its red apples, considered to be the best in Japan, and for Nebuta Matsuri, one of the major summer festivals in Tohoku. Summer is mild but in winter temperatures drop well below freezing and snow becomes a fact of life for months on end. If visiting in the summer, look out for the phone boxes mounted well above street level with steps leading up to them. In winter, the steps – and sometimes much of the phone box – are buried in snow.

Up until just over a decade ago, all rail travellers bound for Hokkaido had no choice but to stop here in order to transfer on to a passenger ferry for the journey across the Tsugaru Straits. It's now possible to avoid the city all together, but it's worth stopping for at least a day, particularly to visit the museum where some of the summer festival floats are displayed year-round (see Side trip, p316) but some can now be seen at Nebuta Wa Rasse right by the station.

What to see and do

A good place to begin a tour of Aomori is at **ASPAM** (Aomori Sightseeing Products Mansion; 1st floor daily 9/9.30am-6.30/7pm, 2nd floor daily 9am-7pm, 10th floor Mon-Fri 10.30am-10pm, Sat & Sun to 8.30pm, 13th floor daily 9am-10pm), the large triangular building (meant to resemble an 'A' for Aomori) by the port 10 minutes on foot from the station. The nicest way to get there is along the walkway by the sea. On the 13th floor there's an observation lounge (¥400) and on the 2nd floor a panorama theatre (¥600) where Aomori prefecture is introduced on a 360° screen. A ticket for both of these is ¥800 (50% off with a Northern Tohoku Welcome Card between 9.30am and 5pm). There are also free shamisen concerts (11am & 2pm) on the 1st floor most days. There are several other ticket combinations – ASPAM and *Hakkoda-Maru* ¥1100; ASPAM, Nebuta Wa Rasse and *Hakkoda-Maru* ¥1300 – and visits can be strung out over several days.

A five-minute walk from ASPAM, and visible across the water, is the **Memorial Ship** *Hakkoda Maru* (daily 9am-7pm, Nov-Mar to 5pm; ¥500), a former JR-operated ferry that ploughed the water between Aomori and Hakodate for 80 years until it was retired in 1987. You can climb aboard, look around and even put on a captain's jacket and cap and pose for photos. The ship has been preserved as it was, except that in the summer there's now a beer garden on the top deck.

Nebuta Wa Rasse (🖥 www.nebuta.jp/warasse; Apr-Aug 9am-7pm, Sep-Mar to 6pm; ¥600), to the left as you exit the station, makes it far easier to see some of the floats used in the Nebuta (see below), especially if you have limited time in Aomori. There's an English leaflet but, sadly, no English labels.

After visiting the fish, fruit and vegetable markets (see p314) in the basement of **Auga Building** and along the road on the east side of the building including **Aomori Gyosai Center**, consider going to **Machinaka-onsen** (daily 6am-11pm; ¥420 plus ¥200 for towel). Turn left at the second set of traffic lights (just before the main road) and the onsen is on your left. Take your shoes off at the entrance and then buy a ticket from the machine. You need a ¥100 coin for the locker. There are several baths, including a Jacuzzi-style one and a *rotemburo* (outdoor bath), as well as a sauna. The ergonomic lilo is a very comfortable way to relax when you are thoroughly clean.

See p316 for details about side trips from Aomori.

PRACTICAL INFORMATION
Station guide
See p288 for details about transferring from Shin-Aomori to Aomori station.

Aomori station is small with two sides, east and west. There are no lifts and only a one-way escalator so you need to carry your luggage when going down to the platforms. The main exit is on the east side.

As you leave the ticket barrier, the **JR ticket office** (daily 5.30am-11pm) is on your right. Go to the adjacent **View Plaza** travel agency (Mon-Fri 10am-6pm, Sat & Sun to 5pm) if you want to make a reservation to stop at Tappi-kaitei station inside the Seikan Tunnel (see box p318).

Aoimori railway's ticket office (daily 6am-10.50pm) is on the left by the station exit. See p286 for details of using the pre-shinkansen line between Aomori and Hachinohe, now operated by Aoimori Railway (🖥 aoimorirailway.com).

There are some **lockers** (including a couple of ¥500 ones) between the station and the entrance to Lovina department store as well as a locker room (daily 5.30am-midnight) with lockers of all sizes on the left as you exit the station.

Tourist information
At the **tourist information desk** (daily 8.30am-7pm) in the bus-terminal office on the left as you exit the station, staff can advise on accommodation. There's another desk on the ground floor of **ASPAM** (daily 9am-10pm).

A useful website for information about Aomori city as well as other towns in the prefecture is 🖥 en.aptinet.jp.

Getting around
The centre of Aomori is walkable but there is also a network of city buses. Nebutan-go (¥500/1-day pass; approx 2/hr) runs in a loop from the station round the main tourist sights.

Festivals
Nebuta Matsuri (1st-7th Aug) is one of the most popular and spectacular festivals in Japan. Every night, giant, colourful floats are paraded through the city and on the evening of the final day a fireworks festival is held in the port area. The atmosphere of the city changes completely during the festival week. Thousands of visitors arrive and accommodation gets booked solid.

Where to stay

Convenient for the station is *Hotel Route Inn Aomori* (☎ 0177-31 3611, 💻 www.route-inn.co.jp; from ¥6000/S, ¥11,700/D, ¥12,600/Tw, inc buffet breakfast). It's not one of the newer hotels in the chain and the beds are firm, which doesn't suit everyone, but the rooms are en suite, some have lovely views over the port, and the hotel also has a common bath so is good value overall.

Nearby is a branch of the ever-reliable Toyoko Inn chain: *Toyoko Inn Aomori-eki Shomen-guchi* (☎ 017-735 1045, 💻 www.toyoko-inn.com; from ¥5480/S, ¥6480/D, ¥7480/Tw, including breakfast).

On a side street near the station is *Iroha Ryokan* (☎/📠 0177-22 8689; ¥4000pp, cash only), offering tatami rooms but no attached bathrooms or meals. It's a small place and gets booked up quickly.

Aomori Grand Hotel (☎ 017-723 1011, 💻 www.agh.co.jp; from ¥6500/S, ¥10,000/D, ¥12,000/Tw, inc breakfast) provides comfortable accommodation and has Western- as well as (pricier) Japanese-style rooms. It's a two-minute walk up Shinmachi-dori from the station.

Aomori Center Hotel (☎ 017-762 7500, 💻 www.aomoricenterhotel.jp; from ¥5250/S, ¥10,500/Tw), on top of Machinaka-onsen (see p313), has mostly single rooms, some of which are pretty compact, but rates include access to the onsen.

Hotel JAL City (☎ 017-732 2580, 💻 www.jalhotels.com/domestic/tohoku/aomori; ¥10,700/S, ¥17,300/Tw, exc breakfast; good online discounts), is more upmarket, with an elegant lobby and large rooms; it is close to the ASPAM building.

A popular budget option is *Super Hotel Aomori* (☎ 017-723 9000, 💻 www.superhoteljapan.com/en; ¥4980/S, ¥6980/D, ¥7980/Tr, inc buffet breakfast). It's a bit of a hike across town but worth the effort. Some rooms are specifically for women.

See pp45-52 for details about accommodation in general and also about facilities at chain hotels.

Where to eat and drink

For a quick packed lunch, the ground floor of the **Lovina** department store (daily 10am-8pm) has lots of options, including a branch of the tonkatsu-chain, *Saboten*, which offers sit-down meals and takeaway lunch boxes.

The basement of the **Auga** building (across the street from the station) has a fresh-fish market (5am-6.30pm). Sushi is naturally on offer at a couple of restaurants adjacent to the market area. Unsurprisingly there is an overwhelming smell of fish, so it's not a place to linger over a slow meal.

There are also **fish and fruit/vegetable markets** along the road to the right of Auga. To create your own sushi/sashimi bowl (*Nokke-don*) go to **Aomori Gyosai Center** (daily 7am-5pm). First get a bowl of rice (¥100/200 small/large) from one of the stands on the left-hand side as you walk in and then go round choosing your fish – there is usually a huge variety to choose from. You can also have miso and pickles; tea is served free. Most of the fish sellers have portions (¥100-250) already prepared.

The **A-Factory** (daily 10am-8pm) is all about promoting local produce. Food options here include a sushi bar, cake shop and soup stand; it would be a good place to get food for a picnic.

Saigon (daily 11.30am-2.30pm & 5.30pm to midnight) is a small, wooden-table restaurant which does excellent Vietnamese, Thai and Indonesian dishes. The set lunch (¥700) is recommended, as is the spicy Thai Red curry (¥750). It's close to Hotel JAL City and has an English sign.

A branch of the Italian chain *Capricciosa* (10am-3pm & 6-11pm) is 12 minutes on foot from the station's east exit along Shinmachi-dori. It's on the corner of a major junction; look for the red-white-and-green veranda. The menu has lots of pasta dishes and pizzas; there's a lunch set for ¥650.

On the 14th floor of the **ASPAM** building down by the port, *Hanafu* (11am-9pm; last orders 7.30pm) serves pasta and curry dishes (around ¥1000) as well as fish or steak sets (¥1800). On the 10th floor, *Nishimura* (11am-10pm), a casual Japanese restaurant with low wooden tables, specialises in local fish dishes.

Aomori
青森

Where to stay
6 Toyoko Inn Aomori-eki Shomen-guchi
東横イン青森駅正面口
7 Iroha Ryokan いろは旅館
8 Hotel Route Inn Aomori ホテルルートイン青森
10 Aomori Grand Hotel 青森グランドホテル
13 Aomori Center Hotel 青森センターホテル
16 Hotel JAL City ホテルJALシティ
18 Super Hotel Aomori スーパーホテル青森

Where to eat and drink
2 A-Factory エーファクトリー
5 Lovina Dept Store ロビンデパート
9 Hanafu; Nishimura (ASPAM)
(はなふ; 西村 (アスパム)
11 Auga Building アウガビル
12 Aomori Gyosai Center 青森魚菜センター
14 Saigon サイゴン
15 Strauss シュトラウス
17 Capricciosa カプリチョーザ

Other
1 Memorial Ship *Hakkoda-maru*
メモリアルシップ八甲田丸
3 Nebuta Wa Rasse ねぶたのワ・ラッセ
4 Tourist Information; Bus Terminal office
観光案内所; バスターミナル
9 ASPAM アスパム
11 Auga Building アウガビル
13 Machinaka-onsen まちなかおんせん

HONSHU

For a decadent treat, try **Strauss**. Downstairs is a cake shop, but upstairs is a very smart café where waitresses in 1920s-style black-and-white uniforms serve slices of rich cake and various coffees. It's as near as you'll get to Vienna in Tohoku – the detail's there right down to the chandeliers and fireplace. There's no better place to escape a freezing Aomori winter than here with a hot chocolate and apple strudel.

Side trips from Aomori

● **Nebuta-no-Sato** Even if you're not here in summer you can get a taste of the annual festival, and see some of the floats, at the huge, indoor Nebuta-no-Sato (⌨ www.nebutanosato.co.jp; daily Apr-Nov 9am-5.30pm, until 8pm in summer; ¥630; Dec-Mar 10am-5.30pm; ¥420).

Four times a day there's a show that introduces some of the flavour of the festival, with performers on stage playing the flute and drums, and visitors pulling one of the floats a few metres along inside the hall. The floats are incredibly heavy; just dragging them along for a few metres makes you wonder how participants manage to do it for two hours during the festival.

To get there, take the JR bus from bus stand No 1 outside Aomori station to Nebuta-no-Sato Iriguchi (30 mins; ¥480, free to JR rail-pass holders).

● **Resort Asunaro** At the weekends and in holiday periods a rail-based side trip is possible round Mutsu Bay either going west on the Tsugaru Line from Shin-Aomori/Aomori to Kanita on the **Resort Asunaro Tsugaru** (Sat, Sun and holidays 1/day round trip) or east on the JR Ominato line from Shin-Aomori/Aomori to Noheji and Ominato on the **Resort Asunaro Shimokita** (Sat, Sun and holidays 2/day round trip). JR rail passes are valid but seat reservations are essential; since the trains only have two cars make your reservation in good time. As with the Resort Shirakami (see p292) there are monitors in the carriages showing the driver's view.

The views, thanks in part to the large windows, are good for both journeys especially as at times the line goes right by the sea, but one reader recommended the Resort Shirakami if time permits only one journey. In reality, if you are going to Hokkaido you will do the route on the Tsugaru line anyhow.

⛩ **Soma-Nomaoi (Soma Wild Horse Chase)**
Soma-Nomaoi (⌨ www6.ocn.ne.jp/~nomaoi and ⌨ www.city.minamisoma. lg.jp/etc/guide/P1718.pdf) is a spectacular 3-day festival (July 23rd to 25th) that has been held in Minami-Soma for over a thousand years. It involves over 500 men, dressed in samurai armour, riding through the streets of the town and out into the countryside where they go to three shrines and also chase and try to catch unsaddled (wild) horses. The devastation in the area caused by the Great East Japan Earthquake meant the festival in 2011 was held on a much smaller scale. Until the railway line is operational the best way to get there is by bus (4/day; approx 2½ hours; ¥1000) from Fukushima.

HOKKAIDO

Hokkaido – route guides

The northernmost of the major islands in the Japanese archipelago, Hokkaido represents one-fifth of the country's land mass but is inhabited by only one-twentieth of the total population.

The island is the largest of Japan's 47 prefectures and is bordered by the Sea of Japan to the west, the Sea of Okhotsk to the north-east and the Pacific Ocean to the south. Hokkaido was colonised by the Japanese only in the middle of the 18th century; prior to that it was known as Ezo and was inhabited almost exclusively by the Ainu, an indigenous people who all but disappeared as more and more Japanese moved north from Honshu (see the box on p356).

Hokkaido is an island of stunning natural beauty, vast national parks with mountain ranges, volcanoes, forests, rivers, crashing water-falls, hot springs, wildlife – and tourists. In the summer months, bikers, backpackers and cyclists descend on the island to feel what it is like to drive on the open road, unclogged by pollution, noise and urban devel-opment. Others come to escape the oppressive heat and humidity found elsewhere in Japan, to see cows, taste fresh Hokkaido milk, yoghurt and even Camembert-style cheese. In winter, when temperatures plum-met and snow falls for months on end, skiers pour on to the slopes.

The bad news for the rail traveller is that parts of the Hokkaido network have closed in the last few decades. Spiralling costs, few passengers on remote lines and the difficulty of track maintenance in areas particularly exposed to the elements mean that some parts are no longer accessible by rail. But enough of the rail network remains to provide more than a glimpse of the spectacular natural environment. You'll be travelling on mostly rural lines, so don't expect lightning-fast services, but few other places in Japan offer such breathtaking scenery from the train window.

Aomori (see pp312-16), on the tip of north-eastern Honshu, is the rail gateway to Hokkaido. The route in this chapter follows a loop around Hokkaido, starting and finishing in Aomori/Shin-Aomori. Three weeks would be enough to enjoy the island without feeling rushed. For a briefer taste of what the island has to offer, the line between Abashiri and Kushiro (see pp336-7) has some of the most impressive scenery. Since Hokkaido

Through fragrant fields of early rice we went beside the wild Ariso Sea
(MATSUO BASHO)

早稲の香や分け入る右は荒磯海

> **⛩ Tunnel vision**
> The 53.85km-long **Seikan Tunnel**, under the Tsugaru Straits between Honshu and Hokkaido, is the longest underwater tunnel in the world. It was built as straight as possible in anticipation of the day (now almost a reality) that shinkansen trains would run through it. Though not recommended for claustrophobics, it's possible to go on a **behind-the-scenes tour** of the tunnel (late Apr to mid Nov 1-2/day; adult ¥2040, children ¥1020; rail passes not valid) at the undersea stop, **Tappi-Kaitei (64km)**. Reservations to stop at Tappi-kaitei should be made in advance at Aomori, Shin-Aomori or Hakodate stations since only one service stops here from Aomori/Shin-Aomori to Hakodate and one as a day trip from Hakodate (see Table 15, pp464-5). However, when the shinkansen service (see box below) starts, it's likely that the chance to stop in the tunnel will end.
>
> At Tappi-Kaitei you are met by a guide who walks you through the service tunnel to a cable car which provides a scary journey up to the surface at Cape Tappi, the very tip of Honshu. There's a small tunnel museum here but there's also time to walk over to the cape, from where there are great views of Hokkaido across the Tsugaru Straits. There's also the chance to make a call from public phones installed at the lowest point in Japan. Luggage can be stored on site for the duration (about 2½ hours) of the tour.

is away from the major tourist areas, most visitors never make it this far but the views, if nothing else, more than repay the distance and effort.

For further information about Hokkaido visit 🖥 en.visit-hokkaido.jp, or 🖥 www.hokkaidoexperience.com.

For details about using the rail route guide see pp8-9.

SHIN-AOMORI/AOMORI TO HAKODATE
[Map 21, p320; Table 15, pp464-5]

Distances from Shin-Aomori. Fastest journey time: 2 hours 25 minutes.

Shin-Aomori (0km) [Aomori, see pp312-16]
From Shin-Aomori or Aomori take the Hakucho or Super Hakucho LEX along the JR Tsugaru Kaikyo line. On the back of every seat is a map and timetable showing when the train will reach particular places; when you are in the tunnel a graphic at the front of each carriage shows how far into the tunnel the train is. If boarding at Shin-Aomori the train will go backwards to **Aomori**.

After Aomori the line runs quite near the coast at first. Most trains stop at **Kanita (30.9km)** after which the line goes slightly inland and passes through

> **⛩ Shinkansen extension to Hokkaido**
> The shinkansen service from Shin-Aomori to Shin-Hakodate is expected to start in 2015. Trains will stop at **Okutsugaru** (near Tsugaru-Imabetsu) on the Honshu side and **Kikonai** on Hokkaido before terminating at **Shin-Hakodate** (currently called Oshima-Ono; H70). Anyone wanting to go to Hakodate will have to transfer to a local line here. Shinkansen trains will also connect here with LEX services to Sapporo.
> The next stage will be the extension of the shinkansen to Sapporo!

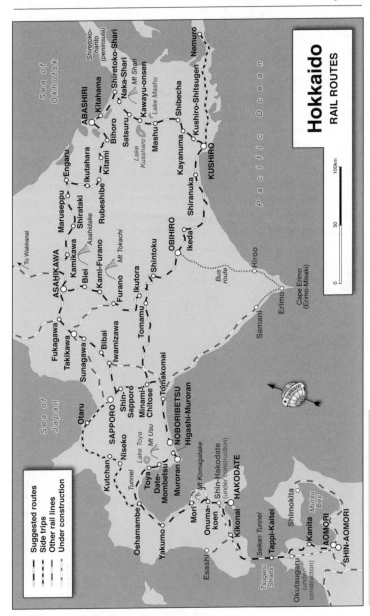

Hokkaido
RAIL ROUTES

Suggested routes
Side trips
Other rail lines
Under construction

0   50   100km

Sea of Okhotsk

Shiretoko-
hanto
(peninsula)

Nemuro
Kushiro-Shitsugen
Shiretoko-Shari
Naka-Shari
Kitahama
ABASHIRI
Kawayu-onsen
Mt Shari
Shibecha
Mashu
Bihoro
Satsuru
Lake Mashu
Lake Kussharo
Kushiro-Shitsugen
KUSHIRO
Engaru
Ikutahara
Kitami
Kayanuma
Maruseppu
Rubeshibe
Shirataki
Shiranuka
To Wakkanai
Kamikawa
Asahidake
Mt Tokachi
OBIHIRO
Ikeda
ASAHIKAWA
Biei
Kami-Furano
Furano
Shintoku
Shimtoku
Fukagawa
Ikutora
Takikawa
Tomamu
Bibai
Iwamizawa
Sunagawa
Hiroo
Bus route
Otaru
Shin-
Sapporo
Tomakomai
SAPPORO
Minami
Chitose
Erimo
Samani
Cape Erimo
(Erimo-Misaki)
NOBORIBETSU
Higashi-Muroran
Kutchan
Niseko
Tunnel
Lake Toya
Mt Usu
Toya
Date-
Mombetsu
Muroran
Shin-Hakodate
(under construction)
Pacific Ocean
Oshamambe
Mt Komagatake
Yakumo
Mori
Onuma-
koen
Shimokita
Mutsu
Bay
HAKODATE
Kikonai
Esashi
Seikan Tunnel
Tappi-Kaitei
Kanita
AOMORI
SHIN-AOMORI
Tsugaru
Straits
Okutsugaru
(under
construction)
Sea of Japan

HOKKAIDO

❑ **Station codes**
To make life simpler for foreigners, JR Hokkaido has given every station a code
number so that when you buy a ticket or make a seat reservation all you need to say
is the code number for the station. This guide also uses these codes, for example
Hakodate is 'H75'.

rural landscapes. Even before Kanita the train runs through some tunnels, easing
passengers gently into the long journey underground through the Seikan Tunnel.
(However, when the shinkansen route is open it is likely that more of the journey
will be in tunnels and also it will be further from the coast.) The opening of the
Seikan Tunnel in 1988 saved nearly two hours on the original journey. Only a
few services stop at **Tappi-Kaitei** (**64km**; see box p318). **Tsugaru-Imabetsu** is
a stop on local services but not on the Hakucho/Super Hakucho.

Kikonai (119km) The first stop in Hokkaido (but not for all limited expresses)
after emerging from the tunnel but it does not have a code (see box above). Just

as you begin to take in the Hokkaido scenery, the train abruptly plunges into a series of tunnels. Once past these, sit on the right side for views over the Tsugaru Straits and, in the distance, the tip of Shimokita Peninsula on Honshu. The train runs close to the coast and the views out to sea are superb.

A few services stop at **Goryokaku (H74; 157km)**.

Hakodate (H75; 160km) [see pp342-8]

Hakodate is the terminus for limited expresses from Aomori and Shin-Aomori.

HAKODATE TO SAPPORO [Map 22, p323; Table 16, p465]

Distances by JR from Hakodate. Fastest journey time: 3 hours.

Hakodate (H75; 0km) The quickest way to Sapporo is along the Hakodate line on the Hokuto or slightly faster Super Hokuto LEX.

Some trains stop at **Goryokaku (H74; 3km)**, see p348. Around 20 minutes after leaving Hakodate, look out to the left for views of Lake Konuma, with its tiny islands scattered across the water.

Onuma-koen (H67; 27km) Not all limited expresses stop here. To the right as you exit the small station is Onuma International Communication Plaza, a wooden building with a glass front, where there's a **tourist information counter** (daily 8.30am-6pm, Nov-Mar to 5.15pm). In the station there are a few ¥400 lockers.

One of the most beautiful, if foreboding, natural backdrops you're likely to come across in Japan is **Mt Komagatake**; it last erupted in a big way in 1640 when it killed more than 700 people. A minor eruption in 2000, which saw nearby areas covered in ash, proved that though Komagatake was dormant it is by no means extinct. There are hiking trails around the volcano, but you may prefer to admire the jagged peak from the safe distance of the lakes. Lake Onuma and two smaller lakes, Konuma and Junsainuma, were created when debris from an eruption of Komagatake settled as a natural dam.

Between April and November pedal boats (¥1400/30 mins), motor boats (¥1300/10 mins) and canoes (¥1400/60 mins) can be hired on the lakes. Alternatively, pleasure boats do 30-minute tours of Lake Onuma for ¥960. However, the best way of seeing the lakes and taking in the spectacular surrounding scenery is to hire a bike (approx ¥500/hour, ¥1000/day. There are rental places in the station area, the most obvious being Friendly Bear, opposite the station. In winter the lakes freeze over and holes are cut in the ice for fishing.

Crawford Inn Onuma (☎ 0120-67 2964, 🖳 crawford.jp; from ¥7500-12,000pp inc breakfast; ¥11,500-15,500pp half-board) is a Japanese-style country-house hotel and it offers a very comfortable overnight stay. No room is the same and each has a different view from the window. If you aren't on a half-board package you can order à la carte: steak or fish of the day (¥2000), or black pork hamburger set (¥1800). Even the humble hamburger is served in silver foil to keep it warm and moist. The restaurant is open 5.30-9pm but last orders are at 7.30pm.

HOKKAIDO

The hotel is named after Joseph Crawford, a professor of engineering who introduced the technology used on American railways to Hokkaido in the 19th century. The trains run nearby but it is lovely to wake up to the sight of trees rather than concrete. If you are already booked they will collect you from the station; the ticket collector will call the hotel for you. Alternatively, it is a relatively short walk. Turn left out of the station, follow the road round till you reach the first turning on the left. Cross over the railway tracks and then also turn left. The hotel (and the TIC) can give you a map showing paths to walk on and viewing spots. Make sure you start the walk around the lake from the turning by the railway crossing rather than the road to the left as you leave the hotel's driveway.

For proximity to the station (right next to it), ***Station Hotel Asahiya*** (☎ 0138-67 2654, 🖳 business2.plala.or.jp/asahiya; from ¥6300/S, ¥7600/Tw, more during the peak summer season) can't be beaten. It has a reasonable in-house restaurant.

As the train leaves Onuma-koen, the line passes between Lake Onuma (on the right) and the smaller Lake Konuma (on the left). It's a fleeting but superb last view of the two lakes. Soon enough, the line becomes enclosed by trees.

Fittingly, the next stop (not all limited expresses call here) is called **Mori (H62; 50km)**; Mori means forest. Just before the station the train passes right by the sea. Mori, despite its name, is actually situated on the coast. The Hakodate-Onuma SL runs between Hakodate and here in the spring (see box p73).

After leaving Mori the line begins to curve around Uchiura Bay. The track runs so close to the sea that you can see the different shades of blue in the water. Not all limited expresses stop at **Yakumo (H54; 81km)**. The train runs further from the sea along this stretch of the line but look out to the left for views of the rolling green hills that are always featured on Japanese TV adverts for Hokkaido milk.

Oshamambe (H47; 112km) Not all limited expresses stop here. Change here for the alternative route to Sapporo, via Niseko and Otaru on the Hakodate line (see below). Hakodate line trains depart from the same platform so transferring is easy, though you may have to wait a while.

For the continuation of the principal route to Sapporo, following the Muroran line, see p325.

Alternative route to Sapporo via Otaru
Oshamambe to Otaru The train from **Oshamambe (H47; 0km)** to Otaru (6-7/day; 198 mins) is a one-car, one-man train. If you don't already have a ticket (or pass) pick up a numbered ticket (the number shows which station you got on at and therefore enables the driver to work our the fare) from the front of the train as you embark. Even though this is a local line announcements are in English; by the end of the journey you will probably be sick of hearing 'This is the local train bound for Otaru. This is a one-man train. Please move forward.'

One of the great features of this journey is that there are few tunnels, at least in the early section. Most of the time you can gaze out at the rural scenery as you gradually get closer to the tree-covered hills and the mountains.

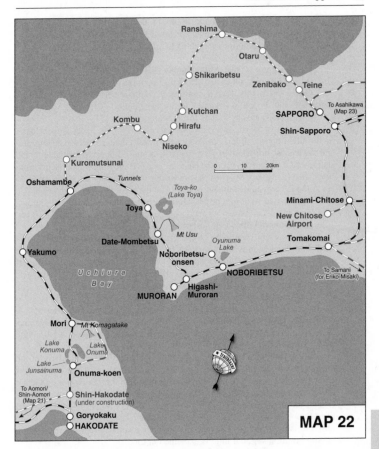

MAP 22

At **Kuromatsunai (S30; 20km)** there is a small ski slope on the right – a sign of the greater things to come.

Just before **Kombu (S26; 58km)**, an onsen resort, you get the first glimpse of snow-clad **Mt Yotei (1898m)**, which resembles Mt Fuji, to the left. It's a long-extinct volcano and the reason for the many hot springs in the area.

Even if you aren't listening to the train announcements, you'll know when you've reached **Niseko (S25; 67.3km)** because of the amazing yellow bridge over its railway track. A year-round activity resort, Niseko has well-developed winter sport facilities and in summer offers white-water rafting, mountain biking, rock-climbing, canyoning and trekking (from around ¥6000/half-day). Contact Niseko Adventure Centre (🖳 nac-web.com), Niseko Hanazono Resort (🖳 hanazononiseko.com/en), or Niseko Outdoor Adventure Sports Club (🖳 noasc.com).

Soon after leaving **Hirafu (S24; 74.3km**; 🖳 www.grand-hirafu.jp), another major ski resort, the urban spread of **Kutchan (81km; S23;** 🖳 www. town.kutchan.hokkaido.jp/town) starts to appear. However, you also get compensatory views of Mt Yotei.

By the time you reach **Shikaribetsu (S20; 111.8km)** the hills are behind you and after **Ranshima (S17; 125.6km)** the train runs near the coast.

Otaru (S15; 140.2km) is a laidback, compact port town surrounded by mountains and the sea. It is known for its stone buildings (former warehouses and banks) and canals as well as for its seafood.

To the right as you exit the ticket gates is a Twinkle Plaza Travel Center (daily 10am-6pm), Midori-no-Madoguchi ticket counter (daily 6.30am-7pm) and the **tourist information** desk (daily 9am-6pm). Maps are available by the station exit if you arrive when the latter is closed. There is also a tourist information office (daily 9am-6pm) on Sakura Bridge in the canal area. There are lockers to the left as you exit the ticket gates and the bus stands are to the right.

It is easy to walk around but **Otaru Stroller Bus** (1-3/hr; ¥210/journey, ¥750/day inc local buses) operates on several routes to the main sights. Alternatively, a rickshaw tour costs from ¥2000 (10 mins) for two people.

Rail fans will want to go **Otaru Transportation Museum** (Otaru Kotsu Kinenkan; Wed-Mon 9.30am-5pm; ¥400, ¥500 for both sites), which is spread over two sites. The Honkan (Railway Museum) is built on the site of Hokkaido's first railway station and is filled with locomotives and carriages. There's even the chance to take a 400m ride on a steam locomotive from one end of the grounds to the other. To reach the museum take a bus from stop No 6 outside Otaru station to Kotsu Kinenkan-mae. The **Canal Building** branch (Ungakan; same hours; ¥300) explores the history of Otaru, the indigenous Ainu people, and the conservation movement in Otaru. It is about a 10-minute walk from the Honkan and is worth allocating some time for.

The **canal area** is lovely at any time of the day but particularly in the evening when the old-fashioned gas lamps are lit. Most of the warehouses have now been converted into shops, restaurants and museums, among them a museum of Venetian Art (daily 8.45am-6pm; ¥700), a Music Box museum (daily 9am-6pm, to 7pm Fri & Sat in summer) and a Bank of Japan museum (Tue-Sun 9.30am-5pm; free) as well as some glass workshops. The Bank museum is interesting in that you can have the chance to feel the weight of a hundred million yen, but little is explained in English.

Conveniently, **Otaru Yuki Akari-no-Michi** (Snow Light Path Festival) is held at the same time as the Sapporo Snow Festival (see p353). Lanterns are lit in two particular parts of town and snow sculptures created (and also illuminated) but everywhere is atmospheric because of the snowy streets.

Dormy Inn Premium Otaru (0134-21 5489, 🖳 www.hotespa.net/busi ness; ¥9500/S, ¥12,000/D, ¥16,000/Tw; ¥1500 breakfast) is on the left at the top of the road down to the canals and sea from the station. It has comfortable rooms as well as an onsen and sauna. *Otaru Green Hotel* (☎ 0134-33 0333; 🖳 www.otaru-green.co.jp/e; Western-style rooms from ¥4200/S, ¥6800/Tw, ¥5900/D; Japanese-style rooms from ¥2800pp; annex ¥3200/S or T, ¥5400/Tr; breakfast ¥800) is further down the road towards the sea. Rooms in the main building, which is set back from the road, are compact but have LAN cables. Register here even if you are staying in the Annex.

Hikari (daily 10.30am-6pm) is an Aladdin's Cave of a coffee shop dating from 1933; it is full of lamps, model ships and tea cups and is furnished with dark wood and velvet-covered seats. A coffee-and-cake set costs ¥680. To reach it walk down the road from the station towards the canal and the sea and turn right when you reach the covered arcade, Miyako-dori. Hikari is the brick building on your left as you walk along.

Sushi fans should head to Sushi-ya-dori (**Sushi St**). To reach it from here continue along Miyako-dori until you reach a crossroads with the main road, Asakusa-dori. Turn left here and then turn right into Sun Mall Ichibangai (another covered arcade. Walk to the end and turn left into Sushi St.

Otaru to Sapporo If you aren't stopping in Otaru you will need to change train here. There are both local and semi-rapid services between Otaru and Sapporo (at least 3/hr); some of the latter continue to Shin-Chitose Airport (2/hr).

Try to sit on the left for the best views of the sea and the coastline, though after **Zenibako (S11; 155.8km)** the line goes inland and the scenery becomes industrial and urban.

At **Teine (S07; 163.4km)** there are views to the hills on the right if you look over the buildings but otherwise there is little of interest until you reach **Sapporo (01; 174km)**, see pp348-54.

There is a long section of tunnels between Oshamambe and Toya, the next major stop.

Toya (H41; 154km) Not all limited expresses stop here. There are lockers at the station.

The attraction hereabouts is **Toya-ko** (Lake Toya; 🖳 www.laketoya.com), a caldera lake formed by the collapse of a mountain following volcanic activity thousands of years ago. However, it lacks the charm of Onuma-koen (see pp321-2) as huge lakeside hotels spoil the scenery and the atmosphere. That said, the lake itself is worth a look and onsen fans might enjoy an afternoon wallowing in a hot spring or two in some of the larger resort hotels.

Turn right out of the station for buses to the lake (daily approx 1/hr; 17 mins; ¥320). **Toya-ko Visitor Center** is near Toya-ko-onsen Bus Terminal and in the same place as the **Volcano Science Museum** (9am-5pm; ¥600).

Politically minded travellers may like to go to the **G8 Hokkaido Toya-ko Summit Memorial Museum** (9am-5pm; ¥400) for a chance to see the round table the leaders sat at in 2008.

Only some limited expresses stop at **Date-Mombetsu (H38; 167km)**, after which it's coast then tunnels then industrial blot then **Higashi-Muroran (H32; 190km)**.

Noboribetsu (H28; 207km) Noboribetsu comes from the Ainu word 'Nupurupetsu', meaning 'a cloudy river tinged with white'. A bus ride away from the station is **Noboribetsu-onsen** (a hot-spring resort) that draws water from **Jigokudani (Hell Valley)**, the centre of which is a volcanic crater where steam rises from the earth. It was only in 1858, when a businessman who was mining sulphur realised there was money to be made from tourism, that the first public bath house was opened using hot water from the crater. Since then tourism has taken off and the resort is now full of concrete hotel blocks and tourist attractions. Despite this, Jigokudani is well worth seeing close up, as is bubbling **Oyunuma Lake**, and a visit here would not be complete without a trip to one of the hot springs in the resort.

From Noboribetsu station, Donan buses run up to the terminal in Noboribetsu-onsen (daily approx 1/hr; 15 mins; ¥330). There is a small tourist office here but if you prefer to keep going there are a couple more before you reach Jigokudani. All can provide a useful English map and guide to the area and advise on accommodation but cannot book it. The first you reach is **Noboribetsu Tourist Association** (🖥 www.noboribetsu-spa.jp; daily 9am-6pm), a couple of minutes up the main road on the left-hand side. Keep walking, past the hotels, until you reach Jigokudani.

In 1924 the area was designated 'Noboribetsu Primeval Forest', a fitting description for the haunting landscape. Though you aren't allowed to walk around Hell Valley (not that you'd want to with the bubbling and smoke rising from the ground), there is a short promenade offering a close-up view. A better walk takes you up into the hills above Hell Valley and down to the volcanic swamp that is Oyunuma Lake, where temperatures reach 130°C. Find the sign for 'Mountain-Ash Observatory' and walk up the path for 20 minutes to reach Oyunuma. Even in the rain the sight is impressive – it's magnificent in autumn.

Having seen the source there are plenty of opportunities to test out the water in one of the onsen hotels. The most popular baths, but also the most expensive (¥2000pp for non residents), are at *Daiichi Takimotokan* (🖥 www.takimoto kan.co.jp/english; daily 9am-5pm; from ¥15,000/S, ¥9150pp half-board), the highlight of which are several *rotemburo* (outdoor hot springs), which even have a drinks service – just pick up the phone in the booth here. Massage and beauty treatments are also available. This hotel is the last before Hell Valley.

Takimoto Inn (☎ 0143-84 2205, 🖥 www.takimotoinn.co.jp; half-board from ¥8550/S, ¥7150pp if sharing), which is right opposite, has none of the grandeur of its neighbour but provides good-value accommodation with free access to Daiichi's baths. To reach them cross the road (it is perfectly acceptable to do this in your yukata), go in the main entrance to the hotel and head left following the signs; it is a surprisingly long walk. There is also an onsen in the basement of the Inn, but no rotemburo. Some of the buses from Noboribetsu station stop right outside Takimoto Inn (and therefore opposite the Daiichi) so it is worth taking one of these to avoid the walk uphill from the bus terminal with heavy luggage.

A less elaborate but much better-value onsen is **Sagiriyu** (daily 7am-9.30pm; ¥390), the only municipal hot spring in the resort. Conveniently it's next door to the tourist office by the bus terminal. Look for the purple hanging curtain and wooden entrance.

Noboribetsu also has more than its fair share of tacky theme-park entertainments, for which there is a combination Noboribetsu Theme Park ticket (¥3300pp/2 parks, ¥4500pp/3 parks). At the station, you can't miss the enormous and kitsch European-style castle; this is **Noboribetsu Marine Park Nixe**

(🖥 www.nixe.co.jp/main.htm; daily 9am-5pm; ¥2400), a large aquarium with dolphin, sea lion and penguin shows plus an aqua tunnel.

Noboribetsu Date Jidaimura (☎ 0143-83 3311, 🖥 www.edo-trip.jp/en; Apr-Oct daily 9am-5pm, Nov-Mar 9am-4pm; ¥2900) is a reproduction Edo-period village. Of particular interest is the Ninja show involving a ninja sword duel, secret doors, a roped descent from the ceiling and a rather unconvincing earthquake scene. In the 'Scary Cat' house you have to be careful of the cat; it appears behind secret panels, its giant furry paw descends from the ceiling and it even hides inside a giant bell ready to pounce! Beware of the cat! The bus from the station to Noboribetsu-onsen stops here (8 mins; ¥330).

Bear Park (Kuma Bokujo; 🖥 www.bearpark.jp; daily Apr-Jun 9am-5pm, Jun-Oct 8am-6pm, Oct-Apr 8.30am-4.30pm; ¥2520 inc ropeway) is home to about a hundred brown bears and three Asiatic black bears as well as a brown bear museum and a village that recreates the daily life of the Ainu. It's at the top of the ropeway (cable car; 7 mins) from Noboribetsu-onsen.

Tomakomai (H18; 248km) Tomakomai is a railway junction and port. About the only reason to stop here would be to transfer to the local Hidaka line, which runs south along the coast towards **Samani** (3-3½ hours), the nearest rail station to Erimo-misaki (Cape Erimo). Irregular buses run to the cape (60 mins; ¥1300) and on to Obihiro (see p338).

Minami-Chitose (H14; 275km) The penultimate limited express stop before Sapporo; change here for **Shin-Chitose (New Chitose) Airport station (AP15;** 🖥 www.new-chitose-airport.jp), three minutes away by local train. This is the nearest airport to Sapporo, handling both domestic and international flights.

Shin-Sapporo (H05; 308km) Some limited expresses make a brief stop here, but stay on the train until the Sapporo terminus.

Sapporo (01; 319km)   [see pp348-54]

SAPPORO TO ASAHIKAWA & ABASHIRI
[Map 23, p328; Map 24, p329; Table 17, p466]

Distances by JR from Sapporo. Fastest journey time to Asahikawa 80 minutes and from Asahikawa to Abashiri 3¾hours.

Note that all the trains on this route from Sapporo stop in Asahikawa but if continuing beyond that you will need to be on the Okhotsk LEX.

Sapporo (01; 0km) The views from the train are less than spectacular as far as **Iwamizawa (41km; A13)**, as it takes some time to leave Hokkaido's capital behind. From here on, the familiar wide green spaces start to open up once more. Some trains stop at **Bibai (A16; 46km)** and **Sunagawa (A20; 64km)**.

The landscape is briefly interrupted by the small city of **Takikawa (A21; 84km)**, known throughout Hokkaido for its extremely heavy snowfall.

About 10 minutes after leaving Takikawa, the train crosses Ishikari-gawa; beyond **Fukagawa (A24; 107km)** is a series of long tunnels.

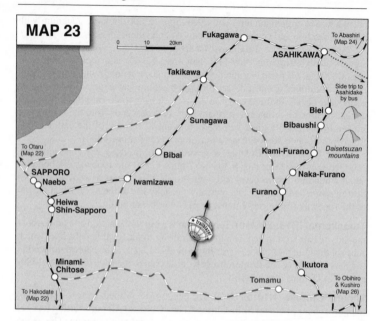

Asahikawa (A28; 137km)   [see pp357-60]

Asahikawa is an important junction station for lines north to Wakkanai, east to Abashiri and south to Obihiro and Kushiro.

For Abashiri continue on, or take, the Okhotsk LEX that runs along the JR Sekihoku line. It's worth making a seat reservation as there is only a limited number of carriages. All the clichés of Japan being a nation of no open space and houses packed together like rabbit hutches collapse on this stretch of the journey. The train travels slowly enough to see some of the tiny stations along the way.

Kamikawa (A43; 185km) Alight here for Sounkyo-onsen (see below).

Side trip by bus to Sounkyo-onsen

In addition to the many ryokan at Sounkyo-onsen (🖳 www.sounkyo.net) there is one **public bath house** (Kurodake no Yu). **Sounkyo Ropeway** (cable car; daily 9am-4pm, longer in peak periods; ¥1850 round trip) and then a chair lift (daily June to mid Oct and mid Nov to Apr; ¥600 round trip) lead to **Mt Kurodake** (1984m). The base of the ropeway is near the visitor centre.

Buses (11/day; 30 mins; ¥770) to the main resort area are timed to meet most trains; enquire at the bus ticket office to the right as you exit the station.

After Kamikawa the predominant scenery is forest rather than open space. The track becomes hemmed in by trees on both sides and there are some semi-tunnels (with windows). There's one long tunnel about 15 minutes before arriving at Shirataki but then the countryside starts to open up again.

Some limited expresses do not stop at **Shirataki (A45; 223km)**, but even when passing through you'll see that the station is supposed to recall the railway of yesteryear, with a clock tower topped by a weathercock.

Most limited expresses make a brief stop at **Maruseppu (A48; 242km)**.

Engaru (A50; 261km) used to be an important rail junction, with a line running up to Mombetsu on the east coast, but as with so many lines JR Hokkaido no longer thought it was profitable so closed it. The train waits a few minutes here as everyone turns their seats around so as to continue facing the direction of travel. If you are feeling hungry there is a soba restaurant in the station.

Shortly after leaving **Ikutahara (A53; 278km)** the train heads into the Jomon Tunnel. The tunnel is very short but achieved notoriety some years ago when human bones (see box below) were discovered nearby.

Rubeshibe (A56, 299km) is home to one of the world's largest cuckoo clocks. In 2006 the town merged to become part of the city of Kitami (see p330).

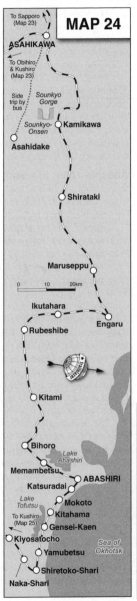

🏮 Human sacrifice?

It was once the practice in Japan, when a new bridge, tunnel or other major public works project was constructed, for an individual to be offered to the site as a human sacrifice.

One Hokkaido resident said that when she was six or seven, human bones were found along the railway line at the Jomon Tunnel. The story goes that, about 30 years before, a railwayman had been supervising the laying of additional track along the line. No doubt he had heard the stories concerning the ghosts that haunted the tunnel. Working alone late one evening he disappeared mysteriously; it was only years later that his skeleton was discovered near the track deep in the tunnel. Locals claim that he'd been pushed by a ghost into the path of an approaching freight train, a sacrifice required because none had been made after the construction of the tunnel.

The wide plains seen during the early part of this journey return, with fields on either side of the track.

During the last few kilometres before **Kitami (A60; 321.5km)**, the final major stop on the line to Abashiri, the surroundings get a little more built up (for Hokkaido) and there's a long tunnel.

Services then call at **Bihoro (A65; 346km)** and **Memambetsu (A67; 358km)**, which lies just at the edge of Lake Abashiri. From here, though the track looks as if it will run right by the lake, trees block out any view and it is only about four minutes before arriving in Abashiri that there is finally a glimpse (on the left) of the northern tip of the lake. Just in case you miss it, the conductor makes an announcement urging passengers to look out of the window and savour the fleeting view.

Abashiri (A69; 374.5km) Abashiri (⌨ www.abashiri.jp/tabinavi_en) is the terminus of the JR Sekihoku line from Asahikawa. In winter, people come here to see blocks of drift ice on the Sea of Okhotsk. Ornate, hand-crafted snow- and ice sculptures are a highlight of the **Drift Ice Festival** in February.

Abashiri station is small but has some **lockers** (all sizes, but only a few ¥500 ones) and a coffee shop, as well as a **tourist information office** (daily 9am-5pm) on your right as you leave the station.

The main sights are around Mt Tento (207m), nationally designated a place of scenic beauty; a bus (daily May to mid Jan; 1-2/hr between 9.30am and 4pm; ¥900 one-day pass) runs on a loop between them, departing from stop No 1, opposite the taxi rank in front of the station.

Taking the bus from Abashiri station, stop first at **Abashiri Prison Museum** (Hakubutsukan Abashiri Kangoku; ⌨ www.kangoku.jp/world; Apr-Oct 8am-6pm; Nov-Mar 9am-5pm; ¥1050), halfway up Mt Tento. Abashiri Prison was first built in the 1890s when Abashiri was a small, remote village. It was modernised in 1984 and the original cells and other buildings were relocated here. Today visitors are allowed to wander around the buildings, which include cell blocks, a court house and bath house, and get an idea of daily life for the prisoners and how tough it must have been, especially during the freezing winters.

The next stop on the bus route is **Okhotsk Ryu-Hyo (Drift Ice) Museum** (Apr-Oct 8am-6pm, Nov-Mar 9am-4.30pm, closed 29th Dec to 5th Jan; ¥520), which has a 'Drift Ice Experience Room', where lumps of ice are supposed to show what the Sea of Okhotsk is like in the dead of winter. Of more interest are the views of Lake Abashiri and the Sea of Okhotsk from the lookout points (Mt Tento Observatory) on the 3rd, 4th and 5th floors.

Next, pick up the bus or walk 800m to the **Hokkaido Museum of Northern Peoples** (Hoppou Minzoku Hakubutsukan; ⌨ hoppohm.org/english; Tue-Sun Jul-Sep 9am-5pm, Oct-Jun 9.30am-4.30pm; ¥450, ¥800 inc temporary exhibitions; English pamphlet available). This museum seems to attract fewer people, which is a pity since it's perhaps the best, with exhibits relating not just to the Ainu but to minorities across the northern hemisphere. The main hall displays everything from snow boots to a recreated winter home. TV screens show footage of reindeer herding and hunting for fish by cutting holes through the ice.

From 20th January to the first Sunday in April the bus also stops at the Aurora Terminal, from where the **Icebreaker Aurora** runs one-hour trips (🖳 ms-aurora.com/abashiri/en; 4-6/day; ¥3300) on the Sea of Okhotsk. 'Feeling the ice cracking beneath the ship's hull defies description,' reads the publicity. This trip is by far the best reason for paying a visit to Abashiri in the dead of winter.

There are two business hotels near the station: ***Toyoko Inn Okhotsk Abashiri Ekimae*** (☎ 0152-45 1043, 🖳 www.toyoko-inn.com; from ¥5480/S, ¥6980/D, ¥7480/Tw, inc breakfast) is on the left as you leave the station.

Alternatively, and just opposite the station, is ***Route Inn Abashiri Ekimae*** (☎ 0152-44 5511, 🖳 route-inn.co.jp/english/pref/hokkaido.html#abashiri; ¥5500/S, ¥9000/D or Tw, inc breakfast).

To reach ***Abashiri Ryuhyo-no-oka Youth Hostel*** (☎/📄 0152-43 8558, 🖳 www.youthhostel.or.jp/English/e_ryuhyo.htm, 🖳 ikeda@seagreen.ocn.ne.jp; ¥3250pp + ¥600 for non members, breakfast ¥630, evening meal ¥1050, or special meal ¥1500; 28 beds), take the bus to Okhotsk Aquarium, from stop No 1 in front of Abashiri station, and get off at the Meiji Iriguchi stop. Look for the youth hostel sign which points you up a road off the main road. Follow this road up for about seven minutes. If booked a pick-up service is available from the station or the bus stop. The hostel is a small, clean friendly place with mostly bunk-bed dorms and a good view over the Okhotsk Sea from outside. Cakes and tea are served at 8pm for anyone who wants to socialise.

ABASHIRI TO KUSHIRO [Map 24, p329; Map 25, p333; Table 18, p466]

Distances by JR from Abashiri. Fastest journey time: 3¾ hours.

Abashiri (A69; 0km) This route has some of the most stunning scenery but is not for anyone in a hurry. Only local trains run along the single-track Senmo line that first heads east along the coast as far as Shiretoko-Shari, before turning south-west through Akan National Park towards the port town of Kushiro.

Once the train has emerged from the short tunnel just after **Katsuradai (B79; 1.5km)** there are great views out to the left of the Sea of Okhotsk.

Mokoto (B77; 9km) is the starting point for an interesting transport experiment (see box below). The station has a coffee shop with views out to sea, though the one at the next stop, Kitahama, is even better.

🚏 Is it a bus? Is it a train?
How about this for a novel form of transport? JR Hokkaido is trialling the first 'Dual Mode Vehicle' (DMV), a bus-like contraption which can operate on roads using conventional tyres but which, at the flick of a switch, turns into a train running on tracks with steel and rubber wheels.

The DMV is being tested along the Senmo line between Mokoto (B77) and Hamako-Shimizu, going one way on rail track (11km) and then returning as a bus on the road (21km). If it proves successful it could serve as a model for other parts of the island. But it's too early to say whether the DMV represents the future of public transport or whether it's just a quirky here-today-gone-tomorrow invention.

HOKKAIDO

Kitahama (B76; 12km) Although only a few minutes out of Abashiri, Kitahama really is worth stopping at. There can be no better location to have a coffee than here, facing the sea, especially in winter when the water becomes a sheet of ice. The old railway seats and battered suitcase make this the ultimate *café* (Wed-Mon 10am to around 8pm) for passing travellers. The menu includes toast, pasta, and a daily set lunch. The station's waiting room is worth seeing as it is covered with old railway tickets and business cards left by travellers.

Bird-watchers may want to stop here as it is only a 10-minute walk to **Lake Tofutsu** in Shirotori Park (daily 9am-5pm). The lake is a popular bird-watching spot in the winter months (particularly October to November and March to April) when the whooper swan and grey heron are here.

After Kitahama, look out to the right for views of Lake Tofutsu (see above). **Gensei-Kaen (B75; 17km)** station is another popular spot for viewing the lake.

If it's not too foggy you should be able to see Shiretoko Peninsula on the left in the distance, though the view is blocked in places by pine trees.

After **Yamubetsu (B73; 26km)** there's a long stretch without any stations.

Shiretoko-Shari (B72; 37km) This is the nearest station to the **Shiretoko Peninsula and Shiretoko National Park**.

Side trip by bus to Utoro for Shiretoko Peninsula/National Park

Shiretoko Peninsula/National Park is considered an idyllic retreat from the man-made world, an unspoilt territory inhabited by wild eagles, brown bears and the world's largest owls; for this reason it was declared a UNESCO World Heritage site in 2005.

Turn left as you exit the station for Shari bus terminal (under the archway that reads 'Welcome to Shiretoko'). Most buses run from here along the peninsula to the bus terminal at **Utoro** (Apr-Oct 8/day, Nov-Mar 5/day; 50 mins; ¥1490, Shiretoko round-trip ticket ¥1800), from where it's about a 10-minute walk to the ferry terminal. The longest **ferry ride** (🖥 ms-aurora.com/shiretoko/en; June-Sep 1/day; 3¾hrs; ¥6500) goes all the way to Cape Shiretoko (inaccessible by road) and back. The Mt Io option (late Apr to late Oct 4-6/day; 90 mins; ¥3100) doesn't go as far.

Note that in winter many of the roads beyond Utoro into the national park are closed because of the amount of snow.

Naka-Shari (B71; 42km) Just after leaving the station a large and unsightly factory looms into view on the right-hand side. This eyesore aside, the journey from here is one of the best in Hokkaido. This is the only line on the island that actually runs through a national park, between Lake Kusshbaro and the smaller but more mysterious Lake Mashu; for both see p334. Neither lake is visible from the train, though there are good access points to both along the way.

After **Kiyosatocho (B69; 49km)** look out for the 1545m **Mt Shari** which, unless the summit is covered in cloud, should be visible out to the left.

There's a long stretch between **Satsuru (B68; 57km)** and **Midori (B67; 65km)** where trees very definitely outnumber people. Midori ('Green') station has a brown roof and blue trees painted on the side, and is the last stop before

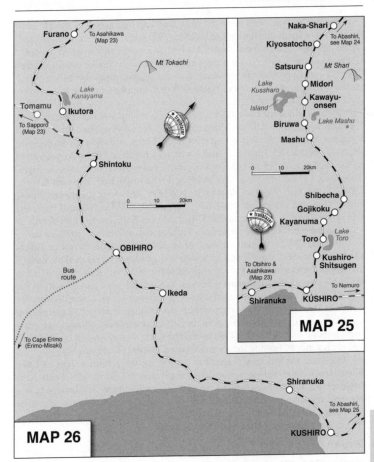

Kawayu-onsen in Akan National Park. The whole area, with the track surrounded by forest, is so lush and green that it is difficult to tell exactly where the national park officially begins. But about 10 minutes after leaving Midori the train passes through a tunnel. Emerging from this you are officially in Akan National Park.

Kawayu-onsen (B66; 80km) Built in 1936, the old station master's office has been turned into an excellent *café*. It's tempting to while away an afternoon right here as there is also a **footbath** at the station, but with such magnificent scenery so close to hand it would be a shame to miss out. **Cycles** can be rented for free (ask at the café) but they must be returned by 5pm. The station has no lockers but you should be able to leave stuff at the café.

HOKKAIDO

From the station, head up to the main road and turn right. Go straight until the first set of lights and turn left onto Route 391. A few minutes down this road, on the left-hand side, is the stunning **Mt Iwo**, still very much an active volcano. If you don't see it first, you'll almost certainly smell it. Smoke pours out from different places around the mountain and the sulphur turns the rock a bright yellow. Most people take a brief closer look at the smoke then rush back, covering their mouths and noses.

Continue along the main road for another 2km until you reach the centre of Kawayu-onsen, known for its 'diamond dust'. This is crystallised water caused by steam from when the hot spring river freezes in the air when the temperature decreases below -20° Celsius (usually seen mid Jan to late Feb). As you arrive in the centre, look for an orange Seicomart convenience store on your right. Then look on the left for a sign pointing to **Kawayu Eco Museum Center** (EMC; Thur-Tue May-Oct 8am-5pm, Nov-Apr 9am-4pm; free); this shows films of the area's flora and fauna, has scale models of Akan National Park, and free tea and coffee. Ask for the *Let's Walk Around EMC* leaflet, with details of walks in the woods around the centre. There is also a free foot bath near here.

Near the EMC is a small museum dedicated to local **sumo wrestler Taiho-san** (daily Oct-May 9am-5pm, Jun-Sep to 9pm; ¥400), who reached the rank of *yokozona*, sumo's highest, and claimed 32 tournament victories, twice winning six consecutive titles. Taiho-san was born in Sakhalin (now part of Russia) but moved to Hokkaido and attended school in Kawayu-onsen before leaving for Tokyo at 16 to begin his sumo apprenticeship. On display are all 32 tournament trophies won up to his retirement in 1971, along with photos and other memorabilia, including one of his oversized suits. Kawayu-onsen continues its link with sumo by hosting the annual Women's Sumo Championship.

Energetic cyclists might consider continuing for a further 3km to **Lake Kussharo**, where Kussie – the local equivalent of Scotland's Loch Ness Monster – is said to live. Around the lake are some outdoor hot springs (a few are free) and summer activities on the lake include canoeing and kayaking. After the cycle tour head back to the station in time to pick up a train to Mashu, as Mashu-ko Youth Hostel (see opposite) is a good place to stay.

Biruwa (B65; 87km) This is more of a portakabin than a station.

Mashu (B64; 96km) A small station with a few ¥300 lockers by the exit and a helpful **tourist information office** (🖳 www.masyuko.or.jp/pc/english; summer only daily 9am-5pm). There is a good **foot bath** on your left as you emerge from the station.

Mashu-ko (Lake Mashu), 20km in circumference, is known as the lake 'of mystery and illusion'. No river flows in or out of it and it is completely surrounded by trees. The only way of seeing the lake is from elevated observation points, but the water is almost always shrouded in a blanket of fog. It's almost as if this mystical natural phenomenon becomes disgruntled by the unwanted attention, so cloaks itself in a mist to avoid the gaze of tourists. Akan Bus (🖳 www.akanbus.co.jp; early Apr to early Oct; ¥540; 20 mins; infrequent services)

⛩ **SL Fuyu-no-Shitsugen**
In the winter months the SL Fuyu-no-Shitsugen (daily mid Jan to mid Mar; 1/ day; free with a JR rail pass but seat reservation essential) operates between Kushiro and Shibecha (some services continue to Kawayu-onsen). The journey through the Kushiro Wetland is worth doing even if you are not a steam fan.

Joe Woodruff (UK) 'saw many a herd of deer, a couple of Hokkaido foxes, assorted birds of prey and a few of the famous Kushiro red-crested cranes. Quite a few of the stations that the SL stops at have foot onsen that you can dip into while waiting for the train to start on its way again. The inside of the carriages is quite interesting too – there's a little coal brazier in each carriage on which people were roasting chestnuts, potatoes and squid during our trip.'

operates from JR Mashu to the two observation decks. If the weather is good take the bus to the less-crowded second observation platform. Another option is to hitch (see p45).

Mashu-ko Youth Hostel (☎ 015-482 3098, 🖥 www.masyuko.co.jp; dorm ¥3000-3500pp, from ¥4500/S, from ¥3700/¥3400/3000pp for 2/3/4 sharing, plus ¥500pp for non-YHA members; closed 1st-20th Dec), situated about halfway to the lake, is an ideal place to stay. Call ahead for a pick-up from the station. Accommodation is Western style and there is a coin laundry and internet access (¥10 per minute). Hostel staff organise summer and winter activities including cross-country skiing and canoeing.

Meals (dinner from ¥1260, breakfast ¥760) are served in *The Great Bear* restaurant (🖥 www2.ocn.ne.jp/~gbear) next to the hostel.

From Mashu-ko Youth Hostel, it's a three-hour walk up the road that runs outside the hostel to the lake but it should be easy to hitch a lift with a fellow hosteller. Alternatively take the bus (see opposite).

Mashu station lies just outside Akan National Park but the views from the train remain tremendous, with long gaps between isolated stations. The next major sight is **Kushiro-Shitsugen National Park**; it's a good idea to plan to spend a whole day on the journey between Mashu and the terminus at Kushiro.

Shibecha (B61; 121km) At the far end of the platform is a monument to SL C11 171, which now only runs along this line in winter (see box above); you can ring the bell in memory of it.

Gojikoku (B60; 130km) This station is on the edge of Kushiro-Shitsugen National Park. The park is mostly marshland, inhabited by Japanese cranes. Though not as well known as Akan National Park it still has some beautiful scenery.

Kayanuma (B59; 135km) During the mating season, between January and March, Japanese cranes perform elaborate mating dances on the snow-covered ground near the station.

Beyond Kayanuma there's a long stretch of track through marshland, so look out for swamp marshes on both sides.

Toro (B58; 142km) Bikes can be rented (¥700/hour) from the *Norroko & 8001* coffee bar in this station. Ask the owner for a map of the area, which includes Lake Toro, the major lake in the marshlands area.

Two minutes on foot from the station is *Kushiro Shitsugen Toro Youth Hostel* (☎ 0154-87 2510, 🖳 www.youthhostel.or.jp/English/e_toro.htm; ¥3360pp plus ¥600 for non-members; breakfast ¥360, dinner ¥1050). It's a homely place with 14 beds, and a good base for exploring the area and bird-watching.

Kushiro-Shitsugen (B56; 152km) All the stations along this stretch of the line are tiny wooden buildings. There are plenty of hiking opportunities around Kushiro-Shitsugen. Views from the train remain impressive until about 10 minutes before Kushiro, where modern life begins to encroach.

Kushiro (K53; 169km) Kushiro is the terminus for the Senmo line from Abashiri and also a stop on the Nemuro line that runs east to Nemuro (see opposite) and west to Obihiro and beyond. Facing the Pacific Ocean, Kushiro is the most easterly city in Japan.

Turn left after the ticket barrier to find lockers (all sizes) and a bakery/café. The staff at the **tourist information booth** (🖳 www.kushiro-kankou.or.jp/english); daily 9am-5.30pm) in the station do not speak English. The horrendously kitsch chapel that sits incongruously outside the station is a fake, rented by couples for a white wedding. Opposite it is an excellent *noodle shop* (under ¥600).

Kushiro was the first station in Japan to open a **Station Museum** (Tue-Sun 10am-5pm; ¥100), which displays the work of local artist Eimatsu Sasaki.

Kushiro City Museum (Tue-Sun 9.30am-5pm; ¥360) is 15 minutes by bus from the station. Here you can get an overview of the city and the Kushiro-Shitsugen marshland you have just travelled through. There are also exhibitions on Ainu traditions and on the Japanese crane (the feathered variety). Several buses go to the museum from the bus terminal to the left as you exit the station. Get off at Kagaku-kan-dori.

Locals often claim that the sunset over the harbour is one of the world's top three sunsets. However, a far nicer place to watch this – and some sunsets are spectacular – is from the **onsen** at Hotel Paco (see below; ¥700 inc towel and yukata). In addition to the selection of baths, there is a rotemburo which faces Kushiro river and offers good views up to the sea and also features a couple of shallow bed-baths that you lie in. Massages are also available. Hotel Paco is on the edge of the entertainment district, Suehiro, next to Nusamai Bridge; it is about a nine-minute walk from the station.

Tokyu Inn (☎ 0154-22 0109, 🖳 www.kushiro-i.tokyuhotels.co.jp/ja; from ¥6600/S, ¥12,000/Tw, ¥12,600/D, breakfast ¥1000) is just to the left across the street as you leave the station.

Hotel Paco (☎ 0154-23 8585; 🖳 www.paco.co.jp/kushiro; from ¥5580/S, ¥8625/D, ¥9380/Tw, ¥13,200/Tr, breakfast ¥1050) is good and guests have free access to the onsen (see above).

ANA Hotel Kushiro (☎ 0154-31 4111, 🖳 www.anahotelkushiro.jp; ¥9500/S, ¥19,000/Tw, ¥16,000/D), directly across the street from MOO, offers the most upmarket accommodation in town. The best budget choice is the youth-hostel at Toro (see opposite).

Kushiro is known for its soba shops, which serve **green soba**. The best are called Azumaya 東家 and usually have big white signs with 東 painted on their traditional facades. To call themselves an Azumaya soba shop, the chefs must have trained at the original restaurant, which is near Harutori Lake. The restaurant is relatively ancient for Hokkaido, having been established over 100 years ago, and Emperor Hirohito once ate there. It also has a lovely bamboo garden. *Nusamai Azumaya* (daily 11am-7pm), a small place across Nusamai Bridge, is not much to look at inside but the quality of the noodles (zarusoba ¥650) is spectacular; their tempura is also excellent.

Fifteen minutes down the main road that leads from the station is **Fisherman's Wharf**, a large waterside shopping and restaurant complex popularly known as MOO. In summer (end of May to end Oct) a big marquée is set up along the riverside here for *robatayaki*. Joe Woodruff (UK) says: 'It's a great experience – you buy a set of tickets at the till as you come in, then find a seat at one of the charcoal barbecues. There are about five stalls, all selling incredibly fresh seafood and meat, with a good selection of vegetables too. Once you've handed over your tickets you take the food over to your barbecue and cook it to your liking, although the wandering waiters will always give you a hand with anything if you need it.'

Side trip to Nemuro, the easternmost tip of Japan
From Kushiro JR Nemuro line extends east to its terminus in Nemuro (⌨ www.nemuro-kankou.com). Nemuro and the surrounding area is known for its delicious seafood, variety of fauna, and for the view of the Habomai Islands, currently disputed territory with Russia. The section of line between Monshizu and Itoizawa is great for seeing the marshland.

Inspired by the many footpaths in the UK, Nemuro has set up its own network. The best access point for these is **Attoko station** (7/day; 90-105 mins). For further details visit ⌨ www.nemuro-foottourism.com.

Trains to Nemuro (7/day) take just over two hours; it's then a further 40 minutes by bus (8/day; ¥1040 one-way) to Cape Nosappu (Nosappu-misaki).

KUSHIRO TO SAPPORO (OR ASAHIKAWA)

Distances by JR from Kushiro. Fastest journey time: 4 hours.

Kushiro to Shintoku   [Map 26, p333; Table 19, p466]

Kushiro (K53; 0km) Pick up the Super Ozora LEX.

There are occasional glimpses of the Pacific Ocean during the first part of the journey. Some trains stop at **Shiranuka (27km)**.

Ikeda (K36; 104km) The first major stop after Kushiro. Joe Woodruff (UK) says: 'Ikeda is famous (in Hokkaido anyway!) for its wine and dairy products and is a nice place to stop in the summer for a few hours. The landscape around the town is Hokkaido down to a tee – wide plains filled with fields and farms, and backed by dramatic mountains. The town is home to **Ikeda Wine Castle**,

HOKKAIDO

where you can sample some of the local tipple. It is not the best and there's not much to the "castle", but it might be worth a quick visit as it's very close to the station. The nicest thing to do in Ikeda, though, is to take a walk alongside the fields to **Happiness Dairy**, which sells excellent ice-cream and cheese made from Tokachi milk. There are a few strange ice-cream flavours which are surprisingly good – the pumpkin and potato flavours were delicious.'

Five or six minutes after leaving Ikeda, the train crosses Tokachi-gawa. Look out for cows – a rare sight – on this part of the journey.

Obihiro (K31; 128km) The Hidaka mountains lie to the south and west of Obihiro. There is a **tourist information office** (🖳 www.obikan.jp/lang/english) on the 2nd floor of the Esta East building in the station, but there is little of interest in Obihiro itself – other than the chance to see a unique version of horse-racing (see box below).

There are two hotels very close to the station. *JR Inn Obihiro* (☎ 0155-28 5600, 🖳 www.jr-inn.jp/obihiro/en; from ¥4000/S, ¥5500/D, ¥6500/Tw) is to the left from the north exit of the station. There is a common bath as well as a lounge area, and you can choose from a wide range of pillows at the Pillow Department if you don't like the one provided in your room. The upmarket *Hotel Nikko Northland Obihiro* (☎ 0155-24 1234, 🖳 www.jrhotels.co.jp/obi hiro/english; ¥13,000/S, ¥22,000/Tw, ¥24,000/D; small discount for rail-pass holders) is right outside the south exit of the station.

Obihiro is known for *butadon* (pork on rice, eaten in a bowl). The dish originated here and lots of restaurants serve it. It's definitely worth checking out the atmospheric *Kita no Yatai* (approx 6pm to midnight), a small alleyway full of superb tiny restaurant-stalls serving traditional Japanese, Korean, Chinese and European food. Each place seats only a few people. The alleyway is about five minutes' walk from the north exit side of the station.

Side trip by bus to Cape Erimo
Obihiro is a distant access point for Cape Erimo (Erimo-misaki), the southern-most point on Hokkaido. The cape is at the base of the Hidaka mountains, known as the backbone of Hokkaido; the cliffs here are about 60 metres high and a lot of seals can be seen from the shore. Be prepared though; it is one of the windiest places in Japan.

Tokachi buses run from the bus terminal outside Obihiro station to Hiroo (two hours; ¥1830), part of the way along the coast to the cape. From Hiroo, a

🏇 Ban'ei racing – with 'draft' horses
Ban'ei Tokachi Obihiro Horse-Race Track (🖳 www.banei-keiba.or.jp; Sat, Sun & Mon from 9.40am, first race 11am; ¥100), in Obihiro, is the only place in the world where you can watch 'draft' horses (like carthorses) racing. The horses are twice the size of thoroughbreds and they race (pulling a weighted sled) on a straight 200m track which has two small hills as obstacles. Races are held throughout the year, even in the snow and at night-time. Success depends on the strength of the horse but also the skill of the 'jockey'. The stadium is about a 15-minute walk from the station.

JR bus runs down to Erimo-misaki (2-4/day; 60 mins; ¥1510) and then to Erimo town. The same bus continues around the cape up to Samani where you can pick up a local train on the JR Samani line that takes three hours to reach Tomakomai (see p327).

Shintoku (K23; 172km) The town of Shintoku is known for buckwheat soba (noodles) and you'll find buckwheat ice cream, buckwheat tea as well as buckwheat soba lunch deals in some of the restaurants.

Shintoku is also at the junction of two lines: to continue to Sapporo stay on the Super Ozora LEX, which travels west along the Sekisho line to **Tomamu (K22; 206km)**, **Shin-Yubari (K20; 261km)**, **Minami-Chitose (H14; 304.5km)** and **Sapporo (01; 348.5km)**, Hokkaido's capital. The section of line between Tomamu and Shin-Yubari is great in the autumn months.

For Asahikawa, change to a local train and continue along the Nemuro line to Furano, as described below, where you'll then need to change again.

▲ Shintoku to Asahikawa
[Map 26, p333; Map 23, p328; Tables 20 & 21, pp466-7]
Stations along this line are spread out and there's a whole series of tunnels, one of the longest being about 25 minutes after leaving Shintoku.

Ikutora (T36; 210km) Ikutora station was the setting for the movie *Poppoya*, a nostalgic story of a stationmaster who loses his young daughter, which grossed at least ¥3 billion at the box office. 'Poppoya' means railroad workers, while 'poppo' is the sound of a steam locomotive's whistle.

After leaving Ikutora, the train runs past **Lake Kanayama** on the right-hand side. The track then crosses the lake before entering a tunnel. After this, it's a pleasant ride through the hills and plains to Furano.

Furano (T30; 254km) Furano is a junction station for the JR Nemuro Line to Shintoku and the JR Furano Line to Asahikawa.

Known for its powder snow in winter (late November to early May; 🖥 www.skifurano.com) and its fields of lavender (see p340) in summer, Furano is one of the most popular tourist resorts in Hokkaido. It feels a little like the south of France and is probably of more interest to the domestic tourist.

There are lockers to the left of the station exit and a soba/udon counter (¥300-400). On the 2nd floor of the white building across the street from the station is **Furano Information Center** (🖥 www.furano-kankou.com; daily 9am-6pm); staff can provide information about the area and accommodation.

The rooms at *Sumire Inn* (☎ 0167-23 4767, 🖥 www4.plala.or.jp/furano-sumire; from ¥3800pp room only, ¥6000pp half-board; ¥300 for heater in winter) may look a bit old and tired but all the facilities are modern – there is even a LAN cable in the rooms; the owner is friendly and keeps cats.

For more upmarket accommodation try *Natulux Hotel* (🖥 www.natulux.com/en; from ¥12,600/S, ¥18,900/D, ¥19,950/Tw; breakfast ¥1260; good-value packages available). The hotel, to the right as you leave the station, has a relaxation spa (guests 5-8.30am & 11am-midnight; non-residents 11am-11pm, ¥630).

HOKKAIDO

Yamadori (11am-3pm & 5-10pm) on the right as you walk to Sumire Inn, serves *yakiniku*. You cook your own meat (pork from ¥600) and vegetables (from ¥420) on a gas charcoal burner. They also do a Furano Cheese fondue (¥1680). *Furano Burger* (🖥 www.furanoburger.com; summer daily 11am-7pm, winter to 5pm though occasionally closed) is near Torinuma Park and is best reached by taxi from the station. It is well known and comes highly recommended for its burgers.

Lavender is big business in Furano; lavender ice-cream is available nearly everywhere and even the JR station has its name painted in purple above the entrance. The main attractions are lavender fields, dairy farms and cheesemaking factories. The official **lavender-viewing season** is June to August; if visiting at this time ensure you have booked accommodation well in advance. During this period the Furano Biei Norokko train (3/day) stops at Lavender Batake, a seasonally constructed station, and it is a short walk from there to Farm Tomita, one of the many lavender farms in the area. JR Hokkaido also operates various Twinkle Bus sightseeing routes (seat reservations essential) from Furano and Biei stations; see the JR Hokkaido website for details.

▲ Transfer here to another local train along the Furano line towards Asahikawa.

Naka-Furano (F42; 262km) The 15-bed *Furano Youth Hostel* (☎/🖨 0167-44 4441, 🖥 www4.ocn.ne.jp/~furanoyh; dorms ¥3360pp; rooms Oct to late Jun: ¥5460/4410/4060pp for 1/2/3 sharing) is six minutes on foot behind the station here. A simple breakfast and supper are included in the rate.

After Naka-Furano, on your left are low hills and fields while in the distance to the right are the more impressive peaks of the Daisetsuzan mountains.

Kami-Furano (F39; 269km) The main reason to stop here, other than in the summer to visit the lavender and flower farms and for the Lavender and Fireworks Festival in July, is to go to one of the hot springs (see below) in Daisetsuzan National Park. For further information visit 🖥 www.kamifurano.jp.

Side trip by bus to Fukiage-onsen & Tokachi-dake-onsen
Kami-Furano Bus goes as far as **Tokachi-dake-onsen** (the stop is called Ryo-unkaku; 3/day; 46 mins; ¥500), but it's better to get off earlier at **Fukiage-onsen** (33 mins; ¥500). This is a completely natural (wild) hot spring where bathing is mixed and there are no admission fees. It's just there in the open for anybody to take a dip.

If mixed bathing in the wild is not your thing, just down the road is *Fukiage-onsen-no-Hakuginso* (☎ 0167-45 4126, 🖥 www.navi-kita.net/shisetsu/hakugin; 10am-10pm; ¥600; no English spoken), with a variety of segregated baths at different temperatures as well as a sauna and rotemburo affording views over the mountains. Buy a ticket from the vending machine in the entrance lobby.

If you fancy a night in the mountains you can stay here, either in a tatami mat room or in bunk-bed dorms (from ¥2600pp). Snacks are available but meals are not provided so bring food with you – there are cooking facilities (nominal charge). Camping is available in the summer.

Bibaushi (F38; 278km) There are opportunities here for a wide variety of outdoor sports. Guide no Yamagoya (☎ 0166-95 2277, 🖥 www.yamagoya.jp; daily May-Nov from 8am but closed in rain), in the wooden building across the street from the station, is an outdoor pursuits centre which arranges canoeing and rafting trips, and guided mountain-bike rides out to Daisetsuzan National Park. From December to March the main activity is cross-country skiing. They also rent out electric bikes (¥600/hr, ¥3000/day) and mountain bikes (¥400/hr, ¥1500/day). Youth hostel guests (see below) get discounted rates. This place also has a café, showers, lockers and laundry.

The bright white house right outside the tiny station is *Bibaushi Liberty Youth Hostel* (☎ 0166-95 2141, 🖥 www.biei.com/liberty; closed early to mid Apr & mid Nov to mid Dec; ¥3780/4380pp), where accommodation is mostly in four-bed dorms. The couple who run the hostel are really welcoming and it's small enough to feel very homely. Evening meals are not available.

Gosh (☎ 0166-95 2052, 🖥 www.gosh-coffee.com; Wed-Mon 10am-5pm), about 800m from the station, is highly recommended for its home-made breads and cakes. It roasts its own coffee and is an atmospheric place, with lots of wood and brickwork, as well. It also serves European-style meals.

Biei (F37; 285km) The extremely helpful **tourist information centre** (🖥 www. biei-hokkaido.jp; daily May-Oct 8.30am-7pm, Nov-Apr to 5pm) is in the green-and-white building to the left outside the station. The lockers here (all sizes; ¥200-500) are available during office hours; bulky luggage can be left with the staff (¥500). Wi-fi is available as well as computers that can be used for free but the internet access is slow. There is a UNO convenience store opposite the station.

If descriptions of 'the greens of the rolling pastures, the delicate pinks of the potato flowers, the rusty yellows of the ripened seeds' appeal, Biei will be the perfect place to stop for an extended cycle ride (outside the snow season). The area is very hilly so be prepared for a bit of legwork, but your efforts will be rewarded with magnificent views. There are also plenty of small cafés and private art galleries to explore in and around the hills above the station.

Matsuura (9am-7pm, closed in wet weather), next to the tourist information centre, rents out mountain **bikes** and ordinary bikes (¥600/200/hour, ¥3000/1000/5 hours), gives out cycling-tour maps and will store luggage.

If cycling sounds like too much work, for a **free view** of the surrounding area go to the top of Biei Town Hall (Shiki-no-Tou). The town hall is on the left at the second set of traffic lights heading straight from the station.

Hotel L'Avenir (☎ 0166-92 5555, 🖥 www.biei-lavenir.com; ¥5000-8000pp half-board) is a concrete-looking building with Western-style en suite rooms a short walk from the station.

Biei Potato-no-Oka Youth Hostel (☎ 0166-92 3255, 🖥 www.potatovillage. com; closed late Nov to late Dec; dorm ¥4960pp; rooms ¥6400-13,860, plus ¥600 for non-YHA members; supper ¥1260, breakfast ¥760) is just over 4km from the station; if you call ahead, someone will pick you up.

Daimaru (daily 11am-3pm & 5-8pm, sometimes closed on summer evenings if food sells out) serves local dishes using local produce as well as

HOKKAIDO

curry-rice and udon (mostly about ¥800). Walk down from the station and then turn first right at the traffic lights. Daimaru is towards the end on the right before the next set of traffic lights.

Side trip by bus to Shirogane Blue Pond

Take a Douhoku bus (5/day; 26 mins; ¥500) to see the unusual Shirogane Blue Pond. This was created by accident as a result of attempts to control landslides in the area after Mount Tokachi erupted in 1989. The local authorities built a dyke to contained the volcanic mudflow and water got trapped here. The aluminium that seeped into the water makes the water look blue in sunlight.

The bus continues to **Shirogane-onsen**, which is part of Daisetsuzan National Park. For further information

From Biei, stay on the train for the rest of the journey along the Furano line to Asahikawa. If you are on a local train there will be lots of stops!

Asahikawa (A28; 309km)   [see pp357-60]
See p328 for routes from Asahikawa (in reverse) back to Sapporo and Hakodate.

Hokkaido – city guides

HAKODATE

The first major stop on a journey through Hokkaido, Hakodate is the third largest city on the island and was one of the first port cities in Japan to open to foreign trade in the 19th century.

The first commercial treaty was signed with the USA in 1858, followed by similar agreements with Holland, Russia, Britain and France. Foreign consulates opened up near the port in order to oversee international trade, red-brick warehouses and churches were built, and many of the original buildings still stand as a reminder of the city's Western influence.

Its proximity to Honshu means Hakodate gets packed out in the summer when tourists come to eat fresh crab and gaze down at the 'milky way floating in the ocean', a lyrical description of the night view of the city from the top of Mt Hakodate.

What to see and do
Outside the station's west exit is the busy **morning market** (*asaichi*; 5am-noon, closed Sun in winter). Early in the morning the market-stall tanks are filled to bursting with fresh catches of crab and squid. Fruit (particularly musk melons) and vegetables are also big business.

Memorial Ship *Mashumaru* (daily Apr-Oct 8.30am-6pm, Nov-Mar 9am-5pm; ¥500). This old JR ferry plied the water between Aomori and Hakodate in the days before the Seikan Tunnel (see box p318). It has a small museum and visitors can tour the bridge and radio-control room, and even put on the captain's jacket and gloves. However, there are better things to see and do in Hakodate.

Motomachi Motomachi is the city's old quarter, where the former consulate buildings were located. It is possible to see four of the 'sights' in the area for ¥840. However, two of these – the museums – have few labels in English and thus may be of less interest. Individual tickets cost ¥300, or ¥500 for two sights. All are open daily 9am to 5pm, to 7pm from April to October.

From Suehiro-cho tram stop cross the road and walk back a bit to reach the **Museum of Literature** (Bungakukan), which has displays on the life and works of novelists, poets and journalists who are connected with Hakodate.

On the same side of the road but a little way past the tram stop, the **Museum of Northern Peoples** (Hoppo Minzoku-shiryokan) is housed in the former branch of the Bank of Japan. Displays include a collection of clothes and accessories worn by the Ainu as well as a number of ceremonial objects and everyday items such as a sled and fishing harpoons.

Five minutes' walk uphill from the museum is the **Former British Consulate** (Kyu-Igirisu-Ryojikan; 🖳 www.hakodate-kankou.com/british), which first opened in 1859. The building that stands today was constructed in 1913 and was used up to the closure of the consulate in 1934. Look out for the rusty 'Dieu et mon Droit' royal crest that used to hang on the consulate gate and for the account of how one consul's wife taught Japanese women the Western way of doing laundry. The video diorama on the 2nd floor is in Japanese but features a lovely scene of American sailors first meeting Japanese people and wanting to take a photo. The gift shop does a roaring trade in old-fashioned British products such as 'Ahmad tea' and 'Simpkins sweets', and the menu at *Victoria Rose Tea Room* (9am-5pm) includes a full tea with cakes and biscuits (¥1260).

A little further up from the consulate is the **former Public Hall** (Kyu-Kokaido), a large Western-style building completed in 1910, with a number of guest bedrooms (look out for the Emperor's toilet and bathroom) and a large hall on the 2nd floor that commands a great view of the harbour. Free concerts are held here occasionally between June and October. Don't be surprised if you see Japanese women drifting around in ball gowns; for ¥1000 they can dress up and be photographed in front of an enlarged photograph of the building that is downstairs in the billiard room.

Highly recommended is a visit to the **former residence of Soma Teppei** (Kyu-Soma-tei; daily 9am-4pm; ¥500). This house was built (1908-11) by Soma Teppei, a very successful merchant, to a design that drew on both Japanese and Western traditions. There is much impressively detailed workmanship, including a handsome dining table and chairs, and make sure you see the wooden lift that was installed so that food could be sent up to the 2nd floor from the kitchen. At the time of writing there was little explanation in English, so if a member of staff offers to guide you round do accept the offer.

Other sights to look out for in the area are **Motomachi Roman Catholic Church** (Motomachi Katoriku-Kyoukai), **Hakodate Russian Orthodox Church** (Hakodate Harisutosu-sei Kyoukai; Mon-Fri 10am-5pm, Sat 10am-4pm, Sun 1-4pm; ¥200) and **Hakodate Episcopal Church** (Hakodate-yohane Kyoukai). *(continued on p346)*

HOKKAIDO

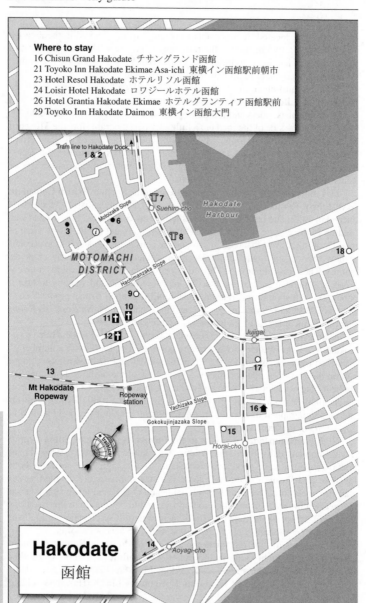

Where to stay
16 Chisun Grand Hakodate チサングランド函館
21 Toyoko Inn Hakodate Ekimae Asa-ichi 東横イン函館駅前朝市
23 Hotel Resol Hakodate ホテルリソル函館
24 Loisir Hotel Hakodate ロワジールホテル函館
26 Hotel Grantia Hakodate Ekimae ホテルグランティア函館駅前
29 Toyoko Inn Hakodate Daimon 東横イン函館大門

Tram line to Hakodate Dock
1 & 2

Motoizaka Slope

7
Suehiro-cho

6
3   4
5

8

Hakodate
Harbour

MOTOMACHI
DISTRICT

Hachimanzaka Slope

9

10
11   12

18

Jujigai

13

17

Mt Hakodate
Ropeway

Ropeway
station

Yachizaka Slope

16

Gokokujinzazaka Slope

15

Horai-cho

14   Aoyagi-cho

Hakodate
函館

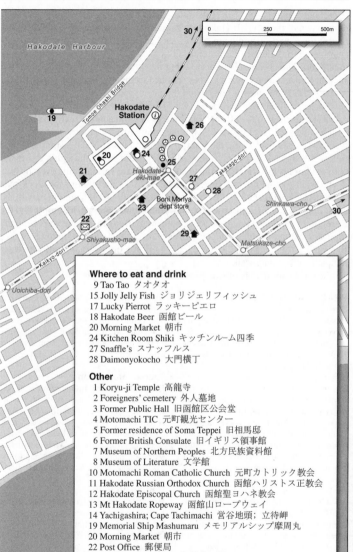

30

0   250   500m

Hakodate Harbour

Tomoe Ohashi Bridge

Hakodate Station ⓘ

26

19

20

24

21

25

Hakodate-eki-mae

Takasago-dori

27

28

Boni Moriya dept store

23

Shinkawa-cho

30

22 ✉

Shiyakusho-mae

29

Matsukaze-cho

Kaikyo-dori

Uoichiba-dori

Where to eat and drink
9 Tao Tao タオタオ
15 Jolly Jelly Fish ジョリジェリフィッシュ
17 Lucky Pierrot ラッキーピエロ
18 Hakodate Beer 函館ビール
20 Morning Market 朝市
24 Kitchen Room Shiki キッチンルーム四季
27 Snaffle's スナッフルス
28 Daimonyokocho 大門横丁

Other
1 Koryu-ji Temple 高龍寺
2 Foreigners' cemetery 外人墓地
3 Former Public Hall 旧函館区公会堂
4 Motomachi TIC 元町観光センター
5 Former residence of Soma Teppei 旧相馬邸
6 Former British Consulate 旧イギリス領事館
7 Museum of Northern Peoples 北方民族資料館
8 Museum of Literature 文学館
10 Motomachi Roman Catholic Church 元町カトリック教会
11 Hakodate Russian Orthodox Church 函館ハリストス正教会
12 Hakodate Episcopal Church 函館聖ヨハネ教会
13 Mt Hakodate Ropeway 函館山ロープウェイ
14 Yachigashira; Cape Tachimachi 營谷地頭; 立待岬
19 Memorial Ship Mashumaru メモリアルシップ摩周丸
20 Morning Market 朝市
22 Post Office 郵便局
25 Bus ticket office バス切符売り場
30 Goryokaku 五稜郭

HOKKAIDO

(Continued from p343) **Mt Hakodate**, 334m above sea level, offers a panoramic view of the city. **Mt Hakodate Ropeway** (🖳 www.334.co.jp/eng; ¥1160 return; times vary according to season; service doesn't operate in windy weather) runs up to the top from Motomachi, or a walking path is open from spring to autumn. The cheapest way of reaching the summit is by bus from Hakodate station. In the summer months a bus service (see below) operates mostly in the evening, when the view is considered the most spectacular.

For great (and free) sea views (with Honshu in the distance) and crashing ocean waves, head out to **Cape Tachimachi** (Tachimachi-misaki), the name of which is derived from words in Ainu meaning 'a rocky point where one waits for and catches fish'. Ride the tram to the terminus at Yachigashira and then follow the signs. It is a 1km walk, partly uphill and partly through a graveyard with memorials to various Hakodate poets. There are various trails over the hills if you want to continue walking. Alternatively take the tram to the Dock-mae terminus on the other side of the peninsula and walk uphill from there, with the coast on your right, for more lovely views and to visit **Koryu-ji Temple** and the **Foreigners cemetery** (Gaijin Bochi); both are a 10- to 15-minute walk from the tram stop and are worth seeing even if they are closed. Another option is to take Bus Line 1 from Hakodate station and get off at Koryu-ji-mae from where the temple is a 3-minute walk.

See p348 for details of side trips from Hakodate.

PRACTICAL INFORMATION
Station guide
Hakodate station is bright, modern and serves as a welcoming gateway to the city. The station is the terminus of the Tsugaru-Kaikyo line from Shin-Aomori and the start of the JR Hakodate main line.

There is only one ticket barrier and it's on the same level as the platforms. Immediately to your left as you leave the ticket barrier are the **JR ticket office** and adjacent Twinkle Plaza **travel agency**. Both can handle rail-pass seat reservations. There is a post office **ATM** on the station concourse. The main exit is the central exit. For the morning market take the west exit, which is to your right as you pass through the ticket barrier.

On the ground floor *King Bake* (daily 7am-7pm) is a decent bakery and *Café St* (daily 6.30am-8pm) serves spaghetti and pizza (¥600-950). Also in this area are some kiosks selling **ekiben** lunch boxes (specialising in crab).

For **lockers** (all sizes; 6am-10pm) take the escalator up from the station concourse. Up here you'll also find *Waka* (10am-9pm),

whose menu includes a tonkatsu curry-rice (¥900) and a tempura set meal (¥1000). It is worth coming up to see the coasters, which illuminate when you put a glass on them, and for the excellent views from here over Mt Hakodate.

Tourist information
Hakodate Tourist Information desk (🖳 www.hakodate-kankou.com; daily Apr-Oct 9am-7pm, Nov-Mar to 5pm) is in the far corner of the Twinkle Plaza travel agency on the station concourse. Staff can provide plenty of information but **Motomachi TIC** (Apr-Oct 9am-7pm, Nov-Mar to 5pm) has a wider range of leaflets in English.

Getting around
Hakodate's **tram (street car) system** has been in operation since 1913 and it's still the best way of getting around the city. A one-day tram pass (¥600) is probably all you need but if you would like to travel on **buses** (except the bus to the airport) as well a one-day pass is ¥1000 (two days ¥1700). This also covers the seasonal bus service (late Apr to late Nov; 2-3/hr; 25 mins; ¥360

one-way) to the top of Mt Hakodate. Purchase the pass from either the tourist information desk or tram drivers. Individual fares (tram or bus) are ¥200-250.

Note that tram stops aren't always opposite each other so ensure you are waiting at the correct one for your destination.

The **bus to Hakodate airport** (2-3/hr; 20 mins; ¥400) goes from Stand 11 in front of the station.

Festivals
The **Hakodate Historical Pageant** (Fri & Sat evening, late July/early Aug; ¥2000, or ¥1800 in advance) is staged at Goryokaku Fort (see p348). It's an astonishing theatrical event that tells the story of Hakodate using dry ice, fireworks, canons, motor boats, stampedes of horses, acrobatics, ballet, dance and an amateur cast of thousands.

Where to stay
Convenient for rail users is *Loisir Hotel Hakodate* (☎ 0138-22 0111; ☐ www. solarehotels.com/english/loisir; ¥13,500/S, ¥16,000/D, ¥23,000/Tw, breakfast ¥1730), which offers upmarket accommodation and is near the west exit of the station.

Hotel Grantia Hakodate Ekimae (☎ 0138-21 4100, ☐ route-inn.co.jp/english/ pref/hokkaido.html#hakodate; ¥5800/S, ¥9900/Tw, ¥12,000/D or family; breakfast from ¥800), part of the Route Inn chain, is to the left as you take the central exit. It has an onsen on the top floor.

Toyoko Inn (☐ www.toyoko-inn.com) has two branches here: *Toyoko Inn Hakodate Ekimae Asa-ichi* (☎ 0138-23 1045; from ¥3980/S, ¥5480/D, ¥6480/Tw) is three minutes on foot from the station, at the edge of the morning market, so you're perfectly placed for an early-morning walk around the stalls. It's also a good place to stay if in need of a haircut since there's a small hair salon attached offering bargain ¥1000, 10-minute cuts. Don't expect to have a long discussion about style. *Toyoko Inn Hakodate Daimon* (☎ 0138-24 1045; from ¥5480/S, ¥6480/D, ¥7480/Tw, inc curry rice supper), is a five-minute walk into town.

Hotel Resol Hakodate (☎ 0138-23 9269, ☐ www.resol-hotel.jp; ¥10,538/S, ¥21,079/Tw, inc breakfast), close to the station, has reasonably spacious rooms and Rakusis, an aromatherapy salon.

Near Horai-cho tram stop is *Chisun Grand Hakodate* (☎ 0138-24 3311, ☐ www.solarehotels.com/chisun/grand-hako date; from ¥14,000/S, ¥18,000/D, ¥26,000/ Tw; buffet breakfast ¥1200). Rooms on the Grand Floor have portable speakers for iPods and bathroom scales! There are no restaurants in the hotel but staff can advise on local alternatives.

See also pp45-52 for general information about finding accommodation.

Where to eat and drink
The **morning market** (see p342) is a good place to hunt around for an impromptu meal; you can be sure that the fish is fresh at the many restaurant stalls.

Kitchen Room Shiki (at Hotel Loisir Hakodate) is an open kitchen and does buffets at lunch (11.30am-2pm; ¥1260) and in the evening (6-8.30pm; ¥2100).

Near to Chisun Grand Hakodate is *Jolly Jelly Fish Bar and Restaurant* (Fri-Wed 11.30am-2.30pm & 5.30pm to midnight; last orders 11pm). Look for the bright pink exterior and the name in English. It does good, simple food (steak pilaf ¥1200, chicken soup curry ¥980) with beer on tap in an American pub-style atmosphere.

Hakodate Beer (daily 11am-10pm) is a lively place where you can try various meat and seafood dishes and wash them down with locally brewed beers. In the summer there's space to sit on a verandah outside. There are also restaurants and shops in the converted old brick warehouses next to Hakodate Beer.

In **Motomachi**, *Tao Tao* (summer daily noon-11pm, winter Tue-Fri 5-11pm and Sat & Sun noon-11pm) is a South-East Asian restaurant serving a range of Asian beers, soft drinks such as guava juice and great spicy food.

Daimonyokocho (daily 6pm to late) is two rows of small, informal shops serving everything from sushi to Asian cuisine. It's a very small area, less than five minutes on foot from the station, and a good place to look around for a bite to eat. There are more than 20 outlets, most with counter or table service.

One of the best cake shops in town is *Snaffle's*, on the main street leading away from the station; choose a cake downstairs, go upstairs to sit and order coffee (from ¥300).

There are several branches of the *Lucky Pierrot* hamburger-and-curry fast-food chain around town. The one most worth visiting, if only for the bizarre year-round Christmas décor, lies close to the Jujigai tram stop. It's easy to spot as it's the only building covered in Christmas trees and Santa Claus faces. The Lucky Pierrot (10am to midnight, Sat to 1am) closest to the station is on the far side of Boni department store. The menu at both includes coffee (¥200), hamburgers (¥350-800) and curry rice (¥700).

Side trip by rail to Goryokaku

About 4km north-east of Hakodate station is Goryokaku, the first Western-style fort in Japan. Built between 1857 and 1864 as a strategic stronghold from which Hokkaido could be ruled, the fort is a pentagonal star shape (called 'the most beautiful star carved on earth'). Warriors from the fallen Tokugawa shogunate escaped from Honshu to Hakodate and occupied the fort in October 1868. Seven months later they gave themselves up to the Imperial Army, bringing Japan's feudal era to a dramatic end.

At the main entrance is the 60m-high **Goryokaku Tower** (🖥 www.goryokaku-tower.co.jp/pdf/leaflet/en.pdf; daily late Apr to late Oct 8am-7pm, late Oct to late Apr 9am-6pm; ¥840). It's a modern-day eyesore but does have an observation platform affording views over the remains of the fort and the city beyond. It is the site of a spectacular Historical Pageant in the summer (see p347). It is also worth coming here in spring to see the blossom on the 1600 cherry trees planted here in the Taisho era.

To reach Goryokaku take the tram to Goryokaku-koen-mae and then walk north along the main road for about 10 minutes. Look for signs to the fort; you'll soon see the concrete tower in front of you. Alternatively take a train from Hakodate to JR Goryokaku. However, the walk from the JR station is longer.

SAPPORO

The biggest city in Hokkaido and venue for the 1972 Winter Olympics, Sapporo is frequently voted the city where most Japanese would like to live. It certainly feels relaxed and cosmopolitan, with green parks, 19th- and 20th-century red-brick buildings and a thriving entertainment district. It's also one of the easiest cities to get around, thanks to the north–south grid layout.

If you need a further incentive to spend a couple of days here, time your visit to coincide with one of the many festivals, the most famous of which is the annual Snow Festival in February. Like the rest of Hokkaido, Sapporo receives a thick blanket of snow in the winter but summer is mild and provides the perfect opportunity for relaxing in the city's central Odori Park.

What to see and do

Akarenga (Red Brick) is the nickname for the **Former Hokkaido Government Office Building** (daily 8.45am-5pm; free). Built in 1888, and modelled on Maryland State House and Massachusetts State House, it was gutted by fire and had to be completely rebuilt in 1911. The main reason to come here would be to see the garden which is a lovely haven from the hustle and bustle. The exhibitions inside are really for people interested in the history of Hokkaido. However, if you have a few moments it is worth strolling around.

One block south and slightly to the east is Sapporo's famous **Clock Tower** (daily 8.45am-5pm except 4th Mon of month; ¥200). If you don't see the clock immediately, you'll no doubt see the tourists lining up at the official photograph point in front of it. The building was originally used by the former Sapporo Agricultural College (now Hokkaido University) for graduation ceremonies and military drills. It has also been used a post office and a library. The tower was constructed in 1878 but had to be redesigned when the clock that arrived from the USA was too big. Inside, the ground floor is used as an exhibition space and on the 2nd floor there is a model of the internal mechanism of the clock as well as a video about it. Concerts are also staged here.

Odori Park (Odori-koen) stretches for 1.5km through the centre of the city between West 1 and West 12. In summer, people come here to relax, play games and hang out. In the eastern corner of the park is the 147.2m-high **TV Tower** (daily 9.30am-9.30pm; ¥700), built in 1957. It has an observatory that's not really high enough for exceptional views. (The JR Tower at Sapporo station is much better; see pp350-1).

West of the Hokkaido Government Building are the **Botanical Gardens** (Apr-Sep Tue-Sun 9am-4pm, Oct-Nov to 3.30pm; ¥400), opened in 1886 and still the perfect place for a summer stroll. The ticket includes entry to a small Ainu museum in the grounds but there's a better museum devoted to preserving Ainu heritage and culture in a building called **Kaderu 2.7** (N2 W7), across the street from the entrance to the gardens. On the 7th floor is a small **Ainu exhibition** (Mon-Sat 9am-5pm; free) with items of Ainu clothing and equipment used in daily life. Pop into the office next door to pick up a leaflet.

Hokkaido Museum of Modern Art (🖳 www.aurora-net.or.jp/art/dokinbi; N1 W17; Tue-Sun 9.30am-5pm; ¥500) has works by Hokkaido artists as well as an exhibition of glass arts by French artists. The easiest way to get here is to take the Burari Sapporo Kanko Bus (see p353).

Sports fans might enjoy the **Okurayama Ski-Jump Stadium** (Okurayama Janppu Kyogijo; ¥500, or ¥900 inc ski-jump chair lift; discount with Burari bus ticket). The ski jump was used in the Sapporo Winter Olympics in 1972 and the chair lift to the top is well worth doing, not least for the stunning views of Sapporo from the observation gallery. The Winter Sports Museum here has few signs in English but has enjoyable simulators for ski-jumping, cross-country skiing, luge, ice hockey and figure skating. The easiest way to get here is to take the Burari Sapporo Kanko Bus (see p353).

The 40,000-capacity **Sapporo Dome stadium** (☎ 011-850 1020, 🖳 www.sapporo-dome.co.jp; tours hourly 10am-4pm; 50 mins; ¥1000 or ¥1200 inc observatory) is home to Consadole Sapporo football team and Hokkaido Nippon-Ham Fighters baseball team and hosted some 2002 World Cup events. The stadium is known for its grass pitch, which grows outside and is brought in on a hi-tech cushion of air when matches are played. Tours take in the stadium, bullpen, locker room and team director's room. An observatory (¥500) at the

🚻 **Toilet in the sky – men only!**
Why not take a comfort break at the top of the city's highest building? The men's toilets at the JR Tower's 38th-floor observation room are 160m above street level and walled with glass. According to the designer, 'one is supposed to do it as if one is taking a leak into a river from the top of a bridge' – well, you can certainly imagine you are taking a leak onto the city below. 'I tried to make men feel as if they were floating in the air while relieving themselves. I finally arrived at this uncompromising design,' revealed Junko Kobayashi, architect and director of the Japan Toilet Association. (You can tell a man designed the loos – the women's loos have no view at all! However, it is possible for women to get an idea of what the experience is like from the disabled toilet).

top of the dome, 53m above the stadium ground, is reached via an 'aerial escalator'. Take the Toho subway line to Fukuzumi station.

The top-floor observation platform inside the 38-storey landmark **JR Tower Sapporo** (🖳 www.jr-tower.com/t38; 10am-11pm; ¥700), 160m above the south exit of JR Sapporo station, offers unparalleled views of the city – and, for men, a possibly unique toilet experience (see box above). Take the lift from

---

HOKKAIDO

MAP KEY – Where to stay

1 JR Inn JR インン
5 JR Tower Hotel Nikko Sapporo
　JRタワーホテル日航札幌
7 Toyoko Inn Sapporo-eki Kita-guchi 東横イン 札幌駅北口
9 R&B Hotel Sapporo
　R＆Bホテル札幌
11 Nakamuraya Ryokan
　中村屋旅館
18 Rasso Iceberg Hotel
　ラッソアイスバーグホテル
19 Sapporo International YH
　サッポロ国際ユースホステル
22 Toyoko Inn Sapporo Suskino-Minami 東横イン札幌
　すすきの南

Where to eat and drink

2 Italian Dining Grazie (JR55)
　イタリアンダイニング
　グラッツェ (JR55)
3 Paul's Café ポールズカフェ
4 The Buffet (Daimaru Dept Store)
　ザブッフェ (大丸デパート)
5 J-Bar, JR Tower Hotel Nikko Sapporo Jバー、JRタワー
　ホテル日航札幌
6 Aji no Tokeidai, Soup Curry Lavi (Esta Dept Store)
　味の時計台、スープカレー
　ラビ (エスタデパート)

Where to eat and drink (cont'd)

11 Nakamuraya Ryokan
　中村屋旅館
14 Aji no Tokeidai 味の時計台
16 Aozora; Lilac (City Hall)
　あおぞら；ライラック
　(市役所)

Other

5 JR Tower Sapporo; Sky Resort Spa Pulau Bulan JRタワー
　札幌；スカイリゾート
　スパプラウブラン
8 Central Post Office
　中央郵便局
10 Former Hokkaido Government Office Bldg 旧本庁舎
12 Botanical Gardens 植物園
13 Kaderu 2.7 かでる2.7
15 Clock Tower 時計台
17 TV Tower テレビタワー
20 Sapporo Dome 札幌ドーム
21 Susukino すすきの
23 Odori Park 大通り公園
24 Hokkaido Museum of Modern Art 北海道立近代美術館
25 Okurayama Ski Jump Stadium; Sapporo Winter Sports Museum 大倉山
　ジャンプ競技場；札幌ウイ
　ンタースポーツミュージアム

Sapporo

札幌

Scale: 0 100 200 300m

- Hokkaido University
- Entrance to JR Tower Sapporo
- To Asahikawa & Historical Village of Hokkaido
- Sapporo Station
- Esta dept store
- Daimaru dept store
- Sumitomo Seimei building
- Former Hokkaido Government Office building
- Botanical Gardens
- Kaderu 2.7 building
- City Hall
- Odori
- Odori-koen
- Nishi-Juitchome
- Nishi-Juhatchome
- Tram line
- Kinokuniya
- ★ trailblazer
- 25 (by Burari-Sapporo Kanko Bus)
- 24

Grid labels: N7, N6, N5, N4, N3, N2, N1, W1, W2, W3, W4, W5, W6, W7, W8, W9, W10, W11, W12, W13, W14, W15, W16, W17, E1, E2, Sapporo Station

Stellar Place Center to the 6th floor of the Tower and then transfer to a special lift to the 38th floor. Elsewhere in the Tower is a department store, spa and multiplex cinema.

If you want to soak weary limbs after a day spent traipsing around the city, **Sky Resort Spa Pulau Bulan** (daily 11am-11pm; ¥2800, hotel guests ¥1500, inc towels) boasts modern and minimalist single-sex hot-spring facilities on the 22nd floor of JR Tower Hotel Nikko Sapporo (see opposite). It has a variety of pools, Jacuzzis, and a Finnish sauna, but best of all is the Karuna air massage bath. Massage and spa-treatment packages are also available (a 40-minute massage plus use of the spa is ¥6500); expect to be in the same room as other customers. Take the lift from the ground-floor hotel lobby.

In the evening, the place to head for an eyeful of Japan by night is the **Susukino** entertainment district. Billed as the 'largest amusement area north of Tokyo', the area boasts between 4000 and 5000 bars and restaurants, all of which rely on the evening trade when the district is flooded by businessmen. It is also the red-light area of Sapporo but in February is also a site for the Snow Festival (see opposite). Take the subway to Susukino.

See pp355-6 for details of side trips from Sapporo.

PRACTICAL INFORMATION
Station guide
The station has two main exits: north and south; take the south exit for all the main sights as well as for the JR Tower Center, buses and taxis. The station itself is divided into two halves, east and west, with JR ticket offices and Twinkle Plaza travel agencies on both sides. You can also access the platforms from both sides. The best bet when leaving a train and wanting to head for the centre of Sapporo (or for the tourist information office) is to leave the platform area and enter the station concourse via the west side. **Lockers** (including enormous ¥600 ones) are located all over the station, but particularly in the passageway which connects the east and west sides.

The station building is full of modern works of art which collectively form part of the JR Tower Art Guide. A full list of all the works of art (all by Hokkaido-commissioned artists), and where they are located, is on a board outside the entrance to Daimaru department store close to the south exit. The aim is to 'explore new possibilities of art for an urban public environment adjacent to a station'.

JR Hokkaido operates an **Information Desk** (daily 8.30am-8pm) in Dosanko Plaza on the west concourse. Rail passes can be exchanged here, rail-pass holders can make seat reservations and you can buy a JR Hokkaido Pass (see p15), as well as the one-day Sapporo/Otaru Welcome Ticket (see p355). Of course you can also use any other JR ticket office or Twinkle Plaza to book tickets/make seat reservations.

The station is home to a flagship **Daimaru** department store, another shopping mall and cinema complex, and the magnificent tower which houses **JR Tower Hotel Nikko Sapporo** (see Where to stay).

Tourist information
The **Tourist Information Corner** (⌨ www.welcome.city.sapporo.jp; daily 8.30am-8pm) is next to the JR Information Desk (see Station guide) in Dosanko Plaza. Pick up a copy of *Bimi* for details about places to eat, drink and shop.

Getting around
Sapporo has a modern **subway** system with three lines – Namboku, Tozai and Toho – that interconnect at Odori station, one stop south of Sapporo station. There is a minimum subway fare of ¥200; one-day subway passes (¥800) are sold at subway vending machines.

❏ Sapporo orientation
Thanks to Sapporo's grid system, it's easy to find your way almost anywhere in the city. Nearly all addresses include a grid reference, so a building at 'N1 W3', for example, is one block north and three blocks west of the grid apex on the eastern corner of Odori-koen in the city centre.

On Saturdays, Sundays and national holidays, you can pick up an unlimited subway pass, called the Donichika, for ¥500. The passes are sold in stations from vending machines that are separate from the usual ticket machines. The 'Common-Use One-Day Card' (¥1000) is valid on the subway, tram (see below) and most buses.

The 8.5km **tram** (street car) line intersects with the subway at Suskino but does not actually go to Sapporo station; it serves the south-west part of the city and is unlikely to be of much use to tourists other than tram/street-car fans.

Burari Sapporo Kanko Bus (13/day; ¥200/journey, ¥500/day pass inc discounted entry to some attractions) operates on a fixed route and stops at the main sights including the Winter Sports Museum. Buses depart from stand 6 in the bus terminal to the left as you leave the station on the south side.

New-Chitose Airport (Shin-Chitose Airport; Airport Express train 2-4/hr; approx 36 mins) is about 30km south of the city centre. The Super Kamui LEX (1/hr) also goes from the airport to Sapporo and on to Asahikawa.

Festivals
The biggest event of the year is the **Snow Festival** (Yuki Matsuri; 6th-12th Feb), when hordes of tourists flock in to see the huge ice sculptures on display in Odori-koen and the main street in Susukino.

Yosakoi Soran Festival (see box below) in June brings together thousands of dancers from all over Japan, who compete in front of a crowd of nearly two million to win over the judges with their own interpretations of a dance rhythm that originated in Kochi (see p420).

In summer the **Pacific Music Festival** (Jul-Aug), which was founded by Leonard Bernstein, draws young musicians from all over the world to stage a series of concerts around the city. Some performances are free.

Where to stay
The plushest place in town is the 350-room *JR Tower Hotel Nikko Sapporo* (also known as Sapporo Sky Resort; N5 W2; ☎ 011-251 2222, 🖳 www.jrhotels.co.jp/tower/english; from ¥18,000/S, ¥26,000/D, ¥34,000/Tw, inc breakfast; rail-pass holders receive a moderate discount). It's part of the JR station and the tower also houses a hot spring spa (see opposite) and an observatory (see p350); the rooms are on the 22nd-36th floors. All rooms come with large windows though it is possible to ask for a corner room (120° view) and/or a room facing the tracks; the views from these are amazing. There will also be a star-gazing chart in your room.

Those on a tighter budget should try *JR Inn* (N5 W6; ☎ 011-233 3008, 🖳 www.jr-inn.jp/en; from ¥4200/S, ¥5200/D, ¥8700/Tw, inc breakfast). The Inn is about a four-minute walk from the station's west exit and offers stylish rooms with full-length

⛩ Yosakoi Soran Festival
This festival is an astonishing spectacle – the vibrant colours of the dancers' costumes twinned with the rhythmic steps and the chanting is a mesmerising sight and I highly recommend catching the festival. Teams come from all over the country, and even from China and Taiwan, to attend and dance their extravagantly-patterned socks off for days on end.   **Joe Woodruff** (UK)

HOKKAIDO

windows. It has a pillow 'library': if you are not happy with the pillow on your bed you can choose from the selection on the ground floor.

Nakamuraya Ryokan (N3 W7; ☎ 011-241 2111, 💻 www.nakamura-ya.com; from ¥6825pp room only; breakfast ¥1575, dinner ¥3150) is a typical Japanese inn with en suite tatami rooms. It's in the city centre, on the road between the Botanical Gardens and Hokkaido government buildings.

Toyoko Inn (💻 www.toyoko-inn.com) has several branches in the city. Most convenient for the station is *Toyoko Inn Sapporo-eki Kita-guchi* (N6 W1; ☎ 011-728 1045; from ¥6480/S, ¥7480/D, ¥8480/Tw, inc breakfast). If you prefer to be closer to the nightlife, *Toyoko Inn Sapporo Susukino Minami* (S6 E2; ☎ 011-551 1045; ¥6600/Tw, ¥11,000/Tr) would be a better bet. There are no single rooms but the rooms are larger than average, and have kitchenettes.

Another good budget bet is *R&B Hotel Sapporo* (N3 W2; ☎ 011-210 1515, 💻 sapporo.randb.jp; from ¥5880/S, ¥7380/Tw, inc breakfast). The rooms have wide beds and check-in is automated (with a key card). *Rasso Iceberg Hotel* (S2 W1; ☎ 011-290 3000, 💻 www.rasso.co.jp/iceberg; from ¥6090/S, ¥9240/D or Tw, inc breakfast) is clean and well located. Rasso stands for Resort and Spending Special Offtime!

The best budget choice by far is *Sapporo International Youth Hostel* (☎ 011-825 3120, 💻 www.youthhostel.or.jp/kokusai; dorm room ¥3200pp, ¥3800pp in private room; breakfast ¥630). The family-size tatami rooms as well as the Western-style dorms are very comfortable and kept spotless. All rooms are equipped with individual lockers; in the basement there's a hot spring bath and coin laundry. From the station, take Toho subway line to Gakuen-mae station and follow the signs for Exit No 2.

See pp45-52 for general details about finding accommodation.

Where to eat and drink

At **Esta**, the department store on the left as you take the south exit of the station, there's a dedicated ramen 'village' on the 10th floor, where you can try the local Sapporo

ramen at *Aji no Tokeidai* (11.30am-11pm; ramen from ¥750); the delicious noodle broth is made from *miso* (fermented soybean paste) and is rich with garlic and butter. There's another branch of *Aji no Tokeidai* opposite Sapporo Grand Hotel (N1 W4), where you can sit at the counter and watch the chefs. The reasonable prices and large portions mean both places gets crowded at lunchtime. An English menu is available. Also on the 10th floor of **Esta** is *Soup Curry Lavi* (5-10pm; from ¥1200), which does the Hokkaido speciality – soup curry.

The 8th floor of **Daimaru** department store, built into the JR station building, is filled with restaurants doing sushi, tonkatsu and Italian food, and there's also the all-you-can-eat *The Buffet* (daily 11am-5pm ¥1490; 5.30-10pm ¥2150).

J-Bar on the 35th floor of JR Tower Hotel Nikko Sapporo (see Where to stay) is a great place for a drink, and if you get there before 8pm the ¥750 cover charge is waived.

JR55, on the way to JR Inn (see Where to stay), offers a variety of Japanese- and Western-style restaurants on the 6th-8th floors including *Italian Dining Grazie* (5pm to midnight), which offers all-you-can-eat meals (eight dishes in two hours ¥2480).

Paul's Café (N5 W5; daily 11.30am-11pm) is an informal bar/restaurant which serves authentic Belgian beer (on tap and in the bottle). The owner is proud of his delicious roast chicken and Belgian pommes frites (¥1500), but he also does rabbit stew and beef stew. Lunch deals cost from ¥700. The café is in the basement of Sumitomo Seimei Building, which houses the Century Royal Hotel.

For a budget lunch with a view, head for **City Hall**, where *Aozora* (N1 W2; Mon-Fri 9am-5pm) on the 19th floor has simple meals such as chicken with rice or noodles for ¥600-700. There's a similar menu at *Lilac* (Mon-Fri 10am-6pm) on the 18th floor.

Nakamuraya Ryokan (see Where to stay; 11.30am-2pm & 5-9pm) offers traditional Japanese meals as well as *bento* that you can take out or eat in; expect to pay from ¥1000.

Side trips by rail from Sapporo

● **Otaru (S15)** The attractive port city of Otaru (see p324) is easily reached in 30 minutes by rapid train west along the Hakodate line.

If you don't have a rail pass, consider buying JR Hokkaido's **One-day Sapporo-Otaru Welcome Pass** (¥1500), which is available only to tourists from abroad and allows unlimited travel on JR services between Sapporo and Otaru, as well as on all subway lines in Sapporo itself. The pass comes with a sightseeing map of Otaru.

● **Asahiyama Zoo** JR Hokkaido (🖳 www2.jrhokkaido.co.jp/global/english/travel) offers an **Asahiyama Zoo Ticket** which includes the journey from Sapporo (¥5900 for unreserved seat on a limited express) to Asahikawa, bus to the zoo and zoo entry (see p357). The ticket is valid for four days.

The Asahiyama Zoo train (weekends and holiday periods 1/day; extra ¥510 for a reserved seat); has five cars (penguin, chimpanzee, lion, wolf and polar bear) and runs between Sapporo and Asahikawa.

● **Heiwa (H04)** The 'No More Hibakusha Kaikan' museum in Heiwa is worth visiting. Kaikan means hall, and Hibakusha is the term used to refer to the victims of the atomic bomb attacks on Nagasaki and Hiroshima who are still alive. Hibakusha are scattered across Japan; a few hundred live in Hokkaido. It's a really small museum (Sun-Fri 10am-4pm, closed on national holidays; free), the size of an ordinary house, and is owned by people who experienced the atomic bombs.

It is nothing like the scale of the museums in Hiroshima (see p253) or Nagasaki (see pp390-1) but it's certainly worth a look if you haven't visited either of these places. Photos of the horrific injuries and burns sustained by victims minutes, hours, days and years after the atomic blasts are accompanied by paintings. Local trains leave Sapporo (on the line to Shin-Sapporo) roughly three times an hour and take 12 minutes to Heiwa. The frequency is the same in the other direction.

To get to the museum head up the flight of steps at Heiwa station. Turn right and walk all the way along the bridge to the end. Right in front of you as you leave the bridge is a red brick building which has a copy of Hiroshima's A-bomb dome on the roof. Ring the bell to be let in.

● **Naebo (H02)** One stop from Sapporo station on the JR Chitose line brings you to **Kura-no-yu** (蔵ノ湯; 🖳 kuranoyu.com; daily 10am-11pm; ¥420; lockers ¥100 which is refunded), a public bath with a rotemburo (one with a partial roof so that you can be seen and one that is fully in the open air).

When you leave the station cross the road and turn right. Kura-no-yu is about two minutes along on the left. Buy a ticket at the vending machine. One of the reasons why the bath is so cheap is that neither soap nor shampoo is provided so bring your own. However, there are vending machines where you can buy whatever you might need.

Side trips by bus from Sapporo

● **Historical Village of Hokkaido** (May-Sep daily 9.30am-5pm, ¥830; Oct-Apr Tue-Sun to 4.30pm; ¥680; 🖳 www.kaitaku.or.jp) in Nopporo Forest Park in the suburbs of Sapporo, since the route is operated by JR Bus and is free to rail-pass holders.

A large number of buildings from the Meiji and Taisho periods (mid 19th to early 20th century) have been restored and moved here. It's a very atmospheric place to wander around and there are explanations in English. The main entrance to the village is through the old Sapporo railway station, in use from 1908 to 1952.

Although the village is the main attraction of Nopporo Forest Park there are also 30km of forest trails to explore. Sapporo tourist office has a map detailing footpaths and distances along various routes.

Three buses a day run to the village from Sapporo station (60 mins; No 3 JR bus), but buses are more frequent from Shin-Sapporo station, where they leave from stop No 10 on the north side of the bus terminal. Some of the return buses from the village continue on to Sapporo station after stopping at Shin-Sapporo, but it's quicker to take the train from Shin-Sapporo back to Sapporo.

⛩ The Ainu: fight for survival

When Kenichi Kawamura visited the National Museum of Natural History in Washington, USA, in April 1999, for an exhibition of Ainu artefacts, he was joined by the late Japanese prime minister, Keizo Obuchi. Kawamura overheard the prime minister enquire of another visitor to the museum, 'Are there still Ainu in Hokkaido?'

One of the world's least-known aboriginal cultures, the Ainu have long been almost invisible to the outside world. In a speech to the United Nations in 1992, a representative of the Ainu people told how the Japanese government had 'denied even our existence in its proud claim that Japan, alone in the world, is a "mono-ethnic nation". The Ainu originally populated parts of northern Honshu as well as Hokkaido, living in small communities of up to 10 families, fishing from the rivers and hunting bear – a sacred animal in Ainu tradition – in the forests.

There was never any question of land rights until the *wajin* (Japanese) moved further north, calling the Ainu 'dogs' (the Japanese word for dog is *inu*) and forcing them off their land. The only work that some could find was manual labour with logging companies – thus the Ainu found themselves in the extraordinary position of having to earn a living by destroying the very land on which they had lived.

In 1899, the Hokkaido Former Aborigine Protection Law was passed, giving the island's governor power to 'manage the communal assets of the Ainu people for their benefit', on the pretext that the Ainu were unable to manage these assets themselves. Almost a century was to pass until the law was repealed in 1997, replaced with a new act to promote Ainu culture and return assets that had been 'managed' by the prefectural government. Endless legal wrangles over the exact amount and how it should be paid suggest a quick resolution is unlikely.

There has been some attempt to revive Ainu traditions and in particular the Ainu language, now spoken by fewer than a dozen elderly people. Weekly Ainu language radio courses have started and storytellers are being trained to continue the Ainu oral tradition. In 1994, Shigeru Kayano became the first Ainu to win a seat in the Upper House of the Japanese Parliament, and in a landmark 1998 ruling a Hokkaido judge recognised the indigenous status of the Ainu people for the first time.

Kayano died in 2006, just short of his 80th birthday and not long before a picture book he wrote about the Ainu, *The Ainu and the Fox*, was published for the first time in English. Kayano wrote the story, based on an Ainu legend, in 1974 for elementary schoolchildren. During his lifetime he also compiled an Ainu-language dictionary and recorded folk tales. Nobody yet knows if all this was too little too late to save the Ainu from cultural extinction.

ASAHIKAWA

Despite the backdrop of the Daisetsu mountain range, Asahikawa is not an attractive place by Hokkaido's standards. The second biggest city in Hokkaido after Sapporo serves mainly as a transport hub and a gateway to Daisetsuzan National Park (see p360). However, it has some attractions, particularly for families.

What to see and do

Asahiyama Zoo (💻 www5.city.asahikawa.hokkaido.jp/asahiyamazoo; late Apr to mid Oct daily 9.30am-5.15pm, early Nov to early Apr Fri-Tue 10.30am-3.30pm, closed for a few weeks in Apr; ¥800, ¥1000 passport, ¥1800 inc Sci-pal) is Japan's northernmost zoo and is a good opportunity to see some of the animals native to Hokkaido, including the brown bear and red fox. An underwater tunnel gives access to the penguin tank. In the aquarium seals swim up through a tunnel into a large tank. To reach the zoo, take an Asahikawa Denkikidou bus (No 41 or 47; 1/hr; 40 mins; ¥400) from stop No 5 outside Asahikawa station. (See also p355).

Asahikawa Science Center, or **Sci-pal** as it is known locally (Tue-Sun 9.30am-5pm; ¥400, planetarium ¥300, both ¥500, ¥1800 inc zoo), is a lot more entertaining than its name suggests. The complex includes a state-of-the-art planetarium and interactive exhibits including the chance to experience zero gravity and feel what it is like to jump on the moon. Take bus No 82 from stop No 5 outside the station and alight at Kagakukan-mae, outside the building.

Kawamura Kaneto Ainu Memorial Hall (Jul & Aug daily 8am-6pm, Sep-Jun 9am-5pm; ¥500) is a very small museum with a few exhibits on Ainu traditions. The museum was founded by Kenichi Kawamura, an eighth-generation Ainu who has campaigned for many years for greater recognition of Hokkaido's indigenous population (see box opposite). It's a 10-minute bus ride (bus No 24; ¥200) from bus stop No 14 outside Seibu department store near the station. Get off at Ainu Kinenkan-mae.

There is little of interest to see in the central area, but if you have time it is worth walking along the main street to **Tokiwa Park** (7-jo-dori, 2-5 chome) – on your way look out for the sculptures, particularly the saxophonist and cat. (If you are keen on sculptures ask at the tourist information office for details of the various sculptures around town.) The park is a pleasant place to stroll in and does have a Museum of Art (Tue-Sun 10am-5pm; ¥100 for the permanent exhibition; additional charge for temporary exhibitions), as well as a small lake on which it is possible to rent a boat in the summer.

See p360 for details of side trips from Asahikawa.

PRACTICAL INFORMATION
Station guide
As of 2011 Asahikawa has a wonderful new station. The supporting columns for the roof are wood and are meant to symbolise trees. In fact there is wood everywhere as the area is known for its wood industry; this makes the station a real pleasure to be in. The walls are even lined with thousands of pieces of wood inscribed with the names of anyone who paid ¥2000. Another great feature of the station is the feeling of space.

The central area has a **post office** (Post Station; Mon-Fri 9am-6pm, Sat & Sun to 5pm) with an **ATM** (same hours).

There is also a **hotel information desk** (daily 2-6pm) here. The north exit has west and east gates and there are **lockers** (all sizes) by both. Take the west gate for Asahikawa Terminal Hotel and the main part of town. There is also free wi-fi.

For sustenance there is a café, an *ekiben* (station lunch box) stand (take away or eat in udon from ¥300), and *Sunny Garden Railway Restaurant* (daily 8.30am-8pm, last orders 7.30pm), which serves pasta, burgers, curry rice and tonkatsu (most ¥600-900).

Tourist information

The **tourist information centre** (daily Jun-Sep 8.30am-7pm, Oct-May 9am-7pm) is on the 1st (ground) floor of the station by the East Gate. There are a lot of leaflets and staff can help with queries.

For information about Asahikawa visit 🖳 www.asahikawa-tourism.com.

Getting around

Walking around Asahikawa is easy as all the roads in the central area are on a grid. The first road going west to east in front of the station is Miyashita-dori but from then on the main roads are numbered 1-jo-dori (No 1 Street) to 10-jo-dori by the river. Each block north to south is a 'chome'; 7-chome is to the left of the main pedestrianised shopping street from the station and on the right is 8-chome.

Buses depart from stops spread around the roads in front of the station. Bus stand No 5 for the zoo and the science museum is on Midoribashi-dori, which runs to the right of Seibu department store.

Festivals

Asahikawa Winter Festival (Asahikawa Fuyu Matsuri; around 8th-12th Feb) is not as vast or commercial as Sapporo Snow Festival (see p353) but it's just as impressive so is worth making time for.

The World Ice Sculpture Competition brings together international teams who compete to build giant sculptures. Some are built along the pedestrianised shopping street (Heiwa-dori) and others are by the river (Asahibashi); a 10- to 15-minute walk from the end of Heiwa-dori. Every year one of these is used as a stage for a variety of performances. A feature of the 2011 festival was a sculpture of the Daisetsuzan Mountains. A fireworks display takes place on the opening night.

Where to stay

The JR-operated *Asahikawa Terminal Hotel* (☎ 0166-24 0111, 🖳 www.asa hikawa-th.com; from ¥4000/S, ¥7400/D or Tw, ¥16,500/Tr, family room ¥25,000; Japanese-style room from ¥6500; rail-pass holders get a discount; breakfast ¥1100) is close to the station but it is not the newest of JR hotels. However, it is a must for any-one with young children as there's a spe-cially outfitted Japanese-style family room complete with kids' play area – soft toys, a mini slide, tunnels lit with LED lights – and a connected sleeping area for adults; it sleeps five. Most of the Western-style rooms offer internet access.

There are two branches of **Toyoko Inn** (🖳 www.toyoko-inn.com) within three minutes' walk of the station. *Toyoko Inn Asahikawa Ekimae Ichi-jo-dori* (☎ 0166-27 1045; from ¥4980/S, ¥6480/D, ¥6980/ Tw, inc breakfast) is at 1-jo-dori, 9-chome and *Toyoko Inn Asahikawa Ekimae Miyashita-dori* (☎ 0166-25 2045; from ¥5980/S, ¥7480/D, ¥7980/Tw, inc break-fast) is at Miyashita-dori, 10-chome.

Hotel Route Inn Asahikawa Ekimae (☎ 0166-21 5011, 🖳 route-inn.co.jp/eng lish; from ¥5300/S, ¥8000/D or Tw), at 1-jo-dori, is a five-minute walk from the station.

See pp45-52 for general details about finding accommodation.

Where to eat and drink

Chaos Heaven (Mon-Sat 11am-9pm, lunch to 3pm; 4-jo-dori, 8-chome) comes highly recommended for its soup curry (¥1000-1300), which comes with a selection of vegetables to which chicken, pork, bacon or frankfurter sausage can be added. Choose the amount of spiciness and also the amount

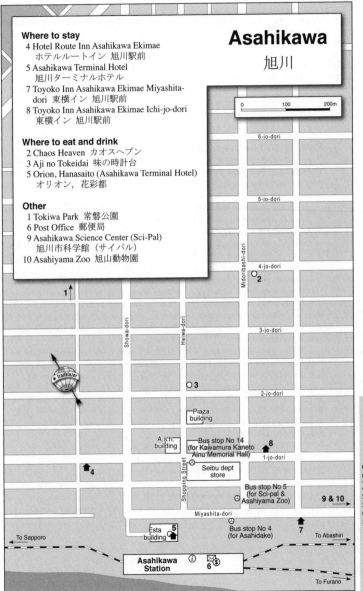

Asahikawa
旭川

Where to stay
4 Hotel Route Inn Asahikawa Ekimae
  ホテルルートイン 旭川駅前
5 Asahikawa Terminal Hotel
  旭川ターミナルホテル
7 Toyoko Inn Asahikawa Ekimae Miyashita-
  dori 東横イン 旭川駅前
8 Toyoko Inn Asahikawa Ekimae Ichi-jo-dori
  東横イン 旭川駅前

Where to eat and drink
2 Chaos Heaven カオスヘブン
3 Aji no Tokeidai 味の時計台
5 Orion, Hanasaito (Asahikawa Terminal Hotel)
  オリオン，花彩都

Other
1 Tokiwa Park 常磐公園
6 Post Office 郵便局
9 Asahikawa Science Center (Sci-Pal)
  旭川市科学館（サイパル）
10 Asahiyama Zoo 旭山動物園

0   100   200m

6-jo-dori

5-jo-dori

4-jo-dori

○2

Midoribashi-dori

3-jo-dori

Showa-dori

Heiwa-dori

★trailblazer

○3

2-jo-dori

Piaza
building

A.shi-
building

Bus stop No 14
(for Kawamura Kaneto
Ainu Memorial Hall)

▲8

1-jo-dori

▲4

Seibu dept
store

Shopping Street

Bus stop No 5
(for Sci-pal &
Asahiyama Zoo)

○

9 & 10

Miyashita-dori

○

Esta
building

▲5

Bus stop No 4
(for Asahidake)

▲7

To Abashiri

To Sapporo

Asahikawa
Station

ⓘ
6

✉$

To Furano

HOKKAIDO

of rice. The coconut-milk sauce is recommended. Also try their mango lassi (¥350).

Asahikawa is proud of its local version of the Sapporo ramen dish, where the pork is stewed in *shochu*. Try it at *Aji no Tokeidai* (11am-11pm; 2-jo-dori, 8-chome), which has a handy picture menu.

Asahikawa Terminal Hotel offers guests who eat in its *Hanasaito* restaurant (6th floor; daily 11am-9pm) a free alcoholic or soft drink with their meal, which makes it good value. The menu ranges from tempura soba sets (¥1100) to more elaborate meals for ¥3465. *Orion* (daily 7am-8pm), a Western-style café/restaurant, is on the ground floor.

There are also several Western-style places on Heiwa-dori, the pedestrianised road heading north from the station.

Side trip by bus to Asahidake

Alpine flowers bloom in spring on the slopes of Asahidake (Mt Asahi) in **Daisetsuzan National Park**, the highest mountain in Hokkaido. In winter, powder snow attracts skiers keen to take advantage of Japan's longest skiing season, from December to early May.

Access to the mountain is by bus from outside Asahikawa station to the resort of Asahidake-onsen (stop No 4; 3/day; 80 mins; ¥1320). Buses terminate at **Asahidake Ropeway** (🖥 wakasaresort.com/eng; 3-4/hr; 9am-5pm, to 4pm in winter, longer in summer; closed 7th-17th May & 30th Nov-10th Dec; Jun-mid Oct ¥2800 round trip, mid Oct-May ¥1800), which takes you up to 1600m.

Before going up the mountain, pop in to **Asahidake Visitor Center** (Jun-Oct daily 9am-5pm, Nov-May Tue-Sun 9am-4pm), on the main street just before the ropeway entrance. Here you can pick up a map and get a weather forecast. From the ropeway's top station a gentle 1km walk brings you to Asahidake's main lookout point, with smoke pouring out from rock turned yellow by the sulphur.

From the lookout point it's a further 2.6km to the **summit** (allow two hours up and one to get back) which, at 2290m, is sometimes covered in cloud. It's advisable to wear strong trainers or hiking boots as the path is rocky.

The 16-bed *Daisetsuzan Shirakaba-so Youth Hostel* (☎ 0166-97 2246, 🖥 park19.wakwak.com/~shirakaba; dorm from ¥5530, private room ¥7940; breakfast ¥760, dinner ¥1260, curry rice ¥630) is less than five minutes on foot down the main road from the ropeway station. Camp-jo-mae bus stop, the stop before the ropeway terminus, is right outside the hostel.

A place that has been highly recommended is *Hotel Bearmonte* (☎ 0166-97 2321, 🖥 www.bearmonte.jp; from ¥7350pp). It has a variety of indoor baths and *rotemburo*; rates depend in part on which way your room faces as some views are better than others.

The hotel is about three minutes' walk from the base of the ropeway. If you have booked at least four days in advance the hotel will offer a free shuttle bus from in front of Esta department store in Asahikawa.

KYUSHU

Kyushu – route guides

Despite its modern-day reputation as something of a backwater, Kyushu's history has been more linked with the West than any of the other main islands. The port of Nagasaki, in particular, was the only place in the country where trading with the outside world was permitted during Japan's nearly 300 years of self-imposed isolation under the Tokugawa shogunate.

Today, the majority of visitors to Kyushu pause briefly in **Fukuoka**, the island's capital, before making a beeline for **Nagasaki**, the second city in Japan to be hit with an atomic bomb in 1945. But if you're prepared to devote more time to seeing the island, it really is worth travelling further south. Perhaps because of its relatively mild climate, Kyushu feels more relaxed and the people more laid back than on Honshu. This may also have something to do with the popularity of *shochu*, a strong spirit found in every bar that becomes even stronger and more popular the further south you go.

A trip down the west coast brings you to the shochu capital, **Kagoshima**, sometimes described as the 'Naples of the East' because of its bay and neighbouring **Sakurajima**, one of the world's most active volcanoes; unlike Naples the city is virtually crime-free. And right in the centre of the island, a perfect side trip by rail from either the east or west coasts, lies formidable **Mt Aso**, where visitors can peer over the top of an active volcanic crater.

Nagasaki can be seen in a couple of days but allow at least a week if you're travelling down either coast and planning to fit in a visit to Mt Aso as well.

Kyushu can be reached easily by rail from Honshu via the Tokaido/Sanyo shinkansen lines, which run from Tokyo to Hakata (for Fukuoka). In spring 2011 the shinkansen line between Hakata and the southern terminus of Kagoshima-chuo was completed; until then it only operated between Shin-Yatsushiro and Kagoshima-chuo. The fastest journey time from Hakata to Kagoshima-chuo has thus been reduced from four to under two hours. There are Green Cars on the Sakura shinkansen but not on either the Mizuho or Tsubame.

Beyond the shinkansen, JR Kyushu runs an efficient network that

Hot spring in the mountains: high above the naked bathers the River of Heaven
(SHIKI MASAOKA)

山の温泉や裸の上の天の川

will take you just about anywhere and uses limited expresses on most of its lines. For details of JR Kyushu's rail pass see pp14-15, for suggested itineraries p25 and for information about using the rail route guide see pp8-9.

SHIN-YAMAGUCHI TO HAKATA/FUKUOKA BY SHINKANSEN
[Map 27, p365; Table 3, pp456-7]

Distances from Tokyo by shinkansen. Fastest journey time from Shin-Yamaguchi: 45 minutes.

Shin-Yamaguchi (1027km) All Kodama, some Nozomi and a few Sakura/Hikari stop here. Shin-Yamaguchi is the point of connection with the route guide around Western Honshu.

All Kodama stop at **Asa (1062km)**. Kodama and some Sakura/Hikari stop at **Shin-Shimonoseki (1089km)** before heading into the tunnel for the journey through the narrow Kammon Straits to Kyushu.

Kokura (1108km) All services stop at Kokura's sleek, modern station. Kokura made the American military's shortlist as the next A-Bomb target following the attack on Hiroshima, but cloud cover over the city on the morning of 9th August 1945 meant the plane carrying the bomb was forced to change direction and headed instead towards Nagasaki.

From Kokura, the shinkansen line continues on to Hakata/Fukuoka and the Nippo line runs along the east coast towards Oita (p375) and Miyazaki (see p380). LEX and local trains to Hakata run on the Kagoshima line. JR West runs the shinkansen tracks at Kokura, so if you're changing from the shinkansen follow the signs for 'JR Kyushu Lines'.

The main station concourse, with a central plaza and large TV screen, is on the 3rd floor. There is good disabled access, with lifts and ramps between the

---

⛩ **How to fillet a fugu**

Two stops west from Shin-Shimonoseki along the Sanyo line, right on the tip of Honshu, is **Shimonoseki**. This city is known for *fugu* (blow fish), the notorious fish that can be fatal if eaten when not correctly prepared. About 70% of Japan's fugu is traded at a fish market in Shimonoseki, where the fisherman and buyer haggle over the price by grasping one another's fingers in a cloth bag.

At the restaurant table, fugu is served raw, as a fish jelly or deep-fried. In a bid to ensure there are no foreign casualties the local government has produced step-by-step instructions in English on how to fillet a fugu. According to the manual, one should 'hit the fugu's head to knock it out', 'put the tip of the knife to the fugu's nostril and cut off the snout', 'scrape out the guts', 'take out the eyes' and 'chop the head'. If you can do or read all this without wincing, it's likely you could apply for a licence to prepare the fish; all would-be fugu masterchefs are required to have a licence before opening a restaurant serving fugu. This requirement should mean there is no risk to diners, though very occasionally reports of death-by-fugu creep into the national press. All the same, it's best not to think too much about the fugu swimming around above you as the shinkansen speeds through the underwater tunnel on its way to Kyushu.

KYUSHU

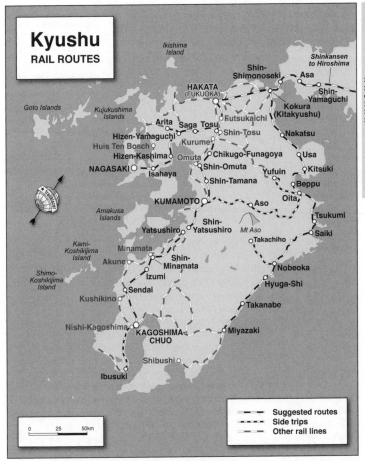

Kyushu
RAIL ROUTES

Ikishima Island

Shinkansen to Hiroshima

Shin-Shimonoseki
Asa
Shin-Yamaguchi

HAKATA
(FUKUOKA)

Goto Islands

Kujukushima Islands

Arita
Saga
Tosu
Futsukaichi
Kokura
(Kitakyushu)

Hizen-Yamaguchi
Shin-Tosu
Nakatsu

Huis Ten Bosch
Kurume
Usa

Hizen-Kashima
Omuta
Chikugo-Funagoya

NAGASAKI
Isahaya
Shin-Omuta
Yufuin
Kitsuki

Shin-Tamana
Beppu

KUMAMOTO
Aso
Oita

Amakusa Islands
Shin-Yatsushiro
Tsukumi

Kami-Koshikijima Island
Yatsushiro
Mt Aso
Saiki

Minamata
Takachiho

Akune
Shin-Minamata

Shimo-Koshikijima Island
Izumi
Nobeoka

Sendai
Hyuga-Shi

Kushikino
Takanabe

Nishi-Kagoshima
KAGOSHIMA-
CHUO
Miyazaki

Shibushi

Ibusuki

0   25   50km

Suggested routes
Side trips
Other rail lines

🎏 **Shinkansen services to Kyushu and within Kyushu**

The only shinkansen which run all the way from Tokyo to Hakata are the Nozomi services for which the Japan Rail Pass is not valid. Mizuho, Sakura and Kodama services to Hakata (the Mizuho and Sakura continue to Kagoshima-chuo) start in Shin-Osaka.

The Japan Rail Pass is valid on all services in Kyushu except the Mizuho. However, the JR Sanyo-Shikoku-Kyushu Rail Pass is valid on all services. For more details see pp14-15.

concourse and street level. The **tourist information counter** (daily 9am-7pm) is on the main concourse. Staff can provide you with an English map, a food-focused walking map (Kokura is synonymous with good food) and a free **Kitakyushu Welcome Card** (see box p64); Kokura is part of a wider area called Kitakyushu. From the main concourse, head towards the shinkansen entrance, next to which is an escalator that leads down to the north exit. Turn right at the bottom of the escalator and the office is in the corner.

The post office has an **ATM** on the main concourse, behind the entrance to the monorail: for cash withdrawals on international cards use the second machine from the right.

There are two **JR ticket offices**: one is to the left as you leave the shinkansen ticket barrier; the other, larger one is on the main concourse. There are **lockers** behind the entrance to the monorail on the main station concourse, but only a very small number of ¥600 ones. More can be found downstairs on the 1st (ground) floor.

New Kitakyushu Airport (🖥 english.kitakyu-air.jp) is a 30-minute bus journey from Kokura, on a man-made island off the Kyushu coast. Currently the only international flights are to/from Incheon, near Seoul, South Korea. Domestic routes include Sapporo, Tokyo and Nagoya.

Monorail buffs might like to take a round trip on the straddle-beam **Kitakyushu monorail**, which departs from Kokura on a 20-minute (8.8km) journey to Kikugaoka (4-6/hr; ¥290) in the suburbs. The entrance and ticket desk is on the main concourse of Kokura station. However, the side trip to Moji (see p366) may be of more interest.

Kokura is of limited appeal to the sightseer. That said, with a couple of hours to spare, it's worth fitting in a trip to the **castle area**, a 15-minute walk from the south exit of Kokura station. Head up the main street, Heiwa-dori, turn right on to Komonji-dori and cross the bridge. The entrance to the castle area is just past City Hall on your right. The castle (daily 9am-5pm, Apr-Oct to 6pm; ¥350, discounted with a Welcome Card) is a 1990 reconstruction of the original 1602 building and now hosts a kitsch puppet show. The only reason to stop here would be for the views from the top floor but you get much better views (for free) from the top floor of City Hall.

It's better to skip the castle and visit **Kokura Castle Japanese Garden** (daily 9am-5pm, Apr-Oct to 6pm; ¥300, discounted with a Welcome Card), the entrance to which is opposite the castle. An Edo-period home has been reconstructed overlooking a small Japanese garden, an unexpected oasis of calm in the middle of an industrial city. The only downside is the view of City Hall that looms overhead. For ¥500 extra, you'll be served a bowl of green tea and a Japanese sweetmeat by shuffling, kimono-clad women and you can briefly imagine yourself transported to a private house in Kyoto.

Families flock to northern Kyushu to visit **Space World** (🖥 www.space world.co.jp; 10am-5pm with seasonal variations; ¥4200, or ¥4000 with the

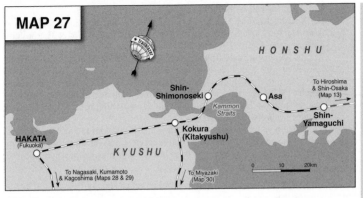

Welcome Card) theme park; it even has its own station (JR Space World) five stops from Kokura along the JR Kagoshima line.

The most convenient place to stay is ***Station Hotel Kokura*** (☎ 093-541 7111, 🖥 www.station-hotel.com; from ¥9009/S, ¥16,170/D, ¥17,902/Tw, 10% discount with a Japan Rail Pass or a Welcome Card), built into the JR station building.

Much cheaper and nearly as convenient is ***Nishitetsu Inn Kokura*** (☎ 093-511 5454, 🖥 www.n-inn.jp/hotels/kokura; from ¥6,200/S, ¥9000/D, ¥12,000/Tw inc a simple breakfast), three minutes from the south exit. Single travellers can upgrade to a double room for an additional ¥800. There is an upstairs onsen.

The 190-room ***Toyoko Inn Kokura Eki Minami-guchi*** (☎ 093-511 1045, 🖥 www.toyoko-inn.com; from ¥5480/S, ¥6480/D, ¥7980/Tw) is also a three-minute walk from the station's south exit.

Kokura's speciality is *yaki-udon* (similar to yakisoba, see p449, but using fried udon), served at several places near the station. One of the best is ***Ishin***, 10 minutes on foot from the south exit. Staff at the tourist information counter can point you in the right direction. If you don't want to leave the station, there are several restaurants on the 6th floor of AMU Plaza department store, including ***Masumasa Shokudo***, which serves yaki-udon.

If you fancy experiencing real local flavours, try making your own *daigaku-don* (student rice bowl) at ***Daigaku-don*** in **Tanga Market**. Buy your rice first in a donburi bowl, then seek out the multiplicity of market stalls outside to purchase toppings from the vocal traders before returning to eat. Unsurprisingly, it was local university students who started this practice.

At ***Yagumo-tei*** (discounts for Kitakyushu Welcome Card holders), a five-minute walk from the station, the raw fish is so fresh, the squid may still be twitching at your table. Eating live squid is a rarity even in this city. Go straight out of the main station exit, turning left at the main junction of Katsuyama street, and look for the restaurant on the right side.

Side trip by rail from Kokura

For **Kyushu Railway History Museum** (Kyushu Tetsudo Kinenkan; 🖳 www
.k-rhm.jp; daily 9am-5pm except 2nd Wed of month & 2nd Wed & Thur in July,
daily in Aug; ¥300, ¥240 with a Sugoca card, see box p44), operated by JR
Kyushu, take a JR Sanyo or JR Kagoshima line (2-3/hr, 5-7 mins) train to **Moji**.

While much smaller than the museums at Omiya (see p270) or Nagoya
(see p160), it is nicely laid out and has mini-trains, modelled on real types,
which visitors can do a circuit on. Moji has a number of historic buildings
(dating from the 1920s and '30s), including the station itself, which is a few
minutes' walk from the museum.

Nearby is the **Mojiko Retro Train** (daily 25th Mar to 3rd Apr, 29th Apr
to 5th May & 21st Jul to 31st Aug; weekends only at other times; 10am-
4.30pm; 25 mins; ¥300), a blue open train, which runs along a line with just
four stations (including termini).

From Kokura it's one more stop by shinkansen to Hakata/Fukuoka. If heading down the east coast (on the route starting on p374), change trains here
rather than at Hakata, otherwise you'll have to backtrack.

Hakata/Fukuoka (1175km)   [see pp381-8]

It's mostly tunnels on the short journey between Kokura and Hakata; in the brief
snatches of daylight it's surprising to see how lush and green the countryside is.

Hakata is the terminus for the Tokaido/Sanyo shinkansen and the starting
point for JR Kyushu's shinkansen service south to Kumamoto and Kagoshima.
It is also the name of the JR station for the city of Fukuoka.

HAKATA/FUKUOKA TO NAGASAKI   [Map 28; Table 22, p467]

Distances by JR from Hakata. Fastest journey time: 1¾ hours.

Hakata (0km) A blueprint for an extension of the shinkansen line to Nagasaki
was drawn up in 1973 and some construction has happened but it is likely to be
years before the extension is operational. For now, the fastest way is on the
Kamome LEX from Hakata along the JR Kagoshima line; if only going to Tosu,
Saga, Hizen-Yamaguchi, or Arita (see p368) you can also take the Midori (1/hr).

Futsukaichi (14km) Some trains make a brief stop at this hot spring resort.

Of far more interest is neighbouring **Dazaifu**, home to the Tenmangu
Shrine and the impressive new Kyushu National Museum; for full details see
p389.

Tosu (29km) There are few facilities at Tosu station, apart from a small
branch of the *Train D'Or* bakery and a convenience store. Exit the station and
you'll see the 'Joyful Town' shopping complex a couple of minutes' walk away.
Here there's a selection of cafés and restaurants and a large department store.

Popular with locals but also of interest to anyone needing a spot of retail
therapy, **Tosu Premium Outlet Mall** (daily 10am-8pm) carries a vast range of
Japanese and international designer brands. Modelled on a southern Californian
town, it is accessed by bus from Tosu station (2/hr, or every 45 mins at weekends; 15 mins; ¥200).

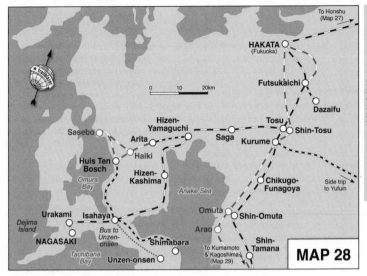

From Tosu, the Nagasaki line heads west towards Nagasaki; this is the route followed here.

For details of the shinkansen services from Shin-Tosu (3 mins on JR Nagasaki line) south to Kumamoto and Kagoshima, see p369.

Saga (54km) Everyone passes through Saga on their way to Nagasaki but few stop here, venue for an **International Balloon Festival** (🖥 www.sibf.jp/e) in November. However, the prefecture is known internationally for its hand-made pottery, exports of which historically left the small town of Karatsu, 80 minutes away on the local Karatsu line. However, much of it was first produced in and around the town of Arita (see p368).

Saga station has north and south exits, **lockers** and a **tourist information office** (daily 8.30am-5/6pm) on the concourse. If you decide to stay, *Toyoko Inn Saga Ekimae* (☎ 0952-23 1045, 🖥 www.toyoko-inn.com; ¥4980/S, ¥6980/D, ¥7480/Tw) is immediately to your right as you take the station's south exit.

In Saga city, the main sight is **Kono Park**, inside which is the **Tea House Kakurintei** (Tue-Sun 9am-5pm; free), a reconstruction of the original built in 1846 by Lord Naomasa Nabeshima, 10th lord of the Saga Clan. It's small but has been faithfully reconstructed with a veranda commanding great views of the surrounding lake (and less impressive views of a concrete water tower). Green tea (¥300) is served.

Hizen-Yamaguchi (68km) This is the junction for the branch line to Sasebo which stops at Arita (see p368) en route. Travelling to Nagasaki there's no need to change trains because the Kamome LEX continues along the Nagasaki line.

Side trip by rail to Arita

The hand-made pottery the prefecture is known for was first produced in and around Arita (🖥 www.arita.jp/en). These milky-white ceramic pieces were highly prized by the Dutch East India company and other European traders.

If not already on a Midori LEX (1/hr; 3/day divide at Haiki and continue to Huis Ten Bosch, see p397) from Hakata transfer at Hizen-Yamaguchi (30 mins), or Saga (40 mins), to Arita and visit **Kyushu Ceramic Museum** (Tue-Sun 9am-4.30pm; free) to view a well-designed history of Japanese porcelain development as well as some fine contemporary pieces. On the walk ahead from the station exit you will cross a bridge festooned with elaborate ornamental pottery. Take the pedestrian overpass and go up the steps on the left to the entrance. The museum's large ceramic clock and unique porcelain toilet cubicles are worth the visit alone.

At nearby **Gallery Arita** (daily 9am-6pm) you can eat reasonably priced lunch sets served on colourful Arita-yaki (Arita ceramics) and buy authentic porcelain souvenirs from the impressive shop. Turn right when you cross back over the green pedestrian overpass; it is on the left-hand side – look for the enormous vase outside.

Arita porcelain fair (29th Apr to 5th May) offers the chance to pick up a variety of bargains as long as you are prepared to jostle with the crowds.

After **Hizen-Kashima (83km)** the line follows the coast, affording great views of the Ariake Sea on the left side. The train briefly comes to a halt along the coast to allow the train returning to Hakata to pass. The view is occasionally blotted out by the odd tunnel and gradually the train moves more inland before arriving at Isahaya.

Isahaya (129km) Isahaya is a gateway to **Shimabara Peninsula**, which juts out east of Nagasaki into the Ariake Sea. Today, people visit for the scenery and to visit the hot-spring resort of Unzen-onsen.

For **Shimabara** turn right out of the JR station; the entrance to the private Shimabara Railway is between Mister Donut and the Joyroad travel agency. Purchase tickets from the ticket machine in the JR station (Isahaya to Shimabara 1-2/hr; approx 65 mins; ¥1330; JR rail passes are not valid).

Buses to **Unzen** are operated by Shimatetsu (🖥 www.shimatetsu.co.jp approx 10/day; 80-90 mins; ¥1300 one way) leave from the bus terminal directly opposite Isahaya station.

Side trips from Isahaya

● **Unzen-onsen** In addition to the many ryokan and public baths in Unzen-onsen (🖥 www.unzen.org/e_ver) people come to see Unzen-Jigoku (Unzen Hell), a place where hot water/steam spurts out of the ground.

About 350 years ago, during the time of religious persecution in Japan, 30 Christians were sent here for refusing to renounce their faith and were thrown into the boiling hot springs. Unzen-onsen and Unzen-Jigoku are at the base of Mt Unzen, an active volcano, that last erupted in 1995; it has over the years also caused lots of deaths but is now deemed safe to go hiking on again.

● **Shimabara** Shimabara Railway runs from Isahaya around the peninsula, stopping at Shimabara (🖥 www.city.shimabara.lg.jp) on the eastern side.

Being a port town it was a place where many Christian missionaries came. It is also a castle town (daily 9am-5pm; ¥520) and has a street with samurai houses (daily 9am-5pm; free) and a neighbourhood, south of the castle, with lots of narrow canals full of bright coloured carp (koi).

For the last ten minutes of the journey to Nagasaki the train goes at full speed and there's one long tunnel about five minutes before arrival.

Urakami (152km) When it first opened in 1897, Urakami was Nagasaki station. But the growth of the downtown port area and land reclamation meant traffic shifted further away so a decision was made to construct a new Nagasaki station; in 1905 the station's name was changed to Urakami.

The atomic bomb exploded at 11.02am on 9th August 1945 over this district; Urakami is the nearest JR stop to the A-Bomb Museum and Peace Park (see pp390-1).

Nagasaki (154km) [see pp389-97

HAKATA/FUKUOKA TO KAGOSHIMA-CHUO BY SHINKANSEN
[Map 28, p367; Map 29, p371; Table 23, p468]

Distances by JR shinkansen from Hakata. Fastest journey time: 79 minutes.

The Tsubame stops at all stations on this route, though some services only go to Kumamoto; the Sakura stops at most stations; and the Mizuho only stops at Kumamoto. The Mizuho can be used with the JR Kyushu Rail Pass but not the Japan Rail Pass.

For the most part there is not much to see on this journey. Though you do get occasional glimpses of flat farm land (mostly rice fields) and wooded hills, for much of the time you are in a tunnel or there is a barrier obscuring the view.

If you get out at the stations between the main towns you will notice how often they seem to be in the middle of nowhere, what vast and impressive structures they are, and how much wood has been used. It is interesting to speculate on what the local farmers feel about the change in their landscape.

Hakata (0km) [Fukuoka/Hakata, see pp381-8]

Shin-Tosu (29km) All Tsubame and most Sakura stop here. There is little of interest other than being a place to transfer to the JR Nagasaki line (especially if coming from Kumamoto or Kagoshima as it saves backtracking all the way to Hakata) for Nagasaki (see pp389-97). When the planned extension of the shinkansen line to Nagasaki is open this will be the junction station.

If you do stop here the **tourist information centre** (daily 8am-8pm) offers free internet access and there is a **Family Mart** in the station as well as **lockers**. The **ticket office** is open daily (5.30am-11.40pm).

If you are keen on shopping you might like to take the bus (10 mins; ¥200) to Premium Outlet (see p366).

Kurume (36km) All Tsubame and most Sakura stop here. Kurume station is the point of interchange for the Kyudai line that cuts across Kyushu (west to

KYUSHU

east), stopping at the hot spring resort of **Yufuin** (see pp376-7) before terminating in **Oita** (see pp375-6). The Yufu and Yufuin no Mori LEX run four times a day to Oita (2 hrs 20 mins) and an additional 2/day as far as Yufuin (96 mins).

It isn't really worth stopping at Kurume unless you want to stay the night before continuing to Yufuin or Oita. If you do, the **tourist information centre** (🖳 www.kurume-hotomeki.jp; daily 9am-7pm), opposite the exit to the shinkansen station, should be your first port of call as they have audio guides which can be borrowed for free (10am-3pm, return by 5pm).

To walk round all 20 places that are covered in the audio guide would take a long time but it is worth doing a circuit starting from the west exit of the station. Turn left there and follow the signs to Suitengu Shrine (about 10 mins). Turn right at the first set of traffic lights and turn right again at the end of Suitengu-dori and walk along parallel to the river.

Suitengu Shrine dates from 1650 and its location by the river means it is a guardian shrine for marine traffic as well as housing the god of safe childbirth.

From here head back along the river towards **Bairin-ji**. You will be able to see it from the riverbank; climb up the rather overgrown steps. The temple is where ascetic (Zen Buddhist) monks come to train and for this reason you can't go into the buildings – indeed the doors are firmly closed – but the grounds are a pleasant place for a stroll. Retrace your steps to the river bank and walk along it, under the shinkansen and local line railway tracks and past the Bridgestone and Asahi factories, then look for another set of overgrown steps. Climb up and join the road heading left; soon you will walk past the remains of **Kurume Castle** and **Sasayama Shinto Shrine**; neither is of particular interest. Turn right here (if you don't go into the castle grounds first) and then right at the traffic lights and from there follow the main road back to the east side of the station. Before you go into the station look out for the **huge tyre** – its diameter is four metres – symbolising the importance of Bridgestone to the town.

The most convenient place to stay is **Kurume Station Hotel** (☎ 0942-36 1122, 🖳 ksth.com; ¥5500-6300/S, ¥8900-14,700/Tw, ¥13,200-18,900/D; Japanese- or Western-style breakfast ¥450); it is on the left if facing the station, behind the bus terminal. A feature of this hotel is the range of massage and other relaxing treatments (from ¥3200/20 mins; discounts available) on offer.

A good place to go for something is eat is **Friesta**, on the 2nd floor by the west exit of the station. There are several restaurants: okonomiyaki (11am-10pm), yakitori (11am-2pm & 5-11pm), udon (11am-11pm) and sashimi (11am-2pm & 5pm to midnight).

⌘ The pre-shinkansen route

The sections of pre-shinkansen railway line (JR Kagoshima line) which run between Hakata and Yatsushiro (via Kumamoto) and from Sendai to Kagoshima-chuo are still operated by JR Kyushu. However, the section between Yatsushiro and Sendai is now run by a private company, Hisatsu Orange Railway, and the fare is ¥2550. JR passes are not valid on this route so it is best to take the shinkansen.

Chikugo-Funagoya (51.5km) Only Tsubame stop here. This station is one of only a few shinkansen stations in a park, in this case **Chikugo Regional Park**, the largest in Fukuoka prefecture.

The only reason to stop here would be to go to one of the **onsen**. One of these is called Suzume-jigoku (Sparrow Hell) because so many sparrows were killed by the hot steam. However, for humans the hot springs can have a healing effect as the water has a variety of minerals.

For details of the various onsen hotels in the area visit 🖥 www.crossroadfukuoka.jp/en.

On the concourse after the first set of escalators down from the shinkansen tracks look out for the large selection of leaflets and the video displays about the attractions of the area. However, sadly none is in English and there is no staffed tourist information centre here.

Shin-Omuta (69km) Only Tsubame stop here; not worth a visit.

Shin-Tamana (90km) Only Tsubame stop here. Shin-Tamana is almost in the middle of nowhere but it is the access point for **Tamana-onsen**. There are several minshuku and ryokan in town and it is possible to go to some for the day (from ¥500) without staying, though if you want to have an onsen experience for free go to the *ashiyu* (foot onsen) in the middle of Tamana.

The staff at the **tourist information centre** (daily 9am-7pm) in the station can help you choose where to go.

A bus (Route 7; ¥160) runs between Shin-Tamana, the onsen area and the original Tamana station several times a day; take the right-hand exit from the station to find the bus stop and the taxi rank (first on the right).

Make the most of the views as soon the train passes through more tunnels with fleeting glimpses of tree-clad hills before you reach the built-up area signalling you are getting near Kumamoto.

KYUSHU

To Hakata
(Map 28) | Tosu 〇〇 Shin-Tosu
Saga 〇
〇 Kurume
To Nagasaki
(Map 28) | Side trip to Yufuin
〇 Chikugo-Funagoya
Omuta 〇〇 Shin-Omuta
Arao 〇 | Shin-Tamana
〇 Tamana
KUMAMOTO 〇
0   10   20km
Shin-Yatsushiro 〇
Yatsushiro 〇
Yatsushiro Bay
Minamata 〇 Shin-Minamata
〇 Izumi
〇 Akune
★ trailblazer
〇 Sendai
KAGOSHIMA-CHUO
(for KAGOSHIMA)
Kushikino 〇
Ijuin 〇
MAP 29 | Nishi-Kagoshima

Kumamoto (118km)   [see pp397-404]

All shinkansen stop here. Kumamoto is a point of interchange for the highly scenic journey across Kyushu to Oita (see pp375-6) on the east coast, via the dramatic Mt Aso caldera.

Side trip by rail to Mt Aso   [Map 31, p377]

A trip to the Aso Tableland with its spectacular mountain scenery and the chance to peer over the edge of a volcanic crater makes an excursion to the centre of Kyushu a highlight of any rail journey in Japan.

An advantage of this journey is that it can be combined with a tour of both Kyushu's west and east coasts.

Access to the tableland is via Aso station on the JR Hohi line. Take the Kyushu Odan Tokkyu LEX (about 67 mins; 4/day; 50km) to Aso station; all other services are local and require several changes of train. In the latter part of the journey the train passes through the Aso valley and its rice fields. In the distance, the craters come into view a while before the train arrives in Aso.

Mt Aso refers not to one particular mountain but to the whole caldera area and all five of its peaks, called Nakadake, Takadake, Nekodake, Kijimadake and Eboshidake. All of these are contained within the enormous outer crater that is the Aso tableland.

The most accessible and impressive is **Nakadake**, the only active volcano, reached by a combination of bus and ropeway. If weather conditions allow you can peer over the edge of this volcanic crater and see the bubbling green liquid below. The last big eruption at Nakadake was in 1979, when a sudden explosion killed three and injured eleven. The ropeway to the crater is often closed because of sulphur gas, and sometimes when it is too foggy.

Aso station is the gateway to Aso National Park. The train only makes a very brief stop here, so be ready to jump off as soon as the doors open. Turn left after leaving the station building to find the **tourist information centre** (🖳 www.asocity-kanko.jp; daily 9am-5pm), whose staff will help book accommodation and provide walking maps and bus timetables for rides to the main hotel area of Uchinomaki (11 mins; ¥280) and to Mt Aso. They can also arrange pick-up services from the station to your hotel. You can store luggage here (daily 9am-5pm; ¥300 per bag) if it won't fit into a locker and even rent a bike (¥900/day).

From the station, seven **buses** a day run up to Nakadake via Asosan-nishi station (no buses after 3pm; 40 mins; ¥540). From Asosan-nishi, a **ropeway** (daily 9am-5pm; every 8 mins; ¥600) completes the journey to the crater. But as the ascent is a rather gentle 108 metres, you might take the terracotta footpath that hugs the roadside instead (20 mins), a relatively quick and physically undemanding opportunity to survey the wondrous landscape.

The ropeway deposits you just beneath the crater. It's an extraordinary experience to stand at the edge of the crater. Some slopes in this area provided exterior shots for Ernst Blofeld's missile silo in the 1967 James Bond film, *You Only Live Twice*. More recently, concrete bunkers have been built in the event of a sudden eruption; experts suggest that at the first sign of danger it's best to run backwards, looking at the crater, so as to dodge pieces of volcanic debris.

If the weather does not cooperate, **Aso Volcano Museum** (daily 9am-5pm; ¥840) displays footage of major eruptions and has real-time cameras for

a close-up of the crater without having to peer over the edge yourself. 7
museum is on the way to Asosan-nishi ropeway and the bus stops in front of it.

The homely and very pleasant *Aso Base Backpackers* (☎ 0967-34-0408,
🖳 www.aso-backpackers.com; ¥2800/dorm; ¥5500/S, ¥6000/D, ¥6600/Tw) is
the newest hostel in Aso and the nearest to the station, located just beyond the
first junction from the station. Facilities are kept spotless, wi-fi is free, there
are mountain views from most rooms and there's an ATM (Mon-Fri 8.45am-
6pm, Sat 9am-5pm, Sun & public holidays 9am-12.30pm) across the street in
the post office's lobby. Check-in is between 4pm and 8pm. Excellent free
walking maps (featuring restaurants and cafés) are available and you also get
a ¥100 discount for the cosy **Yumenoyu** (hot spring; daily 10am-9.30pm;
¥400) near the station. A 24hr Lawson Station convenience store is also
located nearby.

Aso Youth Hostel (☎ 0967-34 0804, 🖳 www.aso-yh.ecnet.jp; ¥2450/
dorm; no meals) is the more established if comparatively scruffier hostel and
still represents good value. There's a kitchen and hiking route maps. The hostel is a 15-minute walk from the station, or you can take the bus bound for
Asosan-nishi station and get off at the first stop; a taxi costs ¥700). Check-in
is also 4-8pm and the front door is closed at 8pm. Call to reserve.

For a hearty meal you can't beat *Sanzoku Tabiji* (Thur-Tue 11am-7pm; no
English spoken). The set menus (from ¥850) are huge and include mountain
vegetables and wild potatoes. Head up the road from Aso station until you
reach Route 57. Turn right on to this main road and the restaurant is a 10- to
15-minute walk along the road on the left. Next door is *Bento no Hirai* (daily
24hr), with a take-out facility which may be of use as many local restaurants
tend to shut early.

To continue from here to Oita, or Beppu (for details on both see p375), get
back on a Kyushu Odan Tokkyu LEX (4/day; about 102 mins).

Shin-Yatsushiro (151km)
All Tsubame and most Sakura stop here.
However, there is no reason to get out.

Unfortunately nearly all the journey from Shin-Yatsushiro to Kagoshima-
chuo is through tunnels. The old JR line skirted Yatsushiro Bay and passengers
enjoyed views out to sea. Bullet-train passengers have to make do with speed
and darkness but they do get on-board comfort.

Shin-Minamata (194km)
The station was constructed for the new shinkansen
and is connected to the Hisatsu Orange Railway (JR passes not accepted), on
your right as you exit. However, there is no real reason to stop here.

If you look carefully, for part of this stretch of the journey – when the train
isn't speeding into tunnels – you can see the old JR track. Keep an eye out also
for a brief glimpse of the sea to your right shortly before the train arrives. What
you might also see – but only between November and March – are Siberian
cranes (see below).

Izumi (210km)
Some services call here briefly. It is a small station also with
a connection to the Hisatsu Orange Railway. Izumi is home to 10,000 Siberian
cranes during the winter months. It's a paradise for bird-watchers and if you're

here in season staff at the local products and **information office** (🖥 www.city.
izumi.kagoshima.jp/english.asp) opposite the station exit can advise on access
to the **Crane Observation Centre** (daily Nov-Mar 9am-5pm; ¥210). A sightseeing excursion bus (Dec-Feb only; 6/day; ¥1000) operates from the west exit,
or take a taxi for about ¥4500.

In the summer months you can see the cranes come to life on the big screen
at the Dome Theater inside the museum at **Crane Park Izumi** (daily Nov-Mar,
Tue-Sun Apr-Oct, 9am-5pm; ¥310). The park is within walking distance from
the station.

An alternative sightseeing spot, 20 minutes on foot from the station or
quicker by bicycle (maps available from the information office), is **Izumi-
fumoto Bukeyashiki-ato**, an area of preserved Edo-period samurai residences.
Cycles can be rented from the station (¥300/3 hours).

Hotel Wing (☎ 0996-63 8111, 🖥 izumi.hotelwingjapan.com; ¥5800/S,
¥7800/D, ¥8800/Tw; ¥700 buffet breakfast) provides Western-style accommodation. To find the hotel, take the escalator for the Hisatsu Orange railway and look
for the 'W' sign on a white building to the left across from the railway track.

After Izumi, some services stop at **Sendai (243km)** before hurtling into
tunnel after tunnel on the way to the Kagoshima-chuo terminal.

Kagoshima-chuo (289km) [see pp404-10]

Kagoshima-chuo station is the main rail terminal for the city of Kagoshima and
the terminus for limited express trains from Hakata.

Kagoshima station is one stop further along but it's small and you'll probably only pass through it if heading towards Miyazaki (see below) on the JR
Nippo line.

Alternative route back to Hakata

Instead of returning to Hakata the same way, it's possible to cut across Kyushu
via the JR Nippo line (120 mins by Kirishima LEX; 10/day) to Miyazaki (see
p380), then follow the route described below in reverse.

The Nichirin Seagaia LEX goes from Miyazaki to Hakata (see Table 24,
p468). If on a Nichirin you will need to change at Oita or Beppu.

KOKURA TO MIYAZAKI [Map 30; Map 32, p379; Table 24, p468]

Distances by JR from Kokura. Fastest journey time: 4 hours 10 mins.

Note: Although it's possible to start a journey down the east coast from Hakata,
if coming from Honshu you'll save a lot of time by changing on to a limited
express at Kokura.

Kokura (0km) The Nichirin Seagaia only goes once a day to Miyazaki so the
chances are you will need to take a Sonic to Oita or Beppu and change there. If
you are on the 883 version you may like the fact that it has headrests that make
you look like Mickey Mouse. Sit on the left side for views of the coast.

The Nichirin Seagaia doesn't stop at Usa or Kitsuki but Sonic services stop
at all or some of the following: **Yukuhashi (25km), Unoshima (45.2km),**

Nakatsu (52km), **Yanagigaura (69km)**, **Usa (76km)** (where American visitors may wish to photograph the tori-framed station signs; Usa is pronounced Oo-sa) and **Kitsuki (99km)**.

Beppu (121km) Infamous as one of Japan's most garish hot-spring resorts, the classic image of the rustic hot spring is shattered by the view as the train arrives in Beppu (🖳 www.city. beppu.oita.jp). It's a sprawling city and somewhere amongst the mass of concrete buildings lie many hot springs that have to be seen to be believed – or simply avoided.

Tacky, overly commercial, a tourist trap – all of these apply. But Beppu sweeps away criticism levelled at it with a confident 'so what?'. It can perhaps justify this attitude as it produces more hot-spring water than any other onsen town in Japan.

As the train pulls away, the left side affords stunning views back across the bay towards the city. Look carefully and you may spot white steam puffing out of the many spas dotting the steep hillside beyond.

Oita (133km) A 'humanistic city with rich greeneries', according to the town guide given out at the **tourist information booth** (🖳 www. oishiimati-oita.jp; daily 9am-5.30pm) just outside the station.

Oita can certainly lay claim to being an international city since it's twinned with Austin, Texas (USA), Wuhan in China, and Abeiro in Portugal, and was also a host city for the 2002 Korea-Japan World Cup. However, the main reason for stopping here now is for a side trip to Yufuin (see pp376-8) or to Aso (see p378).

At the station, turn right after the ticket barrier and walk straight to find **lockers** (mostly ¥300 size but a few large ¥600 ones) at the very end of the concourse.

There are several options for a snack in the station; the **udon** restaurant does good noodle dishes (from ¥380).

MAP 30

KYUSHU

city's **Art Museum** (Tue-Sun 10am-5.30pm; ¥300-800 depending on the exhibition) is 10 minutes by bus (hourly; ¥160) from the station and has temporary exhibitions throughout the year.

The other main attractions in the area are the **Mount Takasaki Monkey Land** (Takasaki Shizen-dobutsu-en; 🖥 www.takasakiyama.jp; daily 8.30am-5pm; ¥500, or ¥2200 inc the Aquarium) and the adjoining **Oita Marine Palace Aquarium 'Umitamago'** (🖥 www.umitamago.jp; Mon-Fri 9am-6pm, Sat & Sun to 9pm; ¥1890, or ¥2200 inc Monkey Land) which are a bus ride from Oita station (¥800 return) but also very close to Beppu if you choose to alight there. At Monkey Land you can roam the 628m-high mountain home of 1300 wild monkeys and watch them feeding – but avoid looking directly into the eyes, as warned in the tourist pamphlet, for they can turn aggressive. The Aquarium features dolphin shows, coral tanks and a variety of other marine creatures.

Comodo Hotel (☎ 097-514-4000; 🖥 www.comodo-hotel.jp; ¥5190/S, ¥7440/D), a minute's walk from the station, offers decent and affordable accommodation with the bonus of an excellent hot spring and sauna on the top floor. After a soak, those brave enough to negotiate the exposed outer stairwell (in full view of Oita city) can wallow in one of three additional rooftop tubs.

Oita Century Hotel (☎ 097 536 2777, 🖥 www.oita-centuryhotel.jp; ¥3850/S, ¥6600/D, ¥7300/Tw), another smart business hotel near the station, is also worth checking out once you have picked up their discount voucher at the tourist office.

If continuing to Miyazaki you will need to change here to a Nichirin LEX.

Side trip by rail to Yufuin [see Map 31]
With Oita prefecture famed for its natural beauty, hiking and abundance of hot springs, the town of Yufuin offers a tranquil and cultural antidote to Beppu's commercial hedonism.

Nestling at the base of Mount Yufu, the town not only boasts a variety of onsen but an assortment of craft shops, koi ponds, art galleries and museums to enrich both soul and body.

The annual *Yufuin Film Festival* (final week in August) further tries to advance the town's cultural credentials.

The Yufu LEX runs to Yufuin (3/day) as does the Yufuin-no-mori LEX (1/day); both take 48 minutes. Local JR Kyudai line trains are more frequent but take around an hour.

The remarkable wooden structure of the station encompasses a **tourist information office** (daily 9am-7pm) on the left of the ticket gate. Staff can provide a walking map, details of public access to private onsens, and information on horse-drawn carriage tours around the town, which depart from the station (50 mins; ¥1500). Another option is a town tour in an English classic car (1/hr; 50 mins; ¥1200) including a look at a local shrine, temple and garden.

There is a small café and small gallery on the left of the station and toilets around to the right.

Visitors wanting a unique museum experience should definitely visit **Yufuin Art Museum** (🖥 www.coara.or.jp/~yufuin; Fri-Wed 10am-5.30pm; ¥600). Inspired by the work and philosophy of the travelling artist and poet Kei

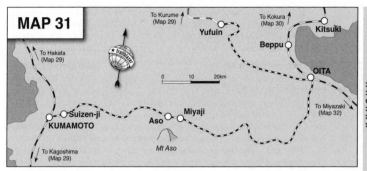

Satoh, the museum breaks with tradition in allowing visitors ample contact with the art itself. Set in a series of small rooms around a circular courtyard, you can peer through oil-based kaleidoscopes, dip your feet in a footbath, or sit and paint the verdant hillsides on a postcard (¥120). Most audacious of all is a grassy mound where the artwork is simply the panorama itself. You can't help but smile. The shop sells good-quality Oita ceramics and other artistic souvenirs. Head up the main street from the station, turn right at the Museum sign by the coffee shop until you reach the river, then left and the entrance is by a large stone on the left side.

A little further along the river you can try the kitsch **Trick Art Museum** (🖳 www.trickart-kyushu.com/yufuin.php; Mar-Sep 9.30am-5.30pm, Oct-Feb 9.30am-5pm; ¥800) where you can literally immerse yourself in masterpieces (by shaking hands with the Mona Lisa, for example) that seem to spill out of the frames for a fun, albeit bizarre, photo opportunity.

Further up the riverside you will eventually hit the pathway around the popular **Kinrinko** lake, filled with koi and birds skimming the clear surface. A great place to admire the lake views or simply relax with a book is the bankside terrace of *Café La Ruche* (11.30am-3pm & 6.30-9pm), which serves good European-style lunch sets (Quiche Lorraine ¥1250) and sandwiches. The superb baked cheesecake and tea/scone sets are both ¥950. If you still don't feel quite relaxed enough, exit the café, turn right twice until you come to the small hut of the **Shitanyu** public hot spring (¥200 honesty box). Theoretically this onsen is unisex, although women seem to steer clear. Undress, wash, plunge in to the sunny bath and enjoy partial views of the lake. Don't forget to bring soap and a towel as it is unstaffed.

A good place to stay is the friendly *Yufuin Country Road Youth Hostel* (☎ 0977-84 3734, 🖳 www.jyh.or.jp, 🖳 yufuincryh@ray.ocn.ne.jp for reservations; ¥3360/dorm, ¥4410pp private room, plus ¥600 non-members; breakfast ¥630; dinner ¥1050). Basic refreshments are free and there's also a shop as well as laundry, internet (¥100/hr) and onsen facilities (onsen tax ¥100-150). Check-in is from 4pm. There are three buses from the station (Mon-Fri 4.48pm, 5.58pm, 6.38pm; 7 mins; ¥200); get off at the Torigoe Iriguchi stop from where it is a three-minute walk. Alternatively, take a taxi (¥900; 5 mins) or walk (2.3km; 35 mins) up the RG17 road. If here at a weekend or a public holiday you can arrange a pick up (6.10pm) at the station itself.

If you were to make one expensive splurge on a ryokan during your trip to Japan, try ***Hotel Kamenoi Besso*** (☎ 0977-84 3166; 🖥 www.kamenoi-bes sou.jp; ¥35,000-40,000pp half-board) near the edge of Kinrinko. It's an idyllic and luxurious retreat, and each room boasts a private natural onsen.

Side trip by rail to Mt Aso [see Map 31, p377]
The main reason for stopping in Oita is to connect up with the JR Hohi line (also known as the Aso Kogen line) that cuts across Kyushu to Kumamoto via the stunning volcanic peaks of **Mt Aso tableland** (see pp372-3). Kyushu Odan Tokkyu (Express) runs (4/day; all JR passes accepted) to **Aso** station (50km; about 67 mins) before terminating in Kumamoto (see pp397-404; 98km; about 102 mins). All other services are local and require several changes of train.

Very soon after leaving Oita the train starts a gradual climb into the mountains and forest scenery takes over. As the train chugs down the single-track line there are long stretches where it passes small clusters of houses separated by fields and mountains.

Heading towards Aso station, the craters that make up the Aso range should be visible in the distance.

Usuki (169km) Usuki's main attraction is the exquisite array of Heian/Kamakura-era Stone Buddha carvings (¥530) tucked serenely away into a remote hillside just 18 minutes by JR bus from the station. Take the bus bound for Miemachi and alight at the Usuki Sekibutsu stop. The statues are a five-minute walk away.

If you don't fancy venturing too far, pick up a tourist map and borrow a free canary-yellow bike from the station master's collection to tour the narrow historic lanes, temples and castle remnants of this charming coastal town before reboarding the next train.

The next stop is **Tsukumi (179km)**.

Saiki (198km) As you approach Saiki there are good views out to sea on the left side. The views become more spectacular as the train leaves the coast and begins to thread its way inland through the hills, where the landscape may remind you of Switzerland.

Nobeoka (256km) There is nothing to see in Nobeoka itself and you may well be disappointed that the verdant landscape enjoyed so far on the journey abruptly disappears as the train pulls in to the station. However, you can transfer here for a side trip to the mountain town Takachiho (see opposite).

Nobeoka was put on the literary map by Japanese author Soseki Natsume, who mentions the place in his most famous novel, *Botchan*.

The refurbished ***City Hotel Plaza Nobeoka*** (☎ 0982-35 8888, 🖥 www.city-h.co.jp; ¥4600/S, ¥6090/D, ¥9800/Tw) is to the left as you leave the station and has a vast range of smart rooms.

Alternatively, a five-minute taxi ride away (¥560) is the more upmarket, business-style ***Hotel Merieges Nobeoka*** (☎ 0982-32 6060, 🖥 www.merieges-n.co.jp; ¥7600/S, ¥12,500/D, ¥14,000/Tw), which has a good Chinese restaurant and a rooftop beer garden (May-Sep only; see pp55-6).

Side trip by bus to Takachiho

The main reason for stopping in Nobeoka is to press on to the mountain town on Takachiho. Formerly, the private Takachiho Railway, one of the most scenic mountain railways in Japan, used to wind travellers along the lush green mountain canopy for the 50km journey; that is until Typhoon Nabi washed away two of its major bridges in 2005, and with it, any chance of the locally funded line resuming business. Now the most practical route is to take the Takachiho bus (80 mins; ¥1740) from Platform 1 of Nobeoka bus centre (outside the train station), whose views en route are equally splendid.

Takachiho is known for *yokagura*, ancient dances which re-enact scenes from Japanese mythology. Traditionally, performances of yokagura take place in local people's homes and tend to last from early evening through to the following morning. Plenty of sake keeps everyone awake into the small hours. Tourists are welcome at these performances, which are organised at the weekend between November and February. Alternatively, a one-hour version is performed at the cedar-lined **Takachiho Shrine** (nightly 8pm; tickets ¥500 at the shrine). From the bus stop, turn right up the slope then left at the main road. The shrine is a 10- to 15-minute walk from the bus stop on the right side.

A high priority is also a visit to **Takachiho Gorge**, formed by the gradual

erosion of lava that once flowed from Mt Aso (see pp372-3). You can rent a boat and row around the gorge (daily 8.30am-5pm; 30 mins, ¥1500), and there's also a 600m walking trail around the summit.

If you have walked to the shrine, a further 15- to 20-minute amble will take you past the prohibitively expensive *Hotel Takachiho* (🖳 www.h-takachiho.com; from ¥42,000/S, or from ¥26,250pp for two or more sharing) and the eventual winding descent to the gorge on the left. Alternatively take a taxi from the bus station (¥720); you can order a return taxi from the ticket booth at the gorge. If the weather is fair, however, rent an electric bike (¥300/day) from the **tourist office** (look for the 'i' sign; daily 8.30am-5.30pm) opposite the bus station. Their quad-bike ('buggy') option (¥1300/hr) offers a more adventurous yet environmentally incongruous alternative. Accommodation and local information is also available here and luggage can be left here all day for ¥300.

The short journey between Nobeoka and **Minami-Nobeoka (260km)** takes you alongside a mass of pipes that connect up the Asahi Kasei factories.

Hyuga-shi (277km) Hyuga has a number of beaches popular with local surfers but isn't really worth stopping at. There are, however, great views of the coast from the train. The line between Hyuga-shi and **Takanabe (314km)** is one of the most rewarding parts of the journey. There are fantastic views of the coastline on the left as the train runs for one stretch just a few metres from the shore.

Miyazaki (340km) The resort city of Miyazaki is known for its long hours of sunshine and mild climate, and pulls in domestic tourists keen to enjoy relaxing weekend escapes from the daily grind.

Miyazaki's modern station is small and easy to find your way around. The staff at the **tourist information counter** (daily 9am-6pm) in the station can provide you with a walking map and there are several options for a snack.

A **Science Center** (Cosmoland; 🖥 www.city.miyazaki.miyazaki.jp/cul/cosmoland/pamplet_english2.pdf; Tue-Sun 9am-4.30pm; ¥520, ¥730 inc planetarium), which focuses on space and has one of the world's largest planetariums, is across the street from the station.

There's only one local speciality you should not leave Miyazaki without trying and that's *chicken nanban*, pieces of fried chicken served with a sweet-and-sour sauce. Ask for the *chicken nanban teishoku* (set meal) at the famous *Ogura Honten* (lunchtimes only), off Tachibana-dori higashi.

JR Kyushu Hotel Miyazaki (nickname Kiten; 🕿 0985-29 8000, 🖥 www.jrk-hotels.jp/Miyazaki; from ¥9500/S, ¥15,000/D, ¥17,000/Tw) could hardly be more convenient as it is above the station. The reception desk (front) is on the 8th floor and the rooms are on floors 9-14. The attractive and spacious public areas make use of traditional local stone, lacquer and cedar wood.

The most luxurious place to stay – indeed, one of the top hotels in Japan – is *Sheraton Grande Ocean Resort* (🕿 0985-21 1133, 🖥 www.seagaia.co.jp; ¥23,100/D or Tw) at **Phoenix Seagaia Resort**. Every room has an ocean view and facilities include numerous restaurants and bars, a fitness centre, spa and pool, and a free shuttle bus service to local beaches such as Jinko beach (good for swimming). Even if you don't stay here, it's worth stopping for an early evening happy-hour shochu cocktail at the hotel's splendid **Pacifica** Cocktail Bar; the 42nd-floor **Skybar** affords unparalleled views of the ocean, coastline and Miyazaki city in the distance – a quite extraordinary experience at dusk.

Part of the same resort but offering cheaper accommodation is *Sun Hotel Phoenix* (🕿 0985-39 3131, 🖥 www.seagaia.co.jp; ¥15,800/Tw); it is set amidst the pine forests along the Hitotsuba coast.

All the Nichirin LEX services to Miyazaki continue to **Miyazaki Airport**, a 9-minute journey.

From Miyazaki, instead of retracing your steps, take a Kirishima LEX (10/day) along the JR Nippo line to Kagoshima (see pp404-10) and then follow the route (in reverse) from p374.

Kyushu – city guides

FUKUOKA/HAKATA

Fukuoka, literally 'Happy Hills', was one of the first areas of Japan to come into contact with foreign culture, due to its proximity to the Asian mainland. Both the city's JR station and the port are called Hakata not Fukuoka, a confusion of names that dates back to the time when the city was divided into the merchants' district (Hakata) and the old castle town (Fukuoka).

For decades Hakata was the terminus for the Sanyo shinkansen running along the length of Honshu from Shin-Osaka. However, with the advent of through shinkansen services from Shin-Osaka to the southern Kyushu terminus of Kagoshima-chuo, there's no longer any need to linger in Fukuoka. But it would be a shame to race through at lightning speed without making even the briefest of stops in Kyushu's capital.

The city has a relentless energy, but feels more laid back and manageable than Tokyo or Osaka. At the weekend, people flock here from all over Kyushu and further afield to take advantage of Fukuoka's abundant shopping and entertainment facilities. There are a good few cultural sights as well, making a stopover in Fukuoka an excellent introduction to the rest of the island.

The city is also a gateway to Japan from South Korea, as Fukuoka is connected by hydrofoil in under three hours to the South Korean port city of Busan (see p387).

What to see and do

Fukuoka City Museum (🖳 museum.city.fukuoka.jp; Tue-Sun 9.30am-5.30pm, to 7pm in Jul & Aug; ¥200, discount with Green Bus Pass) traces the history of Fukuoka, right back to the Yayoi period when the introduction of rice farming led to fights between villages and the beginning of the age of warfare.

The star exhibit is the gold seal of a Chinese Emperor, discovered on nearby Shikanoshima island in 1784. Exhibits examine how and why Fukuoka has always been at the forefront of international exchange in Asia. The number of rusty daggers, spears and swords on display is proof that 'international exchange' has not always been harmonious.

Fukuoka's rapid modernisation after the Meiji Restoration is also covered, including the development of transport network and railway lines. This was the time when streets were paved, ¥1 taxis hit the streets, waterworks were built to improve sanitation and French-style cafés were busy with intellectuals discussing the issues of the day. A typical café has been reconstructed, inside which you can see footage of what the city looked like at the start of the 20th century, before much of it was reduced to rubble in a 1945 American air raid.

Other exhibits in this section include 'replica old Japanese undergarments' and the 'Arrow', the oldest-running automobile in Japan, constructed in 1916 by a Fukuoka resident.

Sadly you can't have a drink in the reconstructed café but there is a coffee shop in the museum with wooden tables overlooking a pond, and decorated with various antiques in glass cabinets. It's a reasonable place for a drink, snack or lunch (beef curry and salad is ¥850).

There are bilingual signs on exhibits and headphones can be rented (free; bring your passport) for an English commentary. To reach the museum, take bus No 306 from stand 6 in the bus centre outside Hakata station to Hakubutsukan kita-guchi (6/hr; ¥220). This bus goes via Fukuoka Dome, Hawks Town and terminates outside Fukuoka Tower. Alternatively take the Green Fukuoka Loop Bus (see p386) to stop 11.

Fukuoka City Museum is in an area called Momochi, built on reclaimed land. Also in this area is **Fukuoka Yahoo! Japan Dome**, home of the city's professional baseball team. Backstage tours of the dome (which boasts the world's first retractable roof) and its locker rooms and practice areas operate daily (hourly 9am-4pm, 9am-noon when a game is on; ¥1000).

Next to the Dome is **Hawks Town**, a shopping and entertainment complex (see box p386).

The skyscraper beyond the dome is the 234m-high **Fukuoka Tower** (🖳 www.fukuokatower.co.jp; daily Apr-Sep 9.30am-10pm, Oct-Mar 9.30am-9pm; ¥800, 20% discounts are available in tourist pamphlets; entry is free if you can prove it is your birthday, give or take three days either side), which has a 123m-high observation deck open to the public. The 3rd floor boasts a designated 'Lovers' Sanctuary' observation area. Those looking up from street level may even arrange (by reservation) to illuminate a large red neon arrow-pierced heart from the glass of the uppermost floors to impress watching partners.

Ohori Park (Ohori-koen) is dominated by a turtle-inhabited boating lake and a Noh theatre. It is home to **Fukuoka Art Museum** (🖳 www.fukuoka-art-museum.jp; Tue-Sun 9.30am-5.30pm, Jul & Aug to 7.30pm; ¥200), whose highlights include works by Salvador Dali and Andy Warhol as well as some superb Buddhist wooden sculptures donated by Hakata's Tokoin temple. Modern art and Blur fans in particular will appreciate Julian Opie's 2nd-floor painting, 'Ruth with Cigarette'.

Next to the museum is a small but pleasant **Japanese garden** (Tue-Sun 9am-5pm; ¥240). To avoid summer mosquitoes the thoughtful staff provide bug repellent. Go by subway to Ohori-koen and take exit No 6.

Fukuoka Asian Art Museum (🖳 faam.city.fukuoka.lg.jp; Thur-Tue 10am-8pm; ¥200) is a modern gallery on the 7th floor of the Hakata Riverain complex. Artists in residence from across Asia display their own works and there is also a small permanent collection of contemporary Asian art. Take the subway to Nakasu-Kawabata.

The **harbour** area is the place to escape from the built-up city centre and get a sense of the historical and modern-day importance of the port to the regional economy. Take bus No 99 (15 mins; ¥220) from bus stop E across the street from the Hakata Exit of Hakata station. The bus drops you close to **Bayside Place Hakata** (🖥 www.baysideplace.jp), the perfect place to start a tour of the port area's trendy shops and waterfront cafés.

From there, head for the tallest building in the vicinity, **Hakata Port Tower**, the ground floor of which is home to the **Port of Hakata Bayside Museum** (daily 10am-5pm; free) and is also the entrance to the lift for the Tower itself (daily 10am-10pm; free). The museum, which has limited English signage, traces the history of shipping in the region, and includes some hand-crafted scale-model boats. Children can dress up in a captain's blue uniform and cap, and learn how to tie sea knots. There is even a machine that lets you simulate the operation of a container crane. The lift whisks you up to the 'View Floor', which is at 70m in the 100m-high tower and offers great panoramas of the port area and nearby islands. At certain times of the day you'll be able to see *Beetle II* (see p387) departing or arriving.

If you need to rest weary limbs, there is a great hot spring next to Hakata Port Tower called **Namiha-no-Yu** (🖥 www.namiha.jp; daily 9am-1am; ¥700, towel rental ¥200).

If you're not in town for Hakata Gion Yamakasa (see p387) it's worth paying a visit to **Hakata Machiya Folk Museum** (🖥 www.hakatamachiya.com; daily 10am-6pm; ¥200), a regional cultural-heritage centre where you can watch a 20-minute film of the raucous highlights.

For an alternative perspective on the city, the **short train/ferry excursion** is recommended. Take a local train on the JR Kagoshima line from Hakata station to Kashii (11 mins). Change on to a local train on the JR Kashii line and travel to the terminus at Saitozaki (20 mins). This is a pleasant ride out along a narrow peninsula but the best part is the boat journey from the ferry terminal at Saitozaki back to Hakata Port Ferry Terminal (¥430 one-way; 1-2/hr). On this short ride there are great views of the skyline and bay area – Fukuoka Dome and Tower are two major landmarks to look out for.

If you need a break and a place to put your feet up, head for **Le Temps** (daily 11am-9.30pm; from ¥1575/15 mins), on the 14th floor of the IMS (Inter Media Station) building in Tenjin, and have a massage and foot reflexology. This is a haven of calm and a million miles from the city-centre bustle below.

See also p389 for side trips from Fukuoka/Hakata.

PRACTICAL INFORMATION
Station guide
Hakata station was completely renovated in 2011 in time for the opening of the Kyushu shinkansen between Hakata and Kagoshima-chuo. It is now called JR Hakata City (🖥 www.jrhakatacity.com). and it is definitely worth exploring.

Hakata Exit is the main exit for the city, while the Chikushi Exit is for JR Kyushu Hotel Blossom Fukuoka. Don't confuse the private Nishitetsu Railway's Fukuoka station with JR's Hakata City station. Nishitetsu Fukuoka station is in Tenjin, the main shopping district.

There are also separate entrances for the shinkansen (2nd floor) and the ordinary lines (ground floor concourse level).

The entrance to the subway for downtown Fukuoka (the Tenjin district) and the airport is via an escalator in the middle of the concourse. *(Continued on p386)*

KYUSHU

Where to stay
18 Washington Hotel Canal City Fukuoka
キャナルシティ福岡ワシントンホテル
19 Grand Hyatt Fukuoka (Canal City)
グランドハイアット福岡
（キャナルシティ）
21 Hotel Active! Hakata
ホテルアクティブ！博多
23 Comfort Hotel Hakata
コンフォートホテル博多
24 Toyoko Inn Hakata-guchi Ekimae
東横イン 博多口駅前
25 Hotel Route Inn Hakata Ekimae
ホテルルートイン博多駅南
27 Hakata Green Hotel Annex
博多グリーンホテル アネックス
28 JR Kyushu Hotel Blossom Fukuoka
JR九州ホテルブラッサム福岡

Where to eat and drink
14 Terrassa, Sushi Isogai (IMS Bldg)
テラッサ，すし磯貝（イムズビル）
15 Daimaru Department Store
大丸デパート
20 Dipper Dan (Canal City)
ディッパーダン（キャナルシティ）
22 Ichiran 一蘭
29 Tonkatsu Hamakatsu (Deitos)
とんかつ浜勝浜勝 （デイトス）
30 37 Pasta, A&K Beer & Food Station
(AMU Plaza Hakata) 37パスタ，
A&K ビア&フード ステーション
（アミュプラザ 博多）

To Saitozaki

6 Fukuoka Kokusai Center

Naka-gawa

7

8

Showa-dori

Tenjin

TENJIN

13

Nishitetsu-Fukuoka Station

IMS building

14

Akasaka Meiji-dori

Tenjin Bus Center

15 Daimaru dept store

9, 10, 11 & 12

DAIMYO

Nishitetsu-Omuta line

Fukuoka / Hakata
福岡 / 博多

KYUSHU

Other

1 Hakata International Ferry Terminal
博多港国際ターミナル
2 Hakata Port Ferry Terminal
博多ポートフェリーターミナル
3 Hakata Port Tower,
Port of Hakata Bayside Museum
博多ポートタワー,
博多港ベイサイドミュージアム
4 Namiha-no-yu 波葉の湯
5 Bayside Place Hakata
ベイサイドプレイス博多
6 Fukuoka Kokusai Center
福岡国際センター
7 Fukuoka Asian Art Museum
(Hakata Riverain)
福岡アジア美術館
（博多リバーレイン）
8 Central Post Office
中央郵便局
9 Fukuoka Art Museum (Ohori Park)
福岡市美術館（大濠公園）

Other (*cont'd*)

10 Fukuoka Yahoo! Japan Dome;
Hawks Town
福岡 Yahoo! JAPANドーム；
ホークスタウン
11 Fukuoka Tower
福岡タワー
12 Fukuoka City Museum
福岡市美術館
13 Tenjin Core 天神コア
14 Le Temps (IMS Bldg)
ル・タン（イムズビル）
16 Hakata Machiya Folk Museum
博多町屋ふるさと館
17 Canal City
キャナルシティ
26 Hakata Station Bus Terminal
博多駅交通ターミナル
30 AMU Plaza Hakata
アミュプラザ 博多
31 Post office 郵便局

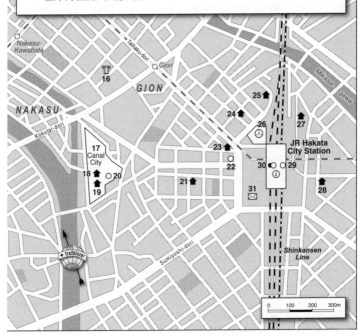

KYUSHU

(Continued from p383) There are several **JR ticket desk**s on the main concourse – all of them can organise (rail-pass) seat reservations.

Next to **JR Kyushu Travel Agency** (Mon-Fri 10am-8pm, Sat & Sun 10am-6pm) on the station concourse and with the same opening times is a special counter marked 'Japan Rail Pass – Kyushu Rail Pass'; rail-pass exchange vouchers should be exchanged here and JR Kyushu passes purchased here rather than in the main travel agency. There are **lockers** all over the station.

One floor below, between the station and the subway, is the **Food Market**, full of cheap places to eat, from Western-style family restaurants to fast food and okonomiyaki, as well as convenience stores.

A central part of the new station complex on the Hakata side is **AMU Plaza Hakata**, with a Hankyu department store (1st-8th floors) and a branch of Tokyu Hands (1st-5th floors). There are restaurants (see Where to eat) on the 9th and 10th floors as well as T-Joy Hakata, a multiplex cinema.

The **roof garden** (Hakata City Tsubame no Mori Hiroba), with over 10,000 painted tiles, is an excellent place to get a view of Hakata and the surrounding area.

There is also a shrine, a miniature train and track, as well as a garden area with some vegetables growing.

Tourist information
The **tourist information centre** (🖥 yokanavi.com/eg; daily 8am-9pm) is on the station concourse (street level). You can pick up *Fukuoka Now!* (🖥 www.fukuoka-now.com), a free monthly English-language guide with cinema listings and reviews of new pubs, clubs, restaurants and shops, and *Fukuoka on Foot*, a very well-researched booklet of city walking tours.

Consider getting a Fukuoka Welcome Card (see box p64) if you plan to do a lot of sightseeing here.

Getting around
The cheapest way of getting into and around the city centre is to take the **Green Fukuoka City loop bus** (Apr-Sep daily 9am-4.30pm; night explorer route 5.30-8pm; Oct-Mar weekends and holidays only; approx 2/hr; ¥250 per ride, ¥700 one-day pass), which departs from bus stop No 1 inside **Hakata Station Bus Terminal** (also known as Fukuoka Bus Center/Fukuoka Kotsu Center) on the right-hand side as you leave Hakata Station's Hakata Exit. An English guide to the loop-bus system is available

---

🏯 Fukuoka – a shopping paradise for some
Fukuoka is Kyushu's shopping capital and **Tenjin** (accessible by subway from Hakata Station) marks its centre. If there was ever an entire department store dedicated to teenage girls, **Tenjin Core** (🖥 www.tenjincore.com; daily 10am-8pm, restaurants 9.30pm) fits the bill although its alternative style in some sections is more typical of Tokyo's Harajuku district. Here boutiques offer teenagers 'baby fashion' in among rows of punk wigs. Most unsettling is the 8th floor soft toy section where you can buy blood-spattered teddy bears; in short, a cultural mecca for maladjusted youth.

Wander just a little way west from here to reach trendy **Daimyo**, a chic enclave of local stores and designer-label shops where you'd be lucky to find anyone aged over 30. Its narrow streets are filled with an eclectic mix of shops selling everything from snowboards to fashion haircuts.

Set away from all this is **Canal City**, a city within a city of shops, restaurants, food courts, thrill rides and multiplex cinema. **Hawks Town**, next to Fukuoka Yahoo! Japan Dome, is where you'll find more shops as well as a United Cinemas multiplex, bowling alleys, Hard Rock Café, cycle rental, karaoke boxes and arcade games.

You don't even have to leave Hakata station to find a shopping paradise: **Hankyu** and **Tokyu Hands** department stores (see Station guide) sell virtually everything.

from the tourist-information desk at Hakata station.

Regular **buses** within Fukuoka city are operated by Nishitetsu Bus; the fare between Hakata station and Tenjin is ¥100. City buses depart from street level and highway buses from the 3rd floor.

There are three **subway** lines (all operate daily 5.30am-12.30am); the most useful is probably the Kuko line which connects the airport with Hakata, Tenjin and Ohori-koen. Fares are either ¥200 or ¥250. If unsure, buy a ¥200 ticket and use the 'fare adjustment' machine when you arrive at your destination. A one-day pass (¥600) gives discounts on some attractions. Fukuoka's subway stations have good facilities for the disabled, with lifts at nearly every station.

Fukuoka Airport (🖳 www.fuk-ab. co.jp) has three domestic terminals and an international terminal serving a number of destinations in Asia. It's two stops on the Kuko subway line (¥250) to Hakata station. Free shuttle buses link the domestic and international terminals.

Both JR Kyushu (🖳 www.jrbeetle. co.jp) and the South Korean company Kobee operate high-speed jetfoils between the **International Ferry Terminal** at Hakata Port and Busan (originally Pusan; 2 hrs 55 mins; from ¥10,000 one-way or ¥15,000 return, plus a fuel surcharge of ¥1500 for Hakata/Fukuoka–Busan or 20,000 won for Busan–Hakata/Fukuoka, payable in cash at the terminals); JR Kyushu's is known as *Beetle II*. Tickets need to be booked in advance (online booking opens three months ahead). Rail passes are not accepted (the point is to encourage travel around Japan, not let you flee to Korea at JR's expense). There are two floors of seating; when checking-in (up to 20 mins before departure) ask for a window seat on the upper deck. From outside JR Hakata City station, take bus No 88 bound for the International Ferry Terminal.

Alternatively, Camellia Line (🖳 www. camellia-line.co.jp) operates an overnight passenger ferry to Busan. The cheapest option is the common tatami area (¥9000 one-way or ¥17,100 return). Private cabins are more expensive.

Festivals and events

The biggest annual event is **Hakata Gion Yamakasa** (1st-15th July), the climax of which is a float race through the city; seven teams carry their respective floats a distance of 5km.

The biggest sporting event is the **Kyushu Grand Sumo Basho**, the last tournament of the annual sumo calendar (see p38). It takes place in November at Fukuoka Kokusai Center.

Where to stay

Fukuoka has some world-class hotels at prices that would be impossible to find in Tokyo, as well as some cheap but clean business hotels.

Hakata Green Hotel Annex (☎ 092-451 4112, 🖳 www.hakata-green.co.jp/ annex; from ¥5700/S, ¥8200/D or Tw) is outside the Chikushi Exit of Hakata station. It's a low-key but smart place with a coin laundry and a Family Mart convenience store next door. There are two more branches nearby if this one is full.

Also near Hakata station, and of similar standard are branches of other popular chains: *Hotel Route Inn Hakata Ekimae* (☎ 092-477 8885, 🖳 www.route-inn.co.jp; ¥6950/S, ¥9500/D, ¥13,500/Tw), *Toyoko Inn Hakata-guchi Ekimae* (☎ 092-451 1045, 🖳 www.toyoko-inn.com; from ¥5480/S, ¥6980/D, ¥7980/Tw inc breakfast) and *Comfort Hotel Hakata* (☎ 092-431 1211, 🖳 www.comfortinn.com/hotel-fukuoka-japan-JP038; ¥6000/S, ¥12,000/ Tw inc continental breakfast).

Hotel Active! Hakata (☎ 092-452 0001, 🖳 www.hotel-active.com/hakata; ¥6980/S, ¥8980/D, ¥9980/Tw inc buffet breakfast), which (like its counterpart in Hiroshima, see p255) has compact modern rooms with a designer feel – great if you like variations on black – plus two single-sex spas. There are also coffee dispensers, drinks vending machines and a coin laundry. To get there from Hakata Station walk down the road with the brick-coloured building on the left. Turn second left (a 7-Eleven store is on the corner) and then first right. The hotel is a little way down on the left.

Rail-pass holders get discounted rates at *JR Kyushu Hotel Blossom Fukuoka* (☎ 092-413 8787, 🖳 www.jrhotelgroup.com; from ¥10,000/S, ¥12,000/D, ¥19,000/Tw). It is more luxurious than a standard business hotel, with larger-than-average rooms and a general feeling of spaciousness; a 2011 refurbishment made use of Hakata-ori, a traditional textile, and the design reflects local architecture. It's only a three-minute walk from the Chikushi Exit of the station: go straight up the main road and it's just past Hotel New Miyako.

Top of the range is *Grand Hyatt Fukuoka* (☎ 092-282 1234, 🖳 fukuoka. grand.hyatt.com; from ¥16,000/S, ¥20,000/D exc breakfast), in Canal City; it's *the* place to stay in Fukuoka if you can afford it. Large bathrooms feature a bath you can definitely sink into and separate shower – and a small TV screen you can watch while soaking in the tub. Hotel facilities include a gymnasium, swimming pool and saunas. Ask about special offers or promotional packages.

Within the same Canal City compound as the Grand Hyatt is a more economical alternative, *Washington Hotel Canal City Fukuoka* (🖳 www.fukuoka-wh.com; ¥7800/S, ¥15,000/D, ¥17,800/Tw), with coin-operated internet terminals in the lobby, automated check-out machines and a coin laundry.

For further details about the facilities at the chain hotels mentioned and guidance on finding accommodation see pp45-52.

Where to eat and drink

Hakata is associated with ramen: there are plenty of places around the station that serve up cheap bowls of the stringy yellow noodles, including the popular *Ichiran* (daily 10am-10pm) on basement level 2 (B2F) of the black building opposite JR Hakata City station (take the Hakata gate), next to the large red-brick building that houses Fukuoka City Bank. It's hidden away in a corner: look for the red curtain with 'Ichiran' in black kanji. Buy a ticket (¥650) from the vending machine and take a seat. You'll then be given a sheet to fill out (ask for the English version), specifying exactly how spicy, how much garlic and what kind of vegetables you want.

Restaurants on the 9th and 10th floors of **AMU Plaza** in the station serve all kinds of cuisine: Japanese, Korean, Chinese, Indian, Mexican and Italian. The best Italian is *37 Pasta* (9th floor; daily 11am-11pm), where a fusion choice could be Itoshima Raizan buta pork and taisho miso bolognese with spinach fettucine (¥1150). Alternatively, try *A&K Beer Restaurant* (daily 10am-11pm), which has a wide range of beers and ¥1000 set meals. The lifts (elevators) up to the restaurants are in the central area to the left of JR Hakata City building.

Deitos by the Chikushi Exit has a Gourmet Street (B1F ie first floor of the basement; daily 11am-11pm) with a range of Japanese and Western dishes, a Japanese-style pub street (1F; 11am-11pm) and a noodle street (2F; 11am-9pm). *Hamakatsu* (B1F; daily 8am-11pm), in Gourmet Street, is a great place to try tonkatsu; it has menus and explanations in English, and they will refill your miso soup and give you extra rice and cabbage free of charge.

Canal City (🖳 www.canalcity.co.jp) has a good selection of restaurants on its basement level, including the popular *Dipper Dan* crêperie-cum-gelateria, whose blueberry cheesecake crêpes and Hokkaido chocolate ice cream are much sought after. On the 5th floor there are several ramen restaurants from around the country; the miso ramen (¥780) is recommended.

At **Daimaru** department store in Tenjin there's take-out food on the 2nd floor of the basement (B2F) and restaurants serving Italian, Chinese, Western and Japanese katsu-style dishes on the 5th and 6th floors.

In the **IMS Building** in Tenjin (restaurants 11am-11pm, many close from 3-5pm) try the smart but relaxed Spanish restaurant *Terrassa* on the 12th floor, which does excellent sherry-braised chicken and fine desserts. On the 13th floor *Sushi Isogai* offers a range of twin-roll plates (¥200-580) and many sushi specialities plus great views across the city.

Side trip by rail to Dazaifu

Once the political heart of Kyushu and the town where the god of learning and literature is enshrined, Dazaifu is an easy day trip from Fukuoka but can equally well be visited en route to Nagasaki, Kumamoto or Kagoshima.

Dazaifu's key draw is the popular **Tenmangu Shrine** complex, which dates from 1591. For ¥100 you can join the hordes of visitors buying an *omikuji* paper to tie on good-luck messages. Photographers will also enjoy the photogenic red Taiko bridge arcing over Shinji pond. The restaurants overlooking the pond are good value (chicken and egg donburi ¥600) for a lunch stop and offer unlimited green tea refills alongside the fine views.

The small **Dazaifu Tenmangu Museum** (daily 9am-4.30pm; ¥300) has some great samurai armour, but not much information in English.

Afterwards, follow the escalators and pulsing light tunnel to reach the striking **Kyushu National Museum** (🖳 www.kyuhaku.com; Tue-Sun 9.30am-4.30pm; ¥420, U18 free; pick up an audio guide on the 4th floor), built in the shape of a blue wave. It aims to provide a 'new perspective on Japanese culture, in the context of Asian history' and highlights include a historical document detailing two battles in the 13th century, known as Genko, in which Japan fought off attacks by the Mongolian empire ruled by Genghis Khan. The special high-definition film screenings are useful for a close inspection of some of the Buddhist artefacts although there is no English commentary.

After you exit the museum, turn left and walk down the slope to the **Komyozen-ji temple** (daily 8am-4.30pm; ¥200), where you can enjoy the tranquility of its rear Zen garden well away from the throbbing crowds. The overhanging trees that shade the upright stones, the mossy perimeters and raked gravel all make for spectacular viewing, especially in the autumn.

From Hakata take a rapid train to **Futsukaichi** (track 7; three stops; 15 mins). From here it's four minutes by bus or ten minutes on foot to the private Nishitetsu Futsukaichi station for the short journey to Dazaifu (every 5-40 mins, most frequently at peak times; ¥150; two stops; rail passes not accepted).

Dazaifu station has a **tourist information counter** on the right after the barriers, as well as large luggage lockers. There is also a bike rental counter (9am-6pm; ¥500, ¥1000/electric).

NAGASAKI

'I cannot think of a more beautiful place. There is a land-locked harbour; at the entrance are islands...the ship winds up the harbour which is more like a very broad river, with hills on either side levelling down towards the extreme end where the town of Nagasaki stands.'

So wrote Elizabeth Alt, wife of William Alt, a 19th-century English merchant who lived and traded in Nagasaki. Nagasaki's history as a centre of international trade and its long period of contact with the West are still the reasons why tourists pour into the city, but it was the dropping of the second atomic bomb here on 9th August 1945 that ensured Nagasaki would become known throughout the world. More people were killed in this one blast than in all the bombing raids on Britain throughout WWII.

Like Hiroshima, Nagasaki is now home to a Peace Park and A-Bomb Museum, both of which record huge numbers of visitors every year.

KYUSHU

> ⛩ **Japan's first railway?**
> Though most history books conclude that the first official railway line in Japan was built between Shimbashi and Yokohama, the estate of the 19th-century Scottish expat Thomas Glover begs to differ. In a corner of Glover's House a sign reveals that in 1865 the Scotsman purchased the 'Iron Duke', claimed to be Japan's first steam locomotive, and laid a 400m-long track in Nagasaki. He used Japanese coal to power the engine and opened the line to an astonished public. It was not until 1872, seven years after the opening of this mini railway, that the Shimbashi–Yokohama line opened for business.
>
> An account of Thomas Glover's life can be found in Alexander McKay's *Scottish Samurai* (Edinburgh, Canongate Press, 1997).

For sightseeing purposes it's useful to consider Nagasaki as a city of two halves. North of the station, in the **Urakami district**, is the Atomic Bomb Museum and Peace Park. Down in the south, on the hills overlooking the harbour, is **Glover Garden**, full of 19th-century Western-style homes. One day would be just enough to visit both parts but it's preferable to allow a couple of days to do everything at a more relaxed pace and incorporate a tour of the central area, including newly restored **Dejima**, the island enclave which was the only point of contact with the outside world during Japan's period of national seclusion (1641-1859).

What to see and do

A good start to a tour of Nagasaki would be to take **Nagasaki Ropeway** (daily Mar-Nov 9am-10pm, Dec-Feb to 9pm; ¥700 one-way, ¥1200 return; ¥200 discount voucher at 🖥 www.nagasaki-ropeway.jp/facility/coupon.php) up Inasa-yama (Mt Inasa) to enjoy a panoramic view of the city. The best time to go is at night when the city is lit up. Look back over the dark hills for a strange and slightly eerie contrast to the bright lights that dazzle below.

Take Nagasaki Bus No 3 or 4 from Nagasaki station and get off at Ropeway-mae, or take tram No 1 or 3 two stops north from the station to Takara-machi. From here, follow the main road underneath the railway line and over Urakami-gawa. Cross the river, turn right and follow the road round until you see a shrine entrance on your left. Walk through the entrance gate and turn left to find the entrance to the ropeway.

Urakami district The atomic bomb dropped on Nagasaki at 11.02am on 9th August 1945 was meant for the city of Kokura (see p362). Poor visibility meant the plane carrying the bomb circled three times over Kokura before changing course for Nagasaki, where cloud also hampered visibility. A chance break in the clouds just after 11am sealed the city's destiny. It's estimated that over 70,000 (of a 240,000 population) were killed either instantly or in the period up to the end of 1945.

The bomb was intended for Nagasaki Shipyard but exploded instead over Urakami, a centre of Christian missionary work in Nagasaki since the latter half of the 16th century. As the bomb was dropped, a service was underway at

Urakami Cathedral; all that's left today is a melted rosary (now on display in the A-Bomb Museum) and one piece of the cathedral wall, in the nearby Hypocenter Park. Today, Urakami is home to the Peace Park and Atomic Bomb Museum.

Nagasaki Atomic Bomb Museum (🖥 www1.city.nagasaki.nagasaki.jp/peace/english/abm; daily 8.30am-5pm, to 6pm in summer; ¥200) is a high priority, though the constant stream of school groups can be wearing. As you pass into the first hall, the scene immediately transforms to the precise moment that the bomb was dropped – a clock ticks and black-and-white images of the devastation appear on screens. Among the most memorable exhibits are the glass bottles melted together from the heat of the blast and the burnt-out remains of a schoolgirl's lunchbox. Directly down the hill from the museum, and next to the main street, is the **Atomic Bomb Hypocenter**, marking the exact spot over which the A-bomb exploded.

The nearby **Peace Park** is filled with statues and memorials given to the city as a gesture of peace from all over the world; many are from former Eastern bloc countries. The centrepiece is a giant **Peace Statue** – a man with his right hand pointing to the threat of the atomic bomb, his extended left hand symbolising peace and his eyes closed, as in prayer, to remember the souls of the dead – erected 10 years after the bombing and now the backdrop for the annual peace ceremony held on 9th August. Throughout the year, visiting school parties hold their own peace ceremonies in front of the statue.

The nearest tram stop for the Peace Park and Atomic Bomb Museum is Matsuyama-machi, eight stops north of Nagasaki station on tram No 1 or 3.

Near Nagasaki station Nagasaki's importance as a historical centre for Christianity in Japan is most apparent at Oura Catholic Church below Glover Garden (see p392) and at the **Site of the Martyrdom of the 26 Saints of Japan** in Nishizaka-machi, a memorial to four Spanish missionaries, one Mexican, one Indian and 20 Japanese Christians who were crucified here in 1597. It's a very simple memorial, a few minutes' walk east from the station, heading up the road to Nishizaka.

Behind the memorial is the **Museum of the 26 Martyrs** (🖥 www.26martyrs.com; daily 9am-5pm; ¥500), which explains the path of Christianity in Japan from Francis Xavier to the Meiji era. The museum is small but its recently renewed displays contain unique religious artworks such as the painting of *Our Lady of the Snows* depicting Mary on Japanese paper.

Very much off the tourist trail is **Oka Masaharu Memorial Peace Museum** (Tue-Sun 9am-5pm; ¥250), which focuses on Japan's actions before and during WWII in Korea, China and south-east Asia. It's not an easy place to visit, some of the photos are shocking, but it provides a very different perspective to that offered at the 'official' A-Bomb Museum. The museum was founded in memory of the late Protestant minister and peace activist Oka Masaharu (1918-94), who devoted much of his life to relief efforts for Korean atomic bomb survivors in Japan. The signs are in Japanese and Korean but there's a detailed ¥300 booklet outlining the history and controversies in English; the photos that line the walls tell their own story. The museum receives few visitors and is not included in any of the tourist guides or brochures produced by the city.

Be aware that the museum is a little hard to find: head for the Site of the 26 Christian Martyrs and you'll find it just past the memorial on the right side of the road as it bends left at the top.

Nagasaki Harbour area **Glover Garden** (💻 www.glover-garden.jp; daily 8am-6pm; ¥600), an area of late 19th-century Western-style houses built on a hill overlooking Nagasaki harbour, is usually swamped with visitors. The harbour views from the hillside repay the ticket cost, even if some of the houses are not overly exciting for Western visitors. The site's Nagasaki Traditional Performing Arts museum screens dynamic footage of October's Nagasaki Kunchi Festival alongside exhibits of the maritime floats that epitomise the city's contact with the West.

Best known of all the 19th-century residents was the man whom the garden is named after, Thomas Glover. Born in Scotland in 1838, Glover moved to Nagasaki in 1859, married a Japanese woman and involved himself in a number of key Japanese businesses, helping to set up the Japan Brewery Company in July 1885, predecessor to today's Kirin Brewery. Look out for the *kirin*, a mythical creature that sports a bushy moustache remarkably similar to Thomas Glover's, on cans and bottles of Kirin beer. Since the area was populated by merchants, it's appropriate that the management of Glover Garden has kept the financial spirit of Glover et al alive by selling Glover shortbread biscuits and the like.

On the way up to the Glover Garden entrance, look out for **Oura Catholic Church** (daily 8.30am-4.45pm; ¥300), built by French missionaries in 1864 and the oldest church in Japan – although any religious solemnity is rather shattered by the loudspeakers' looped explanations in Japanese. Upon exiting, turn left and follow the Glover Garden signs until you reach a two-storey wooden edifice on the right housing an exhibition of Catholic artefacts (including depictions of purgatory) relating to the Christian community in Nagasaki. There is also a small shop.

To reach Glover Garden, take tram No 1 (bound for Shokakuji-shita) from Nagasaki station and change at Tsuki-machi. From here, change to tram No 5 and ride all the way to the terminus at Ishibashi.

Dejima From 1641 to 1859 the island of Dejima, just off Nagasaki, was Japan's sole point of contact with the outside world as the base for trade with the Dutch East India Company.

A reconstruction of the Dutch enclave (daily 8am-5.40pm; ¥500) opened in 2000 to mark the 400th anniversary of relations between Japan and the Netherlands and continues to expand. It currently includes replicas of over 25 19th-century buildings, including the Chief Factor's Residence, and an excellent museum recounting the story of the Dutch traders who were forced to live in isolation on the island. The plan is eventually to recreate Dejima's traditional fan-shape, surrounded by water on all sides.

At Dejima Theatre, in a reconstructed warehouse, an informative and entertaining film (English-audio headphones available) tells the history of Dejima, offering plenty of glimpses into what the place would have been like when the Dutch were trading here. Part of the film dwells on what sort of food the Dutch offered their hosts on special occasions (answer: steamed duck, sausage and castella cake – castella is now a popular souvenir from Nagasaki).

Take tram No 1 three stops south from Nagasaki station to Dejima, which drops you right outside the reconstructed complex.

See p397 for details of the side trip to Huis Ten Bosch from Nagasaki.

PRACTICAL INFORMATION
Station guide
Nagasaki station incorporates a tourist information centre (see below), hotel (see Where to stay), AMU Plaza department store (see Where to eat) and a plaza under a giant canopy. There is only one exit (Central Exit), on the same level as the platforms. For **lockers** turn left after the ticket barrier, skirt around the travel agency and follow the station building round.

Tourist information
Nagasaki City Tourist Information Center (TIC; ⌨ www.at-nagasaki.jp; daily 8am-8pm) is inside the waiting room to your right as you exit the ticket barrier. Pick up a guide to the city tram network.

Getting around
Nagasaki is known for its *chin chin densha*, old-fashioned **trams** that have been trundling around the city since 1915, and which are by far the best means of getting around. One-day tram passes (¥500) are available from tourist offices and some hotels but not on board the trams themselves. Individual rides cost a flat ¥120.

Cycles (daily 9am-5pm; ¥500/2 hours with a JR pass) can be rented from Nagasaki station. Buy a ticket from the JR ticket office (to your left as you exit the ticket barrier) and take it to the rental shop outside the front. Be warned that parking is limited and the city is very hilly!

Shuttle buses (4/hr; 40-50 mins; ¥800, or ¥1200 for a 'pair ticket' if two of you are travelling) to **Nagasaki Airport** (domestic flights only) leave from the ground floor of the bus terminal across the street from the station.

There are **boat trips** from Nagasaki Ferry Terminal to Gunkanjima (50 mins; in Japanese only), which goes past shipyards and islands, and to Hashima (45 mins). Ask at the TIC for details.

Festivals
The main event in Nagasaki is the annual **peace ceremony** on 9th August. However, there are also several festivals in particular **Kunchi Festival** which has been held here on 7th-9th October for over 370 years.

Where to stay
JR Kyushu Hotel Nagasaki (☎ 095-832 8000, ⌨ www.jrhotelgroup.com/eng/hotel/eng148.htm; ¥6900/S, ¥12,600/Tw; breakfast ¥840; 10% discount for JR rail-pass holders) is built into the station complex. Rooms are good value.

Best Western Premier Hotel Nagasaki (☎ 095-820 1801, ⌨ www.bestwestern.co.jp/nagasaki; ¥15,000/S, ¥26,000/Tw) is a top-end hotel with a choice of restaurants, great panoramic views from the bar, and its own hot-spring facilities. The singles and twins are spacious and the more expensive rooms on the executive floor are even larger; there is internet-access in every room. There is also a ladies-only floor.

Three cheaper business-hotel options close to the station are *APA Hotel Nagasaki-ekimae* (☎ 095-820-1111, ⌨ www.apahotel.com/hotel/kyusyu/06_nagasaki-ekimae/english; from ¥7000/S, ¥10,000/D, ¥13,000/Tw; breakfast ¥840; the ever-reliable chain hotel, *Toyoko Inn Nagasaki Ekimae* (☎ 095-825 1045, ⌨ www.toyoko-inn.com; from ¥5480/S, ¥7980/Tw or D) by the Goto Machi streetcar stop; and *Hotel Cuore Nagasaki*

Ekimae (☎ 095-818 9000, 🖳 www.hotel-cuore.com; ¥6300/S, ¥8000/D, ¥10,000/Tw, ¥14,000/3 guests), situated across the street from the station, which offers the usual line in clean, no-frills singles and twins. Solo women travellers can choose a ladies-only floor.

Hotel Dormy Inn Nagasaki (☎ 095-820-5489, 🖳 www.hotespa.net/hotels/nagasaki; ¥3500/capsule (men), ¥8000/S, ¥12000/D, ¥14000/Tr) is one of the newest hotels in the city and very conveniently located for Chinatown, the Peace Park and Glover Garden. It's a two-minute walk from the Tsukimachi tram stop.

The hotel boasts stylishly furnished modern rooms, an excellent spa (including a silky white bath mix) and the chance for male visitors to experience a night in a capsule. There are also free evening noodle buffets.

The nearby *Hotel JAL City Nagasaki* (☎ 095-825-2580, 🖳 www.nagasaki.jalcity.co.jp; ¥6800/S, ¥18,000/D, ¥20,000/Tw) is a more upmarket business option with a good range of facilities and excellent location.

Comfort Hotel Nagasaki (☎ 095-827 1111, 🖹 827 1154, 🖳 www.choice-hotels.jp/nagasaki; ¥5500/S, ¥7,500/D ¥8500/Tw inc simple breakfast) is terrific value.

The modern *Richmond Hotel Nagasaki Shianbashi* (☎ 095-832-2525, 🖳 www.richmondhotel.jp/nagasaki; ¥7800/D, ¥14,200/Tw, plus ¥500 membership) is a short trot along a side street from the Shianbashi tram stop and offers stylish, high-quality rooms. Downstairs is a decent adjoining Italian restaurant.

NAGASAKI – MAP KEY

Where to stay
1 Minshuku Tanpopo 民宿たんぽぽ
6 Best Western Premier Hotel Nagasaki ベストウェスタンプレミアホテル長崎
8 APA Hotel Nagasaki-ekimae アパホテル長崎駅前
11 Hotel Cuore Nagasaki Ekimae ホテルクオーレ長崎駅前
12 JR Kyushu Hotel Nagasaki JR九州ホテル長崎
14 Nagasaki-Ebisu Youth Hostel 長崎ゑびすユースホステル
15 Nagasaki Kagamiya 長崎かがみや
16 Toyoko Inn Nagasaki Ekimae 東横イン長崎駅前
18 Comfort Hotel Nagasaki コンフォートホテル長崎
25 Hotel Dormy Inn Nagasaki ドーミーイン長崎
27 Richmond Hotel Nagasaki Shianbashi リッチモンドホテル長崎思案橋
28 Hotel JALCity Nagasaki ホテルJAL シテイ

Where to eat and drink
12 AMU PLaza アミュプラザ
19 Dejima Wharf 出島ワーフ
21 Hamakatsu 浜勝
22 Tarafuku-Asa 多ら福亜紗

Where to eat and drink (cont'd)
23 Pizzeria Margherita ピッザレーアマーグレータ
24 Ichimaru Sushi 一まる鮨
26 Vida Rosa ヴィダロッサ
27 Yako Hai 夜光杯

Other
2 Peace Park 平和公園
3 Atomic Bomb Hypocenter 原爆落下中心地
4 Nagasaki Atomic Bomb Museum 長崎原爆資料館
5 Nagasaki Ropeway 長崎ロープウェイ
7 Site of the Martyrdom of the 26 Christian Martyrs, Museum of the 26 Martyrs 日本十六聖人殉教地, 日本二 十六聖人記念館
9 Oka Masaharu Memorial Peace Museum 岡まさはる記念長崎平和資料館
10 Ken-ei Bus Terminal 県営バスターミナル
13 Central Post Office 中央郵便局
17 Nagasaki Ferry Terminal 長崎フェリーターミナル
19 Dejima Wharf 出島ワーフ
20 Dejima 出島
29 Oura Catholic Church 大浦天主堂
30 Glover Garden グラバー園

KYUSHU

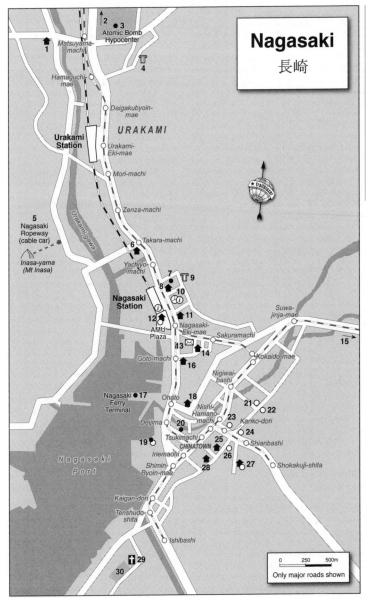

Nagasaki
長崎

1
Matsuyama-machi
2
3 Atomic Bomb Hypocenter
4
Hamaguchi-mae
Daigakubyoin-mae
URAKAMI
Urakami Station
Urakami-Eki-mae
Mori-machi
Zenza-machi
5 Nagasaki Ropeway (cable car)
Inasa-yama (Mt Inasa)
Takara-machi
6
Yachiyo-machi
7
T 9
8
10
Nagasaki Station
12
AMU Plaza
11
Nagasaki-Eki-mae
Sakuramachi
Suwa-jinja-mae
13
14
15
Goto-machi
16
Kokaido-mae
Nigiwai-bashi
Nagasaki Ferry Terminal
17
Ohato
18
21
22
Nishi-Hamano-machi
23
Kanko-dori
Deijima
20
24
Tsukimachi
25
Shianbashi
19
CHINATOWN
26
Iriemachi
27
Shokakuji-shita
28
Shimin-Byoin-mae
Kaigan-dori
Tenshudo-shita
Ishibashi
29
30

0   250   500m
Only major roads shown

Nagasaki Kagamiya (☎ 095-895-8250, ☐ www.n-kagamiya.com; from ¥2300pp/4-bed dorm, ¥4000/S, ¥5600/D; annex Japanese-style rooms 4-7 sharing ¥2500pp) is a delightful family-run hostel that offers an authentic Japanese experience at budget prices. Located just five minutes' walk from Hotarujaya tram stop (six stops east on the red line from Nagasaki station; 12 mins), this small inn and its kimono-clad young owners know the importance of a warm welcome and even offer the chance to rent a kimono for the day (11am-7pm). They speak English and the inn does not operate a curfew. You can check availability online and reserve up to four months ahead. A basic map is available at the TIC but the website has clearer photos for navigation.

If you prefer to be based closer to the Peace Park, the tatami rooms with communal bath at *Minshuku Tanpopo* (☎ 095-861 6230, ☐ www9.ocn.ne.jp/~tanpopo1; ¥4000/S, ¥7000/D or Tw, ¥9000/Tr; breakfast ¥600, dinner ¥1500) are a good choice. The inn is close to Matsuyama tram stop but if you call in advance and arrive at JR Urakami station (last stop before Nagasaki, see pp390-1) you should be able to arrange a free pick-up.

The small *Nagasaki-Ebisu Youth Hostel* (☎/🖷 095-824 3823, ☐ www5a.biglobe.ne.jp/~urakami or ☐ www.jyh.or.jp; ¥2500pp, plus ¥600 for non-members; breakfast ¥500) is a basic but cosy place with 10 beds, five minutes from JR Nagasaki station. Evening meals are not available. Pick up a walking map from the TIC.

For details about accommodation in general see pp45-52.

Where to eat and drink

In the station area the obvious place to head is the 5th-floor Gourmet World (10am-9pm) in **AMU Plaza** department store. Here you'll find *Milan* Indian curry house, a revolving sushi bar, a Korean restaurant, *Royal Host* family restaurant, as well as a flame-grilled steak restaurant.

A *Train d'Or* bakery is on the ground floor and there's also a *Baskin Robbins* ice-cream outlet. The **supermarket** at the back of the ground floor does takeaway sushi and tonkatsu meals.

Popular with Nagasaki residents and visitors alike, *Hamakatsu* (daily 11am-10.30pm, last orders 10pm) is the place to eat tonkatsu. Seating is at tables or along the counter – or a take-out box of tonkatsu sandwiches costs ¥850. The *orandakatsu* set (¥980) of breaded pork and Gouda cheese symbolises the city's international influences. It's a five-minute walk north of Shianbashi tram station. Look for a white building, beige wooden sign and lantern hanging outside.

Just opposite is *Tarafuku-Asa* (daily 5-11pm) whose dark wooden interiors and sunken tables offer an atmospheric setting to sample the daily menu. Try the hoke grilled fish (¥480) or eel (¥740) washed down with a satisfying warm Kiku-Masamune sake (¥370). This is a good-value restaurant even if not geared for English speakers. The nearby *Ichimaru Sushi* (daily 11.30am-10.30pm; ¥400-2000), run by a charming elderly couple, offers mouthwatering and original varieties of sushi. The *anago* (grilled conger sea eel) is an absolute must and less fatty than eel. There is a sushi menu board in English. From Shianbashi tram stop, enter the north end of the arcade, take the first right and the sushi shop is immediately on the right.

For the best wood-fired oven-cooked pizza, go to *Pizzeria Margherita* (daily 11am-10pm; pizzas from ¥980) on the second floor of Hamaya department store, near Kanko-dori tram stop on Harusame-dori.

Adjoining Richmond Hotel is *Yako Hai* (daily 5-11pm), where a broad range of Italian dishes (under ¥1000) is served to customers at stylish banquettes.

Another good area to look for food is **Dejima Wharf**, where you'll find a row of harbourside bars and cafés, including Chinese, Japanese and Italian. It's a good place to watch the sunset over a drink after a hard day of sightseeing in Nagasaki.

Vida Rosa Mexican Kitchen (daily 5-11pm) is a young and lively eatery set on the busy street adjoining the side of JAL City Hotel Nagasaki. It offers standard tacos (¥590), burritos (¥900) and salads along with an inventive array of shochu cocktails. Following your meal you are encouraged to go upstairs to the 'Golf Bar' (2nd/3rd floors), where you can play a computer-aided round before heading to the 4th floor karaoke zone.

Side trip by rail to Huis Ten Bosch
Huis Ten Bosch (🖳 www.huistenbosch.co.jp; hours vary according to the season; one-day passport ¥4900, 12-17 years ¥4200, 4-11 years ¥3200; combination rail-and-passport tickets also available from Nagasaki station), the Dutch theme park overlooking Omura Bay north-east of Nagasaki, is one of Kyushu's most popular attractions for vacationing Japanese.

The idea for this bizarre recreation of tulip fields and windmills came from Yoshikuni Kamichika, who visited Holland in 1979 and decided to build a city in Japan that would combine Dutch city planning with Japanese technology. The aim was to make the site a living, working, eco-friendly city 'to last 1000 years'. What you find is much more of a Disney resort, with hotels, rides and attractions, canals, shops that sell clogs, and a cast of real Dutch who dress up in traditional costume and become walking photo opportunities. As one foreign resident in Nagasaki noted, Huis Ten Bosch can hardly be called authentic when the only grass to be had is in the green fields.

Plan to spend a full day at Huis Ten Bosch. From Nagasaki take a train which runs along the Omura line to JR Huis Ten Bosch station (70 mins).

KUMAMOTO

Halfway down the west side of Kyushu, Kumamoto once flourished as a castle town; today the (reconstructed) castle still rates as the city's biggest tourist draw. Probably Kumamoto's best-known resident was Miyamoto Musashi (1584-1645), an exceptional swordsman and 'expert in tactics' who wrote a book during the last years of his life in which he is said to have 'tempered his samurai way of thinking with more serene views of life'. His serenity did not stop him from being buried in full armour, clutching his sword.

Miyamoto probably approved of the 'Kobori swimming technique', an unusual martial art originating in Kumamoto, which according to city publicity involved the 'art of swimming in the standing posture while attired in armour and helmet'.

What to see and do
To get an overview of the history of Kumamoto and the castle, start with a visit to **Sakuranobaba Josaien** (daily Apr-Oct 8.30am-6.30pm, Nov-Mar to 5.30pm; ¥300, ¥600 with castle entry), a history and culture experience centre. Most signs are in Japanese but look out on the floor for circles where you can stand for an explanation in English, German, Korean and Chinese (one after the other, which is a bit annoying). It is also possible to sit in a sedan, ride a model horse and try on kimonos.

Wakuwaku Za Story Palace, on the 2nd floor, is a theatre where episodes from Kumamoto's history are acted out. The seats at the back are for foreigners who want to listen to a translation but it is hard to hear what is being said as the Japanese version is so loud. However, you can at least enjoy the wonderful smell of the tatami on the seats. Also in the complex are shops and restaurants selling local food and drinks. A meal at **Ginnan Buffet** (daily 11am-2.30pm & 5-9pm; ¥1500/¥2000 lunch/evening) is the best way to try a range of dishes but *Asotei Tamamichaya* specialises in *basashi* (see box p403) and *Yumeakari* serves noodles and light meals. To get to Sakuranobaba Josaien take the tram to Shiyakusho-mae or the loop bus to Kumamoto City Hall bus stop.

It is a short, though uphill, walk from Sakuranobaba Josaien to **Kumamoto Castle** (daily Apr-Oct 8.30am-5.30pm, Nov-Mar 8.30am-4.30pm; ¥500, or ¥640 inc entry to the Former Residence of Hosokawa-Gyobu; enquire at the main gate about free guided tours in English). The castle was completed between 1601 and 1607, but most of its fortifications were destroyed during the civil war of 1877. The structure which exists today is a 20th-century reconstruction and as near as possible to what the original fortification must have looked like. The castle is still an impressive sight, especially when lit up at night (until 11pm). Inside the donjon are displays on the civil war, the cultural history of the region and a scale model of the original castle.

If you prefer to go to the castle from the station, take the Kumamoto Castle loop bus, which drops you off right outside the entrance (stop No 5, Kumamoto Castle Ninomaru Parking Area), or the tram to Kumamotojo-mae (tram No 2 from outside Kumamoto station).

A short walk from the castle (or stop No 7 on the tourist loop bus to Hosokawa's Residence), and set within the vast grounds, is the **Former Residence of Hosokawa Gyobu** (Kyu-Hosokawa-Gyobutei; daily Apr-Oct 8.30am-5.30pm, Nov-Mar 8.30am-4.30pm; ¥300, or ¥640 with castle entry), a samurai residence painstakingly reconstructed during the mid 1990s. Pick up the English leaflet from the ticket booth. It's an elegant building and is worth the entrance fee to walk (or squeak) your way along the wooden corridors that overlook the attractive garden and imagine what it must have been like to live like a samurai.

Just to your right as you leave the house is a **Tea House** (daily 9am-3pm), where kimono-clad staff will serve you green tea with Japanese sweets (¥200) in a small tatami room. It's a nice way to round off a visit to the castle area.

The trendiest art space in town is **Kumamoto Contemporary Art Museum** (🖥 www.camk.or.jp; Wed-Mon 10am-8pm; free). The entrance is on the 3rd floor and the museum is in the same building as Hotel Nikko Kumamoto (stop No 11, Toricho-suji, on the Kumamoto Castle loop bus).

Behind Tsuruya department store in the city centre (stop No 11, Toricho-suji, on the Kumamoto Castle Loop Bus) is the **former residence of Lafcadio Hearn** (Tue-Sun 9.30am-4.30pm; ¥200). Hearn is better known as a one-time resident of Matsue (see pp261-2), from where he moved to Kumamoto in 1891. He lived in a house owned by a local samurai family, now in the middle of the downtown shopping area.

The house is very small but it's still worth going inside, where panels in English tell the story of how Hearn, who was born on the Greek island of Lefkas (Levkas), arrived in Yokohama in 1890 at the age of 40 on an assignment for

Harper's magazine. He spent the rest of his life in Japan, living in Matsue and then spending three years in Kumamoto teaching English. Later he moved to Kobe and in 1896 became a Japanese citizen. Koizumi Yakumo, as Hearn was called after his naturalisation, died suddenly of a heart attack on 26th September 1904.

Flag-waving tour guides lead a constant stream of school parties around Kumamoto's other hotspot, **Suizen-ji Garden** (daily Mar-Nov 7.30am-6pm, Dec-Feb 8.30am-5pm; ¥400), stopping briefly for a mass photo call in front of the main point of interest, a grass mound in the shape of Mt Fuji. The park was constructed in 1632, but since it's much smaller than Kenrokuen (see pp180-1) in Kanazawa it's very hard to enjoy it in tranquility.

Also in the grounds are **Izumi Shrine**, built in 1878 and a popular venue for New Year celebrations, and a **Noh theatre** (firelit performances are staged here during the summer festival, 11th-13th Aug).

It's best to visit Suizen-ji as early as possible to avoid the crowds. Take the tram to Suizenji-koen-mae. Alternatively, rail-pass holders can save a few yen on the tram fare by taking a local train on the JR Hohi line from Kumamoto to Shin-Suizenji (10 mins), from where it's a short walk (follow the tram line) to the garden entrance.

See p404 for details of side trips from Kumamoto.

PRACTICAL INFORMATION
Station guide
The shinkansen station (West Gate) is light, airy and spacious like the others on this line but less wood has been used. As with all the stations there are lifts for disabled access. The shinkansen part is connected to the original station by an underpass. If transferring to the local line take the exit on the left when you reach street level. If heading for Kumamoto go straight ahead.

The sights and hotels are on the Shirakawa/East Gate side so you will almost definitely need to use the underpass. However, as well as places to eat (see Where to eat), convenience stores and all the usual station facilities, there is a small bank of **lockers** opposite the tourist information counter on the non-shinkansen side, and more are available at the end of the concourse, close to the ampm convenience store.

Also at the station is a branch **post office** with an **ATM** which accepts foreign-issued debit/credit cards.

Tourist information
There is a tourist information centre (🖳 www.kumamoto-icb.or.jp/eng and 🖳 www.manyou-kumamoto.jp; daily 8am-8pm) on each side of the station. At both staff can help book accommodation; they also provide city maps and sell the one-day bus/tram passes.

Getting around
One-day passes (¥500) allow unlimited travel on the **tram** and **Shiei buses** (mostly green) within the city centre. Passes are available from the tourist information centres at the station, or on board the trams themselves. Otherwise the flat fare is ¥150.

The **Kumamoto Castle loop bus**, with 'Welcome to Kumamoto' seat covers, does a loop around town (8.30am-5pm; 2/hour; ¥130 flat fare or ¥300 one-day pass) from Kumamoto station, stopping en route at the castle and the Transportation Center (bus stop No 6) in the city centre but not at Suizen-ji. There is a screen at the front of the bus with English information on the castle and other sights. *(Continued on p402)*

KYUSHU

Where to stay
1 Toyoko Inn Kumamoto Ekimae 東横イン熊本駅前
2 JR Kyushu Hotel Kumamoto JR九州ホテル 熊本
6 Hotel New Otani Kumamoto
   ホテルニューオタニ熊本
8 Minshuku-Ryokan Kajita 民宿旅館梶田
15 Hotel Nikko Kumamoto ホテル日航熊本
16 Toyoko Inn Kumamoto-jyo Tori-cho Sujimae
   東横INN熊本城通町筋
20 Comfort Hotel Kumamoto Shinshigai
   コンフォートホテル熊本新市街
22 Richmond Hotel Kumamoto
   リッチモンドホテル熊本新市街
23 Suidocho Green Hotel 水道町グリーンホテル

Where to eat and drink
2 Umaya うまや
3 Hinokuni 本の素材
4 Keika (Fresta) 桂花（フレスタ熊本）
12 Sakuranobaba Josaien 桜の馬場 城彩苑
13 Aoyagi 青柳
14 Ninja 忍者

● 9

Shinmachi

To Hakata/
Fukuoka

7

10

Senbabashi

Nishi-
Karashimacho

8

Keitokuko-mae

Gofukumachi

Kawaramachi

Gionbashi

6
5

4

3

Kumamotoeki-
mae

**Kumamoto
Station**

2

1

To
Kagoshima

Nihongiguchi

0 100 200 300m

KYUSHU

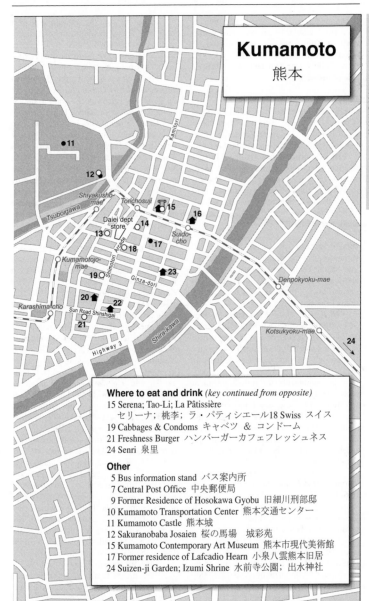

● 11

12 ♀

Shiyakusho-mae

Tsuboigawa

Torichosuji

15

16

Daiei dept store

14

13 ○

Suido-cho

18

17

Kumamotojo-mae

23

19

Ginza-dori

Denpokyoku-mae

20

22

Karashima-cho

Sun Road Shinshigai

21

Shimtori Arcade

Kotsukyoku-mae

24

Shira-kawa

Highway 3

Kamitori

Where to eat and drink *(key continued from opposite)*
15 Serena; Tao-Li; La Pâtissière
　　セリーナ; 桃李; ラ・パティシエール18 Swiss スイス
19 Cabbages & Condoms キャベツ ＆ コンドーム
21 Freshness Burger ハンバーガーカフェフレッシュネス
24 Senri 泉里

Other
　5 Bus information stand バス案内所
　7 Central Post Office 中央郵便局
　9 Former Residence of Hosokawa Gyobu 旧細川刑部邸
10 Kumamoto Transportation Center 熊本交通センター
11 Kumamoto Castle 熊本城
12 Sakuranobaba Josaien 桜の馬場　城彩苑
15 Kumamoto Contemporary Art Museum 熊本市現代美術館
17 Former residence of Lafcadio Hearn 小泉八雲熊本旧居
24 Suizen-ji Garden; Izumi Shrine 水前寺公園；出水神社

(Continued from p399) A healthier, greener alternative would be to rent an electric **cycle** at Kumamoto station, from the JR ticket office (Midori-no-Madoguchi; ¥300/2 hours, ¥600/4 hours) on the non-shinkansen side of the station.

Festivals

The biggest annual event is the **Hi-no-Kuni** (Country of Fire) festival, which takes place 11th-13th August and features a fireworks display and late-night folk dancing.

Aki no Kumamoto Oshiro Matsuri (Kumamoto Oshiro Autumn Festival), held during the first fortnight of October, includes all sorts of events centred around the castle, including *yabusame* (horseback archery; see p39), martial arts, food fiestas, and a Noh performance.

Where to stay

Room rates in the station area are cheaper than in the centre near Kumamoto Castle and it's really not that much of a hassle to get into town – there are regular buses and trams from the station.

JR Kyushu Hotel Kumamoto (☎ 096-354 8000, 🖳 www.jrhotelgroup.com; ¥6500/S, ¥12,600/D or Tw, inc breakfast; rail-pass holders get a small discount), immediately on your right as you exit via the Shirakawa (East Exit) side of the station, is undoubtedly the most convenient place to stay.

If you like watching trains come and go, ask for a room facing the tracks; the sound-proofing is excellent and the windows allow a superb view of the tracks and indeed station life. The baths are also larger than in many hotels.

A more expensive option outside the station is *Hotel New Otani Kumamoto* (☎ 096-326 1111, 🖳 www.newotani.co.jp/en/kumamoto; from ¥11,000/S, ¥18,000/Tw or D), which has all the facilities you'd expect of this top-class hotel chain.

For Japanese-style accommodation, a good bet is *Minshuku-Ryokan Kajita* (☎ 096-353 1546, 🖳 higoshiro@yahoo.co.jp; ¥4000pp, ¥4700pp with breakfast, ¥6000pp half-board) in the city centre and convenient for access to the castle.

If coming from the station the nearest tram stops are either Shinmachi or Urusan-machi, alternatively it is a 20- to 25-minute walk. The minshuku is on the corner of a fairly busy road opposite a small park.

For a cheap night in the downtown area try *Suidocho Green Hotel* (☎ 096-211 2222, 🖳 www.gr-suidocho.com; ¥6090/S, ¥8400/D), part of the Green Hotel chain.

Other alternatives include the two local branches of the Toyoko Inn chain (🖳 www.toyoko-inn.com). *Toyoko Inn Kumamoto Ekimae* (☎ 096-351 1045; from ¥4980/S, ¥6480/D, ¥7480/Tw) is just behind the JR hotel but is best reached by walking on the left side of the taxi rank. Follow the rank round to the right, past the police station and cross the road to the hotel. Since the hotel has 27 floors it's not easy to miss as it's the tallest building in the area. It is worth paying for a panoramic view though sadly none really faces the castle. The breakfast here isn't as good as at many other branches. *Toyoko Inn Kumamoto-jyo Tori-cho Suji* (☎ 096-325 1045; from ¥5480/S, ¥7980/Tw) is in front of Suido-cho tram stop.

Other good business-hotel options include: *Richmond Hotel Kumamoto Shinshigai* (☎ 096-312 3511, 🖳 www.richmondhotel.jp/kumamoto; from ¥13,000/S, ¥23,000/Tw, breakfast from ¥800), and *Comfort Hotel Kumamoto Shinshigai* (☎ 096-211 8411, 🖳 www.comfortinn.com/hotel-kumamoto-japan-JP066; ¥5550/S, ¥10,500/Tw, inc breakfast), which offers all-day coffee in the lobby.

A more luxurious – and expensive – option is *Hotel Nikko Kumamoto* (☎ 096-211 1111, 🖳 www.nikko-kumamoto.co.jp; from ¥17,325/S, ¥31,185/Tw; discount packages often available), considered the best in town. It has larger-than-average rooms (some on the 10th floor with a view of Kumamoto Castle) and a choice of restaurants. Twins have a separate toilet and bathroom. You're ideally placed to visit the Contemporary Art Museum, since it's located on the 3rd and 4th floors of the hotel.

For further details about facilities in chain hotels and finding accommodation in general, see pp45-52.

Where to eat and drink

Branches of **Friesta** (shopping and dining arcades) are on both sides of the station. On the local train side go to the 2nd floor for eat-in restaurants. At *Hinokuni* (11am-9pm), if you would like to try a bit of basashi (see box below) but aren't sure you will like it, have the *kara-age teishoku* (¥1350) as that way there will be other things to eat if you don't like the basashi. The Friesta on the shinkansen side has a ramen shop called *Keika* (11am-9pm). There are plenty of options on the menu; expect to pay ¥800-1000.

Aside from the usual fast-food joints, the best place to eat in the immediate station vicinity is *Umaya* (7am-10/11pm), on your right as you exit the station and attached to JR Kyushu Hotel Kumamoto. It's a modern take on an izakaya, with the option of sitting at the counter and having your food grilled in front of you. Great-value set lunch menus are ¥720.

In the city centre arcades there's a good selection of informal cafés, restaurants and fast-food places. For a lunchtime snack, try *Swiss* (10am-11.30pm), a bakery/café serving simple meals and cake-and-coffee sets. It's in the Shimotori shopping arcade in the city centre.

At *Ninja* (daily 6pm to late) all the staff are dressed as ninjas and entertain guests with ninja magic tricks. The food – fish and meat dishes on skewers – is typical izakaya fare, and there's a good selection of drinks. It's also in the Shimotori Arcade next to a McDonald's and is signed in English.

If you've a big appetite, it's worth considering the all-you-can-eat buffet lunch at *Serena* (11.30am-2.30pm; Mon-Fri ¥1950, Sat & Sun ¥2200), a brasserie-style restaurant on the 2nd floor of Hotel Nikko Kumamoto. On the same floor is an excellent Chinese restaurant, *Tao-Li* (11.30am-3.30pm & 5.30-10pm), where the cheapest lunchtime set menu is ¥1400.

La Pâtissière (daily 11am-8pm) bakery on the ground floor is good for a sweet treat to eat in or take away.

Sakuranobaba Josaien (see pp397-8) also has a variety of options.

An out-of-the ordinary eatery is *Cabbages & Condoms* (daily noon-3pm & 6pm-12.30am), the first franchise of this popular Thai café chain to open outside Thailand. You can't miss the large red Coca-Cola-style sign in English outside, next to a branch of Häagen-Dazs. The entrance is up a flight of stairs on the 2nd floor. The food is authentic and reasonably priced, and as in Thailand, profits are used to fund Aids awareness and other rural-development programmes in Thailand.

At *Freshness Burger* (daily 9am-10pm) the burgers are cooked to order and the freshly squeezed lemonade is very

---

卅 Basashi – an acquired taste

That evening I learned that raw horsemeat was a speciality of the area...I went to a little restaurant near Kumamoto station with my mind made up to try some. It was disappointingly stringy, and having come straight out of the refrigerator, was hard with bits of ice. I sat for a long time sipping beer, waiting for the horsemeat to thaw, while the only customer in the restaurant had a conversation with the owner.
Alan Booth, *The Roads to Sata*, Kodansha International, 1985

Kumamoto's big culinary draw doesn't sound the most appetising of regional specialities; the main problem with *basashi* (raw horsemeat), however, is not so much the taste but that most places offering it are prohibitively expensive. You could easily spend around ¥10,000pp dining at a restaurant specialising in the stuff.

If you decide to try basashi it's best to buy some from a butcher and take it back to your ryokan or minshuku. If you ask, the butcher will prepare it ready to eat and probably include some soy sauce. That way you'll get to try Kumamoto's speciality at a fraction of the prices charged in basashi restaurants. You won't have to wait for it to thaw and nor, hopefully, will you find it stringy.

efreshing. For more of a local flavour try *Aoyagi* (11.30am-10pm), a few steps from Daiei department store; the sashimi is excellent. Expect to pay around ¥2000 per head. Look for the blue curtain hanging outside.

If you're visiting Suizen-ji garden, *Senri* (Thur-Tue 11am-2.30pm & 5-10pm)

has set lunches in private dining rooms starting at ¥2000. Ask for a room with a view on to the park. You can try *basashi* here (see box p403) as part of the set lunch. Dinner courses are more expensive, starting at ¥4500, though you do get to view the park once the tourists have left for the day.

Side trips from Kumamoto on the SL Hitoyoshi and Aso Boy! Kuro

The **SL Hitoyoshi** (Mar-Nov Fri-Sun and national holidays in this period; one round trip a day; 2½hrs each way; ¥2570 one-way) was restored in 2009 in order to celebrate the 100th anniversary of the JR Hisatsu line. This line originally connected Kumamoto and Kagoshima; it was built inland, through the Kirishima mountains and along the Kuma river, so that it couldn't be attacked by any foreign navies. There is no longer a direct service between Kumamoto and Kagoshima on the Hisatsu line but it is still possible to follow the original route. The SL Hitoyoshi goes to Hitoyoshi via Yatsushiro & Shin-Yatsushiro. The three cars have maple and rosewood furnishings and include an observation lounge, a reading area and a buffet counter for snacks and drinks.

The **Aso Boy! Kuro** (most Sat & Sun plus daily in holiday periods; two round trips a day; 80 mins; ¥2380 one way plus ¥200 for a panorama seat) is a Limited Express sightseeing service that started in September 2011. It runs from Kumamoto to Miyaji (see Map 31, p377) and consists of four carriages. Cars No 1 and No 4 have the panorama seating – the driver sits in an elevated position so passengers can reserve the seats at the front and see the driver's usual view – and Car No 3 (Kurochan) is the car for families as it has a play area, a small library and a Kuro Café.

JR rail passes are valid on both services but reserved seats are essential. Since these services are very popular it is worth booking early.

KAGOSHIMA

Kagoshima is on the eastern side of the Satsuma Peninsula, facing Kinko Bay, and is the southern terminus of the Kyushu shinkansen, which runs along the island's west coast from Hakata/Fukuoka. The island of Sakurajima, with its brooding volcano, lies just 4km away. The volcano's proximity means umbrellas are sometimes needed to keep off the dust and ash blown across to the mainland. Don't be surprised to find a thin coating of ash on the streets on some days.

If Sakurajima dominates the skyline, historically it is the Shimazu family who have dominated the political map of Kagoshima. Successive generations of the family remained in power from 1185 through to the Meiji Restoration in 1871. As the southern gateway to Japan, Kagoshima was also the place where missionary Francis Xavier landed on 15th August 1549. As his ship approached the city, Xavier is said to have been filled with excitement on seeing what he thought was the cross of Jesus Christ, but which turned out to be the sign of the ruling Shimazu family. Little of Xavier's legacy is left today since the church he built was bombed during the Pacific War.

What to see and do

Apart from Sakurajima (see p410), Kagoshima's big draw is **Iso-teien**, also known as Sengan-en (🖥 www.senganen.jp/en/senganen; daily 8.30am-5.30pm; ¥1000 garden only, ¥1500 inc tea house and short tour in Japanese). The 50,000-square-metre landscape garden was constructed in 1658 as a residence for Mitsuhisa Shimazu, 19th lord of the ruling Shimazu family. The layout takes full advantage of its Sakurajima backdrop. The City View tourist bus from Kagoshima-chuo station stops outside the main entrance; it's stop No 9 on the Shiroyama/Iso route or stop No 6 on the Waterfront route.

After visiting the garden take a quick look at the adjacent **Tsurugane Shrine**, dedicated to the members of the Shimazu family who reigned over Kagoshima. One of the deities enshrined here is Princess Kameju. Born in 1571 as the third daughter of the 16th Shimazu Lord, Kameju became known as the guardian of female beauty. Legend has it that a woman who prays at the shrine will become even more beautiful.

Tickets for Iso-teien are also valid for **Shoko Shuseikan Museum** (🖥 www.shuseikan.jp; daily 8.30am-5.30pm), across from the entrance to the garden on the site of the former factory used by the Shimazu family to manufacture iron and glassware. Inside, the history of the Shimazu family is told in great detail (with plenty of signs in English).

The main attraction in the **Museum of the Meiji Restoration** (🖥 www. ishinfurusatokan.info; daily 9am-5pm; ¥300) is a waxwork show, during which a model of Saigo Takamori (see box below) rises from the floor/grave and the story of his life is retold in dramatic fashion. The soundtrack is in Japanese only. Take the City View bus from Kagoshima-chuo station; the museum is the first stop on both the Shiroyama/Iso and the Waterfront routes.

The best place for views of Kagoshima and Sakurajima is the observation point (daily; free) on **Mt Shiroyama** (in Shiroyama-koen). *(Continued on p408)*

⛩ **Saigo Takamori**

It's impossible to walk very far around Kagoshima without seeing the name Saigo Takamori on the many statues and monuments around the city. Points of reference such as the 'Birthplace of Saigo', 'Statue of Saigo', 'House where Saigo was resuscitated', 'Cave where Saigo Takamori hid' and 'Place where Saigo Takamori died' can all be seen at one glance on a city map. Laid out around town is the chronicle of one man's life, his journey from humble birth to a glorious if tragic death.

Saigo Takamori (1827-77) was born into a lower-class samurai family in the province of Satsuma (now Kagoshima), the eldest of seven children. In 1868 he became one of the leading figures in the battle to defeat the shogunate and restore power to the Meiji Emperor. It wasn't long before Saigo's loyalties were stretched between support for the new power base and his unerring allegiance to the large numbers of samurai in Satsuma who were being deprived of their status by Imperial edict.

His change of heart reached a dramatic climax in 1877 when Saigo gathered a 15,000 strong army and announced his intention to march on Tokyo. He never even got as far as Honshu and died on Mt Shiroyama in his native Kagoshima at 7am on 24th September 1877 after a defiant last stand against the government he had helped to found.

KYUSHU

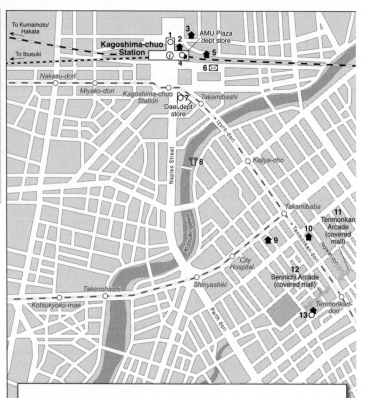

Where to stay

2 JR Kyushu Hotel Kagoshima JR九州ホテル鹿児島
3 Hotel Urbic Kagoshima ホテルアービック鹿児島
5 Toyoko Inn Kagoshima Chuo-eki Nishi-guchi 東横イン鹿児島中央駅西口
9 Toyoko Inn Kagoshima Tenmonkan No 1 東横イン鹿児島天文館1
10 Toyoko Inn Kagoshima Tenmonkan No 2 東横イン鹿児島天文館2
13 Richmond Hotel Kagoshima Tenmonkan リッチモンドホテル鹿児島天文館
18 Nakazono Ryokan 中園旅館

Where to eat and drink

1 Gourmet Yokocho グルメ横町
4 Ichi-Ni-San (AMU Plaza) いちにいさん(アミュプラザ)
7 Daiei Department Store ダイエーデパート
11 Tenmonkan Arcade 天文館アーケード
12 Sennichi Arcade 千日アーケード
13 Yakohai 夜光杯
17 Densuke でんすけ

KYUSHU

Kagoshima

鹿児島

Other
4 Amuran ferris wheel (AMU Plaza)
アミュラン（アミュプラザ）
6 Central Post Office　中央郵便局
8 Museum of the Meiji Restoration
維新ふるさと館
14 Dolphin Port　ドルフィンポート
15 Kagoshima City Aquarium　鹿児島市水族館
16 Sakurajima Ferry Terminal (Kagoshima Port)
桜島フェリーターミナル（鹿児島）
19 Mt Shiroyama (Shiroyama Park)
城山（城山公園）
20 Iso-teien; Tsurugane Shrine;
Shoko Shuseikan Museum
磯庭園；鶴嶺神社；尚古集成館

19

Asahi-dori

City Hall

Izuro-dori

18

Suizokukanguchi

17

Sakurajima
Sanbashi-dori

Kagoshima
Station

14

16

Sakurajima
Pier

15

**Kagoshima
Station**

20

To Miyazaki

Kagoshima Bay

0   100   200m

To Sakurajima

(Continued from p405) From the bus stop walk up past the stalls selling Saigo Takamori T-shirts and trinkets to the observation area, from where there's a great view of the city and of Sakurajima. The colour of the volcano is supposed to change seven times a day, so if it burns bright red and orange for too long, it's at least reassuring to know you're on high ground (107m above sea level). Shiroyama itself consists almost entirely of volcanic deposit and is known as the place where Saigo Takamori died. Take the City View bus from Kagoshima-chuo station to stop No 7 on the Shiroyama/Iso route.

Kagoshima City Aquarium (🖳 www.ioworld.jp; daily 9.30am-6pm, last entry 5pm; ¥1500), next to Sakurajima Ferry Terminal, is in the building with a roof that looks like a rough copy of the Sydney Opera House. Star attractions are the dolphins, though the 3D movie in which you can get wet without having to bring a change of clothes will keep children amused. Take the City View bus from Kagoshima-chuo station to stop No 4 on the Waterfront route, or stop No 11 on the Shiroyama/Iso route. Close by is **Dolphin Port** (🖳 www.dolphinport. jp), where you'll find waterfront restaurants and shops on two levels, and views out to Sakurajima. This is a good place to chill out, have a meal and enjoy the views. Take the City View bus from Kagoshima-chuo station to stop No 12 on the Shiroyama/Iso route or stop No 3 on the Waterfront route.

For a good view of Kagoshima from the station area, head for the 6th floor of **AMU Plaza** department store, where you'll find the entrance to **Amuran**, a bright red ferris wheel (daily 10am-10.45pm; ¥500pp, ¥900/3 people, ¥1000/4 people; tickets from the machine by the entrance). Also on the 6th floor is a 10-screen multiplex cinema and games arcade.

For details of side trips from Kagoshima, see pp410-11.

PRACTICAL INFORMATION
Station guide
The southern terminus for the shinkansen from Fukuoka/Hakata is **Kagoshima-chuo**. It is also a stop on the JR Kagoshima main-line and the JR Ibusuki-Makurazaki line.

Lockers (all sizes) are easy to find on the main concourse. There is also the usual selection of food outlets (see Where to eat) and tourist information (see below). There are two exits: the Nishi-da (west) exit and the Sakurajimaguchi (east) exit; the latter is the main one.

Kagoshima station is the southern terminus of both the JR Kagoshima and the JR Nippo main lines. There is also a small tourist information counter here.

Tourist information
The **tourist information counter** (🖳 www. kagoshima-kankou.com; daily 8am-8pm) is on the main station concourse. Turn right as you exit the ticket barrier (coming from the

platforms) and you'll find it by the East exit.

Staff can provide maps of Kagoshima and Sakurajima, as well as a gourmet map showing restaurants and cafés. They can also assist with accommodation reservations, arrange tickets for Sakurajima sight-seeing tours (see p410) and sell one-day travel passes (see below).

Getting around
Kagoshima's **tram** network is the best way of getting around. There is a flat fare of ¥160. **One-day passes** (¥600) allow you to board all city tram and bus services as well as the retro **City View tourist bus** (daily 9am-5pm; flat fare ¥180), which does two different circuits: the Shiroyama and Iso route (2/hour; 9am-5pm), and the Waterfront route (8/day, roughly hourly 8.40am-5.25pm). Both routes start and end at bus stop No 9 outside the station. Pick up a route map from the tourist information counter.

If you have a rail pass or a valid train ticket you can rent a **bike** (between 9am and 5pm; ¥300/hr, ¥980/day) from JR: ask at the Midori-no-Madoguchi JR ticket desk.

Kagoshima Airport (⌨ www.koj-ab. co.jp; mostly domestic flights) is served by buses (40 mins; ¥1200) from stop No 4 outside Kagoshima-chuo station.

Festivals

Two major festivals are the **Natsu Matsuri** (Summer Festival) at the end of July and **Ohara Matsuri** in early November. Fireworks are a feature of the Natsu Matsuri and the main event at the Ohara Matsuri is a dancing parade which starts from the centre of the city and heads towards the Sakurajima pier.

Where to stay

JR Kyushu Hotel Kagoshima (☎ 099-213 8000, ⌨ www.jrhotelgroup.com/eng/hotel/ eng149.htm; ¥6900/S, ¥12,600/D) is the closest hotel you can get to the train platforms. Turn left as you exit the ticket barrier and follow the sign as you head towards the West Gate exit. The rooms are modern and brightly decorated and check-in is from 2pm (check-out is by 11am). Guests get free internet access in the lobby area.

You can't fault the Toyoko Inn chain (⌨ www.toyoko-inn.com) and there are several branches in Kagoshima. The closest to the station is: *Toyoko Inn Chuo-eki Nishi-guchi* (☎ 099-814 1045; from ¥4980/ S, ¥5980/D, ¥7980/Tw) follow signs for the Nishida (west) Exit and go down the steps to the left of the Friesta arcade. At the bottom turn right taking the Nishida Exit. Follow the signs for JR Kyushu Hotel Kagoshima; this Toyoko Inn is on the right just beyond it. Two other branches are in the main part of town and are best accessed using the tram if you have luggage. *Toyoko Inn Kagoshima Tenmonkan No 2* (☎ 099-224 1045; from ¥4980/S, ¥6480/D, ¥7980/ Tw, inc breakfast) is between Takamibaba and Tenmonkan-dori tram stops. If that is full try *Toyoko Inn Kagoshima Tenmonkan No 1* (☎ 099-219 1045; ¥4980/S, ¥5980/D, inc breakfast), a minute's walk south from Takamibaba stop.

Hotel Urbic Kagoshima (☎ 099-214 3588, ⌨ www.urbic.jp; ¥6900/S, ¥12,600/ Tw, inc breakfast) is a decent business-hotel choice located in front of you as you take the station's Nishida Exit.

Richmond Hotel Kagoshima Tenmonkan (☎ 099-239 0055, ⌨ richmondhotel.jp/en/kagoshima-tenmonkan; ¥7800/S, ¥12,800/D; breakfast ¥900) is an upmarket business hotel in the Tenmonkan shopping district. Hotel staff wear sleek black uniforms, even the single rooms have large double beds, and there is room service (6-11pm) from the hotel restaurant.

Nakazono Ryokan (☎ 099-226 5125, 🖷 226 5126, ⌨ shindon@satsuma.ne.jp; ¥4200pp room only, discount for three people sharing) offers tatami rooms all with TV and telephone, though baths are communal (open 24 hours); there's a coin laundry. Call ahead and if the owner is free he will collect you from the station. Meals are not included but Densuke (see Where to eat) is just around the corner.

For further details about facilities at the chain hotels in Kagoshima and finding accommodation in general see pp45-52.

Where to eat and drink

There are lots of restaurants on the 5th floor (most open 11am-11pm) of **AMU Plaza Kagoshima** department store next to the station complex. Take the Sakurajima (east) exit; you can't miss the building since it's the only one with a large red ferris wheel, protruding from the roof. One of the most popular places here is *Ichi-Ni-San,* which serves a range of Japanese dishes (from ¥750) from shabu-shabu to tonkatsu.

Another good restaurant hub is **Gourmet Yokocho** (restaurants open daily at least 10am-11pm), next to the entrance to JR Kyushu Hotel Kagoshima on the station concourse. Here you'll find a revolving sushi bar (*Mawaru*), a pasta and pizza place (*Trattoria Budonoki*), a coffee and cake shop (*Seattle*) and a ramen place (*Zabon*). Especially interesting is *Ooyama*, which serves tonkatsu and shabu-shabu made with both black and white pork. The pigs are a (now rare) breed from Berkshire, England, and they are fed on a sweet-potato diet; black pork is a speciality of Kagoshima. A very tasty sirloin black pork tonkatsu set is ¥1250. *Yakohai* (daily 11am-3pm for lunch, 3-5pm for snacks, 5pm-1am for dinner), a swish, modern Italian restaurant on the ground floor of Richmond Hotel Kagoshima Tenmonkan, is a great place for lunch. For ¥1980 you get antipasto, soup, salad, pasta, dessert and a soft drink. The cheaper pasta lunch is ¥1200. They also do the Kagoshima speciality, black pork.

Densuke (Mon-Sat 5pm-late) is an *izakaya* close to Nakazono Ryokan. It's chiefly a drinking place, but you can order skewers of meat or fish to accompany your liquid refreshment.

Within the **covered malls** (Sennichi and Tenmonkan arcades) that lead off from Tenmonkan-dori tram stop are some casual eating places with everything from fast-food (Western and Japanese) to a variety of restaurants and also not all on street level.

For **self-catering** try **Daiei** department store opposite the station, or the basement of AMU Plaza, which also has a food court.

Side trips from Kagoshima
By ferry to Sakurajima Smoke, dust and ashes billowing out from Sakurajima are a common-enough sight in Kagoshima but the last major eruption was in 1946. The worst eruption of the 20th century was in 1914, when three million tonnes of lava buried eight villages and turned the island into a peninsula, completely filling a 400m-wide and 70m-deep sea. The worst eruption in recent memory – but tiny in comparison to 1914 – was in March 2009, when Sakurajima spewed debris as far as two kilometres.

The **ferries** (daily 1-6/hr; 15 mins; 24 hours a day; ¥150, bicycle ¥250) to Sakurajima take cars and foot passengers and depart from the ferry terminal near Kagoshima Aquarium – follow the signs to whichever boat will go next. You pay on arrival at Sakurajima. You will need the correct change; there is a change machine by the ticket collector.

The **Sakurajima Island View Tour Bus** (daily 8/day; 60 mins round trip; ¥110-430 per journey or ¥500/one-day pass) departs from Sakurajima port and stops at the main sights on the western side of the island, including the Visitor Centre and several lookout points. The bus stops at the lookout points for 5-15 minutes so it is possible to stay on the same bus rather than waiting for another. Tickets are available on the bus or at TICs in the area. Alternatively, take the **Sakurajima Nature Sightseeing Tour** (in Japanese only). You can either join this at Kagoshima-chuo station (bus stand 8; departs 9am & 1.40pm; 3½hrs; ¥2200) or on the island (9.40am & 2.20pm; 2hrs; ¥1700). Just one main road circles the island; on the way round look out for lava fields and the *daikon* (giant radishes) that can grow up to 30kg in weight on the fertile slopes.

Before leaving the ferry terminal on the Sakurajima side, go to **Sakurajima Information Centre** (daily 8.30am-5pm) for a map and cycle rental (¥300/hour). However, the better source of information is **Sakurajima Visitor Centre** (Tue-Sun 9am-5pm; free). Turn right out of the ferry terminal and follow the road round the coast for about 10 minutes. The centre has a model of Sakurajima, an explanation of the ecosystem, displays of volcanic rock and footage of previous eruptions. There are labels in English and the film (11 mins) is subtitled in English. In the park outside there is a foot spa – walk out of the door opposite the one you came in by and head towards the sea but slightly to the left. Towels are not provided but it shouldn't take long for your feet to dry after a soak. It is certainly a relaxing experience and will set you up for the walk back.

Onsen fans may like to make their way to **Furusato-onsen** (Fri-Wed 8am-6pm for non-residents; ¥105), a seaside hot spring located in *Furusato*

Kanko Hotel (☎ 099-221 3111, 💻 www.furukan.co.jp; rooms from ¥9450). Located right by the sea, this onsen ranks as one of the most impressive places to bathe in Japan. At the hotel someone will direct you to the ticket-vending machine, where you collect a yukata and head downstairs. Eventually you'll find the door that leads outdoors and down some steps to the hot spring. Everyone has to wear their yukata in the water because the spring is part of a shrine. The hotel runs a free shuttle bus service to/from stop No 4 outside the ferry terminal at Sakurajima Port (at least hourly 9am-5pm).

Sakurajima Youth Hostel (☎ 099-293 2150, 💻 www.e-yh.net/kagoshima; ¥2650pp; breakfast ¥510, dinner ¥710) is about 10 minutes on foot uphill from the ferry terminal.

By rail to Ibusuki A day trip to Ibusuki combining a journey on the **Ibusuki-no-Tamatebako** train (also known as Ibutama; 3/day; 50 mins; ¥2070 each way; free with a Japan Rail or JR Kyushu rail pass; seat reservation essential) with a unique natural hot-sand bath (a Japanese-style sauna) at Ibusuki Sunamushi-onsen is highly recommended.

Both the train's name, which means Ibusuki Treasure Box, and its paintwork – the side that faces the sea is painted white and the land side black – are inspired by a folk tale. In this tale, a character called **Taro Urashima** opens a treasure box, whereupon white mist curls out of the box and his own hair turns from black to white. As you enter the train white mist duly comes out above the doors. The train has an area where children can play as well as books to read. Some seats face out to the sea and some the traditional way so specify which you would prefer when you make a reservation; since the train only has two cars and each is designed differently ask to be in one on the way out and the other on the return.

Once the train has left the Kagoshima suburbs the scenery improves; if the weather is good, Sakurajima is visible most of the time. The Ibusuki station **tourist information centre** (daily 9am-5pm) has a map of the area.

A session at **Sunamushi-onsen hot-sand bath** (Mon-Fri 8.30am-noon & 1-8.30pm, Sat, Sun & hols all day; ¥900, towel rental ¥200) is meant to improve circulation and relieve conditions such as arthritis, asthma, rheumatism, 'alimentary disorder' and 'sensitivity to cold', but should be avoided if you're pregnant or have high blood pressure. To reach the onsen from the station, either take the bus (1-2/hr; ¥130) or walk (15-20 mins): follow the road straight ahead and turn right at the first traffic lights. The sand bath building is a little way along on the left. Take the escalator up to the 2nd floor and go to the ticket office to collect a yukata and a towel if you haven't brought one.

Having undressed and put on your yukata, follow the signs to the sand bath on the beach. You will be allocated a space and staff will cover you with the hot black sand. You are recommended to stay for only 10 minutes, after which you get up (not an entirely easy process) and shake yourself down before heading back in for a shower followed by a bath in the onsen. There is a *café* on the top floor as well as a viewing platform.

If you are already missing the onsen effect by the time you get back to Ibusuki station, join the locals at the foot onsen in front of the station. Ibusuki is rather rundown so it is unlikely you would want to stay here. Also, other than *Casa Vecchio* (11.30am-2.30pm & 6-10pm), which serves a pasta lunch (¥950) or pizza (¥1000), there are few places offering food in the station area.

SHIKOKU

Shikoku – route guides

Shikoku ('Four Provinces') takes its name from the provinces into which the island was once divided. The old provinces of Sanuki, Tosa, Iyo and Awa are known today as the prefectures of Kagawa, Kochi, Ehime and Tokushima.

Predominantly rural, Shikoku has everything that the current image of Japan does not: wide open spaces, forests, country villages and a dramatic natural landscape. However, the island is not just a provincial backwater. There's plenty to see and it's worth devoting at least a week to completing the loop route described below.

The route passes through all four prefectures and includes stops in the capital cities of three of them. Though a number of road bridges link Shikoku with Honshu, the only entry/exit point by rail is across the Inland Sea via the Seto-Ohashi Bridge (see p414).

This route starts in **Okayama**, taking the Marine Liner train across the bridge to **Takamatsu** where you can savour a trip to Ritsurin-koen, one of the largest gardens in Japan.

From Takamatsu there is an additional loop that continues east to **Tokushima**, known in particular for its summer dance festival, then returns to the main route at Awa-Ikeda, before heading south to **Kochi** where you can visit Yokoyama Ryuichi Manga Museum.

Alternatively, from Takamatsu, the route heads south to Kochi via **Kotohira**, home to an interesting shrine, Kompira-san. The route continues in a clockwise direction to **Uwajima**, known for its bull fights and sex museum, then on to **Matsuyama**, the largest city on the island and a good access point for a visit to Dogo-onsen, Japan's oldest spa town. The last part of the journey covers the route from Matsuyama back towards Okayama on Honshu.

See p15 for details of the passes available in Shikoku and see p25 for itinerary ideas. It's worth noting that though plenty can be accomplished on a rail tour of Shikoku, the more isolated parts of the island, including the two southern capes at Muroto and Ashizuri, can be reached only by infrequent buses or by hiring a car.

On most weekends between April and September (except in June, because of the rainy season) open-air carriages (*torokko*) are attached to some of the most scenic rail lines

冬星の旅青鷺は番なり

*Winter stars –
just two grey herons
as I journey by*
(MINAKO KANEKO)

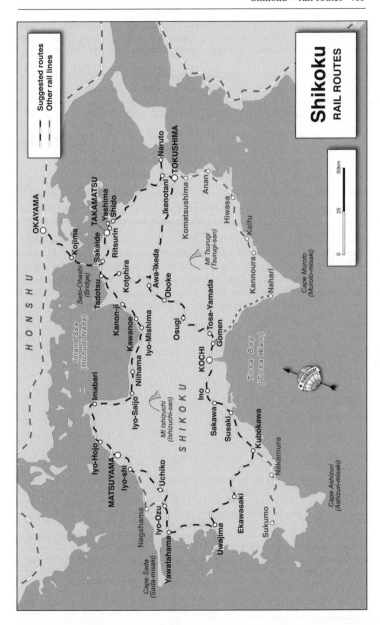

Shikoku
RAIL ROUTES

Suggested routes
Other rail lines

0   25   50km

OKAYAMA
HONSHU
Kojima
Seto-Ohashi (Bridge)
Inland Sea (Hichudi Nada)
Tadotsu
Sakaide
TAKAMATSU
Yashima
Ritsurin
Shido
Naruto
TOKUSHIMA
Ikenotani
Komatsushima
Anan
Hiwasa
Mt Tsurugi (Tsurugi-san)
Kaifu
Kotohira
Awa-Ikeda
Oboke
Kannoura
Nahari
Cape Muroto (Muroto-misaki)
Kanon-ji
Kawanoe
Iyo-Mishima
Osugi
Tosa-Yamada
Gomen
Niihama
Iyo-Saijo
Mt Ishizuchi (Ishizuchi-san)
KOCHI
Tosa Bay (Tosa Wan)
Imabari
SHIKOKU
Ino
Sakawa
Susaki
Iyo-Hojo
MATSUYAMA
Iyo-shi
Uchiko
Kubokawa
Nakamura
Cape Ashizuri (Ashizuri-misaki)
Nagahama
Iyo-Ozu
Ekawasaki
Sukumo
Cape Sada (Sada-misaki)
Yawatahama
Uwajima

in Shikoku. These carriages carry an additional charge which is not covered by the rail pass. One of the most popular torokko services runs every year between Tokawa and Ekawasaki on the Yodo line (see p422). Apart from this the routes change annually to take in a variety of railway lines, so check in advance through JR Shikoku's website or the JR East helpline (☎ 050-2016 1603). Seat reservations (¥310) should be made in advance (from any JR ticket office) anyhow.

A useful resource for planning a trip is 🖥 www.tourismshikoku.org.

See also pp8-9 for details about using this guide.

OKAYAMA TO TAKAMATSU [Map 33, p417; Table 25, p468]

Distances by JR from Okayama. Fastest journey time: 60 minutes.

Okayama (0km) [see pp247-52]
Take the Marine Liner rapid train along the Seto-Ohashi line, which runs direct to Takamatsu across the Seto-Ohashi Bridge. On its way to the bridge the train calls at **Senoo (8km)**, **Hayashima (12km)** and **Chaya-machi (15km)**.

Kojima (28km)
Last stop on Honshu before the train crosses **Seto-Ohashi**. The bridge, or rather series of bridges, spans 9.4km and took nearly a decade to build, opening in 1988 with a construction bill of ¥1120 billion. The view from the train as it crosses the bridge is certainly impressive, though eclipsed by the scale and design of the bridge itself. However, one reader wrote that it was a 'disappointing journey because it was hard to see through the safety barriers'.

Sakaide (Y08; 51km)
First stop after crossing the bridge. Towards Honshu lies **Seto-Ohashi Commemorative Park**, with a museum and observation tower; outdoor concerts are held here occasionally. Change here if planning to visit the pilgrimage temple of Kokubun-ji (see opposite).

🙏 Shikoku 88 temple pilgrimage

Pilgrims who embark on the circuit of Shikoku's 88 temples are following in the steps of Kobo Daishi, the Buddhist saint who first walked around the island and who now lies in eternal meditation at Koya-san on Honshu, home to the Shingon sect of Buddhism founded by him in the 9th century.

Most *henro* (pilgrims) visit Koya-san (see pp223-5) either before or after completing the Shikoku pilgrimage. It's not necessary to follow precisely in Kobo Daishi's steps by walking between the temples. There are no rules to prevent modern-day pilgrims using public or private transport. Indeed, many of the pilgrims you see in the temples today, dressed in traditional white and carrying sticks to help them along the way, have a minibus waiting in the car park ready to whisk them off to their next destination.

The pilgrimage does not have to be completed in one visit, so many make return trips to Shikoku over a number of years. Some, however, such as the Buddhist monks who walk the circuit for spiritual cleansing, do it the hard way. Sakaide station (see above) offers a large interactive computer screen which displays images and maps of the various temples on the route to aid pilgrims on their journey, but it is only in Japanese.

In the station are **lockers** (up to ¥500), a convenience store, coffee shop, udon restaurant and, slightly hidden, a **tourist information office** (daily 9am-5.30pm), where only Japanese is spoken. There are elevators between the concourse and platforms. Opposite one side of the station is the SATY shopping complex with a variety of restaurants.

♦ **Kokubu (Y04; 60km)** Only local trains stop here; services operate approximately every 30 minutes from Sakaide (11 mins) and from Takamatsu (15 mins). It's a five-minute walk from the station to **Kokubun-ji**, the 80th temple on the Shikoku pilgrimage. If coming from Takamatsu cross the overhead bridge, exit the station and walk straight ahead to the main road that runs parallel with the rail track. Turn right and about three minutes down this road on the left is a sign pointing towards the temple. The entrance is just off the main road on the left. Despite the numbers of pilgrims, the temple is a tranquil place.

To the right of the main temple, Japanese music plays, guiding you into a store where you can buy assorted lucky charms and various pieces of the pilgrim's outfit, including the white shirt and walking stick.

Takamatsu (Y0, T28; 72km)   [see pp428-33]

TAKAMATSU TO TOKUSHIMA   [Map 33, p417; Table 25, p468]

Distances by JR from Takamatsu. Fastest journey time Takamatsu to Tokushima: 57 minutes.

Takamatsu (Y0, T28; 0km) For those looking for a more leisurely route around Shikoku, Tokushima makes an excellent cultural diversion before you rejoin the Takamatsu to Kochi route at Awa-Ikeda (see p418).

From Takamatsu take a Uzushio LEX bound for Tokushima. All of these stop at **Ritsurin (T25; 4.3km)**, but only local trains stop at Ritsurin-koen Kitaguchi, the closest station to Ritsurin-koen. Most then call at **Yashima (T23; 9.5km)** and all at **Shido (T19; 16.3km)**. From **Sambommatsu (T12; 38km)** the already impressive scenery gets even better as the train weaves through the isolated forested slopes. Some trains stop at **Hiketa (T10; 45.1km)**.

After **Itano (T07; 58km)** most trains stop at **Ikenotani (T04, N04; 64.2km)** where you may consider changing for the Naruto whirlpools (see pp438-9). The next stop is **Shozui (T03; 66.9km)**.

Tokushima (M0, T0; 75km)   (see pp435-8)

If continuing to travel around Shikoku it is sensible to go to **Awa-Ikeda** (**D22, B25; 74km**; see p417), from where you can pick up the route guide to Kochi, rather than returning to Takamatsu. The Tsurugisan LEX (6/day) takes 76 mins from Tokushima but the local trains take around two hours to wend their way alongside Yama-gawa to Awa-Ikeda.

TAKAMATSU TO KOCHI   [Map 33; Table 26, p469]

Distances by JR from Takamatsu. Fastest journey time: 130 minutes.

Takamatsu (Y0, T28; 0km)   Pick up the Shimanto LEX heading south towards Kochi along the Dosan line.

All services stop at **Sakaide (Y08; 22km**; see pp414-15), **Utazu (Y09; 26km**; see p427), **Marugame (Y10; 29km**; see pp426-7). Since the number of Shimanto LEX services is limited, consider taking an Ishizuchi LEX to Marugame and changing there on to a Nanpu LEX to Kochi.

The line divides at **Tadotsu (Y12, D12; 33km**; see p426): the Yosan line heads west towards Matsuyama (see pp439-43); the Shimanto LEX continues south along the Dosan line to Kochi.

Zentsu-ji (D14; 39km)   Zentsu-ji is the birthplace of Kobo Daishi, the Buddhist monk who made a pilgrimage on foot around Shikoku (see box p414). The temple here is the 75th on the 88-temple circuit and one of the busiest because of its link with Daishi. It's also the place for Hadaka Matsuri (see box below).

Inside the temple precincts are a 45m-high five-storeyed pagoda, completed in 1884 for the 1050th anniversary of Kobo Daishi's death, and Mie-do Hall, said to be the very spot where Kobo Daishi was born in 774. The temple is a 20-minute walk west along the main road which runs away from the station.

Kotohira (D15; 44km)   Kotohira has an interesting shrine and is the ideal place to break your journey for a few hours. JR Kotohira station has **lockers** (¥600) but it's cheaper (¥400) to leave large luggage with the staff. There's also a small *udon restaurant*. You can pick up a pictorial map of the local sights. Walk straight up the main road from the station to find the steps leading up to the shrine.

The shrine of Kotohira-gu is better known as **Kompira-san**, the affection-ate name for the guardian deity of seafarers. Kompira-san clings to the slope of

---

☖ Naked Festival
   The highlight of February's **Hadaka Matsuri** (Naked Festival) at **Zentsu-ji** is *fukubai*, the 'scrambling for good-luck sticks'. Hundreds of young men, wearing only a loincloth, battle to grab the sticks and ensure they enjoy good fortune for the rest of the year. A local guidebook suggests that, even though participants are wearing next to nothing, 'the fierce fights make participants steaming hot. Nakedness signifies innocence like a newborn baby, while the white of the loincloth represents the purity of its wearer.' Check with the tourist office in Takamatsu (see pp429-30) for the exact date of the festival, which changes every year.

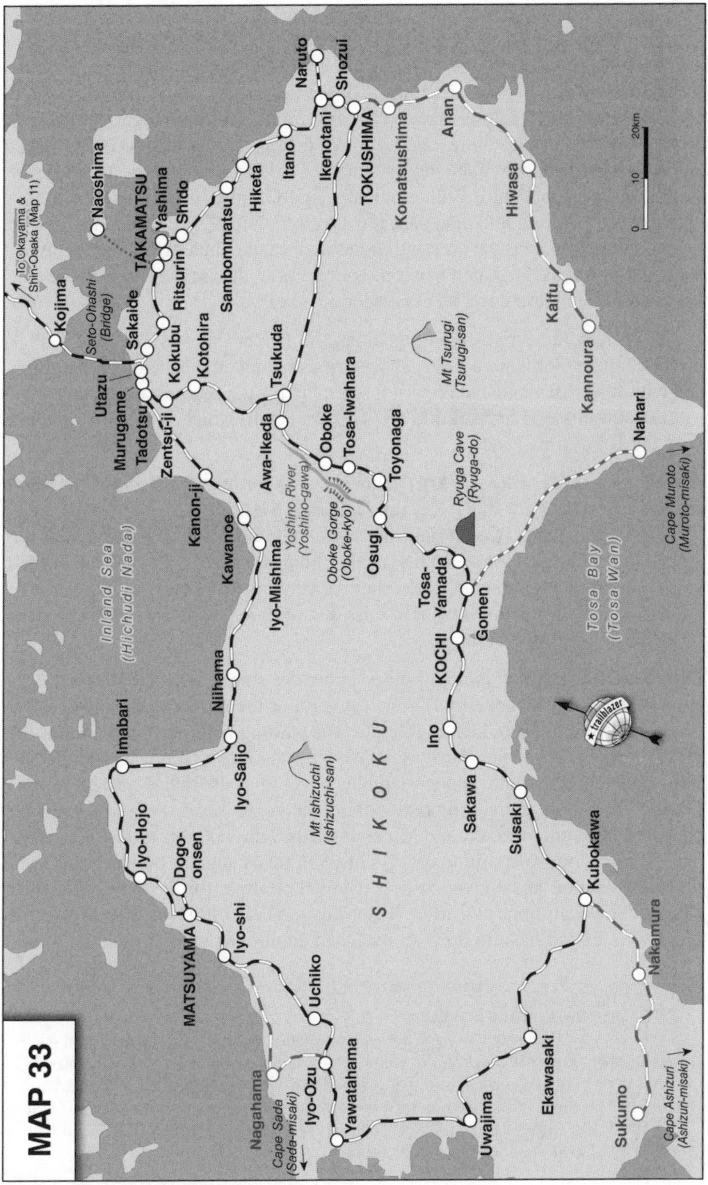

MAP 33

To Okayama &
Shin-Osaka (Map 11)

Naoshima

Kojima

Seto-Ohashi
(Bridge)

TAKAMATSU

Yashima

Shido

Ritsurin

Sakaide

Utazu

Kokubu

Kotohira

Murugame

Tadotsu

Zentsu-ji

Kanon-ji

Kawanoe

Iyo-Mishima

Awa-Ikeda

Tsukuda

Sambommatsu

Hiketa

Itano

Ikenotani

TOKUSHIMA

Komatsushima

Naruto

Shozui

Anan

Mt Tsurugi
(Tsurugi-san)

Oboke

Tosa-Iwahara

Toyonaga

Yoshino River
(Yoshino-gawa)

Oboke Gorge
(Oboke-kyo)

Osugi

Ryuga Cave
(Ryuga-do)

Hiwasa

Kaifu

Kannoura

Nahari

Cape Muroto
(Muroto-misaki)

Inland Sea
(Hichudi Nadai)

Niihama

Imabari

Iyo-Saijo

Mt Ishizuchi
(Ishizuchi-san)

S H I K O K U

Tosa-
Yamada

Gomen

KOCHI

Ino

Sakawa

Susaki

Tosa Bay
(Tosa Wan)

Kubokawa

Nakamura

Cape Ashizuri
(Ashizuri-misaki)

Iyo-Hojo

Dogo-
onsen

Iyo-shi

MATSUYAMA

Uchiko

Iyo-Ozu

Yawatahama

Nagahama

Cape Sada
(Sada-misaki)

Uwajima

Ekawasaki

Sukumo

S H I K O K U

20km

10

0

S H I K O K U

Mt Zozu ('Elephant's Head'); the reward for making it up the first 785 steps to the main shrine is a view over the valley below and across the Inland Sea. It's a further 583 steps to Okusha Shrine, the Inner Sanctuary. Along the way are stalls that sell walking sticks, drinks and noodles.

Before or after making the ascent, drop in at **Kanamaru-za** (☎ 0877-73 3846; 🖳 www.town.kotohira.kagawa.jp; Wed-Mon 9am-4pm; ¥500), the oldest kabuki theatre in Japan. Take the road that leads left from the foot of the shrine steps and up a small hill. Built originally in 1835, the theatre later became a cinema before falling into disrepair. It was restored in 1976 and you can now go behind the scenes, tour the dressing rooms and wander underneath the revolving stage itself. Kabuki is staged here only once a year, during the spring, when the best seat in the house costs an eye-watering ¥12,000.

From Kotohira, trains continue along the Dosan line towards Kochi. Pick up the Shimanto or Nanpu LEX. Reservations are recommended as some trains run with fewer carriages, making it a scramble for the non-reserved seats.

Local trains stop at **Tsukuda (B24, D21; 72km)** which is the first junction with the Tokushima Line.

Awa-Ikeda (D22, B25; 77km) This is a stop for most LEXs so is the main interchange station for the Tokushima line (see p416).

From Awa-Ikeda, the Dosan line continues south towards the area's big sight, Oboke Gorge. Unfortunately, many of the passengers who use the limited express train to commute to Kochi shut the curtains and sleep through some of the best views. If you don't want to miss out, reserve a window seat (both sides of the train have superb views).

Oboke (D27; 99km) Not all limited expresses stop here, so plan ahead.

Oboke gorge (Oboke-kyo) – or 'canyon', as the Japanese signposts call it – is one of Shikoku's hidden highlights. The starting point for boat tours of the gorge is about 1km from the station. Walk up to Oboke Bridge above the station, cross it, turn right and go straight. A short walk brings you to '**Lapis Oboke**', in a modern building overlooking the gorge. Inside is a café, souvenir shop and Museum of Rocks and Minerals (daily 9am-4.30pm; ¥500). This is not an essential stop, so continue past it until you reach another building that contains a restaurant and souvenir shop. The ticket office for the 30-minute **boat tours** (daily 9am-5pm or earlier if not busy; ¥1050) is inside. No rowing is required – all you have to do is sit back and admire the view.

Borrowed from Belgium
One less well-known sight not far from Oboke Gorge is a copy of Brussels' best-known statue, Mannekin Pis (Shoben Kozo in Japanese). The naked boy is perched precariously on a clifftop looking down into the gorge, quietly relieving himself. The cliff-top vantage point is considered a place to prove your bravery. If you can stand next to the statue and look down at the gorge directly below, it's said that nobody will ever again question your courage.

If the weather is fine and you fancy something more adventurous, get off the limited express here and take a local train to Tosa-Iwahara (7 mins).

♦ **Tosa-Iwahara (D28)** Less than 100m from the station is Australian-run **Happy Raft** (🖳 www.happyraft.com), which offers whitewater rafting (¥10,000pp/day, Jul-Sep ¥15,500pp/day) and canyoning adventures (Jul-Oct ¥9000pp/half-day) on the Yoshino River.

If you need to stay the night, a good choice is the homely and friendly B&B-style *Pension Murata* (☎ 0887-75 0010, 🖳 www.murata-p.jp; ¥4725pp room only, or ¥7350pp half-board), three minutes on foot from **Toyonaga (D29)** station, one stop further south by local train from Tosa-Iwahara.

To continue your journey south from Tosa-Iwahara or Toyonaga, take a local train to Osugi (see below) and pick up the limited express for the final stretch of the journey to Kochi.

Osugi (D32; 120km) Not all limited expresses stop here. Osugi means 'Big Cedar'; the place is named after a nearby tree which some people claim is 3000 years old. Most of the next 5km are spent in tunnels.

The next stop is **Tosa-Yamada (D37; 144km)**.

Gomen (D40; 149km) Change here if you plan to visit an incredibly faithful copy of the garden of Claude Monet, the French impressionist (see below).

Side trip by rail to see Monet in Japan
Shakespeare's home town was painstakingly recreated years ago in Japan, so it should not come as a surprise to discover that an attempt has been made to do the same for French impressionist Claude Monet (1840-1926), whose garden in Giverny has been recreated almost blade by blade, lily by lily, in the small village of **Kitagawa**, accessed via the private Tosa-Kuroshio Railway (🖳 www.tosakuro.co.jp) from Gomen.

Le jardin de Monet Marmottan au Village de Kitagawa (🖳 www. kjmonet.jp; Mar-Dec Wed-Mon 10am-5pm; ¥700), to give the place its full French name, is hugely popular. If you've been to Giverny, it's still worth seeing the Japanese version and playing spot the difference. If you haven't seen the original, think of this as an opportunity to take a trip to France without leaving Shikoku.

To reach the garden, change at Gomen onto the private Tosa-Kuroshio Railway's Gomen-Nahari line and ride the train all the way to the terminus at **Nahari** (64 mins; ¥1040; rail passes not accepted). A shuttle bus runs from Nahari and drops you off outside the main entrance (10 mins, ¥230).

Kochi (D45, K00; 160km) Bordered in the north by the Shikoku mountain range and to the south by the Pacific Ocean, Kochi is known for its mild climate, long days of sunshine, and relaxed, friendly atmosphere.

Arriving at the impressive new structure of Kochi station, you will find **lockers** (including large ¥600 ones) in the far right corner after going through the exit barrier. JR **buses to Matsuyama** (see p421) depart from platforms to the right of the station's left-side exit. The **tram terminus** is on the main road that runs parallel to the front of the station (right exit).

Kochi's well-informed **tourist information counter** (🖳 www.attaka.or.jp; daily 9am-8pm, English-speaking staff guaranteed until only 5pm) is housed in the wooden edifice to the right side of the station's central exit.

Kochi's old but efficient **tram system** comprises two lines which intersect at Harimaya-bashi in the city centre. City-centre rides cost a flat ¥190 and a one-day pass, available from the bus centre ticket office at Kochi station, is ¥500. If changing tram lines at Harimaya-bashi, ask for a *norikae-kippu,* which allows you to transfer without paying again. Look out for the trams that have been brought from Germany, Portugal, Austria and Norway, each with a different design and interior layout.

Completed in 1611, **Kochi Castle** (Kochi-jo; daily 9am-5pm; ¥400) at the end of Otesuji-dori, is the city's big sight and one of a dozen original Japanese castles remaining. Among its many defensive elements (ironically never used) are holes for dropping stones on assailants. There's a fine view from the top floor of the donjon. Take the tram from the station to Kochijomae (¥190).

Chikurin-ji, on the Shikoku pilgrimage (see box p414), is accessible by bus from Kochi station or from the bus terminal. Take a bus marked 'Godaisan Chikurin-ji'.

Yokoyama Ryuichi Memorial Manga Museum (🖳 www.bunkaplaza. or.jp/mangakan; Tue-Sun 9am-6pm; ¥400) celebrates the work of one of Japan's most famous cartoonists, the late Yokoyama, who died in 2001. His best-known comic-strip character, Fuku-chan, made his debut in a national newspaper in 1936 and was only retired in 1971. Comics fans will be in heaven in the attached **manga library** (free entry). The museum is in Kochi City Culture Plaza (3rd-5th floors), a three-minute walk from Saenbacho tram stop.

Yosakoi Festival (🖳 www.yosakoi.com) is a high-energy dance event involving over 14,000 people divided into teams. Each team can choreograph their own dance so the festival has a contemporary feel. The festival (9th-12th Aug) is held on streets in central Kochi, approximately 15 minutes' walk south from the station. A similar event is held in Sapporo (see p353).

If you want to stay near the station try *Comfort Hotel Kochi* (☎ 088-883 1441, 🖳 www.comfortinn.com/hotel-kochi-japan-JP032; ¥5400/S, ¥7200/D, ¥9000/Tw). Rooms are very spacious, with free internet access, and there are laundry facilities. A good budget option is *Hotel Los Inn* (☎ 088-884 1110, 🖳 losinn.co.jp; ¥4500/S, ¥7350/D, ¥ 7600/Tw; breakfast ¥400) a little further down from Comfort Hotel but still near the station. The lobby may be slightly dated but you'll get an effusive welcome, and free internet in your room. Meals at the adjoining restaurant, *Hannah no Ren* (5-10pm), where the speciality is local Tosa-seared bonito, can be added to your hotel bill.

A short way up the main road that heads away from the station towards the Harimaya-bashi crossing is *Kochi Pacific Hotel* (☎ 088-884 0777, 🖳 www. kochi-pacific.co.jp; ¥7700/S, ¥17,300/Tw), an upmarket business hotel (note the grandfather clock in the lobby), with a 2pm check-in. Close to the centre of town in the covered arcade next door to *Doutor Coffee, Richmond Hotel* (☎ 092-739 2055, 🖳 www.richmondhotel.jp; ¥5400/S, ¥8700/D, ¥10,700/Tw, plus

¥500 membership; breakfast ¥880) is a trendy outfit near lots of bars, with fashionably tailored staff, modern décor and pleasingly spacious rooms.

Freshly caught sea bream is popular and, according to one local gourmet guide, 'prepared so that it is still alive and in one piece before eating'. Less upsetting would be a bowl of *dorome* – tiny, clear fish that are the local special-ity; they are served at many places, including the popular **Tosa Ichiba** (Tue-Sun 11am-9.50pm), on Obiyamachi shopping arcade (look for the picture of the whale on the sign outside), which has a feast of plastic window-display models and does well-priced set meals.

Beyond Tosa Ichiba, **Tsukasa** (11.30am-2.30pm & 4.30-10pm, to 9.30pm at weekends) is a showcase for 'Sawachi' cuisine (large platters of food, best for groups) such as *saba* (mackerel) sushi; the seafood is certainly impressive, but the prices are a little high (tempura set ¥1800, tuna set ¥1260), possibly to cover the cost of the wonderful interiors and kimono-clad staff. Similar is **Tosahan** (11.30am-10pm), diagonally across the arcade from Tosa Ichiba. It's an atmos-pheric place with low wooden tables. Note the large fish tank on your way in and the extensive array of plastic food models outside.

In the centre, on the south side of the Ohashi-dori shopping arcade, base-ment izakaya **Futsuwauchi** (5.30-11.30pm; last orders 10.30pm) offers a quiet but pleasant dining experience. The okonomiyaki (Japanese omelette) is very good and the young owners will try to keep you entertained.

At **Hirome Market**, an indoor food mall on Otesuji-dori, you can sit at picnic tables and enjoy snacking on a cornucopia of food and drink from the hundreds of densely packed stalls.

KOCHI TO UWAJIMA

Distances by JR from Kochi. Fastest journey time: 3 hours 5 mins.

Kochi to Kubokawa   [Map 33, p417; Table 27, p469]
If you're in a hurry and want to skip the next (slow!) part of the journey from Kochi to Matsuyama via Uwajima, consider taking a direct JR bus (6/day, 2½ hours; ¥3500/one-way, rail-pass holders free) between the two cities.

Kochi (K00, D45; 0km) From Kochi, pick up the Nanpu LEX, which con-tinues along the Dosan line to Kubokawa.

Ino (K07; 11km) has been a paper-making town for over a thousand years, using water from Niyodo-gawa. Ino is the terminus for one of Kochi's tram lines, so streetcar enthusiasts might consider a trip by tram between here and Kochi station.

After **Sakawa (K13; 28km)** there are rice fields everywhere you look on this stretch of the journey. Kochi's mild weather and heavy rainfall means that it's the first place in Japan to harvest the year's crop.

Approaching **Susaki (K19; 42km)** it's something of a shock to come across factories, concrete buildings and industry; not the most attractive part of the journey. The next stop is at **Tosa-Kure (K22; 53km)**.

SHIKOKU

Kubokawa (K26, TK26; 72km) The JR Dosan line terminates here. From here, the private Tosa Kuroshio Railway runs further south to **Nakamura (TK40)**, the nearest station to **Ashizuri-misaki**. The JR Nanpu LEX continues along this private line, though rail-pass holders have to pay between Kubokawa and Nakamura.

▲ To follow the next part of this rail route, change trains here and connect with the rural Yodo line, which runs along Shimanto-gawa before terminating in Uwajima. Pick up a Yodo line train from platform 4. If you don't have a rail pass take a ticket when boarding the train and pay the fare when you get off. No limited expresses run along this line.

Kubokawa to Uwajima [Map 33, p417; Table 28, p469]

The Yodo line is one of the most scenic and rural in Shikoku; most of the stops are barely stations – just places where the train pulls up, often on the edge of a field. In theory, since the line between Kubokawa and **Wakai (5km**; the first stop after Kubokawa) runs on private track, rail-pass holders should pay a ¥200 supplement. However, since nobody checks your ticket until you arrive in Uwajima, it seems that this additional fare is forgotten.

It takes around two hours for the train from Kubokawa to pull in to Uwajima. En route it occasionally fills up with schoolchildren but then just as quickly empties again. For part of the way the line follows the course of Shimanto-gawa, claimed to be the 'last great virgin river in Japan'. No man-made dams have been built near it; unimpeded by mechanical barriers, the water is probably the clearest you'll see anywhere. Trout and *ayu* (sweetfish) are popular catches.

Even though the chugging of the train can be sleep-inducing, the scenery is worth staying awake for, as you'll see farmers working in the fields and storks in water-logged rice paddies. More often than not, the rail line has been cut between fields, so you can stare right down at the cauliflowers, cabbages and individual rice plants.

Between 2nd July and 31st August a *torokko* (see p414) is added between **Tokawa (G32; 103km)** and **Ekawasaki (G34; 115km)**. After Ekawasaki the line leaves Shimanto-gawa and winds its way towards the Pacific Ocean, crossing into Ehime prefecture on its way to Uwajima.

Uwajima (G47, U28; 150km) Uwajima station has platforms on the same level as the exit. The station itself is very spartan. Only small **lockers** are available but the staff at the ticket barrier may allow you to store large luggage. The **tourist information office** booth (daily 9am-6pm) is inside the station and has maps but little English is spoken. To find an English speaker, turn right out of the station and trot 15 minutes along the palm-lined main street to **Kisaiya Hiroba** information centre by the port. The window is around the left facing the courtyard.

As a staging post between Kochi and Matsuyama, Uwajima has a few attractions. Top of the bill is **Taga-jinja (Shrine)** and its **Sex Museum** (daily 8am-5pm; ¥800). The museum is wall-to-wall penises, in various shapes and sizes, though the emphasis is on the huge. The phallic models, pictures and works of art that leave nothing to the imagination are crammed into a three-storeyed building in one corner of the shrine. All the signs are in Japanese but it's not as if much explanation is needed.

Uwajima's other big attraction is **bull fighting** (*togyu*). These contests are strictly bull against bull – no human risks getting hurt – and take place a few times a year at the Municipal Bull Fighting Ring (2nd Jan, first Sun in Apr, 24th Jul, 14th Aug, second Sun in Nov; ¥3000). At other times, a film of the fighting is shown (Mon-Fri 8.30am-5pm; ¥500). The following extract from the promotional literature gives an idea of what to expect: 'Bouts between two bulls weighing nearly one tonne are quite dynamic. The bulls crash so hard against each other trying to push their opponent out that you may possibly hear the sound of their pant'.

Uwajima Castle (Tue-Sun 9am-4pm; ¥200) is about a 15-minute walk from the station (turn right out of the station, then left on Highway 56 at the main junction). It is called a *hirayamashiro* (a castle on a hill surrounded by a plain) as it was build on a 80m-high hill in Shiroyama Park, near Shiroyama history building. The three-storey structure dates from the Edo period and the *tenshukaku* (donjon; main keep) is one of twelve in Japan that is still an original but there is no exhibition to speak of inside the castle. Nearby is **Tensha-en garden** (daily 8.30am-4.30pm, closed Mon mid Dec to Feb; ¥300).

If you need somewhere to stay, the JR-operated *Hotel Clement Uwajima* (☎ 0895-23 6111, 🖳 www.jrhotelgroup.com; ¥6930/S, ¥11,550/D, ¥12,127/Tw; tatami rooms ¥17,325/D or Tw; 10% off all rates with a JR rail pass) is immediately above the station. Standard rooms have modern furnishings, bilingual TV, and fridge and there are also a couple of attractive tatami rooms. A rooftop beer garden (summertime only, 6-9.30pm) offers an unlimited food-and-drink deal for ¥3000 (¥3500 for non-guests), with a wide variety of hot buffet dishes. Signs discourage drunkenness.

Kodoya (11am-2.30pm & 5-9pm) is a well-known local sashimi restaurant on the main strip (Nishiki-machi) as you leave the station. As the road doglegs, go straight on and the restaurant is on the right-hand side after you cross the first side street. Dishes include pork tonkatsu, tempura sets (both ¥1480), sashimi sets (from ¥1980) and steak sets (¥2200). A few doors back on the station side of Kodoya is the cheaper *Tomiya* restaurant (Thur-Tue 11am-4pm & 6-9pm), whose plastic displays reflect its modest interior (look out for the rope entrance curtain). It does provide good, hearty portions however: tamago-udon (¥450), basic sushi-sets (¥450), curry rice (¥550) and prawn sets (¥1400).

UWAJIMA TO MATSUYAMA [Map 33, p417; Table 29, p470]

Distances by JR from Uwajima. Fastest journey time: 1¼ hours.

Uwajima (U28, G47; 0km) From Uwajima, pick up the Uwakai LEX, which runs along the Yosan line to Matsuyama. The first stop is **Unomachi (20km)**.

Yawatahama (U18; 35km) Home to one of the region's largest fishing communities, Yawatahama is the nearest station to Cape Sada peninsula. At 50km, the cape is the longest and narrowest in Japan; from Cape Sada Lighthouse at the tip there are good views of the Seto Inland Sea. The best way to reach the cape is by car: enquire about car-hire prices at the JR ticket counter.

Iyo-Ozu (U14, S18; 48km) This castle town is just one of three remaining spots in Japan where traditional **cormorant fishing** can be seen (on Hiji-kawa, Hiji river; June to mid Sep). In season, a nightly boat trip (7pm; 2hrs, ¥3000 inc dinner) enables tourists to watch the birds dive and deliver their freshwater *ayu* sweetfish in the glow of flaming torchlight. Take a taxi from the station to the river (6 mins) or, if too early for the fishing, take the taxi instead to the nearby **Garyu Sanso** mountain villa (daily 9am-5pm; ¥500), high above the river. Recently restored, its beautiful thatched roof and traditional Japanese garden showcase the area's former prosperity.

The rail line divides at Iyo-Ozu, with a choice of either the **inland route**, which this guide follows (served by limited express or local train), or the **coastal route** (served by local trains only). If you're on a limited express and want to follow the coastal route, this is the last place you can change before the lines diverge. Taking the coastal route, the line follows Hiji-gawa to the sea, then heads slowly up the coast before converging with the inland line at Iyo-shi station; services operate roughly hourly and take approximately 70 minutes.

Uchiko (U10; 59km) There are elevators from platforms 1 and 2 down to street level. The station has small **lockers** only but you can leave you bags at the adjoining café for ¥200 and also pick up leaflets there as well as a map if you haven't already downloaded one from the website (🖳 www.we-love-uchiko.jp). In the square outside the station is a **steam locomotive** that ran on the Uchiko Line from 1969 to 1970, transporting cargo between Uchiko and Iyo-Ozu. Built in 1939, its accumulated mileage would be enough to circum-navigate the globe 33 times.

Between the Edo and Meiji periods, Uchiko prospered as a manufacturing centre for Japanese paper and wax. Today it is known for the **Yokaichi Historical Area**, a street of preserved old houses, some of which are open to the public as museums or upmarket coffee shops. From the station, walk ahead to the second set of lights, then turn left into town along Honmachi street, then left again at Iyo Bank. Walk uphill to find the old street.

Uchiko even boasts its own kabuki theatre, **Uchiko-za** (daily 9am-4.30pm; ¥300; 60 performances/year). Built in 1916 and restored in 1985, it is similar in design to the theatre at Kotohira (see p416), with a revolving stage and seats for up to 650. Look for signs to the theatre on your way into town from the station. Good photo opportunities can be had from upstairs.

To find the **Museum of Commercial and Domestic Life** (also known as Uchiko History Museum; ¥200), a folksy recreation of a 1920s family-run pharmaceutical business, look for the mannequins staffing the pharmaceutical counter on the right as you head up Honmachi street. Inside, you can wander freely among the wax figures seated on the upstairs tatami mats, but it's more atmospheric than instructive.

At the more informative **Japanese Wax Museum** (¥400 inc entry to Kami-Haga) in the heart of the Yokaichi area, the production cycle and international role of Uchiko's wax industry is proudly outlined (in English) through an interesting variety of dioramas, artefacts and local products.

Adjoining the wax museum, the recently renovated **Kami-Haga Residence** beautifully illustrates the prosperity the industry brought to one of the major producer families in the early 1900s. All are open daily 9am-4.30pm.

Poco a Poco, an Italian trattoria on Honmachi street, serves reasonably priced spaghetti lunch sets and salads. Alternatively, just past the left turning for Uchiko-za, try the tatami-floored *Rinsuke*, which does good, traditional Japanese dishes from ¥500.

Iyo-shi (85km) This is the point at which the coastal and inland rail lines reconverge for the final part of the journey to Matsuyama.

Matsuyama (U0, Y55; 97km) [see pp439-43]

As the train pulls in to Matsuyama, look out to the left for the silver Botchan Stadium. A location for city baseball games, the stadium is named after one of Matsuyama's most famous honorary citizens, the character, Botchan, from Soseki Natsume's novel of the same name. 'Botchan' also visited Dogo-onsen hot-spring baths (see pp444-5), still one of the city's biggest draws.

MATSUYAMA TO OKAYAMA [Map 33, p417; Table 30, p470]

Distances by JR from Matsuyama. Fastest journey time: 2 hours 35 mins.

Matsuyama (U0, Y55; 0km) The final part of the journey around Shikoku; the Shiokaze LEX runs direct from here back to Okayama. If returning to Honshu, make sure you're sitting in cars 4-8 as cars 1-3 split off at Tadotsu and head to Takamatsu (if you have a seat reservation, you'll already be in the right part of the train).

Between Matsuyama and **Iyo-Hojo (18km)**, the line roughly parallels the main 196 trunk road but there are occasional views of the Inland Sea out to the left. About 20 minutes after Iyo-Hojo you should see, also out to the left, the Nishi-Seto Highway linking Shikoku with Honshu.

Imabari (Y40; 50km) Imabari is the starting point for the **Nishi-Seto Highway**, which connects Shikoku with Honshu via a road bridge. Completed in 1999, the bridge uses six small islands as staging posts and runs across the Inland Sea to Onomichi. This is the third road bridge connecting Shikoku with Honshu. Imabari's other claim to fame is that it's the number one towel-producing city in Japan.

Iyo-Saijo (Y31; 80km) If you happen to be passing this way around 14th-17th October, drop in on the town's autumn **festival**. The highlight is a parade of portable shrines through the city on the morning of the 15th. For more details see 🖳 www.city.saijo.ehime.jp/english/kankou/kankoutop.htm.

Conveniently, Niihama (see p426) holds a festival at around the same time.

SHIKOKU

On the way between the two stations, there's some mountain scenery out to the right.

Niihama (Y29; 91km) Expect **Niihama's Drum Festival** (16th-18th Oct) to be a noisy event. The drums that get paraded through the town (🖥 www.city.niihama.lg.jp/english) weigh around two tonnes each, and require 150 people to carry them.

The limited express next calls at **Iyo-Mishima (116.8km)** and **Kawanoe (122km)**, which is the last stop before the train crosses the border from Ehime back to Kagawa prefecture.

Kanon-ji (Y19; 138km) This is the best stop for Kotohiki Park, known for its massive and mysterious coin shape called **Zenigata** (see box below), carved about 2m deep in the sand. The park is a 20-minute walk north-west of the station, across Saita-gawa.

Between **Takuma (Y14; 152km)** and Tadotsu there are great views of the many tiny islands in the Inland Sea.

Tadotsu (Y12, D12; 162km) Tadotsu is a junction for the Yosan line between Matsuyama and Takamatsu, and the Dosan line to Kochi. This is where the railway network on Shikoku began in 1889, when the first steam locomotive ran 15.5km from Marugame to Kotohira via Tadotsu.

As soon as the Shiokaze LEX stops, a lightning-fast decoupling takes place, allowing the front half (cars 4-8) to continue on to Okayama, while the remainder wait a couple of minutes before starting off for Takamatsu.

Marugame (Y10; 166km) Marugame is a former castle town with a couple of attractions. Take the south exit for **tourist information** (🖥 www.city.marugame.kagawa.jp; Mon-Fri 9.30am-6pm, Sat-Sun 10am-5pm), just to the right as you exit the station. No English is spoken, but the place is well stocked with leaflets.

The Zenigata – a coin shape carved in the sand

There are several stories about how the Zenigata came to be in Kotohiki Park (see Kanon-ji above). Some claim the coin carving is at least 350 years old, while others say it only dates back 130 years. However, the common consensus is that it was completed in just one night by locals in 1633 as an unusual gift to the feudal lord of the area, Ikoma Takatoshi, who was to arrive the next day on a tour of inspection. Everybody knew that his lordship had to be pleased and a huge coin in the sand seemed the perfect answer. Another theory is that the coin was and remains to this day a UFO base (a Japanese version of crop circles?), while others attribute it to the miracle-working of Kobo Daishi (see box p414). With a circumference of 345m, the biggest mystery is why the design does not disappear in the rain or wind.

Twice a year the coin is reshaped by a group of volunteers who have orders shouted to them by one person commanding a bird's eye view. A two-day **Zenigata Festival** is held around 20th July (Maritime Day), with a fireworks display and dance contest in Kotohiki Park.

Marugame Castle (daily 9am-4.30pm; ¥200) was built in 1597 on a hill overlooking the city. Thus, like Uwajima Castle (see p423) it is called a *hiraya-mashiro* (a castle on a hill surrounded by a plain). Its design may not be unusual but the mason who built the ramparts certainly was: legend records that he always worked naked. To reach it walk for about 10 minutes down the main road which runs away from the south exit.

Right outside the station in a striking modern building is **Marugame Genichiro Inokuma Museum of Contemporary Art (MIMOCA)** (🖥 www.mimoca.org; daily 10am-6pm, occasional holidays; ¥300). The permanent exhibitions on the 2nd floor display the works of Genichiro Inokuma (1902-93), who attended school in Marugame before eventually settling in New York for 20 years and then Hawaii. His works are unusual in that most are on paper rather than canvas. The shop sells a good selection of quirky T-shirts and books for a more original souvenir. The arty museum *café* on the 3rd floor is a great place to relax and much better than anywhere in the station: Earl Grey tea (¥600/pot) and delicious homemade scones with jam (¥500) are on the menu as well as sandwiches and the normal chicken, fish and curry options.

Marugame is also known for its *uchiwa* (non-bending fans), which have been produced here since the Edo era. The town now churns out 80,000,000 uchiwa every year – 90% of the domestic market – and you see how they're made at the **Uchiwa no Minato Museum** (🖥 kougeihin.jp; Tue-Sun 9.30am-5pm; free), a 15-minute walk north-east from the station.

Utazu (Y09; 169km) Heading out of the station you can't miss **Play Park Gold Tower** (🖥 www.goldtower.co.jp; daily 10am-10pm, some areas open until 3am). It looks tacky from the outside and is even more so inside, filled with amusement arcades and attractions aimed chiefly at younger children. Aside from electronic games, you'll find a bowling alley, karaoke booths (where you can burn a recording of your efforts), a children's play area and 'Wan Wan Land' – a small space where children can pet a selection of cute furry animals ('wan wan' is the Japanese equivalent of 'woof woof'). A novel experience for adults, now replicated in spas around the world, is *'Doctor Fish'* (noon-5pm; ¥500/10mins) on the 1st floor. Stick your feet into a small tub and tiny fish will, without prompting, swarm over your hardened soles and toes, nibbling away at any dead skin. This natural treatment feels slightly ticklish but oddly satisfying. About the only other thing worth doing here is to take the elevator to the top of the tower (¥840), where you'll find a 127m-high observation gallery with views of the Seto-Ohashi Bridge.

Utazu is the final stop in Shikoku before the train turns to cross the Seto-Ohashi Bridge and heads for Okayama. If you're not returning to Honshu and haven't yet changed trains, this is the last chance to do so.

Kojima (187km) First stop back on Honshu, and the point where JR Shikoku staff are replaced by their counterparts from JR West.

Okayama (214km)   [see pp247-52]

Shikoku – city guides

TAKAMATSU

Capital of Kagawa Prefecture for over a century and a former castle town, Takamatsu has transformed itself into a major business and tourism centre for the 21st century with the regeneration of the port area behind JR Takamatsu station. The hugely ambitious decade-long land reclamation project, dubbed 'Sunport Takamatsu', is still ongoing and has changed the face of the city beyond recognition. The skyline is dominated by the Symbol Tower, Shikoku's tallest building.

Kagawa may be the smallest prefecture in Japan but high-rise developments such as the Symbol Tower and the new Prefectural Office skyscraper suggest that it's probably not one of the poorest. The biggest attraction for tourists is Ritsurin-koen, a large park 2km south of the station area.

Takamatsu feels very international – you might be surprised to see how many foreigners there are in town – and has several sister-city relations around the world, including Tours in France. This outward-looking approach might explain why the city took the very unusual (for Japan) step of banning smoking in city centre streets from April 2010 (apart from in designated areas).

What to see and do

You can't miss **Takamatsu Symbol Tower**, looming over everything else in the station vicinity. It's on your left as you exit the station. Take the elevator up to the 30th-floor viewing platform (⌨ www.symboltower.com; daily 10am-8pm; free). On a cloudless day you'll get unparalleled views of the city and out over the Inland Sea. Once you've got your bearings, and before you head into the city centre, consider taking a leisurely stroll out to **Red Lighthouse** (Aka-todai; located just beyond Mikayla restaurant (see p433). It's a popular place to hang out in the summer.

Tamamo-koen (daily 5.30am-7pm in summer, 9am-5pm in winter; ¥200), by the harbour and next to Takamatsu-Chikko station (Kotoden Kotohira line), is a large park where Takamatsu Castle once stood. It was built in 1590 and some of the original turrets remain but what makes the castle noteworthy is its unusual proximity to the sea. Waves crashed against the northern ramparts until 1900, when land was reclaimed to construct a new harbour. An air raid on Takamatsu on 4th July 1945 killed more than 1300 people and destroyed over 18,000 buildings, including most of what remained of the castle. One reader commented that the ruins are worth visiting 'to fill time but are otherwise not very exciting'.

Located on the far side of Tamamo-koen, **Kagawa Prefectural Museum** (daily 9am-5pm, last entrance 4.30pm; ¥400) charts the history of Kagawa from the Stone Age to the modern period through collections of fossils, scrolls, maritime artefacts, pagodas and fine prints. An English audio-guide is provided for the more interesting 3rd floor History Gallery, where you can enjoy dioramas of a Yayoi period pit dwelling and an early 20th-century school classroom. The special exhibitions are often drawn from the national museums in Tokyo.

If you fancy a bird's-eye view while in the downtown area, make for the **Prefectural Office**, which has a free observatory on the top floor and is a good place to orientate yourself.

Ritsurin-koen (💻 ritsuringarden.jp; daily 5.30am-7pm in summer, 7am-5pm in winter; ¥400), Takamatsu's biggest draw, enjoys a dramatic setting at the foot of Mt Shiun. It's very large and has plenty of narrow paths and observation points that give an impressive overview of the grounds, which are divided into two: the Hokutei (Northern Garden) and Nantei (Southern Garden). The 'wild ducks' in the duck pond are disappointingly tame – perhaps they realise they will no longer be shot as sport, which they were about 400 years ago when the gardens were part of the local feudal lord's villa residence. Look out for turtles along the paths, apparently oblivious to the hordes of tourists storming by. Kikugetsu-tei (Moon-Scooping Cottage) is a restored teahouse where it's thought that moon-viewing parties were once held. The teahouse is sometimes open to the public for tea ceremony demonstrations (an extra ¥710 including tea and cake; check times with the tourist office).

Also within the park grounds is the small **Sanuki Folkcraft Museum** (Thur-Tue 8.45am-4.30pm, to 4pm on Wed; free), containing a model portable shrine and various ceramics and masks. To ensure you have as much peace as possible, go early. To get to the park take a local train from JR Takamatsu (on the Kotoku line towards Tokushima) two stops to Ritsurin-koen Kitaguchi, just by the park's north gate.

Takamatsu City Museum of Art (Tue-Fri 9am-7pm, Sat-Sun until 5pm; ¥200), housed in a modern building downtown, has a worthwhile permanent collection of mostly contemporary Japanese art. The galleries are small but exhibits are changed every few months. The museum occasionally stages classical and folk music concerts.

See also pp433-4 for details of side trips from Takamatsu.

PRACTICAL INFORMATION
Station guide
The station was completely rebuilt as part of the redevelopment of the port area and it has a spacious atrium interior.

You may also notice that the station has a nickname: **Sanuki Udon station**. The udon is named after Sanuki region in Kagawa Prefecture so the additional name for the station is of course to promote this udon, which is known for its smooth texture and strong body. So, don't be surprised if you see Sanuki Udon on your ticket.

There are many restaurants on the 2nd floor including a reasonably priced *UCC Café Plaza* serving lunch sets from ¥600.

Immediately to your left as you exit the ticket barrier are **lockers** (including large ¥600 ones). To your right is the JR ticket office.

Tourist information
The tourist information desk (💻 www.takamatsu.or.jp; daily 9am-6pm) is in an office on the left side of the square in front of the main station exit. The helpful staff

> ⛩ **Kotoden – trainspotters' paradise**
> The private Kotoden rail company operates three lines around Takamatsu and Kagawa, with its main Kawara-machi station beneath Tenmaya department store in the city centre. Particularly among trainspotters – called *tetsudo mania* (railway enthusiasts) in Japanese – Kotoden is known as a good place to photograph some of Japan's oldest trains still in service. The company has bought old rolling stock from cities such as Tokyo and Osaka and put them back into service on local lines. The oldest train dates back to 1925.

can advise on trips to the islands and on accommodation in Takamatsu, but booking is at a separate desk.

Getting around
As well as JR train services, you can use the private **Kotoden Railway** (see box above), which operates in and around Takamatsu. Though you may want to take a train to Ritsurin-koen, the best way of seeing the city centre is on foot.

    Cycles are available for rent outside the station. On the right side of the square (opposite the tourist information office) as

you exit the station, take the stairs by the grey building down to the basement level for the cycle rental counter (¥100/day). It's very good value and you can drop off the cycles at a couple of other locations (the tourist information office has a map marked with the bicycle drop-off points).

Festivals
The biggest annual event is **Takamatsu Festival** (12th-14th Aug), when thousands of costumed locals dance through the main streets (anyone is welcome to join in) and there are large-scale fireworks on the 13th.

TAKAMATSU – MAP KEY

Where to stay
5 JR Hotel Clement Takamatsu
JR ホテルクレメント高松
8 Hotel Fukuya ホテル福屋
9 Toyoko Inn Takamatsu Hyogomachi
東横イン 高松兵庫町
11 Rihga Hotel Zest Takamatsu
リガホテルゼスト高松
12 Hotel Sakika ホテルサキカ
17 Dormy Inn Takamatsu
ドーミーイン高松
21 Toyoko Inn Takamatsu Nakajincho
東横イン 高松中新町

Where to eat and drink
2 Mikayla ミケイラ
3 Alice; Freshness Burger; Nakamura Komei; Szechwan (Symbol Tower)
アリス；フレッシュネスバーガー；中村孝明；スーツァン
（シンボルタワー）
5 Bar Astro; Karin; Vent
バーアストロ；花梨；ヴァン
13 Ten Yasu てんやす
15 Takamatsu City Hall 高松市役所

Where to eat and drink (cont'd)
19 Zucca ズッカ
20 Tenmaya Department Store
天満屋デパート

Other
1 Takamatsu 'Red' Lighthouse
高松港の赤灯台
3 Takamatsu Symbol Tower
高松シンボルタワー
4 Ferry Terminal (to Megijima, Naoshima) フェリーターミナル
（女木島、直島）
6 Tamamo-koen 玉藻公園
7 Kagawa Prefectural Museum
香川県立ミュージアム
10 Post Office 郵便局
14 Takamatsu City Museum of Art
高松市美術館
16 Prefectural Office 県庁
18 Post Office 郵便局
22 Sanuki Folkcraft Museum
讃岐民芸館
23 Ritsurin-koen 栗林公園

1 →
2 ○

Takamatsu Symbol Tower

Takamatsu Port

3 ○
4 ⛴

Mizuki-dori

Takamatsu-chikko

6 Tamamo-koen
7

Remains of Takamatsu Castle

Takamatsu Station
5

JR Kotoku, Yosan & Dosan lines

Seto ohashi-dori

Kotoden Kotohira line

9 ▲
10 ✉
Hyogomachi

Katahara-machi

8 ▲
11 ▲

12 ▲ Katahara-machi

13 ○

14

Chuo-dori

Marugamemachi

Raion-dori

Ferry-dori

15
Il Gosen

Chuo Park

Covered arcade
17 ▲

To Yashima

16 ●

Shido line

18 ✉
19 ○

Minamishinmachi

Kikukichan-dori

Kawara-machi
20 ○ Tenmaya dept store

Kanko-dori

Nagao line

21 ▲

JR Kotoku line

Kotoden Kotohira line

Ritsurin-koen Kitaguchi

To Yashima by JR

22

23
Ritsurin-koen

0 100 200 300m

Takamatsu
高松

SHIKOKU

SHIKOKU

Where to stay

Right outside the station, *JR Hotel Clement Takamatsu* (formerly ANA Hotel Clement Takamatsu; ☎ 087-811 1111, 💻 www.jrclement.co.jp; ¥12,474/S, ¥23,100/D, ¥24,255/Tw), centrepiece of the redeveloped port area, is dwarfed by the neighbouring Symbol Tower but is still a skyscraper by Takamatsu standards. It's easily the most de luxe place to stay in town, and since it's operated by JR Shikoku, rail-pass holders receive a modest discount.

Away from the station area there are two branches of the popular Toyoko Inn chain (💻 www.toyoko-inn.com). The newer *Toyoko Inn Takamatsu Hyogocho* (☎ 087-821 1045; ¥5980/S, ¥7480/D, ¥7980/Tw, inc hot Japanese breakfast), is five minutes on foot from the station. The original *Toyoko Inn Takamatsu Nakajincho* (☎ 087-831 1045; ¥4980/S, ¥6090/de luxe S, ¥8400/D or Tw) has especially good de luxe single rooms, which are very spacious and include a separate seating area.

Hotel Fukuya (☎ 087-851 2365, 💻 www.hotel-fukuya.com; ¥6720/S, ¥11,550/Tw, tatami rooms: ¥12,705/D or Tw, ¥17,325/Tr) is a 10- to 15-minute walk from the station. The open-plan lobby sets the tone and rooms are also veering on the spacious, particularly the tatami ones – the bathrooms remain tiny though.

For a taste of luxury, try *Rihga Hotel Zest Takamatsu* (☎ 087-822 3555, 💻 www.rihga.com/kagawa; ¥6800/S, ¥13000/D, ¥15000/Tw, ¥25,000/de luxe Tw, ¥25,000/sleeps four). The rooms in the main building are adequate, but those in the newer annex are de luxe and there's a combination Western/tatami room that can sleep four; the hotel also has three restaurants.

As a member of the YHA/HI, *Hotel Sakika* (☎ 087-822-2111, 💻 www.hihostels.com; ¥4095-5025/S, ¥9450/Tw, ¥12,600/Tr, ¥21,000 max/sleeps 5) is a good budget option (and not a bunk bed in sight). It mixes Japanese- and Western-style accommodation and is spacious and has more character than a business hotel. Wi-fi and washer/dryer facilities are available. Note that reception (front) is not always well attended, check-in closes at 11pm and they don't store luggage. Book in advance as there are only 21 rooms. Meals are served in the New Grand Mimatsu building, two mins away on foot. Follow the left-side path to the hotel entrance.

Hotel Dormy Inn (☎ 087-832-5489, 💻 www.hotespa.net/hotels/takamatsu; ¥7500/S, ¥13,000/D, breakfast ¥600) is a new, upmarket but reasonably priced business hotel. Guests can use the attractive spa for free and there's free internet in the rooms.

For details about accommodation in general see pp45-52.

Where to eat and drink

There are a few reasonable restaurants on the 2nd floor of the station building. For more upscale dining try **ANA Hotel Clement Takamatsu**, which has a good-value all-you-can-eat buffet lunch in its informal brasserie café *Vent* (7am-3pm & 5-9pm) for ¥2500 including soft drinks. The evening buffet is ¥4000 and includes alcohol. The 2nd-floor Chinese restaurant *Karin* (11.30am-3pm & 5-9.30pm) has sets from ¥1700 and an all-you-can-eat meal for a rather pricier ¥4500. For take-out food, try the hotel's own **bakery** on the 1st (ground) floor and for a drink with a view try the 21st-floor *Bar Astro* (5pm to midnight), where you can sip cocktails (from ¥900) while admiring the sunset over the harbour area.

A few floors higher in the adjacent **Symbol Tower** is *Alice* (☎ 087-823 6088; 11.30am-9.30pm), a French restaurant where you pay for the stunning views as much as the excellent nouvelle cuisine (set dinner menus from ¥6000). One floor below is *Szechwan* (11am-3pm & 5-10pm), a good Chinese place, and *Nakamura Koumei* (11am-3pm & 5-9pm), serving quality food from Japan's renowned 'iron chef'. Prices start at ¥1000 for basic dishes and ¥3500 for lunch and dinner sets. Both have tables next to large bay windows. Inside Maritime Plaza on the 2nd floor you'll find a branch of fast-food joint *Freshness Burger* (10am-10pm), where all the burgers are made to order and include vegetarian options.

Mikayla (☎ 087-811 5357; daily 11am to midnight, last orders 9.30pm), also part of the **Sunport** complex, is out on the pier and has a terrace café which affords great views over the Inland Sea. The evening menu is a little pricey (¥1200 for a basic chicken dish) but the food (pasta, salads, fish and meat dishes) is excellent. There are cheaper set deals in the afternoon (a pasta set costs ¥1500) and the terrace is a great place to relax with a cocktail at sunset as people stroll along the promenade. Booking is advisable in the evening. The glass entrance is easy to spot as the name, Mikayla, is written above the entrance. It's a five-minute walk from JR Takamatsu station, close to the ferries.

In the city centre there are several good restaurants on the 10th floor of **Tenmaya** department store (10am-10pm), including places serving tonkatsu and Italian food.

Zucca (Mon-Fri 11.30am-1.30pm, daily 5-11pm), a small Italian place off the 2nd floor of a concrete stairwell on your left as you walk west from Kawaramachi station on Kikuchikan-dori, before you reach the post office. It dishes up a Japanese take on modern Italian cuisine from ¥950 for a main course and a four-course meal for ¥2380.

Ten Yasu (11am-9pm) is a delightfully traditional tempura house with dishes from ¥1200 and sets from ¥2800. Look out for the large Japanese tree at the entrance.

Finally, for cheap food with a great view, try the canteen inside **Takamatsu City Hall** (Mon-Fri lunchtimes only, busiest 1-2pm). It's on the 13th floor; though it's supposed to be for City Hall staff, it's open to anybody. Plastic models of the meals (from ¥450) make selection easy and you can get a window table with great views of Takamatsu.

Side trips from Takamatsu

By rail to Yashima To the north-east of Takamatsu lies Yashima (Roof-top Island), a plateau made of volcanic lava jutting out 5km into the Inland Sea. The plateau gained its place in national history as the site of a decisive battle between the Minamoto and Taira clans (see pp32-3), both of which were vying to rule Japan in the 12th century.

The plateau, accessed by **cable car** (funicular; daily 8am-5.30pm; ¥1300 return), affords great views of the Inland Sea and is home to the 84th temple on the Shikoku pilgrimage, **Yashima-ji**. Below the plateau is **Shikoku Mura** (daily 8.30am-5.30/6pm; ¥800 or ¥1000 inc gallery), an open-air museum of traditional homes and workshops gathered from all over Shikoku. It includes an art gallery, vine bridge and outdoor kabuki theatre with occasional performances.

After visiting Shikoku Mura the done thing is to stop for a bowl of *sanuki udon*, a traditional noodle dish, at *Waraya* (daily last orders 6.30pm). The restaurant is in the building next to the water mill, by the entrance to Shikoku Mura. Alternatively, as you leave Shikoku Mura, look out for a traditional British-style building with red phone- and pillar-boxes outside. Inside is a *café* (daily 9am-6pm) which serves tea and cakes.

Yashima can be reached from Takamatsu station by JR on the Kotoku line but it is more fun to travel on the private Kotoden line; this takes longer but drops you closer to the start of the cable car up to the plateau.

From Takamatsu-Chikko station (close to JR Takamatsu station) to Yashima, the fare is ¥310 (change at Kawara-machi). As you leave Kotoden Yashima station you'll see the cable car (funicular) going up the plateau. Shikoku Mura is a few minutes' walk east of the cable car entrance.

SHIKOKU

By boat to Megijima, Shodoshima and Naoshima Takamatsu is also an access point for some of the islands on the Inland Sea; check with the tourist office for ferry/hydrofoil departure times and fares.

Megijima, also known as Onigashima, has a huge cave said to have been used as a pirate den. Close to its port is a small village full of atmospheric narrow streets that also borders the sandy Megijima beach, an attractive and popular refuge for Takamatsu locals.

Shodoshima is much larger and is known as an island resort. Attractions here include a miniature version of the 88 temples on the Shikoku pilgrimage, useful for anyone in need of a fast-track spiritual cleansing.

Naoshima is a place of pilgrimage for fans of James Bond. James Bond is no stranger to Japan: most of *You Only Live Twice*, starring Sean Connery opposite the characters Tiger Tanaka and Kissy Suzuki, was set and filmed in the country. But it may come as a surprise to learn that there is a small museum – **007: The Man With the Red Tattoo Museum** (💻 www.007museum.jp; daily 9am-5pm; free) – devoted to Ian Fleming's British secret-service agent on the island of Naoshima, near Takamatsu. The museum focuses on one of American author Raymond Benson's 007 novels, *The Man With the Red Tattoo* (Hodder & Stoughton, 2002), which was set in Japan, much of it on Naoshima itself. The museum displays information on Benson and other authors who have contributed to the Bond legacy, as well as memorabilia connected to the 007 franchise.

To reach the museum, take a 50-minute ferry ride (¥970 return) from Takamatsu port (the entrance is across the street from JR Hotel Clement Takamatsu) to Naoshima. The ferry drops you off at Miyanoura port, less than a minute's walk from the museum.

> ❏ **The name's Bond-san**
> Tiger Tanaka: *Rule number one: never do anything yourself when someone else can do it for you.*
> James Bond: *And rule number two?*
> Tiger Tanaka: *Rule number two: in Japan, men come first, women come second.*
> James Bond: *I just might retire here.*
> *You Only Live Twice*
> (Eon Productions, 1967)

Naoshima is also home to an impressive art and cultural complex called **Benesse Art Site Naoshima**, the centrepiece of which is the superb Benesse House (💻 www.benesse-artsite.jp; daily 8am-9pm; ¥1000), a contemporary art museum designed by leading architect Tadao Ando. You can even stay the night here in super-swanky purpose-built rooms overlooking the Inland Sea; see the website for details.

Before you leave, don't forget to enjoy an artistic soak in the gloriously eccentric bathhouse **I♥湯(Yu)** (Tue-Fri 2-9pm, Sat, Sun & holidays 10am-9pm; ¥500), a very short stroll up the narrow lane that bisects the village opposite the ferry. Created by artist Shinro Otake, the architecture reverses notions of interior and exterior and may explain why your hot bath takes place in the shadow of a giant elephant called Sadako.

TOKUSHIMA

You might not immediately think of Rio when you see Tokushima, but the city believes its annual dance festival is as big as Brazil's carnival. Quiet for most of the year, Tokushima comes alive in August when it hosts the Awa-Odori. If you miss the festival itself, you can experience its highlights year-round at Awa-Odori Kaikan. Tokushima is also a useful staging post for a side trip to the spectacular Naruto whirlpools (see pp438-9).

What to see and do

Head down the main thoroughfare leading away from the station until you come to **Awa-Odori Kaikan**, home to both the Awa-Odori Museum and a hall where there are regular performances of the festival dance. The ropeway (cable car) up to Mt Bizan is also here (ropeway plus the museum or the dance hall ¥1100, ropeway plus both ¥1500).

The **Awa-Odori Museum** on the 3rd floor (🖥 www.awaodori-kaikan.jp; daily 9am-5pm, closed every 2nd and 4th Wed; ¥300) presents the history, costumes and instruments of the Awa-Odori dance, even providing an electronic dance mat so you can perform the dance steps to the famous Yoshikono rhythm (you may be humming this when you leave!). You might be lucky enough to catch the Awanokaze team perform the dance for real in the 2nd-floor dance hall (¥500 afternoon, ¥700 evening; check with the TIC for timings). From the 5th floor, take **Bizan Ropeway** (daily 9am-5.30pm, to 9pm in summer; 6 mins; ¥1000 round trip) to Mt Bizan, from where there are impressive views of the city.

Also at the top here is the small but quirky **Moraes Museum** (9.30am-5pm; ¥200), which is dedicated to the Portuguese Consul-General who retired to the city then wrote books about both his Japanese wives and (of course) the Awa-Odori festival. The museum is in Japanese but the irrepressible curator can provide written as well as a verbal English explanation. If you find yourself at the top of Bizan on a summer evening, the viewing terrace also becomes a beer garden (see p55; 5.30-9pm).

On your way back into town, turn right immediately after crossing the river, walking along **Shinmachi Riverside Park** promenade, to find Hyotanjima Cruise Boat Pier. From here you can take a very good-value **boat trip** (dep daily every 40 mins 1-3.40pm, in Jul & Aug 5-7.40pm as well; ¥100) along the Shinmachi and Suketoh rivers, with fine perimeter views of Tokushima's island centre; the tourism information office keeps advance schedules.

Tokushima Castle Museum (Tue-Sun 9.30am-5pm; ¥300), within **Tokushima Central Park**, charts the 267-year history of the Tokushima clan's castle under the leadership of Lord Hachisuka until his fall in the modern period. Entrance is worth it just to see the full-length Senzan-Maru cruising vessel from feudal Japan's civil war period, the only Daimyo vessel left in Japan. Entrance includes admission to the **Omotegoten Garden** (¥50 on its own), constructed for Hachisuka and featuring an impressive pond and rock garden that you can clamber over. Look out for turtles and the occasional snake. From the station, turn left and hug the railway line until you see a little pedestrian bridge crossing the tracks which takes you into the park. Turn left for the museum.

Even if you are not staying there if you fancy an **onsen**, head to *Hotel Sunroute* (see Where to stay; non-residents ¥500 7am-noon, ¥700 noon-8pm).

See pp438-9 for details of side trips from Tokushima.

PRACTICAL INFORMATION
Station guide
Walk down to the basement level for large **lockers**. The Clement Plaza shopping complex is built above the station; there are several restaurants on the 5th floor.

Tourist information
Pick up a map and guide from the small tourist information office (🖥 www.city. tokushima.tokushima.jp; daily 10am-6pm; little English spoken) towards the right side of the station square.

Getting around
Tokushima is easy to navigate on foot. However, city **buses** leave from the main terminal to the right as you exit the station. **Bike rental** is available at Awa-Odori Kaikan (daily 9.30am-4pm; return bike by 5pm; ¥500 per bike); ID is required.

Festivals
The city's fame lies squarely with its 400-year-old **Awa-Odori dance festival**, staged during the O-bon celebrations (Aug 12th-15th; be sure to book accommodation in advance if arriving in this period). The festival encapsulates the city's cultural identity, and has a relaxed vibe.

Where to stay
For accommodation with style, and part of the JR Hotel group (see box p49), *Hotel Clement Tokushima* (☎ 088-656-3131, 🖥 www.hotelclement.co.jp;   ¥10,164/S, ¥20,790/D, ¥19,735/Tw) is a convenient choice, plus you can check-in at 1pm and check out at 11am. Rates for online reservations can be much less. It is located just to the right of the station as you exit.

Another decent and recently renovated option is *Agnes Hotel* (☎ 088-626-2222, 🖥 www.agneshotel.jp; ¥6300/S, ¥12,600/Tw,

inc good buffet breakfast), which has free internet access in the room and boasts a patisserie and café.

Tokushima Tokyu Inn (☎ 088-626-0109, 🖥 www.tokyuhotels.co.jp; ¥7600/S, ¥13,000/D, ¥12,600/Tw) is part of the reliable business hotel chain, for more on which, see p48. Head for the first junction out of the station, walk to the next major traffic lights, then turn right.

Hotel Sunroute (☎ 088 653 8111, 🖥 www.sunroute.jp/HotelInfoSVE; 6825/S, 12,600/D 13650/Tw) offers stylish and comfortable accommodation. A particular feature is enjoy the tranquil 11th-floor *Bizan no yu* hot spring bath.

Where to eat and drink
Hotel Clement has a Japanese and Chinese restaurant plus an 18th-floor adjoining bar affording great views across the city. Do sit at the bar if you want to avoid the ¥700 table fee on top of your cocktail (¥924). The 6th floor also offers an all-you-can-eat-and-drink 'Viking' beer garden (May to mid Sep daily 5.30-9pm; ¥3800/men, ¥3500/women).

Sogo department store in the far right corner of the station square has a medley of restaurants including Italian and Chinese on the 9th floor (11am-9pm). The blandly named but very popular *Family Restaurant* offers the best value with a vast range of rice, udon and spaghetti sets for under ¥900. Don't be put off by the long queues outside as the cavernous restaurant has brisk service.

Whatever the time of day, there is always a queue for *Menou*, but such is its reputation for delicious ramen that locals feel it is always worth the wait. You purchase a ticket from the machine outside (ramen ¥480, gyoza ¥380) then await a free seat in the narrow eatery. From the JR exit,

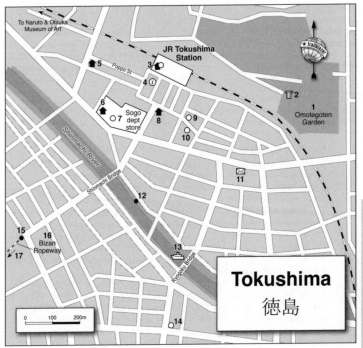

Where to stay

3 Hotel Clement Tokushima
ホテルクレメント徳島
5 Agnes Hotel アグネスホテル
6 Tokushima Tokyu Inn 徳島東急イン
8 Hotel Sunroute
ホテルサンルート徳島

Where to eat and drink

3 Hotel Clement Tokushima
ホテルクレメント徳島
7 Sogo Department Store そごう徳島店
9 Menou 麺王
10 Copa コパ
14 Grasp グラスプ

Other

1 Omotego-ten Garden 表御殿庭園
2 Tokushima Castle Museum
徳島城博物館
4 Tourist Information Office 観光案内所
11 Central Post Office 中央郵便局
12 Shinmachi Riverside Park
新町川水際公園
13 Hyotanjima Cruise Boat Pier
ひょうたん島周遊船乗降口
15 Awa Odori Kaikan 阿波おどり会館
16 Bizan Ropeway 眉山ロープウエイ
17 Moraes Museum モラエス館

head to the top left of the station square, and it is a few doors down the side street on the left. Look for the bamboo at the entrance. Next door is another restaurant that does sushi and noodle sets for just ¥840.

For a quiet drink, try the friendly *Copa* bar, which has interesting photo pastiches of arty/Euro-culture on the walls and serves a decent choice of beer (¥600) and spirits as well as unorthodox cocktails such as beer and tomato juice (¥600). The atmosphere is intimate and conducive to conversation and it's handy if you don't want to walk as far as the central area.

Go past Menou (see p436) and keep walking until you see the English sign on the right side of the road.

For livelier options, continue then turn right at Tokyu Inn, cross the bridge, then head into Akitamachi where the city's student community gather. Here, *Grasp* (closes 3am) is a bar with a chic, mellow atmosphere, a modern interior and a jazz-background vibe, all of which adds up to a pleasant and unhurried evening. All cocktails are ¥700 and there are also interesting seafood dishes (Hong Kong-style shrimp ¥850). The bar is on the 2nd floor, on the left side (look for outside steps), just before the second big traffic junction on the main strip.

Side trip by rail to Naruto

Guaranteed to get your fellow mariners gasping with delight, the phenomenon of the colliding Pacific Ocean and Seto Inland Sea currents, whipping the waters of the narrow Naruto straits into a series of frothy vortexes, is an experience best seen by boat.

Tours of the **Naruto Whirlpools** (🖳 www.uzusio.com; 9am-5pm, closed every 2nd Mon) are best enjoyed during the faster spring tidal periods, when they can measure 20 metres across and 2 metres deep. Failing that, ensure you are there during the 90-minute morning or evening low/high tide to see them at their most active. See the website (Japanese only) or visit Tokushima tourist information office for daily tide times.

Ferry tours on *Wonder Naruto* ferry leave from the departure pavilion (every 40 mins; 30 mins; ¥1530), or there's *Aqua Eddy*, a smaller (and more cramped) vessel whose lower level allows for an underwater view of the spinning eddies (25 mins; ¥2200; book online at least four days ahead). Above the whirlpools, the Onaruto bridge offers a ¥500 glass-floor-viewing-walkway (9am-5pm) but the experience is comparatively unexciting.

From JR Tokushima take the local train to Naruto (40 mins), then hop on a Naruto Kohen-bound bus outside the station (¥270; 20 mins), exiting opposite the grey departure pavilion on your right. Alternatively take a direct bus from platform 1 outside Tokushima station (No 27; 55 mins; ¥690). Pick up return bus timetables and advance tickets at the adjoining bus information booth.

Located in handy proximity to the whirlpool tours pavilion (about a 15-min walk), **Otsuka Museum of Art** (🖳 www.o-museum.or.jp; Tue-Sun 9.30am-5pm, last admission 4pm; ¥3150) is a must for art lovers. It contains over one thousand impressive reproductions of Western masterpieces, all recreated on specially manufactured ceramic boards.

The museum is the largest permanent exhibition space in Japan, spread over five chronological floors (Antiquities to 20th Century) and contains its very own full-scale Sistine and Scrovegni chapels. You will also find the *Mona Lisa*, *Last Supper*, Van Gogh's *Sunflowers* and even Picasso's *Guernica* hanging on the walls. It is a rare opportunity to take in some of the world's most famous pieces of art under one roof. Comfortable footwear is strongly recommended as a total circuit can involve a 4km walk. Regular gallery talks are held, some even provided by 'Art', a diminutive robot who speaks four languages and points his own professorial laser beam!

The Otsuka Museum of Art bus stop (look out for the car park sign) is the one before the Naruto whirlpool tour pavilion as you come from Naruto station (ask for Otsuka Kokusan Bijutsukan-mae). The museum entrance is up and around the adjacent road-turning on the left. If also going on to the whirlpool tours, take the next bus (or simply walk 15 minutes up the road). Do check against the whirlpool's low/high tide viewing times when deciding what to see first when planning your trip.

MATSUYAMA

Matsuyama, the largest city on the island, became prominent as a castle town in the 17th century. In recent years the city has benefited greatly from the opening of new road links with Honshu, in particular the Nishi-Seto Highway, which links nearby Imabari with the main island.

Matsuyama is keen to project itself as an international city and has established sister-city relations with Sacramento, California, and Freiburg, Germany.

What to see and do

Two priorities are Matsuyama Castle and nearby Dogo-onsen (see pp444-5). Both could be done in one day, but an overnight stay in either Matsuyama or neighbouring Dogo would be more relaxing.

Matsuyama Castle (daily 9am-5pm; ¥500, joint admission/ropeway ticket ¥1000) is at the top of Katsuyama Hill in the city centre. Construction of the castle was completed in 1627 but, like other castles in Japan, it has suffered various misfortunes since. Struck by lightning on New Year's Day 1784, the donjon burnt to the ground.

The castle was reconstructed in 1854, only to suffer bomb damage during WWII. Today, the castle is reached by taking either the **ropeway** (cable car) or a cutesy chair lift (daily 8.30am-5.30pm; ¥600 return). It's difficult to imagine what the castle lords who occupied this fortification would have made of the sight of people gliding up the hill in moving chairs but it's safe to assume that as intruders they'd have been easy targets.

Even if you avoid the cost of the ropeway/chair lift by walking up the hill there's still a fair way to go before you reach the donjon (132m above sea level), let alone climbing up inside it which is probably the main purpose of your journey. However, the views of the city and surrounding area, with mountains on one side and the Inland Sea coastline on the other make the effort worthwhile. But since the donjon is invariably jam-packed with tour parties and school groups you may prefer to admire the view from outside. The nearest tram stop for the ropeway up to the castle is Okaido.

The French-style building lower down the hill is **Bansui-so** (Tue-Sun 9am-6pm) and was built in 1922 by a former feudal lord. Today it functions as an annex to the Prefectural Art Museum (see below). Entry to the ground floor is free but the 2nd floor houses temporary exhibitions for which the charge varies. The nearest tram stop is Okaido.

A couple of minutes north of Minami-Horibata tram stop is **Ehime Prefectural Art Museum** (Tue-Sun 9.40am-6pm; ¥300) which houses a permanent collection of Japanese and Western art alongside special exhibitions (¥1000). In amongst the traditional scrolls depicting cormorant fisherman are some intriguing sculptures such as Jean Arc's 'Gur'. At the opposite end of the upper floor gallery, significant space is devoted to local artwork, although the quantity of displays from local schoolchildren suggest the curators may be in need of further acquisitions.

Popular with couples in search of a romantic view of Matsuyama is the **ferris wheel** (Kururin or Kanran-sha; 10am-9.30pm last ride; ¥500/ride or ¥1000 per 4-seat gondola), an unmissable landmark (eyesore?) perched on top of Iyotetsu Takashimaya department store, above Matsuyama-shi station. This addition to Matsuyama's skyline is worth a go for the views of the city. The best time is at dusk, when you'll witness the sun setting over the city. Tickets are purchased from vending machines on the 9th floor.

See pp444-5 for details of a side trip from Matsuyama.

PRACTICAL INFORMATION
Station guide

Access to the platforms at **JR Matsuyama** is by stairs only. However, if you walk to the end of platform No 1 (turning left after passing through the ticket barrier), you can cross over the tracks to the other platforms without having to use the stairs.

The **JR ticket office** (daily 5am-11pm) is combined with the travel agency. On the 2nd floor of the station is a large souvenir shop. **Lockers** (all sizes) are to the right of the station exit.

There's an *udon and soba* place by the ticket barrier, and a *restaurant* on the 2nd floor of the station building which does a

SHIKOKU

MATSUYAMA – MAP KEY

Where to stay
1 Terminal Hotel Matsuyama ターミナルホテル松山
2 Sky Hotel スカイホテル
3 Hotel JAL City Matsuyama ホテルJALシティ松山
12 ANA Hotel Matsuyama 全日航ホテル松山
15 Matsuyama Tokyu Inn 松山東急イン
18 Hotel Top Inn ホテルトップイン
19 Toyoko Inn Matsuyama Ichibancho 東横イン松山一番町
20 Super Hotel Matsuyama スーパーホテル松山

Where to eat and drink
2 Handai, Sky Hotel 飯台, スカイホテル
3 La Terrazza テラッツァ
5 Amitie アミティイエ
6 Shoya ショヤ
8 Toriyakyube とりや久兵衛
10 Mitra ミトラ

Where to eat and drink (cont'd)
12 Provence Dining; Provence Bar プロヴァンス ダイニング; プロヴァンスバー
15 Pinomonte ピノモンテ
16 Flying Scotsman フライングスコッツマン
17 Oiritei 大入亭

Other
4 Ehime Prefectural Art Museum 愛媛県美術館
7 Matsuyama-shi bus terminal 松山空港ターミナルビル
9 Ferris wheel 大観覧車
11 Central Post Office 中央郵便局
13 Matsuyama Castle 松山城
14 Bansui-so 萬翠荘
21 Dogo-onsen 道後温泉

Matsuyama

松山

SHIKOKU

Katsuyama Hill

Ropeway (cable car)

- Sekijuji byoin-mae
- Kami-ichiman
- Keisatsusho-mae
- Katsuyama-cho
- Heiwa-dori
- Honmachi 4 chome
- Honmachi 3 chome
- Honmachi 3 chome
- Nishi-Horibata
- Ichibancho-dori
- Nibancho-dori
- Okaido shopping arcade
- Okaido
- Mitsukoshi dept store
- Sanbancho-dori
- Chifune-mach-dori
- Kencho-mae
- Shiyakusho-mae
- Minami-Horibata
- Hanazo-no-dori
- Iyotetsu Takashimaya dept store
- Matsuyama-shi Station
- Matsuyama-shi-Eki
- Nishi-Horibata
- Otemachi
- Iyo Railway (Takahama line)
- Tomita-cho
- Matsuyama-Ekimae
- JR Matsuyama Station

20
19
18
17
16
15
14
13
12
11
10
9
8
7
6
5
4
3
2
1

21

0 100 200 300m

variety of cheap set meals, but otherwise there's little in the way of places to eat.

Do not confuse JR Matsuyama station with **Matsuyama-shi station** which is the main station in Matsuyama for services operated by Iyotetsu.

Tourist information

The **tourist information booth** (🖳 www. city.matsuyama.ehime.jp; daily 8.30am-5pm), to the left as you exit the ticket barrier, has maps but the staff may not speak much English. A quirk of this place is that from 8.30am to 5pm it functions only as a tourist information office and cannot help with accommodation reservations. However, from 5pm to 8.30pm hotel reservation staff take over. If you time your arrival for around 4.30pm you may get the best of both worlds. Another **tourist office** is across the street from the tram terminus at Dogo-onsen (see pp444-5).

At either of these, as well as in some hotels, you should be able to pick up a copy of *What's Going On?*, a monthly guide to events in Matsuyama.

Getting around

The easiest way of travelling around Matsuyama is on one of its five **tram** lines – they're regular, cheap (¥150 flat fare, ¥400/1-day pass) and go past all the major places in town. Enter at the back and pay as you leave at the front.

Passes can be bought either from the tourist office at JR Matsuyama station or at Matsuyama-shi station, or at the central tram terminal in the city centre. The tram driver may also have them if you ask.

Festivals

The highlight of **Matsuyama Festival** (11th-13th Aug) is a night-time parade of samba dancers. The event is kicked off by a fireworks display on 10th August.

Where to stay

The station area is not so convenient for sightseeing, though if you've got an early start and need to be close to the JR station, *Terminal Hotel Matsuyama* (☎ 089-947 5388, 🖳 www.th-matsuyama.jp; ¥5775/S,

¥9450/D, ¥10,500/Tw), a JR hotel (see box p49) has functional rooms and free bicycle rental. It is also just by the tram stop for trips into town. Look for it to the left as you exit the station. Beside the entrance is a small coin laundry.

Also near JR station is *Sky Hotel* (☎ 089-947 7776, 🖳 www.shikoku-sky.com; ¥6800/S, ¥11,400/D, ¥11,800/T; extra bed ¥3500; buffet breakfast ¥840), a reliable option with comfortably sized rooms. Exit the station, turn right at the traffic lights, then left at the next set and you will see the tall grey building immediately on your right.

Hotel JAL City Matsuyama (☎ 089-913 2580, 🖳 matsuyama.jalcity.co.jp; ¥9820/S, ¥18,480/D, ¥19,060/Tw) is within walking distance of the JR station, handily placed for the tram lines and a cut above the standard business hotel. Reception staff are friendly and pro-active.

As Shikoku's biggest city, Matsuyama is not short of top-class hotels. *ANA Hotel Matsuyama* (☎ 089-933 5511, 🖳 www. anahotelmatsuyama.com; ¥6930/S, ¥19,635/D, ¥21,368/Tw) has the best location, opposite the castle and in the centre of town. The spacious rooms have wide-screen TVs, mini bars and room service.

Across the street is *Matsuyama Tokyu Inn* (☎ 089-941 0109, 🖳 www.tokyuho tels.co.jp; ¥7200/S, ¥16,300/D, ¥17,300/ Tw), with a bright interior and smartly decorated rooms, some with views of Bansui-so.

A good budget option a short way from the Okaido shopping arcade is *Hotel Top Inn* (☎ 089-933 3333, 🖳 www.top-inn.com; ¥3980/S, ¥8400/D; frequent special offers). A basic business hotel with simple rooms (and room service), this is near the sights and tram stops. Japanese-style rooms (sleeping up to three people) are also available.

Toyoko Inn Matsuyama Ichibancho (☎ 089-941 1045, 🖳 www.toyoko-inn. com; ¥5480/S, ¥6980/D, ¥7980/Tw, inc breakfast and a curry-rice supper), a branch of the reliable chain hotel, is in the city centre; the Katsuyama-cho tram stop is outside the hotel.

About three minutes further along the

road is *Super Hotel Matsuyama* (☎ 089-932 9000, 💻 www.superhoteljapan.com/en/s-hotels/matsuyama; ¥4980/S, inc breakfast), a cash-only, no-frills business hotel.

For details of accommodation at Dogo-onsen see pp444-5 and for information about accommodation in general and facilities at the chain hotels see pp45-52.

Where to eat and drink

In *Oiritei* (daily 6-11pm) izakaya, a cramped little eatery specialising in sashimi, you can try what a regular claimed was fresher and better-quality fish than that served in Michelin-starred Tokyo restaurants.

Ask for the *otoshi* (appetiser) set to sample a few various starters including egg, spinach and carrot mix, sea slugs and grilled-fish paste. Your main however, should be the *o-sashimi mori awase*, a splendid plate of up to 15 types of sashimi. The menu is in Japanese and prices vary according to the daily catch, but expect to pay an absolute minimum of ¥1500 per person for the main sashimi course.

Be aware that this place is very hidden. Walk south down the covered Okaido arcade from Okaido tram stop, turn immediately left after passing McDonald's, then follow the narrow alley as it doglegs right than left. Look for the white kanji entrance sign low on the right side. You may have to sit at the bar as early reservations are recommended.

At the alley entrance lies the mock railway carriage of the *Flying Scotsman* diner, a fine choice for a lunchtime sandwich. Hamburger sets (¥650) and toasted sandwich sets (¥850) complement the cold choices. Find a peaceful booth to munch away in and let the period interiors turn your thoughts back to the golden age of steam.

Toriyakyube (5pm to midnight), with its wooden exterior, serves a variety of yakitori (¥120-250) as well as various grilled vegetables including aubergines, potatoes and onions. Donburi (¥650) is also available for non-meat eaters. It is by Gate 8 of the bus terminal.

To the west side of the square in front of Matsuyama-shi station lie several more mainstream izakaya, including *Shoya*, which serves pork udon (¥460) and cheap sushi (¥600 for 18 pieces) in booths and has menus with pictures.

Opposite Ehime Art Museum on the main road is *Amitie* (lunch 11.30am-2pm, tea 2-4.30pm, evening meals 5.30-10pm), an odd cross between an antique shop and French bistro. Seated in the cluttered arty interior, diners enjoy a good choice of grilled fish, lasagne and continental desserts from a changing daily menu. Mains start at ¥1200.

On the eastern edge of Matsuyama-shi station square lies *Mitra* (Tue-Sat 11.30am-2pm & 6pm-2am; Sun 11.30am-2pm & 6pm to midnight), a ground-floor dining bar that tries to bring an edge of European sophistication to a young demographic. Its menu offers Italian fare such as creamy pasta (¥880) and pizza (¥800) as well as fried rice (¥900). Drinks are a standard ¥500 (¥380 if ordering food) and there is an excellent range of wines. All-you-can-eat-and-drink deals are also available (¥2000 women, ¥3000 men, for 2hrs). The terrace is pleasant in the summer and offers a nice oasis in the city. A 'soft darts' board complements the relaxed atmosphere.

Many of the hotels have restaurants: ANA Hotel Matsuyama (see Where to stay) has a good choice of restaurants including *Provence Dining*, an Italian restaurant serving dishes from ¥2000. Also on the 14th floor is *Provence Bar* which provides a panorama of the neon cityscape as you sit and reflect on the day's discoveries over a cocktail (¥1080).

Tokyu Inn's 2nd-floor *Pinomonte* restaurant offers a ¥1200 breakfast buffet (6.45-10am), an all-you-can-eat ¥1200 feast (11am-2pm), and an unlimited food-and-drink 'beer festa' (5.30-9pm; women ¥3000, men ¥3500).

Hotel JAL City's adjoining *La Terrazza* restaurant does good pizzas (¥1000), seafood and hamburgers. *Handai* (daily 11.30am-2pm & 5-10pm), on the 11th floor at Sky Hotel, offers set menus at lunch (from ¥1260) and is an izakaya-style place in the evening. A beer hall (daily 5-10pm; ¥3800/2hrs) is open May to early October on the hotel's rooftop terrace.

SHIKOKU

Side trip to Dogo-onsen

Twenty minutes by tram from Matsuyama is the ancient spa town of Dogo. Today, Dogo is geared up to the tourist trade but a trip to the bath house is an excellent way to unwind after a day's sightseeing. Don't plan on doing any serious hiking after a trip to the baths though, since a visit here can leave you feeling extremely lethargic.

The hot spring dates back 3000 years and according to legend was discovered when a white heron put its injured leg into hot water flowing out of a crevice in some rocks. The main wooden bath house was built in 1894 and is said to be the inspiration for the bathhouse of the Gods in Miyazaki's animated classic *Spirited Away*. The hot spring is now deemed one of the three most famous in Japan (see p247).

For the best atmosphere and views of the illuminated Dogo bath house (daily 6am-10pm, last entry 9pm; ground floor open until 11pm, last entry 10pm), schedule an evening visit. Tickets for the no-frills ground-floor bath, called **Kami-no-yu** (Water of the Gods), cost ¥400. For ¥800 you are given a yukata and served Japanese tea and a rice cracker afterwards on the 2nd floor. The 2nd floor also has its own bath, the more exclusive **Tama-no-yu** (Water of the Spirits), which costs ¥1200 including yukata, tea and cracker, or ¥1500 with a **private room** (with balcony) for relaxing in. This option also includes Botchan Dango, dumpling-shaped sweetmeats, that Soseki Natsume, author of *Botchan*, used to eat when he was a teacher at Matsuyama Junior High School. Read the English pamphlet to avoid making any onsen faux-pas such as stumbling into the wrong changing rooms. A towel can be hired for ¥50. Don't worry about the lockers, you can safely deposit items alongside your clothes in the free wooden lockers at the bath entrances. Wear the key on your wrist as you enter the baths.

Take a tram (No 5) from Matsuyama station bound for Dogo-onsen. The old-fashioned terminal here is a 1986 reconstruction of the original (1911) European-style building. From the tram station, walk through the covered shopping arcade to reach Dogo bath house, turning right when you reach the locally popular but less well known (and less crowded) **Tsubaki-no-yu** bath house (¥360) on your left. Dogo bath house will be straight in front of you at the exit to the arcade.

Back near the tram stop, be sure to stop and observe the exquisite workings of the Botchan Karakuri Dokei clock on each quarter hour. The roof rises to reveal traditionally clad figures from a bathhouse scene in Soseki's novel as they gently spin to a playful musical score. You can also dip your feet into the adjoining footbath.

If you decide to stay in the area there are several options: the facilities and welcome make staying at *Matsuyama Youth Hostel* (☎ 089-933 6366, 🖳 www.matsuyama-yh.com; reception closed 10am-4pm; dorm ¥2625pp, private room from ¥3360pp; evening meal ¥1050, breakfast ¥525) worthwhile. From the tram terminal head for the steps that lead up to Isaniwa Shrine. Take the uphill path to the right of these stairs, following the green signs before turning right just before the tennis courts.

The youth hostel is in an unmissable bright yellow building on the right. The dorms are cosy (3-4 beds per room) rather than bland while the timbered construction and snug interiors lend the hostel the comforting aspect of an alpine chalet. Free internet and wi-fi plus laundry facilities and a beer-vending machine are available to guests.

The somewhat bizarre activities on offer to hostel guests from the eccentric proprietor, Hirano-san, include a spoon-bending course (¥300, minimum two people) and an opportunity to 'take a photograph of your "aura"' (¥2500 for a photograph of 'your whole living body' and ¥1000 'for your fingers only'). For a further ¥950, guests can also enjoy the hostel's Ganbanyoku sauna, in which small bags of hot stones are spread along your spine as part of a relaxing wind-down.

Other places in the area include *Hotel Patio Dogo* (☎ 089-941 4128, 🖳 www.patio-dogo.co.jp; ¥7665/S, ¥11,550/D, ¥14,700/Tw according to season, see website for discounts; breakfast ¥750), which has Western-style accommodation right across from the bath house. But *Yamatoya Honten* (☎ 089-935 8880, 🖳 www.yamatoyahonten.com; from ¥19,050pp half-board; room-only rates on request) is definitely the place to stay if you can afford it. It's all kimonos and shamisen music in this upmarket ryokan, which even stages daily performances at its own Noh theatre. The hotel also has its own attractive outdoor hot spring. Most rooms are tatami style though there are 28 Western singles and two twins. Advance booking is highly recommended.

One of the newest places in Dogo is *Old England Dogo Yamanote Hotel* (☎ 089-998 2111, 🖳 www.dogo-yamanote.com; ¥11,700/S, ¥21,300/D, ¥23,400/Tw, inc breakfast; half-board also available). This place exudes luxury and impresses from the moment you approach it, as top-hatted bellboys compete to unburden you of your luggage and a line of smart receptionists stand behind the desk of the wood-panelled lobby. This is a place which tries and to some extent succeeds in recreating the atmosphere and décor of an Edwardian English country house. Don't come here for an authentic Japanese experience although do come for an insight into how much interest the Japanese find in historical notions of British social deference. If you can't be bothered to walk around the corner to Dogo-onsen hot spring, you can soak in the hotel's own spa. It's great for an unusual one-night escape.

SHIKOKU

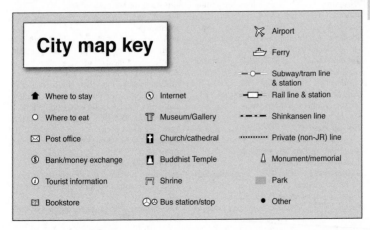

APPENDIX A: GLOSSARY

GENERAL

Asa-ichi 朝市 morning market

Ashi-yu 足湯 foot bath

-basho 場所 place where a sumo tournament is held

-bashi 橋 bridge

Bento 弁当 lunch box (see also ekiben)

Bunraku 文楽 puppetry

Cosplay コスプレ costume play ie dressing as a character from anime or manga

Daimyo 大名 feudal lord

Depachika デパチカ department store food hall

-dori/odori -道リ street

Ekiben 駅弁 station lunch box (see also bento)

Front フロント reception desk in a hotel

Gaijin 外人 foreigner

-gawa 川 river

Geisha 芸者 person (usually a woman) trained to entertain at a party

Geta 下駄 wooden clogs

-gu 宮 Shinto shrine

Hanabi 花火 fireworks

Haiku 俳句 poem of 17 syllables

Hanami 花見 cherry-blossom viewing

Hanten 半纏 or はんてん a jacket worn over a yukata (see opposite) in the winter

Henro 遍路 pilgrims

Hibakusha 被爆者 A-bomb survivors

Hiragana ひらがな syllabary for writing Japanese words (see p450)

Ikebana 生け花 flower arranging

Izakaya 居酒屋 Japanese-style pub/bar

-ji 寺 Buddhist temple

Jidohan-baiki 自動販売機 vending machine

-jinja 神社 Shinto shrine

Jinrikisha 人力車 pulled (cycle) rickshaws, common in tourist areas

-jo 城 castle

Kaiseki-ryori 懐石料理 a traditional multi-course meal each course of which will be small but aesthetically pleasing

Kaisoku 快速 rapid train

Kaiten-zushi 回転ずし conveyor-belt sushi restaurant

Kami 神 spirit/deity in Shinto

Kanji 漢字 Chinese characters used to write the Japanese language

Katakana カタカナ syllabary for writing non-Japanese words (see p451)

Kissaten/manga kissa 喫茶店 a coffee shop where morning sets (see below) as well as tea, coffee, cakes, sandwiches and light meals are served. A manga kissa is a café with manga/video games.

-ko 湖 lake

Koban 交番 police box

-koen 公園 park

Koi 鯉 a carp (fish)

Konbini コンビニ convenience store

Koto 琴 Japanese harp

Koyo 紅葉 autumn leaves

Kyuko 急行 express train

Maiko 舞子 trainee geisha; often called a *geiko* (芸子) in Kyoto

Manga 漫画/マンガ comic

Matsuri 祭 festival

Meishi 名刺 business card

Mikoshi 神輿 portable Shinto shrine particularly used in festivals

Minshuku 民宿 place to stay, similar to a B&B (see p47-9)

Morning set/service モーニングセット/サビス a coffee shop's breakfast; usually coffee, boiled/fried egg and toast

Noren 暖簾 split curtain in front of Japanese-style restaurant or shop that shows it is open for business

Onsen 温泉 hot-spring resort (see also rotemburo)

Oshibori おしぼり or お絞り hot (or cold) wet towel used to refresh yourself before/after a meal

Robatayaki 炉端焼き/ろばたやき a kind of izakaya but where the food is displayed in front of the customer and they point to what they want cooked on a grill

Rotemburo 露天風呂 open-air hot-spring bath (see also onsen)

Ryokan 旅館 Japanese-style hotel (see pp50-1)

Sento 銭湯 public bath

Shamisen 三味線 wood instrument covered in cat skin with three strings made of silk

Shinkansen 新幹線 super express or bullet train

Shohizei 消費税 consumption tax (5%)

Shoji 障子 sliding paper screens

Shojin ryori 精進料理 vegetarian food served and eaten by monks in temples

Shokudo 食堂 canteen, dining hall

Taiko 太鼓 drum

-taisha 大社 shrine

Tatami 畳 traditional Japanese mat made from rice straw and used as flooring

-teien 庭園 garden

Teishoku 定食 set meal

Tenshukaku 天守閣 donjon; the tower or keep of a castle

Tetsudo mania/otaku 鉄道マニア/オタク railway enthusiast

Togyu 闘牛 bullfighting

Tokkyu 特急 limited express train

Tokonoma 床の間 alcove (in a room) containing a Japanese fan, vase or scroll

Torii 鳥居 gate at entrance to Shinto shrine

Torokko トロッコ open-air carriage on a train

Ukai 鵜飼 cormorant fishing

Yabusame 流鏑馬 horseback archery

Yakuza やくざ Japanese mafia

-yama 山 mountain

Yokozuna 横綱 grand champion in sumo tournament

Yukata 浴衣 cotton garment worn as a dressing gown; also a summer kimono

Zazen 座禅 Zen meditation

FOOD AND DRINK

Food

Basashi 馬刺し Raw horsemeat (see box p403).

Butadon 豚丼 See Donburi.

Curry rice (kare raisu) カレーライス A Japanese take on the Indian curry. The sauce is more like gravy than curry but it's a cheap, filling meal.

Dango 団子 Dumpling-shaped sweetmeat or confection.

Donburi 丼 A bowl of rice topped with chicken and egg (*oyako-don;* 親子丼), strips of beef (*gyudon;* 牛丼), or pork *(butadon;* 豚丼*)* cooked in a slightly sweet sauce. These restaurants are easy to spot as the counter is usually full of businessmen and meal tickets are bought from vending machines at the entrance; a very cheap meal.

Edamame 枝豆 Soy beans, often served as a snack in izakaya.

Fugu 河豚 or 鰒 A kind of fish (see box p362).

Gunkan-zushi 軍艦巻 Rice surrounded by dried seaweed and shaped into a container which is filled with fish such as *ikura* (salmon roe; イクラ), *uni* (sea urchin; うに、ウニ) and *natto* (see Natto).

Gyutan-yaki 牛タン焼き Grilled beef/ox tongue.

Gyudon 牛丼 *See* Donburi.

Inari-zushi 稲荷寿司 The cheapest kind of sushi; rice is covered with *abu-rage* (deep-fried tofu; 油揚げ).

Kaki-fry カキフライ Deep-fried oysters; also popular is *ebi-fry* (deep-fried prawns).

Kakigori かき氷 Crushed ice served with different fruit flavours, similar to Slush Puppy.

Kani 蟹 Crab, which is usually served in dedicated crab restaurants, recognisable from the giant crab with moving pincers above the entrance.

Kare raisu カレーライス See Curry rice.

Katsudon (カツ丼) A bowl of rice with tonkatsu (see p448) on top, covered with a slightly sweet sauce (see also donburi).

Katsuobushi かつおぶし A kind of fish (bonito) which is smoked and dried and then used to make dashi, a stock for soup.

Kitsune-udon きつねうどん Udon (see p449) served with deep-fried thinly sliced tofu.

Kushikatsu 串カツ Deep-fried bits of meat on a skewer (like a kebab).

Meron pan メロンパン Melon-flavoured buns.

Misoshiru みそしる、みそ汁 Miso soup; served with practically every Japanese dish, miso (soybean paste) is a staple ingredient in Japanese cuisine. In Nagano there's even a shop where you can try miso-flavoured ice cream (see p168).

Mochi 餅 A rice cake; a special type of mochi is eaten to celebrate New Year.

Nabe 鍋 A kind of Japanese hot pot; chicken, beef, pork or seafood mixed with vegetables and cooked in a large pot at your table.

Natto 納豆 Fermented soy beans. Foreigners are often asked if they like *natto*. Answering yes will shock your listener since gaijin are supposed not to like it.

Nigiri-zushi 握り寿司 Slices of fresh fish, shellfish, or a sweet Japanese-style omelette (*tamago-yaki*, 卵焼き) on small, oval-shaped rice balls.

Nori/nori-maki 海苔巻き Dried seaweed/seaweed-covered sushi.

Okonomiyaki お好み焼き Japanese savoury pancake with vegetables and meat, cooked on a grill and served in front of the customer.

Onigiri おにぎり Triangles of rice wrapped in a sheet of nori (seaweed) with fillings such as salmon, tuna or pickled plum (see Umeboshi). A popular convenience-store snack.

Oshi-zushi 押し寿司 Rice in a box covered with a mixture of fish, pickles, seaweed and other delights; common as a bento/ekiben (see box p82).

Oyako-don 親子丼 See Donburi.

Ramen ラーメン Stringy yellow noodles, served in a soup/broth with vegetables, and a popular late-night snack. Some restaurants offer 'challenge ramen' which is incredibly hot, but which you don't have to pay for if you can finish it without exploding.

Sashimi 刺身 Slices of raw fish such as tuna, eel (see Unagi), mackerel (*saba;* さば、鯖), prawn (*ebi*) and salmon roe (see Ikura); not to be confused with sushi (see below).

Shabu-shabu しゃぶしゃぶ Thinly sliced beef cooked at your table with vegetables and served with a special sauce.

Shoyu しょうゆ 醤油 Soy/soya sauce; fermented soy/soya beans with water and salt; an essential condiment for most meals.

Soba そば Thin buckwheat noodles eaten hot in a soup/broth, or cold when the noodles are dipped into a separate sauce made from soy, mirin (rice wine for cooking) and sake.

Somen そうめん Noodles served cold and eaten only in the summer.

Soup curry スープカレー The name is pretty clear; this is a popular dish in Hokkaido and the advantage is that you can say how spicy you want your soup to be. It is served with a variety of meat and vegetables.

Sukiyaki すき焼き Sliced beef with vegetables grilled in a special iron pan at your table.

Sushi すし、寿司 The general name for slices of fresh fish, particularly prawn (*ebi*; えび、海老) and tuna (*maguro*; マグロ) on a bed of rice. The most common kind is nigiri-zushi but other common ones are temaki-zushi, nori-maki and inari-zushi (see relevant entry). Add soy sauce (and wasabi) to taste and eat with a few slices of pickled ginger.

Takoyaki たこ焼き Pieces of octopus in batter; popular at summer festivals.

Temaki-zushi 手巻寿司 A cone shape of dried seaweed filled with rice, fish and vegetables such as avocado, that is big enough to hold in your hand.

Tempura 天ぷら Prawns/fish/vegetables deep fried in batter; served with a dipping sauce.

Tendon 天丼 Tempura served on a bowl of rice.

Teppanyaki 鉄板焼き Meat and fish cooked on an iron griddle.

Tofu 豆腐 Soybean curd, delicious when dipped in soy sauce.

Tomorokoshi (焼き)ともろこし (Grilled) corn on the cob.

Tonkatsu トンカツ A pork cutlet, dipped in breadcrumbs and deep fried. Always served with a mountain of shredded cabbage, miso soup and rice (which can be refilled on demand). Comes as either hirekatsu (ヒレカツ; pork fillet) or rosukatsu (ロースカツ; pork tenderloin). It is acceptable to ask for more cabbage or rice.

Udon うどん Wheat-flour noodles, much thicker than soba, served hot in a broth.

Umeboshi うめぼし、梅干し Sour, pickled plums. Some restaurants have bowls of umeboshi on the table for diners to pick at before/after a meal.

Unagi 鰻 Eel, basted in soy and sake sauce, cooked over a charcoal fire and served on a bed of rice. Traditionally eaten in the summer as stamina food for beating the heat.

Viking バイキング The Japanese word for a buffet meal.

Wanko soba わんこそば Bowls of good-quality soba, served with side dishes and traditionally eaten in a competition where diners race to scoff the most noodles; a speciality of the Morioka area.

Wasabi わさび Hot mustard, similar to horseradish, served with sushi and sashimi.

Yaki-imo ヤキイモ、焼き芋 Baked sweet potato.

Yakisoba 焼きそば Pork mince and vegetables with fried (but soft) soba; popular at summer festivals. The soba can also be served crunchy ie deep-fried (*kata-yakisoba* 固焼きそば). Also served with udon (*yakiudon* 焼きうどん).

Yakitori 焼き鳥 Chunks of chicken (wing, leg, heart, liver) and/or vegetables (usually leeks and pepper) on a skewer, dipped in a sauce made from sake, mirin (rice wine for cooking), stock and soy sauce and cooked over a charcoal fire. Usually served in small Japanese bars called *izakaya*.

Drink

● **Beer** *Asahi Superdry* (アサヒスーパードライ) and *Kirin* (キリン; see p392) are rivals for the title of 'nation's favourite beer'. See p55 for details about beer gardens (ビアガーデン).

● **Soft drinks** *Calpis* (カルピス) is a milk-based soft drink popular with children. Its name was changed to 'Calpico' when launched overseas. *CC Lemon* (CCレモン) is a fizzy drink which claims to have 'a hundred lemons' worth of Vitamin C' in every can. *Pocari Sweat* (ポカリスエット) is an energy drink. *Yakult* (ヤクルト) is a 'lactic acid bacteria beverage' or, if you think it sounds more appealing, a fermented milk drink. Either way it is very popular in Japan.

● **Sake** (酒) Often refers generally to alcoholic drinks, while 'Nihonshu' (日本酒) is more specifically what is known in the West as sake (pronounced sa-kay). Made from particular kinds of white rice (not the rice which is eaten) which has been fermented. Sake is served hot or cold and, as with wine, comes in a range of qualities. Amazake (甘酒) is a sweet form of sake and is usually less alcoholic.

● **Shochu** (焼酎) A strong spirit, particularly popular in Kyushu, made from grain/potato. *Chu-hai* (チューハイ) is shochu served with carbonated water and lemon or lime.

● **Tea** Cups of *o-cha* (お茶; green tea) or *houji-cha* (ほうじ茶; brown tea) are served free in some Japanese restaurants. *Ko-cha* (紅茶) is Western-style tea; Earl Grey and English Breakfast are common in many hotels, while fruit- and peppermint -flavour tea infusions are also widely available. *Mugi-cha* (麦茶; barley tea) is particularly popular as a cooling drink in the summer when it is served cold but it is also served hot.

● **Whisky** (ウイスキー) No karaoke bar would be without bottles of Suntory whisky, the leading domestic brand. But really high-class establishments only serve imported Scotch (particularly Johnny Walker).

APPENDIX B: USEFUL WORDS AND PHRASES

General words and phrases

Good morning	*ohaiyoo gozaimasu*	Good evening	*kombanwa*
Good night	*oyasumi nasai*	Hello	*konnichiwa*
Please*	*dozo, onegaishimasu* or *kudasai*	Goodbye	*sayonara*
Thank you	*domo arigato*	Yes (see p60)	*hai*
(very much)	*(gozaimashita)*	No	*iie*
No thanks	*kekko desu*	I don't understand	*wakarimasen*
Excuse me / I'm sorry	*shitsureishimasu/sumimasen* or *gomen nasai*		

What's your name?	*O-namae wa nan desu-ka*
My name is	*Watashi wa .... desu*
Where do you live?	*Doko ni sunde imasu ka*
I'm from Britain / America / Canada / Australia / New Zealand	*Igirisujin / Amerikajin / Kanadajin / Australiajin / New Zealandjin desu*
Do you speak English?	*Anata wa eigo ga hanasemasu ka*
Please write it down for me	*Sore o kaite kudasai*
Could you repeat that please?	*Mo ichido itte kudasai*
How much does it cost?	*Ikura desu ka*
Where is an ATM?	*ATM (genkin jodo azukebaraiki) wa doko desu-ka*

*Note: *onegaishimasu* and *kudasai* are used with a noun or when requesting/receiving something; *dozo* can be used without a noun and when giving something away.

Day/time

Monday	*getsuyobi*	月曜日	yesterday	*kino*	昨日
Tuesday	*kayobi*	火曜日	morning	*asa*	朝
Wednesday	*suiyobi*	水曜日	afternoon	*gogo*	午後
Thursday	*mokuyobi*	木曜日	evening	*yoru*	夜
Friday	*kinyobi*	金曜日	day	*hi / nichi*	日
Saturday	*doyobi*	土曜日	month	*gatsu / tsuki*	月
Sunday	*nichiyobi*	日曜日	year	*nen/toshi*	年
today	*kyo*	今日	hour	*ji*	時
tomorrow	*ashita*	明日	minute	*fun / pun*	分

Hiragana chart

a あ	ka (ga) か(が)	sa (za) さ(ざ)	ta (da) た(だ)	na な	ha (ba/pa) は(ば/ぱ)	ma ま	ya や	ra ら	wa わ
i い	ki (gi) き(ぎ)	shi (ji) し(じ)	chi (ji) ち(ぢ)	ni に	hi (bi/pi) ひ(び/ぴ)	mi み		ri り	
u う	ku (gu) く(ぐ)	su (zu) す(ず)	tsu (zu) つ(づ)	nu ぬ	hu (bu/pu) ふ(ぶ/ぷ)	mu む	yu ゆ	ru る	(w)o を
e え	ke (ge) け(げ)	se (ze) せ(ぜ)	te (de) て(で)	ne ね	he (be/pe) へ(べ/ぺ)	me め		re れ	
o お	ko (go) こ(ご)	so (zo) そ(ぞ)	to (do) と(ど)	no の	ho (bo/po) ほ(ぼ/ぽ)	mo も	yo よ	ro ろ	n ん

Numerals and counting systems

1	ichi	一	*11*	ju-ichi	十一	*21*	ni-ju-ichi	二十一
2	ni	二	*12*	ju-ni	十二	*22*	ni-ju-ni	二十二
3	san	三	*13*	ju-san	十三	*100*	hyaku	百
4	shi/yon	四	*14*	ju-shi/yon	十四	*101*	hyaku-ichi	百一
5	go	五	*15*	ju-go	十五	*200*	ni-hyaku	二百
6	roku	六	*16*	ju-rokku	十六	*1000*	sen	千
7	shichi / nana	七	*17*	ju-shichi / nana	十七	*1001*	sen-ichi	千一
8	hachi	八	*18*	ju-hachi	十八	*2000*	ni-sen	二千
9	kyu / ku	九	*19*	ju-kyu	十九	*10,000*	ichi-man	一万
10	ju	十	*20*	ni-ju	二十	*20,000*	ni-man	二万

There are many different counting systems in Japanese. The most useful to know are (based on counting from one to five):

● **People:** hitori (pronounced shitori) / futari / san-nin / yon-nin / go-nin
● **Nights (stay in a hotel/minshuku etc):** ippaku / nihaku / sanpaku / yonpaku / gohaku
● **Flat thin objects such as tickets:** ichimae / nimae / sanmae / yonmae / gomae
● **Cylindrical-shaped objects such as bottles of beer/wine or glasses (of drink):** ippon / nihon / sanbon / yonhon / gohon
● **Floors of a building:** ikkai / nikai / sankai / yonkai / gokai

Directions

North	*kita*	北	West	*nishi*	西	(Go) left / right	*hidari / migi (itte)*
South	*minami*	南	East	*higashi*	東	(Go) straight on	*massugu (itte)*

Where is ...?	*... wa doko desu ka*	... はどこですか
the train station	*Eki ...*	駅 ...
the ticket office	*Midori-no-Madoguchi ...*	みどりの窓口 ...
the bus stop	*Basu noriba ...*	バスのりば ...
a tourist information office	*Kanko annaijo ...*	観光案内所 ...
the tram stop	*Romendensha noriba ...*	路面電車のりば ...
a toilet (see also box p51)	*O-tearai* (polite) / *toire* (informal)	お手洗い ／ トイレ...
(male / female)		(男 ／ 女)
a taxi stand	*Takushi noriba ...*	タクシーのりば ...

Katakana chart

a	ka (ga)	sa (za)	ta (da)	na	ha (ba/pa)	ma	ya	ra	wa
ア	カ (ガ)	サ (ザ)	タ (ダ)	ナ	ハ (バ/パ)	マ	ヤ	ラ	ワ
i	ki (gi)	shi (ji)	chi (ji)	ni	hi (bi/pi)	mi		ri	
イ	キ (ギ)	シ (ジ)	チ (ヂ)	ニ	ヒ (ビ/ピ)	ミ		リ	
u	ku (gu)	su (zu)	tsu (zu)	nu	hu (bu/pu)	mu	yu	ru	(w)o
ウ	ク (グ)	ス (ズ)	ツ (ヅ)	ヌ	フ (ブ/プ)	ム	ユ	ル	ヲ
e	ke (ge)	se (ze)	te (de)	ne	he (be/pe)	me		re	
エ	ケ (ゲ)	セ (ゼ)	テ (デ)	ネ	ヘ (ベ/ペ)	メ		レ	
o	ko (go)	so (zo)	to (do)	no	ho (bo/po)	mo	yo	ro	n
オ	コ (ゴ)	ソ (ゾ)	ト (ド)	ノ	ホ (ボ/ポ)	モ	ヨ	ロ	ン

Railway vocabulary

adult / child	*otona / kodomo*	大人 ／ 子供
aisle (seat)	*tsuro (gawa no seki)*	通路（側の席）
arrival	*tochaku*	到着
berth	*shindai*	寝台
conductor	*shashosan*	車掌さん
departure	*shupatsu*	出発
entrance / exit	*iriguchi / deguchi*	入り口 ／ 出口
express train	*kyuko*	急行
fare adjustment office	*ryokin seisanjo*	料金精算所
Green car	*guriin-sha*	グリーンカー
handicapped person	*karada no fujyu na hito*	身体の不自由
limited express train	*tokkyu*	特急
local train	*futsu*	普通
luggage	*nimotsu*	にもつ
no-smoking car	*kin-en-sha*	禁煙車
ordinary class car	*futsu-sha*	普通車
platform	*platthomu*	プラットホーム
railway line	*sen*	線
railway lunchbox	*ekiben*	駅弁
rapid train	*kaisoku*	快速
refund	*haraimodoshi*	払い戻し
reservation	*yoyaku*	予約
reserved seat	*shitei-seki*	指定席
sleeper train	*shindaisha*	寝台車
smoking car	*kitsuen-sha*	喫煙車
station	*eki*	駅
ticket / transfer ticket	*kippu / norikae-kippu*	きっぷ ／ 乗り換えきっぷ
ticket gate	*kaisatsu-guchi*	改札口
timetable	*jikoku hyo*	時刻表
Travel Service Center	*ryoko senta*	旅行センター
trolley	*wagon service*	ワゴンサービス
underground / subway / metro	*chikatetsu*	地下鉄
unreserved seat	*jiyu-seki*	自由席
window (seat)	*madogawa no seki*	窓側の席

Railway phrases

How can I get to [Kyoto] from here?	*Koko kara [Kyoto] niwa made dousureba ikemasu ka*
I'd like to reserve a seat on the next train to [Kyoto]	*Tsugi no [Kyoto] iki ressha no zaseki o yoyaku shitai'n desu ga*
What time does the train to [Kyoto] leave?	*[Kyoto] iki densha wa nan ji ni shuppatsu demasu ka*
Which platform does the train to [Kyoto] leave from?	*[Kyoto] iki no densha wa nan ban sen kara shuppatsu shimasu ka*
Excuse me, does this train go to [Kyoto]?	*Kono densha wa [Kyoto] ni ikimasu ka*
Can you tell me where my seat is on this train?	*Watashi no seki wa doko desu ka*

Accommodation (see also Numerals and counting systems, p451)

I'd like to book a single / double / twin room (Western-style hotel)	*Singuru / daburu / tuin no heya o yoyaku shitai'n desu ga*

(Since in Japanese-style accommodation the number of people who can share a room depends on how many futon can be laid out it is best to say how many people want to share.)

I'd like a Japanese-/Western-style room	*Washitsu / Yoshitsu onegaishimasu*
I'd like a room but no meals	*Sudomari onegaishimasu*
What is the rate?	*Ryokin wa ikura desu ka*
Does it include breakfast / supper?	*Choshoku / Yushoku wa tsuite imasu ka*
Where is the reception desk?	*Front wa doko desu ka*
Where is the (Japanese-style) bath?	*O-furo wa doko desu ka*
Can I check-in?	*Check-in dekimasu ka*
I'd like to check out	*Check-out onegaishimasu*
Do you accept Amex / Visa card?	*Amekkusu / Viza kaado wa tsukaemasu ka*
Can I leave my luggage here?	*Nimotsu wa koko azuketemo ii desu ka*
Can I borrow a LAN cable?	*Lan cable karitemo ii desu ka*
What time is breakfast?	*Choshoku (or Asa-gohan) wa nan-ji desu ka*
What time is supper?	*Yushoku (or Ban-gohan) wa nan-ji desu ka*

Restaurant

Resutoran

I'd like to make a reservation	*Shokuji no yoyaku o shitai'n desu ga*
Do you have a menu in English?	*Eigo no menyuu wa arimasu ka*
What is this?	*Kore wa nan desu ka*
I'd like this, please	*Kore o kudasai*
What time does the restaurant open/close?	*Resutoran wa nan ji kara/nan ji made desu ka*
Can I have some more water/tea?	*O-mizu/o-cha morae masu ka.*
Can I have some more cabbage/rice please? (for a tonkatsu meal, see p448)	*Kyabetsu/gohan morae masu ka*
I don't eat meat / I am a vegetarian	*Niku wa tabemasen / Bejitarian desu*

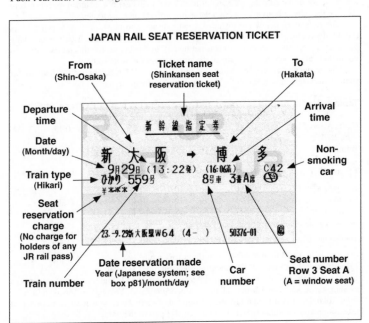

JAPAN RAIL SEAT RESERVATION TICKET

From (Shin-Osaka)

Ticket name (Shinkansen seat reservation ticket)

To (Hakata)

Departure time

Arrival time

Date (Month/day)

Non-smoking car

Train type (Hikari)

Seat reservation charge (No charge for holders of any JR rail pass)

Date reservation made Year (Japanese system; see box p81)/month/day

Train number

Car number

Seat number Row 3 Seat A (A = window seat)

APPENDIX C: TIMETABLES

THE JAPANESE RAILWAY TIMETABLE

Even though the timetables contained in this appendix will give you an idea of the services available, the Japanese Timetable (see pp78-9) and online versions (see box p75) will always be the most up to date and also provide information for all the services.

How to use the Japanese Timetable

The route maps on the colour pages at the front of the Japanese timetable use kanji so you need to know the kanji for where you are and where you want to go – a selection is provided in the timetables in this guide, or you can look at JNTO's *Tourist Map of Japan*. In the timetable find the route map which covers the area you are travelling in and then the places you want to travel between. Finally, look for the number which appears immediately above or below it. This refers to the corresponding page in the timetable. For major services two numbers are given – one for each direction.

At the beginning of every timetable the names of all stops on a particular route appear in hiragana as well as kanji. Thus, even if the kanji you want isn't in this guide, by using the hiragana syllabary on p450 you could work out the hiragana.

Working your way around the Japanese timetable can take time but is rewarding and also it is by far the most reliable way of checking train times.

USING THE TIMETABLES IN THIS GUIDE

Timetables for shinkansen and limited express (LEX) services for most routes described in this book are provided below. Times for local/rapid trains are not included (except where they are the only option) even though these also operate on most routes.

The timetables below are included as an assistance to planning your trip but times should **always** be checked before heading to the station. Most services listed operate daily but weekend services can differ (this is not noted). In most cases the timetables shown do not include all the services; nor are all the stops shown for every route.

The frequency of services can also vary seasonally. The timetables given here are for summer services; in winter months these may be less frequent.

Table 1: Narita Airport to Tokyo and Yokohama via Narita Express (N'EX)
1a: Narita Airport to Tokyo and Yokohama

Narita Airport Terminal 1 成田空港ターミナル1	07.44	08.13	08.50	09.15	09.45	10.15[1]	13.45[2]
Terminal 2 ターミナル2	07.46	08.16	08.53	09.18	09.48	10.18	13.48
Tokyo[3] 東京	09.03[3]	09.27[3]	09.52[3]	10.17[3]	10.44[3]	11.14[3]	14.44[3]
Shinagawa 品川	09.16	09.36	10.01	10.26	10.53	11.23	14.52
Shibuya 渋谷	09.25	09.49	10.13	10.40	11.05	11.34	
Shinjuku 新宿	09.31	09.55	10.19	10.46	11.11	11.39	
Ikebukuro 池袋		10.02				11.48	
Yokohama 横浜		09.59	10.26	10.51	11.14	11.44	15.14

[1] Hourly until 19.15 though subsequent times vary a bit.

[2] Hourly from 14.45 until 21.45 though subsequent times vary a bit.

[3] Trains divide at Tokyo – part goes to Shibuya, Shinjuku and Ikebukuro, the other part goes to Shinagawa, Musashi-Kosugi (11 mins from Shinagawa), Yokohama, Totsuka (12 mins from Yokohama) and Ofuna (18 mins from Yokohama). Since you have to have a seat reservation you should definitely be in the correct part of the train.

Table 1: *(cont'd)*

1b: Yokohama and Tokyo to Narita Airport

Yokohama 横浜		06.40	06.56	07.28	08.26	09.29[1]	12.59[2]
Ikebukuro 池袋	06.00	06.43				09.32	13.03
Shinjuku 新宿	06.07	06.51	07.06			09.39	13.10
Shibuya 渋谷	06.12	06.57	07.12			09.45	13.16
Shinagawa 品川	06.21	07.02	07.18	07.51	08.49	09.50	13.20
Tokyo[3] 東京	06.31[3]	07.15[3]	07.31[3]	08.00[3]	09.00	10.03[3]	13.33[3]
Narita Airport Terminal 2 成田空港ターミナル2	07.26	08.08	08.33	08.58	09.54	10.54	14.23
Terminal 1 ターミナル1	07.30	08.10	08.36	09.01	09.58	10.58	14.27

[1] Hourly until 16.29 and also at 18.29 & 19.29 but arrival times may vary by up to 15 mins.
[2] Hourly until 17.59 though subsequent arrival times may vary a little.
[3] Trains join up at Tokyo – one part comes from Ikebukuro, Shinjuku and Shibuya; the other part comes from Ofuna (18 mins to Yokohama), Totsuka (12 mins to Yokohama), Yokohama, Musashi-Kosugi (11 mins to Shinagawa) and Shinagawa.

Table 2: Kansai Airport to Shin-Osaka/Kyoto via Haruka LEX

	2a: Airport to Osaka/Kyoto				2b: Kyoto/Osaka to airport			
Kansai Airport 関西空港	06.33[1]	07.55	08.46[2]	09.16[3]	07.11	07.41	08.54	11.03
Tennoji 天王時	07.17	08.40	09.20	09.50	06.38	07.07	08.08	10.32
Shin-Osaka 新大阪	07.38	09.07	09.37	10.07	06.17	06.48	07.47	10.15
Kyoto 京都	08.03	09.32	10.02	10.31	05.46[4]	06.22	07.15[5]	09.45[6]

[1] Also at 07.27; arr 09.03   [2] Also at 09.46 & 16.46-20.46.   [3] Hourly until 20.16
[4] Also at 06.45; arr 08.17   [5] Hourly until 20.15   [6] Also at 16.45-19.45

Note: For all services subsequent departure/arrival times vary by a few minutes from those given here.

Table 3: Tokyo to Hakata (Fukuoka) by Tokaido/Sanyo shinkansen

Note: The **Hikari/Sakura** and **Kodama** services listed on pp456-7 generally operate daily and hourly until approximately 20.00. The details given are accurate for the services shown but subsequent trains may not make all the same stops and some make additional stops. This therefore affects departure/arrival times. In addition this list is only a sample of the many services available.

Kodama services operate from Tokyo to Nagoya/Shin-Osaka and from Shin-Osaka to Hakata, Hikari services from Tokyo to Shin-Osaka/Okayama, and Sakura from Shin-Osaka to Hakata/Kagoshima-chuo. Sakura (and Kodama) services from Shin-Osaka to Hakata are shown here but Sakura services from Shin-Osaka to Kagoshima-chuo are shown in Table 23 on p468. However, the 09.20 Sakura from Shin-Osaka continues to Kumamoto (13.42) and Kagoshima-chuo (13.40) and the 10.04 from Hakata starts in Kagoshima-chuo (08.37) and Kumamoto (09.25).

Nozomi services operate approximately every ten minutes (6/hr from Tokyo to Shin-Osaka and 3/hr to Hakata) but the Japan Rail Pass is not valid and it is not possible to pay a supplement to use them. If travelling without a rail pass, note that all Nozomi services have three non-reserved carriages (and therefore no compulsory seat-reservation charge).

The **Mizuho** (valid with a JR Kyushu Pass but not a Japan Rail Pass) services from Shin-Osaka to Kagoshima-chuo are shown in Table 23 on p468.

Table 3: *(cont'd)*   **3a: Tokyo to Hakata (Fukuoka)** (See note p455)

	To Shin-Osaka (Hikari)	To Okayama (Hikari)	To Hakata (Nozomi)	To Shin-Osaka (Kodama)	To Nagoya (Kodama)
Tokyo 東京	06.26	07.03	06.50	06.56	07.26
Shinagawa 品川	06.34	07.10	06.57	07.04	07.34
Shin-Yokohama 新横浜	06.46	07.22	07.09	07.16	07.46
Odawara 小田原	07.04			07.36	08.03
Atami 熱海				07.46	08.12
Mishima 三島				07.58	08.25
Shin-Fuji 新富士				08.12	08.40
Shizuoka 静岡		08.11		08.26	08.57
Kakegawa 掛川				08.41	09.11
Hamamatsu 浜松		08.37		08.56	09.28
Toyohashi 豊橋	07.59			09.14	09.45
Mikawa-Anjo 三河安城				09.32	10.03
Nagoya 名古屋	08.21	09.10	08.35	09.45	10.14
Gifu-Hashima 岐阜羽島	08.34			09.56	
Maibara 米原	08.54			10.15	
Kyoto 京都	09.16	09.48	09.13	10.38	
Shin-Osaka (arr) 新大阪	09.30	10.03	09.27	10.50	
		Shin-Osaka to Hakata (Sakura)		**Shin-Osaka to Hiroshima (Kodama)**	
Shin-Osaka (dep) 新大阪	09.20	10.05	09.29	09.38	
Shin-Kobe 新神戸	09.34	10.19	09.42	09.53	
Nishi-Akashi 西明石		10.32		10.11	**Okayama to Hakata (Kodama)**
Himeji 姫路	09.50	10.47	09.58	10.28	
Aioi 相生		11.06		10.43	
Okayama 岡山	10.11	11.22	10.19	11.00	10.05
Shin-Kurashiki 新倉敷				11.14	10.19
Fukuyama 福山	10.27			11.33	10.34
Shin-Onomichi 新尾道				11.42	10.49
Mihara 三原				11.52	10.59
Higashi-Hiroshima 東広島				12.07	11.12
Hiroshima 広島	10.51		10.56	12.19	11.23
Shin-Iwakuni 新岩国				12.34	11.47
Tokuyama 徳山				12.48	12.01
Shin-Yamaguchi 新山口				13.10	12.17
Asa 厚狭				13.23	12.37
Shin-Shimonoseki 新下関	11.37			13.43	12.52
Kokura 小倉	11.47		11.43	14.02	13.04
Hakata (Fukuoka) 博多	12.04		11.59	14.21	13.24

Table 3: *(cont'd)*   **3b: Hakata (Fukuoka) to Tokyo** (See note p455)

	To Tokyo (Nozomi)	To Okayama (Kodama)		To Shin-Osaka (Sakura)	To Shin-Osaka (Kodama)
Hakata (Fukuoka) 博多	07.00	07.12		10.04	11.23
Kokura 小倉	07.17	07.30		10.22	11.41
Shin-Shimonoseki 新下関		07.39			11.54
Asa 厚狭		07.59			12.09
Shin-Yamaguchi 新山口		08.10		10.41	12.25
Tokuyama 徳山	07.47	08.29			12.49
Shin-Iwakuni 新岩国		08.54			13.03
Hiroshima 広島	08.10	09.11		11.15	13.21
Higashi-Hiroshima 東広島		09.23			13.39
Mihara 三原		09.39			13.53
Shin-Onomichi 新尾道		09.48			14.03
Fukuyama 福山		10.00	**Okayama to Shin-Osaka (Hikari)**	11.40	14.17
Shin-Kurashiki 新倉敷		10.23			14.33
Okayama 岡山	08.49	10.33	09.27	11.58	14.52
Aioi 相生			09.51		15.13
Himeji 姫路			10.01		15.25
Nishi-Akashi 西明石			10.15		15.40
Shin-Kobe 新神戸	09.22		10.25	12.31	15.50
Shin-Osaka 新大阪	09.35 (arr)		10.38 (arr)	12.44	16.05
		Shin-Osaka to Tokyo (Kodama)		**Shin-Osaka to Tokyo (Hikari)**	
Shin-Osaka 新大阪	09.37 (dep)	08.53	10.40 (dep)	09.13	
Kyoto 京都	09.53	09.09	10.56	09.29	
Maibara 米原		09.34		09.55	
Gifu-Hashima 岐阜羽島		09.48		10.11	**Nagoya to Tokyo (Kodama)**
Nagoya 名古屋	10.30	10.00	11.34	10.24	11.28
Mikawa-Anjo 三河安城		10.13			11.44
Toyohashi 豊橋		10.33		10.45	12.02
Hamamatsu 浜松		10.50	12.11		12.20
Kakegawa 掛川		11.03			12.32
Shizuoka 静岡		11.19	12.37		12.48
Shin-Fuji 新富士		11.36			13.07
Mishima 三島		11.50			13.20
Atami 熱海		11.58	13.02		13.28
Odawara 小田原		12.11			13.42
Shin-Yokohama 新横浜	11.54	12.28	13.22	11.51	13.58
Shinagawa 品川	12.06	12.39	13.33	12.03	14.09
Tokyo 東京	12.13	12.47	13.40	12.10	14.17

Table 4: Tokyo to Nagano by Nagano (Asama) shinkansen

Note. The services shown below are only a sample of the many on this route. During the day there are at least two an hour to/from Tokyo and one an hour to/from Ueno, thus the table should be used as a guide only.

Even though Honjo-Waseda (本庄早稲田) is on this route it is served mostly by Toki, Tanigawa and Max-Tanigawa services to Niigata, rather than the Asama shinkansen.

4a: Tokyo to Nagano

Tokyo 東京	07.52	08.36	09.52	10.44	12.24	13.04[1]	15.44	16.24
Ueno 上野	07.58	08.42	09.58	10.50	12.30	13.10	15.50	16.30
Omiya 大宮	08.18	09.02	10.18	11.10	12.50	13.30	16.10	16.50
Kumagaya 熊谷	08.31			11.23				
Takasaki 高崎	08.51	09.29		11.39	13.15	13.55	16.34	
Annaka-Haruna 安中榛名	09.00			11.48	13.24			
Karuizawa 軽井沢	09.13	09.46	10.56	12.01	13.37	14.12	16.51	17.28
Sakudaira 佐久平	09.22	09.55	11.05	12.10	13.46	14.21	17.00	17.37
Ueda 上田	09.32	10.05	11.15	12.20	13.56	14.31	17.10	17.47
Nagano 長野	09.45	10.18	11.28	12.33	14.09	14.44	17.23	18.00

[1] Also at 14.04 and 15.04

4b: Nagano to Tokyo

Nagano 長野	08.55	09.26[1]	11.09[2]	13.03	13.50	14.26[3]	16.18	17.26
Ueda 上田	09.08	09.39	11.22	13.16	14.03	14.39	16.31	17.39
Sakudaira 佐久平	09.19	09.50	11.33	13.27	14.14	14.50	16.42	17.50
Karuizawa 軽井沢		09.59	11.43	13.36	14.24	15.00	16.52	18.00
Annaka-Haruna 安中榛名				13.48		15.11	17.03	18.11
Takasaki 高崎		10.17	12.00	13.58		15.21	17.13	18.21
Kumagaya 熊谷		10.32		14.13			17.32	
Omiya 大宮	10.06	10.46	12.26	14.26	15.06	15.46	17.46	18.46
Ueno 上野	10.26	11.06	12.46	14.46	15.26	16.06	18.06	19.06
Tokyo 東京	10.32	11.12	12.52	14.52	15.32	16.12	18.12	19.12

[1] Also at 10.26; the next service leaves at 10.08 but only calls at Omiya (11.08) and Tokyo (11.12).   [2] Also at 12.09.   [3] Also at 15.26

Table 5: Nagano to Nagoya via Matsumoto on Wide View Shinano LEX[1]

	5a: Nagano to Nagoya				5b: Nagoya to Nagano				
Nagano 長野	08.12	09.00	14.00	18.11	10.01	11.52	13.53	20.39
Shinonoi 篠ノ井	08.20	09.08	14.09	18.19	09.54	11.44	13.45	20.31
Hijiri-Kogen 聖高原		09.40	14.53	18.51				20.13
Matsumoto 松本	09.04	09.52	15.03	19.06	09.09	11.05	13.05	19.46
Shiojiri 塩尻	09.15	10.03		19.19	08.58	10.54	12.54	19.36
Kiso-Fukushima 木曽福島	09.44	10.30	15.30	19.48	08.29	10.25	12.25	19.07
Nagiso 南木曽			15.55		08.01			
Nakatsugawa 中津川	10.24	11.07	16.07	20.26	07.49	09.49	11.49	18.30
Tajimi 多治見	10.51	11.35	16.34	20.54	07.23	09.22	11.23	18.04
Chikusa 千種	11.08	11.53	16.52	21.13	07.06	09.06	11.06	17.48
Nagoya 名古屋	11.16	12.00	17.01[2]	21.20	07.00	09.00	11.00[3]	17.40

[1] Generally one service an hour, on the hour, from both Nagano and Nagoya.
[2] Continues to Kyoto (18.48) & Osaka (19.18). [3] Comes from Osaka (08.58) & Kyoto (09.25).

Table 6: Nagano to Toyama (and Kanazawa) via Naoetsu

6a: Nagano to Naoetsu[1]

Nagano 長野	08.12
Toyono 豊野	08.25
Kurohime 黒姫	08.46
Myoko-Kogen 妙高高原	08.55
Sekiyama 関山	09.03
Nihongi 二本木	09.10
Arai 新井	09.19
Takada 高田	09.32
Naoetsu 直江津	09.41

6b: Naoetsu to Toyama/Kanazawa[2/3]

	Ho[4]	Ha[5]	Ha[5]	Ho[4]	Ha[5]
Naoetsu 直江津	09.37[4]	10.10	12.31	14.57[4]	17.01
Itoigawa 糸魚川	10.01	10.33	12.54	15.13	17.26
Tomari 泊		10.53			17.44
Nyuzen 入善					17.49
Kurobe 黒部	10.29	11.02		15.40	17.57
Uozu 魚津	10.34	11.07	13.24	15.46	18.02
Namerikawa 滑川	10.40				
Toyama 富山	10.53	11.23	13.41	16.03	18.19
Takaoka 高岡	11.05	11.35	13.53	16.16	18.32
Isurugi 石動					18.42
Tsubata 津幡					
Kanazawa 金沢	11.31	11.59	14.18	16.41	18.59

6c: Kanazawa/Toyama to Naoetsu[2/3]

	Ha[5]	Ho[4]	Ha[5]	Ho[4]	Ha[5]
Kanazawa 金沢	07.10	10.34[4]	12.07	13.37[4]	17.17
Tsubata 津幡		10.44			
Isurugi 石動	07.25	10.53	12.31		
Takaoka 高岡	07.35	11.03	12.38	14.03	17.41
Toyama 富山	07.47	11.16	12.43	14.16	17.53
Namerikawa 滑川	07.59				
Uozu 魚津	08.06	11.32	12.59	14.32	18.09
Kurobe 黒部		11.38		14.38	18.14
Nyuzen 入善	08.17				18.22
Tomari 泊				14.49	
Itoigawa 糸魚川	08.38	12.06		15.08	18.43
Naoetsu 直江津	09.00	12.32	13.53	15.31	19.05

6d: Naoetsu to Nagano[1]

Naoetsu 直江津	08.10
Takada 高田	08.20
Arai 新井	08.44
Nihongi 二本木	08.53
Sekiyama 関山	09.03
Myoko-Kogen 妙高高原	09.12
Kurohime 黒姫	09.19
Toyono 豊野	09.39
Nagano 長野	09.53

Ho = Hokuetsu   Ha = Hakutaka   Not all stops are shown

1 There are no limited express services between Nagano and Naoetsu; the local service generally operates once an hour though at irregular times.

2 The times shown are a sample of the almost hourly service (in each direction) between Naoetsu and Kanazawa.

3 See Table 8 for details of other services between Toyama and Kanazawa.

4 Hokuetsu services (5/day in all) start in/continue to Niigata. The 09.37 service from Naoetsu starts in Niigata at 07.55 and the 14.57 starts in Niigata at 13.02.

The 10.34 service from Kanazawa arrives in Niigata at 14.19 and the 13.37 service arrives in Niigata at 17.19.

5 Hakutaka services (12/day) operate between Kanazawa and Echigo-Yuzawa; 1/day continues to/starts in Wakura-onsen and 1/day continues to/starts in Fukui.

Table 7: Toyama/Takayama to Nagoya[1,2] on Wide View Hida LEX

	7a: Toyama to Nagoya					7b: Nagoya to Toyama			
Toyama 富山	08.00	13.02	15.10	17.10	▲	12.26	14.44	16.42	18.52
Hida-Furukawa 飛騨古川	09.18	14.19	16.25	18.26		11.13	13.27	15.23	17.29
Takayama 高山	09.37	14.39	16.44	18.45		11.00	13.14	15.10	17.13
Gero 下呂	10.26	15.25	17.27	19.28		10.14	12.27	14.23	16.26
Mino-Ota 美濃太田	11.19	16.19	18.19	20.20		09.23	11.29	13.28	15.29
Gifu 岐阜	11.39	16.39	18.39	20.42		09.03	11.08	13.08	15.08
Nagoya 名古屋	12.02	17.02	19.02	21.02	▼	08.43	10.48	12.48	14.48

Note:
[1] Between Toyama and Nagoya some of these services stop at Hayahoshi, Etchu-Yatsuo, Inotani, Kuguno, Hida-Osaka, Hida-Hagiwara, Hida-Kanayama, Shirakawa-guchi, Unuma and Owari-Ichinomiya.
[2] Services for Nagoya that start in Takayama (and vice versa) are not given but generally operate once an hour during the day.

Table 8: Toyama to Osaka on Thunderbird LEX

	8a: Toyama to Osaka					8b: Osaka to Toyama			
Toyama 富山	08.18	10.10[1]	14.19[1]	17.11	▲	11.58	12.59	15.01	17.07
Takaoka 高岡	08.30	10.22	14.31	17.24		11.46	12.47	14.47	16.54
Kanazawa 金沢	09.03	10.55		17.56		11.22	12.19	14.23	16.25
Komatsu 小松			14.57	18.13			14.05	16.06	
Kaga-onsen 加賀温泉		11.20	15.23				11.53	13.56	15.58
Awara-onsen 芦原温泉		11.30		18.31				13.45	15.47
Fukui 福井	09.47	11.42	15.44	18.43		10.31	11.33	13.35	15.36
Sabae 鯖江				18.51					15.27
Takefu 武生		11.54		18.55				13.22	15.22
Tsuruga 敦賀		12.16		19.15				13.02	15.02
Kyoto 京都	11.09	13.09	17.07	20.09		09.10	10.10	12.10	14.10
Shin-Osaka 新大阪	11.32	13.32	17.30	20.32		08.46	09.46	11.46	13.46
Osaka 大阪	11.37	13.37	17.34	20.37	▼	08.42	09.42[2]	11.42[2]	13.42[2]

[1] Hourly until 17.11   [2] Hourly until 18.42

Services operate hourly but note that the departure/arrival times and stops vary slightly so it is essential to check.

The Thunderbird services shown are ones that go from Osaka to Toyama. Additional services (starting in Wakura-onsen; 4/day) operate from Kanazawa to Osaka via Hakui.

Table 9: Nagoya to Shingu/Kii Katsuura on Wide View Nanki LEX[1]

	9a: Nagoya to Shingu/Kii-Katsuura				9b:Kii-Katsuura/Shingu to Nagoya			
Nagoya 名古屋	08.08	10.00	12.58	19.45	▲ 09.39	12.38	16.07	20.44
Kuwana 桑名	08.29	10.23	13.20	20.04	09.16	12.14	15.44	20.23
Yokkaichi[2] 四日市	08.40	10.35	13.35	20.15	09.03	12.02	15.32	20.11
Suzuka[2] 鈴鹿	08.48	10.43	13.43	20.23	08.54	11.52	15.24	20.02
Tsu[2] 津	09.01	10.59	13.58	20.37	08.41	11.40	15.11	19.49
Matsusaka 松阪	09.16	11.14	14.14	20.52	08.26	11.24	14.55	19.35
Taki 多気	09.24	11.27	14.21	20.59	08.19	11.17	14.46	19.27
Misedani 三瀬谷	09.46	11.49	14.45	21.21	07.57	10.55	14.22	19.05
Kii-Nagashima 紀伊長島	10.13	12.17	15.13	21.48	07.30	10.28	13.55	18.37
Owase 尾鷲	10.34	12.38	15.36	22.09	07.08	10.01	13.33	18.15
Kumano-Shi 熊野市	11.02	13.06	16.03	22.41	06.41	09.33	13.06	17.48
Shingu 新宮	11.21	13.25	16.22	23.01	06.21	09.13	12.43	17.28
Kii-Katsuura 紀伊勝浦	11.39	13.46	16.40	▼		08.55	12.23	17.10

[1] These are the only limited express services on this route. Local trains (at least 1/hr) may involve changing train at Yokkaichi but some services are direct.

[2] Rail-pass holders have to pay an additional fare (¥490) between Yokkaichi and Tsu.

Table 10: Shingu to Shin-Osaka (and Kyoto) on Kuroshio LEX[1,2]

	10a: Shingu to Kyoto				10b: Kyoto to Shingu			
Shingu 新宮	08.37	10.31	12.44	15.42	▲ 13.09	14.55	16.58	19.02
Kii-Katsuura 紀伊勝浦	08.54	10.46	13.01	15.57	12.53	14.40	16.43	18.47
Taiji 太地	09.01	10.52			12.46		16.36	18.40
Koza 古座	09.18	11.10	13.23	16.20	12.29	14.19	16.20	18.24
Kushimoto 串本	09.26	11.19	13.31	16.29	12.21	14.11	16.11	18.16
Susami 周参見	09.57	11.58	14.02	17.00	11.50	13.37	15.39	17.43
Tsubaki 椿	10.09							17.29
Shirahama 白浜	10.31	12.30	14.30	17.32	11.30	13.17	15.19	17.19
Kii-Tanabe 紀伊田辺	10.42	12.43	14.42	17.43	11.13	13.05	15.07	17.07
Gobo 御坊	11.10	13.10	15.08	18.10	10.44	12.38	14.39	16.40
Wakayama 和歌山	11.49	13.49	15.47	18.50	10.06	12.00	14.01	16.02
Hineno 日根野				19.09				
Tennoji 天王寺	12.34	14.34	16.29	19.34	09.21	11.17	13.17	15.17
Shin-Osaka 新大阪	12.50	14.50	16.50	19.51	09.03	11.00	13.00	15.00
Kyoto 京都			17.17	20.17 ▼	08.36			

[1] Not all stops are shown.

[2] The Kuroshio operates 7/day in both directions between Shingu and Shin-Osaka; two of these services continue to/start in Kyoto.

Additional services (8/day) operate between Shirahama and Shin-Osaka. Most of these services call at every station listed in the suggested route.

Table 11: Shin-Yamaguchi to Matsue (and Tottori) on Super Oki LEX[1]

	11a: Shin-Yamaguchi to Matsue					11b: Matsue to Shin-Yamaguchi			
	SO[1]	SM[2]	SO[1]	SO[1]		SO[1]	SO[1]	SM[2]	SO[1]
Shin-Yamaguchi 新山口	08.51		12.53	16.48	▲	10.13	14.57		18.51
Yuda-onsen 湯田温泉	09.02		13.03	16.57		10.04	14.48		18.42
Yamaguchi 山口	09.07		13.07	17.01		10.00	14.44		18.39
Mitani 三谷	09.34		13.33	17.26		09.34	14.19		18.12
Tokusa 徳佐	09.45		13.43	17.37		09.24	14.09		18.02
Tsuwano 津和野	09.58		13.56	17.49		09.11	13.56		17.49
Nichihara 日原	10.08		14.07	18.00		09.01	13.46		17.39
Masuda (arr) 益田	10.29		14.28	18.23	(dep)	08.40	13.25		17.18
Masuda (dep) 益田	10.31	12.08	14.32	18.48	(arr)	08.37	13.22	14.52	17.15
Mihomisumi 三保三隅			14.51	19.04		08.21	13.05		16.56
Hamada 浜田	11.03	12.41	15.06	19.21		08.05	12.50	14.19	16.41
Hashi 波子	11.14		15.22				12.39		16.31
Gotsu 江津	11.19	12.56	15.31	19.32		07.44	12.31	14.03	16.21
Yunotsu 温泉津			15.43	19.44				16.07	
Oda-Shi 大田市	11.45	13.23	15.51	19.50		07.11	12.05	13.35	15.51
Izumo-Shi 出雲市	12.11	13.50	16.14	20.13		06.40	11.36	13.12	15.28
Shinji 宍道	12.22					06.28			
Tamatsukuri-onsen 玉造温泉		14.10	16.33	20.32		06.20	11.17		15.10
Matsue 松江	12.37	14.17	16.42	20.39	▼	06.15	11.11	12.48	15.04
Tottori 鳥取		15.44	18.16				09.46	11.27	13.43

[1] The services shown are the only Super Oki (SO) services each day.

[2] The Super Matsukaze (SM) operates 4/day between Masuda and Tottori via Matsue.

Table 12: Tokyo to Sendai, Morioka and Shin-Aomori by shinkansen

Notes: The services shown are only a selection of the many available.

Seat reservations are essential for Hayate and Hayabusa services.

Not all stops are shown

HAY = Hayate   Hb = Hayabusa   N = Nasuno   Y/MY = Yamabiko/Max-Yamabiko

	12a: Tokyo to Sendai/Morioka/Shin-Aomori							
	HAY	HAY	Hb	N	Y	Y	MY	Y/MY
Tokyo 東京	08.56[1]	09.56[2]	09.36[3]	08.20[4]	08.40[5]	09.16[5]	09.00[5]	11.08[5]
Ueno 上野	09.02	10.02		08.26	08.46	09.22	09.06	11.14
Omiya 大宮	09.22	10.22	10.01	08.46	09.06	09.42	09.26	11.34
Oyama 小山				09.03		09.58		
Utsunomiya 宇都宮				09.18	09.30	10.13	09.51	11.59
Shin-Shirakawa 新白河				09.50				
Koriyama 郡山				10.03	09.58	11.09	10.22	12.31
Fukushima 福島					10.12	11.24	10.41	12.51
Sendai 仙台	10.38	11.38	11.14		11.42	11.46	11.08	13.17
Ichinoseki 一ノ関					11.14			
Kitakami 北上					11.33			

Table 12: *(cont'd)*   **12a: Tokyo to Sendai/Morioka/Shin-Aomori**

	HAY	HAY	Hb	N	Y	Y	MY	Y/MY
Shin-Hanamaki 新花巻					11.41			
Morioka 盛岡	11.26	12.26	11.57		11.52			
Iwate-Numakunai いわて沼宮内	11.39							
Ninohe 二戸	11.53							
Hachinohe 八戸	12.05	12.55						
Shichinohe-Towada 七戸十和田	12.18							
Shin-Aomori 新青森	12.33	13.19	12.46					

1 Hayate: Also at 10.56, 12.56, 14.56, 16.56 & 18.56

2 Hayate: Also at 11.56, 13.56, 15.56 & 17.56 though stops and times vary for some services

3 Hayabusa: Also operates at 08.12 arriving in Shin-Aomori at 11.22 and in the evening at 21.36 but to Sendai only (arr 23.12).

4 Nasuno: Also at 10.20, 12.20, 13.20 and 15.20

5 Yamabiko/Max Yamabiko: the services at 8 and 40 minutes past the hour operate hourly until 18.08; the other two services listed also operate hourly but the times vary by up to ten minutes and the stations called at also change so check in advance.

12b: Shin-Aomori/Morioka/Sendai to Tokyo

	Hb	HAY	HAY	N	Y/MY	Y	Y	Y
Shin-Aomori 新青森	06.10[1]	08.28[2]	09.42[3]					
Shichinohe-Towada 七戸十和田		08.43						
Hachinohe 八戸	06.34	08.57	10.06					
Ninohe 二戸		09.09						
Iwate-Numakunai いわて沼宮内		09.22						
Morioka 盛岡	07.04	09.41	10.41		10.10[5]			
Shin-Hanamaki 新花巻					10.22			
Kitakami 北上					10.29			
Ichinoseki 一ノ関					10.48			
Sendai 仙台	07.49	10.26	11.26		08.44[5]	11.21	09.13	09.19[5]
Fukushima 福島					09.19	11.47	09.37	09.47
Koriyama 郡山				11.05[4]	09.34	12.01	09.55	10.01
Shin-Shirakawa 新白河				11.19			10.15	
Utsunomiya 宇都宮				11.50	10.06	12.31	10.50	10.31
Oyama 小山				12.01			11.01	
Omiya 大宮	08.59	11.42	12.42	12.18	10.30	12.58	11.18	10.58
Ueno 上野		12.02	13.02	12.38	10.50	13.18	11.38	11.18
Tokyo 東京	09.24	12.08	13.08	12.44	10.56	13.24	11.44	11.24

HAY = Hayate   Hb = Hayabusa   N = Nasuno   Y/MY = Yamabiko/Max-Yamabiko

1 Hayabusa: Also operates at 18.14 arriving in Tokyo to 21.24.

2 Hayate: Also at 10.28, 12.28, 14.28 and 16.08 though stops and times vary for some services

3 Hayate: Also at 11.42, 13.42, 15.42 and 17.33 though stops and times vary for some services

4 Nasuno: Also at 13.05, 15.05, 16.05 and 18.05

5 Yamabiko/Max Yamabiko: the services at 10 and 44 minutes past the hour operate hourly until 14.10/18.48 but the times vary by up to ten minutes; this also applies for the other two services listed and the stations called at also change so check in advance.

Table 13: Aomori to Akita on Tsugaru LEX

	13a: Aomori to Akita				13b: Akita to Aomori			
Aomori 青森	05.44[1]	10.04	13.35	16.09	11.25	15.47	20.08	22.08
Shin-Aomori 新青森	05.50	10.11	13.42	16.15	11.19	15.42	20.02	22.02
Hirosaki 弘前	06.17	10.43	14.09	16.43	10.51	15.14	19.35	21.32
Owani-onsen 大鰐温泉	06.27	10.53	14.20	16.54	10.40	15.03	19.24	21.21
Ikarigaseki 碇ヶ関	06.36	11.02	14.28	17.03	10.32	14.55	19.17	21.14
Odate 大館	06.55	11.21	14.47	17.23	10.14	14.36	18.58	20.55
Takanosu 鷹ノ巣	07.10	11.36	15.03	17.39	09.58	14.20	18.42	20.38
Higashi-Noshiro 東能代	07.35	12.01	15.27	18.03	09.34	13.56	18.18	20.14
Hachirogata 八郎潟	07.59	12.25	15.54	18.33	09.09	13.32	17.54	19.49
Akita 秋田	08.24	12.48	16.18	18.57	08.46	13.08	17.30	19.26

Note: The services shown are the main direct services on this route; the Resort Shirakami (3-4/day) operates at weekends and holidays. Local trains also operate on this line but, for the most part, only for short sections of the route.

Table 14: Akita to Niigata[1] on Inaho LEX

	14a: Akita to Niigata				14b: Niigata to Akita			
Akita 秋田		09.10	13.00	16.34	12.04		16.10	19.15
Kisakata 象潟		10.08	13.53	17.27	11.12		15.16	18.22
Sakata 酒田	08.54	10.44	14.26	18.00	10.41	13.07	14.45	17.50
Amarume 余目	09.02	10.53	14.34	18.09	10.30	12.58	14.34	17.37
Tsuruoka 鶴岡	09.14	11.05	14.46	18.20	10.20	12.47	14.24	17.26
Atsumi-onsen あつみ温泉	09.33	11.25	15.05	18.39	09.58	12.27	14.03	17.06
Murakami 村上	10.14	12.09	15.45	19.21	09.15	11.45	13.21	16.23
Sakamachi 坂町	10.23	12.18	15.54	19.30	09.06	11.36	13.12	16.15
Niigata 新潟	11.01	12.57	16.33	20.09	08.25	10.58	12.30	15.31

[1] The services shown between Akita and Niigata are the only direct ones; an additional 4/day (one of which is shown) operate between Sakata and Niigata. Not all stops are shown.

Table 15: Shin-Aomori/Aomori to Hakodate on Hakucho/Super Hakucho LEX

15a: Shin-Aomori/Aomori to Hakodate)

	SH	SH	SH	SH	H	H	SH	SH
Shin-Aomori 新青森	09.13	10.16	11.34	13.03[1]	14.41	15.35	16.41	18.41
Aomori 青森	09.28	10.30	11.51	13.17	14.56	15.51	16.54	18.56
Kanita 蟹田	10.00	10.56	12.20	13.41	15.22	16.22	17.21	19.20
Tappi-Kaitei 竜飛海底				14.04	15.48[2]	16.46[1]		
Kikonai 木古内	10.56	11.44	13.08	14.34	16.19	17.13	18.10	20.10
Goryokaku 五稜郭							18.48	20.42
Hakodate 函館	11.38	12.22	13.44	15.10	17.01	17.54	18.53	20.47

H = Hakucho   SH = Super Hakucho

[1] **Tappi 1 Course** (see box p318) dep Shin-Aomori 13.03 and then dep Tappi-Kaitei at 16.46 for Hakodate.

[2] **Tappi 2 Course** dep Hakodate 12.04 (see opposite), dep Tappi-Kaitei at 15.48 for Hakodate.

Table 15: *(cont'd)* **15b: (Hakodate to Aomori/Shin-Aomori)**

	SH	SH	SH	H	SH	SH	SH	SH
Hakodate 函館	08.08	10.17	11.19	12.04[2]	13.56	15.55	17.07	18.19
Goryokaku 五稜郭	08.13	10.21						
Kikonai 木古内	08.47	10.56	11.59	12.47	14.34	16.31	17.44	18.56
Tappi-Kaitei 竜飛海底				13.14				
Kanita 蟹田	09.39	11.44	12.53	13.40	15.23	17.22	18.32	19.50
Aomori 青森	10.10	12.14	13.22	14.10	15.54	17.51	19.05	20.22
Shin-Aomori 新青森	10.15	12.19	13.27	14.15	15.59	17.56	19.11	20.27

Table 16: Hakodate to Sapporo on Hokuto/Super Hokuto LEX

16a: Hakodate to Sapporo

	SH	H	SH	SH	H	SH	H	SH
Hakodate 函館	08.30	09.30	10.40	12.30	14.00	15.18	16.28	17.11
Goryokaku 五稜郭	08.34	09.34	10.44	12.34	14.04	15.22		17.16
Onuma-koen 大沼公園	08.49	09.53	10.59	12.49	14.21	15.37		17.33
Mori 森	09.06		11.15	13.05	14.39	15.53		17.54
Yakumo 八雲	09.25	10.30	11.35	13.24	15.00	16.12		18.14
Oshamambe 長万部	09.43	10.49	11.54	13.42	15.19	16.30		18.35
Toya 洞爺	10.05	11.14	12.17	14.04	15.44	16.52		19.00
Date-Mombetsu 伊達紋別	10.15	11.25	12.26	14.14	15.55	17.02		19.10
Higashi-Muroran 東室蘭	10.30	11.42	12.41	14.29	16.12	17.17	18.15	19.27
Noboribetsu 登別	10.41	11.53	12.52	14.40	16.23	17.28		19.39
Tomakomai 苫小牧	11.03	12.15	13.14	15.02	16.45	17.50	18.47	20.03
Minami-Chitose 南千歳	11.19	12.31	13.29	15.17	17.01	18.05	19.02	20.19
Shin-Sapporo 新札幌	11.39	12.50	13.50	15.35	17.21	18.26	19.20	20.40
Sapporo 札幌	11.47	12.59	13.58	15.44	17.29	18.35	19.28	20.49

16b: Sapporo to Hakodate

	H	SH	SH	SH	SH	H	SH	SH
Sapporo 札幌	07.30	08.34	09.19	10.37	12.22	13.17	14.52	16.52
Shin-Sapporo 新札幌	07.39	08.43	09.28	10.45	12.30	13.25	15.00	17.00
Minami-Chitose 南千歳	08.00	09.04	09.47	11.05	12.48	13.45	15.18	17.19
Tomakomai 苫小牧	08.18	09.19	10.03	11.20	13.04	14.01	15.33	17.34
Noboribetsu 登別	08.42	09.40	10.26	11.42	13.25	14.23	15.55	17.59
Higashi-Muroran 東室蘭	08.56	09.52	10.38	11.53	13.37	14.36	16.07	18.12
Date-Mombetsu 伊達紋別	09.12	10.06	10.54	12.07	13.51	14.52	16.21	18.26
Toya 洞爺	09.22	10.16	11.04	12.17	14.00	15.02	16.30	18.36
Oshamambe 長万部	09.50	10.39	11.30	12.40	14.24	15.28	16.53	18.59
Yakumo 八雲	10.10	10.57	11.49	12.58	14.42	15.47	17.11	19.17
Mori 森	10.31	11.16	12.10		15.01	16.08	17.29	19.35
Onuma-koen 大沼公園	10.50	11.31	12.28	13.30	15.17	16.26	17.47	
Goryokaku 五稜郭	11.09	11.49	12.47	13.47	15.34	16.45	18.04	20.07
Hakodate 函館	11.11	11.53	12.51	13.52	15.38	16.49	18.09	20.12

H = Hokuto   SH = Super Hokuto

Table 17: Sapporo to Asahikawa & Abashiri on Okhotsk LEX

	17a: Sapporo to Abashiri				17b: Abashiri to Sapporo			
Sapporo 札幌	07.21[1]	09.41	15.08	17.30	11.46	14.45	18.47	22.38
Iwamizawa 岩見沢	07.49	10.10	15.37	17.58	11.18	14.17	18.16	22.10
Bibai 美唄	08.01			18.09	11.06			21.58
Sunagawa 砂川	08.14			18.22	10.53			21.45
Takikawa 滝川	08.20	10.37	16.04	18.29	10.47	13.49	17.49	21.39
Fukagawa 深川	08.37	10.53	16.20	18.44	10.31	13.34	17.34	21.22
Asahikawa 旭川	09.01	11.19	16.42	19.08	10.11	13.13	17.13	21.00
Kamikawa 上川	09.42	12.01	17.31	19.52	09.25	12.31	16.32	20.20
Engaru 遠軽	10.57	13.22	18.45	21.13	08.09	11.16	15.17	19.05
Kitami 北見	11.57	14.19	19.45	22.08	07.12	10.19	14.19	18.08
Bihoro 美幌	12.20	14.43	20.10	22.32	06.49	09.56	13.55	17.44
Abashiri 網走	12.46	15.09	20.37	22.58	06.23	09.30	13.29	17.18

[1] The Okhotsk services shown are the only direct services from Sapporo to Abashiri. The Super Kamui (1-2/hr) operates from Sapporo to Asahikawa. However, one service an hour (10.19 to 20.19 as well as at 21.16) starts at New Chitose Airport and also one an hour continues to the airport (08.00 to 19.00).

Table 18: Abashiri to Kushiro[1]

	18a: Abashiri to Kushiro				18b: Kushiro to Abashiri			
Abashiri 網走	06.41	10.01	16.15	18.50	09.18	12.05	18.49	21.25
Kitahama 北浜	06.57	10.15	16.33	19.08	09.02	11.51	18.33	21.08
Shiretoko-Shari 知床斜里	07.27	10.46	17.30	19.36	08.34	11.25	18.07	20.43
Kawayu-onsen 川湯温泉	08.17	11.40	18.25	20.36	07.46	10.36	17.23	19.59
Mashu 摩周	08.37	11.55	18.48	20.54	07.29	10.21	17.06	19.42
Toro 塘路	09.36	12.48	19.37	21.51	06.37	09.36	16.20	18.53
Kushiro 釧路	10.07	13.19	20.07	22.53	06.06	09.05	15.50	18.20

[1] The services shown are the only direct services between Abashiri and Kushiro. Not all stops are shown.

Table 19: Kushiro to Shintoku (and Sapporo) on Super Ozora LEX[1,2]

Kushiro 釧路	08.39	11.29	13.25	16.17	13.03	15.44	18.14	19.45
Ikeda 池田	09.47	12.45	14.39	17.28	11.51	14.30	16.55	18.31
Obihiro 帯広市	10.04	13.01	14.56	17.44	11.35	14.14	16.39	18.15
Shintoku 新得	10.31	13.29	15.25	18.15	11.07	13.46	16.09	17.41
Minami-Chitose 南千歳	11.48	14.45	16.48	19.42	09.32	12.17	14.47	16.17
Shin-Sapporo 新札幌	12.06	15.06	17.09	20.05	09.12	11.59	14.28	15.58
Sapporo 札幌	12.14	15.15	17.17	20.13	09.04	11.51	14.20	15.50

[1] Not all stops are shown.

[2] In addition to the four Super Ozora services shown (out of 7/day) the Super Tokachi LEX operates from Obihiro to Sapporo five times a day.

Table 20: Shintoku to Furano [All services shown are direct and local]

23a: Shintoku to Furano

Shintoku 新得	05.51	08.04[1]	10.12[2]	11.33[3]	14.17[4]	19.16[5]	20.55[6]
Furano 富良野	07.19	09.45	11.34	13.03	15.46	20.35	22.29

23b: Furano to Shintoku

Furano 富良野	07.20	09.20	11.08	16.45	19.10	22.00
Shintoku 新得	08.56[7]	10.44[8]	12.46[9]	18.09	20.49[10]	23.26

[1] Starts in Ikeda at 06.05   [2] Starts in Kushiro at 05.45   [3] Starts in Obihiro at 10.13
[4] Starts in Obihiro at 13.05   [5] Starts in Obihiro at 18.28   [6] Starts in Ikeda at 18.51
[7] Reaches Obihiro at 10.03   [8] Reaches Obihiro at 11.28   [9] Reaches Kushiro at 17.39
[10] Reaches Ikeda at 22.44

Table 21: Furano to Asahikawa

A steam train, SL Furano Biei, operates between Asahikawa and Furano in the summer months; check locally for details.

21a: Furano to Asahikawa

Furano 富良野	09.57	11.45	13.12	15.34	16.55	18.00	19.07	20.44[1]
Naka-Furano 中富良野	10.07	11.52	13.22	15.45	17.05	18.11	19.17	20.51
Kami-Furano 上富良野	10.17	11.59	13.33	15.54	17.21	18.21	19.30	20.58
Bibaushi 美馬牛	10.26	12.15	13.42	16.10	17.31	18.30	19.39	21.08
Biei 美瑛	10.34	12.23	13.50	16.28	17.39	18.38	19.47	21.15
Asahikawa 旭川	11.05	12.55	14.25	17.02	18.16	19.09	20.19	21.41

[1] Starts in Obihiro at 18.28 and departs Shintoku at 19.16 (see Shintoku to Furano above).

21b: Asahikawa to Furano

Asahikawa 旭川	07.42	09.34	11.30	13.38	15.25	16.30	17.46	18.34
Biei 美瑛	08.20	10.08	12.08	14.16	16.01	17.03	18.20	19.13
Bibaushi 美馬牛	08.27	10.26	12.16	14.23	16.09	17.11	18.30	19.20
Kami-Furano 上富良野	08.37	10.36	12.25	14.33	16.19	17.21	18.40	19.30
Naka-Furano 中富良野	08.44	10.44	12.33	14.41	16.28	17.29	18.48	19.38
Furano 富良野	08.51[2]	10.54	12.40	14.51	16.38	17.39	18.55	19.48

[2] Departs Furano at 09.20 and reaches Obihiro at 11.28 and (see Furano to Shintoku above).

Table 22: Hakata/Fukuoka to Nagasaki on Kamome LEX

	22a: Hakata to Nagasaki		22b: Nagasaki to Hakata	
Hakata/Fukuoka 博多/福岡	09.55[1]	10.15[2]	10.52	11.12
Futsukaichi 二日市		10.27	10.41	
Tosu 鳥栖	10.15	10.38	10.31	10.52
Saga 佐賀	10.33	10.56	10.13	10.36
Hizen-Yamaguchi 肥前山口	10.42			10.26
Hizen-Kashima 肥前鹿島	10.53	11.16	09.54	10.16
Isahaya 諫早	11.32	12.04	09.09	09.38
Urakami 浦上	11.45	12.19	08.51	09.23
Nagasaki 長崎	11.48	12.21	08.48[3]	09.20[4]

[1] Hourly until 17.55   [2] Also at 11.15 and 15.15, 16.15, 17.15 and 18.15
[3] Also at 09.51, 10.53, 14.53, 15.53, 16.53 and 17.52   [4] Hourly until 20.23.

Table 23: Shin-Osaka and Hakata/Fukuoka to Kagoshima-chuo by shinkansen

	M	S	T	S	T	M	S	S
Shin-Osaka 新大阪	08.59[1]	09.59[2]				10.44	13.44	
Shin-Kobe 新神戸	09.13	10.13				10.31	13.31	
Okayama 岡山	09.46	10.46				09.58	12.58	
Hiroshima 広島	10.23	11.29				09.22	12.15	
Kokura 小倉	11.09	12.22				08.36	11.22	
Hakata (Fukuoka) 博多 (福岡)	11.27	12.41	08.40[3]	13.09[4]	08.54	08.17	11.02	11.36
Shin-Tosu 新鳥栖			08.54	13.23	08.40			11.24
Kurume 久留米		12.56	08.59		08.35		10.48	
Chikugo-Funagoya 筑後船小屋			09.06		08.28			
Shin-Omuta 新大牟田			09.12		08.22			
Shin-Tamana 新玉名			09.20		08.14			
Kumamoto 熊本	12.01	13.18	09.29	13.46	08.04[5]	07.44	10.26	11.00
Shin-Yatsushiro 新八代				13.59				10.47
Shin-Minamata 新水俣				14.13				10.33
Izumi 出水				14.20				10.25
Sendai 川内		13.53		14.32			09.51	10.13
Kagoshima-chuo 鹿児島中央	12.44	14.05		14.44		07.00[6]	09.38[7]	10.00[8]

M = Mizuho   S = Sakura   T = Tsubame

[1] Also at 06.00, 07.53 & 19.59 though departure/arrival times vary
[2] Hourly until 19.59   [3] Hourly until 20.48 though times vary by up to 10 minutes
[4] Hourly until 17.09   [5] Hourly until 20.03   [6] Also at 08.00, 16.00, 18.00 & 19.55
[7] Hourly until 18.27 though departure times vary by up to 10 minutes
[8] Hourly till 19.00; services between 15.00 and 19.00 continue to Shin-Osaka

In both directions subsequent departure/arrival times sometimes vary by a few minutes.

Table 24: Hakata/Fukuoka & Kokura to Miyazaki on Sonic/Nichirin (N) & Nichirin Seagaia (NS)

	24a: Hakata to Miyazaki				24b: Miyazaki to Hakata			
	NS	Sonic	Sonic	Sonic	Sonic	Sonic	Sonic	NS
Hakata/Fukuoka 博多 (福岡)	07.33	09.02	09.21[1]	09.57[2]	11.28	11.48	12.47	20.57
Kokura 小倉	08.34	09.48	10.09	10.40	10.42	11.05	12.05	20.09
Nakatsu 中津	09.08	10.18	10.42	11.10	10.05	10.29	11.32	19.34
Usa 宇佐			10.57		09.49			
Beppu 別府	09.51	10.57	11.28	11.50	09.19	09.47	10.53	18.51
Oita 大分 (arr/dep)	10.02	11.06	11.38	11.59	09.10[3]	09.39	10.45[4]	18.42
		N	N	N	N	N	N	
Oita 大分 (dep/arr)	10.07	09.10	11.12	12.06[5]	12.39	13.39	14.40	18.39
Usuki 宇宿	10.36	09.42	11.42	12.36	12.04	13.08	14.08	18.09
Saiki 佐伯	11.04	10.08	12.11	13.07	11.37	12.41	13.40	17.39
Nobeoka 延岡	12.08	11.06	13.09	14.09	10.39	11.41	12.42	16.41
Miyazaki 宮崎	13.08	12.10	14.13	15.14	09.37	10.31	11.37[6]	15.37

Not all stops shown; in both directions subsequent times sometimes vary by a few minutes. All the services continue to Miyazaki Airport (a 9-minute journey)

[1] Hourly until 20.20   [2] Hourly until 19.59   [3] Hourly until 20.12   [4] Hourly until 19.42
[5] Hourly until 18.10   [6] Hourly until 18.42

Table 25: Okayama to Takamatsu to Tokushima on Marine Liner & Uzushio

	25a: Okayama to Takamatsu				25b: Takamatsu to Okayama			
Okayama 岡山	09.32	09.54	10.23	10.53	▲ 10.17	10.48	11.03	11.32
Kojima 児島	09.55	10.20	10.47	11.19	09.53	10.22	10.40	11.10
Sakaide 坂出	10.10	10.35	11.02	11.34	09.37	10.06	10.24	10.55
Takamatsu 高松	10.25	10.51	11.17	11.49 ▼	09.22	09.51	10.10	10.40

The Marine Liner is a rapid train rather than a LEX but it is the easiest way to get from Okayama to Takamatsu. The service operates at least twice an hour in both directions; subsequent times vary by a few minutes from those shown.
Note: not all stops are listed.

	25c: Takamatsu to Tokushima[1]				25d: Tokushima to Takamatsu[1]			
Takamatsu 高松	09.10	12.06[2]	13.11	20.05[3]	▲ 09.31[4]	10.32	11.37	17.44[5]
Ritsurin 栗林	09.15	12.11	13.16	20.10	09.25	10.27	11.32	17.39
Yashima 八島	09.19		13.21	20.15	09.19	10.22		
Itano 板野		12.51	14.01	20.59	08.40	09.38	10.43	16.59
Ikenotani 池谷	10.09		14.08	21.05	08.34	09.31	10.35	
Tokushima 徳島	10.17	13.04	14.16	21.14 ▼	08.24	09.22	10.28	16.46

[1] Uzushio LEX; hourly in both directions; times vary by up to 10 minutes from those shown.
[2] Starts in Okayama at 11.05.   [3] Starts in Okayama at 19.05.
[4] Arrives in Okayama at 10.33.   [5] Arrives in Okayama at 18.46.
Note: not all stops are listed.

Table 26: Takamatsu to Kochi/Kubokawa on Shimanto/Nanpu LEX

	26a: Takamatsu to Kochi				26b: Kochi to Takamatsu			
	S/N	S	S/N	S/N	S/N	S/N	S/N	S
Takamatsu 高松	07.20	08.25	16.24	20.25	▲ 09.20	19.25	21.41	23.24
Sakaide 坂出	07.37	08.39	16.37	20.38	09.06	19.11	21.27	23.11
Utazu 宇多津	07.48		16.48	20.49	09.00	19.06	21.23	
Marugame 丸亀	07.51	08.45	16.51	20.52	08.55	19.01	21.17	23.05
Tadotsu 多度津	07.56	08.50	16.56	20.58	08.51	18.57	21.13	23.01
Zentsu-ji 善通寺	08.01	08.55	17.02	21.08	08.44	18.51	21.08	22.56
Kotohira 琴平	08.06	09.00	17.07	21.13	08.40	18.46	21.03	22.51
Awa-Ikeda 阿波池田	08.29	09.24	17.34	21.37	08.13	18.23	20.40	22.27
Oboke 大歩危	08.49	09.42	17.52	21.56	07.52	18.05	20.23	22.09
Osugi 大杉	09.07	10.03		22.16	07.32	17.47	20.05	21.51
Tosa-Yamada 土佐山田	09.27	10.25	18.31	22.36	07.12	17.28	19.46	21.32
Gomen 郷免	09.31	10.29	18.36	22.40	07.07	17.21	19.42	21.28
Kochi 高知	09.53	10.37	18.58	22.48 ▼	07.00	17.13	19.34	21.20
Kubokawa 窪川	10.55		20.07			15.51	18.23	

Some Shimanto (S) services from Takamatsu join the Nanpu (N) from Okayama at Utazu.

Table 27: Kochi to Kubokawa on Ashizuri/Nanpu LEX

	27a: Kochi to Kubokawa[1]				27b: Kubokawa to Kochi[1]			
	A	N	A	N	N	A	N	A
Kochi 故知	08.20	11.39	13.50	15.44	▲ 11.06	13.03	15.03	18.32
Ino 井野	08.34	11.53	14.01	15.57	10.55	12.50	14.53	18.19
Kubokawa 窪川	09.27	12.48	14.54	16.51 ▼	10.04	11.57	14.01	17.29

[1] See also Table 26

Table 28: Kubokawa to Uwajima on local train

	28a: Kubokawa to Uwajima				28b: Uwajima to Kubokawa			
Kubokawa 窪川	10.04	13.28	15.01	16.57	11.47	13.51	17.49	19.44
Tokawa 十川	10.42	14.10	15.46	17.36	11.06	12.54	17.05	19.03
Ekawasaki 江川崎	10.58	14.23	16.37	17.48	10.54	12.40	16.52	18.48
Uwajima 宇和島	12.11	15.28	17.44	19.00	09.38	11.32	15.30	17.36

Table 29: Uwajima to Matsuyama on Uwakai LEX

	29a: Uwajima to Matsuyama[1]				29b: Matsuyama to Uwajima[1]			
Uwajima 宇和島	08.39	09.53	12.54	14.56	09.30	10.26	11.30	15.51
Uno-machi 卯之町	09.01	10.12	13.14	15.16	09.11	10.04	11.12	15.32
Yawatahama 八幡浜	09.16	10.24	13.29	15.28	08.59	09.52	11.00	15.16
Iyo-Ozu 伊予大洲	09.28	10.36	13.41	15.40	08.46	09.40	10.48	15.04
Uchiko 内子	09.39	10.50	13.51	15.52	08.35	09.27	10.38	14.55
Iyo-shi 伊予市	09.57	11.06	14.07	16.08	08.16	09.10	10.22	14.36
Matsuyama 松山	10.07	11.16	14.17	16.18	08.08	09.02	10.14	14.27

[1] Services in both directions operate approximately hourly but the departure/arrival times vary by a few minutes.

Table 30: Matsuyama to Okayama on Shiokaze LEX[1]

30a: Matsuyama to Okayama[2]

Matsuyama 松山	09.15	10.20	11.24	12.19	13.25	14.23	15.28	16.28
Imabari 今治	09.56	10.58	11.59	12.57	14.04	15.01	16.06	17.04
Iyo-Saijo 伊予西条	10.20	11.22	12.25	13.24	14.26	15.26	16.27	17.29
Niihama 新居浜	10.30	11.30	12.33	13.32	14.34	15.34	16.35	17.37
Kanon-ji 観音寺	11.05	12.06	13.07	14.07	15.08	16.08	17.10	18.10
Tadotsu 多度津	11.20	12.22	13.23	14.23	15.23	16.24	17.25	18.26
Marugame 丸亀	11.25	12.26	13.28	14.28	15.28	16.29	17.30	18.30
Utazu 宇多津	11.32	12.34	13.34	14.34	15.34	16.35	17.35	18.35
Sakaide 坂出	*11.38*	*12.40*	*13.39*	*14.40*	*15.40*	*16.39*	*17.40*	*18.40*
Takamatsu 高松	*11.54*	*12.55*	*13.54*	*14.55*	*15.55*	*16.55*	*17.54*	*18.55*
Okayama 岡山	12.11	13.11	14.09	15.11	16.11	17.11	18.11	19.11

[1] The Shiokaze LEX (12/day) operates from Matsuyama to Okayama. However, the train divides at Utazu; part of it becomes the Ishizuchi LEX and goes to Takamatsu.

30b: Okayama to Matsuyama[2]

Okayama 岡山	09.24	10.34	11.34	12.35	13.35	14.35	15.35	16.35
Takamatsu 高松	*09.40*	*10.47*	*11.50*	*12.50*	*13.50*	*14.50*	*15.50*	*16.50*
Sakaide 坂出	*09.55*	*11.01*	*12.03*	*13.04*	*14.04*	*15.03*	*16.05*	*17.05*
Utazu 宇多津	10.05	11.12	12.13	13.14	14.14	15.14	16.15	17.15
Marugame 丸亀	10.08	11.16	12.17	13.17	14.17	15.18	16.19	17.19
Tadotsu 多度津	10.13	11.20	12.21	13.22	14.22	15.23	16.24	17.25
Kanon-ji 観音寺	10.28	11.36	12.37	13.37	14.38	15.38	16.39	17.40
Niihama 新居浜	11.00	12.08	13.09	14.09	15.10	16.11	17.13	18.13
Iyo-Saijo 伊予西条	11.08	12.17	13.17	14.17	15.19	16.19	17.22	18.21
Imabari 今治	11.33	12.39	13.38	14.43	15.41	16.45	17.45	18.46
Matsuyama 松山	12.10	13.13	14.12	15.17	16.16	17.24	18.25	19.23

[1] The Shiokaze LEX (12/day) operates from Okayama to Matsuyama. However, the Ishizuchi LEX from Takamatsu joins up with it at Utazu.

[2] Services in both directions operate hourly though departure times vary by a few minutes.

INDEX

TRAILBLAZER TITLE LIST

Adventure Motorcycling Handbook
Australia by Rail
Australia's Great Ocean Road
Azerbaijan
Coast to Coast (British Walking Guide)
Cornwall Coast Path (British Walking Guide)
Corsica Trekking – GR20
Cotswold Way (British Walking Guide)
Dolomites Trekking – AV1 & AV2
Dorset & S Devon Coast Path (British Walking)
Exmoor & N Devon Coast Path (British Walking)
Hadrian's Wall Path (British Walking Guide)
Himalaya by Bike – a route and planning guide
Inca Trail, Cusco & Machu Picchu
Indian Rail Handbook
Japan by Rail
Kilimanjaro – the trekking guide (inc Mt Meru)
Mediterranean Handbook
Morocco Overland (4WD/motorcycle/mtnbike)
Moroccan Atlas – The Trekking Guide
Nepal Trekking & The Great Himalaya Trail
New Zealand – The Great Walks
North Downs Way (British Walking Guide)
Norway's Arctic Highway
Offa's Dyke Path (British Walking Guide)
Overlanders' Handbook – worldwide driving gde
Peddars Way & Norfolk Coast Path (BWG)
Pembrokeshire Coast Path (British Walking Gde)
Pennine Way (British Walking Guide)
The Ridgeway (British Walking Guide)
Siberian BAM Guide – rail, rivers & road
The Silk Roads – a route and planning guide
Sahara Overland – a route and planning guide
Scottish Highlands – The Hillwalking Guide
Sinai – the trekking guide
South Downs Way (British Walking Guide)
Tour du Mont Blanc
Trans-Canada Rail Guide
Trans-Siberian Handbook
Trekking in the Annapurna Region
Trekking in the Everest Region
Trekking in Ladakh
Trekking in the Pyrenees
Walker's Haute Route – Mont Blanc to Matterhorn
West Highland Way (British Walking Guide)

For more information about Trailblazer and our
range of guides, for guidebook updates or
for mail order sales visit our website:

www.trailblazer-guides.com

Trans-Siberian Handbook *Bryn Thomas*, 8th edn, £14.99
ISBN 978-1-905864-36-1, 512pp, 90 maps, 22 colour photos
First edition short-listed for the Thomas Cook Guidebook Awards.
Eighth edition of the most popular guide to the world's longest
rail journey. How to arrange a trip, plus a km-by-km guide to the
routes. Updated and expanded to include extra information on
travelling independently in Russia. New mapping. Now includes
Siberian BAM Railway *'The best guidebook is Bryn Thomas's
"Trans-Siberian Handbook"'* **The Independent** (UK)

Trans-Canada Rail Guide
Melissa Graham, 5th edn, £12.99
ISBN 978-1-905864-33-1, 256pp, 34 maps, 30 colour photos
Comprehensive guide to Canada's trans-continental railroad. Cov-
ers the entire route from coast to coast with information for all
budgets. Mile-by-mile route guides. City guides and maps – ten
major stops including Quebec City, Montreal, Toronto, Winnipeg,
Jasper and Vancouver.

Indian Rail Handbook *Nick Hill & Royston Ellis*, 1st edn, £12.99
ISBN 978-1-873756-87-4, 256pp, 80 maps, 30 colour photos
India has the most comprehensive railway network in the world,
with almost all tourist attractions accessible by rail. For most visi-
tors travel by train is the preferred means of transport, the ideal way
to see the country. This new book is a wholly inclusive guide for rail
travellers in India. Foreword by Sir Mark Tully.
• Fully-indexed rail atlas of 80 maps with all 7326 railway stations
• Rail travel for all budgets, special trains and railway history
• Timetables, suggested itineraries and how to book tickets

The Silk Roads *Paul Wilson*, 3rd edn, £14.99
ISBN 978-1-905864-32-4, 448pp, 60 maps, 40 colour photos
The Silk Road was never a single thread across Asia but an intricate
web of shorter trade routes – Silk Roads – which together linked
Asia and Europe. City guides & maps – the best sights, places to
stay and restaurants for all budgets in 55 stopovers along the way.
Includes Turkey, Syria, Iran, Turkmenistan, Uzbekistan, Kyrgyz-
stan, Pakistan, China. Plus lesser-known routes – Southern Takla-
makan, Karakorum Highway, Marco Polo's route to Xanadu.

Siberian BAM Guide – Rail, Rivers & Road [Stocks low]
Athol Yates & Nicholas Zvegintzov, 2nd edn, £13.99
ISBN 978-1-873756-18-8, 384pp, 60 maps, 22 colour photos
Comprehensive guide to the BAM Zone in NE Siberia. Includes
a km-by-km guide to the 3400km Baikal Amur Mainline (BAM)
railway which traverses east Siberia from the Pacific Ocean to
Lake Baikal. How to take the train and where to go in the BAM
Zone. *'An encyclopaedic companion'* – **The Independent**

Australia by Rail *Colin Taylor*, 5th edn, £12.99
ISBN 978-1-873756-81-2, 290pp, 65 maps, 30 colour photos
With 65 strip maps covering all rail routes in Australia, city guides
(Sydney, Melbourne, Brisbane, Adelaide, Perth, Darwin and Can-
berra), and includes the Ghan line from Alice Springs to Darwin.
'Benefiting from Taylor's 30 years of travel on Australia's trains.'
The Sunday Times

Colour section
● **(Opposite) Some typical Japanese dishes**   [For more information see pp447-9]
Clockwise from top left

1: Katsudon – deep-fried breaded pork cutlet (tonkatsu; see below) served on rice and covered with a slightly sweet sauce made with eggs and soy sauce.
2: Sashimi (raw fish) served with a shiso leaf, shredded daikon (radish) and wasabi.
3: Sushi – the main kinds are nigiri-zushi (on rice) and maki-zushi (wrapped in seaweed).
4: Unadon – eel (unagi) served on rice in a lacquerware box.
5: Ramen noodles with a miso-based sauce, a speciality of Hokkaido.
6: Somen noodles are served cold and are popular in the summer months.
7: Tonkatsu (deep-fried breaded pork cutlet) with shredded cabbage. Plastic models like this are often displayed in a restaurant's window to show customers what is available.
8: Yakitori – pieces of chicken on a bamboo stick, cooked over a charcoal fire.

(Photo credits for food photos: Nos 1, 4 and 8 © JNTO; 3 © Kanazawa City/© JNTO; 5 © Hokkaido Tourism Organization/© JNTO; 6 © Saga Prefecture/© JNTO; Nos 2 and 7 © Kazuo Udagawa).

● **(Overleaf) The diversity and style of Japan's trains never fails to impress**
Photos from left

Row 1: Yamanote Line train, the line operates in a circular route around Tokyo (© JRL); **linked trains** – Yamabiko/Max Yamabiko services are sometimes coupled with the Tsubasa between Tokyo and Fukushima (© AU); the **Super Hokuto** runs from Sapporo to Hakodate (© AU); the **Komachi shinkansen** runs from Morioka to Akita (© KU); **500-series shinkansen** used by JR West (© KU).

Row 2: Resort Asunaro trains operate around Mutsu Bay, Aomori (© KU); one of the **steam locomotives** operating on the Oigawa Railway (© AU); a **700-series shinkansen** passing through Atami station (© KU); the **Hikari Rail Star** operates between Shin-Osaka and Hakata/Fukuoka (© JRL).

Row 3: At the start and end of routes it is common to see **cleaners** waiting for a train to arrive so they can clean it and get the seats facing the right direction before it leaves on its next journey (© JRL); **announcements** about train arrivals and departures are often made in English at major stations (© AU); the **Narita Express (N'EX)** operates between Narita Airport and various stations in the Tokyo area (© AU); the **N700** (upper picture) is the fastest train between Tokyo and Hakata (© CJRC); **Dr Yellow** (lower picture) is the nickname for the trains that test the condition of the track and overhead cables on shinkansen lines (© AU).

Row 4: An **ekiben** (station lunch box) for the journey from Honshu to Hokkaido: the details on the cover say both the day and time by which it should be eaten and the contents reflect local produce and are designed to be visually pleasing (© AU); the **Kumagera train** is one of three operating on the Resort Shirakami service (© AU); the **Aizu Liner** runs from Koriyama to Aizu-Wakamatsu (© AU); a **Hokuto train** at Onuma-koen station, Hokkaido (© AU).

(Photo credits for train photos: (© JRL) J&R Leslie; (© AU) Anna Udagawa; (© KU) Kazuo Udagawa; (© CJRC) courtesy Central Japan Railway Company)